MUSEUM PRACTICE

Museum Practice

Edited by
Conal McCarthy

General Editors
Sharon Macdonald and Helen Rees Leahy

WILEY Blackwell

Registered Offices
John Wiley & Sons, Inc., 111 River Street, Hoboken, NJ 07030, USA
John Wiley & Sons Ltd, The Atrium, Southern Gate, Chichester, West Sussex, PO19 8SQ, UK

Editorial Office
The Atrium, Southern Gate, Chichester, West Sussex, PO19 8SQ, UK
For details of our global editorial offices, customer services, and more information about Wiley products visit us at www.wiley.com.

Library of Congress Cataloging-in-Publication Data

Museum Practice – The international handbooks of museum studies /
edited by Conal McCarthy / general editors: Sharon Macdonald,
Helen Rees Leahy. – First edition.
    pages   cm
  Includes bibliographical references and index.
  ISBN 978-1-4051-9850-9 (cloth) | ISBN 978-1-119-64207-7 (pbk.)
1. Museums.   2. Museum exhibits.   I. Macdonald, Sharon.   II. Leahy, Helen Rees.
  AM5.I565 2015
  069–dc23

                                                                      2015003407

Cover Design: Wiley
Cover Image: Tiger and conservator. Photo: Courtesy of Manchester Museum, The University of Manchester

Set in 11/13 pt Dante by SPi Global, Pondicherry, India

Printed and bound by CPI Group (UK) Ltd, Croydon, CR0 4YY

10 9 8 7 6 5 4 3 2 1

CONTENTS

LIST OF ILLUSTRATIONS

Color plate section

Chapter illustrations

EDITOR

Conal McCarthy is Professor and Director of the Museum and Heritage Studies program at Victoria University of Wellington, Aotearoa New Zealand. Conal has degrees in English, Art History, Museum Studies, and Māori language and has worked in galleries and museums in a variety of professional roles: educator, interpreter, visitor researcher, collection manager, curator, and exhibition developer, as well as sitting on the boards and advisory groups of a number of institutions. He has published widely on museum practice, including the books *Museums and Māori: Heritage Professionals, Indigenous Collections, Current Practice* (2011), and *Curatopia: Museums and the Future of Curatorship* (2019).

Professor Conal McCarthy
Director Museum & Heritage Studies programme
Stout Research Centre
Victoria University of Wellington
Wellington
New Zealand

GENERAL EDITORS

Sharon Macdonald is Alexander van Humboldt Professor in Social Anthropology at the Humboldt University Berlin where she directs the Centre for Anthropological Research on Museums and Heritage – CARMAH. The centre works closely with a wide range of museums. Sharon has edited and coedited volumes include the *Companion to Museum Studies* (Blackwell, 2006); *Exhibition Experiments* (with Paul Basu; Blackwell, 2007); and *Theorizing Museums* (with Gordon Fyfe; Blackwell, 1996). Her authored books include *Behind the Scenes at the Science Museum* (Berg, 2002); *Difficult Heritage: Negotiating the Nazi Past in Nuremberg and Beyond* (Routledge, 2009); and *Memorylands: Heritage and Identity in Europe Today* (Routledge, 2013). Her current projects include *Making Differences. Transforming Museums and Heritage in the 21ˢᵗ Century.*

Professor Sharon Macdonald
Alexander van Humboldt Professor in Social Anthropology
Institute for European Ethnology
Humboldt University of Berlin
Berlin, Germany

Helen Rees Leahy is Professor Emerita of Museology at the University of Manchester, where, between 2002 and 2017 she directed the Centre for Museology. Previously, Helen held a variety of senior posts in UK museums, including the Design Museum, Eureka!, The Museum for Children, and the National Art Collections Fund. She has also worked as an independent consultant and curator, and has organized numerous exhibitions of art and design. She has published widely on practices of individual and institutional collecting, in both historical and contemporary contexts, including issues of patronage, display and interpretation. Her *Museum Bodies: The Politics and Practices of Visiting and Viewing* was published by Ashgate in 2012.

Professor Emerita Helen Rees Leahy
Centre for Museology
School of Arts, Languages and Cultures
University of Manchester
Manchester, UK

CONTRIBUTORS

Ken Arnold, Wellcome Collection, London, UK

Rosmarie Beier-de Haan, German Historical Museum, Berlin, Germany

Piotr Bienkowski, independent consultant, and Co-Director, International Umm al-Biyara Project, Petra, Jordan

Graham Black, Nottingham Trent University, UK

Malcolm Chapman, University of Glasgow, UK

Derrick Chong, Royal Holloway, University of London, UK

Elizabeth Crooke, University of Ulster, Northern Ireland, UK

Lee Davidson, Victoria University of Wellington, New Zealand

Stuart Davies, Stuart Davies Associates, UK

David K. Dean, Texas Tech University, USA

Gail Lord, Co-President, Lord Cultural Resources Inc., Canada

Jocelyn Dodd, University of Leicester, UK

David Fleming, National Museums Liverpool, UK

James B. Gardner, US National Archives, Washington, DC, USA

Rina Gerson (née Zigler), Canada

Kerry Jimson, Victoria University of Wellington, New Zealand

Ceri Jones, University of Leicester, UK

Barry Lord, Co-President, Lord Cultural Resources Inc., Canada

Janet Marstine, University of Leicester, UK

Nick Merriman, Manchester Museum, UK

Eithne Nightingale, independent consultant, writer, and researcher, UK

Halona Norton-Westbrook, Toledo Museum of Art, Ohio, USA

Gillian Oliver, Victoria University of Wellington, New Zealand

Michael Pickering, National Museum of Australia, Canberra, Australia

John Reeve, University of London, UK

Carol A. Scott, Director, Carol Scott Associates, UK

Sara Selwood, independent cultural analyst and consultant, UK

Anthony Alan Shelton, Museum of Anthropology at the University of British Columbia, Vancouver, Canada

Ted Silberberg, Senior Principal, Lord Cultural Resources Inc., Canada

John E. Simmons, Museologica, USA

Dan Spock, Minnesota History Center, USA

Dean Sully, University College London, UK

Shannon Wellington, Victoria University of Wellington, New Zealand

Anne Whitelaw, Concordia University, Montreal, Canada

Vicky Woollard, consultant and researcher, UK

Linda Young, Deakin University, Melbourne, Australia

ACKNOWLEDGMENTS

Ahakoa he iti te matakahi, ka pakaru i a ia te tōtara
[Although the wedge is small, it fells the great *tōtara* tree]

(Māori proverb)

A book of this size and complexity is the work of many hands, and I would like to acknowledge everyone who helped me complete it.

Thanks to the general editors, Helen Rees Leahy and Sharon Macdonald, for the opportunity to tackle the topic, the support to compile the contents, and the encouragement to get it completed.

Thanks to all the contributors who have made this volume possible by writing these diverse and accessible chapters on the contemporary museum at work – your labour, patience, and commitment have made a persuasive case for current museum practice.

In particular I would like to thank Gill Whitley, the Project Editor, for her many efforts large and small, which made it all happen.

Lastly, thanks to my partner Bronwyn Labrum for waiting for me to finish the project. Now we can get on to our book!

Conal McCarthy
January 2015

EDITORS' PREFACE TO *MUSEUM PRACTICE* AND *THE INTERNATIONAL HANDBOOKS IN MUSEUM STUDIES*

Museum Practice

As general editors of *The International Handbooks in Museum Studies,* we – Sharon Macdonald and Helen Rees Leahy – are delighted that *Museum Practice* is now appearing in paperback, as a self-standing volume. So too are the other volumes, which is testament to the strength of these volumes individually, as well as collectively, and to the importance of the issues that they each address. *Museum Practice* clearly concerns a fundamental area of museum studies – without such practice, there would be no museums. Nevertheless, there has not yet developed an established consensus on precisely what might be covered under the label 'museum practice', and, in particular, more extensive and theorised accounts and analyses of practice – going beyond 'how to' guides – are still far from numerous. One reason for this is the relative recency of museum studies as a field. A second reason is that museum studies draws on a wide range of disciplines, each themselves renewing their toolkits in various ways, resulting in new impulses for thinking about museum practice – so challenging the formation of a fixed canon. In addition, and perhaps of most significance, is the fact of changing museum practice in response to wider challenges and opportunities, be they in relation to issues of funding, communities or new media possibilities, to name but a few. This results in the need to think afresh about practice – to take a critical perspective on how things are done, as well as to take inspiration from the most intriguing and promising instances of practice in order to develop new modes of working.

In light of the considerable change underway, the editor of *Museum Practice*, Conal McCarthy, in consultation with us as general editors, faced a task of how to achieve a volume that would cover topics that have become central to consideration of museum practice, while also being sure to include as much as possible of the new directions and ideas that have been emerging in recent years. That this was achieved so well is evident from the resulting volume. The range of topics included and the ways in which they are tackled, provide a sound and also cutting-edge coverage of museum practice.

The International Handbooks in Museum Studies

Collectively, *The International Handbooks in Museum Studies* include over a hundred original, state-of-the-art chapters on museums and museum studies. As such, they are the most comprehensive review to date of the lively and expanding field of museum studies. Written by a wide range of scholars and practitioners – newer voices as well as those already widely esteemed – *The International Handbooks* provide not only extensive coverage of key topics and debates in the museum field, but also make a productive contribution to emerging debates and areas, as well as to suggest how museum studies – and museums – might develop in the future.

The number of excellent contributors able and willing to write on museum topics is itself testimony to the state of the field, as was recognition by the publishers that the field warranted such a substantial work. Bringing together such a range and quantity of new writing about museums was accomplished through the deep knowledge, extensive networks, and sheer labour of the volume editors – Andrea Witcomb and Kylie Message, *Museum Theory*; Conal McCarthy, *Museum Practice*; Michelle Henning, *Museum Media*; and Annie E. Coombes and Ruth B. Phillips, *Museum Transformations*. All enthusiastically took up the mandate to go out and recruit those they thought would be best able to write useful and timely essays on what they defined as the most important topics within their area of remit. Their brief was to look widely for potential contributors, including unfamiliar, as well as familiar, names. We – and they – were especially interested in perspectives from people whose voices have not always been heard within the international museum studies conversation thus far. This breadth is also a feature of the expanded and expanding field itself, as we explain further below.

Diversification and democratization

The editors of the four volumes that constitute *The International Handbooks* are based in four different countries – Australia, New Zealand, the United Kingdom, and Canada; and contributors have their institutional homes in over a dozen more. Yet these numbers alone do not fully convey the trend to diversification that we see in these volumes, and in museum studies more widely. "Internationalization" is a term that might be used but does not, we think, adequately characterize what is involved. Certainly, there is more traffic between nations of ideas about museums and about how to study them. Debates travel from one part of the globe to another, with museums and exhibitions in one location being used as models for emulation or avoidance in another. The massive expansion of professional training in museum studies that has taken place over the past three decades helps establish a shared discourse, not least as many students study away from their home countries or those in which they will later work. So too do texts in and about the field, certain key ones often being found on reading lists in numerous countries and also republished in successive readers. Such developments establish the basis for a conversation capable of transcending borders.

It is evident from the contents of *The International Handbooks of Museum Studies*, however, that the democratization runs deeper than the traffic of discourse and practice across national borders, and, in particular, that the traffic is more multi-directional than it was previously. Not only do contributors have their primary work bases in a range of different countries, and not only do many have experience of training or working in others, they also often give attention – sometimes through the direct engagement of collaborative work or study – to a wide range of groups and populations in a variety of countries, including their own. In doing so, they strive not merely to incorporate but also to learn from and be challenged by people and perspectives that have not been part of mainstream museological debate. The attention to the (not unproblematic) category of the indigenous is especially marked in these *International Handbooks*, most notably in the *Transformations* volume, although it also finds its way into the others. Like attention to other forms of absence from the existing mainstream museum conversation, this is symptomatic of a broader move toward finding alternative ways of seeing and doing, ways that both add to the range of existing possibilities and also, sometimes, unsettle these by showing how, say, particular theorizing or practice relies on unspoken or previously unrecognized assumptions.

Diversification takes other forms too. These volumes are not organized by type of museum – a format that we think restrictive in its lack of recognition of so many shared features and concerns of museums – and do not use this as a classification of content. Nevertheless, it is easy to see that the volumes include a great range of museum kinds, and even of forms that might not always be considered museums, or that challenge the idea of the museum as a physical space. Museums of art, history, and ethnography – and also those more general and eclectic museums that have sometimes been described as encyclopedic – have powered a good deal of museum theorizing and debate, and they are amply represented here. But they are accompanied also by examples from museums of natural history, science, technology, and medicine, as well as heritage sites and out-of- gallery installations. Alongside national museums, which were the backbone of much important theorizing of the role of museums in the making of national identity and citizenship, are numerous examples of smaller museums, some of which are devoted to a specific topic and others of which have a regional or local foundation and focus. These museums may be less well endowed with staff, buildings, or funds, but are nevertheless doing important, even pioneering, work that deserves attention from museum studies. That attention contributes not only to extending the range of types and cases but also helps to illuminate the variety of specific features of museums that need to be taken into account in formulating more comprehensive approaches. As many chapters across the volumes show, one size does not fit all – or, to put it better perhaps, one theoretical perspective or set of guidelines for practice, one apt choice of media or transformative activity, does not fit all types and sizes of museums. Adding more to the mix does not just provide greater coverage or choice but also helps to identify better what is at stake and what might be possible in different kinds of situations, constellations, or conjunctures (to use a word favored in *Museum Theory*). As such, it helps those of us engaged in and with museums to get a better grasp on what is and what might be shared, as well as on what is distinctive and needs to be understood in more fine-grained ways.

Another feature of diversification that deserves comment here is the temporal. There has been a considerable amount of outstanding historical research undertaken in museum studies and the *International Handbooks* both review some of this and contribute further to it. Such work is important in its own terms, helping us to understand better the contexts in which museums emerged and have operated, and the concerns, constraints, personalities, and opportunities in evidence in particular times and places. It also contributes in vital ways to contemporary understandings, both by adding to the range of cases available for analysis and by showing the longer historical trajectories out of which various current approaches and practices emerged. Sometimes – and there are examples in all of the volumes here – their message is salutary, showing that what seemed like an innovation has been tried before, and perhaps with the distance of time allowing a more critical perspective than might feel comfortable today. The past shows change but also continuities and the re-emergence, or even repackaging, of what has gone before.

Disciplinarity and methodology

Research on past museum innovation and practice shows the importance of historical method, and of history as a discipline, within museum studies. This brings us to the wider issue of disciplinarity and methodology. To talk of museum studies as interdisciplinary has become a truism. The volumes here are a clear illustration that those involved in museum studies have been trained in and may have primary institutional locations in a wide range of disciplines and areas of study, including anthropology, archaeology, architecture, area studies, cultural studies, economics, education, geography, literature, management, media studies, political science, and sociology, as well as history and art history. Beyond that, however, they are also carving out new niches, sometimes institutionally recognized, sometimes not, in areas such as digital curation and creative technologies, as well as in art gallery, museum, and heritage studies, in various combinations or alone. Moreover, in addition to disciplines and a multitude of academic specialisms, practitioner contributors bring diverse professional expertise in areas including exhibition design, community engagement, conservation, interpretation, and management.

Alongside the diversity of concepts and methodologies offered by various disciplines and diverse forms of practical expertise, is also the distinctive feature of museum studies – its engagement with the past, present, and future world of museums. Such work, to varying extents, confronts researchers and academics with the actual concerns, predicaments, objects, spaces, media, and people all, in various ways, involved in museum collections and exhibitions. Increasingly, this means actual collaboration, and the development of methodological approaches to enable this. Examples in these volumes include those who consider themselves to be primarily academics, artists, or activists being directly involved in the production of collections, media (e.g., new media apps or forms of display), and exhibitions. The nature of museum work is, inevitably, collaborative, but in some cases it also involves more explicit attempts to work with those who have had little previous engagement in museum worlds and draws on methodology and ethical insight from disciplines such as social and cultural anthropology to do so. Such actual engagement – coupled with what we see as more fluid traffic between academia and museums also powers new forms of theorizing and practice. This productive mobility affords museum studies its characteristic – and, in our view, especially exciting – dynamic.

Organization of the *International Handbooks*

As we originally planned these *International Handbooks*, dividing their coverage into the four volumes of Theory, Practice, Media, and Transformations made good sense as a way of grouping key areas of work within the field. Our idea was that *Theory* would bring together work that showed central areas of theorizing that have shaped museum studies so far, together with those that might do so in the future. We envisaged *Practice* as attending especially to areas of actual museum work, especially those that have tended to be ignored in past theorizing, not in order to try to reinstate a theory/practice division but, rather, to take the opportunity to transcend it through theorizing these too. We saw *Media* as the appropriate label to cover the crucially important area for museums of their architecture, spaces, and uses of diverse media primarily, though not exclusively, for display. *Transformations* was intended to direct its attention especially to some of the most important social, cultural, political, and economic developments that are shaping and look likely to reshape museums in the future.

In many ways, what has resulted fits this original remit. We always knew that there would inevitably be areas of convergence: in particular, that theory can derive from practice, and vice versa; that the development and expansion of social media is propelling some of the most significant transformations in museums, and so forth. Yet it is probably true to say that there are more synergies than we had imagined, perhaps because museum work has itself become more open to change, new ideas and practice, and unconventional practitioners and participants, from what would previously have been considered outside. To make distinctions between practitioners and theorists continues to make sense in some contexts. What we see, however, is an increasing band of critical practitioners and practice-based researchers – those who operate in both worlds, drawing inspiration for new practice from areas of theorizing as well as from adaptations of cases from else-where. Equally they use practice to think through issues such as the nature of objects, the role of media, or sensory potentials.

It is interesting to note that at an analytical level, the volumes all contain chapters that give emphasis to specific cases and argue for the importance of paying close attention to grounded process – what actually happens, where, who, and what is involved. Although not all are informed by theoretical perspectives of actor network theory or assemblage theory, there is much here that recognizes the significance of material forms not just as objects of analysis but as agents in processes themselves. There is also much work across the volumes that gives explicit attention to the affective dimensions of museums, exploring, for example, how different media or spaces might afford certain emotional engagements. The sensory is also given new levels of consideration in what we see as, collectively, a more extensive attempt to really get to grips with the distinctiveness of museums as a medium, as well as with their sheer variety.

Various forms of collaborative engagement with specific groups – sometimes called communities – as well as with individual visitors, is also a notable theme cutting across the various volumes. Certainly, the idea of a generic "audience" or "public" seems to be less present as a central but abstract focus than in the past. Divisions along lines of gender or class are made less frequently than they might have been in earlier critical perspectives – though when they are, this is often done especially well and powerfully, as, for example, in some contributions to the discussion of museum media. Interestingly, and this is a comment on our times as well as on social and political developments in which museums are embroiled, the work with "communities" is framed less in terms of identity politics than would probably have been the case previously. No longer, perhaps, is the issue so much about making presence seen in a museum, increasingly it is more about mutually enriching ways of working together, and about pursuing particular areas or issues of concern, such as those of the environment or future generations. Yet politics is certainly not absent. Not only is the fundamental question about whose voice is represented in the museum a thoroughly political one, the chapters also show political concerns over relatively subtle matters such as methodology and reformulations of intimacy, as well as over questions of sponsorship, money-flow in the art world, the development of mega-museums in Gulf states, environmental destruction, and so forth. Indeed, there is a strong current of work that positions the museum as an activist institution and that shows its potential as such – something perhaps indicative of at least one future direction that more museums might take.

One thing that is clear from these volumes, however, is that there is no single trajectory that museums have taken in the past. Neither is there a single track along which they are all heading, nor one that those of us who have contributed would agree that they should necessarily all take. The diversity of museums themselves, as well as of those who work in, on, and with them, and of the perspectives that these volumes show can be brought to bear upon them – as well as their very various histories, collections, contexts, personnel, publics, and ambitions – has inspired the diversified museum studies represented in these *International Handbooks*. Our hope is that this more diversified museum studies can contribute not only to new ways of understanding museums but also to new, and more varied, forms of practice within them – and to exciting, challenging futures, whatever these might be.

Acknowledgments

Producing these *International Handbooks of Museum Studies* has probably been a bigger and more demanding project than any of us had anticipated at the outset. Assembling together so many authors across four different volumes, and accommodating so many different timetables, work dynamics, styles, and sensitivities has been a major task over more years than we like to recall for both us as general editors, and even more especially for the editors of our four volumes: Andrea Witcomb, Kylie Message, Conal McCarthy, Michelle Henning, Annie E. Coombes, and Ruth B. Phillips. As general editors, our first thanks must be to the volume editors, who have done a remarkable task of identifying and eliciting so many insightful and illuminating contributions from such a wide field, and of working with authors – not all of whom were experienced in academic writing and many of whom were already grappling with hectic schedules – to coax the best possible chapters from them. We thank our volume editors too for working with us and what may sometimes have seemed overly interventionist assistance on our part in our push to make the volumes work together, as well as individually, and for all contributions, as well as the *International Handbooks* as a whole, to be a substantial contribution to the field. We also thank our volume editors for sharing so much good humor and so many cheering messages along the way, turning what sometimes felt like relentless chasing and head-aching over deadlines into something much more human and enjoyable. All of the contributors also deserve immense thanks too, of course, for joining the convoy and staying the journey. We hope that it feels well worth it for all concerned. Without you – editors and contributors – it couldn't have happened.

There is also somebody else without whom it couldn't have happened. This is Gill Whitley. Gill joined the project in 2012 as Project Editor. In short, she transformed our lives through her impeccable organization and skillful diplomacy, directly contacting contributors to extract chapters from them, setting up systems to keep us all on track with where things were up to, and securing many of the picture permissions. She has been a pleasure to work with and we are immensely grateful to her.

The idea for a series of *International Handbooks of Museum Studies* came from Jayne Fargnoli at Wiley Blackwell and we are grateful to her for this and being such a great cheerleader for the project. She read a good deal of the work as it came in and knowing that this only increased her enthusiasm for the project boosted everyone's energy as we chased deadlines. We also thank other staff at Wiley Blackwell for their role in the production processes, including, most recently, Jake Opie, for helping to at last allow us to bring out the individual volumes in paperback format.

Because of its extended nature and because things don't always happen according to initial timetables, editorial work like this often has to be fitted into what might otherwise be leisure time or time allocated for other things. Luckily, both of our Mikes (Mike Beaney and Mike Leahy) were sympathetic, not least as both have deeply occupying work of their own; and we thank them for being there for us when we needed them.

Lastly, we would like to thank each other. We have each benefited from the other's complementary expertise and networks, from the confidence of having that insightful second opinion, and from the sharing of the load. Having somebody else with whom to experience the frustrations and joys, the tribulations and amusements, has made it so much more fun. Not only has this helped to keep us relatively sane, but it has also made *The International Handbooks of Museum Studies* so much better than they would otherwise have been.

Sharon Macdonald and Helen Rees Leahy,
August 2014 and July 2019

INTRODUCTION
Grounding Museum Studies: Introducing Practice

Conal McCarthy

Practice, broadly speaking, is what we do, and more specifically what we as practitioners do in particular practice communities and how others engage with this practice.

Higgs 2010, 1

When a collection manager documents an object, a curator writes a label, an educator leads a tour group, a director attends a board meeting, or a visitor walks through an exhibition – these are the forms of museum practice with which the public are familiar. But there are other kinds of museum practice hidden from view, taking place at different levels of the institution: for example, the policy framework, the marketing campaign, the collection catalog, the exhibition design, the funds development plan, the conservation lab, the public program, or the mission statement.

This book is about all these kinds of museum practice – the visible and the hidden – or "what we as practitioners do" (Higgs 2010, 1). "Museum practice" refers to the broad range of professional work in museums, from the functions of management, collections, exhibitions, and programs to the varied activities that take place within these diverse and complex organizations, as well as indicating a recognizable sphere of work. Museum "practice" is also sometimes differentiated from museum theory – as is the case in the volumes that make up these *International Handbooks of Museum Studies* – drawing especial attention to what actually goes on in museum work. As do the other volumes, including *Museum Theory*, however, *Museum Practice* recognizes the inevitable – and productive – overlap between theory and practice.

Gerard Corsane proposes that museum work can be thought of as a *process* of communication moving from resources at one end to public outputs at the other (Corsane 2005, 3, figure 1.1). This functional process model of museums has been employed in the organization of this book in four parts as follows.

Part I: Priorities

In this first part we hear from contributors, most of them experienced professionals, who discuss how museums go about deciding what it is they are going to do through the "top" level of museum management, policy frameworks, and ethical guidelines. The chapters consider issues to do with setting the strategic direction of museums through mission, vision, leadership, and governance, changing ideas about ethics and what museums should do, debates about the measurement of performance, and shifts in legislation and policy guidelines. This section also contains a chapter on audience development, a critical dimension of museum work that increasingly shapes how institutions today set their priorities.

Part II: Resources

In Corsane's process model of museum, gallery, and heritage work, "resources" refers broadly to the "stuff" that professionals collect, use, and research, which they then subject to various processes of interpretation (Part III) before they are communicated to the public in the form of various outputs (Part IV). In this section, then, contributors discuss those objects, collections, and other materials that can be understood as the "resources" that museums contain, whether it is the objects at the heart of collecting institutions or the curators, collection managers, and other staff who acquire, research, care for, and manage them. Here readers will find several chapters on collections in one form or another: collections planning, collections care and management, collection development, and collections management systems, and a chapter reviewing recent shifts in conservation practice. This section also considers the financial resources that make all this work possible – museum economics – plus a chapter on critical issues to do with sponsorship, marketing, and branding.

Part III: Processes

In Part III, the focus is the internal "processes" of various kinds within museums that develop and deliver the resources discussed above into outputs or products delivered to the publics considered in the last part of the book. A group of chapters considers the development of exhibitions, trends in permanent and temporary museum exhibitions, and exhibition design and display. Two chapters survey developments in curatorial theory and practice, seen here as connected to but not limited by collections and exhibitions, in which curators acquire, select, arrange, research, present, and interpret things for people to look at. This section also considers repatriation and restitution, including of human remains, a process that is assuming increasing importance for museum practice, raising, as it does, questions about the very nature of museums, the ethics of collections and displays, and relationships with source communities.

Part IV: Publics

In the last part of *Museum Practice* we come to the space in which the products, created by the contemporary museum at work, circulate in the public realm. Though the exhibitions considered in the previous section could also be seen as one of the most obvious of museum outputs, in "Publics" we look at a more diverse and diffuse range of topics – from visitor research and community, to interpretation, learning and public programs, and digital heritage – which explore how these are used, consumed, mediated, and responded to by the audiences that the museum addresses.

It should be clear from the outline above that this volume is structured as an anatomy of the contemporary museum in terms of its conventional organizational divisions and roles. When people learn how to work in a museum, they have to master knowledge and skills considered necessary according to current professional guidelines. This takes various forms, such as workplace-based training, university courses, International Council of Museums (ICOM) curricula, and manuals and books.[1] The professionalization of museum work has expanded considerably over the past two decades, and training programs for museum professionals are not only increasing in number but are also diversifying and adapting in response to a "changing museum landscape" (Livingstone and Davis 2013, 12–13). Professional museum bodies often talk of "best practice" as a clear set of rules of dos and don'ts: do wear gloves; don't allow board members to make management decisions; don't sell collections items; and so forth. Codes of ethics attempt to establish the essentials of "good" museum practice.[2]

An historical overview of professionalization in museums has been provided by Patrick Boylan (2006), who also gives an overview of the role played internationally by ICOM, and nationally by professional organizations: the Museums Association in the United Kingdom, the American Alliance of Museums in the United States, and their equivalents elsewhere.[3] Any account of museum practice has to take into account the membership associations and professional bodies that are such an important part of the framework within which museums operate, as well as legislation, policies, and regulatory environment. We should, however, be wary of definitions, codes, and laws, useful as they are for raising standards and monitoring performance. As Simon Knell cautioned, these "artifacts of professionalism" can restrict practice, instead of advocating a "creative professionalism" that is more open to change (Knell 2013). Different professionals in different kinds of museums in different parts of the world do not always agree on what museum practice consists of, and might even see the setting of standards, processes of accreditation, and other bureaucratic guidelines as exclusive boundaries that may stifle responsiveness to change. There may be disagreement over specific aspects of museum work or even over basic principles, as well as over what universal best practice might be.

Rather than viewing museum practice simply as the best way of doing things in museums, then, this volume seeks to recognize the diversity of perspectives, to open up questions and to show a variety of ways in which they might be addressed. To introduce it, I provide some background to how museum practice has been dealt with in museum studies thus far and suggest how it might be better integrated into research on and in the museum. Then I consider the relationship between theory and practice and argue that together the university and museum sectors can collaborate in teaching, research, training, and practice. In the third section I review recent "practice theory" and assess its value for an integrated model of museum studies that is grounded in current museum practice, a model showcased in this volume. Lastly I briefly preview the contents of the four parts of the book – Priorities, Resources, Processes, Publics – which describes the contemporary museum at work.

The place of practice within museum studies

While there has been much useful academic research on contemporary museums, there is much less coverage of museum practice – especially of the practicalities of museum work – in the museum studies literature. The incorporation of social and cultural theory into museum studies from the 1980s was necessary for strengthening the field, and has produced much work of a high quality that has added immeasurably to the breadth and depth of the subject (Macdonald and Fyfe 1996), though it has been suggested that the introduction of more theoretical perspectives has contributed to a disconnect between research and practice (Grewcock 2013). Some critics have even claimed that the explosion of academic and critical writing on museums has produced little that is directly useful to those who work in them or to those who use them (Spiess 1996; Rice 2003; Starn 2005; McCarthy 2007); and others argue that university museum studies courses with an emphasis on academic theory may be a poor preparation for the workplace (Davies 2007; Duff, Cherry, and Sheffield 2010).

Much of the academic work on museums has been written by university scholars who may have little experience working in the sector. Unfortunately not nearly as much has been written about their work by professionals themselves (who are perhaps so busy doing it that they do not have time to write about it). Some commentators point out that there is little incentive for professionals to read widely and write critically about their practice, and that many museums lack a research culture, let alone a framework to define, fund, and manage research as universities now do. They argue that museums can gain much from the strategic and structured way in which university-based scholars go about their research, just as the academy would learn a great deal by working with museums and galleries whose collections, education, and interpretation programs, not to mention their demonstrable social impact, offer a model for engaged public service (McCarthy 2012; Boddington, Boys, and Speight 2013).

One of the key benefits that university research in museum studies *can* offer museums is critical analysis. Much institutional discourse continues to present museums as if they were innocent of social, political, and economic forces. As academic writing on museums – as well as the experience of numerous cases – has made clear, however, much of what goes on in museums is unavoidably embroiled in power relations. They are so, though, in specific, localized ways in which actual ongoing practice matters. This is well recognized by Anthony Shelton, who provides an afterword in this volume, in his recent manifesto for critical museology. This takes what he calls "operational museology" as its object of study. According to Shelton, such museology tends to "construct ... the museum's institutional authority on an uncritical acceptance of empirical methodologies anchored in theories of objectivity" (2013, 11). Drawing on Pierre Bourdieu's field theory, Shelton argues, by contrast, that "museological practices should be understood in relation to the field in which they unfold." This would mean paying more attention to institutional concerns and work practices, thus leading, he suggests, to "establishing a theory of practice ... from which a practice of theory can emerge" (2013, 14). "Continued separation between the academy and museum and between their different traditions of scholarship is no longer justifiable or desirable," writes Shelton (this volume), "and the division between practice and theory needs to be flatly rejected." For museum practice, he adds, the problem is not too much theory, but "working through the implications of theory and criticism to help re-define museum operations, purposes, resources, as well as ... providing perspectives on new issues" (Shelton this volume).

It is precisely this task that the current volume sets itself, to provide a bottom-up outline of current practice throughout the contemporary museum from govern-ance, management, and policy, to collections, exhibitions, and programs. In order to ground museum studies in the everyday work of museums, we need more research within all areas of the museum across its varied roles and functions – lead-ership practice, repatriation practice, collection management practice, community engagement practice, interpretation practice, and so on. The chapters in this book make a start on this, as authors conceive of each of these sub-topics as *practices* in their own right, allowing us to build up a detailed empirical picture of the contem-porary museum.

Reviewing the literature: the state of the art

The most influential readers, anthologies, and edited collections that have defined the field of museum studies over the past 20 years have been preoccupied with issues such as the politics of representation in collecting and display, giving some attention too to the history and theory of collections and collecting (Karp and Lavine 1991; Karp, Lavine, and Kreamer 1992; Preziosi and Farrago 2004; Carbonell 2004; Karp et al. 2006). These works, and much of the material pub-lished in the major journals in the field, tend, however, to talk generally about cultural practices *in* museums, rather than *professional practice* as such. A small amount of work provides insight into the specifics of process and internal condi-tions of museum work (Gillespie 2001; Macdonald 2002); with some prominent positions, such as that of the director/CEO (Janes and Sandell 2007) or curator (Marincola 2001; Townsend 2003; Graham and Cook 2010), receiving extensive attention. Even this, however, tends to be directed primarily toward the content of collections/exhibitions, or individual experience, than the actual *practice* of curating/exhibiting/managing itself; though there are some notable exceptions, such as anthropologist Christina Kreps, who describes curatorship as a "social practice" (2003).

More recently, there has been an attempt to bring academic work on a more comprehensive cross-section of museum practice together with research in the form of readers (i.e., volumes of work already published on a topic, with chapters not all necessarily directly concerned with museums): see for example, Caple (2011) on conservation, Parry (2010) on digital media, Watson (2007) on communities, Knell (2007) on material culture and Janes and Sandell (2007) on management and marketing. Texts by Corsane (2005) and Marstine (2005) pay some attention to practice in selected chapters (e.g., Stam 2005) though Marstine focuses more on art galleries and Corsane on heritage management than on museums broadly speaking.

Nevertheless, for many areas of museum practice, we do not yet have a developed body of literature, and significant gaps remain. For example, there is scant attention to collections care and management, despite the fact that these are critical functions in most museums. This volume sets out to build a research base in some of these areas, establishing a foundation for further work. This includes chapters on museum economics (Silberberg and Lord, Chapter 7), marketing and sponsorship (Chong, Chapter 8), audience development (Black, Chapter 6), and museum value (Scott, Chapter 5; Chapman, Chapter 12). Some areas of museum work do, of course, have extensive literatures – including interpretation, education, and learning, and of course visitor studies – perhaps because they are linked to well-established traditions of professional practice in the fields of education, teaching, and leisure studies (Hirsch and Silverman 2000; Hooper-Greenhill 2006; Hein 2006; Falk, Dierking, and Foutz 2007). Museum educators have long conceived of their work as a distinctive practice, and have always explored ways to theorize it (Rice 2000; Hein 2012), for example, Kevin Coffee (2007) who analyzes the visitor experience as a "social practice." In this volume Reeve and Woollard (Chapter 24) provide an authoritative overview of this extensive research in museum education and learning, identifying current and breaking trends in the field.

It should also be acknowledged that outside of "museum studies" narrowly defined, work in art history and curatorial studies, and art criticism, gives attention to "practice," often referring to the artistic work(s) of an artist/artists (Schjeldahl 2011, 105), or to the activities of curators in relation to the content of exhibitions, rather than to the explicit ways in which they go about collecting, selecting, interpreting, or displaying art. Arnold and Norton-Westbrook (this volume, Chapter 14 and 15, respectively) draw on this literature in their chapters on curatorial theory and practice but interrogate more closely the how and the why as well as what curators do in the museum.

Another recent trend in the existing museological literature is the documentation of radical social practice in museums (Goodnow and Skartveit 2010; Sandell and Nightingale 2013), or what museums *should* be doing, a trend that Carbonell has referred to, somewhat skeptically, as the "prescriptive turn" in museum studies (2012, 11). We do not yet know how far these interventions have gone beyond the front-of-house areas where they are usually found, though other *International Handbook* volumes suggest that inroads have been made in transforming museums as a whole.

The best coverage to date of museum practice as such can be found in Gail Anderson's collection *Reinventing the Museum* (2004; see also Anderson 2012), which includes shorter pieces from experienced professionals covering a wide range of subjects. Literature with a more practical focus includes a useful survey by Kavanagh (1994), handbooks by Edson and Dean (1994), and by Ambrose and Paine (2012), and the manuals of Barry Lord and Gail Lord and colleagues (2002; 2007; 2009). Then there is the "gray" literature made up of unpublished internal induction materials, and a few published guidelines and manuals, which give a step-by-step account of particular technical tasks such as registration and conservation (Thompson 1984; Buck and Gilmore 2011). This small body of writing on museum practice falls somewhere between the practical material that is produced and used within the sector, and academic museum studies. As I explain below, *Museum Practice* is positioned alongside this literature, but with a critical edge; it aims for a synthesis of museum studies and practice, what Rice calls the "useful middle-ground" between theory and experience resulting in "more nuanced theory and a more thoughtful practice" (Rice 2003, 77). As examples in this volume the chapters by Barry Lord on governance (Chapter 2), Ted Silberberg and Gail Lord (Chapter 7) on museum economics, and David Dean on exhibition project management draw on this kind of material and bring it into the frame of museum studies.

In this book I set out to bring together the two strands of writing about museums: academic museum studies and writing about museum practice. *Museum Practice* is therefore an academic project that reaches out to the museum sector. My goal is to avoid a hypertheorized critique of museums from the outside, aiming instead for an informed internal account from professionals, academics, and critics in touch with the realities of everyday work in museums. In her Introduction to the *Companion to Museum Studies*, the inspiration for this volume and series, Sharon Macdonald describes an expanded museum studies that brings together the academy and the museum and combines the new museology's emphasis on theory with the old museology's practical concerns (2006, 8). She calls for both "expansion and specificity," and a "reconnecting of the critical study of the museum with some of the 'how to' concerns that the new museology saw itself as having superseded" (2006, 8). Likewise Rhiannon Mason in the same book argues that we need an integrated "theoretical museology" (Mason 2006, 29). Research located "at the *intersection* of theory and practice, as opposed to a mode of critique which stands outside looking inward," she argues, "is best suited to the complexity of museums as cultural phenomena"

(Mason 2006, 29). Theory and practice are "anything but separate spheres," Mason continues, but are "mutually informing and intimately connected." She adds: "Recognition of the importance of research to practice and vice versa will only enrich both academics' and practitioners' understanding of museums" (Mason 2006, 30). It is the aim of *Museum Practice* to provide such enrichment.

Understanding practice

The bringing together of theory and practice in order to enrich and understand the latter, requires attention to both analytical models and also to modes of knowledge transmission. In museum studies, there has been a discernible movement toward *integrated* models for the study of museum processes (Corsane 2005, 3). In one of the most successful readers of museum studies, which reaches across the divide between academics and professionals, and between museums, galleries, and heritage, Gerard Corsane provides a model of museum work as an overall process which I employ in this book (2005, 3). Corsane proposes that museum work can be thought of as a process of communication moving from resources at one end (objects, collections, information) to outputs at the other (exhibitions, programs, publications), with the central flow of decisions and activities performed as processes of meaning making and interpretation. The value of this model is not only its simplicity, but also the way it brings together different areas of the institution into a public-facing continuum. Heritage, museum, and gallery studies, writes Corsane, are not just cross-disciplinary but postdisciplinary (Corsane 2005, xiii). This fruitfully suggests that the study of, and work in, museums needs to be focused on the institutions themselves as a site of analysis, and not simply applied *from* university *to* museums in the old theory/practice dualism.

Other scholars have taken up the challenge to return to empirical research on and in the museum. The authors of *Post-critical Museology* argue that "museum professionals are rightfully wary of academic researchers who often know little of the practical pressures and exigencies of making an art museum 'work' successfully" (Dewdney, Dibosa, and Walsh 2013, 16). This leads to an "epistemic fault line between the museum and the academy" where the museum is seen merely as a "concrete operational sphere considered as the object of abstract reflection by the academy" (2013, 221). According to them, museum staff are often anti theory because it seems that academic theory only produces more theory, but professionals are equally locked into a "reproduction of professional operational practices without end" which lacks "criticality and reflexivity." For Dewdney, Dibosa, and Walsh, the solution to this impasse is a radical one. Museum studies is limited, they argue, because the insights offered by the critique of the museum and the politics of representation are now "exhausted." Critical museology is "problematic" because it emerged from a "distanced elaboration of theory rather than from an embedded working through of museum practices"

(2013, 224). In contrast, their research project at Tate, London was situated in the "space between the production of knowledge about the museum produced by the academy and the reproduction of knowledge in the practices of the museum" (2013, 16), including the "know-how of operational practices and know-why of strategic knowledge" (2013, 221).

Developing a postcritical museum studies for the twenty-first century, one that incorporates practice as an integral element in the study of museums, involves not only (re)fashioning theoretical frameworks, and particularly the social and cultural dimensions of theory, but also taking account of the diversity of current practice. Alongside the theorizing of museum work, in this volume scholars attempt to take current practice seriously as an object of analysis in its own right and produce work that reflects the inside view of practitioners.

Also important for developing a new museum studies is the training of museum practitioners in partnership with academic museum studies. As Lois Silverman and Mark O'Neill (2012, 195) point out, some traditionalists working in museums do not appreciate the value of theory at all, seeing it as the abstract product of ivory-tower academics with little relevance to the demands of their working day. Yet, because museum work often leaves little opportunity for reflection on practice, the challenge is for academia to help provide this in order to produce a "deeper and more complex understanding of the museum experience" (2012, 193–194). Part of the problem is how and where the learning takes place – is it best configured as training located in the museum or scholarship in the university? John E. Simmons (2006) writes that in the United States museum studies has matured as a form of university-based training, but there is still a need for standards in professional training that are endorsed by professional museum organizations – a point demonstrated by his chapter in this volume, which sketches out the history, theory, and practice of collection care and management. Simmons believes this problem can be overcome by implementing Suzanne MacLeod's conceptual model which combines these elements (Simmons 2006, 124, figure 2). This model has been visualized in a diagram below (see Figure 0.1).

The longstanding tension between theory and practice has therefore been partially resolved by an "integrated understanding of museum studies as training, education, research, and practice … in relation to the profession as a whole" (MacLeod 2001, 53). University-based museum studies (and other disciplines) and museum-based practice should form a single hinge between town and gown. MacLeod points out that theory/practice is a false split; in its place she advocates theory-as-practice and vice versa:

> The museum practice dimension of museum studies suggests both the incorporation of research findings and training and education (however formal or informal) into the day-to-day practices of the museum as well as the integration of practice-based research findings into training, education and other types of research projects. (2001, 57)

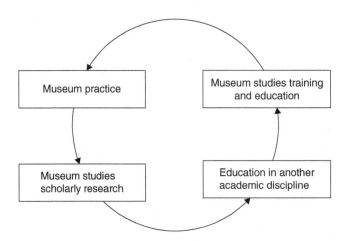

FIGURE 0.1   Integrated model of museum studies incorporating research, practice, training, and education (after Simmons 2006, 124).

This model allows for flexible relationships between the museum sector and training providers – professionals in the field become researchers, and academics are immersed in practice – so that everyone collaborates in the service of common goals. An appealing synthesis of research-led practice and practical theory, it demonstrates that museum studies is "more than the study of museums" (MacLeod 2001, 58). There is strong potential for synergies that can fill the apparent gap: university courses can be aligned with sub-degree industry training, so that short courses and workshops in museums can link up to and count toward degree programs with their placements and internships. This strategic positioning of sector and tertiary provider is in line with international moves to identify standards, core competencies, and a central body of knowledge in order to provide uniformity of skills across art galleries, museum, and heritage organizations (see n. 1 below), and also museums, libraries, archives, and similar organizations (Salzburg Curriculum 2013). There is the potential here – already being realized in Canada, for example (see Carter, Castle, and Soren 2011; Dubuc 2011; Teather 1991; 2009) – for universities and the museum sector to work together in partnership to provide a continuous and embedded learning stream that goes all the way from introductory skills in museum-based training to postgraduate degrees, much as teacher-training for the education sector is integrated within universities.

Practice theory: rethinking professional work

We need to be mindful while focusing on professional practice not to naturalize it as an activity that is somehow beyond the level of inquiry. Evidence-based practice – trying to build future approaches on "what works" – is a defensible approach to "developing" the work of museum professionals, but it risks reproducing the status quo and is often applied in technocratic ways that fail to address the complexity of museum culture. Sometimes unfettered professionalism can be self-interested and lacks the longer view afforded by history and theory. Ironically, untrained "amateurs" are more open to doing things a different way because they are unrestricted by professional guidelines, as was demonstrated in the New Zealand case by the museum resistance to incorporating Indigenous Māori perspectives on the collecting and display of their ancestral culture (McCarthy 2011).

Too often professional practice in museums is seen in somewhat narrow terms as a set of established working methods or ways of doing things that is officially sanctioned and formally described. Here, I want to draw on broader understandings of the term "practice," as reflected in dictionary definitions, which describe the *practicing* of a profession as the ongoing pursuit of a craft, or the practicing of a skill to become proficient in it; and to extend this through a critical framework of practice theory that sees practices as the *things that people do* (Turner 1994). This emphasis on practices (plural) is important in the following chapters where professionals critically reflect on aspects of their practice in the contemporary museum.

To help to denaturalize practice and recognize its plurality, there is some useful academic work that might be drawn upon. What is now called "practice theory" has a long academic genealogy with the work of sociologists such as Bourdieu, who sought to balance the study of people and structures by paying more attention to human action. Bourdieu talked about the "field" of practice, structured social spaces in which agents act according to their "feel" (habitus) for the "game" (Bourdieu 1977). For anthropologists, analyzing cultural practices provided a more complete account of the social world, showing that people are not simply victims of social and economic structures but exercise agency (Sahlins 2005). As Sherry Ortner argues, practice theory situates cultural processes in the grounded social relations of people and institutions, revealing the dialectical connections between the practices of social actors on the ground and the systems that constrain them but which are also capable of being transformed by them (Ortner 2006, 16).

The work of several scholars, responsible for the "practice turn" in contemporary social theory, also provide building blocks for a more theorized model of museum practice. For example, Theodore Schatzki calls practice a "set of actions," but also a "nexus of doings and sayings" which combines the things that people say and write as well as do (Schatzki, Cetina, and Savigny 2001, 48, 53). This "block" or complex of "body/knowledge/things" is understandable not just to those carrying out the practice but also to observers as "a routinized way in which bodies are moved, objects are handled, subjects are treated, things are described and the world is understood" (Reckwitz 2002, 249–250). As Reckwitz puts it: "Practice theory 'decentres' mind, texts and conversation. Simultaneously, it shifts bodily movements, things, practical knowledge and routine to the centre of its vocabulary" (2002, 259).

The turn to practice, seen in much recent work in science and technology studies, has much to offer the study of museums by tempering the preoccupation of cultural theory with discourse, language, and meaning. Attention to practice, seen as emergent and performative (Pickering 1995), allows scholar-practitioners to be more attentive to the complex organizational interplay of things, people, and organizations with their constantly changing networks of social and material agency. Analyzing scientific practice in laboratories as the "specific, repeatable sequence of activities on which scientists rely in their daily work" (1995, 4), Pickering highlights "the emergence in time of resistances," and "the success or failure of 'accommodations' to resistances." This "temporal structuring of practice as a dialectic of resistance and accommodation" is called the "mangle of practice" (1995, xi). A broad relational approach to museum practice as a messy process of modeling, planning, failures, compromises, and solutions, a back-and-forth "dance" of agency between human and nonhuman actors, can be seen in many of the contributions to this volume. Chapters by several authors (see especially Jimson on interpretive planning, Chapter 23; Dean on exhibition production, Chapter 16; and Pickering on repatriation processes, Chapter 20) speak of trials, experiments, and successive phases of development, grounded in specific sites and circumstances, in which people, objects, and institutions are mangled together in complex, ongoing struggles to realize their goals in the midst of all manner of social, economic, and environmental forces.

What does practice theory have to offer the study of professional practice/s? Theorizing museum work as a *social practice* brings a more diverse range of professional activities into view as important arenas of analysis. The chapters in this volume explore a wide array of practice, from the public relations, community engagement, visitor research, exhibitions, and public programs found "front of house" (Chong, Davidson, Young, Whitelaw, and Beier-de Haan, Reeve and Woollard, Jimson) to the planning, collections, conservation, and curatorial practice that go on "back of house" (Gardner, Simmons, Merriman, Arnold, Norton-Westbrook, Sully). Some of the chapters deal with topics behind the scenes that are perhaps not appreciated by outside viewers or visitors: for example, exhibition development (Dean), exhibition design (Spock), and repatriation and restitution (Bienkowski; Pickering), as well as others previously mentioned, such as economics and finance (Silberberg and Lord), and value and measurement (Scott), while others touch on topics that are vitally important but not widely scrutinized in museum studies, such as policy and legislation (Selwood and Davies), mission and purpose (Fleming), and collection management systems (Chapman).

Practice theory also helps us see how the everyday doings and sayings of professionals in museums is not simply a codified activity but a constantly evolving, lived phenomenon that is bound up with unequal social relations. An awareness of the social and political responsibility of museum work is essential so that museum practice does not become atomized, self-interested, and conservative. The museum profession still requires standards and structured professional development, but a grounded theory of museum practice provides a more balanced, flexible, and fluid counter to the tendency to freeze professional work in rules, and a reminder of the world beyond the workplace. Politics is at least implicit in many of the chapters in this volume but is more central to some, including Selwood and Davies on regulatory frameworks, Chong on arts marketing, and Jimson on exhibition interpretation, concept development, and writing. Both Nightingale and Shelton highlight the politics of practice in their Afterwords, Nightingale in particular reviewing the "continuing struggle for diversity and equality."

By foregrounding action and performance, and by exploring human patterns of behavior in the workplace, practice theory reveals embodied actions, meaning formed by doing, and the performance of everyday work. This has the capacity to make practitioners aware of aspects of their practice that they might have overlooked or deemed inconsequential. While much research remains to be done, this volume begins to address this for several areas of museum work: see for example the chapters by Wellington and Oliver (Chapter 25) on the practice of digital heritage in museums and related sectors, Merriman's strategy for reviving disciplinary collecting (Chapter 11), the models for new ethics-based museum practice presented by Marstine, Dodd, and Jones after collaborative research with practitioners (Chapter 4), and the points raised by Arnold (Chapter 14) and Norton-Westbrook (Chapter 15) concerning "new" curatorial practice (based on seminars, surveys, and interviews). It seems to me that there is an urgent need for this engaged practice-based research because the sector in many countries, especially outside of Canada, the United States, and the United Kingdom, is still rather fragmented with workforces who come to museums from different backgrounds (usually without degrees in museum studies) and with little sense of unified professional identity.

As well as the traditional focus on the *content* of museum collections and *style* of exhibitions, then, we need more research on *what people do*: in-depth empirical studies of staff at work in a greater variety of jobs and functions within the museum, not just directors, curators, and educators (on this point see: Higgs, McAllister, and Whiteford 2009). In the chapters that follow, contributors fill in these gaps in museum practice: including fundraising, retail and entry charges, trust boards and local government, registration, collection care and storage, project management, exhibition design and display, leadership and management, learning and public programs, and many other roles, jobs, and processes *across* the organization.

One way of advancing this agenda is to reconceive aspects of current museum practice as research.[4] This need not be restricted to the typically self-directed, historical or theoretical academic inquiry, or to the rather limited internal desktop "research" and reporting conducted within museums, but should be directed at the *whole* of the operations of the institution, and conducted in ways that are accessible, strategic, and relevant to a broad audience of professionals, stakeholders, and public. Good examples are provided in this volume by Merriman (Chapter 11), who talks about disciplinary research and collecting as a strategic and thematic exercise for the whole museum, by Gardner (Chapter 9) who puts a case for an intellectual rationale for developmental collections planning, and by Davidson (Chapter 22) who sees visitor research underpinning all the museum's work rather than as simply a crude marketing exercise. If museums are the site of research and analysis, and if the findings of this research inform university teaching and professional development programs, then practice will become a more important part of museum studies, grounding and consolidating it to serve better academics, students, professionals, and indeed museums themselves. It is hoped that the chapters in this volume are a step toward this goal.

Notes

1   ICOM provides guidance on professional education through ICTOP (International Committee for the Training of Personnel), which was founded in 1968. See http://network.icom.museum/ictop/L/10, accessed September 12, 2014. See also "Special Report: Training Museum Professionals." *ICOM News* 66 (2013): 12–23.
2   For the ICOM code of ethics, see http://icom.museum/the-vision/code-of-ethics, accessed September 12, 2014.
3   See Boylan 2006. For the Museums Association see http://www.museumsassociation.org. For the American Alliance of Museums see http://www.aam-us.org. For the Canadian Museums Association see http://www.museums.ca. For Museums Australia see http://www.museumsaustralia.org.au/site. For Museums Aotearoa see http://www.museumsaotearoa.org.nz. All accessed September 12, 2014.
4   On the question of museums and research see Poulot 2013. For ideas on museum exhibitions as research see Herle 2013, and on collections and collecting, see Gosden and Larsen 2007.

References

Ambrose, Timothy, and Crispin Paine. 2012. *Museum Basics*, 3rd ed. London: Routledge.

Anderson, Gail, ed. 2004. *Reinventing the Museum: Historical and Contemporary Perspectives on the Paradigm Shift*. Lanham, MD: AltaMira.

Anderson, Gail. 2012. *Reinventing the Museum: The Evolving Conversation on the Paradigm Shift*. Lanham, MD: AltaMira.

Boddington, Anne, Jos Boys, and Catherine Speight, eds. 2013. *Museums and Higher Education Working Together: Challenges and Opportunities*. Farnham, UK: Ashgate.

Bourdieu, Pierre. 1977. *Outline of a Theory of Practice*. Translated by R. Nice. Cambridge: Cambridge University Press.

Boylan, Patrick J. 2006. "The Museum Profession." In *A Companion to Museum Studies*, edited by Sharon Macdonald, 415–430. Malden, MA: Blackwell.

Buck, Rebecca A., and Jean Allman Gilmore. 2011. *Museum Registration Methods*, 5th ed. Chicago: American Library Association.

Caple, Chris, ed. 2011. *Preventive Conservation in Museums*. London: Routledge.

Carbonell, Bettina Messias, ed. 2004. *Museum Studies: An Anthology of Contexts*. Malden, MA: Blackwell.

Carbonell, Bettina Messias, ed. 2012. *Museum Studies: An Anthology of Contexts*, 2nd ed. Malden, MA: Wiley-Blackwell.

Carter, Jennifer, Christine Castle, and Barbara Soren. 2011. "Introduction: Taking Stock – Museum Studies and Museum Practices in Canada." *Museum Management and Curatorship* 26(5): 415–420.

Coffee, Kevin. 2007. "Audience Research and the Museum Experience as Social Practice." *Museum Management and Curatorship* 22(4): 377–389.

Corsane, Gerard, ed. 2005. *Heritage, Museums and Galleries: An Introductory Reader*. London: Routledge.

Davies, Maurice. 2007. "The Tomorrow People: Entry to the Museum Workforce." Report to the Museums Association and the University of East Anglia. Accessed September 12, 2014. http://www.museumsassociation.org/download?id=13718.

Dewdney, Andrew, David Dibosa, and Victoria Walsh. 2013. *Post-critical Museology: Theory and Practice in the Art Museum*. London: Routledge.

Dubuc, Elise. 2011. "Museum and University Mutations: The Relationship between Museum Practices and Museum Studies in the Era of Interdisciplinarity, Professionalisation, Globalisation and New Technologies." *Museum Management and Curatorship* 26(5): 497–508.

Duff, Wendy, Joan Cherry, and Rebecka Sheffield. 2010. "'Creating a Better Understanding of Who We Are': A Survey of Graduates of a Museum Studies Program." *Museum Management and Curatorship* 25(4): 361–381.

Edson, Gary, and David Dean. 1994. *The Handbook for Museums*. London: Routledge.

Falk, John, Lynn D. Dierking, and Susan Foutz. 2007. *In Principle, in Practice: Museums as Learning Institutions*. Lanham, MD: AltaMira.

Gillespie, Richard. 2001. "Making an Exhibition: One Gallery, One Thousand Objects, One Million Critics." *Meanjin* 60(4): 118–119.

Goodnow, Katherine, and Hanne-Lovise Skartveit, eds. 2010. *Changes in Museum Practice: New Media, Refugees and Participation*. London: Berghahn.

Gosden, Chris, and Frances Larsen. 2007. *Knowing Things: Exploring the Collections at the Pitt Rivers Museum*. Oxford: Oxford University Press.

Graham, Beryl, and Sarah Cook. 2010. *Rethinking Curating: Art after New Media*. Cambridge, MA: MIT Press.

Grewcock, Duncan. 2013. *Doing Museology Differently*. London: Routledge.

Hein, George E. 2006. "Museum Education." In *A Companion to Museum Studies*, edited by Sharon Macdonald, 340–352. Malden, MA: Blackwell.

Hein, George E. 2012. *Progressive Museum Practice: John Dewey and Democracy*. Walnut Creek, CA: Left Coast Press.

Herle, Anita. 2013. "Exhibitions as Research: Displaying the Technologies that Make Bodies Visible." *Museum Worlds* 1: 113–135.

Higgs, Joy, 2010. "Researching Practice: Entering the Practice Discourse." In *Researching Practice: A Discourse on Qualitative Methodologies*, edited by Joy Higgs, Nita Cherry, Rob Macklin, and Rola Ajjawa, 1–8. Rotterdam: Sense Publishers.

Higgs, Joy, L. McAllister, and G. Whiteford. 2009. "The Practice and Praxis of Professional Decision Making." In *Understanding and Researching Professional Practice*, edited by B. Green, 101–120. Rotterdam: Sense Publishers.

Hirsch, Joanne S., and Lois Silverman. 2000. *Transforming Practice: Selections from the Journal of Museum Education*. Indiana University: Museum Education Roundtable.

Hooper-Greenhill, Eilean. 2006. "Studying Visitors." In *A Companion to Museum Studies*, edited by Sharon Macdonald, 362–376. Malden, MA: Blackwell.

Janes, Robert, and Richard Sandell, eds. 2007. *Museum Management and Marketing*. London: Routledge.

Karp, Ivan, and Steven D. Lavine, eds. 1991. *Exhibiting Cultures: The Poetics and Politics of Museum Display*. Washington, DC: Smithsonian Institution.

Karp, Ivan, Steven D. Lavine, and Christine Mullen Kreamer, eds. 1992. *Museums and Communities: The Politics of Public Culture*. Washington, DC: Smithsonian Institution.

Karp, Ivan, Corinne A. Kratz, Lynn Szwaja, and Tomas Ybarra-Frausto, eds. 2006. *Museum Frictions: Public Cultures/Global Transformations*. Durham, NC: Duke University Press.

Kavanagh, Gaynor, ed. 1994. *Museum Provision and Professionalism*. London: Routledge.

Knell, Simon J., ed. 2007. *Museums in the Material World*. London: Routledge.

Knell, Simon J. 2013. "Thinking Outside the Box: Considering How Museums, Objects and Collections Change." Keynote address, ICOM New Zealand Conference, Dunedin, October 25.

Kreps, Christina. 2003. "Curatorship as Social Practice." *Curator* 43(1): 311–323.

Livingstone, Phaedra, and Joy Davis. 2013. "Changing Curricula: Adapting Education Programmes to a Changing Museum Landscape." *ICOM News* 66: 12–13.

Lord, Barry, and Gail Dexter Lord, eds. 2002. *The Manual of Museum Exhibitions*. Lanham, MD: AltaMira.

Lord, Barry, and Gail Dexter Lord. 2009. *The Manual of Museum Management*. Lanham, MD: AltaMira.

Lord, Gail Dexter, and Kate Markert. 2007. *The Manual of Strategic Planning for Museums*. Lanham, MD: AltaMira.

Macdonald, Sharon. 2002. *Behind the Scenes at the Science Museum*. Oxford: Berg.

Macdonald, Sharon. 2006. "Expanding Museum Studies: An Introduction." In *A Companion to Museum Studies*, edited by Sharon Macdonald, 1–16. Malden, MA: Blackwell.

Macdonald, Sharon, and Gordon Fyfe, eds. 1996. *Theorizing Museums: Representing Identity and Diversity in a Changing World*. Malden, MA: Blackwell.

MacLeod, Suzanne. 2001. "Making Museum Meanings: Training, Education, Research and Practice." *Museum Management and Curatorship* 19(1): 51–62.

Marincola, Paul, ed. 2001. *Curating Now: Imaginative Practice/Public Responsibility*. Philadelphia: Philadelphia Exhibitions Initiative.

Marstine, Janet, ed. 2005. *New Museum Theory and Practice: An Introduction*. Malden, MA: Blackwell.

Mason, Rhiannon. 2006. "Cultural Theory and Museum Studies." In *A Companion to Museum Studies*, edited by Sharon Macdonald, 17–32. Oxford: Blackwell.

McCarthy, Conal. 2007. "Review Article: Museum Factions – The Transformation of Museum Studies." *Museum and Society* 5(3). Accessed September 12, 2014. http://www.le.ac.uk/ms/museumsociety.html.

McCarthy, Conal. 2011. *Museums and Maori: Heritage Professionals, Indigenous Collections, Current Practice*. Wellington: Te Papa Press.

McCarthy, Conal. 2012. "The Theory of Practice or Practice Theory? Some Thoughts on Museums and the Future of Research." Seminar presented in the series *Thinking Through Museums*, Te Papa, Wellington, April 23.

Ortner, Sherry. 2006. *Anthropology and Social Theory: Culture, Power and the Acting Subject.* Durham, NC: Duke University Press.

Parry, Ross, ed. 2010. *Museums in a Digital Age.* London: Routledge.

Pickering, Michael. 1995. *The Mangle of Practice: Time, Agency and Science.* Chicago: University of Chicago Press.

Poulot, Dominique. 2013. "Museums and Research: A Few Thoughts." Originally published as "Musées et recherche: quelques perspectives" in *Musées* 31 (2013): 4–11, 18–23. Accessed September 12, 2014. https://www.academia.edu/4937973/Museums_and_research_a_few_thoughts.

Preziosi, Donald, and Claire Farrago, eds. 2004. *Grasping the World: The Idea of the Museum.* Aldershot: Ashgate.

Reckwitz, Andreas. 2002. "Towards a Theory of Social Practices." *European Journal of Social Theory* 5(2): 243–263.

Rice, Danielle. 2000. "Constructing Informed Practice." In *Transforming Practice: Selections from the Journal of Museum Education*, edited by Joanne S. Hirsch and Lois Silverman, 222–225. Indiana University: Museum Education Roundtable.

Rice, Danielle. 2003. "Museums: Theory, Practice and Illusion." In *Art and Its Publics: Museum Studies at the End of the Millennium*, edited by A. McClellan, 77–95. Oxford: Blackwell.

Sahlins, Marshall. 2005. *Culture in Practice: Selected Essays.* New York: Zone Books.

Salzburg Curriculum. 2013. Accessed September 12, 2014. http://salzburg.hyperlib.sjsu.edu.

Sandell, Richard, and Eithne Nightingale, eds. 2013. *Museums, Equality and Social Justice.* London: Routledge.

Schatzki, Theodore R., Karin Knorr Cetina, and Eike von Savigny. 2001. *The Practice Turn in Contemporary Theory.* London: Routledge.

Schjeldahl, Peter. 2011. "Of Ourselves and Our Origins: Can We Speak Sensibly about What We Like about Art?" *Frieze* 137: 104–105. Accessed September 12, 2014. http://www.frieze.com/issue/article/of-ourselves-and-of-our-origins-subjects-of-art.

Shelton, Anthony. 2013. "Critical Museology: A Manifesto." *Museum Worlds* 1: 7–23.

Silverman, Lois, and Mark O'Neill. 2012. "Change and Complexity in the 21st-Century Museum." In *Reinventing the Museum: The Evolving Conversation on the Paradigm Shift*, edited by Gail Anderson, 193–201. Lanham, MD: AltaMira. Originally published 2004 in *Museum News* 83(6): 36–43.

Simmons, J.E. 2006. "Museum studies training in North America." In *Museum Studies: Perspectives and Innovation*, edited by S. L. Williams and C. A. Hawks, 113–128. Washington DC: Society for the Preservation of Natural History Collections.

Spiess, P. D. 1996. "Museum Studies: Are They Doing Their Job?" *Museum News* 75(6): 32–40.

Stam, Deirdre C. 2005. "The Informed Muse: The Implications of 'The New Museology' for Museum Practice." In *Heritage, Museums and Galleries: An Introductory Reader*, edited by Gerard Corsane, 54–70. Oxford: Routledge.

Starn, R. 2005. "A Historian's Brief Guide to New Museum Studies." *American Historical Review* 110(1): 68–98.

Teather, Lynne. 1991. "Museum Studies: Reflecting on Reflective Practice." *Museum Management and Curatorship* 10(4): 403–417.

Teather, Lynne. 2009. "Critical Museology Now: Theory/Practice/Theory." *Muse* 27(6): 23–32.

Thompson, John M. A., ed. 1984. *Manual of Curatorship: A Guide to Museum Practice*. London: Museums Association/Butterworths.

Townsend, Melanie, ed. 2003. *Beyond the Box: Diverging Curatorial Practices*. Banff, Canada: Banff Centre Press.

Turner, Stephen. 1994. *The Social Theory of Practices: Tradition, Tacit Knowledge and Presuppositions*. Chicago: University of Chicago Press.

Watson, Sheila, ed. 2007. *Museums and Their Communities*. London: Routledge.

Associate Professor Conal McCarthy is Director of the Museum and Heritage Studies program at Victoria University of Wellington, New Zealand. Conal has degrees in English, Art History, Museum Studies, and Māori language and has worked in galleries and museums in a variety of professional roles: educator, interpreter, visitor researcher, collection manager, curator, and exhibition developer, as well as sitting on the boards and advisory groups of a number of institutions. He has published widely on museum practice, including the book *Museums and Māori: Heritage Professionals, Indigenous Collections, Current Practice* (2011).

PART I

Priorities

1 THE ESSENCE OF THE MUSEUM
Mission, Values, Vision

David Fleming

I once began a new job, and asked the museum director a couple of starter questions. What happens when you aren't here? Answer: "Nothing, absolutely nothing." What are the big things coming up next? Answer: "I've done everything." This was in the dark days – not that long ago – when museums were run by an amateur cadre of egotistical directors who had no truck with accountability, or social value, or even with the notion of management, if that meant anything other than issuing orders. I have known very good museum directors. But I have also known directors lacking in spirit, courage, judgment, and integrity – and the one thing they had in common was their failure to have any vision.

Why does a museum exist? What is its purpose? What is it trying to achieve? What are its goals? Nothing is more important for a museum to sort out than its *mission*. The answers to these questions are to be found in the museum's *values*. Add together the mission and the values, project forward, and you identify the museum's *vision*.

These are not just clichés, management-speak jargon, used by different people in different ways, so that none of us is altogether clear about exactly what each of the words means. They capture the essence of the museum, its worth, its social value. They define for museum staff, and for others, exactly what it is they are trying to achieve: a shared sense of purpose. This is of fundamental importance in that museums are (mostly) non-profit organizations, and so they do not have the aim of making money as their ultimate goal.

Museums are not profit-driven, but *value-driven*. We are here to deliver services to customers, not profits, nor dividends to shareholders. Our work is not solely about our financial performance, and is, as a consequence, hard to measure and judge. Missions in the non-profit sector are complex, the values are profound, the visions are, or should be, inspiring.

It follows that being clear about a museum's mission, values, and vision is the primary responsibility of the museum's governing body, and, therefore, of the museum

The International Handbooks of Museum Studies: Museum Practice, First Edition.
Edited by Conal McCarthy.
© 2015 John Wiley & Sons Ltd. Published 2020 by John Wiley & Sons Ltd.

management team. It is this clarity that enables museums to demonstrate their success, to set themselves apart from others, to offer themselves as worthy of support, to earn and win dedication and commitment from their staff and other interested parties. In this chapter I consider these issues, drawing upon the experience of the corporate (profit-driven) sector as well the non-profit sector, including detailed reference to Tyne and Wear Museums and National Museums Liverpool, so as to throw light upon what museums are for, and how best they might promote their value in a world that is changing at a remarkable speed, and which remains largely ignorant, even skeptical, of the worth of museums. In doing so, it should be pointed out that I have been closely involved in both these institutions and offer this personal view of the internal process of revising mission and vision in order to show how this work can be carried out practically on the ground. I also wish to stress the need for the museum to understand its context before setting out its mission, and the importance of the research necessary for a museum to understand that context.

Mission statements

There is nothing especially new-fangled about mission statements. The first mission statement, it is often claimed, can be found in the Bible (Genesis 9:7 – "be fruitful and multiply"). The Preamble to the US Constitution is also cited frequently ("We the People of the United States, in Order to form a more perfect Union, establish Justice, insure domestic Tranquility, provide for the common defence, promote the general Welfare, and secure the Blessings of Liberty to ourselves and our Posterity, do ordain and establish this Constitution for the United States of America").

Today the world is full of mission statements. Look up "mission statements" on the internet and you will find a mass of references. Here are the first three American business examples from the alphabetical list of the Fortune 500 companies (Missionstatements.com 2011):

Advanced Auto Parts, Inc.

It is the Mission of Advance Auto Parts to provide personal vehicle owners and enthusiasts with the vehicle related products and knowledge that fulfil their wants and needs at the right price. Our friendly, knowledgeable and professional staff will help inspire, educate and problem-solve for our customers.

Aflac (an insurance company)

To combine aggressive strategic marketing with quality products and services at competitive prices to provide the best insurance value for consumers.

AGCO Corporation (a manufacturer and distributor of agricultural equipment)

Profitable growth through superior customer service, innovation, quality and commitment.

These missions are typical of the American corporate sector. They speak of maximizing sales/profits, and are rather more targeted at internal staff than at the outside world, such as, customers. As a consumer of insurance services, I am not likely to be influenced by Aflac's claim that they conduct "aggressive marketing," or that AGCO are pursuing "profitable growth," though as a member of staff I am being given a clear message about for whom I'm working, and why the company exists. The mission statements contained in Jeffrey Abrahams' book *101 Mission Statements from Top Companies* are littered with references to profit-making (e.g., Denny's Corporation: "to profitably grow the company"; Chiquita Brands International, Inc.: "consistently delivering sustainable, profitable growth"; Ecolab: "aggressive growth and a fair return for our shareholders"). Abrahams makes the point that the term "mission statement" may include vision and values, but that in broad terms the mission is an assertion of a company's reason for existence; employees, customers, partners, and the community being among the primary audience (Abrahams 2007, 3). There are, indeed, lots of different ways that companies choose to express their missions – as "aims," "objectives," "philosophies," "beliefs," "values," "visions," "principles," "purpose," "aspirations," "credo," or "our way."

Here are some examples featuring a group of non-profit organizations that sent participants to attend the *Strategic Perspectives on Non-profit Management* program at Harvard Business School in July 2008. The program faculty collected together a number of succinct mission statements for study, including these:

Habitat for Humanity Quad Cities

Habitat for Humanity Quad Cities works in partnership with God and people from all walks of life to build simple, decent, affordable housing and improve our community so all people can live as God intended. (Habitat for Humanity Quad Cities 2011)

Unlad Kabayan Migrant Services Foundation

To promote social entrepreneurship and social enterprises by mobilising migrant workers, the marginalized in the community and their resources to build a sustainable local economy. (Unlad Kabayan Migrant Services Foundation 2011)

A fuller "statement of purpose" came from the Rainbow Centre in Singapore:

Vision: Leading in Special Education, Making a Difference

Mission: We are committed to enhancing the quality of life of children with special needs through education and training to enable them to achieve their fullest potential by:

- providing a holistic developmental educational programme for our children
- collaborating with parents, the public and private sectors
- committing to the professional development and personal fulfilment of our staff

- contributing to the training and development in the field of special education locally and regionally; and
- engendering greater public awareness, understanding and acceptance of children with special needs

Core Values:
We serve with DEDICATION, INTEGRITY and COMPASSION, and strive to achieve EXCELLENCE in our services for the betterment of our special children. We believe in TEAMWORK and RESPECT for our clients, their parents and those we work with. (Rainbow Centre 2011)

In contrast to the company missions quoted above, these non-profit missions send a message to outsiders, at least as much as to staff. This is because in the non-profit sector, a prime function of the mission is to advocate the organization to supporters and potential supporters, including potential donors and partners. The mission statement is an external public relations and advocacy tool as well as an internal, motivational "call to arms" for staff.

Of course, we must never underestimate the power of the non-profit mission to attract staff. Salaries in the non-profit sector are invariably lower than in the corporate sector, and in order to attract talented people away from the big money non-profits have to emphasize the *social* value they are capable of creating. Creating social value – doing a job that is socially worthwhile – motivates many people far more than accumulating money ever will.

V. Kasturi Rangan writes: "Most of the nonprofits operating today make program decisions based on a mission rather than on a strategy" (Rangan 2004, 1). It is worth exploring more carefully the distinction he is making. Rangan writes of the tendency for non-profits to become victims of "stick-and-stretch syndrome" (2004, 2). He describes how a non-profit may fail to respond to changing conditions, such as a changing market, and to fall behind the times, by sticking too rigidly to their original, motivational mission, dubbing this "mission stickiness" (Rangan 2004, 1).

On the other hand, non-profits are pulled by market forces, and, as Rangan puts it, "[t]he need to attract new donors often compels nonprofits to take on programs that don't fit their existing capabilities and expertise well." He calls this tendency "stretchiness to market demands" (Rangan 2004, 2). Combining "mission stickiness" with "stretchiness" can undermine a non-profit's effectiveness, resulting in either a slow-moving bureaucracy that survives because of mission legitimacy rather than mission performance, or a busy organization that suffers from action paralysis because it never steps back to consider the full implications of its actions.

The problem, as Rangan points out, is that it is all very well having a mission, but you also need a strategy. As he puts it:

What most nonprofits consider strategy is really just intensive resource allocation and program management activity ... Nonprofits don't have the discipline of the bottom line and of performance-obsessed capital markets, so they can go for years without having to make strategic choices. Moreover, because neither the nonprofits nor their funding sources are especially skilled at measuring results, it's easy for them to fall into a vicious cycle of ineffectiveness that can take years to become apparent. Only a grave crisis, a visionary leader, or an outsider (such as a board member) would be able to highlight the need for strategic deliberation and redirection. (Rangan 2004, 3)

This is a salutary warning. Being clear about the mission, values, and vision won't amount to much unless an organization is capable of turning these notions into appropriate, and preferably measurable, activity that is responsive to changes in the environment in which the organization operates.

Museum missions

There is a literature on mission in the not-for-profit sector, and a few publications on museum missions (Drucker 1990; Scott, Jaffe, and Tobe 1993; Davies 1999; Lord and Lord 1999; Anderson 2000). In the museum world the importance of mission statements has long been known, though perhaps rather better in US museums than elsewhere. In the United States, the management of "nonprofit organizations" was recognized long ago as requiring specific approaches and skills that are different from those needed in business. "Non-profit institutions exist for the sake of their mission," wrote Peter Drucker, "They exist to make a difference in society … They exist for the sake of their mission, and this must never be forgotten" (Drucker 1990, 45).

Gail Anderson stressed the point that museums operate in a fast-changing world, and that they must therefore be "agile" (Anderson 2000, v). I have come to realize that remaining agile, by watching social, economic, political, and technological trends very carefully, and molding museum activity to suit new circumstances (trying to anticipate change before it happens), has long been at the core of my own work. This contrasts with the traditional museum approach of keeping one's head down until things have stabilized so that museums can go back to their "real" work of research, collecting, preservation, and so on. In my view, the constant re-examination needed for museums to remain viable leads inevitably to the requirement for their missions to underpin the change process. The mission statement has to be a lot more than a mere description of the functions performed by a museum, which, Anderson noted, had been common in the sector (2000, v).

Acknowledging that the mission is actually a central and inspirational part of modernizing a museum, and of ensuring it remains relevant, is a key to understanding how change can be brought about in the museum industry. Needless to say, the world outside the museum changes at a faster and faster rate, so the need for museum staff to understand these changes and to keep up with them becomes ever more pressing (Knell, MacLeod, and Watson 2007). Recognizing the need for constant change in museums, and implementing this change, is the most important role of the modern museum director, and a huge challenge for his or her leadership skills (Fleming 1999). Managing change lies at the heart of the contemporary museum.

In this chapter I present two case studies which demonstrate the process of bringing about change, and in which I have been involved over the past two decades. In each case I was the new director of a museum service which was in need of a major overhaul in order to realize its potential. Bringing about sustainable change within these two services was my primary leadership challenge. I felt that my staff and I had to reshape the services so that they had a healthy and productive future. So, I needed to ensure that we re-envisioned ourselves, based upon an agreed set of values, captured in a set of statements that made it absolutely clear within the museum service what we were about, and which also served to announce to the outside world how we saw ourselves.

Case study 1: Tyne and Wear Museums

My experience with missions, values, and vision began in earnest in the early 1990s, when I became Director of Tyne and Wear Museums (TWM) in the northeast of England. TWM was, and remains, essentially a major local authority museum service, which has responsibility for a group of museums that hold collections of regional, national, and international significance (Tyne and Wear Archives and Museums 2011).[1] Its funding and governance arrangements are unusual, and the service currently is funded by the five Tyne and Wear local authorities (Gateshead, Newcastle upon Tyne, Sunderland, North Tyneside, and South Tyneside), by the University of Newcastle, and by the Department for Culture, Media and Sport, part of the UK Government. Balancing the interests of the various funding bodies has always been a challenge, and this necessarily under-pinned the ways in which I approached the management of TWM.

I had been Assistant Director at TWM for just over a year when, in late 1991, I was appointed director. I was fully aware, therefore, that TWM was an organiza-tion that was failing to inspire the public, the politicians who provided the majority of the museum service's funding, or its staff. It was made clear to me by the politi-cians who voted the funding for TWM that the service was being given its last chance to put its house in order, or dire consequences would follow – in effect, the probable collapse of the "joint service" arrangement entered into by the five Tyne and Wear local authorities.

The febrile atmosphere at the time was captured in a *Museums Journal* article enti-tled "Lifting the Fog on the Tyne" (Davies 1991). Having been created as a joint local authority service in 1986, TWM was unstable, and had already been condemned by the Museums and Galleries Commission in 1988 as "unworkable." I recall one north-east museum director described TWM at the time as a "critically injured patient."

Nonetheless, a series of attempts had been made to stabilize the beleaguered museum service, which led to a new staff structure in 1990, though this had been done in such a way that a senior member of TWM staff commented that "someone had a vision of how it's all supposed to work, but they didn't tell me."

Within weeks of this article appearing in print, a second *Museums Journal* article appeared entitled "All Change at Tyne and Wear Museums Service" (Murdin 1991). This described the latest upheavals that resulted in my appointment as director. While this is all now seems like ancient history, the point is that TWM was able to go on from the unhappy situation in 1991 to become, over the next ten years, argu- ably, the most successful of all UK local authority museum services. The potential that many observers recognized in TWM needed to be unlocked. How did this happen, and what role was played in the TWM saga by a new mission, new values and a re-envisioning?[2] First and foremost, I believed that what TWM needed was a change in its "culture": namely, "the shared assumptions, beliefs, values and norms of an organisation, which shape patterns of behaviour" (Fleming 1993). In an address to the Museums Association Conference in 1993, I explained that TWM had had "a major change of philosophy" that meant we saw "the museum as an agent of social change" (1993).[3] In a 1994 lecture, I said:

> I believe that museums should play an active role in society, and engage with as many people as possible. This means breaking down those barriers, which museums themselves have erected, which dissuade too many people from using museums …
> I believe that museums in towns and cities have an important role to play in combating societal decay, in encouraging disadvantaged groups of people to increase their understanding of their environment. Because I believe this, I have made it my business to change the culture of Tyne and Wear Museums. (Fleming 1994)

It seems obvious to me now that, at the time, we were groping toward a new mission for TWM, but my instinct was that what we really needed was a change in attitudes and behaviors, which I described as "culture." I spoke of using the reorganization of a museum to "change culture," of recruiting new staff, and promoting others, who would "carry the new culture," of using modern manage- ment techniques to "lever in culture change" (Fleming 1994).

I still believe this. There is nothing more pointless than a mission that is not based on attitudes and behaviors, as well as beliefs and values. Without culture change a demoralized museum service such as TWM could never have thrived. One member of TWM staff wrote to me on the eve of his retirement and referred to the "amazing job" we had done at TWM, which, he wrote "was doomed without your intervention. The apathy was writ large for all to see."[4] The prob- lems that had to be confronted were insularity, departmentalism, negativity, lack of ambition, and lack of realism. I felt that we had to reinvigorate TWM, and give it a new sense of purpose and direction. We had to learn how to cope with change, and take control of our destiny. We needed a mission.

But in order to create a workable and worthwhile mission, we had to understand the context in which TWM was operating. The Tyne and Wear area was characterized by widespread urban poverty, arising out of the post-industrial collapse of the local economy: coalmining, shipbuilding, and heavy engineering were all things of the past. Museums do not exist in vacuums; rather they are functions of contemporary society, and need to key into what is going on around them. This is why it is so important to conduct research on audiences, existing and potential. Consider the question: "If you do not understand the audience, how do you know what to do tomorrow?" This is a rhetorical question I have posed a number of times at National Museums Liverpool (NML), where at the beginning of the twenty-first century it seemed to me that we had not done sufficient to learn about our audience.

It took time to crystallize a mission at TWM. It always does, if it's done with rigor. More urgent was the need to improve morale and bring about behavioral change. This involved a range of changes; breaking down of artificial barriers; creating new staff structures, new line management, some new posts; and switching resources between operational areas. In the early days of effecting culture change, the senior management team had to be dictatorial. There was nothing optional about the changes, although there were people who resisted it. My new management team had to steam ahead, as we felt we had no time to spare if we were to save TWM. This concentrated our minds wonderfully. Nonetheless, this approach can only be sustained for a limited period, and sensing the right time to ease off and adopt a more inclusive style of management is crucial to the successful implementation of culture change.

The importance of supportive governance needs to be stressed. Museums always have governing bodies, whether they are local authorities or a board of trustees, and culture change is impossible without their agreement. At TWM our governing body was the Joint Museums Committee, a body made up of elected councillors from the five local authorities of Tyne and Wear. It was the potential threat of these five authorities ending the joint funding agreement that always hung over TWM like the Sword of Damocles.

In fact, the Committee could not have been more supportive.[5] The councillors welcomed the improvements that the new culture brought about. In particular, they could hardly fail to notice that visitor numbers began to increase as we invigorated the museum service with education work, capital developments, an increasingly varied exhibitions program, and a new emphasis on attracting non-traditional audiences and on professional marketing and fundraising.[6] In 1994 TWM was cited as a success in that year's Newcastle Labour Party Election Manifesto: an extraordinary turnaround, and proof that successful museums can prosper even in the most skeptical political environment.[7] Anecdotal evidence and independent evaluation has confirmed that the revamped museum service has been successful in terms of social impact and other factors (Calzia et al. 2005).[8]

Committee support meant that we could take risks. And one of our biggest risks was to take over the management of the Hancock Museum from Newcastle

University, which subsequently became the core of the Great North Museum. This was a major undertaking that could have gone wrong in so many ways, but in fact the new arrangements led to significant gains for the Hancock (including increased profile, audience growth, several awards, and improved fundraising) and a huge amount of credit for TWM (Great North Museum 2013). Moreover, assuming management responsibility for the Hancock meant that TWM staff were exposed to all manner of new practices and issues, and our success in turning around the museum's fortunes acted as a demonstration of how good TWM could be, and a motivational example. It became a catalyst for change elsewhere in TWM.

During the 1990s, as TWM developed into a radical and effective museum service, we developed a written set of documents that culminated in our *Statement of Purpose and Beliefs*. Along the way we wrote a number of mission statements. The (rather clunky) one from 1995 reads: "Tyne and Wear Museums assembles and protects evidence of human and environmental development in Tyne and Wear and, where appropriate, elsewhere; and provides the fullest access to that evidence to people of all ages, background and abilities." While the 1995 mission acknowledges the core collections-based role of TWM, significantly it follows this with the statement that "the fullest access" should be provided to these collections. In the TWM 1996 Corporate Plan this mission statement had been amended to read: "Tyne and Wear Museums assembles and protects evidence of human and environmental development, and, in making these fully accessible, strives to improve the quality of people's lives in Tyne and Wear." The 1996 mission statement was supported by a list of "aims," which elaborated upon the brief mission, and included the express aim that TWM should act "as an agent of social change."

What was happening was that TWM was edging away from the traditional view of the role of museums as defined by, for example, the UK Museums Association and ICOM, toward a position where the right of the public to access and benefit from collections becomes the overriding mission.[9] This is a subtle but important distinction that reflects the need for museums to be acutely conscious of their socioeconomic environment, whatever their collections-based needs and priorities.

In May 1996 TWM's senior managers held a "Strategy Day," something we did on a frequent basis. We noted at that meeting that, in 1991, we had been suffering from political hostility, low staff morale, a low professional profile, declining funding, no strategy, and low visitor numbers. By 1996 we had become politically popular, staff morale was "quite good" (although members of staff were "tired"), our professional profile was strong, our fundraising was successful, we were now very strategic, and visitor numbers had more than doubled from 500,000 to 1.2 million since 1990 (Tyne and Wear Museum Annual Reports 1990–1998). We also noted that we had become far more cost-effective and ambitious, the funding from the National Lottery had changed our landscape dramatically, and that a possible Labour Government was on the political horizon.

High visitor numbers suggested that our focus on being relevant to local communities was working, but we could not rest on our laurels. In April 1998, I sent a note to TWM staff: "If ever we forget that our single most important performance indicator is the level of public support we enjoy (and earn) then our present Golden Age will be finished." There was a growing acknowledgment within TWM that the primary purpose of museums is to provide a service to the whole of the public. This belief sat at the heart of TWM's philosophy by the end of the 1990s, and was captured in our *Statement of Purpose and Beliefs* (mentioned above), a document worked on by scores of TWM managers and endorsed by the Department for Culture, Media and Sport in its Policy Guidance on social inclusion for museums, galleries, and archives in May 2000 (DCMS 2000, 29). This *Purpose and Beliefs* was clearer than had been our previous mission statements about TWM's social role. Here is an extract:

> Our Mission is:
> > To help people determine their place in the world and understand their identities, so enhancing their self-respect and their respect for others.
>
> We Believe that:
> > We act as an agent of social and economic regeneration.
>
> We Pursue our Mission by:
> > Exposing our public to ideas, thus helping counter ignorance, discrimination and hostility.
>
> Our Vision for the Future of TWM is for:
> > Total inclusion.

Thirteen years later, the current TWAM (now Tyne and Wear Archives and Museums) mission reads: "Our mission is to help people determine their place in the world and define their identities, so enhancing their self-respect and their respect for others" (Tyne and Wear Museums and Archives 2011).

It would be fair to note that the advent of the New Labour Government in 1997 had encouraged our explicit commitment to social inclusion at TWM, because social inclusion was a key government policy which shaped and was shaped by important research on social inequality (Fleming in Dodd and Sandell 2001). We felt able to be more expansive about our social aims, and when the Government decided to use the TWM *Purpose and Beliefs* in its policy guidance for all museums and archives, we felt vindicated in our approach. In letters written to me by the outgoing Government Ministers in 2001, both Secretary of State Chris Smith and Culture Minister Alan Howarth made reference to the example TWM had provided to the museum sector. Howarth wrote:

> I have very much admired the way in which you have flown the flag not just for Tyne and Wear Museums, but for regional museums in general. You have demonstrated that first class practice is not confined to the national museums, and indeed you have blazed several of the trails that as Ministers we very much wanted the museums system to pursue.[10]

Case study 2: National Museums Liverpool

My most recent experience of redefining a mission and organizational values has been at National Museums Liverpool (NML), where I became director in October 2001. NML has been a national museum service since 1986. It is a group of museums in Liverpool and Wirral that hold world-class collections across the range of museum disciplines (National Museums Liverpool 2013). It is a bigger service than TWM and, unlike TWM, there is no local authority control. Again my perspective on this case study is colored by my own involvement, but I believe the value of this autobiographical sketch is to provide a personal account of organizational change from the inside.

On becoming director of, as it was known at the time, National Museums and Galleries on Merseyside (NMGM), like all new directors I needed to get beneath the skin of the organization, and one of the ways of doing this was to find out what the NMGM managers thought of their service. A "Vision Away Day" in November 2001, entitled "Reinventing NMGM," threw up a great many issues, as senior managers raised long-held frustrations.

Among the more serious concerns about NMGM that were expressed by the senior team were: the museum had no shared vision, it was fragmented, risk averse, not strategic, and, far from having a team culture, had a *blame culture*. Having worked at TWM, of course, none of this was altogether shocking. All museums need to refresh their thinking every now and again in order to prevent this kind of perceived staleness. NMGM's Mission Statement read in 2001:

> To use effectively the staff, buildings and resources of NMGM to promote the public enjoyment and understanding of art, history and science by:
>
> - adding to, caring for and preserving the collections
> - studying and researching the collections
> - exhibiting the collections
> - and by other appropriate means.

The mission was backed up not by a set of values or beliefs, but by a schedule of "services provided to the public" and a list of "national standards achieved or aspired to." This was hardly a motivational mission. Dry, descriptive, and functional, it had been in use for a number of years, and spoke volumes about the need for a new approach at NMGM.

NMGM was certainly not in the parlous state that TWM had been in 1991, but it did need a renewed sense of purpose, wherein the service was able to identify what it was good at, but then go on to fulfill its potential in terms of audience-building and social impact; audiences were too low, invariably a sign that all is not well. When I worked at TWM, we used to compare our visitor numbers with those of NMGM, which had far bigger budgets but smaller audiences. I was determined to do something about this: at my job interview with the NMGM trustees, I had argued that NMGM needed a new primary aim, which was "to be a social, cultural and educational powerhouse, through audience development." In a report for trustees in 2005, I wrote that in 2001:

> Our culture was slow-moving and bureaucratic, and energies and boldness were suppressed by anxieties and fear of failure … NMGM was tribal, racked by departmental agendas, with loyalties to individual venues. Central services, such as marketing and finance, were held in low regard by venue managers, and therefore by their staff. Curators often saw themselves as superior beings rather than as part of a team. Others simply kept their heads down so as to avoid, as they perceived it, unnecessary bureaucracy and interference.

And so, together with senior staff, I set out together on a long journey to reinvent NMGM. In an early address to staff entitled "First Impressions" in December 2001, I set the scene: despite having talented and experienced staff, great collections and buildings, and other capabilities, we were poor at internal communications, at forward planning, at prioritization. I said that:

> Over and above all this, and causing many of these problems, is the issue of NMGM CULTURE, or corporate personality, which in turn is the result of a lack of a shared and articulated VISION. We have, to a degree, failed to be clear about why we exist, what we are here for, and what we want to be.

Furthermore, I argued that NMGM needed a vision "of a learning organisation which is ambitious, generous, exciting and successful; which is founded on a bedrock of scholarship and excellence; wherein different talents are valued and respected; which is geared up for operating in a rapidly-changing world." It was at this address that I first set a target for NMGM to attract 2 million visitors a year by 2010. The number visiting in 2001 was around 700,000 a year (Brown 2006). It was also in this speech that I explained my belief that museums are, first and foremost, educational organizations, and that NMGM must strive to attract the broadest audiences.

Much discussion and debate followed, involving staff and trustees, and out of these discussions arose an early symbolic change of name from National Museums and Galleries on Merseyside, which the service had been called since 1986, to National Museums Liverpool. This may not seem such a big deal, but it was a conscious decision to shorten our name and acronym, and drop the rather indeterminate "Merseyside" in favor of the much stronger, if somewhat controversial, city brand "Liverpool."[11] Names can be important signifiers of intent, style, and value, which is why many organizations spend so much on branding (see Chong, this volume).

Meanwhile, we restructured NML in order to improve strategic focus, try to kill off a rampant departmentalism, enable us to bring in some new talent, and promote existing talent. We continued a process of "visioning," which included an illuminating discussion in February 2003 at a workshop for 30 managers. We were seeking "a shared sense of purpose," and specifically we wanted to develop a new mission, values, and vision. During the course of this workshop, members of staff were asked to imagine NML as a person, as a car, as a dog, and to suggest whom or what we would rather be. The responses were rather alarming: they saw NML as nonagenarian romantic novelist Barbara Cartland ("seen better days"), Tory Prime Minister John Major ("safe, old fashioned"), and Coronation Street's Ken Barlow ("stuffy, staid, a bit embittered"). Similarly, as a car we would be a safe family car like a Volvo or a Rover ("old and reliable, past its time"), and as a dog we would be an old English sheepdog ("big, cuddly, lumbering, wants to be loved") or a cross-breed ("so in-bred, not sure what it is"). In aspiration terms staff wanted NML to be like Halle Berry ("stylish, elegant, sexy, racy"), a Mini Cooper ("nippy, sporty, cool"), and a young Border collie ("boundless energy, enthusiastic, fun, friendly, hard working").

The comment about being "a bit embittered" struck a real chord. What was obvious was the degree of *frustration* among the managers at NML's stately pace and demeanor, lack of excitement, and the distance between where we were and where the managers wanted us to be. As a newcomer at both TWM and NML, I discovered that many staff understood that something was wrong with the museum service, and they were often clear about what it was. They were frustrated that those with the power to change things for the better seemed unable to do so. As the new director, I saw it as my job to erase this frustration.

However, there was a problem in addressing the issues revealed in this workshop; namely that the staff did not always feel that our ambitions for modernizing NML were matched by the ambitions of our trustees. Staff felt that we were way ahead of trustees, who were regarded as staid, traditional in their thinking, risk-averse, and rather nervous, which is obviously problematic in the fast-changing twenty-first century.

At a joint session with staff to discuss possible name changes, one trustee forcibly expressed the opinion that museums weren't about education at all. This was both irritating and ironic, in that the central role of education in museum work was precisely what staff were trying to implant in our corporate thinking. Trustees took an age to allow us to change NMGM's name, and, for a number of years, they insisted on watering down the new mission statements that staff had drafted, so that they became less radical than we would have liked. We had to wait a while until the governance environment was more positive, enlightened, and enabling (on governance see Lord, Chapter 2 in this volume).

This situation was compounded by a distinct sense among members of staff that some long-serving trustees actually resented the reforms and improvements to NMGM, in that they felt they were being implicitly criticized for faulty stewardship of the organization. Trying to effect radical change in an atmosphere of defensiveness and denial is not easy. At the beginning of 2004, I wrote a status report on NML entitled "Picking Up Speed" that expressed the belief that our new "Aims and Beliefs" fell somewhat short of what we wanted to say (see Appendix B below).

> One of the hardest things to change in a complex organisation is its culture. What I found when I came to NML was a culture of rivalry and finger pointing, compliance and deference, with a bureaucratic overlay which made decision-making and prioritisation difficult. This is not a recipe for an organisation to be able to improve its performance in a fast-changing and demanding environment.
>
> I do not pretend that all is yet well, though I do believe we are on the mend. I sense widespread support for our new Aims and Beliefs which, while imperfect, does a decent job of outlining what we need to do – and with what attitude – in order for us to move onward successfully, i.e. to be a people- and service-orientated organisation rather than an insular and procedurally-minded one.
>
> We have gone some way towards freeing up the collective mindset of NML, causing us to be less risk averse and more creative, more confident in sharing information, more relaxed, easier to engage with. Of course, such a transformation is facilitated by obvious successes such as the steep rise in visitor numbers, in turn the result of changed ways of doing things.

Nonetheless, we were making progress. These are some of the changes we implemented during the five-year period from 2002 to 2006:

- overhauled our financial structure and got a grip on our finances;
- brought in some key new staff and made some judicious promotions to ensure a positive approach to a change agenda;
- strengthened our Board of Trustees with some key appointments;
- placed a new emphasis on education work;
- placed a new emphasis on work with local communities;
- increased our volunteer workforce;
- implemented a number of capital projects that helped break down internal barriers and motivate staff;
- introduced free admission to all venues, events, and activities;
- introduced an improved exhibitions management regime;
- greatly increased our media profile.

These changes enabled us to build audiences: the annual number of visitors rose to more than 2 million by 2007, three years ahead of the target I set (purely speculatively) in 2001, and almost three times as many as that year. By 2011, the annual visitor total was 3 million, up 330 percent, and by 2012 the NML had its most successful year ever with 3.3 million visitors, five times as many as a decade before (National Museums Liverpool 2013). These audiences were more diverse than before, and more diverse than most other national museums in the United Kingdom (*Changing Lives* 2012, 21). Meanwhile new iterations of our Aims and Beliefs appeared annually over the years, arising out of regular discussions among staff and trustees, culminating eventually in the current version:

Who we are and what we do

National Museums Liverpool (NML) is one of the world's great museum organisations. We hold in trust and safeguard some of the world's most important museum collections, which are universal in their range.

We are core-funded by central government and we are the only national museum service in England based wholly outside London, so we have a unique fourfold role – we are the main museum service for Liverpool and Merseyside; we are the region's largest cultural organisation; we operate at national and at international levels.

Having played a pivotal role in the cultural, educational and economic life of Liverpool and the North West for more than 150 years, our success can be measured in terms of how well we combine this local and regional role with our national and international responsibilities.

NML currently comprises eight museums: International Slavery Museum, Lady Lever Art Gallery, Merseyside Maritime Museum, Sudley House, UK Border Agency National Museum, Walker Art Gallery, World Museum Liverpool, and the Museum of Liverpool.

Our mission

We change lives and enable millions of people, from all backgrounds, to engage with our world-class museums.

Our values

- We believe that museums are fundamentally educational in purpose.
- We believe that museums are places for ideas and dialogue that use collections to inspire people.
- We are a democratic museum service and we believe in the concept of social justice: we are funded by the whole of the public and in return we strive to provide an excellent service to the whole of the public.
- We believe in the power of museums to help promote good and active citizenship, and to act as agents of social change (National Museums Liverpool 2010).

The "who we are and what we do" statement of mission and values is supplemented by a "Strategy Statement" (see Appendix A below). This approach to capturing values and writing a mission, but also citing the social and economic contexts in which we work, seems to me to be the best way for a museum service to stress its non-profit nature. Readers may not be surprised that we try to run NML efficiently; they may be more surprised to find that we are quite so aware of, and tenacious about, our social role.

This is particularly important to NML because we see ourselves as an organization that carries a very weighty social responsibility, and we have to capture this in our mission statements, values, and vision. Before the arrival in 2008 of Phil

Redmond, the current Chair of NML, the atmosphere among our trustees was at best indifferent, at worst hostile to this kind of socially oriented mission statement, even though members of staff were committed to this approach.

In July 2011, we opened a new museum, the Museum of Liverpool (Museum of Liverpool 2013). I have often described this as a "democratic museum," in that it has been conceived and created by people who adhere to what I see as NML's democratic mission (Fleming 2011). Indeed, the Museum of Liverpool in many ways embodies NML's values: it is people- and story-led; it is emotional; it sets out to engage local people first and foremost. The museum is the culmination of ten years of re-visioning the purpose and value of NML, and of the ways in which we work. So far the museum has proved to be extremely popular with Liverpudlians. In 2012, ALVA reported it was the most visited museum in the United Kingdom outside London with over 1 million visitors (ALVA 2013).

The current Aims and Beliefs statement is now just about where we want it to be. It will be revised for our Strategic Plan 2012–2015, because our external environment has shifted with the election of a Conservative-led Coalition Government in May 2010, and the subsequent reduction in our budgets. Thousands of public sector jobs have already been lost in Merseyside, including scores at NML, as government spending cuts bite deep; the think-tank Centre for Cities has forecast that cuts will damage Liverpool more than any other city in the United Kingdom (Centre for Cities 2011). Nonetheless, we will adhere to our values. As the world around us shifts on its axis once more, our values are what make us what we are.

Conclusion

The way that NML's mission, values, and vision are expressed is always a work in progress, even though these things do not change in essence, whatever the external environment might throw up. There is always external change, so there is always more to do within the museum. No museum can afford to stand still. Political, social, economic, technological, and environmental changes mean the museum must continually rethink what it is doing and how it does it. But the mission, values, and vision will remain constant.

Recent data indicates NML's success in pursuing our social justice agenda. The audience continues to grow and become more diverse ("Liverpool's Museums and Galleries Celebrate a Rise in Visitor Numbers" 2013). In 2010/2011 the number of visits made to NML museums by adults from NS-NSC groups 5–8 (i.e., those from lower-income groups) exceeded that of any other DCMS-funded museum, and was far greater than the numbers recorded for the British Museum, Tate Gallery, and Victoria and Albert Museum *combined* (*Changing Lives* 2012, 21).

This kind of achievement results from a determined adherence to our mission and values, added to the ability to anticipate and respond to external change. I have learned that clarity about mission and values must accompanied by: the courage to challenge the status quo; adapting to local circumstances and avoiding generic solutions to problems; motivating staff as well as outside stakeholders; and a determination not to be bland and procedural in this crucially important area of our work.

NML now has less money to spend than for the past few years and has lost staff, and it is difficult to plan for the future when there is something of a political policy vacuum nationally where culture is concerned. Museum professionals need to be very aware of these things or we shall lose our way. Nonetheless, mission, values, and vision provide a reference point and an anchor for a museum, even in the most troubled of times.

APPENDIX A
NML Strategy Statement

The brutal reality of austerity Britain will begin to be felt in earnest in England's most deprived city this week, as Merseyside's five local authorities collectively deliver the harshest public spending cuts the region has seen for generations.

The five councils – Liverpool, Knowsley, Wirral, Sefton and St Helens – will from tomorrow formally ratify plans that will see their budgets slashed by a fifth (£200 m) shrinking or axing hundreds of services and shedding thousands of jobs.

The Guardian, February 28, 2011

National Museums Liverpool operates in a city which remains the most deprived in the UK. Employment rates, local educational attainment and skills levels are still well below the national average; the welfare bill *per capita* is the highest in the UK. As the whole country suffers the consequences of a deep recession, and now severe cuts in public expenditure, fragile cities like Liverpool are threatened anew by adverse and profound social consequences.

This is a hugely challenging environment for NML. Locally, people are at risk of suffering from social tensions, lack of social cohesion, anti-social behaviour, loss of confidence and aspiration, pressure on families and relationships, high stress levels.

NML carries a very great responsibility in terms of delivering first class museums that, as part of a wider pattern of cultural provision, can help create "social capital" in the area, enhancing well being, confidence and social connectedness. In a period of recession and public spending cuts this responsibility grows even greater, and NML can help mitigate the social consequences of adverse economic conditions.

We are committed to facing up to this social responsibility, and our determination to provide free access to all of our exhibitions, events and activities, allied with the highest quality standards and enormous variety, is at the core of this commitment.

In doing all this we will:

- widen participation in our activities, thereby fulfilling our **social objectives**, especially by attracting diverse audiences
- ensure that we offer **educational opportunities** to people of all ages and backgrounds
- as the major cultural business in the region which is also a prime tourist asset, achieve **economic benefits** through developing cultural tourism, and by helping build a strong image for Liverpool and the city region
- pursue **research programmes** that lead to greater knowledge about our collections, and promote the exceptional quality of our collections
- improve our **visitors' experience** by upgrading our buildings, displays, and facilities, offering quality and variety
- strive to create an **organisational culture** that motivates our team and enables us to work effectively and in harmony, acknowledging that it is only through the commitment of staff that we achieve success
- seek actively to increase the **diversity of our workforce**
- be alert to **social, economic and technological change** to ensure we remain focussed and relevant
- work in **partnership** with other agencies – education, arts, business, public bodies
- behave in an **ethical manner** at all times, promoting sustainable practices
- manage **risk** in a positive and effective manner
- use our **resources** wisely and augment them wherever we are able, providing real value for money.

In pursuing a strategy of combining significant audience growth and diversity with the highest levels of professionalism, we acknowledge that this has radically changed the culture of NML, and has created a challenging working environment. This environment is characterised by regular review of the way we do things, by the pursuit of new ideas and methods, and by the constant re-examination of traditional museum practices.

Recent successes in terms of massive audience growth, combined with rising standards of collections care, demonstrate the validity of this approach, and we are determined to continue to pursue this strategy.

Despite current and future funding uncertainties, notably in terms of government finances, it is in our capacity to manage ourselves bravely and imaginatively, and to move forward on many fronts at the same time, that our future value and success lies.

Extract from National Museums Liverpool Strategic
Plan 2010–11, issued 23 July 2010.

APPENDIX B
Version of NML Vision and Beliefs Approved by Trustees

Vision and Beliefs

NML is one of the world's great museum services. We are active locally, regionally, nationally and internationally, reflecting our unique status as a national institution based in a major regional city

Vision: We will be progressive and outward looking, exciting and inspiring people in ways that are inclusive and challenging

We believe that:

NML has a responsibility to the whole of society. Everyone, regardless of age, identity, ability or background, has a right to expect that we will be enjoyable and welcoming, providing routes to discovery, awareness and learning for all

NML is committed to study, care for and enhance our world-class collections, making them accessible to all.

NML is a creative, energetic and dynamic organisation which must be managed imaginatively and effectively. We are prepared to identify and embrace opportunities, to experiment, take risks and use innovative approaches to achieve our aims.

NML must always be modern, radical and responsive. We will build on our strengths, but we thrive on change. We believe in continuous assessment, transparency and openness, listening and reacting to our users, and in improvement of all that we do

Teamwork and co-operation is valued and inherent in all that NML does. We will create a working environment where respect for different roles and talents is paramount, and all staff feel motivated, promoting quality, trust and integrity

NML grows stronger through partnerships, community, cultural, educational and business. We will build such relationships wherever it helps us achieve our aims, while helping others achieve theirs.

Author's own collection

Notes

1 Now TWAM, having added responsibility for Tyne and Wear Archives.
2 The principal architects of the extraordinary changes at TWM during the 1990s were John Millard, Neil Sinclair, John Wilks, Sharon Granville, Alex Saint, and Alec Coles, though many others made important contributions. I should like to acknowledge all

TWM staff of that period for their remarkable contribution to helping change the nature of British museums.

3 I gave a paper with the title of "The Museum as an Agent of Social Change" at the Annual Conference of the Museums Association in Liverpool in September 1993, to an audience of fewer than 10 people.

4 Letter, Joe Ging to the author, March 3, 1993.

5 I should like to record my thanks to the Chairs of Tyne and Wear Museums during my directorship, especially Newcastle councillors Barney Rice and Don Price, to the Vice-Chairs throughout this period, Sunderland councillor Ralph Baxter, and to David Cobb of Newcastle City Council, the Clerk to the Joint Museums Committee. Our achievements at Tyne and Wear Museums would have been much thinner without the unflagging support of these people.

6 See the series of 10 Tyne and Wear Museums Annual Reports that cover this period for details of changes in staff structures, exhibition programs, new permanent displays, visitor numbers etc. (Tyne and Wear Museums Annual Reports. 1991/2–2000/1). See also "Visitor Services Case Study" (1998) and "Education Case Study" (1999).

7 Museums Association (1995). In a letter, a prominent Newcastle Labour councillor referred to herself as "Past President: Philistines for Labour" after having discovered that, contrary to her expectations, museums were not merely a place for elitist activities. Letter, Councillor Gina Tiller to the author, April 1, 1994. In another letter, the outgoing Leader of Newcastle City Council wrote that management of TWM had "improved immeasurably" compared with "the rather dreary days" of former times. Letter, Councillor Sir Jeremy Beecham to the author, December 5, 1994. Another endorsement came from the Chief Executive of the Tyne and Wear Development Corporation, who wrote of "the revolution you are engaged in making the Museums service more accessible." Letter, Alastair G. Balls to the author, October 5, 1994.

8 See also Watson (2012: 19).

9 See ICOM (2014) and Museums Association (2014).

10 Letter, Rt. Hon Alan Howarth CBE, MP, to the author, August 13, 2001.

11 At that time the word "Liverpool" was still rather synonymous in the UK with urban decay, deprivation, unemployment, and crime. Not all trustees were comfortable with these associations, and although those of us who believed in adopting the new name eventually prevailed, it was not before we had to endure considerable delay in trustees finally agreeing to implement the new name. The decision has been more than justified since then, not least when Liverpool won the accolade of becoming the European Capital of Culture in 2008.

References

Abrahams, Jeffrey. 2007. *101 Mission Statements from Top Companies*. Berkeley, CA: Ten Speed.

ALVA (Association of Leading Visitor Attractions). 2013. "Latest Visitor Figures." Accessed September 14, 2014. http://alva.org.uk/details.cfm?p=423.

Anderson, Gail, ed. 2000. *Museum Mission Statements: Building a Distinct Identity.* Washington, DC: American Association of Museums.

Brown, Mark. 2006. "Visitor Numbers Soar at Britain's Free Museums and Galleries." *The Guardian*, December 2. Accessed September 14, 2014. http://www.theguardian.com/uk/2006/dec/02/arts.politics.

Calzia, Carolyn, Luke Davidson, Chris Lorway, and Holly Sidford. 2005. *Tyne and Wear Museums, Bristol's Museums, Galleries and Archives: Social Impact Programme Assessment.* London: AEA Consulting. Accessed September 14, 2014. http://tynewear2.sumodesign.co.uk/about/corporatedocuments/documents/Social_Impact.pdf.

Centre for Cities. 2011. "Cities Outlook." Accessed September 14, 2014. http://www.centreforcities.org/assets/files/Cities%20Outlook%202011/CITIES%20OUTLOOK_2011.pdf.

Changing Lives. 2012. *Changing Lives: Economic Impact and Social Responsibility at National Museums Liverpool.* Liverpool: National Museum Liverpool. Accessed September 14, 2014. http://www.liverpoolmuseums.org.uk/about/corporate/reports/NML-Changing-Lives-social-eco-impact-report.pdf.

Davies, Maurice. 1991. "Lifting the Fog on the Tyne." *Museums Journal* 91(7): 29–32.

Davies, Stuart. 1999. "Visionary Leadership and Missionary Zeal." In *Management in Museums*, edited by Kevin Moore, 108–132. New Research in Museum Studies 7. London: Athlone.

DCMS (Department for Culture, Media and Sport). 2000. "Centres for Social Change: Museums, Galleries and Archives for All." Accessed September 20, 2014. http://webarchive.nationalarchives.gov.uk/20090903013156/http://www.cep.culture.gov.uk/images/publications/centers_social_change.pdf.

Dodd, Jocelyn, and Richard Sandell, eds. 2001. *Including Museums: Perspectives on Museums, Galleries and Social Inclusion.* Leicester: Research Centre for Museums and Galleries, Museum Studies Department, University of Leicester.

Drucker, Peter F. 1990. *Managing the Nonprofit Organization: Principles and Practices.* New York: HarperCollins.

"Education Case Study: Tyne and Wear Museums." 1999. *Museum Practice.* November 12: 47.

Fleming, David. 1993. "The Museum as an Agent of Social Change." Unpublished paper given at the Museums Association Conference, Liverpool. September 15.

Fleming, David. 1994. "Planning, Performance and Prosperity: A Framework for Museums." Unpublished lecture given at a meeting on Strategic Planning for Senior Managers organized by the Area Museum Council for the South West, Guildhall, Bath, May 16.

Fleming, David. 1995. "Planning: An Anarchist's Guide." *MPG Transactions*, 29.

Fleming, David. 1999. "Leadership." In *Management in Museums*, edited by Kevin Moore, 93–107. New Research in Museum Studies 7. London: Athlone.

Fleming, David. 2011. "The Democratic Museum." In *The Radical Museum: Democracy, Dialogue and Debate*, edited by Gregory Chamberlain, 1–15. Milton Keynes: Museum ID.

Great North Museum. 2013. Website. Accessed September 14, 2014. http://www.twmuseums.org.uk/great-north-museum.html.

Habitat for Humanity Quad Cities. 2011. "Mission." Accessed September 14, 2014. http://www.habitatqc.org/?page_id=52.

ICOM (International Council of Museums). 2014. "Museum Definition." Accessed September 14, 2014. http://icom.museum/the-vision/museum-definition.

Knell, Simon J., Suzanne MacLeod, and Sheila Watson, eds. 2007. *Museum Revolutions: How Museums Change and Are Changed*. London: Routledge.

"Liverpool's Museums and Galleries Celebrate a Rise in Visitor Numbers." 2013. *Liverpool Echo*. March 12. Accessed September 20, 2014. http://www.liverpoolecho.co.uk/news/liverpool-news/liverpools-museums-galleries-celebrate-rise-3009490.

Lord, Gail, and Barry Lord. 1999. *The Manual of Museum Planning*. Lanham, MD: AltaMira.

Missionstatements.com. 2011. Accessed September 14, 2014. http://www.missionstatements.com/fortune_500_mission_statements.html.

Murdin, Lynda. 1991. "All Change at Tyne and Wear Museums Service." *Museums Journal* 91(10): 5.

Museum of Liverpool. 2013. Website. Accessed September 14, 2014. http://www.liverpoolmuseums.org.uk/mol.

Museums Association. 1995. *Museum Briefing, 9: Advocacy for Museums*. September. London: Museums Association.

Museums Association. 2014. "About." Accessed September 14, 2014. http://www.museumsassociation.org/about/frequently-asked-questions.

National Museums Liverpool. 2010. *Strategic Plan 2010–2011*. July 23. Liverpool: National Museums Liverpool.

National Museums Liverpool. 2013. Website. Accessed September 14, 2014. www.liverpoolmuseums.org.uk.

Rainbow Centre, Singapore. 2011. "Vision, Mission and Core Values." Accessed September 14, 2014. http://www.rainbowcentre.org.sg/index.php?id=21.

Rangan, V. K. 2004. "Lofty Missions, Down-to-Earth Plans." *Harvard Business Review* 82(3). Accessed September 14, 2014. http://hbr.org/2004/03/lofty-missions-down-to-earth-plans/ar/1.

Scott, Cynthia D., Dennis T. Jaffe, and Glenn R. Tobe. 1993. *Organisational Vision, Values and Mission*. Menlo Park, CA: Crisp Publications.

Tyne and Wear Archives and Museums. 2011. Website. Accessed September 14, 2014. www.twmuseums.org.uk.

Tyne and Wear Museums Annual Reports. 1991/2–2000/1. Newcastle: Tyne and Wear Museums.

Unlad Kabayan Migrant Services Foundation. 2011. "Vision and Mission." Accessed September 14, 2014. http://www.unladkabayan.org/vision-mission.html.

"Visitor Services Case Study: Tyne and Wear Museums." 1998. *Museum Practice*. March 7: 49–55.

Watson, Ian. 2012. "How Museums Can Make a Difference." *Museums Journal* 112(4): 19.

Further Reading

Chamberlain, Gregory. 2009. "National Museum Liverpool: The Great Museum Experiment of our Time?" *Museum Identity: Museums Galleries Heritage* 1: 24–33.

Fleming, David. 1997. "The Regeneration Game." *Museums Journal* 97(4): 32–33.

Fleming, David. 1999. "A Question of Perception." *Museums Journal* 99(4): 29.

Janes, Robert R. 1997. *Museums and the Paradox of Change: A Case Study in Urgent Adaptation.* Calgary, AB: Glenbow Museum, University of Calgary Press.

Janes, Robert R., and Richard Sandell, eds. 2007. *Museum Management and Marketing.* London: Routledge.

Kotler, Neil, and Philip Kotler. 2004. "Can Museums Be All Things to All People? Missions, Goals and Marketing's Role." In *Reinventing the Museum: Historical and Contemporary Perspectives on the Paradigm Shift*, edited by G. Anderson, 167–186. Walnut Creek, CA: AltaMira.

Kotler, Neil, Philip Kotler, and Wendy Kotler. 2008. *Museum Marketing and Strategy: Designing Missions, Building Audiences, Generating Revenue and Resources.* San Francisco: Jossey Bass.

David Fleming has been Director, National Museums Liverpool, since 2001. During his time there, he has completed major projects including the opening of the Slavery Museum, the Museum of Liverpool, and the project Into the Future, which involved the refurbishment of the Walker Art Gallery and World Museum. Before that he was Director, Tyne and Wear Museums for 11 years, and before that Principal Keeper at Hull Museums. David has spoken at many international conferences and published widely on museum management and leadership, city history museums, social inclusion, and human rights.

2 GOVERNANCE
Guiding the Museum in Trust

Barry Lord

Museums seem to be about objects, but they are really about people. Museums seem to be buildings with things in them, but they are really means of communication between people – people of all countries, people of the distant past, and the people of future generations. The three-dimensional objects in museum collections are the ways in which people of all times and places communicate with each other.

The governance of museums is therefore a trusteeship. Those who are given the honor and responsibility of governing our museum institutions hold the objects through which we communicate to each other over time and place in trust. The people of past generations and foreign countries must trust those who govern our museums to preserve the heritage held in them. Those museum governors are equally entrusted to hand down the legacy of the past and the present to future generations.

In order to fulfill this trusteeship, museum governors have a duty of loyalty and a duty of care. The duty of loyalty means that they put the interests of their institution ahead of any personal interests. The duty of care extends not only to the preservation of the heritage, but to its effective presentation and interpretation to museum users today. This trust is fiduciary, meaning that those charged with the responsibility should exercise the same care in managing its assets as a prudent person normally would for his or her own possessions.

Literature on governance

Most of the current literature about museum governance focuses on the role of boards and trustees (Fisher 1995). Marie Malaro's 1994 text on mission, ethics, and policy, John Carver's well-known book (1997), and the collections that Gail Anderson has edited (2000, 2004) are typical examples of studies that share this preoccupation. In fact, however, boards of trustees are by no means the most frequently encountered form of museum governance. Throughout most of the world, museums are line departments of national, state, provincial, county, or

The International Handbooks of Museum Studies: Museum Practice, First Edition.
Edited by Conal McCarthy.
© 2015 John Wiley & Sons Ltd. Published 2020 by John Wiley & Sons Ltd.

civic governments. Even where boards are operating, they may be advisory only, or may function only with a limited mandate established by the relevant government department. The contributions that my partner Gail Dexter Lord and I have made to the literature, such as our *Manual of Museum Management* (2009), while amply discussing the role of boards and trustees, have attempted to reflect this reality.

Modes of museum governance

Broadly, despite the multifarious ways in which museums are established and maintained around the world, there are only four modes of governance:

- line departments;
- "arms-length" institutions;
- independent not-for-profit associations;
- private ownership.

Those museums in the last category that are operated for profit are excluded from the definitions of museums by the United Nations Educational and Scientific Organization (UNESCO), the Museums Association of Great Britain (MA), and the American Association of Museums (AAM), all of which define museums as not-for-profit. Not-for-profit privately owned museums are included in the definitions, but do not constitute a separate category since these museums, many of which are corporate institutions, may be operated under any of the other three modes of governance: thus a corporate museum may be a line department of its parent corporation, or may be established under a governing board established at arm's length from the corporation, or may even be set up as a completely independent institution to which the corporation contributes grants. Thus it is sufficient here to consider the first three modes of governance, which characterize all those institutions that satisfy the internationally accepted definition of a museum.

Line departments

Line departments, by far the most numerous, are in most cases government museums administered by a department of the national, state, provincial, county, or municipal government. However, line department museums also include most university museums – such as a geology museum that is administered by the university's earth sciences division – and corporate museums, such as the automotive museums maintained by each of Germany's car manufacturers. In governance terms, all these museums have in common that they are administered as a line department of a larger organization that owns their buildings and collections.

Government line departments may report to a minister responsible for culture, education, tourism, or other government sectors. Although the Director of the National Palace Museum in Taipei is an appointed member of Taiwan's governing cabinet, all other government line department museums around the world report through the relevant government hierarchy.

Specialized museums may report to ministers of their relevant departments – thus an agricultural museum may be part of a federal or provincial department of agriculture, and many postal museums and communication museums are an integral part of national postal or telecommunication services. Among the most numerous museum types in many countries (including the United States) are the military museums governed by the unit of the armed forces that they represent – regimental museums.

If line department museums have boards of trustees, they are usually advisory only. Sometimes called visiting committees, these advisory boards may have a broader or a more narrowly specified scope, but in any case they remain advisory to the governing body, which retains authority and responsibility for the institution. The mission, mandate, goals, objectives, and policies of these museums are established within guidelines set by the organizations of which they are a part – government departments, university disciplines, or divisions of a corporation. The larger organization owns the buildings and the collections, while staff, including the director, are employees of that organization – civil servants in the case of government line departments, university or corporate employees in the other examples. Recruitment, evaluation, and disciplinary processes are all subject to the policies of the larger organization – meaning civil service procedures for government line department museums – often resulting in a relatively static institution with limited capacity for change. Few of these museums have membership programs, and volunteers are usually scarce, since the public perception of many of these museums is that all tasks should be accomplished by paid employees, especially if these are taxpayer-supported, as in the case of government line department museums.

Funding for the operation of line department museums is in most cases a line item in the budget of the government, university, or corporate department of which they are a part. They may also qualify for grants, but their primary financial support comes from regular appropriations. Most line department museums offer free admission, but even if admission is charged, self-generated revenue – whether from ticket sales, retail, rentals, or food services – in most cases does not benefit the museum directly, with profits (sometimes all revenue) going into the general funds of the government, university, or corporation, not benefiting the museum directly; in the worst instances, government appropriations may even be reduced commensurate with any increase in self-generated funds. Such a financial structure has two obvious drawbacks:

1. The museum has no motivation to enhance visitor services that could generate additional revenue. As a result, visitor services in government line department museums around the world are often notoriously poor.

2. Annual appropriations are subject to periodic cutbacks, especially affecting government line department museums in times of economic difficulty. Since these cutbacks usually constrain the funds available for programs that may or may not be offered by the museum, rather than the salaries of relatively fixed civil service positions, over many years the salaries tend to creep up as a proportion of the budget, resulting in a dearth of operating resources for programming.

More complex systems

Some governments responsible for multiple museums have established museum systems, adding an administrative layer in the form of a national, provincial, civic, or state museums authority, in the hope of obtaining efficiencies of scale due to the centralization of such services as conservation, documentation, purchasing, security, accounting, or human resources. One result is often the erection of a non-public building in which many of these support functions can be maintained. Singapore's Heritage Conservation Centre in Jurong is an outstanding example, which our company, Lord Cultural Resources, helped to plan. The individual museums, which usually retain their specific curatorial, education, and exhibition departments, may struggle to assert their identities in such a system, but in general these disadvantages are outweighed by the gains in efficiency due to centralization of other functions. In the case of Singapore, these include the Singapore Art Museum, the Singapore History Museum, and the Asian Civilization Museum, all of which benefit from the storage, conservation, and documentation services of the state-of-the-art Centre in Jurong; the entire complex is governed by the government-appointed National Heritage Board, which is currently proceeding with the renovation and expansion of two heritage buildings into a new National Gallery of Singapore.

Further complexity in governance can arise when the museum is part of a cultural complex. A cultural district may be simply an area within a city where a number of independent cultural attractions are located; or it may be a deliberately planned complex, as on Abu Dhabi's Saadiyat Island in the United Arab Emirates, or in Hong Kong's West Kowloon Cultural District. The Louvre Abu Dhabi, the Guggenheim Abu Dhabi, and the National Zayed Museum are currently under construction on Saadiyat Island, with a Maritime Museum also planned, while at West Kowloon a multidisciplinary museum named M+ is planned, along with an exhibition center and a range of performing arts venues.

The governance of each component of a complex – which may individually be line departments, "arm's length" institutions, not-for-profit organizations, or private sector attractions – may need to be planned in relation to a central authority for the complex, if there is to be one. The concern is to respect the independence of each constituent while realizing advantages due to their association, such as common marketing, joint purchasing, security, or in some cases shared facilities. Our company has assisted with both the Abu Dhabi and Hong Kong projects, where final decisions as to governance are still under consideration, as government agencies – the Tourism

Development and Investment Corporation (TDIC) of the United Arab Emirates (UAE) and the West Kowloon Cultural District Authority in Hong Kong – serve as at least interim, possibly longer-term governance for these developing projects.

Collaboration to realize advantages of scale can even be negotiated among the governing bodies of long-standing independent institutions. Several years ago our firm helped the Cleveland Museum of Natural History, the Cleveland Botanic Garden, and the Western Reserve Historical Society, all of which were independent not-for-profit associations located in one sector of Cleveland's Museum Circle, to form the Cleveland Cultural Collaborative, aimed at achieving efficiencies of scale by combining purchasing, support staff, and services where possible.

Still another governance challenge arises for museums that are also responsible for colleges or schools. Every variety of relationship may be observed here: from the complete integration of staff appointments where curators are also professors at the American Museum of Natural History and its graduate school in New York; over to complete separation, as at the Portland (Oregon) Art Museum, which founded the school that became the Pacific Northwest College of Art in 1909 but separated from it in 1994, with the college relocating four years later so that the museum could expand. Even where the museum and the school are in the same building or physically connected, as at the Art Institute of Chicago, museum and college may have separate governance. At the time of writing our firm was working with the Corcoran Gallery and College of Art and Design[1] in Washington, DC, which formerly had separate boards for each, but for some years now has been trying to administer both gallery and college with the board of one independent not-for-profit association. State or provincial university museums in the United States, Canada, and elsewhere can often simplify these relationships, since both college and museum usually report as line departments to a central university board or senate. Such university museums often benefit by receiving allocations that are part of a much larger state education budget.

Whether operating independently or as part of a larger system, however, government line department museums around the world too often suffer from cutbacks in funding, inadequate programming resources, virtually no acquisition budgets, and top-down administrations that may be ill-informed about or indifferent to the museum's needs. Such an institution has great difficulty answering the call to participate as an economic generator of cultural tourism, or even as an educational resource. As a result, the past few decades have seen a worldwide trend toward setting many government line department museums at a distance sufficient to facilitate other means of revenue generation – creating the second common governance type, often called "arm's-length" museums.

"Arm's-length" museums

Arm's-length museums are so called because they operate at some distance from the "head," the central governing agency. This "arm's length" may be longer or shorter, but in all cases is intended to encourage greater financial independence and freedom from political or corporate control, even though the "head" organization retains ultimate authority. The "arm's length" may be established in various ways:

- Boards of trustees for arm's-length institutions may be given real authority and responsibility as governing boards, sometimes within certain limits. The governing authority – government department, university administration, or corporation – is usually represented on the board, with the rest of its members appointed to include collectors, concerned interest groups, or the general public. Although the collection and buildings are still publicly owned, the board is said to hold the collections in a public trust.
- Budgets are usually based on annual grants (as distinguished from departmental budget allocations), with the understanding that these grants will not meet all costs, so that the board of trustees has responsibility for raising the balance, through private donations, self-generated revenues, and grants from other levels or branches of government.
- Museums are enfranchised to benefit directly from their self-generated revenues – admission fees, retail, rentals, food services, or other sources of funding.
- Staff may remain civil servants, or may be employed directly by the museum, often granted status and benefits equivalent to or better than civil service conditions of employment.
- Arm's-length institutions are usually more successful than government line department museums at attracting donations, developing membership programs, recruiting Friends' organizations and enlisting volunteer activities.

Not all of these features are found in every arm's-length institution. During the 1980s in the United Kingdom Margaret Thatcher's government gave a great impetus in this direction to Britain's national museums, with most of the emphasis on the individual institution's responsibility for its own fund-raising and ability to profit from its own enterprise. In Paris the Louvre is now solidly established as an arm's-length institution, having developed a series of *grands projets* and currently participating, along with eight other French national institutions, in *France Museums*, a consortium that is providing long-term loans and short-term exhibitions from their collections to the Louvre Abu Dhabi on Saadiyat Island, in exchange for substantial funds that are being used primarily for conservation of France's national collections. In 2003 the Prado in Madrid became an arm's-length institution, still strongly linked to government but with its own board and a long-range goal of reducing its reliance on government funding from 80 to 50 percent of its budget. Several years ago we undertook a study for Hong Kong's Leisure and Cultural Services Department that considered the extent to which an arm's-length model might benefit government-operated museums there.

Independent not-for-profit associations

The independent not-for-profit association, the governance model that is almost exclusively the subject of much of the literature on the subject, is found in its most typical form in the United States, and to a lesser degree in Canada, Australia, and elsewhere. In most jurisdictions these museums qualify for exemption from taxes on the grounds that they are dedicating their earnings to charitable or educational purposes. Their governing boards, with new trustees recruited and appointed by the present board, assume legal and financial responsibility for the museum, and are responsible for several key functions:

- establishment, approval, and revision of the museum's foundation statements – mission, vision, mandate, and statement of purpose;
- ensuring that the museum's collections are preserved, studied, documented, and made accessible to as wide a range of museum visitors and users as possible;
- approval of long-range plans for development of the museum;
- recruitment, appointment, evaluation, and (if necessary) dismissal of the museum's director, who is responsible for all other hiring, evaluation, and dismissal of staff;
- fund-raising for capital projects and development of the museum;
- approval of budgets, review of regular audits, and maintenance of the fiscal stability of the museum;
- approval of policies submitted by staff, or directions for their revision;
- public advocacy for community involvement in the museum to governments, foundations, corporations, educational institutions, and other organizations;
- collegial loyalty among trustees, and avoidance of conflicts of interest.

The key recurring term in the above list of responsibilities is "approval." The focus of the board of trustees must be on consideration of foundation statements, plans, policies, and budgets prepared by their staff and submitted by their director for their consideration. The goal is approval: if the board is not satisfied they may withhold approval and direct revisions or reconsideration, but in order to support their director (who may or may not be a member or a secretary of the board) they should not yield to the temptation to begin generating these documents themselves.

In our practice we usually recommend a rota of policies to be submitted for consideration and possible revision each month, so that every policy is reconsidered at some time during the year; this practice helps to prevent unwitting lapses – in security policy, for instance – that may otherwise be left unexamined until a crisis erupts. Board members must learn to limit their role to the approval of policies and their revisions prepared for their consideration by staff, yet retain an active role in the development and monitoring of these policies. On the one hand boards must refuse to apply a "rubber stamp" to whatever the director submits to them, but on the other they must refrain from meddling in the museum's day-to-day operations, which should implement the policies they approve, and report back to the board regularly on their success or lack of it in implementation, together with any suggested revisions in policies to make them more realistically applicable.

The role of the board is usually established by a constitution or deed, and may be further interpreted in bylaws or rules passed by the board. Constitution and bylaws are likely to address the number and tenure of trustees, an executive and committee structure and the reporting relationships of their officers, the frequency, location, quorum, and minuting of meetings, provision for expenses or remuneration of trustees, and the extent or limitation of trustees' financial, legal, and ethical responsibilities. In addition to an Executive Committee, which is empowered to make necessary decisions between board meetings, there is usually a need for a Nominating or Recruitment Committee, a Long-range Planning Committee, a Finance Committee (concerned with operating funds), and a Development Committee (focused on capital fund-raising). In an art museum an Acquisition Committee may be useful as a means to raise funds for large-value purchases, but in general board committees concerned with the daily work of the museum – such as a Collections Committee, an Exhibitions Committee, or an Education Committee – are signs of dysfunction, indicating that the board may be too much involved in daily operations.

Conflicts of interest are inherent among trustees because boards often seek to recruit among persons who are interested in the museum's subject matter, and therefore may be themselves collecting or professionally involved in the field. Some "insider trading" is impossible to avoid, as when trustees know in advance of the general public when their museum is planning a major retrospective of an artist whose works they may hold or decide to acquire. This is the ethical area where the "duty of care" and the "duty of loyalty" must be respected. Trustees are enjoined to state conflicts of interest when they arise, and to refrain from voting (usually avoiding even participation in the discussion) on issues with real, potential, or perceived conflicts. Most boards adopt a Code of Ethics to guide trustees in these matters.

Independent not-for-profit associations and incorporated societies are far better placed than any other mode of governance to establish membership programs and to benefit from the support of volunteers – indeed, some of these museums are highly reliant on volunteerism. Some associations and societies – such as many of those concerned with vintage transport museums – begin as groups of like-minded volunteers, who may have difficulty managing the transition to serving on a board that hires a director to operate a professional museum with paid staff. Particularly challenging is the role of the trustee who also serves as a volunteer operating a heritage steam train or scraping paint off a vintage automobile under the direction of the museum's conservator.

In order to maintain their tax-exempt status all not-for-profit independent museums have to apply for registration, file annual financial statements and comply with the relevant regulations of their governments. In the United States, for example, the tax exemption applies only to those activities that are related to their educational mission – so the shop must keep separate accounts for the sale of items that are judged to be unrelated.

Funding for these museums is always a mixture of private donations, foundation grants, and self-generated revenue, but government grants also play a major role on most of their balance sheets. Board members are expected to make annual donations to operations – with minimal amounts often set in advance for incoming trustees – and in addition may be asked to "get, give, or get off" the board during fund-raising campaigns for capital projects or other development programs. An important feature of many of these museums' finances, especially in the United States, is an endowment fund to which museum supporters are encouraged to donate or bequeath contributions that are not spent directly but are invested so that the interest earned by the Fund is expended on annual operations. Difficulties arise when beleaguered trustees spend more than the interest earned, or even worse "borrow" from the fund to replenish the operating budget. Some endowments are restricted so that only their earnings can be used, whereas unrestricted endowments offer more flexibility. As much as 20 percent and more of the budgets of many large US museums consists of endowment fund earnings; the economic crisis of 2008–2009 sharply reduced these earnings by 20 to 30 percent, resulting in cutbacks to staffing, salaries, or operations in many places.

Another temptation for hard-pressed boards of trustees is to consider deaccessioning works of art or artifacts as a means to shore up their depleted treasuries. The statement of professional ethics of the International Council of Museums (ICOM) requires that any proceeds of deaccessioning must be used for new acquisitions; AAM agrees, with the qualification that proceeds may in some cases be used for the conservation of the remaining collection. In addition, museums considering deaccessioning must also consider the terms of wills or gift agreements before they can legally avail themselves of the proceeds of auctions or other sales. Nevertheless, economic necessity obliges many trustees to consider their legal and ethical options closely; it is particularly tempting to place revenues resulting from deaccessioning in an "acquisitions fund," but then to "borrow" from that fund for operational expenses, committing the board to replenish the fund at some time in the future. Internal "loans" of this kind, as with those obtained from restricted endowment funds, are not recommended, but may in some situations be inescapable as government appropriations and private contributions become more and more difficult to obtain in times of economic crisis.

The greater vitality of independent not-for-profit associations has prompted moves to introduce them in jurisdictions where museums have traditionally been governed as line departments. The transition is often difficult. In Hong Kong, for instance, the West Kowloon Cultural District Authority has had the disconcerting experience of seeing its first two directors (one local, the other imported) resign, allegedly for "personal" or "health" reasons, within a few days of their appointments. Such *contretemps* occur as boards accustomed to obedient civil servants within government line departments encounter directors who must be given freedom to operate an independent association. Considering all these issues, it is not surprising that incoming trustees are usually presented with a Board Manual, and may be expected to undergo an orientation program. When museum board meetings make bad news, it is usually due to an ill-prepared or only partially understood relationship between the director and some or all of the board members.

New directions in the governance of civil society institutions

Any discussion of museum governance today must be conducted in the context established by the late Stephen Weil (1928–2005), the renowned American museologist who introduced the term "civil society institutions" in much of his writing and speaking toward the end of his life (Weil 2004). By this phrase he was referring to the emergence of museums that are far more involved in their communities – culturally, economically, and socially – so that their governance calls out for the active participation of public and private sectors, individuals and organizations with a sense of responsibility to and for the maintenance of a healthy, creative, innovative society. This movement can be clearly seen in science centers that get involved in public/private partnerships to encourage innovation, in art museums aiming to stimulate creativity in the public school system, or in natural or cultural history museums that are courageous enough to present exhibitions on controversial topics.

Ironically, this trend has been intensified by government financial cutbacks, as even line department museums have reached out to become more involved in the economic realities of their communities. The increasingly important role of museums in the vital cultural tourism industry has also supported this direction. Museums' contributions to social cohesion in an age of rapid social change, their often decisive role in urban regeneration, and their ability to contribute to the "brand" of their cities are all further factors encouraging this direction. Perhaps most important has been the growth in importance of what economist Richard Florida has called "the creative class," in other words people working in or around the "knowledge economy"; as scientific, cultural, and heritage institutions, museums are integral to the knowledge economy, and their governance must be adapted to reflect this position (Florida 2003).

Not surprisingly, the resultant tendency among line department museums has been to move to arm's-length status, while among those museums already at "arm's length" there has been pressure for greater autonomy. Among independent not-for-profit associations greater civil society engagement points to the need for boards that are more representative of the diverse populations the museums are serving, with concomitant attention to increasing access for all sectors of society.

Consider the following statement of a museum board's responsibilities that we recently wrote in the executive summary of a Board Development Strategy for a museum of contemporary art:

> It is recommended that the board's roles and responsibilities be two-fold: the board will be responsible both to the museum and the public. The board will work to ensure institutional sustainability, continuity and evolution. It will also represent the ethnic and social diversity of the community that it represents.

Exactly how museum governance of civil society institutions will evolve will form the narrative of the coming decades. Nina Simon may have pointed the way in her recent book, *The Participatory Museum* (2010). Governing boards will need to find ways to encourage greater public participation without weakening museum professionalism. Hopefully this greater engagement with the museum's community may result in a civil society institution that is not dependent on any one source of funding but reflective of the broad public support its professionals will work hard to deserve. All of us may then directly and consciously hold our heritage in trust.

The following case study, drawn from our firm's work with the governing board of the Museum of Contemporary Canadian Art (MOCCA) in Toronto, illustrates the development of a civil society institution. Interestingly, it traces an evolution that has included aspects of all three types of governance discussed here. Currently, as an arm's-length institution, MOCCA continues to evolve as a civil society institution. Its aspirations may serve as a signal example of how museums in the present century will be entering more and more into every aspect of the economic and social as well as cultural life of their communities. The future of museum governance may be uncertain, but it can certainly be bright, and challenging, if our institutions collectively have the courage to genuinely serve the societies they live in.

Case study: Becoming a civil society museum – the Museum of Contemporary Canadian Art (Toronto, Canada)

Rina Gerson

The Museum of Contemporary Canadian Art and its governance structure is an exemplary model of an institution making the transition into a "civil society museum." Today it is a thriving anchor for the contemporary art community in Toronto's Arts + Design District. However, the museum was born of a complex relationship between a corporation and a municipality, neither of which now exist, and has fought for survival under changing governance and leadership. Over its two-decade history, the museum has continuously adapted to meet the needs of its constituency, fulfilling its mandate to further the careers of living Canadian artists. The museum has undergone tremendous transformation and continues to grow. Its survival is a testament to exceptional civic, political, and institutional leadership, as well as a responsive and evolving approach to governance.

Background

MOCCA was constituted in 1999 from the former Art Gallery of North York, which was founded five years earlier. In its original incarnation, the Art Gallery of North York was a 5000 sq. foot (465 m²) gallery in the back of the North York Performing Arts Centre (NYPAC), a state-of-the-art theater complex built in 1993 by what was then called the City of North York, which is now a suburb of Toronto.

The driving principle behind the Centre was that it would be an incubator for the arts without requiring additional tax dollars. This was accomplished through a 10-year deal between the City of North York and Live Entertainment Corp. (Livent), according to which Livent paid the City an annual fee from the profits it made by operating NYPAC as a commercial venture. Through this deal, Livent paid the staff salaries and other operating costs at the Centre. It also allocated a portion of the surcharge on ticket sales toward building a contemporary Canadian art collection for the City of North York. While Livent operated the Centre, NYPAC was nevertheless governed by the North York Performing Arts Centre Corporation, a city-appointed body responsible for running the Centre. The Gallery and its advisors reported directly to this NYPAC Corporation board.

The Art Gallery of North York was an exciting, novel, and important venue for living Canadian artists. When it opened on June 21, 1994 with an ambitious exhibition entitled *Future Traditions in Canadian Art: Seven Artists Selected by Seven Curators*, it became the only institution in Toronto dedicated exclusively to showcasing the work of living Canadian artists. For the next four years the Gallery built its collection, which in 1999 was reported to be worth CDN$3 million and welcomed 70,000 visitors at its peak – many of whom were also theater patrons at Livent productions.

This was an unprecedented and unique deal for a public art gallery. Livent's agreement to build a public art collection for North York had made them an attractive tenant for the venue. However, collecting, displaying, and preserving works of visual art were neither the core business nor a priority of NYPAC. Therefore, the Gallery's operations were of minimal consequence to the overall governance of the Centre, so the curator was endowed with virtual freedom to collect and exhibit at his discretion. The audience was largely captive, since it consisted almost entirely of theater patrons awaiting performances or between acts. Therefore, an educational, public-oriented mandate was not the primary driver for attendance or for keeping the Gallery afloat.

Unfortunately, the deal proved to be too good to be true, and in 1998 Livent went bankrupt. Simultaneously, North York and other municipalities amalgamated to join what became "the mega city" of Toronto. The greatly enlarged City of Toronto was left with a multimillion dollar complex to operate and, without funding, the Gallery was left on life support.

Going public

The metropolitan amalgamation of Toronto and the collapse of Livent meant change for the Centre and for the Gallery. First came branding: the Centre was renamed the Toronto Centre for the Arts, and the Art Gallery of North York became the Museum of Contemporary Canadian Art (MOCCA). While the ownership of the collection and governance of the Gallery had technically always remained under the control of the City, the shift in circumstances left the Gallery somewhere between being an arm's-length institution and a line item in the City's cultural budget. While the City had always been in charge of funding the Gallery, without the Livent surcharge funds, the new MOCCA needed direct funding from the City to survive. Without Livent in the middle, the City also was now directly responsible for the Gallery.

For the 1998–1999 season the City underwrote the costs of concerts, exhibitions, maintenance, and salaries at the Centre, but grappled with the Centre's and the Gallery's fate for 2000 and beyond. An ad-hoc "Save MOCCA" committee anticipated forthcoming struggles, acknowledged that ultimately MOCCA needed to be its own entity, and began to petition City Council and raise funds for exhibitions.

This early fight for independence proved successful, and by February 1999 the committee produced a petition of 1300 signatures in favor of keeping MOCCA. Throughout the year it raised enough momentum and funds to convince the City that MOCCA was a worthy cause. Its success culminated that September when MOCCA successfully opened a major retrospective exhibition. In a letter to the committee, the City Hall Culture Commissioner wrote: "I cannot stress enough the important role … the ad-hoc committee [has] played in providing a focus that is specific to MOCCA and its future … I encourage you to continue this work." Another official in the culture division commended MOCCA: "It has forced itself to separate from the [NYPAC and] to define itself. And it has brought people and money. You know, when people commit money, that's when politicians sit up and take notice" (Ross 1999, 62). Following this effort the ad-hoc committee disbanded, morphing into an Advisory Board, and MOCCA began reporting to both the NYPAC board and the City, ushering in MOCCA's transition over the next decade into what we have called a "civil society museum."

MOCCA downtown

In 2005, MOCCA relocated to the Queen Street West Art & Design District in downtown Toronto. In an almost unanimous vote, the City Council funded this move and signed the museum's 10-year lease on a former textile factory that was renovated to serve as a gallery. Between 1999 and 2004 the MOCCA Advisory Board and the people of Toronto fought hard and successfully raised the museum's profile and proved its value, not only to the arts and cultural community, but also to the overall cultural landscape of the City of Toronto.

As a line department in the City's Culture division, the City used MOCCA to realize its plans to revitalize and brand distinct neighborhoods in downtown Toronto. With MOCCA as an anchor, the Queen Street West neighborhood has developed its character as an epicenter for art, design, and creativity in Toronto, Canada, North America, and the world. The relationship is one of mutual benefit.

After ten years in its downtown location, MOCCA continues to grow. Its visibility and presence has attracted important partnerships: in November 2010 the National Gallery of Canada launched a three-year program under which that Ottawa institution will co-organize and co-present exhibitions of art from its collection in partnership with Toronto's MOCCA.

Following its move downtown, MOCCA's relationship with the City shifted to more of an arm's-length status, providing MOCCA with discretion to administer and allocate its budget. MOCCA staff report to the City through the managing director. The City provided operating funds and a number of "in-kind" services for the museum. The museum could do some fund-raising; however, it did not have the liberty to issue its own tax-deductible receipts (the City issued the tax receipts), and at times was restricted in terms of the types of donations that it could receive. Finally, in 2012 MOCCA changed its status once again, becoming an independent not-for-profit institution in order that it could do its own fund-raising and issue its own tax-deductible receipts for donations. This new status is expected to give MOCCA more organizational freedom to grow into a world-class center for contemporary art.

MOCCA's Advisory Board has therefore become a Governing Board. It has been a driving force in enabling the museum to become a successful growing arm's-length institution as opposed to a passive line item department as it was in its original incarnation in North York. In 2008, under the stewardship of the managing director, the Board introduced strategic and governance planning exercises (which our firm assisted with) to gear the museum up for its next major change in governance: initially something between an "arm's length" institution and an independent not-for-profit, which they called a "hybrid model." Under these circumstances, MOCCA would have more freedom in terms of its fund-raising and revenue generating activities. Its Advisory Board transitioned into a Governing Board, with fiduciary responsibility and more accountability to the public. Through this process, MOCCA was once again evolving to become more independent. The City continued to provide off-site collection storage space, but as of 2012 MOCCA acquired a fully independent status.

As its Board has undergone this change, MOCCA has gone to great lengths to consider what it means to represent, build, and lead a museum. During the Livent days, the Gallery's Director and Curator did not have to report to a Board. While exhibitions at the Art Gallery of North York spoke to and represented Toronto's diverse public, it was not a requirement of Livent's in order for the Gallery to receive funding. The museum's new status relies heavily on support and buy-in from the public. Consequently, the MOCCA board is considering the museum's broad pool of stakeholders as potential resources for funding, audience, and over-all support. Their presence and participation are essential to the gallery's opera-tions and survival, whereas before they were passive patrons.

Toronto has been defined as the most diverse municipality on the planet, with the largest number of communities of 20,000 people or more speaking a language other than English. More than half of Toronto's population was born elsewhere. As the Board prepares to recruit new members and strengthen its leadership, it is addressing the need to include the city's ethnographically diverse communities, diverse professional backgrounds, and developing adequate, transparent proce-dures in order to be accountable to the public. The museum's programs will also need to draw in broader audiences to attract a strong membership.

MOCCA is indeed transforming into a civil society museum, acknowledging that every area of its governance and operations require diverse participation from the pub-lic at large. The future of this still-evolving institution is full of challenge, and of hope.

Note

1 The Corcoran has subsequently negotiated an agreement to transfer its collections to the ownership of the National Gallery of Art in Washington, while another educational institution is taking over the Art College.

References

Anderson, Gail, ed. 2000. *Museum Mission Statements: Building a Distinct Identity*. Washington, DC: American Association of Museums.

Anderson, Gail, ed. 2004. *Reinventing the Museum: Historical and Contemporary Perspectives on the Paradigm Shift*. Lanham, MD: AltaMira Press.

Carver, John. 1997. *Boards that Make a Difference: A New Design for Leadership in Non-profit and Public Organizations*. San Francisco: Jossey-Bass.

Fisher, H. 1995. *Welcome to the Board: Your Guide to Effective Participation*. San Francisco: Jossey-Bass.

Florida, Richard. 2003. *The Rise of the Creative Class: And How It's Transforming Work, Leisure, Community and Everyday Life*. New York: Basic Books.

Lord, Barry, and Gail Dexter Lord. 2009. *The Manual of Museum Management*, 2nd ed. Lanham, MD: AltaMira.

Malaro, Marie. 1994. *Museum Governance: Mission Ethics Policy*. Washington, DC: Smithsonian Institution.

Ross, V. 1999. "Big City Gallery: What Happens When You Pull the Rug Out from Under an Art-World Success Story?" *Canadian Art* 16(4): 62.

Simon, Nina. 2010. *The Participatory Museum*. Santa Cruz, CA: Museum 2.0.

Weil, Stephen. 2004. "Rethinking the Museum: An Emerging New Paradigm." In *Reinventing the Museum: Historical and Contemporary Perspectives on the Paradigm Shift*, edited by Gail Anderson, 74–79. Lanham, MD: AltaMira.

Further Reading

Cornforth, Chris. 2005. *The Governance of Public and Non-profit Organisations: What Do Boards Do?* Routledge Studies in the Management of Voluntary and Non-Profit Organisations. London: Routledge Psychology Press.

Falk, John. 2006. *Thriving in the Knowledge Age: New Business Models for Museums and Other Cultural Institutions.* Lanham, MD: AltaMira.

Lord, Barry, Gail Dexter Lord, and Lindsay Martin. 2012. *Manual of Museum Planning: Sustainable Space, Facilities, and Operations.* Lanham, MD: AltaMira.

Lord, Gail Dexter. 2007. "Museums Outside-In." *Conference Proceedings of the 21st ICOM General Conference*, 90–97. Vienna: ICOM. Accessed September 20, 2014. http://icom.museum/fileadmin/user_upload/pdf/ICOM_2007/2007_Proceedings_eng.pdf.

Macdonald, Sharon, ed. 2011. *A Companion to Museum Studies.* Oxford: Blackwell.

Oster, Sharon, and William Goetzmann. 2003. "Does Governance Matter? The Case of Art Museums." In *The Governance of Not-for-Profit Organizations*, edited by Edward L. Glaeser, 71–99. Chicago: University of Chicago Press, National Bureau of Economic Research. Accessed September 20, 2014. http://www.nber.org/chapters/c9966.pdf.

Suchy, Sherene. 2004. *Leading with Passion: Change Management in the 21st Century Museum.* Lanham, MD: AltaMira.

Barry Lord is Co-President of Lord Cultural Resources, the world's largest firm specialized in the planning and management of museums and other cultural institutions. With his wife and partner, Gail Dexter Lord, he is co-author of *The Manual of Museum Management* (2nd ed. 2009), co-editor of other volumes in their *Manual* series, and most recently author of *Art & Energy: How Culture Changes* (The AAM Press, 2014).

Rina Gerson (née Zigler) was a Research Consultant in the Management Consulting Group at Lord Cultural Resources between 2008 and 2011. Rina worked with MOCCA's Board and Staff, guiding it through Strategic and Governance Planning initiatives and later became the founding Co-Chair of MOCCA's young leadership committee, the Moccamigos. She holds a BA with Honours in Art History from McGill University and an MBA from the Rotman School of Management at the University of Toronto.

3 POLICIES, FRAMEWORKS, AND LEGISLATION
The Conditions Under Which English Museums Operate

Sara Selwood and Stuart Davies

The conditions within which English museums currently operate tend to be associated with the three successive New Labour governments of May 1997 to May 2010. New Labour issued unprecedented levels of policy guidance, introduced a "new cultural framework" and substantially increased funding to the cultural sector. In one of his valedictory speeches, former Prime Minister, Tony Blair, referred to having achieved "a golden age" for the arts and museums (Tempest 2007). But, of course, museums' modus operandi goes back considerably further and many interventions were not targeted at museums, but intended to reform the public sector more broadly. Their impact on museums was secondary and unintentional.

Policies change over the course of 13 years. Not only did New Labour improve many of the programs it inherited, but, over the course of the 2000s, retracted much of the cultural framework it had itself put in place. And, in the wake of the 2008 recession, its successor government, the Conservative and Liberal Democrat Coalition, has rescinded even more. It abolished New Labour's Museums, Libraries and Archives Council (MLA) in what was known as its "bonfire of the quangos" (the abolition of a number of quasi-autonomous non-governmental organizations) and withdrew funding from many museum-related initiatives. These included Strategic Commissioning, an education program which linked museums and schools, and Creative Partnerships, launched in 2002 to bring creative workers such as artists, architects, and scientists into schools to work alongside teachers to inspire young people's learning.

The sustainability of policies and legislation depends on various factors – including economic stringencies; ideologies; and effectiveness. This chapter explores three of the most iconic manifestations of English museums' regulatory

The International Handbooks of Museum Studies: Museum Practice, First Edition.
Edited by Conal McCarthy.
© 2015 John Wiley & Sons Ltd. Published 2020 by John Wiley & Sons Ltd.

frameworks introduced over the past 20 years: the National Lottery, launched in 1994; free admission to the national museums (from 1999); and Renaissance in the Regions (from 2001). It examines their original intentions, their development over the long term, and their perceived significance.

The chapter is presented in six sections. The first provides background to the nature of legislation and regulation governing museums in England; the second sets out the major reforms introduced by the Thatcher and Major governments up to 1997; the third describes New Labour's policies and frameworks, including prescribed modes of delivery and accountability, as they applied to museums, 1997–2010; the fourth focuses on the current Coalition Government from 2010; the fifth traces the evolution of three particular initiatives, introduced by Conservative and Labour governments, as illustrated by case studies; and the last offers some observations drawn from the above.

The chapter explores the position of English museums from both macro- and micro-perspectives, by considering the wider picture, as well as that which is sector specific. While it is accepted that case studies have their limitations (not least that they may not be representative), they are nevertheless grounded in lived reality. Each case study presented here sets out its subject's original intentions against a background of government policies; describes the nature of its administrative and delivery mechanisms; and considers changes introduced over time and its perceived effect. The chapter draws on a variety of sources. Primary sources include reports from the Department for Culture, Media and Sport (DCMS), other policy documents, and autobiographies. It also refers to secondary sources, including the academic literature, sectoral reports, and political biographies, and the first-hand experiences and observations of the authors, both of whom, in different ways, worked for government agencies during the New Labour years.

Intentional and unintentional legislation and regulation

Museums and galleries in the United Kingdom are relatively lightly legislated or regulated. A number of Acts of Parliament deal with individual museum's issues, but these relate mostly to the governance or constitutional arrangements of the national museums. For example, it is under the terms of the *Museums and Galleries Act 1992* that the Trustees of the National Portrait Gallery maintain a collection of portraits in all media of the most eminent persons in British history from the earliest times to the present day. Other types of legislation affecting museums include amendments to existing legislation and the unintended consequences of legislation. This section considers all three types.

Recent examples of intentional legislation include the *Holocaust (Return of Cultural Objects) Act 2009* which granted the trustees of named British national institutions the power to de-accession any artifacts or cultural objects currently held in their collections that were stolen by or on behalf of the Nazi regime between 1933 and 1945, so that these could be returned to their lawful owners or heirs.

More often, legislation comprises amendments to existing legislation. The *Regulatory Reform (Museum of London) (Location of Premises) Order 2004*, for example, permitted the Museum of London to operate a museum anywhere within the confines of Greater London, rather than within the limits of the City of London. This made it legally possible for the Museum of London to merge with the Museum in Docklands. Legislation may also serve to enable policy-led changes to the infrastructure. Following its review of non-departmental public bodies (September 2010; UK Parliament 2010), the government proposed to abolish, merge, and modify the constitution and the functions of a number of quangos including MLA, which was abolished. This became law under the *Public Bodies Act 2011*.

Local authority museums, core funded from taxation, make up nearly half of accredited museums throughout the UK.[1] Until the explosion of independent museum foundations in the 1960s and 1970s, these constituted the backbone of regional and local museum provision. The most important local authority museums often originated from the Victorians' enthusiasm for the educational power of culture, art, and artifacts. A series of Acts that were passed over a period of 50 years from 1845 authorized them to spend money on establishing, collecting for, and running museums. The *Museums Act 1845* enabled authorities in places with populations of 10,000 people or more to levy a halfpenny rate; the *Public Libraries and Museums Act 1855* allowed for a one penny rate to buy specimens; the *Public Libraries (England and Scotland) Amendment Act 1866* allowed authorities with libraries to open museums; the *Museums and Gymnasiums Act 1891* allowed all urban authorities to provide support for museums from rates except London (until 1901); and the *Public Libraries Act 1892* transferred responsibility for museums to new library authorities.

The *Public Libraries and Museums Act 1964* replaced all the previous legislation. It confirmed that local authorities could fund and run museums if they wished but they were not statutorily obliged to do so. The benefits of this are still disputed. Although museums benefit from not being tied down by the inflexible regulation that inevitably accompanies statutory obligations established by Parliament, they remain very vulnerable to funding cuts because the statutory services have priority when resources are tight. Many museum professionals, therefore, consider that securing statutory status should be the top policy objective for the sector. But it is very unlikely that local authorities would willingly add to their statutory obligations and the costs that go with it.

Arguably, more importance is attached to the unintended consequences of legislation. Museums are subject to the law in the same way as any other institution or individual. Many Acts of Parliament are passed which impact upon museums although they were not in the mind of the legislators. There are numerous examples. The *Town and Country Planning Act 1990*, for example, covers many aspects of strategic development planning which may affect the building of new museums and conservation-led regeneration. The *Disability Discrimination Act 1995* (amended 2005) makes it unlawful to discriminate against disabled persons, as well as making provision about the employment of disabled persons. This has had a major impact on museums in historic buildings where accessibility and authenticity can conflict. It adds to a situation created by the *Health and Safety at Work etc. Act 1974*, where health and safety issues have dominated the management of many museum buildings, at considerable cost and occasionally in a way that seriously compromises interpretation.

In some cases the legislation has no particular impact on museums other than bringing significant additional costs which museums may ill afford. The *Employment Rights Act 1996*, for example, sets out detailed processes and conditions which employers must respect, regardless of cost or bureaucratic inconvenience. The *Freedom of Information Act 2000* enables a person to make a request for information to a public authority and entitles them to be informed in writing whether that information is available. The costs of Freedom of Information inquiries are considered almost prohibitive.

Other legislation aimed at a much wider sector will challenge museums to be clear about their purpose. The *Charities Act 2006* expands the existing four categories of "charitable purpose" (the relief of poverty, the advancement of education, the advancement of religion, and other purposes beneficial to the community) developed by courts over the years. There are now 13 categories in total, including "the advancement of arts, culture, heritage or science." All charities must demonstrate that their purposes are for public benefit. This affects private museums, which may seek tax concessions, but whose purpose may not be for public benefit.

Conservatives, 1979–1997

Over the past 20 years, a major factor in the development and realization of English museums' policies, frameworks, and legislation is the degree to which the sector is regarded, or regards itself, as delivering on government objectives. During the four Conservative administrations, 1979–1997, the way in which government perceived its relationship with the organizations that it funded changed considerably. As Prime Minister between 1979 and 1990, Margaret Thatcher had little interest in the arts or museums. She regarded the promotion of culture as indicative of a nation's international standing, and thought that support for it should broadly involve "the private sector raising more money and bringing business acumen and efficiency to bear on the administration of cultural institutions" (Thatcher 1993, 634). This is pretty much the same line that the current Coalition is taking too.

Not surprisingly, the museums sector had little obvious connection to the center of government and appeared to contribute little to its objectives, and within government responsibility for the arts vacillated between several departments. Its aims were simultaneously myopic and broad-based, aspiring to encourage public access to, and the appreciation and enjoyment of, the arts and the nation's cultural heritage. Several of its initiatives were intended to contribute to the maintenance and enhancement of the national museums' collections and the preservation of objects of historic importance. The Office of Arts and Libraries (OAL) regarded private sector support, sponsorship in particular, as the most likely way of expanding the resources available to its sectors, developing initiatives such as the Business Sponsorship Incentive Scheme, launched in 1984, which matched funding from private sponsors.

Restrictions in public expenditure across the board meant that the whole emphasis of the government's cultural policy was on plural funding, via sponsorship, marketing, charges, and trading. Thatcher's introduction of entrepreneurialism to the public sector prompted major reform. Through the Financial Management Initiative, launched in 1982, her government called for greater accountability efficiency, effectiveness, and "value for money" at central and local government levels. It brought about change in the culture of the civil service and government-funded agencies, with budget-holding and -planning regularly impinging on the lives of those who had never previously been required to consider issues of costs and benefits. The implementation of the Financial Management Initiative was largely scrutinized through the Audit Commission and the National Audit Office, both of which were set up in 1983. The former had responsibility for examining the management of local authority auditing in England and Wales and the latter, for reporting on public spending programs in England, Scotland, and Wales. While neither body was, or is, specifically responsible for cultural services, yet museums, galleries, and the arts nonetheless fall within their remits and have been subject to the philosophy that they represent.

These changes impacted on national museums as well as local authority museums in England. They were hit by a series of initiatives designed to introduce a basic understanding of the principles of business managerialism as far down their structures as possible. The introduction of competitive tendering in the early 1980s brought indirect pressure to bear as costs were everywhere scrutinized and tested. The Audit Commission's report, *The Road to Wigan Pier* (1991) reminded local authorities "first to be clear about why they are supporting museums, to set objectives for them and then to devise a business or development plan for the service," and that that their "[s]ervices should be targeted at chosen customers" (Audit Commission 1991, 3). Other indirect reforms included the Citizens' Charter. This initiative, launched by Thatcher's successor John Major in 1991, promised better-quality public service provision through the publication of service standards, the right of redress, performance monitoring, penalties, tighter regulation of privatized utilities, and the increased pressures resulting from competition and privatization. "Charter marks" were awarded to the most successful service providers, including several museums.

Following Major's 1992 election victory, and in response to what he perceived as having been a fragmentary approach to support for culture, he replaced the OAL with the Department for National Heritage (DNH). Unlike its predecessor departments, the DNH was headed by a Secretary of State with Cabinet status, which brought a greater political influence to bear on its sectors. The new department's agenda was visibly shaped by the interests of government. In 1996, DNH published *Treasures in Trust* (DNH 1996a), described as the first major statement of government policy toward museums since the 1930s. It was intended to provide a new framework for museums, which increased emphasis on collection care, public participation, and quality of service. It proposed to help to raise standards in museums and galleries, using the existing Museum Registration Scheme as a basis; underline the importance of museum education, especially as part of lifelong learning; address the opportunities provided by new technologies, especially to make collections more widely accessible; and give museums and galleries access to funding from the National Lottery for a wide range of projects. It also commissioned David Anderson's report *A Common Wealth* (1997) which made the case for museums offering much better services to learners of all kinds (and was subsequently republished by Labour).

In the longer term, the most important innovation under Major was undoubtedly the creation of the National Lottery through the *National Lottery Act 1993*. Heritage was one of the five good causes identified to receive lottery income and museums have benefited enormously over the years since (see case studies below). By 1997, DNH was increasingly guiding its sectors' strategic direction, which it articulated as being to encourage high quality and diversity; safeguard existing creative achievements and promote understanding of the past; extend opportunities to enjoy and appreciate rewarding leisure opportunities; promote the contribution all our sectors make to the national prosperity and prestige; and carry out these activities with proper stewardship of the resources available (DNH 1996b, 3). It had seemingly embraced the importance of access (Bottomley in DNH 1996b, 8) and had possibly learned from what Labour local authorities had achieved during the years of opposition. The way was perhaps smoothed for the arrival of New Labour and an unprecedented proactive approach to cultural policy.

New Labour, 1997–2010

New Labour won three successive elections: 1997, 2001, and 2005. Over the period within which it was in power, its policies were broadly consistent. Before winning the 1997 election, Labour described the cultural sector as of fundamental importance to its operation as the incoming government, with the capacity "to promote our sense of community and common purpose" and as being "central to the task of re-establishing a sense of community, of identity and of civic pride, the undermining of which has so damaged our society" (Labour Party 1997, 9). New Labour's establishment of DCMS, and the publication of *A New Cultural Framework*

(DCMS 1998), the most detailed statement of any government's plans to reform the sector, made explicit the extent to which culture was envisaged as being an instrument of government.

DCMS was committed to "reducing bureaucracy; making sure that money is spent on direct services, and putting a new emphasis on the public rather than the producer." The reward would be substantial increases in funding. DCMS was also committed to "joined-up government." It worked, for example, with the Social Exclusion Unit, Home Office, Department of Education, and Department of the Environment, to explore the connections between crime, schooling, poor housing, and culture, an area where museums felt that they had something positive to offer.

DCMS's policy preoccupations, as reported in its Annual Reports from 1998–2009, remained largely consistent, even if their emphases shifted and the ways in which they were articulated changed. Little distinguishes its original desire to promote "access for the many not just the few" (a standard Labour mantra of the time); pursue "excellence and innovation"; nurture "educational opportunity"; and foster the creative industries (DCMS 1998) from its final objectives – to encourage more widespread enjoyment of culture, media, and sport; support talent and excellence in culture, media, and sport, and realize the economic benefits of the department's sectors.

DCMS's actions were based on New Labour's belief in the increased effectiveness of greater public expenditure attached to its modernization agenda (Chief Secretary to the Treasury 1998). Having initially adhered to the Conservative's spending plans, Labour's expenditure grew at an average of 4.4 percent per annum in real terms, which was significantly more than the Conservatives' 0.7 percent per annum average between 1979 and 1997. While this largely reflected increases in spending on the National Health Service, education, and transport, increases in culture were far from insignificant. Between 1998 and 2010, support to the cultural sector rose by about 98 percent, and for museums by around 95 percent. That is quite apart from the billions of pounds that came from the National Lottery. Such investments reflected a period of steady public growth in the economy from 37 percent in 1999–2000 to 42 percent by 2007–2008.

New Labour's primary mechanisms for allocating expenditure, cost control, and performance measurement were the Biennial Spending Reviews (2000, 2002, 2004), which set fixed three-year departmental expenditure limits, and the Comprehensive Spending Reviews (1998, 2007), which represented longer-term and more fundamental reviews of government expenditure. The Spending Reviews defined "the key improvements that the public can expect from these resources" through Public Service Agreements, which marked individual departments' agreements with Treasury. These agreements played "a vital role in galvanizing public service delivery and driving major improvements in outcomes" (HM Treasury 2010), and were conceived in terms of "evidence-based policy" (Cabinet Office 1999), that is to say the subsequent development of informed public policy on the basis of rigorously established objective evidence.

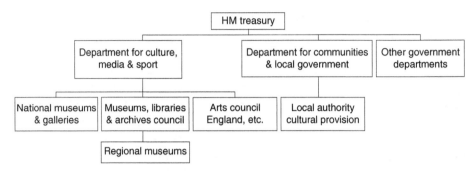

FIGURE 3.1   Policy, funding, and accountability cascade: a map of central government's support for the cultural sector.

This unprecedented commitment to deliver necessarily impinged on DCMS's sponsored bodies (see Figure 3.1). Their Funding Agreements obliged them to deliver on departmental objectives, and meet measurable efficiency and effectiveness targets. The desire to improve management across the sector was closely related to the government's concern to enhance the integrity of official statistics. By 2007, DCMS was supporting 63 non-departmental public bodies, which accounted for the vast majority of its annual spend. In practice, these were also responsible for the outcomes of the department's programs and, as such, were subject to unprecedented levels of scrutiny and accountability. Whereas, under the arm's-length principle, performance measurement was previously considered inappropriate for cultural provision, after 2000 it became the norm, although in Blair's second government some felt that the DCMS had to be about "going beyond targets" to "best capture the value of culture" (Jowell 2004). This theme was further developed by the McMaster Review of 1998 into concepts of excellence, and although this generated much debate it never materialized into sustained action (McMaster 2008).

From about 2002 New Labour increasingly referred to the notion of public value, borrowed from the standard work, Mark Moore's *Creating Public Value* (1995). This focused on what might constitute "public" value – how the working practices of public servants might contribute to particular sorts of benefits found only in public services. This might simply comprise

> new public services (extended library opening hours …); increased trust in public institutions, ("I trust my library service more") or a contribution to an established public good ("the library is open longer so I can read more books and be better educated"). (Oakley, Naylor, and Lee 2011, 3)

Public value appears to refer to public goods; services which are non-rivalrous and non-excludable, such as defense or street lighting, which are in the public interest or in the public domain. This has, in particular, informed its attitude to local government reform.

The *Local Government Act 1999* introduced the best value service delivery regime and scrapped the widely disliked compulsory competitive tendering. Best value was designed to ensure continuous improvement in local government services by creating a series of performance indicators and associated targets, which could both, measure the progress of an individual service and compare it with others across the country. It is the bedrock of a commitment to making services transparently accountable to local people. The *Local Government Act 2000* was the controversial piece of legislation that introduced mayors and cabinets alongside a new legal framework that allows councils to do anything that will contribute to the social, environmental, or economic well-being of their communities, which might of course include supporting museums or museum initiatives.

New Labour was the party of regionalism. It reintroduced regional development agencies and generally claimed that it wished to devolve powers to the English regions and the nations. There was, however, never complete agreement upon how regionalism and the need for strong central government to drive New Labour election-winning policies could be successfully reconciled. The issue focused around the distinction between "regional government" and "government in the regions." Regional Development Agencies were launched in eight English regions in 1999; the ninth in London in 2000, following the establishment of the Greater London Authority. They were intended to coordinate regional economic development and competitiveness. A number of other regional bodies advised them or looked to them for funding – including government regional offices, English Partnerships, and the Rural Development Commission. For museums with ambitious capital projects they were to be key sources of funding.

A *New Cultural Framework* introduced regional Cultural Consortiums in 1999 – non-executive advisory bodies for each of the English regions, except London where the function sat with the Cultural Strategy Group, established by the mayor. The consortiums included representation from all cultural activities including museums. Each was charged with producing cross-cutting strategies for each region, which were expected to inform the Regional Development Agencies. Regional support structures were highly important to the museums sector, where the majority of local museums were small and often had no paid professional staff. Area Museum Councils, collaborative bodies sustained by subscriptions and a small grant from MLA's predecessor, the Museums and Galleries Commission, were very influential. But from 2001 they were replaced by cross-cutting MLA's regional agencies, intended to reflect and be more controllable by MLA itself.

Regional government reached its high-water mark in 2004 when a referendum about the creation of a Regional Assembly was held in the Northeast. The rejection of the offer of devolved power in one of the most partisan of all the English regions effectively killed off regional government as a policy objective and left its organs vulnerable to retrenchment or changes in central government. After New Labour lost power in 2010, virtually all the English regional bodies were disbanded, though the devolved Scottish Parliament and Welsh Assembly survived.

New Labour had high expectations of museums and galleries, given that a sizeable percentage of DCMS's operational spend and activity was dedicated to museums. Most of the policy initiatives were either applied to museums or they were indirectly deeply affected by them (as in local government, for example). Specific initiatives identified in *A New Cultural Framework* (DCMS 1998) included the creation of a new strategic agency for museums, archives, and libraries (Resource, subsequently MLA), the imposition of public service agreements, and the establishment of a watchdog, QUEST (the Quality, Efficiency and Standards Team). But it was two other initiatives, discussed below, that headlined: the introduction of free admission to all national museums and galleries and the unprecedented funding of regional museums following the *Renaissance in the Regions* report (RMTF 2001).

The Coalition Government, 2010–

Previous sections have highlighted the evolution of museum policy, the sector's regulatory frameworks and the impact of legislation over the past 30 or so years. Many of the changes introduced appeared to have been driven by ideological differences. Access-for-all policies (as manifest in free admission) have been promoted by planning for a better society, while an absence of policy reflects a belief in allowing the market to determine what happens. However, the increasing centrism of British politics means differences between the Left and Right are now much less stark than they once were – something that is perhaps reflected in the current Coalition's cultural policies and the case studies that follow.

One year into its first term of office, the absolute priority of Britain's Coalition Government, the first for over 50 years, remains the national debt. At the end of December 2010 general government debt was £1105.8 billion, equivalent to 76.1 percent of GDP – the largest budget deficit in the UK's post-war history. In practice, the Conservative and Liberal Democrat partnership's recovery strategy has significantly accelerated the previous government's plans to reduce the budget deficit. Its main instruments are the cutting of all government departments' spending (with the exceptions of health and overseas aid), and the introduction of savings and reforms to welfare, tax, environmental levies, and public service pensions.

Museums anticipated serious reductions in public funding following the 2010 Spending Review. In the event, the sector has been subject to cuts of around 15 percent stemming from decreases in DCMS's own budget and local authorities' funding.[2] They are also affected by declining support from charitable foundations and corporate sponsorship, which had been falling since 2007/2008. The government's response was to call upon museums to be more entrepreneurial, though the barriers are easy enough to identify:

> We expect museums to operate like businesses and yet we are handicapped by our funding structures and regimes. In Local Authorities the restricted ability to trade, the central recharging, the lack of ability in some to even control catering contracts

plus over bureaucratic systems of pay, recruitment and procurement make it impossible to change in any reasonable time frame. Finance controls on end of year flexibility, use of reserves, cost of employment etc., have all created organisations with ever increasing fixed costs and ever decreasing public service despite huge fundraising efforts. (Lees 2009, unpaginated)

The sector's default position has been, as ever, to do the best it can with the hand it is dealt. Museums are trimming and shrinking their operations. In July 2011 it was claimed that one-fifth of museums had suffered cuts of over 25 percent (Newman and Toule 2011). But there is also a greater sense of crisis. More local authorities are not just talking about converting their museum services to trusts, running services jointly with neighbors, mothballing whole museums, or introducing admission charges – they are actually doing it. Birmingham, Carlisle, Derby, and Bournemouth are all local authorities where these measures are occurring. Whether such moves will escalate into a longer-term sectoral change remains to be seen.

In contrast to New Labour, the Coalition's announcements on cultural policy have been few and far between. To date (July 2011), DCMS's major preoccupation has been with funding, the abolition of several of its quangos, including MLA, and its plans to boost philanthropy and increase Lottery funding available to the good causes. The Coalition's "programme for government" (HM Government 2010, 14), and subsequent DCMS Structural Reform Plan (DCMS 2010) placed an emphasis on philanthropic and corporate investment. "Support to the sector is regarded as a way to 'redress the balance' where the market fails to deliver, and as contributing to conditions for growth in the cultural economy" (DCMS 2011, 1). More specifically, DCMS has undertaken to preserve museum collections and continue free entry to national museums and galleries (see case studies below). Other priorities recall those of previous Conservative administrations: cutting spending on administration, encouraging philanthropic giving, and reducing the dependence of museums on government funding (DCMS 2011, 4). Cameron also claims a vision for greater citizen engagement in government, calling for a "Big Society" where citizens have a greater say in what and how public services are delivered. Ultimately this goes beyond the volunteerism that is already essential to many museums. In acknowledging that GDP is an "incomplete way" of measuring the country's progress, current Prime Minister Cameron charged the Office of National Statistics to develop measures around well-being and life satisfaction to inform social and economic policy:

From April next year we will start measuring our progress as a country not just by how our economy is growing, but by how our lives are improving; not just by our standard of living, but by our quality of life (Cameron 2010).

The indicators were due to be announced in late 2011, but museums have begun to lobby for public participation in museums to be acknowledged as contributing to national happiness (Thompson et al. 2011).

Other than continuing reports of serious budget cuts, the main focus of discussion over the winter of 2011/12 was how the Arts Council would assimilate Renaissance funding into its existing programs and who would benefit from it. Arts Council England (ACE) agreed that Renaissance would retain its own identity for the short term but that fewer museums would be funded directly. In effect the Hub system was dismantled and museums were invited to apply for direct funding under the new regime. Sixteen museums were duly accepted as "major partner museums" (there had been 42 Hub museums) on the basis of criteria allegedly about excellence. There were relatively few surprises; Sheffield Museums Trust lost out and the East Midlands "region" is unrepresented. (Regionalism is once again out of favor with Conservative-led governments.)

On the whole, the museums sector seems to have accepted the slimming down of the regional English premier league. Those who lost out have had the pill sweetened by the offer of transitional funding (for one year) to help them scale down, and sector favorites, the Museum Development Officers,[3] have survived while a Strategic Support Fund is going to be available for all English regional museums to bid into. It is too early to say anything sensible about culture change within ACE, which is bound to find it difficult to remain unchanged if it is to successfully bring museums into the fold (not to mention libraries). In March 2012 the government announced that the much respected Liz Forgan was not going to be offered another term as Chair of ACE. Forgan had been appointed under New Labour and was strongly associated with them, but she had also served at Heritage Lottery Fund (HLF) and had a good understanding of museums. The government talked of the future challenges of philanthropy and technological change, raising the specter of Forgan being succeeded by a digital entrepreneur rather than someone who can relate to arts and museums. In the event, she was succeeded on January 31, 2013 by Sir Peter Bazalgette, formerly creative director of Endemol, the company behind the television series *Big Brother*.

Case study 1: The Heritage Lottery Fund

Intentions

As part of the development of the National Lottery, the Heritage Lottery Fund (HLF) was set up by the *National Lottery Act 1993* to give grants to a wide range of projects involving the local, regional, and national heritage of the United Kingdom. The HLF distributes a share (determined by the government, currently 18 percent) of the money raised by the National Lottery for "good causes." The trustees currently have three core aims for HLF, which define in broad terms how they are trying to improve quality of life through the heritage. These are to:

- conserve the UK's diverse heritage for present and future generations to experience and enjoy;

- help more people, and a wider range of people, to take an active part in and make decisions about their heritage;
- help people to learn about their own and other people's heritage.

At the beginning there was a reluctance to either define "heritage" or lay out clear aims and objectives. Its emphasis focused on conservation, and particularly the conservation of historic buildings and their contents. But in addition to eventually agreeing on these aims – which are as good a summary of New Labour policy toward the heritage as you are likely to find – the government issues HLF with policy directions under the 1993 Act. The current directions took effect in 2008. As before, these are matters "to be taken into account" when distributing money.[4] They include:

- asking HLF to assess the needs of the heritage when deciding upon priorities;
- involving the public in making policies, setting priorities, and distributing money;
- increasing access and participation;
- inspiring children and young people;
- fostering initiatives that bring people together;
- supporting and encouraging volunteering;
- encouraging skills development; and
- reducing economic and social deprivation.

The HLF has to report back to government on these policy directions, detailing how they are addressing them, evidenced by statistics where applicable. A brief summary of HLF responses may be found in the HLF Annual Reports.

Administration and delivery mechanisms

HLF is administered by the Trustees of the National Heritage Memorial Fund (NHMF), the fund of last resort for the UK's heritage, coming to the rescue by funding emergency acquisitions. NHMF allocates around £10 million of government grant-in-aid money per year to our national heritage. But since it first allocated grants in 1995, HLF has had far greater impact on museums and galleries than its parent body. It has distributed about £1.3 billion in capital and revenue grants, which have touched the majority of accredited museums, enabling them to invest in buildings, renew their displays, and develop new or improved educational and outreach programs.

Achieving a careful balance between income, awards, and commitments is a constant source of concern for HLF. Table 3.1 shows how even over a short period (five years) it is impossible to assume stability. Trustees can make awards in a year greater than one year's income, because they have held back funds in the bank. The sudden fall in awards in 2008/2009 and 2009/2010 is mostly explained by developing a new system of assessing applications in two rounds: Round One

TABLE 3.1   Heritage Lottery Fund financial and staffing profile 2005/6–2009/10

Financial year	Trustees' awards (£m)	Income from National Lottery (£m)	NLDF investment income (£m)	Total income (£m)	Average number of employees
2005/2006	n/a	230.4	39.7	270.7	245
2006/2007	285.4	201.0	30.0	231.7	247
2007/2008	283.9	200.4	15.4	217.0	238
2008/2009	150.9	208.2	9.9	209.1	230
2009/2010	85.5	246.7*	2.0	205.5	226

*However, from this, £43.4m was transferred to the Olympic Lottery Distribution Fund. £10.8m had been taken in the previous year.
Source: HLF Annual Reports

passes are not committed awards and therefore do not count. The figure will rise again in 2010/2011 because most of the projects passed at Round One will by then have passed Round Two and will have been awarded a grant.

Income from the National Lottery derives from ticket sales. Interest in playing the games seems to have fallen in the mid-2010s, but revived again as recession set in – it seems that poorer people gamble more when economically threatened. Unfortunately all of the increase (and more) in 2009/2010 was lost because £43.4 million was "stolen" to help fund the 2012 London Olympics (see Table 3.1).

Investment income from the National Lottery Development Fund (which holds lottery income, maximizing investment income, and releases it to the distributing bodies as required) crashed spectacularly over the past five years because of significant reductions in market interest rates and gilt yields. So, overall, annual income into the HLF fell by a quarter because of an increasingly challenging economic climate and a raid to support the Olympics. However, as the recession continues to bite, the number of lottery tickets sold has been increasing. As of February 2012, projections suggested that the HLF is likely to see its share of funding rise over the next five years. £1.42 billion is expected to be available between 2011/2012 and 2015/2016 – a 14.7 percent increase on 2010 projections (Kendall 2012).

Legislation and amendments

During the earliest years of HLF's distribution of funding, discussion of its grant awards was dominated by three questions:

1. Were the trustees allocating huge grants to the big heritage institutions and neglecting "grass roots" heritage?
2. Were some regions (usually a euphemism for London and the South East) getting a disproportionate slice of the lottery cake?
3. Were some heritage sectors doing rather better than others?

TABLE 3.2   Heritage Lottery Fund – distribution of awards by size of grant

Financial year	% by total value of awards going to grants of under £1m	% of total value of awards going to grants of £5m and over
2002/2003	35.9	33.0
2003/2004	37.4	26.3
2004/2005	36.6	28.8
2005/2006	39.7	28.7
2006/2007	40.8	25.6
2007/2008	44.0	21.7

Source: HLF Annual Reports

The government issues "policy directions" to the lottery distributors, steering them toward ensuring that their independent policies and grant criteria take full account of the government's own policy. DCMS used policy directions to intervene on the first question, trying to ensure that HLF recognized that the heritage can be tangible (e.g., a church) and intangible (e.g., oral histories); that it is owned and supported by millions, not just an elite few; and that access to lottery funding must indeed be "for the many not just a few."

The 1997 Act empowered Trustees to assist projects (revenue as well as capital) directed to increasing public understanding and enjoyment of the heritage, and to interpreting and recording important aspects of the nation's history, natural history, and landscape. Similarly, responding to policy directions meant eventually that a much broader definition of "heritage projects" was accepted and small grants for small community organizations for what they considered to be heritage was encouraged and enabled. The impact of its intervention can be seen in Table 3.2, which shows that the percentage of grant money being allocated to smaller projects increased and the amount allocated to large capital projects fell.

The second and third questions were closely monitored by HLF themselves. With the coming of New Labour in 1997 and a wider definition of what heritage was, it became easier to ensure that grants were not skewed toward major museums or the most well-known heritage sites (Table 3.2). Grants could be mapped against population densities and "cold spots" identified. HLF also set up development teams in each region who actively helped potential applicants to reach the point where they could submit a proposal. In these ways HLF tried to ensure a fair distribution of lottery money back into the communities that had funded it.

The 1998 Act enabled HLF to "regionalize" by setting up 12 committees in the nations and English regions to which decisions (up to a certain grant size ceiling) could be delegated. It also meant the setting up of regional offices which helped HLF counter complaints that HLF was too London-focused, and not sufficiently in touch with grass-roots heritage across the UK. It also helped ensure a greater degree of fairness in geographical distribution, as discussed above.

Effects

All in all, New Labour may be able to claim that its interventions democratized the distribution of lottery grants to the heritage. On its part, HLF may be equally justified in feeling that it has retained its integrity and not deviated from only supporting heritage that merited it.

Case study 2: Renaissance in the Regions

Since 2003, groups of museums in each of the English regions have been receiving funding from the government to improve and extend their services, as part of a program called Renaissance. Renaissance is the most significant development in English non-national museums since the *Museums Act 1845*, which empowered cities to set up Free Museums. It builds on the achievements of the HLF and the Designation Challenge Fund, which identified the most significant collections built up by non-national museums over the past 150 years.

Intentions

Renaissance was designed to respond to the state of England's regional museums. By the 1990s many of the country's largest regional museums were suffering from ongoing funding cuts, leaving them unable to meet the expectations of their users. In 2000, Chris Smith, then Secretary of State for Culture, convened a Regional Museums Task Force to look into the problems facing regional museums, and to propose solutions for their future development. Their report, *Renaissance in the Regions: A New Vision for England's Museums* (2001), proposed that regional museums could be:

- an important resource and champion for learning and education;
- promote access and inclusion encouraging social inclusion and cultural diversity, acting as focal points for their local communities, and providing public spaces for dialogue and discussion about issues of contemporary significance;
- contribute to economic regeneration in the regions;
- collect, care for and interpret (on a foundation of research and scholarship) the material culture of the UK and use it to encourage inspiration and creativity;
- ensure excellence and quality in the delivery of their core services.

(RMTF 2001, 21)

In order to achieve that the Task Force proposed an innovative structure, with a "hub" for each of the nine English regions, made up of a group of the largest and most significant museums. Each museum remained the responsibility of its existing governing body but the structure created a channel for significant funding contributions from central government, something which had been recommended in various reports since the 1920s but which was now to be achieved for the first time.[5] The report not only highlighted funding difficulties but also demonstrated how relatively small sums of government investment could create a real improvement in the number of people who could be reached by better services. Furthermore, the hubs would be working together to improve museums across the whole region.

Administrative and delivery mechanisms

In the 2002 Spending Review, the government allocated £70 million to the Renaissance program, about one-third of that recommended by the report. In order to demonstrate what the impact of full funding could be, the Task Force recommended that it should be implemented in phases. The government agreed and tasked Resource (subsequently MLA) with the management and delivery of Renaissance.

In the first phase, three hubs (North East, South West, and West Midlands) were given the majority of the money they needed to implement the Renaissance vision and the other six received small sums of money for development and planning. The government allocated further funding for Renaissance in the Spending Review of 2004. Although this was again less than the sum requested (only 60 percent of what was needed), it did mean that significant funding could be allocated in a second phase to the other six hubs.

The regional museum hubs have developed business plans according to MLA guidelines. All have an obligation to increase visits, particularly from non-traditional museum users and to extend their work with schools. In other respects, the hubs pursued priorities they had identified for their region. In particular this allowed them to develop areas other than simple audience increases, including strategic reviews to identify how museums can be sustained in the future, as well as collections management and workforce development.

Regional museum hubs are the main strand of Renaissance but the program has many other elements. For example, more funding has been made available for museum development officers to support smaller museums, enabling more officers to be employed and boosting the budgets of existing services. Renaissance has also provided funding for the Museum Association's Diversify program (encouraging minorities into museum careers) and its Effective Collections initiative; and for Subject Specialist Networks, one of the ideas in the *Renaissance in the Regions* report. Indeed, Renaissance has worked in partnership with virtually every museum sector initiative since 2002 and has been, with the HLF, the mainstay of museum development for nearly 10 years.

Legislation, amendments, and effects

It was inevitable that the implementation of Renaissance would depart from the Task Force's proposals. There was no formal, forward plan for it, and Renaissance was subject to a number of factors – most importantly, the amount of funding available, government priorities, and choices made by MLA. The Renaissance Review, written seven years after the publication of the 2001 Regional Museums Task Force Report, and in anticipation of nearly £300 million having been spent on the program by 2011, tracked the program's achievements. Regional museums had come a long way since 2001: they had a political profile; were more capable of levering in other funding, and their capacity to contribute to regional regeneration agendas was better understood and recognized. Regional museums were noticeably more confident in the management and presentation of their collections than previously. Research and evaluation had become an increasingly standard part of their work; they were increasingly modernized; have introduced greater cultural diversity; and were reaching more audiences through learning projects with children, young people, and adults. Volunteering has not only added to the value of museums, it has also enabled hubs to engage more effectively with members of the local community, as well as helping volunteers to develop their own skills and self-confidence. Beyond the hubs, the Museum Development Officer structure was regarded as achieving "real change" (RRAG 2009, 11). The Review also made recommendations for the future priorities, management, and delivery of the Renaissance.

With the abolition of MLA, Arts Council England assumed a number of MLA's functions for museums. Following a review as to how its strategic goals could best reflect the museums and libraries sectors alongside the arts (Morris 2011), it published *A Review of Research and Literature on Museums and Libraries* (ACE 2011b) and a 10-year strategic framework for the sector (ACE 2011a). ACE's principal museum responsibilities include the Renaissance in the Regions program; the regional museums' improvement and development agenda, including the Accreditation Standard and Designation Scheme; the protection of cultural objects; export controls; tax incentives and projects relating to the 2012 Cultural Olympiad. In January 2012 it announced its funding decisions for the Renaissance major grants program, valued at £20 million a year.

Case study 3: Free admission

Free admission had been a manifesto pledge and most strongly represented New Labour's commitment to access-for-all to culture, especially in the national museums.

Intentions

New Labour assumed that museums were "an essential platform for learning for all and lifelong learning" (HoC 2002, summary 1). Consequently, free admission, promised in both New Labour's pre-1997 election manifesto (Labour Party 1997) and its *A New Cultural Framework* (DCMS 1998) was intended to broaden access by "the many not just the few" and to encourage visits by people from "hard to reach" social groups in particular.

Administrative and delivery mechanisms

New Labour's strategy on free admission involved the trustees of government-sponsored museums, who had previously charged for entry, dropping their admission fees. In "exchange" for this, the department would increase its funding (HoC 2002, summary 4). A special VAT rebate scheme was introduced in 2001 for museums and galleries offering free access. The introduction of free admission was incremental: free admission for children was introduced in April 1999; for the over-60s in April 2000, and for everyone in December 2001. Free admission to university museums followed in August 2005.

Perceived effect

DCMS's press releases presented free admission as a spectacular success on the basis of visit numbers at the formerly charging museums having escalated.

Alongside Lottery funding, which enabled existing museums and galleries throughout the UK to be extended and extensively refurbished, free admission contributed considerably to the increased profile of British museums: the policy itself has become iconic. For the arch spin-doctor of New Labour, Peter Mandelson, the government got off to a good start by keeping to campaign commitments and implementing quick wins, which included announcing free entry to museums.

DCMS's reporting on free admission has, however, been opaque. It has compared visit numbers against a baseline indicative of the situation before entry charges were scrapped, but it also presented aggregated visit numbers, and converted visits into visitors. Although free admission clearly prompted millions of extra visits, by a larger percentage of the population (HoC 2002, evidence p. 33 para. 79), the department has never publicly reflected on whom was encouraged to visit, and whether or not they were its original target audience. Ministerial statements, nevertheless, implied that DCMS's strategy was working to plan claiming that free admission has democratized the nation's treasures making them accessible to all; that the removal of such barriers as admission charges was a clear rebuttal to those who had said that people were not interested in "serious" culture and learning. The figures were said to disprove the contention that the initiative was all about the same people visiting more often: that half of all visits were by "new visitors" – "new visitors" being defined as those who had not visited in the previous 12 months.

Yet, other reports suggested that DCMS's target audience for free admission, originally identified as those whom the department initially classified as C2DEs (the half of the population comprising skilled, semi-skilled, and unskilled manual workers, state pensioners etc., with no other earnings) did not necessarily account for the increases in visit numbers.[6] Within a year of the introduction of universal free admission, it was apparent that while attendance was increasing across all social groups, the most significant rises in visit numbers were among those who had always been well represented amongst museum and gallery visitors (Martin 2002). The same kind of people were still going, and the profile of a typical population of museum visitors remained relatively stable. Indeed a government inquiry, *National Museums and Galleries: Funding and Free Admission*, concluded that "Emerging trends and previous research indicate that free admission on its own is unlikely to be effective in attracting significant numbers of new visitors from the widest range of socio-economic and ethnic groups" (HoC 2002, para. 60). DCMS's 2003–2006 agreements with its sponsored museums and galleries, as well as with MLA regarding Renaissance-funded museums, required an overall increase of 8 percent between April 2003 and March 2006 by adult visitors in socioeconomic group C2DE. Each museum would undertake specific activities depending on its own circumstances. DCMS's 2006 Annual Report declared this target as having been met. The 2007 target was to increase the number of people from priority groups (defined as those with a social disability, people from lower socioeconomic groups and ethnic minorities by 2 percent). But, its 2008 Annual Report reported slippage across arts, museums and galleries, and historic environment. Evidence drawn from DCMS data, including its monthly museum visit figures, suggests that many of DCMS-funded museums experienced difficulties in increasing their numbers of adult visitors from socioeconomic group C2DE. This may, however, highlight some of the problems with the department's methods of data collection and its clarification of the definitions used which produced a number of anomalies. The apparent decline in the percentage of C2DE visits also reflects the fact that prior to 2005/2006, a number of the museums had included under 16-year-old C2DEs in their performance indicators, although these were specifically meant to refer to people of 16 and over. The totals for 2005/2006 have been adjusted to exclude children.

Strictly speaking, it is impossible to read across the data that the department has collected or to assume consistencies. Given the number of caveats that apply, it could be argued that this data is incapable of demonstrating trends in attendance by target groups to museums and galleries. However, the consistent data generated after the mid-2000s, indicates that the percentage of visits by adults from social groups NS-SEC 5–8 has marginally declined since 2006/2007. This suggests that free admission has not succeeded in attracting the groups for whom it was originally intended, which raises questions about the integrity of the most basic performance indicators; government's concerns with efficiency and value for money; its seriousness about evidence-based policy; and its commitment to extending access to the many, not just the few.

It is, perhaps, significant that under the Coalition, free admission is now considered central to the position of museums in the UK visitor economy. The UK is home to three of the five most visited art museums in the world, all three of which are free: the British Museum, Tate, and the National Gallery (*Art Newspaper* 2011, 24), and nearly 60 percent of visitors to the UK visit the free DCMS-sponsored museums. By 2010/2011 there were 17.7 million overseas visits to DCMS-sponsored museums (ONS 2010), accounting for over one-third of all visits.

Conclusions

> Labour bequeathed a public realm that shone. They renovated, restocked and rebuilt schools, hospitals and clinics, arts and sports venues, parks and museums. JK Galbraith once talked about private affluences and public squalor; now there are plenty of the former, despite the recession, but much less of the latter. Public spaces no longer felt second best or the shabby poor relations of commerce. Sober academics talked of a renaissance of England's northern cities, and you could say the same of Glasgow and Belfast. For years to come, civic buildings will stand as monuments to the Labour era ...
>
> But... the social state we are in now is not much different from 1997. The broad judgment has to be that not enough altered in the fabric of our country, given Labour's commitments on equality and fairness. The country remains strongly defined by class, regional disparity, inequality and individual and business under-achievement.
>
> Toynbee and Walker 2010, 297

Money evidently wasn't everything. Seen against its objectives, the effectiveness of recent museums policy initiatives is questionable. The plethora of policy directives over the past 20 years may have been as functionally related to the growth of the economy as it was to a belief in the ethos of the public sector. The greater transparency of the terms of government's engagement in museums policy opened the door to more detailed criticism. In retrospect, museums, and culture in general, were of less importance to New Labour than its rhetoric suggested. The flourish of autobiographies published around the time of the 2010 election devote little space to the subject.

And how important was New Labour policy to museums, museum professionals, and museum practice? The short answer is that it was of considerable importance if it brought paychecks with it. So for the 60 or so National or Hub museums that received direct funding from DCMS or via MLA, understanding and keeping abreast of policy was essential. But many hundreds of museums were also indirectly touched by government policy. The resources put into Museum Development Officers and Subject Specialist Networks, for example, reached deep into the sector. It also influenced the Heritage Lottery Fund and therefore all those who applied for a grant.

Policy certainly endorsed the actions of those museums – or more specifically, those museum leaders – who sought a wider role in society, through social inclusion and purposefully working with the disadvantaged. But policy-engaged people are not that common in the museums sector. At best even the more able museum managers are primarily and selfishly partisan for their own institutions and see any benefits of government policy as somehow being "accidental windfalls." Government initiatives encouraging museums to do different things and do things differently are usually regarded as being just another set of criteria to which lip service must be paid if you want the financial benefits. Policy rarely stimulates serious discussion within the sector. But then neither does the DCMS energetically promote such discussions.

This chapter reveals something of the vacillations of government policy, and the unpredictable durability of particular initiatives. Certain preoccupations remained consistent: museums registration (subsequently, Accreditation Scheme); funding and governance; relationships within the UK and internationally; use of new technologies – although these may not have progressed according to plan. Other concerns proved less predictable. Museum admission charges, for example, are often regarded as the battleground between Conservative versus Labour ideologies (Wilkinson 2003). While different Conservative administrations introduced charges, their reasons for doing so were different. Thatcher's predecessor, Edward Heath, refused to accept the principle that museum access should be free, whereas Thatcher was concerned to make the public sector less dependent on state support. A more meaningful indicator of the consistent evolution of conditions affecting British museums' operations might therefore be the degree to which the sector delivers, or is expected to deliver, on government objectives.

Other museum-related enterprises can be seen to have manifestly fallen by the wayside. These include the watchdog, QUEST, which may have part of a ruse by DCMS's first Secretary of State to increase funding to the sector from the Treasury (Smith 2003). It was abolished by New Labour's second Secretary of State on taking up office. Other matters were clouded by political argument. After the think-tank, Demos, first raised the specter of cultural value as a reprieve from instrumentalist value in 2003, DCMS responded by describing culture as synonymous with "transformative power," a greater sense of well-being, connectedness, confidence, and aspiration, and giving a greater sense of personal meaning. But it still associated culture with the development of more aspirant individuals and better communities, in short, the production of a more thriving economy. The debate has now become the subject of academic research partnerships (O'Brien 2010), as interrogation of subjective well-being has taken over from economic and social impact, represented for example, in MLA's attempt to promote SORI (Social Return on Investment), following the Cabinet Office's lead.

Elsewhere the persistence, if not the transience, of policy reflected broader trends within government. Evidence on the development of evidence-based policy is slight. The vast amount of evidence collected on museums either proved insufficient for the generation of evidence-based policy, or it may have simply proved surplus to the requirements of policy-making (as with free admission). But DCMS's declining emphasis on targets reflects a withdrawal from a target-driven culture across government more generally. However, when it came to it DCMS exerted no scrutiny over MLA, which never produced annual reports or accounts – not even on Renaissance, its most substantial museums program for over 150 years.

This sort of laxity should be unacceptable to museum professionals and should provoke outrage. But to earn the respect of government and be treated more seriously, they must engage more critically with government policy. There is often a resignation about museums – worldwide, not just in the UK – and their relationship with almost everything that ought to matter to them. It is David and Goliath, but worse odds. Museums have a support base in society. They need to work harder to have a place in policy-making so that they have just a little more say in what happens to them rather than rolling over and becoming hapless victims.

Notes

1   Those that are recognized as working to nationally agreed standards for museums. See the accreditation section originally set up by the Museums Libraries and Archives Council and now administered by Arts Council England; see also ACE 2014a. The relationship between DCMS, its UK and English remits is complex, and beyond the scope of this chapter. National museums in Scotland, Wales, and Northern Ireland are funded by those countries' devolved governments.
2   One study concluded that whereas national museums had a uniform 15 percent cut, other museums were affected to varying degrees, with 20 percent of respondents reporting cuts of more than 25 percent (Newman and Tourle 2011, 3).
3   Their job is to "drive development and deliver sustainability resilience and innovation in England's regional museums" (ACE 2014b).
4   At the same time, the Welsh Assembly Government issued policy directions related to money distributed in Wales; these complement the UK-wide directions.
5   See Sir H. A. Miers. 1928. *A Report on the Public Museums of the British Isles (other than the National Museums)*. Edinburgh; S. F. Markham. 1938. *The Museums and Art Galleries of the British Isles*. Edinburgh; Standing Commission on Museums and Galleries. 1963. *Survey of Provincial Museums and Galleries*. London (the Rosse Report); Standing Commission on Museums and Galleries. 1979. *Framework for a System of Museums*. London (the Drew Report).
6   This refers to a demographic classification system derived from the British National Readership Survey (NRS), used in market research, in which C2 are skilled manual workers; D are semi-skilled and unskilled manual workers, and E are state pensioners, casual or lowest grade workers, unemployed with state benefits only (Ipsos Media CT 2009).

References

ACE (Arts Council England). 2011a. "Culture, Knowledge and Understanding: Great Museums and Libraries for Everyone." Accessed September 15, 2014. http://www. artscouncil.org.uk/media/uploads/pdf/culture_knowledge_and_understanding.pdf.

ACE (Arts Council England). 2011b. "A Review of Research and Literature on Museums and Libraries." Accessed September 15, 2014. http://www.artscouncil.org.uk/publication_archive/museums-and-libraries-research-review.

ACE (Arts Council England). 2014a. "Accreditation Scheme." Accessed September 15, 2014. http://www.artscouncil.org.uk/what-we-do/supporting-museums/accreditation-scheme.

ACE (Arts Council England). 2014b. "Arts Council England Announces Successful Recipients of the Renaissance Strategic Support and Designation Development Funds." Accessed September 20, 2014. http://press.artscouncil.org.uk/Press-Releases/Arts-Council-England-announces-successful-recipients-of-the-Renaissance-Strategic-support-and-Design-846.aspx.

Anderson, David. 1997. *A Common Wealth*. London: HMSO.

The Art Newspaper. 2011. No. 223, April.

Audit Commission. 1991. *The Road to Wigan Pier? Managing Local Authority Museums and Art Galleries* (Local Government Report). London: HMSO.

Cabinet Office. 1999. *Modernising Government*. London: HMSO.

Cameron, David. 2010. Transcript of a speech given by the Prime Minister on well-being. November 25. Accessed September 15, 2014. http://www.number10.gov.uk/news/pm-speech-on-well-being.

Chief Secretary to the Treasury. 1998. *Public Services for the Future: Modernisation, Reform, Accountability. Comprehensive Spending Review: Public Service Agreements 1999–2002.* Accessed September 20, 2014. https://www.gov.uk/government/uploads/system/uploads/attachment_data/file/260759/4181.pdf.

DCMS (Department for Culture, Media and Sport). 1998. *A New Cultural Framework.* London: Department for Culture, Media, and Sport.

DCMS (Department for Culture, Media and Sport). 2010. *Structural Reform Plan.* Accessed September 20, 2014. https://www.gov.uk/government/uploads/system/uploads/attachment_data/file/78503/SRP_DCMS_150710.pdf.

DCMS (Department for Culture, Media and Sport). 2011. *DCMS Business Plan 2011–2015.* May. Accessed September 20, 2014. https://www.gov.uk/government/uploads/system/uploads/attachment_data/file/78430/DCMS-Business-Plan-2011-2015.pdf.

DNH (Department of National Heritage). 1996a. *Annual Report 1996.* London: HMSO.

DNH (Department of National Heritage). 1996b. *Treasures in Trust: A Review of Museum Policy.* London: HMSO.

HM Government. 2010. *The Coalition: Our Programme for Government.* Accessed September 15, 2014. http://www.cabinetoffice.gov.uk/sites/default/files/resources/coalition_programme_for_government.pdf.

HM Treasury. 2010. "Spending Review 2010." Accessed September 15, 2014. http://www.hm-treasury.gov.uk/spend_index.htm.

HoC (House of Commons Culture, Media and Sport Committee). 2002. *National Museums and Galleries: Funding and Free Admission.* First report of Session 2002–2003. HC 85. London: HMSO.

Ipsos Media CT. 2009. *Social Grade. A Classification Tool. Bite Sized Thought Piece.* Accessed September 15, 2014. http://www.ipsos-mori.com/DownloadPublication/1285_MediaCT_thoughtpiece_Social_Grade_July09_V3_WEB.pdf.

Jowell, Tessa. 2004. *Government and the Value of Culture*. London: Department for Culture, Media, and Sport.

Kendall, Geraldine. 2012. "Lottery Sales Boom Could Benefit ACE and HLF." *Museums Journal*, February 17. Accessed September 15, 2014. http://www.museumsassociation.org/news/14022012-160m-lottery-funding-ace.

Labour Party. 1997. *Create the Future. A Strategy for Cultural Policy, Arts and the Creative Economy*. London: Labour Party.

Lees, Diane. 2009. "Out of the Ashes." Keynote address at Museums Association Conference, London, October 5. Accessed September 15, 2014. http://www.museumsassociation.org/about/37272.

Martin, Andy. 2002. "The Impact of Free Entry to Museums." *Cultural Trends* 47: 1–12.

McMaster, Brian. 2008. *Supporting Excellence in the Arts. From Measurement to Judgment*. London: Department for Culture, Media and Sport.

Moore, Mark H. 1995. *Creating Public Value: Strategic Management in Government*. Cambridge, MA: Harvard University Press.

Morris, Estelle. 2011. *Review of the Arts Council's Strategic Framework*. Arts Council England. Accessed September 20, 2014. http://www.artscouncil.org.uk/media/uploads/pdf/strategic_framework_review_120711.PDF.

Newman, K., and P. Toule. 2011. *The Impact of Cuts on Museums*. London: Museums Association.

Oakley, Kate, Richard Naylor, and David Lee. 2011. "'The Public Gets What the Public Wants': The Uses and Abuses of 'Public Value' in Contemporary British Cultural Policy." *International Journal of Cultural Policy* 17(3): 289–300.

O'Brien, David. 2010. *Measuring the Value of Culture: A Report to the Department for Culture Media and Sport*. Department for Culture Media and Sport. Accessed September 15, 2014. http://www.culture.gov.uk/images/publications/measuring-the-value-culture-report.pdf.

ONS (Office of National Statistics). 2010. *Travel Trends 2010*. Accessed September 15, 2015. http://www.ons.gov.uk/ons/rel/ott/travel-trends/2010/index.html.

RMTF (Regional Museums Task Force). 2001. *Renaissance in the Regions: A New Vision for England's Museums*. Museums Association. Accessed September 15, 2014. http://www.museumsassociation.org/download?id=12190.

RRAG (Renaissance Review Advisory Group). 2009. *Renaissance in the Regions: Realising the Vision. Renaissance in the Regions, 2001–2008*. Museums Libraries and Archives Council.

Smith, Charles Saumarez. 2003. "Valuing Culture." DEMOS website. Accessed September 15, 2014. http://www.demos.co.uk/files/File/VACUCSmith.pdf.

Tempest, Matthew. 2007. "Blair Pledges to Protect Arts Funding." *The Guardian*. March 6. Accessed September 20, 2014. http://www.theguardian.com/politics/2007/mar/06/politicsandthearts.uk.

Thatcher, Margaret. 1993. *Downing Street Years, 1979–90*, vol. 1, *Memoirs of Margaret Thatcher*. London: HarperCollins.

Thompson, Sam, and Jody Aked, with Bridget McKenzie, Chris Wood, Maurice Davies, and Tony Butler. 2011. *The Happy Museum: A Tale of How It Could Turn Out All Right*. Happy

Museum Project. Accessed September 15, 2014. http://www.happymuseumproject. org/wp-content/uploads/2011/03/The_Happy_Museum_report_web.pdf.

Toynbee, Polly, and David Walker. 2010. *The Verdict. Did Labour Change Britain?* London: Granta.

UK Parliament. 2010. "Public Bodies Bill." Accessed September 15, 2014. http://www. publications.parliament.uk/pa/jt201011/jtselect/jtrights/86/8604.htm.

Wilkinson, Helen. 2003. "To Charge or Not to Charge: Museum's Admission Dilemma." *Insights* 14: A145–A150. London: English Tourism Council.

Further Reading

Craik, Jennifer. 2007. *Re-visioning Arts and Cultural Policy: Current Impasses and Future Directions*. Canberra: ANU EPress.

Miller, Toby, and George Yudice. 2002. *Cultural Policy*. London: Sage.

Museum International. 2006. Special Issue: *Museums and Cultural Policy*. 232 58(4). Accessed September 20, 2014. http://onlinelibrary.wiley.com/doi/10.1111/muse.2006.58. issue-4/issuetoc.

O'Brien, Dave. 2014. *Cultural Policy: Management, Value and Modernity in the Creative Industries*. London: Routledge.

Sara Selwood is an independent cultural analyst and consultant who has worked in museums, galleries, and cultural management for many years in various capacities as a curator, director, trustee, and academic (http://saraselwood.co.uk). She was formerly Professor of Cultural Policy and Management at City University, London, and is currently an Honorary Professor, Institute of Archaeology, University College London. She edits the journal *Cultural Trends* and has published widely on the relationship between the expectations of UK cultural policy, its implementation, funding, and the public's experience of cultural provision. Her books include *The Benefits of Public Art: The Polemics of Permanent Art in Public Places* (1995), and *The UK Cultural Sector: Profile and Policy Issues* (2001).

Stuart Davies has over 25 years' experience of working in, and with, the museums, galleries, archives, and heritage sectors. He is currently Director of Stuart Davies Associates (SDA; http://www.sdaconsultants.co.uk) which delivers support for museum and galleries, arts organizations, historic houses, heritage sites, historic landscapes, archives, development agencies, and local authorities throughout the UK. He worked for several government agencies during the New Labour years, including the Heritage Lottery Fund (1997–2000) and the Museums, Libraries and Archives Council (2000–2004), and authored the government Task Force report, *Renaissance in the Regions* (2001). Stuart was also President of the UK Museums Association (2008–2010).

4 RECONCEPTUALIZING MUSEUM ETHICS FOR THE TWENTY-FIRST CENTURY
A View from the Field[1]

Janet Marstine, Jocelyn Dodd, and Ceri Jones

In our rapidly changing world museums face increasing demands to engage with complex ethics issues, and to behave ethically. However, the predominant late twentieth-century approach to ethics as professional practice, which relies on ethics codes revised perhaps once a decade and authored by like-minded individuals to produce and implement these codes, has proven to be a constraining factor, rather than an enabling process. In order for museums effectively to negotiate difficult issues as well as ethical opportunities that arise, novel approaches to ethics are required in which the museum sector actively pursues a dynamic ethics-based museum practice. Over the past five years a new model of museum ethics has emerged; it reconceptualizes ethics as a discourse contingent upon transformations in the social, political, technological, and economic domains. Where these transformations interact with museum practice, a new sphere for ethics debate results. Through discussions among diverse stakeholders with divergent viewpoints, ethical issues are identified, considered, and acted upon. Conceptualizing museum ethics as a discourse acknowledges both the intellectual inquiry and social practice that are integral to communications. In addition, our focus on discourse aims to refute the fragmentation of ethics into distinct and overly reductive protocols for professional practice.

The new museum ethics has been shaped by scholarship in several key areas, most notably: the postmodern critical theories of post-colonialism, feminism, and neo-Marxism; new thinking in applied ethics across disciplines; and current

The International Handbooks of Museum Studies: Museum Practice, First Edition.
Edited by Conal McCarthy.
© 2015 John Wiley & Sons Ltd. Published 2020 by John Wiley & Sons Ltd.

research on new museum theory and practice. Encouraging museums to look outward and engage with the wider world through the lens of ethics, it maintains that transparency and self-reflexivity toward the processes and authority that museums hold, helps them to build trust with communities. The new museum ethics advocates placing social responsibility at the heart of museums so as to reinvigorate their mission and values toward contributing to the wellbeing of society (Marstine 2011a).

In order to map the twenty-first-century ethical terrain that museums must negotiate, and to explore how the new museum ethics can be translated effectively into practice, the Research Centre for Museums and Galleries (RCMG), based in the School of Museum Studies at the University of Leicester, embarked in 2011 on a research project with partners the Museums Association (MA) and the Inter-Disciplinary Ethics Applied Centre for Excellence in Teaching and Learning (IDEA CETL) at the University of Leeds. The unique cross-disciplinary nature of the collaboration created a rich environment for new thinking: RCMG researches the social role of museums and engages in knowledge exchange with the museum sector; IDEA CETL helps professionals across disciplines identify, analyze, and respond effectively to ethical issues they encounter in their careers; and the MA is a membership organization for UK museum, gallery, and heritage professionals and sets ethical standards for the sector.

Funded by the UK's Arts and Humanities Research Council (AHRC) under the "Care for the Future" initiative, the project took the form of a research network which brought together some 26 museum leaders, including museum directors, policymakers, senior practitioners, and academics (RCMG 2013), to identify and analyze key ethics issues with which museums are grappling and to test the potential value of the new museum ethics to address these issues. The primary aim of the project was to build a network of expertise in the new museum ethics. While the parameters of the grant dictated that the scale of the network remain modest, with most participants based in the UK, British contributors were joined by a number from Europe, the United States, Australia, and New Zealand. Together, they represented a cross-section of museum practitioners and researchers active in social and ethical initiatives; group members expressed a range of political perspectives, but shared a set of values rooted in the belief that museums have the potential to play an important social role in addressing inequalities. Many of the conversations could be characterized as encompassing an Anglo-American perspective, but nonetheless raise important questions about ethics in other contexts. Two members of the network are representatives of the MA's ethics committee, including Nick Merriman, the ethics committee convener. Other network members did not necessarily think of themselves as ethicists, but recognized that they were working to model ethical leadership in their practice.

Led by Janet Marstine and Jocelyn Dodd from RCMG, the research network met during five day-long workshops over 18 months (late 2011 to early 2013). Each workshop was devoted to a specific theme chosen by RCMG in consultation with partner organizations. These themes were: social engagement; transparency; shared guardianship of collections; moving beyond canonicity; and sustainability. Approximately half of the participants were core group members who attended all five workshops, creating a sustained conversation. The other half consisted of guest speakers who attended a single workshop as provocateurs.

This chapter discusses the findings from the research network and presents preliminary ideas about how the new museum ethics might be shared and implemented within the wider museum sector. Support for the model of new museum ethics was unanimous among participants; all agreed that the model represents a powerful and productive framework through which to re-envision museums in the twenty-first century. While many questions persist about the practical implications of the new museum ethics that will require further research, responses from participants affirm the significance of the five ethics themes on which the network focused. Responses from contributors also emphasize the value for museums in forging new relationships with communities, built upon participation, mutual understanding, and joint decision-making. Through incorporating unpublished group discussions, the chapter captures the distinct voices of network participants as they collaborate, speaking freely and experimenting with new ideas. In this way, we hope to model one strand of how new museum ethics discourse might develop to chart a course for change in the museum. Comments made by contributors to the five workshops are quoted throughout the text; the Appendix provides a full list of contributors for each workshop. Where appropriate, references have been made to publications that further extend or elucidate the themes discussed.

The new museum ethics: why is change needed, and why now?

As Marstine has described, museums are facing some of the most serious challenges in their history but the sector is unable to adapt or respond effectively to these challenges (Marstine 2011b, xxiii). New opportunities to become socially responsible are going unrecognized and unmet. Many museums are currently under-resourced and, as a result, innovative agendas to promote social engagement are often abandoned in favor of conventional approaches to practice. Financial pressures are forcing museum leaders to make choices in the short term that may compromise the work of institutions in the longer term.

Of great concern is the sector's inadequate engagement with the shifting ethics landscape. Museum professional bodies and the museums they represent have long relied on ethics codes to define their policy and practice. Introduced by the American Association of Museums in 1925, the Museums Association in the 1970s, and the International Council of Museums in 1986 (Besterman 2006, 433–435), such codes remain the touchstone of museum ethics today. This dependence, in turn, reflects the prioritization of skill development and standard setting that characterized the museum and museum studies sectors for much of the last century. The focus on professional ethics has played a significant role in distinguishing public service from personal gain and political interests. Ironically, it has also insulated museums from social concerns in the world around them. Gary Edson's seminal volume *Museum Ethics* advanced this notion of ethics as an inward looking process of professionalization; "Museum ethics is not about the imposition of external values on museums, but about an understanding of the foundations of museum practices" (Edson 1997, xxi). By contrast, the shifting terrain around museums drives a critique of common practice: change is needed to address the current and future needs of society.

The understanding of ethics as a code has led to a "legalistic" approach that too often produces reactive and incremental change instead of the responsive and holistic thinking for which the new museum ethics argues. While there are increasingly strident calls for stronger reinforcement of ethics codes and legal interventions, the question remains: are ethics codes fit for purpose (Marstine 2011a)?

Recent social, economic, political, and technological trends have sparked a developing discourse about the moral agency of museums that contests the authorized view of ethics. Richard Sandell has argued persuasively that objectivity is an elusive stance that imparts value through the invoked authority of the institution. Sandell uses the term "moral activism" to suggest a direction for museums to realize their potential as agents of social change both inside and outside the museum (Sandell 2007, p. x). Hilde Hein identifies what she calls an "institutional morality," asserting that, while museums may not have a conscience, they do have moral agency (Hein 2000, 91–93, 103). Moving beyond personal and professional ethics, institutional morality suggests that, while museum staff may come and go, their activities across time and place create an institutional, and also a sectoral, ethics.

When asked why new thinking is required in museum ethics now, participants in the research network cited both short- and long-term trends in policy and practice. Figure 4.1 shows that these factors included: the shifting political climate in the UK; pressures for museums to be more accountable; and the need to make fundamental changes to the model of the museum itself, including how knowledge is conceived, notions of "who" owns what and "who" has a say in the interpretation and use of collections. However, for some participants this question only raised more questions, including what is meant by "change" and what is meant by "now."

A premise that underpins the development of the new museum ethics is that professional ethics codes alone do not suffice; as a default instrument of ethical practice, they do not adequately equip museums to deal sensitively and fairly with the shifting ethical terrain. Exploring this premise in the first workshop, John Jackson, Science Policy Advisor at the Natural History Museum, London, asserted that traditional ethics codes represent a particular set of values intended to prescribe how museum professionals should "properly" behave. Nick Merriman, MA

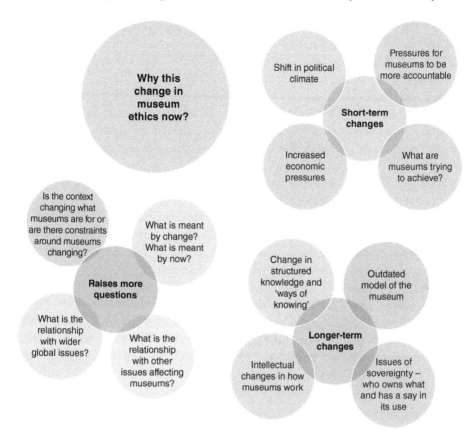

FIGURE 4.1   Participant responses to the question: "Why this change in museum ethics now?"

project partner and Manchester Museum Director, stressed that each ethics code encapsulates the moment or context in which it is written so that it effectively becomes "fixed" in time. Director of Policy and Research, Glasgow Life, Mark O'Neill, added that the underlying values of a particular code become less relevant as its original context shifts over time. In a later workshop, Michael Pickering, Head of Curatorial and Research at the NMA, noted that national, international, discipline-based, and institution-based ethics codes and conventions too often contradict one another, leaving practitioners in a muddle about how to proceed (Pickering 2011).

In the UK, the focus of museum ethics has waxed and waned as the profession has developed. Merriman pointed out that the MA first produced a code of conduct as late as the 1970s, and it was directed solely at curators. It was not until the 1990s that the MA produced a code relevant to the profession as a whole. By 2001, a revised code referenced a range of ethics issues across many areas of the museum, including responsibilities for public engagement; however, in today's economic climate, the focus has shifted back to collections and disposal issues (Museums Association 2008). Participants in the research network, including Nick Poole of the Collections Trust, voiced concern that this shift back to collections has driven museums to become too inward-looking, at the expense of putting equal emphasis on their social roles.

The new museum ethics offers a pathway to redirect this inward focus and to recognize codes as part of a larger body of ethics guidance. It draws on a range of disciplines, including philosophy, sociology, political science, and information technology, to provide museums with the tools and confidence to respond proactively to the challenges and opportunities they face. The key idea is that ethics is a dynamic social practice that encourages dialogue and critical thinking, with the aim of developing socially purposeful museums. And, as IDEA CETL project partner James Dempsey explained, ethics discourse emerges from a triad of three distinct, overlapping spheres: case studies (both from within and outside the sector); ethics codes; and values and principles (Figure 4.2).

What is the value of case studies for the new museum ethics? IDEA CETL Director, Christopher Megone, explains that the use of applied ethics case studies from a range of disciplines – medical ethics to media ethics – can help museums to negotiate difficult issues; for example, by encouraging them to move away from the polarized positions of stakeholder groups toward finding points of similarity which can advance equitable solutions. Indeed, the new museum ethics does not settle for consensus that may exclude minority or radical views, but instead welcomes conflicting perspectives as a constructive contribution (Lynch 2011). This is

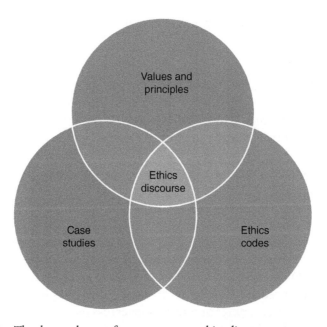

FIGURE 4.2   The three spheres of contemporary ethics discourse.

not an easy process, nor will case studies from across disciplines give museums all the answers, but it does provide a model for ethics leadership and practice.

What is the significance for museum ethics discourse of identifying and applying values and principles? In network conversations, an embrace of museum activism was juxtaposed with the dangers of accepting the continued absence of value-based ethics in sector debates. For network participants such as David Anderson, Director General, Amgueddfa Cymru – National Museum Wales, ethical thinking was a "way of being" which permeated the whole museum; however, the group identified fractures in the museum sector, including inequalities of resource and action, that could mitigate against the adoption of the new museum ethics. For example, Anderson drew attention to the geographical hierarchy entrenched in UK museum funding, with London institutions receiving the majority of private contributions.

Some of the participants mooted the impact of a personal ethics code for museum professionals in response to institutional silence on issues of social responsibility, thereby effectively protecting structures of cultural authority derived from the eighteenth and nineteenth centuries. David Fleming, Director, National Museums Liverpool, argued that the existence of an "unspoken set of values" enabled museums to prioritize their collections over social engagement. According to many in the network, vested interests in maintaining the status quo could present a challenge to the new museum ethics.

The research network expressed a compelling need for change in museums through the framework of new museum ethics. Participants were receptive to the premise of the research network: namely, that new methods, new ways of thinking and a more strategic approach are required to effect organizational change and to ensure that museums are adequately equipped to develop responsive ethical policies, procedures, and decision-making, now and in the future. There is need for an ethics that enables museums to be nimble and adapt to changing circumstances. We are currently on the threshold of change in which the social role and value of museums will become increasingly significant (Museums Association 2013). The research network viewed the new museum ethics as a catalyst that can help museums to step over this threshold.

Analysis and discussion: key ideas from the network workshops

In this section, we explore the key findings from each of the workshops and identify the patterns that emerged. Throughout the process, participants used the workshop themes – social engagement; transparency; shared guardianship of collections; moving beyond canonicity; and sustainability – to raise ethics issues at the core of *what* and *whom* museums are for. Overarching threads of discussion called for: a radical overhaul of museums in terms of structure, purpose, and values;

embedding social responsibility as a core value alongside care and research of collections; and collaborative action across the sector in order to meet the above aims. The group was critical of UK museums' longstanding silence on ethical issues beyond the use of codes; in fact, many participants agreed that ethics codes are used as a justification for museums to avoid more complex ethics discussions, particularly around social responsibility. They welcomed evidence that aspirations such as shared guardianship can be translated into practice, while acknowledging that this was not easy work and required museums coming to terms with complexity and uncertainty.

Members of the network characterized ethics as an expensive (in terms of human resources) but powerful tool in its capacity to function as a set of lived values which connects ideas with actions and consequences. Thus, self-reflective practice and long-term collaborative relationships with communities, on which the new museum ethics depends, each require an additional investment in time. It is not enough to "bolt on" the new museum ethics to current museum structures because these structures are fundamentally undemocratic, underpinned by outdated values and hierarchies that perpetuate inequalities. Network participants voiced their concern that museums' focus on ownership of "property" (collections) encourages work in isolation from their communities, at the expense of developing relations among people. They also embraced interdisciplinary articulations of values and principles; for example, Article 27 of the Universal Declaration of Human Rights (United Nations 1948) was cited as a strongly worded, inalienable principle and persuasive statement of intent (Anderson 2012). Similarly, the Physicians Charter and the Hippocratic Oath each articulates principles that necessitate action. Network participants also identified empathy as being as important as legislation in fostering social engagement. These threads of discussion form the backdrop to specific issues debated in the respective workshops, which we consider next.

Social engagement

Participants in the workshop on social engagement concluded that social responsibility defines the twenty-first-century ethical museum, in which "democratic pluralism, shared authority and social justice are distinct but convergent areas of policy" (Marstine 2011a, 10). Workshop contributors agreed that, in order to realize the potential of social responsibility in museums, radical change was necessary, but achievable. Director of Policy and Research, Glasgow Life, Mark O'Neill critiqued what he called a "welfare model," which he described as the dominant approach to social engagement whereby museums offer educational services to the public in order both to defend the core (collections) work of the organization and also to "correct" the perceived knowledge deficiencies of both visitors and non-visitors for their own benefit. Instead, he championed a social-justice model which prioritizes: the removal of barriers to engagement; respect for human rights; strategic thinking; long-term goals; and quality learning

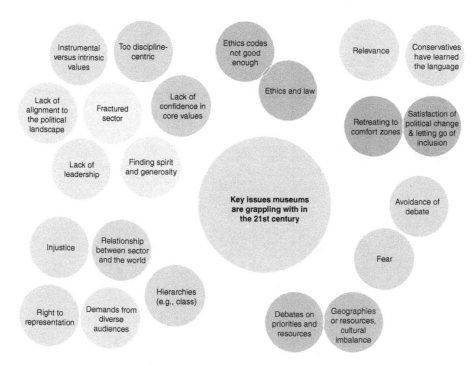

FIGURE 4.3   Participant responses to "Key issues that museums are grappling with in the twenty-first century."

and content. This model also acknowledges and subverts power hierarchies as it generates co-creation and facilitates informed debate. Meanwhile, Fleming argued that the National Museums Liverpool's mission "to change lives" through its commitment to social justice, makes it a unique national museum which views its citizens as agents of social change (National Museums Liverpool 2013).

Both O'Neill and Fleming acknowledged that moving from current models of museum operation to a social-justice model is not a straightforward process. Figure 4.3 shows some of the obstacles to change identified by participants, including: a fractured museum sector that is too discipline-centric and lacks leadership; inadequate codes of ethics that also exclude certain groups from the decision-making process; an avoidance of debate; and continuing global injustice. Figure 4.4 represents some of the major hurdles to museums' realization of their potential moral agency, namely the need for museums to: admit their vulnerability and remove "fear of failure"; be led by values rather than finances; and embed a focus on social justice across the organization.

The group acknowledged that the commitment to moral agency varies across the museum spectrum, from municipal to national museums. Participants O'Neill and Anderson discussed the apparent disparity between local and regional museums that focus strongly on social engagement, but receive relatively little media

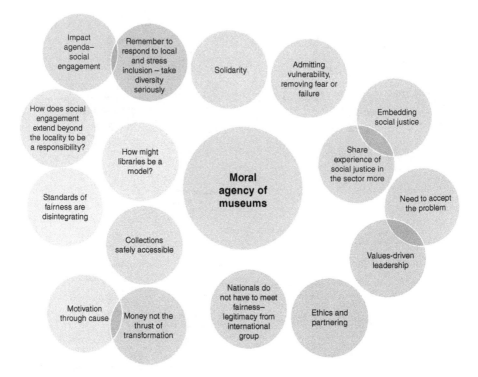

FIGURE 4.4   Participant responses to "The moral agency of museums."

attention and resources, and the national museums that frequently evade the social responsibility agenda by comparing themselves with their international peers and by securing media coverage and funding for their global reach. What is needed to change this situation? Head of Diversity and Strategy at Victoria and Albert Museum, Eithne Nightingale, asserted that funding alone was not the answer. Generous resources from previous UK governments for social inclusion work had led to changes at the margins, but not to the core values of museums (Nightingale and Mahal 2012). Participants agreed that the challenge is to convince museums that do not already share the values of social justice to become socially responsible, and that the discourse of ethics should be activated in order to effect this change.

Network contributors accepted that, in order to nurture a discourse of ethics, museum staff and trustees must develop the tools to identify and evaluate ethical issues and make appropriate ethical decisions. James Dempsey argued that the power of applied ethics does not rely on one method to resolve ethical issues, but draws upon a range of approaches, namely case studies, ethics codes, and values and principles (Figure 4.2). In the workshop, participants discussed the relative merits of each approach (summarized in Table 4.1). Of these methods, codes of ethics and values and principles were readily accepted by participants, although the use of non-museum case studies raised questions. However, over the course

TABLE 4.1   Methods used in applied ethics: their benefits and challenges

Method	Description	Benefits	Challenges
Case study	Analyzes a specific ethical issue. Invites discussion and practical thinking about how the issue can be resolved.	Practical and relevant, can help work through a specific problem.	Case studies often lack clear guidance, framework or structure. May be too specific to be applied to other contexts.
Ethics codes	Prescriptive set of rules for "how to do ethics." Levels of specificity over "how to behave."	Provide very clear guidelines in particular situations.	Prescriptive approach can be alienating as it does not explain why. Imposes rules formed by the few on the many. Sees practice as unchanging. Works against creative practice. Tends to be cited for one-off controversies and then forgotten.
Values and principles	Set of high level ideas to adhere to such as honesty, fairness, integrity.	Positive and inclusive, can provide guidance for action.	Can be abstract and difficult to describe in practice. Can embody political positions.

of the five workshops, IDEA CETL partners convinced the network of the efficacy of ethics discourse developed through case studies and of the complementary, interlinked nature of the three methods as a means of empowering individuals to make informed and responsive ethical decisions.

Transparency

The second workshop took up the theme of transparency, recognizing both the ubiquitous and slippery usage of the term today. Marstine argued that the tensions between exposure and withholding warrant new approaches to museum transparency as an integral component of twenty-first-century museum ethics. She called for a transparency that makes the disclosure of data meaningful for constituents through contextualization, translation, and mediation, by identifying the agendas and perspectives of those "experts" responsible for framing the data. She asserted that, through equitable knowledge sharing, museum transparency has the capacity to critique and redistribute power and resources (Marstine 2012).

Three strong examples of museum transparency in action served as our case studies. Esmé Ward, Head of Learning and Engagement at Manchester Museum, took participants on a tour of the museum (the venue for the workshop) to demonstrate the efforts directed at making the institution's values and agendas transparent to audiences. Ward showed how interpretation, permanent collection displays, and social media are used to examine issues of power and ethics around collecting and to encourage reciprocal exchange between the museum and its publics. Audiences are encouraged to be researchers and to draw on what they have learned in the museum to take action in the wider world. Then Michael Pickering explored how the context of repatriation and restoration of cultural rights to Indigenous peoples in Australia had created, by necessity, an environment of transparency at the National Museum of Australia in Canberra. He explained that, although enacting transparency was a non-negotiable response to Indigenous activism and related government policy, it had now become part of the museum's culture because it was "the right thing to do." In our third case study, Jan Ramirez, Chief Curator and Director of Collections at the National September 11 Memorial Museum, New York, presented both the challenges and imperatives of embedding transparency into the processes and policies of the organization at a time when diverse stakeholders (including families, survivors, first responders, and neighborhood groups) are emotionally invested in the site and when political and media scrutiny are high.

Against the backdrop of these examples, Marstine presented for debate two distinct, but overlapping, models of transparency: "dashboard" (or transactional) and radical. Network participants agreed that dashboard transparency, defined as transparency demonstrated through statistics that benchmark performance outcomes, prioritizes the needs of the institution over obligations to communities. Many critiqued dashboard transparency as too carefully managed; providing an array of data without explaining *why* the data is important. By contrast, contributors viewed radical transparency, described as equitable knowledge sharing that empowers consumers of information to make critically informed choices and to take action, as a more effective tool for advancing participatory practice, but also more costly in terms of human resources.

Despite the examples highlighted in the case studies, participants concurred that workshop discussions on transparency raised more questions than they answered. Many believed that museums were rarely transparent about their processes and practices, but that radical transparency as a basis for ethical practice had transformative potential. However, Jette Sandahl, Director of the City Museum of Copenhagen, warned against allowing transparency to subjugate more politically difficult issues in the new museum ethics discourse, warning: "The concept of transparency has the capacity to usurp other issues such as power, equal access, reciprocity and democracy which might be more robust and relevant." Other contributors underscored the link between transparency and trust, while Pickering singled out empathy as a particularly "under-rated" professional stance in museums.

Some network participants were unsure whether audiences were really interested in transparency in museum processes and values; for instance, Merriman suggested that transparency is often a way for museums to justify their own structures and processes, while Ramirez emphasized that transparency may be particularly significant to communities at highly contested flashpoints. It was agreed that there is no endpoint of complete transparency; transparency is a continual negotiation. Marstine referred to the image of glass as a relevant metaphor, that is to say, something which is both clear and opaque at the same time (Marstine 2012). Returning to the practice of transparency at the NMA, Pickering noted that some objects need to be kept hidden from public view because of the sacred or secret beliefs attached to them; however, the museum explains to visitors why they cannot be shared. And while Marstine held that transparency was an instrumental, rather than an intrinsic value, other network members disagreed, asserting that transparency could be an end unto itself.

Shared guardianship of collections

Shared guardianship, described as respecting the dynamic, experiential, and contingent qualities of heritage and distributing the rights and responsibilities to this heritage in new ways (Marstine 2011b, 17), strongly resonated with participants at the third workshop. A particularly challenging notion for conventional museum structures, the concept of shared guardianship required critical reflection and problem-solving in the network. It also led to creative and aspirational thinking about the need to reject the conventions of museum possession/ownership of collections so as to embrace a concept of joint stewardship with communities. In a 2008 essay, Haidy Geismar argued that the Māori principle of shared guardianship (*kaitiakitanga*), based on the concept of a "dynamic link between people and things" (Geismar 2008, 116; Tapsell 201, 86–93), has the capacity to transform Western proprietary notions of museum collections. During the workshop, Poole suggested that shared guardianship "represents a shift from museums conceived as gatekeepers of culture to enablers of culture" and, as a result, "museums become part of a cultural commons with shared rights of access and shared responsibilities for stewardship." Technology increases this potential, Poole explained, opening up a fluid way of thinking about collections, while shared guardianship reminds museums that they acquire title to collections on behalf on the public.

An exciting finding from the workshop was that senior museum leaders want to see museums develop policies and practices of shared guardianship. This was clear from a group provocation in which participants were asked to identify their aspirations for shared guardianship of collections at the end of the twenty-first century (Figure 4.5). Contributors hoped for greater access to collections for all possible interest groups and redistribution of collections to where "they are most loved."

The majority of participants agreed that aspirations toward shared guardianship depend on museums valuing the many different ways of knowing that exist within communities. Accordingly, valuing community expertise helps to promote personal connections to objects, develop mutual understanding in connection with tangible and intangible heritage, and encourage collaborative collecting with communities, sometimes called "relational collecting" (Gosden and Larson 2007). The

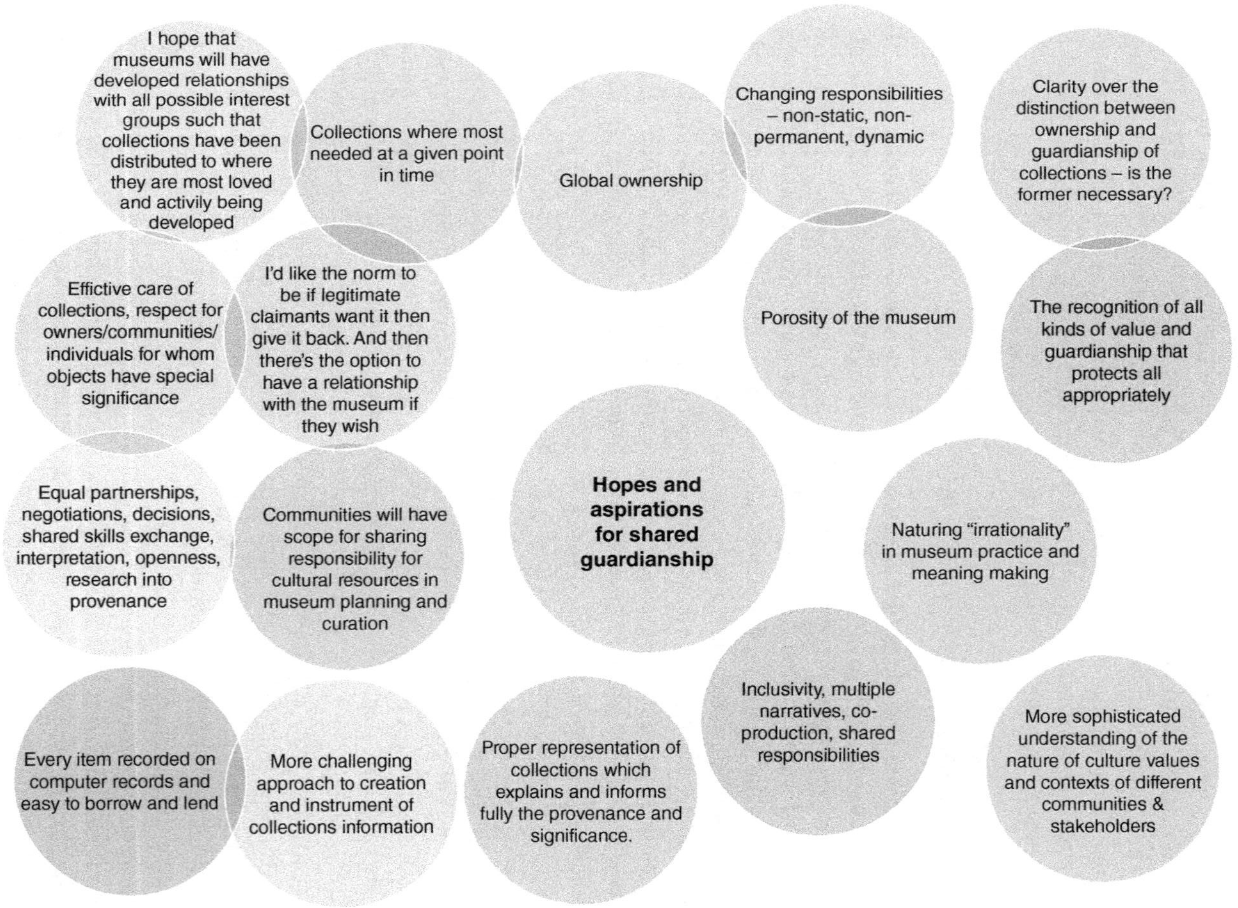

FIGURE 4.5 Participant responses to "Hopes and aspirations for shared guardianship."

discussion also made clear that conventional museum structures are holding back change, because their underpinning principles were formed at a time of confidence in Western cultural superiority when it was thought the world could be known in its entirety through empirical research. These principles and structures evidently conflict with the concept that communities hold knowledge about collections of equal status and value to that of the museum, and that authority should be shared. Within the context of shared guardianship, facilitation is a form of expertise, although, as Poole suggested, this idea may be threatening to curators who prioritize research over public engagement.

Marstine remarked that the ethics of museum collecting and collections is a highly contested area that often leads to polarization between economic and cultural rights. Janet Ulph, Professor of Law at the University of Leicester, discussed how contrasting legal and ethical approaches to collections have contributed to these oppositions. She explained that, from a legal perspective, objects are viewed as property and are assigned economic value, but from an ethical perspective, objects are seen in terms of the relationships they produce among stakeholders and the "social good(s)" that these relationships generate. The group agreed that the concept of "social good" in the context of collections needs to be explored further, as do the values (such as aesthetic and nationalistic) that museums attach to objects that may mitigate against shared guardianship.

Megone argued that case studies of repatriation debates demonstrate that disagreement is fundamental to applied ethics and that conflict should be explored as a means of overcoming polarized positions. A process of identifying how and why clashing positions develop can facilitate a shared understanding of common ground. Megone showed how the protagonists on either side of an argument might desire the same outcome, but disagree on how to reach it. Alternatively, they might articulate the same view, but frame it within different political or belief systems. There was general support for the idea of unpacking conflict in order to identify potential points of connection as a fruitful and constructive approach that could be developed in the museum sector, although some participants felt that certain views may be too entrenched to be reconciled. Several contributors remarked that the difficult work of reconciliation hinges on transparency in communicating organizational values and agendas. MA Head of Policy and Communications, Maurice Davies, added that in the UK government policy is also key. When museums encounter legal imperatives to rethink ownership of collections (for example, in cases of Nazi spoliation), they respond with a coordinated and successful approach; however, when government policy is more ambiguous (for example, in cases of the possession and display of human remains), museum responses are less clear and consistent (on these topics see chapters by Bienkowski and Pickering in this volume).

Paul Tapsell, Dean of Te Tumu, School of Māori, Pacific and Indigenous Studies at the University of Otago, New Zealand, elucidated policies and practices of shared guardianship from a Māori perspective and discussed how these policies and practices have shaped the bicultural society of New Zealand, including its museums (Tapsell 2011). He presented a persuasive argument from a rights per-spective for implementing shared guardianship across the museum sector.

Paul Basu and Nick Merriman presented case studies of shared guardianship in a UK context. Basu, Reader in Material Culture and Museum Studies at University College London, discussed an initiative on "reanimating cultural heritage" through a digital access initiative among five UK museums and archives and collaborating institutions in Sierra Leone. (See Chapter 15, "Reanimating Cultural Heritage: Digital Curatorship, Knowledge Networks, and Social Transformation in Sierra Leone," by Paul Basu, in *Museum Transformations*.) The project speaks to broader agendas of access, inclusion, capacity-building, and knowledge sharing. Merriman outlined the Manchester Museum's work on relational collecting. He described a collaboration with local communities on collecting trees as a means both to pro-mote sustainability and to apply a different lens to the legacies of colonialism within the permanent collection, including botanical collections, live collections of animals, and trees in mythological and symbolic representation (see Merriman, this volume). Both Basu's and Merriman's examples illustrated the importance of producing a "social good" by enabling communities to reconnect with their cul-ture and heritage. Jette Sandahl, who has worked in museums in New Zealand and Europe, argued that, so as to avoid becoming mausoleums, museums need to keep collecting, and that relational collecting is an ethical practice. She voiced a powerful reminder that we need to "keep remembering the violence sitting beneath the surface of museum collections" as well as the "loneliness of exile and life as a thing" when alienated from their communities.

What else emerged from the robust discussions about the challenges and opportunities of shared guardianship? Questions arose about how an aspiration to shared guardianship could be implemented in practice. Some participants described challenges in identifying who can represent or speak for a community and in building trust within groups that museums have wronged in the past. Overall, there is a need for museums to develop more sophisticated ways of understanding cultural value, and to think more deeply about how and why museums collect and display objects. Manchester City Galleries conservator Amanda Wallace remarked that museums have become overly obsessed with the materiality of objects. Many contributors concurred that relational collecting could play a significant role in shared guardianship, with museums developing their collections in relation to important themes to their communities. Poole expressed the idea that if museums do not open up their collections toward shared guardianship, they risk becoming irrelevant in an era that values participation and agency. Davies suggested that the new museums ethics is, first and foremost, about deconstructing power issues, and that the area of collections is highly con-tested because collections represent both economic and cultural control. Others countered that, within the context of shared guardianship, there is the potential to think about collecting as an ethical good.

Moving beyond canonicity

The fourth workshop took a narrow lens to focus on ethics in one particular type of museum – the art museum. Marstine asserted that many of the ethical challenges endemic in art museums and galleries stem from the principles and assumptions of canonicity. She explained how judgments of quality, based on subjective and culturally relative factors including aesthetics, originality, and influence, determine a canon; a canon is thus an exclusionary sifting device that delineates boundaries between insiders and outsiders, the core and the margins. This discrimination leaks from the artistic to the social sphere: in perpetuating canonicity, art museums and galleries implicitly also perpetuate social inequalities that create barriers to participation. Marstine argued that canonicity encourages art museums to extend themselves financially to develop costly blockbuster exhibitions and to acquire high-priced works by canonical artists, and, as a result, many art museums make ethical compromises, from accepting funding from ethically tainted corporations to overlooking conflicts of interest. Despite the focus on art museums, the workshop raised issues relevant to other types of museums, particularly the ways in which canonicity translates to history, science, anthropology, and natural history museum settings. Participants acknowledged that canonicity in these other settings often operates through hierarchies attached to factors such as provenance, gender, sexual orientation, ethnicity, race, and class. Poole asserted that the canon reinforces the founding identity of the museum as a means of organizing and structuring the world: "it's difficult to take institutions founded as such and transform them into reflective and responsive spaces."

Issues of canonicity illuminate a crisis of values that dissuades museums from tackling inequalities. John Jackson, from the Natural History Museum in London, was critical of the ways in which museums naturalize canonicity without explaining how, and by whom, it is constructed. Matt Smith, a Brighton-based artist and curator, discussed the burdens of canonicity from a queer perspective. He explained how narratives of canonicity exclude LGBT experiences and discussed examples from his own work that refute and unsettle this exclusivity. David Anderson argued that museums invest very little in meaningful social participation and staff assume that the institution itself has intrinsic, rather than instrumental, value. Rather, he said, "[i]t is the objects within them, rather than the organizations themselves, that have intrinsic value." Basu added that the nineteenth-century notion of the art museum as a "civilizing institution" is alive and well. Merriman championed working with artists to develop imaginative and creative approaches to collections and exhibitions, but Sandahl and Nightingale voiced frustration that one-off artist-driven initiatives too often enable museums to ignore the potential of such projects to produce organizational change.

Professor Richard Sandell of the School of Museum Studies at the University of Leicester explored BP's sponsorship of Tate and the powerful protest art of activist group Liberate Tate in critiquing this partnership (see Chong, this volume). When questions arose about the assumption that corporate funding is tainted while public money is always free from compromise, Megone cautioned that it is always challenging to analyze the ethical practices of any organization and its supply chains. Jackson asked whether the ethical practices of individual donors should be scrutinized before their contribution is accepted. Merriman admitted that the UK MA ethics committee does not consider cases concerned with museum sponsorship; almost all of its work involves collections issues. Jackson remarked that most museums make funding decisions based on risk assessment, not on ethics.

Overall, there was no consensus that art museums are particularly weak in addressing ethical issues. Some discussants were concerned that the critique of canonicity was not more widespread and that most practitioners believed that art museums are valuable spaces of creativity, inquiry, and reflection. Sandell declared that quality and social justice are not mutually exclusive. Jocelyn Dodd shared the findings from a long-term RCMG project that evaluated the impact of art works on the perceptions, feelings, and attitudes of young people. Though unfamiliar with art museums, the sample respondents had the opportunity for sustained engagement with a particular painting: Raphael's *Madonna of the Pinks* (National Gallery, London). The research showed that age, ability, and previous knowledge of art are not prerequisites for engaging with such canonical works; the experiences of the young people involved were enjoyable, thought-provoking, and in many cases enabled self-reflection and considerable skills to be developed (RCMG 2007). Do projects like this challenge canonicity or legitimize it through public funding? Merriman pointed out that some art museums have taken significant steps to deconstruct canonicity; he cited Kelvingrove in Glasgow, which challenges canonicity by treating artworks like all other museum objects. He also expressed some concern with the "missionary zeal" with which social responsibility was thrust upon museums and galleries, believing it was also important for people to have the choice to resist museums. Others countered that, for many people, resisting is not a choice because the power structures in place do not equally empower diverse publics to exercise their cultural rights.

What would it mean to exercise ethical leadership in the art museum? IDEA CETL took the lead in asking how the museum sector might find common ground. Megone suggested that museums could look to universities, which grapple with many of the same ethical dilemmas of participation and access, but also acknowledge their moral agency as they challenge traditional hierarchies of disciplines and "ways of knowing." Partnerships between art museums and museum studies departments could offer new ways to think beyond canonicity. IDEA CETL lecturer Jamie Dow advocated a role for museum professionals, in conjunction with museum studies researchers, to define more rigorously the "social good" that museums promote. David Anderson suggested we re-examine the values of public service, which are rarely discussed, as a way of thinking. The workshop as a whole revealed that alternative ways of valuing artistic practice beyond the hierarchies of canonicity can help art museums and galleries to generate shared authority more successfully and become, as Jackson put it, "social actors beyond matters of taste and cultural capital."

Sustainability

The fifth and final meeting of the network examined the theme of sustainability and, like many of the other workshops, raised ethical debates that were not easily resolved. Nick Poole, who opened the discussions, identified the need to decide the parameters of sustainability in museums; specifically, what should be sustained, why, and who decides. Poole characterized sustainability as "managing a dynamic equilibrium between consumption and production by establishing priorities." He acknowledged the many conflicting definitions of perpetuity: from 100 years, which is how many museum professionals frame long-term impact, to thousands and millions of years, which is how environmentalists commonly measure actions. Poole asked if it is ethical to sustain some elements of museum activity, such as collections, at the expense of others, such as the experience of culture. He suggested that, in museums, sustainability concerns "educating individuals about their mutual obligation to others." Megone noted that the ancient Greeks did not have a concept that could be identified as sustainability; instead, our relatively greater control over our world today has generated the idea of sustainability as an ethical value. Others added, however, that it remains difficult to determine exactly what we do, and do not, control.

Tony Kendle, Creative Director of the Eden Project, Cornwall, and Robert Janes, Editor-in-Chief of *Museum Management and Curatorship*, agreed on the need for collective action among museums to help define and develop the parameters of sustainability. Kendle discussed the interconnectedness of the "three pillars" of sustainability: environmental, economic, and social. He argued for the benefits of understanding how these work together, rather than focusing on each at the expense of the others. Kendle warned that views on sustainability too often "protect particular versions of the future" that create difficult ethical dilemmas. Poole proposed that museums could justify a commitment to sustainability by balancing their economic costs with the social good they create: "the opportunity to live good and reflective lives."

Janes claimed that addressing sustainability is dependent upon recognizing the synergies between museums and wider society: if economic growth is no longer tenable, how will museums adapt to a non-growth economy? He identified three issues of sustainability facing museums: negative environmental impacts; government and private debt; and resource depletion. Museums can only become sustainable when they engage with people and issues outside, including both professional "outreach" activities and personal experiences beyond their own self-interest.

The role of museum professionals in leading change sparked a debate about the agency of individuals within an organization. Janes remarked that senior management often feels threatened by the idea of individual agency and, as a result, does not cultivate it; this is a wasted opportunity to strengthen museum ethics. The model of the lone museum CEO is not working, and, as Farson has argued, "leadership is the property of the group, not an individual" (1996, 144). David Anderson called for the museum sector to develop a statement of personal ethics that could accede greater agency to individuals, citing medicine as a profession that cannot ignore the social context in which it operates. Responding to this, Eithne Nightingale advocated the alignment of personal and organizational ethics. Poole, however, questioned the wisdom of conflating ethics for the sector with individual ethics, and suggested that revisions to organizational structures and pathways of authority can also generate greater individual agency among museum staff. Similarly, Kendle critiqued the environmental movement's focus on personal behavior to the detriment of larger, but more disruptive, social changes; while collective action toward sustainability is essential, individuals have to be inspired to hope in a "future possible."

Acknowledging the dilemmas of sustainability in twenty-first-century ethics, Poole remarked that tackling the issue was "like looking through a veil" and not knowing what was on the other side. He noted that it is possible to address very limited areas of sustainability, but much harder to resolve the broader issues. Kendle stated that some impacts might not be known or measurable, even if we do know they exist. Janes added that sustainability could be understood as a process of coming to terms with the paradoxical nature of museums and the need to manage an unknown future. Participants were certain that it was no longer acceptable for museums to remain silent, but that they must become activist organizations in pursuit of a sustainable world. They also acknowledged that the route toward change was slow and that the discourse around radical change is weak, but, as Sandahl remarked, the route backward is much faster.

In conclusion, Janes reinforced the need for individual *and* institutional action to develop the socially engaged museum. However, some participants argued that, in their experience, institutions were likely to impede or compromise ethical decision-making. Poole asserted that currently there was a "moral leadership vacuum" in the museum sector that needed to be addressed. Citing the example of the UK's Leveson Inquiry, the public investigation into the practices and ethics of the British press after the revelation of the phone-hacking scandal by News International in 2011, Megone considered its implications for redefining ethics in the media, drawing attention to the tension between public interest and freedom of the press (over which there is a lack of clarity), and the need for an active code of ethics alongside regulation. It was suggested that examples such as this relevant to museums would help to define the cultural contexts for museum ethics. Finally, Poole noted that Kendle had used three aspirational phrases to capture the spirit of network conversations on sustainability and museum ethics: "hope," "change you can believe in," and "future possible."

Reflections on the processes of the research network: what was most valuable?

Involvement in the workshops had a significant impact on participants. It gave them a new language to discuss ethics in the wider sector and brought them into contact with other colleagues who advocate progressive ethical models for museums. Participants were asked to indicate what issues from the five workshops they found to be most insightful (Figure 4.6) and most challenging (Figure 4.7). Insightful issues included: co-production; the interdependence of museums and the wider world; and the need for a personal ethics in the sector. Challenging issues ranged from: mapping the relationships between personal and institutional ethics; distinguishing between theoretical and applied ethics; and acknowledging the diversity of approaches to ethics within the museum sector. Contributors reflected that there was often a connection between the most insightful and the most challenging issues: for example, co-production was an insightful issue for some participants, but also raised challenges in in terms of definition and the reinterpretation of expertise. One participant questioned whether ethics was the most appropriate framework through which to address the most pressing issues facing museums, such as the structures of power and inequality.

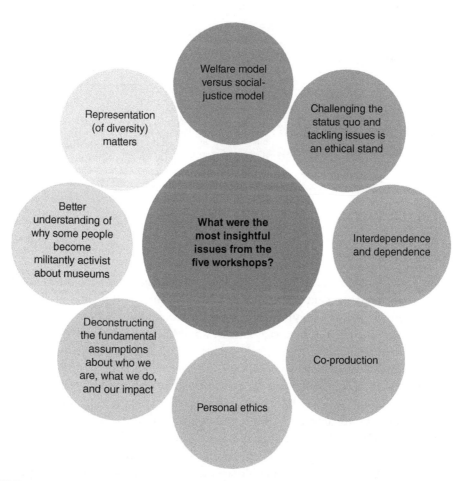

FIGURE 4.6 Reflections on the most insightful elements of the five workshops.

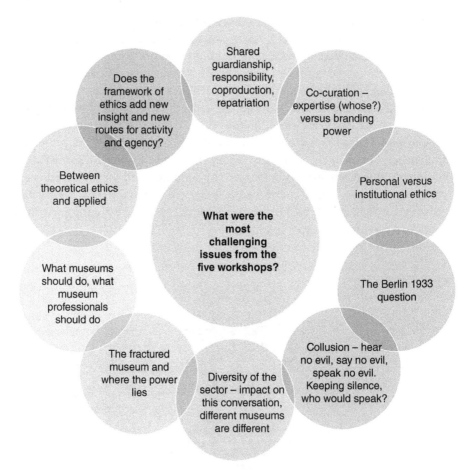

FIGURE 4.7   Reflections on the most challenging issues from the five workshops.

When asked what major questions had been left unanswered by the research network, participants wanted more time to unpack further the ideas of the new museum ethics. Issues to explore in greater depth included: whether ethics is a set of principles and values, a discipline, or a method; and the multiple ways in which ethics is framed – by "universal" values or principles such as human rights or culturally relative practices – and might be negotiated within conflicting systems of values. The network would have benefited from the involvement of more international and non-Western contributors, and from more time to consider how ethics intersects with power and politics. Members also said that they would have welcomed more discussion of case studies outside of the museum sector, such as the Leveson Inquiry into media ethics. A few participants wanted more exposure to speakers who could articulate a conservative perspective on museums so as to challenge the formation of a consensus within the workshop and to help prepare for conversations within the sector.

Finally, contributors wanted to look at a range of new initiatives to advance twenty-first-century museum ethics. Some contributors championed the possibility of developing an independent body that would stand as an intermediary between institutions and museum professionals, to ensure that museum staff who disagreed with the ethical position of their institution would have a voice; the body would provide support for dissensus, as well as a space to reflect and think critically about ethics in museums. Other participants advocated the establishment of a research and development fund for museums to experiment with socially engaged projects. A few hoped to see an integrity auditing or monitoring tool that could be piloted in the museum sector. Participants were eager to put their ideas into action. Clearly, the research network created momentum among the group to keep conversations flowing.

Conclusion

The AHRC research network tested the value of the new ethics to address key ethics issues with which museums are grappling and its relevance to developing socially purposeful museums. The conversations that emerged from the network argued that reconceptualizing ethics as a discourse, informed by both intellectual engagement and social practice, is integral to museums' continued relevance and sustainability. Understanding the significance and confluences among values, case studies, and codes has the potential to help museum practitioners recognize the benefits of self-reflective practice through the lens of the new museum ethics. Clearly, building a strategic approach to embed the new museum ethics is challenging work. But regulation per se is not an adequate response to the ethics quandaries of the twenty-first century. In fact, the reliance on codes alone too often becomes a justification for museums to avoid difficult ethics conversations, particularly around values, principles, and social responsibility. The new museum ethics represents an opportunity for growth, rather than a burden of compliance.

Engaging in the new museum ethics is a twenty-first-century skill that museum and museum studies leaders must build among students, professionals, and communities. The new ethics is a powerful tool to effect organizational change and work toward social responsibility. It has the capacity to strengthen public trust by equipping museum practitioners to deal sensitively and fairly with the shifting ethical terrain, now and in the future. To develop a level of comfort with ethical decision-making based on a range of social concerns, is to accept the complexity and dynamism of ethics discourse that both reflects and shapes the real issues that museums encounter.

APPENDIX: LIST OF CONTRIBUTORS TO THE MUSEUM ETHICS NETWORK BY EACH WORKSHOP

Workshop, date, and venue	List of contributors
AHRC Ethics Research Network Workshop 1: Social Engagement December 5, 2011 School of Museum Studies, University of Leicester	David Anderson Paul Basu James Dempsey Jocelyn Dodd David Fleming Graeme Gooday John Jackson Ceri Jones Janet Marstine Nick Merriman Eithne Nightingale Mark O'Neill Nick Poole Jette Sandahl Amanda Wallace
AHRC Ethics Research Network Workshop 2: Transparency March 1, 2012 Manchester Museum, Manchester	James Dempsey Jocelyn Dodd John Jackson Ceri Jones Rob Lawlor Janet Marstine Christopher Megone Eithne Nightingale Mike Pickering Nick Poole Jan Ramirez Jette Sandahl

Workshop, date, and venue	List of contributors
AHRC Ethics Research Network Workshop 3: Shared Guardianship of Collections June 28, 2012 Natural History Museum, London	Paul Basu Maurice Davies James Dempsey Jocelyn Dodd Graeme Gooday Ceri Jones Janet Marstine Christopher Megone Nick Merriman Eithne Nightingale Nick Poole Jette Sandahl Paul Tapsell Janet Ulph Amanda Wallace
AHRC Ethics Research Network Workshop 4: Moving Beyond Canonicity October 18, 2012 Victoria and Albert Museum, London	David Anderson Paul Basu Patricia Cronin Jocelyn Dodd Jamie Dow John Jackson Ceri Jones Megan Kime Janet Marstine Christopher Megone Nick Merriman Eithne Nightingale Nick Poole Jette Sandahl Richard Sandell Matt Smith
AHRC Ethics Research Network Workshop 5: Sustainability February 21, 2013 National Museum of Wales, Cardiff	David Anderson Jocelyn Dodd Robert Janes Ceri Jones Tony Kendle Megan Kime Janice Lane Christopher Megone Eithne Nightingale Nick Poole Jette Sandahl

Note

1   The authors are grateful to the Arts and Humanities Research Council for its support of the research network. We thank our partner institutions, the Museums Association and IDEA CETL, University of Leeds, and the participants in the network. We also very much appreciate the helpful comments on this chapter from our colleague Simon Knell.

References

Anderson, David. 2012. "Creativity, Learning and Cultural Rights." In *Museums, Equality and Social Justice*, edited by Richard Sandell and Eithne Nightingale, 216–226. London: Routledge.

Besterman, Tristram. 2006. "Museum Ethics." In *A Companion to Museum Studies*, edited by Sharon Macdonald, 431–441. Malden, MA: Blackwell.

Edson, Gary. 1997. "Introduction." In *Museum Ethics*, edited by Gary Edson, xxi–xxiii. London: Routledge.

Farson, Richard. 1996. *Management of the Absurd: Paradoxes in Leadership*. New York: Simon and Schuster.

Geismar, Haidy. 2008. "Cultural Property, Museums and the Pacific: Reframing the Debates." *International Journal of Cultural Property* 15(2): 109–122. doi:10.1017/S0940739108080089.

Gosden, Chris, and F. Larson. 2007. *Knowing Things: Exploring the Collections at the Pitt Rivers Museum, 1884–1945*. Oxford: Oxford University Press.

Hein, Hilde. 2000. *The Museum in Transition: A Philosophical Perspective*. Washington, DC: Smithsonian Institution.

Janes, Robert R. 2009. *Museums in a Troubled World: Renewal, Irrelevance or Collapse?* London: Routledge.

Lynch, Bernadette T. 2011. "Collaboration, Contestation, and Creative Conflict: On the Efficacy of Museum/Community Partnerships." In *The Routledge Companion to Museum Ethics*, edited by Janet Marstine, 146–163. London: Routledge.

Marstine, Janet. 2011a. "The Contingent Nature of the New Museum Ethics." In *The Routledge Companion to Museum Ethics*, edited by Janet Marstine, 3–25. London: Routledge.

Marstine, Janet. 2011b. "Preface." In *The Routledge Companion to Museum Ethics*, edited by Janet Marstine, xxiii–xxv. London: Routledge.

Marstine, Janet. 2012. "Situated Revelations: Radical Transparency in the Museum." In *New Directions in Museum Ethics*, edited by Janet Marstine, Alexander Bauer, and Chelsea Haines, 1–23. London: Routledge.

Museums Association. 2008. "Code of Ethics for Museums." Accessed September 23, 2014. http://www.museumsassociation.org/ethics/code-of-ethics.

Museums Association. 2013. "Museums Change Lives: The MA's Vision for the Impact of Museums." Accessed September 23, 2014. http://www.museumsassociation.org/download?id=1001738.

National Museums Liverpool. 2013. "Mission, Values and Strategic Plan." Accessed September 23, 2014. http://www.liverpoolmuseums.org.uk/about/corporate/strategic-plan.

Nightingale, Eithne, and Chandan Mahal. 2012. "The Heart of the Matter: Integrating Equality and Diversity into the Policy and Practice of Museums and Galleries." In *Museums, Equality and Social Justice*, edited by Richard Sandell and Eithne Nightingale, 13–37. London: Routledge.

Pickering, Michael. 2011. "Dance through the Minefield: The Development of Practical Ethics for Repatriation." In *The Routledge Companion to Museum Ethics*, edited by Janet Marstine, 256–274. London: Routledge.

RCMG (Research Centre for Museums and Galleries). 2007. "The Madonna of the Pinks." Accessed September 23, 2014. http://www2.le.ac.uk/departments/museumstudies/rcmg/projects/madonna-of-the-pinks.

RCMG (Research Centre for Museums and Galleries). 2013. "Developing a Research Network to Advance 21st-Century Museum Ethics in Theory and Practice." Accessed September 23, 2014. http://www2.le.ac.uk/departments/museumstudies/rcmg/projects.

Sandell, Richard. 2007. *Museums, Prejudice and the Reframing of Difference*. London: Routledge.

Tapsell, Paul. 2011. "Aroha mai: Whose Museum? The Rise of Indigenous Ethics within Museum Contexts: A Maori Perspective." In *The Routledge Companion to Museum Ethics*, edited by Janet Marstine, 85–111. London: Routledge.

United Nations. 1948. "Article 27: The Universal Declaration of Human Rights." Accessed September 23, 2014. http://www.un.org/en/documents/udhr/index.shtml#a27.

Janet Marstine is Academic Director and Programme Director of Art Museum and Gallery Studies in the School of Museum Studies at the University of Leicester. Her research focuses on museum ethics and on the ways that contemporary art advances ethics thinking. Among her publications are *The Routledge Companion to Museum Ethics: Redefining Ethics for the Twenty-First Century Museum* (editor, 2011), *New Directions in Museum Ethics* (co-editor, 2012), and a monograph on artists' interventions as reconciliations between museums and communities (*Critical Practice: Artists, Museums, Ethics* (forthcoming, 2015)).

Jocelyn Dodd is Director of the Research Centre for Museums and Galleries (RCMG), School of Museum Studies, University of Leicester. She joined RCMG in 2000 after her extensive experience in the museum sector of museum education, community engagement, consultation, exhibition development, and museum management: she held a number of senior management roles including Manager of Nottingham City Museums and Galleries. Jocelyn was appointed Director of RCMG in 2006, and leads team-based, collaborative, funded research which explores the social role, agency, and impact of museums. She has project-managed and directed a number of large research projects with multiple partners. Jocelyn has disseminated research findings nationally and internationally. She was Co-investigator for the AHRC-funded Research Network to Advance 21st-Century Museum Ethics in Theory and Practice (2011–2013).

Ceri Jones joined the Research Centre for Museums and Galleries (RCMG) at the School of Museum Studies, University of Leicester in September 2002. As a Research Assistant and Research Associate she has worked in collaboration with colleagues, researchers, and practitioners on a wide variety of research projects exploring the social role, agency, and impact of museums, galleries, and cultural organizations. She recently completed her doctoral research which looked at the impact of living history performances in museums and historic sites on the historical consciousness of young people in the UK.

5 MUSEUM MEASUREMENT
Questions of Value

Carol A. Scott

As the result of increased calls on the public purse, there are not enough funds to go round, so how do we allocate them?

O'Brien 2010, 13–14

Measurement has developed as part of a wider agenda of public sector reform, introduced to ensure accountability for funding within declining public sector budgets and the collection of evidence with which to develop policy and make decisions about resource allocation. It is worth beginning this chapter, therefore, with a reminder of the meanings attached to the terms "public services" and the "public sector." The existence of public services reflects a social consensus that certain services are valued, provide identifiable benefits for end-users, and should be equally available to all members of a population. The provision of these services (social security, healthcare, education, national defense, arts, and cultural heritage) is authorized by governments and delivered through a government-financed public sector. The public sector works outside the free market and is funded through income earned by taxation and redistributed by governments to agencies and institutions over which it has legislative, judicial, or executive authority (ABS 2002, Cat. No. 1218.0, 7). This grant-enabled financial base allows public services to be provided to individuals and communities, either free of charge, or at prices that allow purchase to remain accessible to the majority of the population.

From the late 1970s, governments within the Organisation for Economic Co-operation and Development (OECD) family of countries (which includes the United Kingdom, the United States, Australia, and New Zealand)[1] introduced a "modernizing" program of public sector reform with accountability for the receipt of public monies at its core. The financial implications of this reform agenda are important for the subject of this chapter. On the one hand, in seeking to ensure that the potential benefits of a policy outweigh its costs, governments subject the

The International Handbooks of Museum Studies: Museum Practice, First Edition.
Edited by Conal McCarthy.
© 2015 John Wiley & Sons Ltd. Published 2020 by John Wiley & Sons Ltd.

potential costs of a policy to cost–benefit analysis (CBA). This monetized approach to valuing potential benefits has privileged quantitative and numerical data over other forms of evaluative information.

Quantitative and numerical assessments have been preferred by governments for monitoring the efficient use of public resources through balancing outputs (activities) and outcomes (results of activities) against inputs (funds received). However, measurement based on quantitative data alone has been contested by the cultural sector which considers it to be deficient in capturing other valued outcomes. These other, less tangible effects are perceived by the cultural field to be at the core of cultural value. The debates of the past two and half decades have coalesced around these main points of "whose values" and "which values" should provide the basis for assessing the worth of culture, determining policy and allocating resources (Matarasso 1996; Mason 2002; Owen 2006).

Setting the agenda

To begin this discussion, we have to go back to another time and another global financial crisis. In the late 1970s and early 1980s, the major concern for governments within the OECD was also economic stability and sustainability. Following the global oil crisis of the 1970s, OECD governments found themselves unable to maintain the policies of expansionism that had characterized public spending following World War II. Sweeping economic and structural reforms were introduced with the common objectives of reducing public expenditure and making public services more responsive, transparent, and efficient in meeting the needs of citizens (OECD 2005a).

To this end, public sector agencies were expected to provide evidence that they were using public funds efficiently, effectively, and economically amid a growing focus on the performance of public services rather than their simple conformity with law (OECD 2005b, 3). Under the broad reform agenda of "modernizing," OECD governments introduced the "New Public Management" (NPM) to control the public service through an integrated system of budget regulation, management by results, and performance evaluation. For two decades, these three features constituted the framework within which the relationship between government and the public sector was conducted.

Budget cycles assumed a central role in the process of reviewing financial probity, efficiency, and performance. As well as being a financial tool, budgeting became a management tool for governments to ensure accountability. The result was the centrality of budgets as a key element of control, with greater demands on managers to show that they had used public money efficiently. Audit scrutiny increased and audit offices with mandates to provide regular, independent reviews of financial management, performance, and compliance became a feature within most OECD governments (OECD 2005b, 2).

Another major tenet of the modernizing agenda was public sector performance, controlled through systems of performance management and evaluation. Performance management served to focus attention on results (OECD 2004, 1) and goals, targets, indicators, and measures were introduced into the formal management and incentive systems of government organizations and public employees. Integrated with performance management, performance evaluation enabled governments to assess progress against policy objectives, targets, and benchmarks (OECD 1997, 10).

In the ensuing decades, provision of performance information assumed a central role in managing and controlling public services, monitoring value for money and meeting public pressures for accountability. With the subsequent introduction of "evidence-based policy," the centrality of performance data, to determine whether a policy had achieved its intended outcomes, increased.

A culture of accountability

Although the UK, New Zealand, and Australia differ in terms of the number of tiers of government, they each took a similar approach to implementing the modernizing agenda.[2] In all three countries, a total-system approach, mandating change across government (OECD 2004, 4) was adopted. This model of fiscal control and accountability had a profound impact on the relationship between governments and the public sector in these three countries. Governments set the rules of engagement, aligned them to economic and social policy, and consequently linked the value of the sector to its contribution to and compliance with this agenda.

Demands for increased compliance with government policy progressively paved the way for the decline of the "arm's-length" principle and greater intervention by government in the work of sponsored agencies (Selwood 2002a). In 1998, the Department for Culture, Media, and Sport (DCMS) in Britain established three-year funding agreements tied to the achievement of government objectives, particularly with regard to a key New Labour policy of social inclusion. The Rt. Hon. Chris Smith, then Secretary of State for Culture, Media, and Sport, described the "new relationship" between government and the recipients of public funding as part of the modernization and reform agenda which sought returns on public investment in line with government policy:

> Three year funding will be accompanied by three year funding agreements and all recipients of funding from DCMS will have a clear responsibility to deliver against demanding output and outcome based targets … The advent of resource accounting across Government will ensure that DCMS ties its expenditure to its objectives, and we will need to be assured that public money is being used appropriately to meet public objectives. (DCMS 1998, 3)

A similar approach was evident in Australia where service and resource allocation agreements moved to a "greater degree of performance control" (APSC 2003, 95).

From 1999, the Commonwealth moved from direct performance reporting (what an agency had done and what services it had delivered) to an outcomes framework focusing on what results had been achieved by delivering those services. Importantly, Australian governments at both Commonwealth and state level sought agency "outcomes" that directly reflected government policy and the allocation of resources based on the achievement of prescribed outcomes:

> The framework focuses on the outputs the public sector is producing and their contribution to the outcomes set by government, and is aimed at assisting the tracking of results and progress towards targets ... Importantly, appropriations are now made at the outcomes level. Outcomes, and the supporting administered and departmental outputs, therefore form the basis of an agency's operating budget and external reporting framework. (APSC 2003, 95)

Though the modernizing agenda originated in the need for economic reform of the public sector, the "outcomes" that governments in both countries sought shifted significantly in the 1990s to encompass social as well as economic objectives. This change was influenced by a broader international debate which criticized models for measuring the health of communities based solely on economic determinants such as Gross Domestic Product (GDP) and Gross National Product (GNP). The debates encouraged a shift from the dominance of the economic paradigm toward a more balanced approach for measuring the health of communities linked to social capital, well-being, and quality of life.

The development of wider social indicator frameworks revealed the importance of cultural vitality to sustain communities and highlighted the contribution that culture makes to building social capital. Policy development began to focus on the intersection of culture with other social areas including education, crime prevention, health, and community building. Within this larger world of national indicator frameworks, arts and culture gained prominence (Duxbury 2003; CMC 2010).

Building social capital and social cohesion in communities was a subject under much discussion during the mid to late 1990s. When New Labour won the British general election in 1997, the incoming government saw opportunities for cultural solutions to resolve the country's socioeconomic problems (Selwood 2002b). Accordingly, museum contributions to rectify social exclusion, achieve social cohesion, and contribute to life-long learning, and community regeneration were embedded into funding agreements as objectives against which museums were expected to report progress.

In Australia, the role of arts and cultural heritage in achieving wider social development goals was particularly identified in state policies where governments developed strong commitments to reducing exclusion, improving individual self-esteem, providing opportunities for life-long learning, and contributing to community health (CMC 2010). In short, in both the UK and Australia, museums were required to "justify their spending in broader social and economic terms, rather than the simple development of their portfolio activity" (CMC 2010, 44).

Challenge

Driven by governments' reform and policy agendas, pressed into delivering a number of government objectives, and forced to justify their existence in terms specified by funding bodies, the sector became adept at articulating its purpose around what became known as the "instrumental" purposes cast for them by governments which entailed "going beyond function … to contribute to a wider agenda of social change" (Davies 2008, 260).

Critics of the instrumental agenda argued that preoccupation with its implementation deflected the attention of museum leadership away from developing a strong and articulate position with which to defend the sector (Ellis 2002, 8). However, another opinion, expressed by Belfiore and Bennett (2006, 2) argues that "the existence of cultural policy … is to a large extent responsible for public discussion of their value." In other words, the very vigor with which governments have pursued their agenda has been a catalyst to stimulate discourse within the cultural sector itself around notions of value and ways to prove it. The museum sector has been at the forefront of these discussions.

Though required to comply, and work within an instrumental agenda, the museum sector challenged both the model of structural reform and its mode of implementation. From the early 1990s critics in the museum profession questioned the appropriateness of applying a system that originated in the profit-making, commercial sector, where a financial bottom line lends itself to quantitative measurement, to the more complex environment of the public sector where multi-dimensional briefs and a wide range of stakeholders make meaningful performance assessment a much more complex issue (Ames 1991; Bud, Cave, and Haney 1991; Walden 1991).

Of particular concern was performance evaluation which required tangible evidence of achievements measured against predetermined targets. Holden criticized performance targets "expressed in terms of efficiency, cost-per-user and audience diversity, rather than discussed in terms of cultural achievement" (2004, 14). From the perspective of the expressive and creative arts, Tusa (2007, 11) argues that "measurable" does not necessarily mean "valuable" and that applying a performance measurement model to a sector defined by innovation and creativity is to limit the very risk taking on which it is based. These arguments are echoed in Selwood's report (2010) on the cultural impact of museums in which she quotes Barton:

> The problem lies in the fact that there is little or no space built into the system to allow "different" work. Put another way, "good work" becomes that which is covered

by the PI [performance indicator], can be externally evaluated in a quantitative manner and can supply hard data. As a result, some types of work and some types of professional practice becomes seen as "difficult" because they are not susceptible to this form of evaluation ... [T]his places pressure on certain groups of professionals to change their working practices or become marginalized within the system and thus risk a reduction or cessation in funding for no other reason than the fact that their work does not fit the requirements of audit and therefore cannot be "trusted" in the same way as more structured professional practice. For many professionals who fall into this group the choice is stark: change working practices or risk extinction. (Barton 2008, 275; qtd. in Selwood 2010, 7)

When, in the late 1990s, governments began to shift to social objectives and evidence-based policy development, the corresponding shift in evaluation model from performance measurement to impact evaluation added another layer of complexity. Impact evaluation concerns itself with the outcomes of applying policy to a target population with the aim of determining whether the intended objectives were achieved (Davies 2003; Owen 2006). It was a logical choice for governments interested in realizing social objectives as it addresses the central question of evidence-based policy evaluation: "Did it make a difference?"

However, vague terminology, failure to define success indicators, problems with isolating direct causality, and the inconvenient fact that measuring social impact is a long-term proposition (Burns Owen Partnership 2005; Levitt 2008, 224) combined to generate more criticism of the model than acceptance. O'Brien (2010, 36) and Jones (2010, 79) also observe that impact evaluation has too retrospective a focus, seeking to evaluate programs after the fact and then constructing a case for the value of culture based on those evaluations. Other philosophical challenges were also emerging.

By the beginning of this century, a debate was gaining momentum in Britain that openly contested the instrumental paradigm as a basis for measuring the worth of arts and cultural heritage. While the application of museum purposes and functions to wider social issues is not a new phenomenon (O'Neill 2008, 293), the concept of instrumentalism had become associated with an agenda imposed from above, diverting museums' and others' cultural activity from core purposes and relegating the intrinsic benefits of cultural experience to the sidelines. Most importantly, however, the predominance of the instrumental paradigm in evaluating the worth of the arts and cultural heritage was perceived to be a narrow and incomplete estimation of their value. The sector was seeking an alternative paradigm to instrumentalism and found it initially in its opposite – intrinsic value. In Britain, these debates became the catalyst for a sector-organized event which significantly altered the discourse, helped to change the relationship between the government and the cultural sector, and reset the agenda on measuring cultural value.

Introducing value

In June 2003, Demos (a think tank for the arts and cultural industries in England)[3] in partnership with the National Gallery, the National Theatre, and AEA Consulting organized the *Valuing Culture* forum to which arts and cultural heritage leadership and government ministers and policymakers were invited. Speakers from the arts and cultural heritage sectors openly criticized the "lopsided attempt" of the then British government to define the cultural in terms of wider social and economic goals leaving "underarticulated and, given an environment where there is a strong bias towards the quantifiable, undervalued, the intrinsic worth of these organisations and their activities" (Ellis 2003, 3).

Valuing Culture had an impact. Within two months of attending the forum, the UK Secretary of State for Culture, Media, and Sport, Tessa Jowell, penned her personal essay *Government and the Value of Culture* (DCMS 2004). In it, the minister acknowledged the need for a wider frame of reference for determining value and appropriate systems to measure it (DCMS 2004, 9–10). As importantly, her essay heralded a discernible shift toward greater inclusiveness in decision-making calling for "consensus across government and the sector to develop a more strategic overall vision" (DCMS 2004, 31). Moreover, it distanced itself from the New Public Management. Government, stated the minister, was not "a piece of top down social engineering, but a bottom up realisation of possibility and potential" (DCMS 2004, 10).

The following year, a consultation paper *Understanding the Future: Museums and 21st-Century Life – The Value of Museums* (DCMS 2005) was published with a foreword by Tessa Jowell and a personal introduction by the Minister for the Arts, Estelle Morris, acknowledging the need for a wider frame of reference with which to measure museum value and the need to seek this in conversation with the museum sector: "Government needs to look beyond an instrumental framework. Government and museums need to articulate better the sector's worth, in response to a clearer understanding of the benefits for users and non-users, as well as their own needs" (DCMS 2005, 32–33). When *Understanding the Future: Priorities for England's Museums* was published by the DCMS in October 2006, it was "the result of collaboration between DCMS officials and a group of informed advocates for museums, conscious of and committed to the need for further change for the benefit of museum audiences" (DCMS 2006, 4) and recognized the contribution of the Museums, Libraries, and Archives Council,[4] the Museums Association, the National Museum Directors Conference, the Association of Independent Museums, the University Museums Group, and Arts Council England.

A more strategic and proactive position emerged from the cultural sector itself. Led by the National Museum Directors' Conference (NMDC), Arts Council England, the Museums, Libraries, and Archives Council, the Association of Independent Museums, the Group for Large Local Authority Museums, the Museums Association, and the University Museums Group, it articulated its position in a joint document titled *Value and Vision: The contribution of culture* (NMDC 2006). The document called for a "new settlement" between the government and the cultural sector that would "place the cultural sector closer to the heart of public policy making" and invest sustainable funding for the next 10 years (NMDC 2006, 2). Importantly, the sector based its position on a broad spectrum of value including intrinsic as well as instrumental outcomes and citing the power of culture to enrich people's lives, position Britain as a world player, encourage creativity, maintain standards of excellence and quality, engage young people, extend learning opportunities, celebrate diversity, connect communities, and forge partnerships. Recent fora organized by the DCMS with the arts and cultural heritage sectors indicate that this culture of consultation is now embedded in departmental practice.[5]

This shift from compliance to discussion and dialogue between governments and the arts and cultural heritage sectors was also evident at the Commonwealth and state levels of government in Australia. In the 1990s there were instances when bureaucrats at both levels brought arts and cultural heritage sector professionals together with arts departments (and, on one occasion with Commonwealth Treasury) to develop qualitative and quantitative performance indicators to measure impact (Scott 1991). Processes of consultation to inform cultural planning are now embedded in most state and territory arts and cultural ministries (Scott 2010). At the state level, consultation with the arts and cultural heritage sectors includes evaluating progress against state cultural objectives, setting new directions for state cultural plans and developing measures around these directions (Scott 2010). There is evidence that the results are taken seriously:

> In response to the feedback received from arts industry stakeholders in reviewing the current Plan and to take forward the conversation about an updated Queensland Arts Industry Sector Development Plan for 2010 to 2012, the vision and goals of the Plan have been recast. (Queensland Government 2009, 11)

At a national level, cultural measurement was part of the remit of the Cultural Ministers' Council (CMC),[6] an intergovernmental forum consisting of federal, state, and territory arts ministers from Australia and counterparts from New Zealand. The CMC met regularly to discuss issues of broad concern to arts and cultural ministries and departments across different levels of government and between the two countries. One of its major priorities was the collection of data to inform cultural policy and planning with the Statistics Working Group (SWG) of the CMC taking a particularly active role in this area.

Working to a brief from the CMC, the Australian Bureau of Statistics (ABS) through the National Centre for Culture and Recreation Statistics (NCCRS), has published a series of documents to guide data collection. One of the first was *Arts and Cultural Heritage in Australia: Key Issues for an Information Development Plan* (IDP) published in 2006 as a starting point for industry-wide discussion about priority needs for data collection in the arts and cultural heritage sectors. Following consultation with "320 government arts agencies [including museums], peak bodies, community arts networks, city councils, regional bodies and researchers across Australia" a subsequent iteration was published in 2008 (ABS 2008a, 1, cat. 4915.0.55.002).

Importantly, the IDP acknowledged that the question of "value" is at the heart of evidence collection, for what we choose to collect as evidence reflects the much larger question: "What is the value of arts and cultural heritage?" (ABS 2008a, 8, cat. 4915.0.55.002). Within this overarching value question the IDP also recognized the issue of what *kind* of value is created by arts and cultural heritage referring to intrinsic as well as instrumental value and acknowledging that "[m]any Australian public arts and cultural heritage programs provide multiple aims, which encompass both instrumental and intrinsic values, and in this IDP, both aspects of value are considered relevant" (ABS 2008a, 9, cat. 4915.0.55.002).

Although this chapter focuses on the UK and Australasia, it is worth noting that the theme of an encompassing range of values in the assessment of culture and museums is reiterated elsewhere. *Gifts of the Muse*, a report commissioned by the Wallace Foundation and published in the United States by the Rand Corporation in 2004, argued for consideration of the "full range of effects" that participation in arts and culture can afford individuals and communities (McCarthy et al. 2004, xi) and Selma Holo and Mari-Tedi Alvarez's series of essays by museum leaders (2009) highlight the four values needed to sustain museums in the long term – relevance, creativity and experimentation, inclusion, and public trust.

Questions of value

In the early part of this century, a shift to greater dialogue and discussion between governments and the cultural sector, a widening of the discourse around notions of "value," acknowledgment of intrinsic as well as instrumental dimensions of culture, and modification of the strict regime of compliance imposed by the New Public Management as part of the modernizing agenda became apparent. However, the major issue about how to measure cultural value remains unresolved and is the subject of ongoing discussion and debate. In part, the reasons are to be found within the paradigm that held out hope for a resolution. Value, it turns out, is a tricky concept.

Economics and value

Critics continue to question the paradigm upon which policy development and cultural funding are based. Holden (2004, 10) calls for "a wholesale reshaping of the way in which public funding of culture is undertaken," sharing with Matarasso (1997),

Hawkes (2001), and Throsby (2002) a view that governments have adopted a narrow interpretation of economics focused on financial bottom lines and market forces which ignores non-market values and obscures the deeper meaning of economics such as the management of a society's resources:

> Economic value is determined by the extent to which something enhances or detracts from our well-being. Something has economic value if its benefits to the well-being of society (including future generations) are greater than or outweigh its costs. Though it encompasses commercial value – as expressed through monetary exchange within markets – economic value is not restricted to values that are revealed through markets. The full schema of economic value incorporates commercial (or market) value; use values not captured within markets; and non-use values. (Holden 2004, 31)

"Use" is an important principle when considering both the financial and the non-financial benefits of culture (Mourato and Mazzanti 2002; McCarthy et al. 2004). "Use" in the economic context has been seen as important for cultural policy development because, in economic terms, use values are market values and can be assigned a price. Use can also be measured. Use value is found in Willingness to Pay, or willingness to give up time and make an effort. When people give time and effort to visit a museum, work as a volunteer, and pay an entrance fee or the cost to see a temporary exhibition, they are demonstrating a calculable value:

> Use values of material heritage refer to the goods and services that flow from it that are tradable and priceable in existing markets. For instance, admission fees for a historic site, the cost of land, and the wages of workers are values. Because they are exchanged in markets, these values can be easily expressed in terms of price, and they are susceptible to economists' many analytical tools based on neoclassical theory. (Mason 2002, 13)

But many of the qualities described as sociocultural and intrinsic values are non-use values. These non-use values are not traded in or captured by markets and are therefore difficult to express in terms of price. They can, however, be classed as economic values because individuals would be willing to allocate resources (spend money) to acquire them and/or protect them, as has been proven through Contingent Valuation studies (Pung, Clarke, and Patten 2004; Aabo 2005).

Mourato and Mazzanti (2002, 51) argue that, this "non-market" dimension of cultural heritage can work against it when it comes to making decisions for sustainable funding. Though the non-financial benefits of culture are valued by society, they remain outside markets and are not valued against any market price. This form of "market failure" can result in under-funding, leaving the conservation of many important cultural assets at the mercy of political whims and overstretched government budgets.

Throsby (2002, 101) suggests *cultural capital* as an approach to viewing the economic value of culture because it takes account of non-use values. Heritage, Throsby argues, brings with it "stores of cultural value – that is, things that have been inherited from the past which are valuable in themselves and which yield value to those who enjoy them, both now and in the future" (2002, 101). These accumulated stores of cultural value can generate a flow of services that provide continuing benefits for individuals, communities, and the economy and which, combined, constitute the cultural capital of a heritage asset. In Throsby's view, the economic value of a heritage asset or of the goods and services to which it gives rise, is reflected in both use and non-use values. He provides the example of Venice:

> The different types of economic values identified above can be illustrated with reference to Venice … A significant proportion of these direct use values is generated by tourism, which provides the tangible revenue base upon which the local economy is sustained. In addition, Venice gives rise to all three of the nonmarket benefits noted above: people all over the world care deeply about the continued existence of Venice, even if they have never been there; many would be willing to pay something simply to preserve the option of visiting it at some time; and the city is surely regarded as part of Italy's and the world's cultural patrimony, which must be passed on intact to future generations. (Throsby 2002, 104; qtd. in de la Torre and Mason 2002)

Moreover, within a wider interpretation of economics as sustainable resource management, critics are of the opinion that the purpose of culture is not to create wealth but to contribute to a stable, confident, and creative society through public planning that integrates cultural, social, economic, and environmental factors to create a quadruple bottom line (Hawkes 2001). This is a view shared by Jones (2010) who argues that culture should be funded on the basis that it is fundamental to developing the cultural capabilities which enable citizens to operate effectively within contemporary society, negotiating cultural difference and becoming cultural producers themselves:

> The public realm can only be public if people take part in shaping and forming it, and so it not only comprises but is also based on the values that people hold. It is a foundational concept of democratic society, comprising the common set of assets to which people can relate and contribute. As a result, it is a space in which different values meet, merge and mingle and in which the development of society is negotiated. Culture is the expression of these values and so the forms in which it is manifest are the currency of the public realm and society itself. (Jones 2010, 33)

In Jones's opinion, the public are cultural creators. This is also the view of Public Value, a theory and model of public sector management which argues that the public should not only be recognized for their role as cultural producers but should also be acknowledged as the ultimate authorizers of what constitutes cultural value.

Public Value

The concept of Public Value emerged as an alternative to the New Public Management through the writings of Mark Moore, a Harvard professor who published *Creating Public Value: Strategic Management in Government* in 1995. Unlike the top-down, compliance model of the New Public Management, Public Value proposes a relationship between government policymakers and funders (the authorizing environment) and public managers (the operational environment) which is strategic, intentional, and collectively focused on making "a positive difference in the individual and collective lives of citizens" (Moore and Moore 2005, 17). It focuses attention on the "good" that can be created with the assets with which the public sector is entrusted and "is rooted in the ethos of public service" (Holden 2006, 17).

> Through its concern for the public an institution can achieve such public goods as creating trust and mutual respect among citizens, enhancing the public realm, and providing a context for sociability and the enjoyment of shared experiences. (Holden 2006, 17)

Public Value has been an influential idea, permeating thought and discourse, particularly in the English-speaking world. It was adopted by researchers interested in its potential for public sector reform during the years of British government under New Labour (Kelly, Mulgan, and Muers 2002; Blaug, Horner, and Lekhi 2006; Horner, Lekhi, and Blaug 2006) and provided a conceptual framework for the Australian Bureau of Statistics' 2008 Information Development Plan for the arts and cultural industries. It has resonated with cultural providers because of its focus on end-users and the role of the public as co-producers and authorizers of culture at a time of changing perceptions that recognize the public as active, autonomous, co-creators of messages and meaning (Scott 2007; ACE 2008; Radbourne, Glow, and Johanson 2010).

> The public may play as large a part in determining the outcome as the institution – and perhaps this is as it should be in a publicly funded sector such as ours? If we aspire to cultural influence, we must be open to more influences too. (NMDC member qtd. in Selwood 2010, 51)

Public Value was introduced to the cultural sector by Holden (2006) when he proposed a tripartite model encompassing instrumental, intrinsic, and "institutional" dimensions for mea0suring cultural value. It is worth reviewing the dimension of intrinsic value as its absence in cultural assessment has served to dominate discussions on value discourse over the past two decades.

Measuring intrinsic value

Intrinsic value is predominantly associated with individual and community experiences that are less tangible, often expressed in affective language (McCarthy et al. 2004) and described by Holden as "the set of values that relate to the subjective experience of culture intellectually, emotionally and spiritually" (2006, 14). While the cultural sector has argued that intrinsic value is fundamental to appreciating cultural impact (Holden 2004; McCarthy et al. 2004) and has had some success in shifting the discourse to the point where intrinsic value is now acknowledged by governments, measuring intrinsic value continues to be a contested area.

Parts of the cultural sector, Hewison (2003) and Tusa (2007) among them, have maintained "a longstanding skepticism" toward measurement applied to culture (O'Brien 2010, 12). Bakhshi et al. have little patience with this position, pointing out that there

> is a contradiction between the plea that the intrinsic value of art should be accounted for, and the idea that it is beyond accounting. If art really is beyond valuation, there is no point complaining that it has been valued improperly. If it really cannot be assigned a value, it cannot sensibly also be argued that policymakers can properly take this value into account. (Bakhshi, Freeman, and Hitchen 2009, 10)

The dilemma, in O'Brien's view, is that funding decisions must be made that "are acceptable to both central government and the cultural sector" (O'Brien 2010, 5) and while he acknowledges that narrative accounts of cultural value are important, argues that they fail to represent the benefits of culture in a manner that is commensurable with competitive bids from other sectors with calls on the public purse:

> Narrative accounts remind us of the need to make the case for culture in a variety of ways. Political decisions are not merely technocratic exercises in economic valuation, and nor should they be. However, without the data offered by economic valuation techniques the richness of the narratives of cultural value are likely to be less influential. (O'Brien 2010, 9)

Bakhshi and his colleagues have argued that intrinsic benefits *can* be captured using economic valuation techniques that analyze subjective preferences. They cite the success of methods such as Contingent Valuation and Willingness to Pay that do not "merely record the fact that the public like the arts, but allow a figure to be placed on it" (Bakhshi, Freeman, and Hitchen 2009, 6).

Bakhshi's position addresses three issues important to this discussion. Firstly, Contingent Valuation and Willingness to Pay methods enable decisions to be made about the allocation of public funds using "a commensurable estimate of intrinsic value – one that permits comparisons between alternative uses of public funds" (Bakhshi, Freeman, and Hitchen 2009, 10). Secondly, these methods allow the *public* to allocate a numerical value to cultural activities and services and, thirdly, Contingent Valuation and Willingness to Pay also capture the value placed on culture by *non-users*. Bakhshi et al. (2009, 2) are of the opinion that the reluctance to use rigorous economic methods to capture cultural value has hindered rather than helped the case for funding. "If we can stop insisting that intrinsic benefits cannot be measured, and start demanding that they should be, then there is no reason not to extend artistic influence in decision making well beyond its present relatively narrow reach" (Bakhshi, Freeman, and Hitchen 2009, 13).

Other approaches to measuring different types of value have been surveyed by Selwood (2010) and O'Brien (2010), who both note the process undertaken by the UK Film Council on measuring the cultural impact of 400 British films using criteria such as influence on British culture, box office and DVD performance, citations and quotations in media and culture, notoriety or levels of censorship, and "whether the film captured a 'zeitgeist' moment or reflected broader, longer term changes in British society." O'Brien is of the opinion that this type of evaluation produces "a robust narrative of cultural value" that "is important as it allows us to make sense and contextualize economic valuations" (O'Brien 2010, 41–42).

However, although there are typologies of cultural value and approaches to measuring them (Scott 2007; Selwood 2010), decisions on viable measurement frameworks that encompass both government needs and cultural sector conviction have been slow in gestation. Nevertheless, national projects that measure the impact of cultural value across a range of indices are an emerging trend. These national approaches differ but they are addressing some of the issues formulated through the debates of the past two decades.

National approaches to measuring value

What constitutes cultural value, how to measure it, and what evidence is required for different purposes are of concern to both governments and the museum sector. From the perspective of governments, measuring value is aimed at providing comparable evidence to determine funding allocations and develop public policy. For the museum field, evidence is needed to support value claims, to advocate for the sector, and to argue for a sustainable future.

National models for measuring value are being developed at both these levels; museum value is being measured within government-initiated meta-evaluations of culture and through the accountability requirements tied to funding.

The United Kingdom

In the contemporary United Kingdom the constituent nation states exercise degrees of autonomy over some areas of "home" policy and public funding. The devolved nations of Scotland, Wales, and Northern Ireland each have their own cultural policies but this section will focus on England where the situation in terms of measuring cultural value is going through a complex and, in some cases, seemingly contradictory period. Following the election of the Conservative Coalition in 2010, it seemed that some of the lessons about the holistic nature of value had carried over to the new government. Not long after the election, the new Conservative Secretary of State for Culture, Media, and Sport, Jeremy Hunt, was quoted as saying: "For me culture is not just about the economic value of our creative industries – it is what defines us as a civilisation. Culture helps us understand the world around us, explain it, and sometimes escape from it" (qtd. in Jones 2010, 23).

In a relatively short space of time, however, the economic crisis has precipitated a policy return to a familiar focus on instrumental value. In April 2013, Maria Miller, Hunt's successor, announced in a speech at the British Museum that

> when times are tough and money is tight, our focus must be on culture's economic impact. To maintain the argument for continued public funding, we must make the case as a two-way street. We must demonstrate the healthy dividends that our investment continues to pay. (Hon. Maria Miller, British Museum, April 24, 2013)

While a sluggish British economy and its implications for public spending dominate discourse at government level, other initiatives on identifying and measuring value are focused on different objectives. One of these is the *Taking Part* survey. The *Taking Part* survey was an initiative inherited from New Labour which has been maintained under the Coalition. It has been continuously interviewing adults over 16 since 2005 (and children since 2006) to identify the links between individual engagement, subjective well-being, and social capital building in communities. By contrast with government, which has reduced cultural impact to economic contributions, *Taking Part* continues to explore social and personal outcomes.

Subjective Well-Being is described as an individual's assessment of his/her own well-being and is elicited through numeric or qualitative scales by asking respondents to rate their well-being on scales of 1–10, 1–7, or by stating life satisfaction from "not at all satisfied" to "completely satisfied." Advocates of the approach (Bakhshi, Freeman, and Hitchen 2009; DCMS et al. 2010, 36) see Subjective Well-Being as a generation beyond Contingent Valuation and Willingness to Pay, arguing that Subjective Well-Being captures people's experiences directly, rather than requiring a proxy such as willingness to pay or to commit time and effort. The results provide policymakers with a picture of the short-term, individual value of engagement, with specific reference to the improvement in Subjective Well-Being

TABLE 5.1   Benefits generated by engagement in culture and sport

Individual	Community	National
Achievement	Bequest value	Citizenship
Continuity with the past	Community cohesion	International reputation
Diversion	Community identity	National pride
Escape	Creativity	
Expression	Employment	
Health	Existence value	
Income	Innovation	
Knowledge of culture	Option to use	
Self-identity	Productivity	
Skills/competency	Reduced crime	
Solace/consolation	Shared experience	
	Social capital	

Source: DCMS et al. 2010, 36

generated by participation in culture (and sport; DCMS et al. 2010, 33). Subjective Well-Being is then cross-referenced with the development of social capital in communities, focusing on the creation of networks of trust and reciprocity offered by the opportunities for socialization that result from participation in cultural and sporting activities.

In 2008, the *Taking Part* data was used to explore the drivers, impacts, and value of cultural and sporting engagement through evidence that government investment in these sectors was providing value for money. As part of the Culture and Sport Evidence (CASE) project, a stakeholder engagement exercise was undertaken to identify the benefits of engagement in culture and sport from the perspective of respondents. The results of the exercise revealed many of the perceived benefits to be closely associated with intrinsic values (see Table 5.1).

The most recent development associated with the debate about cultural value in the UK context is a two-year funding grant (2013–2015) from the Arts and Humanities Research Council (AHRC) to establish a framework aimed at advancing the way that cultural engagement is conceptualized, to identify the methods by which it is evaluated, and to suggest a way forward in terms of its future measurement. The AHRC recognizes that "recent years have seen many attempts to capture that value in straightforward ways, not least in order to make the case to governments for public funding, but none have commanded widespread confidence" (AHRC 2013).

In spite of the instrumentalism that is creeping back into UK government policy, the starting point for the AHRC project is the user's perspective on the cultural experience "rather than the ancillary effects of this experience." A critical review of two decades of museum literature, funded by the Cultural Value Project, was conducted by Scott, Sandell, and Dodd in 2014. The review found that users express their personal museum experiences in positive terms, describing feelings of well-being, connectedness, and sophisticated cognitive engagement with objects and exhibitions. In spite of positive outcomes cited by users, evidence that these outcomes subsequently accrue to the public realm, with resulting social impact beyond the museum walls, remains under-researched and elusive.

Australia

Like the UK, government measurement of museum value in Australia occurs at several levels. In 2008, the Australian Bureau of Statistics published *Towards Comparable Statistics for Cultural Heritage Organisations*, a statistical digest aimed at improving the overall quality and comparability of key data collected by the cultural heritage sector for benchmarking, planning and policymaking (ABS 2008b, vii, cat. 4916.0). Its publication followed an extensive consultation process with industry stakeholders to develop the measures. Forty-one cultural institutions (all the major national and state museums, galleries, archives, and libraries) across Australia and a range of relevant peak bodies including the Statistical Working Group of the Cultural Ministers' Council (SWG CMC), the Council of Australasian Museum Directors, the Collections Council of Australia, the National and State Libraries Australasia, the Council of Australasian Archives and Records Authorities, and the Council of Australian Art Museum Directors, among others, were engaged in the process of identifying and refining the indicators. The indicators are presented as "guidelines" and were developed after an analysis of existing data collection systems within Australian museums to facilitate compatibility and ease of collection.

The five statistical categories cover direct and indirect use (the number of on-site visits by general and educational visitors and unique website visits), reach and inclusion (a range of demographics focusing on age, gender, educational attainment, and employment), visitor satisfaction (measured against an immediate, on-site visit experience), the type of investment required to support cultural heritage (financial dependence on government support compared with other forms of finance and expenditure), the existing human resource quotient (particularly, the distribution of employed against volunteer workers) and the significance of collections in terms of their size, growth, method of acquisition, and number of loans.

Another Australian initiative is seeking to provide a basis for measuring the contribution that culture makes to the public good and to inform evidence-based decision-making and the evaluation of public policy (CMC/ABS 2004, 6). The project, *Vital Signs*, is currently being developed by the SWG CMC and the Australian Bureau of Statistics National Centre for Culture and Recreation Statistics. The project is an ambitious one, distinguished by its overall objective to bring together a wide range of data sets under one system to aggregate, analyze, and use data related to the public value of the cultural sector.

Much of the data is available from other work conducted by the ABS. Data on cultural employment has been sourced from the *National Census*, *Household Expenditure* surveys identifying cultural spend across the population, *Time Use* surveys revealing the amount of time that Australians spend on cultural activities, and *Tourism Research Australia* surveys providing information on participation and expenditure by overseas and domestic tourists in arts and cultural activities. The ABS collects information about public funding to arts and culture from all three levels of government and the Australia Business Arts Foundation, which "includes all monetary and in-kind sponsorship, corporate donations, grants from foundations and trusts, and contribution from individual members of the community in its sample surveys of arts and cultural organisations" (CMC/ABS 2004, 26).

The *Vital Signs* classification framework comprises three broad themes: economic development, cultural value, and engagement and social impact. Although research into other international models was undertaken, the draft document acknowledges that "this Australian report ... takes Cultural Indicators for New Zealand as a key reference point" (CMC/ABS 2004, 8). The New Zealand cultural statistics program has been in existence since 1993 and has been refining its approach to cultural value measurement over two decades (Ministry for Culture and Heritage 2009). Especially within areas of measuring "cultural value," the CMC/ABS report *Social Impacts of Participating in the Arts and Cultural Activities* acknowledges that existing data sets can only go so far to provide information.

> Some of these matters – such as the contribution of cultural industries to employment – are already measured and monitored. Others, such as those relating to cultural strength and impact, are more qualitative, and it will take time to develop and refine both the measures and the relevant research and data gathering processes to enable them to be used. Over time, we expect the project will provide feedback into the work of the NCCRS. (CMC/ABS 2004, 3)

The draft plan acknowledges that qualitative data is needed "for the interpretation of cultural phenomena" (CMC/ABS 2004, 7) and also recognizes the need to consult with and take account of the "interests of stakeholders." The consultation process will hopefully include the Australian equivalent of the UK's NMDC. The Council of Australasian Museum Directors has been conducting their own yearly survey of museum value since 1989 and has built a considerable (though not always comparable from year to year) evidence base about the contribution that museums are making economically and socially. The comprehensive Council of Australasian Museum Directors survey collects data about general attendances, school use of museums, partnerships with other educational bodies, the number of research projects that are collection based, the number of Australian Research Council Grants received, the number and type of publications, the number of public inquiries answered, attendances to new exhibitions, loans to other institutions, visitors to traveling exhibitions, repatriation of indigenous material, participation in outreach activities, engagement through volunteering, membership, and affiliated societies as well as evidence of economic value through employment, capacity to attract investment through sponsorship, bequests and donations, level of self-generated revenue, and the number of tourists attracted.

These initiatives appear to be part of a worldwide trend in the English-speaking democracies toward creating national systems for identifying indicators of museum value, collating the evidence, and using it for advocacy, funding, and policy. It is worth noting that similar initiatives are currently underway in the United States where the national agency for policy and grant-making, the Institute of Museums and Library Services, has initiated a national museum data collection project. Ultimately available as a web portal, the *Museums Count* project is conducting a census of all museums in the United States, developing standard data definitions in collaboration with the museum field and collating an evidence base that will identify museums' impact and their contribution to public value.

A crucial issue surrounding this activity is the degree to which there will be consensus and integration. Ultimately, both governments and the museum sector are challenged to find common ground across approaches to describing and measuring the value of museums so that they can direct their collective energies to "make a positive difference in the individual and collective lives of citizens" (Moore and Moore 2005, 17).

Conclusion

In the past two decades, the field of cultural measurement has progressed. Museums as cultural heritage institutions within a wider cultural remit have been at the forefront of the discourse as debaters, advocates, and recipients of the developments that have occurred within wider cultural measurement frameworks. Current approaches to cultural measurement are generally more consultative and transparent than they were when the New Public Management enforced policies and systems in the late 1980s and early 1990s. The need for more holistic approaches to cultural value has achieved some recognition and the discussion has moved to considerations of how best to capture intrinsic values within appropriate measurement systems rather than whether they should be included at all.

However, economic valuation methods continue to predominate. On the one hand, this is indicative of the monetized approach to policy formulation and evaluation still in use in governments in the United Kingdom, Australia, and the United States and the need for comparable bases with which to make funding decisions among competing priorities.

We find ourselves in the middle of the second decade of this new millennium with a model for museum measurement that is still "developing." Some progress has been made and the role of the museum sector in forcefully rejecting the reductionist model of the instrumental paradigm and arguing for a more holistic model has been fundamental to this shift. But the hard work of building dialogue and striving for consensus needs to be continued and, in many ways, the next major step has yet to be taken.

In spite of a body of evidence generated by the museum sector on economic value (Travers and Glaister 2004; Travers 2006), social value (Bryson, Usherwood, and Streatfield 2002; CMC 2010), intrinsic, instrumental, institutional, and use values (Scott 2007), and cultural value (Selwood 2010), museums have yet to distil this into a convincing narrative:

> The museum sector believes that it makes a real difference to peoples' [*sic*] lives. It is a line that is frequently used to advocate and promote our work to stakeholders; but what does it mean and how might we investigate it? What is the nature of the impact that museums have on the individual and how does this play out in communities, societies and even nations? (Unidentified NMDC member qtd. in Selwood 2010, 4)

And, though still critical of evaluation models adopted by governments, the museum sector has yet to propose a viable alternative. As a result, in the absence of a clearly articulated position about the value of museums and viable options for measurement acceptable to parties, governments faced with the necessity of making decisions, among competing needs in a time of economic limitations, have tended to fill the void and opt for systems aligned with economic valuation. Pragmatically, O'Brien concludes that "the question of valuing culture becomes how best to make the case for culture within the framework of central government decision-making" (O'Brien 2010, 21). This pragmatism is endorsed by Mourato and Mazzanti, who feel that not to do so is a risky option:

> If the alternative to economic valuation is to put cultural heritage value equal or close to zero, the cultural sector would, as a result, be severely damaged. Ignoring economic preferences can lead to undervaluing and under pricing of cultural assets. This, directly and indirectly, reduces the amount of financial resources available to cultural institutions relative to other public priorities. (Mourato and Mazzanti 2002, 68)

But there are others who feel that the work on measuring value is incomplete and that

> measuring and articulating the value and impact of the sector is more than an academic exercise: given the policy, financial and business structures in which most cultural organizations operate …, rightly selecting, rigorously measuring and powerfully articulating the value and impact of the sector is one of the key pre-requisites for its sustainability. (Stanziola 2008, 317)

Notes

1   The OECD was formed in 1961 and comprises 30 countries including Australia, Austria, Belgium, Canada, Czech Republic, Denmark, Finland, France, Germany, Greece, Hungary, Iceland, Ireland, Italy, Japan, Korea, Luxembourg, Mexico, Netherlands, New Zealand, Norway, Poland, Portugal, Slovak Republic, Spain, Sweden, Switzerland, Turkey, the United Kingdom, and the United States. One of its prominent roles is fostering good governance in the public service of OECD countries.

2   The UK and New Zealand have two tiers of government (national and local) while Australia has three (Commonwealth/federal, state/territory, and local) with responsibility for cultural policy and spending apportioned across each level.

3   Demos describes itself as a cross-party think tank concerned with policy debate and "with an overarching mission to bring politics closer to people."

4   Many of the functions of the Museums, Libraries and Archives Council were absorbed into Arts Council England in October 2011.

5   The cultural sector was: (a) invited to review and assess the usefulness of *Taking Part* (August 19, 2010); (b) introduced to the findings from the Culture and Sport Evidence (CASE) programme (July 21, 2010); (c) invited to discuss ways in which policy outcomes are evaluated (October 8, 2010).

6   Under Australia's federal system of government, matters which fall within the jurisdictions of both state and federal governments are coordinated through a series of Ministerial Councils. The CMC has been one of these coordinating bodies. Following a series of recent reforms to this system, the CMC ceased to exist in June 2011, although cross-jurisdictional coordinating continues. The body responsible for *Vital Signs*, the Statistics Working Group, has agreement from all jurisdictions for its work to continue. Personal communication with Leigh Tabrett, Chair SWG, June 15, 2011.

References

Aabo, Svanhild. 2005. "Are Public Libraries Worth Their Price? A Contingent Valuation Study of Norwegian Public Libraries." *New Library World* 106: 487–495.

ABS (Australian Bureau of Statistics). 2002. *Standard Economic Sector Classifications of Australia (SESCA)*. Cat. 1218.0. Canberra: Australian Bureau of Statistics.

ABS (Australian Bureau of Statistics). 2008a. *Arts and Cultural Heritage-an Information Development Plan*. Cat. 4915.0.55.002. Canberra: Australian Bureau of Statistics.

ABS (Australian Bureau of Statistics). 2008b. *Towards Comparable Statistics for Cultural Heritage Organisations*. Cat. 4916.0. Canberra: Australian Bureau of Statistics.

ACE (Arts Council England). 2008. *What People Want from the Arts*. London: Arts Council England. Accessed September 24, 2014. http://www.artscouncil.org.uk/publication_archive/what-people-want-from-the-arts.

AHRC (Arts and Humanities Research Council). 2013. *The AHRC Cultural Value Project*. Swindon, UK: AHRC.

Ames, Peter. 1991. "Measures of Merit?." *Museum News* September/October: 55–56.

APSC (Australian Public Service Commission). 2003. *The Australian Experience of Public Sector Reform.* Canberra: Australian Public Service Commission Occasional Paper. Accessed September 30, 2014. http://www.apsc.gov.au/publications-and-media/archive/publications-archive/history-of-reform.

Bakhshi, Hasan, Alan Freeman, and Graham Hitchen. 2009. *Measuring Intrinsic Value (How to Stop Worrying and Love Economics).* Accessed September 30, 2014. http://www.labforculture.org/en/resources-for-research/contents/publications/measuring-intrinsic-value-how-to-stop-worrying-and-love-economics.

Barton, Adrian. 2008. "New Labour's Management, Audit, and 'What Works' Approach to Controlling the Untrustworthy Professions." *Public Policy and Administration* 23(3): 263–77.

Belfiore, Elenora, and Oliver Bennett. 2006. *Rethinking the Social Impacts of the Arts: A Critical-Historical Review.* Centre for Cultural Policy Studies, University of Warwick. Accessed September 30, 2014. http://wrap.warwick.ac.uk/53054.

Blaug, Ricardo, Louise Horner, and Rohit Lekhi. 2006. "*Public Value, Politics and Public Management: A Literature Review.*" London: The Work Foundation. Accessed September 30, 2014. http://www.theworkfoundation.com/Reports/117/Public-value-politics-and-public-management-A-literature-review.

Bryson, Jarod, Bob Usherwood, and David Streatfield. 2002. *South West Museums, Archives and Libraries Social Impact Audit.* Sheffield: Centre for Public Libraries and Information in Society, Department of Information Studies, University of Sheffield.

Bud, R., M. Cave, and S. Haney. 1991. "Measuring a Museum's Output." *Museums Journal* January: 29–31.

Burns Owen Partnership. 2005. *New Directions in Social Policy: Developing the Evidence Base for Museums, Libraries and Archives in England.* London: Museums Libraries and Archives Council. Accessed September 30, 2014. http://webarchive.nationalarchives.gov.uk/20111013135435/research.mla.gov.uk/evidence/documents/ndsp_developing_evidence_doc_6649.pdf.

CMC/ABS (Cultural Ministers' Council Statistics Working Group). 2004. *Social Impacts of Participating in the Arts and Cultural Activities: Stage Two Report: Evidence, Issues and Recommendations.* Prepared by the Australian Expert Group in Industry Studies at the University of Western Sydney.

Cultural Ministers' Council, 2010. *Vital Signs: Cultural Indicators for Australia (first edition for consultation)* Meeting of Cultural Ministers, Canberra. Viewed January 30, 2011. http://mcm.arts.gov.au/sites/default/files/vital-signs-2010_0.pdf

Davies, Philip. 2003. *The Magenta Book Chapter 1: What Is Policy Evaluation? Background Document.* London: Government Chief Social Researcher's Office Cabinet Office Strategy Unit. Accessed September 30, 2014. http://www.civilservice.gov.uk/wp-content/uploads/2011/09/the_complete_magenta_book_2007_edition2.pdf.

Davies, Stuart. 2008. "Intellectual and Political Landscape: The Instrumentalism Debate." *Cultural Trends* 17(4): 259–265.

Department for Culture, Media and Sport. 1998. *A new cultural framework.* DCMS, London; viewed 10 February 2011. http://webarchive.nationalarchives.gov.uk/+/http:/www.culture.gov.uk/images/publications/dept_spending_review.pdf..

DCMS (Department for Culture, Media, and Sport). 2004. *Government and the Value of Culture.* London: Department for Culture, Media, and Sport. Accessed October 1,

2014. https://www.gov.uk/government/uploads/system/uploads/attachment_data/file/77934/measuring-the-value-culture-report.doc.

DCMS (Department for Culture, Media, and Sport). 2005. *Understanding the Future: Museums and 21st-Century Life – The Value of Museums*. London: Department for Culture, Media, and Sport. Accessed October 1, 2014. http://webarchive.nationalarchives.gov.uk/+/http:/www.culture.gov.uk/images/publications/understanding_the_future_responses.pdf.

DCMS (Department for Culture, Media, and Sport). 2006. *Understanding the Future: Priorities for England's Museums*. London: Department for Culture, Media, and Sport.

DCMS (Department for Culture, Media, and Sport), Arts Council England, English Heritage, Museums, Libraries and Archives Council, and Sport England. 2010. *The Culture and Sport Evidence (CASE) Programme: Understanding the Drivers, Impact and Value of Engagement in Culture and Sport*. London: Department for Culture, Media, and Sport. Accessed September 24, 2014. http://www.culture.gov.uk/case.

de la Torre, Marta and Randall Mason. 2002 *"Introduction."* In *Assessing the Values of Cultural Heritage: Research Report*, edited by Marta de la Torre, 3–4. Los Angeles: Getty Conservation Institute. Accessed September 24, 2014. http://www.getty.edu/conservation/publications_resources/pdf_publications/pdf/assessing.pdf.

Duxbury, Nancy. 2003. "Cultural Indicators and Benchmarks in Community Indicator Projects: Performance Measures for Cultural Investment?" Paper prepared for the "Accounting for Culture Colloquium," Strategic Research and Analysis and Analyses stratégiques International Comparative Research Group, Montreal, November 15, 2003.

Ellis, Adrian. 2002. "Planning in a Cold Climate." Lecture at the Getty Leadership Institute (July 21–26). Los Angeles: Getty Center.

Ellis, Adrian. 2003. "Valuing Culture." Paper presented at the Valuing Culture event held at the National Theatre Studio, June 17. Demos in partnership with the National Gallery, National Theatre and AEA Consulting. Accessed September 24, 2014. http://www.demos.co.uk/files/File/VACUAEllis.pdf.

Hawkes, Jon. 2001. *The Fourth Pillar of Sustainability: Culture's Essential Role in Public Planning*. Victoria, Australia: Common Ground.

Hewison, Robert. 2003. "Money for Values." Paper presented at the Valuing Culture event held at the National Theatre Studio, June 17. Demos in partnership with the National Gallery, the National Theatre and area Consulting. Accessed September 24, 2014. http://www.demos.co.uk/files/File/VACURHewison.pdf.

Holden, John. 2004. *Capturing Cultural Value: How Culture Has Become a Tool of Government Policy*. London: Demos. Accessed September 24, 2014. http://www.demos.co.uk/files/CapturingCulturalValue.pdf.

Holden, John. 2006. *Cultural Value and the Crisis of Legitimacy: Why Culture Needs a Democratic Mandate*. London: Demos. Accessed September 14, 2014. http://www.demos.co.uk/files/Culturalvalueweb.pdf.

Holo, Salma, and Mari-Tere Alvarez, eds. 2009. *Beyond the Turnstile: Making the Case for Museums and Sustainable Values*. Lanham, MD: AltaMira.

Horner, Louise, Rohit Lekhi, and Ricardo Blaug. 2006. *Deliberative Democracy and the Role of Public Managers: Final Report of the Work Foundation's Public Value Consortium*. London: Work Foundation.

Jones, Samuel. 2010. *Culture Shock*. London: Demos. Accessed September 24, 2014. http://www.demos.co.uk/files/Culture_shock_-_web.pdf.

Kelly, G., G. Mulgan, and S. Muers. 2002. *Creating Public Value: An Analytical Framework for Public Service Reform*. London: Strategy Unit, Cabinet Office. Accessed September 24, 2014. http://www.cabinetoffice.gov.uk/strategy/downloads/files/public_value2.pdf.

Levitt, R. 2008. "The Political and Intellectual Landscape of Instrumental Museum Policy." *Cultural Trends* 17(4): 223–231.

Mason, Randall. 2002. "Assessing Values in Conservation Planning: Methodological Issues and Choices." In *Assessing the Values of Cultural Heritage: Research Report*, edited by Marta de la Torre, 5–30. Los Angeles: Getty Conservation Institute. Accessed September 14, 2014. http://www.getty.edu/conservation/publications_resources/pdf_publications/pdf/assessing.pdf.

Matarasso, François. 1996. "Defining Values: Evaluating Arts Programmes." *Social Impact of the Arts*, working paper 1. Stroud, UK: Comedia.

Matarasso, François. 1997. *Use or Ornament? The Social Impact of Participation in the Arts Programmes*. Stroud, UK: Comedia.

McCarthy, Kevin F., Elizabeth Heneghan Ondaatje, Laura Zakaras, and Arthur Brooks. 2004. *Gifts of the Muse: Reframing the Debate about the Benefits of the Arts*. Santa Monica, CA: Rand Corporation. Accessed September 24, 2014. http://www.wallacefoundation.org/knowledge-center/audience-development-for-the-arts/key-research/Documents/Gifts-of-the-Muse.pdf.

Ministry for Culture and Heritage. 2009. "Cultural Indicators for New Zealand/Tohu Ahurea mō Aotearoa." Accessed September 24, 2014. http://www.mch.govt.nz/research-publications/cultural-statistics/cultural-indicators-new-zealand-2009.

Moore, Mark. 1995. *Creating Public Value: Strategic Management in Government*. Cambridge, MA: Harvard University Press.

Moore, Mark, and Gaylen Moore. 2005. *Creating Public Value through State Arts Agencies*. Minneapolis: Arts Midwest.

Mourato, Susanna, and Massimiliano Mazzanti. 2002. "Economic Valuation of Cultural Heritage: Evidence and Prospects in Heritage Conservation." In *Assessing the Values of Cultural Heritage: Research Report*, edited by Marta de la Torre, 51–76. Los Angeles: Getty Conservation Institute. Accessed September 24, 2014. http://www.getty.edu/conservation/publications_resources/pdf_publications/pdf/assessing.pdf.

NMDC (National Museum Directors' Conference). 2006. *Values and Vision: The Contribution of Culture*. London: National Museum Directors' Conference. Accessed September 24, 2014. http://www.nationalmuseums.org.uk/media/documents/publications/values_and_vision.pdf.

O'Brien, David. 2010. *Measuring the Value of Culture: A Report to the Department for Culture, Media, and Sport*. London: DCMS.

OECD (Organisation for Economic Co-operation and Development). 1997. "In Search of Results: Performance Management Practices." Accessed September 24, 2014. http://www.oecd.org/dataoecd/18/12/36144694.pdf.

OECD (Organisation for Economic Co-operation and Development). 2004. "Public Sector Modernisation: Governing for Performance." Policy brief. Accessed October 1, 2014. http://www.oecd.org/site/govgfg/39044817.pdf.

OECD (Organisation for Economic Co-operation and Development). 2005a. "Public Sector Modernisation: The Way Forward." Policy brief. Accessed October 1, 2014. http://www.oecd.org/gov/modernisinggovernmentthewayforward.htm.

OECD (Organisation for Economic Co-operation and Development). 2005b. "Public Sector Modernisation: Modernising Accountability and Control." Policy brief. Accessed October 1, 2014. http://www.oecd.org/site/govgfg/39044829.pdf.

O'Neill, Mark. 2008. "Museums, Professionalism and Democracy." *Cultural Trends* 17(4): 289–307.

Owen, John M. 2006. *Program Evaluation: Forms and Approaches*, 3rd ed. Sydney: Allen and Unwin.

Pung, Caroline, Ann Clarke, and Laurie Patten. 2004. "Measuring the Economic Impact of the British Library." *New Review of Academic Librarianship* 10(1): 79–102.

Queensland Government. 2009. *Building on Success – Queensland Arts Industry Sector Development Plan 2010–2012: A Consultation Paper for the Arts Industry*. Brisbane: Queensland Government.

Radbourne, Jennifer, Hilary Glow, and Katya Johanson. 2010. "Measuring the Intrinsic Benefits of Arts Attendance." *Cultural Trends* 19(4): 307–324.

Scott, Carol A. 1991. "Report on the Outcomes of a Consultancy to Develop Performance Indicators for National Collecting Institutions." Unpublished report prepared for the Cultural Heritage Branch of the Department of the Arts, Sports, the Environment, Tourism, and Territories, Canberra.

Scott, Carol A. 2007. "Assessing Value: Australian Museums in the 21st Century." Unpublished PhD thesis, University of Sydney.

Scott, Carol A. 2010. "Searching for the Public in Public Value: Arts and Cultural Heritage in Australia." *Cultural Trends* 19(4): 273–289.

Scott, Carol A. R. Sandell, and J. Dodd, 2014. *Cultural Value. User Value of Museums and Galleries: A Critical Review of the Literature*. Research Centre for Museums and Galleries, University of Leicester, Leicester. Accessed January 30, 2015. http://www2.le.ac.uk/departments/museumstudies/rcmg/publications/cultural-value-of-museums

Selwood, Sara. 2002a. "What Difference Do Museums Make? Producing Evidence on the Impact of Museums." *Critical Quarterly* 44(4): 65–81.

Selwood, Sara. 2002b. "The Politics of Data Collection: Gathering, Analysing and Using Data about the Subsidised Cultural Sector in England." *Cultural Trends* 12(47): 13–97.

Selwood, Sara. 2010. "Making a Difference: The Cultural Impact of Museums." National Museums Directors' Conference website. Accessed September 24, 2014. http://www.nationalmuseums.org.uk/media/documents/publications/cultural_impact_final.pdf.

Stanziola, Javier. 2008. "Developing a Model to Articulate the Impact of Museums and Galleries: Another Dead Duck in Cultural Policy Research." *Cultural Trends* 17(4): 317–321.

Throsby, David. 2002. "Cultural Capital and Sustainability Concepts in the Economics of Cultural Heritage." In *Assessing the Values of Cultural Heritage: Research Report*, edited by Marta de la Torre, 101–117. Los Angeles: Getty Conservation Institute. Accessed September 24, 2014. http://www.getty.edu/conservation/publications_resources/pdf_publications/pdf/assessing.pdf.

Travers, Tony. 2006. *Museums and Galleries in Britain: Economic, Social and Creative Impacts*. Report commissioned by the Museums, Libraries, and Archives Council and the National Museums Directors' Conference. Accessed September 24, 2014. http://www.nationalmuseums.org.uk/media/documents/publications/museums_galleries_in_britain_travers_2006.pdf.

Travers, Tony, and Stephen Glaister. 2004. *Valuing Museums: Impact and Innovation among National Museums*. Report commissioned by the National Museum Directors' Conference. Accessed October 1, 2014. http://www.nationalmuseums.org.uk/media/documents/publications/valuing_museums.pdf.

Tusa, John. 2007. *Engaged with the Arts: Writings from the Frontline*. London: Tauris.

Walden, I. 1991. "Qualities and Quantities." *Museums Journal* January: 27–28.

Further Reading

de la Torre, Marta, ed. 2002. *Assessing the Values of Cultural Heritage: Research Report*. Los Angeles: The Getty Conservation Institute.

Gray, Clive. 2008. "Instrumental Policies: Causes, Consequences, Museums, Galleries." *Cultural Trends* 17(4): 209–222.

Jacobsen John, 2013. *"Museum Indicators of Impact and Performance." MIIP Research Project Description*. Marblehead, MA: White Oak Institute.

Scott, Carol A. 2013. *Museums and Public Value: Creating Sustainable Futures*. Farnham: Ashgate.

Carol A. Scott has had extensive experience as a museum professional, scholar, and consultant (http://carolscottassociates.com). She lives in London and has worked with museum leaders in the UK, Europe, North America, and Australasia on planning, branding, audience engagement, measurement, and funding. Carol has become widely known for her work on museum value, and has published extensively in this area in the journals *Curator, Museum Management and Curatorship, Cultural Trends*, and the *International Journal of Arts Management*. In 2013 she published a major book on the topic titled *Museums and Public Value*.

6 DEVELOPING AUDIENCES FOR THE TWENTY-FIRST-CENTURY MUSEUM

Graham Black

Responding to audiences that increasingly look, think, behave, and process information differently requires museums to not only get to know these audiences better, but to be willing to make bold changes in marketing, programming, and infrastructure to meet future visitor needs.

OP&A 2007a, 15

For four years in a row, from 2009 to 2012, a majority of museums in the United States reported an increase in on-site attendance, with museum directors putting this down to "better exhibits and marketing" (AAM 2013). No one can feel complacent however. While museums have been through difficult times since the start of the recession in 2007–2008, the future is even more unpredictable due not least to the constantly shifting and changing nature of audiences (see Crooke in this volume). Audience development is an important part of contemporary museum practice, and, while working with the public through public programs was traditionally something of an add-on, it is now increasingly seen as central to the museum's mission and purpose (Figure 6.1). The underlying theme of this chapter – the challenge museums face in remaining relevant to twenty-first-century audiences – sets the future of museums in the context of the rapid societal developments that we are all part of. The chapter argues that, as a result, museums should prioritize equally rapid changes in their public practice. It explores the development of museum practice toward both traditional and new audiences. Importantly, it emphasizes that there is not a choice to be made between the two – museums need both.

The International Handbooks of Museum Studies: Museum Practice, First Edition.
Edited by Conal McCarthy.
© 2015 John Wiley & Sons Ltd. Published 2020 by John Wiley & Sons Ltd.

FIGURE 6.1   Music in the foyer at Tel Aviv Museum of Art, Israel. A regular program of events is an important element in building a loyal audience in museums. (For a color version of this figure, please see the color plate section.)
Photograph courtesy of Yael Borovich.

The "traditional" museum visitor is changing

Any discussion of future audiences for museums must begin with what we know of current audiences. While museum audience research has a history stretching back to the late nineteenth century (see Kelly 2007), its substantial development only began in the United States in the 1960s, and it was not until 1988 that the First Annual Visitor Studies Conference was held in Jacksonville, Alabama, while the USA Visitor Studies Association was formally incorporated in 1992. The Visitor Studies Association in Canada was established in 1991, the Evaluation and Visitor Research Special Interest Group (EVRSIG) of Museums Australia in 1995 and the Visitor Studies Group in the United Kingdom in 1998. It is, therefore, a relatively new activity and a sophisticated and complex research base has taken time to develop.

Not surprisingly, initial research concentrated on quantitative data associated with attendance, zipcode, and the segmentation of audiences by demographics (age, gender, family status, education), geography (local, day tripper, or tourist), and socioeconomic status. Segmentation is a market research approach that breaks audiences down into distinct groups that are supposed to behave in similar ways.

Characteristics of the traditional museum visitor revealed by such segmentation includes the fact that, for most users, a visit represents an occasional leisure-led event; the family group is frequently the largest audience characteristically making up from 40 percent to 55 percent of total visitor numbers; and the two genders are relatively equally represented, but this is dependent on the nature of the site. The most striking evidence, however, is that the largest group, and the most over-represented in comparison to their percentage within the general population, consists of the better educated, more affluent, white professional classes, with education the most important factor. Hood (1993) summarized the traditional US audience as "in the upper education, upper occupation and upper income groups ... This social class factor applies across the spectrum of museums – from zoos, science-technology centres and children's museums to historical sites, botanical gardens and art museums" (Hood 1993, 17).

In the USA, among adults who visit an art gallery or art museum at least once a year, 80 percent have some college education, including 52 percent of those with graduate degrees visiting (NEA 2009). In the UK, 65 percent of people with a university degree or above visited museums while only 19 percent of people with no qualifications did (MLAC 2004). At the Canadian Museum of Civilization some 48 percent have some university education or higher, 22 percent pre-university college, 22 percent high school, and only 8 percent with no more than elementary school (Rabinovitch 2003). Visitor studies at the Australian Museum, Sydney, suggest 50 percent of their audience have a university education or above (AMARC 2003). Those with higher educational levels are also significantly more likely to attend regularly than those with other or no qualifications (Bunting et al. 2007, 25).

Such surveys, however, do no more than explore mass demand within defined market segments and, from this, attempt to generalize the nature of users and their expectations. A closer look at museum audiences reveals a more complex picture. Central to this is motivation – why the choice is made to visit a museum. Individuals, families, and social groups are audience segments in their own right and it is their personal needs which motivate their choice of site and, once there, of what to engage with. If museums are to support visitors who seek such a personalized experience, based on individual motivations and interests, they must develop a much more sophisticated understanding of audiences.

A central issue, for example, is whether the make-up of the traditional museum audience is limited not by constraints but rather by choice. To what extent do the professional and/or highly educated classes see their use of an important element of their leisure time as comprising goal-oriented activities, and does this go some way to explaining their disproportionate use of museums and heritage sites? As Hood put it:

> they are attracted to the kinds of experiences museums offer and they find those offerings and activities satisfying ... These folk emphasise three factors in their leisure life: opportunities to learn, the challenge of new experiences, and doing something worthwhile for themselves. (Hood 1993, 17)

This is similar to discussions on cultural heritage tourists and the importance or otherwise of the motivation to build cultural capital. But these discussions must be placed in a wider context of societal change. Taking the United Kingdom as an example, on Christmas Day 1986, 30.15 million people watched the soap opera *EastEnders* on television – the top viewing figure of that day. *EastEnders* also came top on Christmas Day 2012, but with 9.4 million viewers, despite the fact that television viewing has increased substantially since 1986, with much more choice and more competition for how people exercise that choice. Meanwhile, in April 2012 at a UK inquiry into the behavior of newspaper journalists, the magnate Rupert Murdoch predicted that hard-copy newspapers will cease to exist by 2030. People still want news, but are getting it in different ways. Similarly much of the High Street is in disarray, with predictions that up to 20 percent of shops in the UK will disappear. Amazon now claims to sell more e-books than print ones while CD and DVD shops are going out of business, and HMV, the last major music and DVD retail chain in the UK, was in administration. People are still accessing music and film, but differently.

Museums are not immune. To remain relevant to their future audiences, they require long-term strategies in response to a perfect storm of three related elements:

- demographic change
- generational shift
- the rise of new media.

Demographic change. We are witnessing the global movements of peoples on an unprecedented scale. There are an estimated 214 million migrants worldwide, potentially rising to 405 million by 2050 (IOM 2010, xix). The populations of Western cities in particular are in the midst of rapid demographic change, with immigration and a rise in birth rates radically altering the ethnic and racial make-up. Furthermore, as the Wallace Foundation put it, "diversity is becoming more and more diverse" (Wallace Foundation 2009, 15). The UK, for example, has seen a dramatic influx of people from Eastern Europe, with Polish now the second most commonly spoken language in the country. In this environment, issues around identity, sense of belonging, and community cohesion are high on the agenda for individuals, communities, and political leaders. The impact of demographic change on museums will be explored in the second half of the chapter.

Generational shift. The tastes, interests, and behavior of those born since the 1960s are beginning to dominate (see Table 6.1). These generations have very different expectations to their baby-boomer predecessors. For example by 2030 the digital natives mentioned in Table 6.1 – the first generation to grow up with new technology – will hopefully be bringing their children to our museums. What will they expect?

The impact of new media. Web 2.0 has meant that people engage differently with the world. They communicate differently, learn differently, and have new opportunities for creativity and collaboration. WITNESS – RECORD – SHARE has become the norm (Vargas 2007, qtd. in OP&A 2007a, 2). Facebook estimates that each

TABLE 6.1   Generational shift

Silent generation, born 1927–1945	Shaped by economic depression and war.
Baby boomers, born 1946–1964	Shaped by social upheavals of 1960s. Witnessed impact of mass media. Lived through economic boom. **Slowly relinquishing power.**
Generation X, born 1965–1978	Smaller numbers. Rise in dual income families. Family splits. Higher debt burdens than boomers. Expansion of women in higher education. **Increasingly in power.**
Generation Y, born 1979 – mid-1990s: "Millennials"	Increased birth rate. Increasingly diverse. Filter the world through new media. **By 2015/2016 will make up more of the workforce than baby boomers.**
Generation M, post-mid-1990s)	"Digital natives."

(after Wilkening and Chung 2009, 8–10; Rainie 2006, qtd. in OP&A 2007a, 9–10)

month approximately 7.5 billion photographs are uploaded on to its servers. It is also increasingly a mobile world. By 2020 mobile technologies will be the main means of access to the web. For museums, on-site, online, and mobile provision must converge because that is what audiences will expect.

Cultural commentators such as Charles Leadbeater argue that the web and use of new media are changing what people want from a cultural experience. He suggests that arts and cultural venues have always sought an overlapping "mix of three different experiences" – Enjoy, Talk, Do – but that the balance is changing from Enjoy to Talk and Do.

Box 6.1   Enjoy, Talk, Do: Three Forms of Cultural Engagement

Enjoy: To enjoy being entertained and served; to watch, listen, read. Inside their heads, enjoy experiences which can be intensely engaging.
Talk: Experiences in which the content provides a focal point for socializing and interacting. The value lies in part in the talk that the content sets off.
Do: Some people also want experiences that allow them to be creative, to get involved, to contribute.

(after Leadbeater 2009, 11)

What one could perhaps surmise is that generational shift and the growing use of new technology and the web are together leading to an increased expectation of a profoundly different, much more participatory and personalized museum experience. This represents a remarkable opportunity to create new and meaningful opportunities for engagement, and to build loyalty among users, on-site and online. But this will involve planning for and sustaining a multiplatform museum experience.

> **Box 6.2**   A Multi-platform Museum Experience
>
> **Enjoy:** Watch, listen, read.
> **Engage:** More pro-actively involved, talk about the experience.
> **Participate:** Use participative exhibits. Take part in programs.
> **Contribute:** User-generated content (on-site, online). Crowd-sourcing (including community and niche-sourcing).
> **Co-create/co-curate:** Associated particularly with community engagement.

The challenge, as the quote at the beginning of this chapter makes clear, is to "get to know our audiences better" and then plan and implement change for the long term. The case studies below on the National Trust and Dallas Museum of Art show two ways forward, but first comes a brief examination of a core and growing part of the traditional audience: the cultural heritage tourist.

The tourist as museum visitor

There is a symbiotic relationship between museums, heritage sites, and the leisure and tourism industry. Museums worldwide depend on tourism, both domestic and international, to generate visitor numbers and income. And, for the tourism industry, the cultural heritage tourist is a key figure – growing in numbers, and likely to both stay in an area longer and to spend more money (US Department of Commerce and the President's Committee on the Arts and Humanities 2005). Some 57 percent of tourists to Australia visit museums and/or art galleries (Tourism Research Australia 2008). Both the Travel Industry of America and the State of the American Traveller Survey 2008 (Destination Analysts 2009) suggest that cultural tourism is growing, with 81 percent of leisure travelers in the United States defined as cultural tourists, a considerable growth from the 61 percent recorded in 1998 and the 65 percent of 2001.

There is a remarkable similarity between analyses of the cultural heritage tourists and of traditional museum visitors. This should not be surprising as they are many of the same people (US Department of Commerce and the President's Committee on the Arts and Humanities 2005, 5; Richards 2001). Following a major research project that spanned Western Europe, Richards concluded:

- The proportion with a higher education qualification is almost double the EU average.
- More than 40 percent of were aged 50 or over.
- Almost 60 percent had managerial or professional jobs.
- Their average incomes were significantly higher than the European average.

- A major motivating factor lies in their desire to gain a deeper understanding of the culture and heritage of a destination.
- Households headed by "baby boomers" are more likely to engage in cultural activities.

(Richards 2001, ch. 3)

In a report looking specifically at city cultural tourism in Europe, important given the concentration of museums in cities, the conclusions were:

- Museums were by far the most popular attractions for all visitors.
- Visitors tend to be highly educated with professional of managerial occupations and relatively high incomes.
- Cultural tourism in cities is an activity followed by all age groups, with the peak age group in terms of participation between 20 and 30.
- Those over the age of 50 tend to visit more cultural attractions than younger tourists.
- Culture is the single most important motivation for city trips, although relatively few visitors view themselves as "cultural tourists."
- Demographic developments in Europe during the coming 10 to 15 years strongly favour cultural tourism as the group of potential travellers older than 55 years will grow significantly.
- With increasing globalization and mass production leading to greater uniformity worldwide, the value of authenticity … will become increasingly important.

(ETC Research Group 2005, vii, viii, ix)

The wide age range, the quest for "authenticity," and the demographics all bode well for future visitor numbers to museums in tourist areas. The tourism economy in the UK is projected to grow by 2.6 percent a year until 2018 (HLF 2010a, 8) and heritage is the mainstay of UK non-business tourism (HLF 2010a, 3). In 2012 the top 10 most visited free attractions in the UK were all museums, and seven of the top 10 paid attractions were heritage sites (ALVA 2013).

In the USA, the increase in visits identified by tourism research seems to contradict the evidence from the National Endowment for the Arts (NEA) survey of participation in the arts, which continues to suggest declining attendances:

After topping 26 percent in 1992 and 2002, art museum attendance slipped to 23 percent in 2008 … For the first time in the SPPA [*Survey of Public Participation in the Arts*], women reduced their rate of attendance … The proportion of US adults touring parks or historical buildings (25 percent) has diminished by one third since 1982. (NEA 2009, 2)

A possible explanation is that people are visiting museums and heritage sites while on a leisure trip, but are reducing the amount they do so while at home. If this is the case, it suggests future problems for museums in non-tourist areas.

Given the importance of cultural heritage tourism, there have been attempts to develop segmentation as a means of analyzing likely impact, with the most commonly referred to example outlined in Box 6.3.

> ### Box 6.3   A Segmentation of Cultural Heritage Tourists
>
> **The purposeful cultural tourist:** Cultural tourism is the primary motive for visiting a destination and the tourist has a very deep cultural experience.
> **The sightseeing cultural tourist:** Cultural tourism is a primary reason for visiting a destination, but the experience is less deep.
> **The serendipitous cultural tourist:** A tourist who does not travel for cultural reasons, but who, after participating, ends up having a deep cultural tourism experience.
> **The casual cultural tourist:** Cultural tourism is a weak motive for travel and the resulting experience is shallow.
> **The incidental cultural tourist:** This tourist does not travel specifically for cultural tourism.
>
> (McKercher and du Cros 2002, 144)

An area of research that is more immediately relevant to museums has investigated what the tourism field sees as the three core drivers in cultural heritage tourism – prior knowledge, motivations, and the building of cultural capital – which together define visits and levels of engagement. Prior knowledge and experience of target attractions and/or subject matter has a strong influence on choice of destination (e.g. Prentice 2004). Bourdieu (1984, 2) argued that to appreciate cultural products, people must first build the cultural competence, or capital, to interpret them. Questions remain about the extent to which museum visitation is based on the ambition to build cultural capital by those from higher social strata and/or with higher levels of education (e.g. DCMS et al. 2010; Hood 1993; NEA 2009), and how much it has to do, rather, with individuality (Cohen-Gewerc and Stebbins, 2013). Overall, the analysis of motivation within the tourism field has tended to break down into "push" and "pull" factors: push being motivations that drive interest, and pull understood as attractiveness of the destination (see Baloglu and Uysal 1996).

From this base, tourism researchers have explored the impact of these drivers on the levels of engagement of cultural tourists to museums and heritage sites. While museum advocates focus on learning, cultural and social capital, and identity as key motivators for engagement, the tourism and leisure field has added the concept of "serious leisure" (e.g. Stebbins 2009) – actively participating in something that the participant wants to do at a level that not only satisfies but also gives a sense of progress which can, in turn, lead to even higher levels of engagement.

Finally, one must also note what is expected by a global tourist audience of a quality leisure experience. This emphasizes the continuing requirement for museums to respond to the demands of recreational visitors alongside regular users, and to ensure the quality of the overall visitor experience, not just the collections and displays.

Learning sustained focus from the National Trust

The National Trust for England, Wales, and Northern Ireland is Europe's largest conservation body. Its responsibilities include caring for over 350 historic houses, gardens, parks, and major ancient monuments. In February 2010, it launched a new national strategy – *Going Local*. At its heart was an ambition to devolve more power and responsibility to individual properties and to "try to make sure that the unique spirit of each property can come alive in the hearts and minds of visitors" (National Trust 2010b, Introduction). This commitment involved a fundamental change in the way each property was presented – "always the same" could no longer apply.

Under the theme of "bringing the house to life," early initiatives included visitors being able to sit on chairs and play the piano (Dunham Massey), and even play billiards (Upton House), but interpretation rapidly concentrated on spirit of place. Approaches taken have included long-established techniques such as costumed interpreters and conservation volunteering opportunities, but also a new emphasis on stories about the properties and their inhabitants, engaging visitors with conservation in action (Figure 6.2),

FIGURE 6.2   National Trust conservation in action: people watch while one of the sixteenth-century Gideon Tapestries is rehung at Hardwick Hall, Derbyshire. Whereas previously the gallery would have been closed to the public, now the Trust ensures that members and visitors are aware of the conservation work it carries out as part of its commitment to involving people in its work. (For a color version of this figure, please see the color plate section.)
Reproduced with permission of the National Trust.

extended opportunities to go behind the scenes, the use of local produce in tea-rooms, and also a new partnership with Arts Council England, bringing contemporary art and artists-in-residence to properties. In 2011, the Trust extended its initiative out of doors, with new walking routes opened at its properties and a Walking Festival during school half-term in October that incorporated 1036 walking events targeted at all abilities (National Trust 2012, 29). For children, there is "Fifty Things to Do before You Are 11¾."

Underpinning the initiative was the Trust's *2020 Vision*: "Everyone will feel like a member; five million will be" (National Trust 2010a). At the time, the Trust had 2.5 million members, itself a huge number, and doubling this to 5 million was seen as quite a challenge. A core reason for concentrating interpretation on what was distinctive about each property was to build loyalty and encourage return visits. To support the new interpretation, the Trust used previous audience research to develop a segmentation based on motivation. Each property was then expected to define three target segments and mold its interpretation to meet their needs. The segmentation proved essential in focusing the whole organization on the idea that not all audiences are the same or have the same expectations. This shift was crucial to the Trust's workforce as a whole accepting the need for change. It was reinforced by a renewed commitment to regular visitor satisfaction surveys with each property expected to increase the percentages describing their visit as "very enjoyable."

Box 6.4   National Trust Segmentation by Motivation

- **Out and About:** Spontaneous, prefer chance encounters to firm plans. Love to share their experiences with friends.
- **Young Experience Seekers:** Open to challenge; they make and take opportunities in their journey of personal discovery.
- **Curious Minds:** Active thinkers, always questioning and making connections between the things they learn. They ensure a continual flow of intellectual stimuli in their lives.
- **Live Life to the Full:** Self-driven intellectuals, confident of their own preferences and opinions and independent in their decision-making.
- **Explorer Families:** Actively learn together, the adults will get as much out of their experience as the children.
- **Kids First Families:** Put the needs of the children first and look for a fun environment where children are stimulated and adults can relax; they're looking for a guaranteed good time.
- **Home and Family:** Broad groups of friends and family who gather together for special occasions. They seek passive enjoyment of an experience to suit all tastes and ages.

National Trust, unpublished, edited by the author

Museums have much to learn from the way the Trust approached audience development. The strategy was underpinned by necessary managerial and operational change. Interpretation was developed around the unique spirit of place of each individual property. It then focused directly on the visitor experience, using segmentation by motivation to develop this and simple satisfaction surveys to evaluate impact. Perhaps most importantly, the Trust recognized that achieving its ambitions depended ultimately on sustained drive over a considerable timeframe, and required regular evaluation against targets. By late 2013, the Trust already had over 4 million members.

Dallas Museum of Art: Using Visitor-Profiling to Transform the Museum Offer

To date, the best published examples of visitor-profiling leading to a transformation of the museum offer come from the USA, particularly Denver Art Gallery, Oakland Museum of California, and Dallas Museum of Art. At the latter, a seven-year study of visitor preferences and behaviors, from 2003 to 2009, led to the identification of four related "visitor clusters," what the museum calls its "Levels of Engagement with Art Framework" (Table 6.2).

Putting this research into action led to fundamental change in all aspects of the museum's public practice – from exhibition and programming development to new marketing strategies and interpretation tools. This has resulted in attendance figures doubling, and it motivated more than 50 percent of the museum's visitors to participate in its educational and public programs. New initiatives have included the establishment of a Centre for Creative Connections, interactive exhibitions, a much-enhanced online presence and late-night events. The latter have included both DJs in the galleries and bedtime stories for young visitors.

The redesigned website has been developed as an integral part of gallery provision. Online and mobile users can download not only high-resolution digital images of artworks and associated documentation, but also video clips of artists, curators, scholars, and education resource materials, as well as related links.

TABLE 6.2   Dallas Museum of Art levels of engagement with art framework (summary)

Observers	Tentative, least confident, high proportion of males.
26% of on-site visitors	
Participants	Enjoy learning and the social aspects of their experience.
24% of on-site visitors	Have a strong knowledge of and interest in art.
Independents	Like to view works independently.
20% of on-site visitors	Are confident about their knowledge and seek intense interactions with art.
Enthusiasts	Confident, enthusiastic, knowledgeable, and comfortable.
30% of on-site visitors	Actively participate in a wide variety of museum programming.

Source: after Pitman and Hirzy 2011

Crucially, the museum is integrating on-site, online, and mobile provision for what it is calling its Arts Network System. This is now providing audiences with smart-phone tours and interpretive materials they can customize to their own needs, as well as general information about exhibitions, special events, and programs.

Reaching out to new audiences

it is clearly more challenging in hard times for arts organizations to take the long view and continue to devote time and effort to building new audiences, but that work and the resulting lessons are also more vital than ever to the long-term health of arts organizations and the entire arts sector.

Wallace Foundation 2009, 2

The Museums Association declares that "Museums belong to everybody. They exist to serve the public" (Museums Association 2008, *Code of Ethics* 2.0). If museums are to be for everybody, then, on both ethical and business grounds, the development and retention of new audiences should be at the core of what museums do. Ethically, museums hold the cultural memory of humankind and access should not be the exclusive right of an educated elite, nor should its content exclude the contributions made by large sectors of the population. And, of course, everyone should have the right to benefit from the life-affirming impact that museums can have. In business terms, demographic change means the audience base of many museums is changing. In the medium to long term, museums must reach out successfully to these new audiences or die. In the shorter term, sustainably developing a wider audience both increases income and creates the political goodwill essential to maintaining public funding. However, it will be difficult enough for museums to retain their relevance among "traditional" audiences. It is much more challenging to diversify the user base by engaging with new audiences. This is a complex area and museum thinking on it has developed considerably over the past 20 years. In the space available, it is impossible to do full justice to the subject. Instead, an approach has been taken here that seeks to illustrate some of elements under consideration.

Getting to know the non-visitor

The *Taking Part Survey 2005/6* (Aust and Vine 2007), in revealing that up to 60 percent of the population of England at that time did not visit a museum, suggested three central reasons for non-visiting:

- They do not know the museum exists.
- They know it exists but do not see any relevance to their lives.
- Poor health was also a significant issue.

TABLE 6.3   Arts Council England: non-user segments (edited by author)

Time-poor dreamers	Busy, short-term-oriented, living in the moment. They engage with popular culture and the arts are not for them.
A quiet pint with the match	Content with life and not seeking change.
Older and home-bound	In their senior years. They enjoy a slower pace of life and like spending a lot of their free time at home. Some of them report poor levels of health, which restricts their activities.
Limited means, nothing fancy	For them, their leisure time is all about having a break and chilling out, within their limited means.

Source: ACE 2011, 46, 50, 54, 58

The first two reasons highlight an urgent need for better and more targeted marketing – not only in terms of making people aware of a museum's existence but in persuading non-users to put aside their preconceptions of museums. An example of such targeted marketing can be seen in Arts Council England's segmentation of users and non-users into 13 groups, based on their engagement with the arts rather than traditional demographics (ACE 2011). In this they defined their non-user segments (or, as they put it, "not currently engaged") (see Table 6.3).

The fourth of these segments reflects a body of literature that has sought to define criteria by which people judge their leisure experiences. For example, the core attributes Hood listed were, in alphabetical order:

- being with people, or social interaction
- doing something worthwhile
- feeling comfortable and at ease in one's surroundings
- having a challenge of new experiences
- having an opportunity to learn
- participating actively.

(Hood 1983, 51)

Hood's research contrasted the desire of highly educated users to have an opportunity to learn, do something worthwhile and have new experiences, discussed above, with the characteristics that museum non-visitors valued most highly – being with people, participating actively, and feeling comfortable and at ease – and concluded that these latter three leisure attributes are frequently not present in people's mental image of museums:

> They perceive museums to be formal, formidable places, inaccessible to them because they usually have had little preparation to read the "museum code" – places that invoke restrictions on group social behaviour and on active participation. Sports, picnicking, browsing in shopping malls better meet their criteria of desirable leisure activities. (Hood 1983, 54)

In these circumstances, focus on the projection of an engaging image and on the creation of a user-friendly museum environment may be the first, essential, steps in reaching out to non-users. Yet, not all highly educated people visit museums. Equally, many less well educated people visit museums regularly. So other factors must play an important role. For example, childhood and adolescent exposure to museum-visiting, and the arts in general, appears to be a major factor in adult leisure choices (DCMS et al. 2010; McCarthy and Jinnett 2001; OP&A 2007b; Orend 1989).

In general terms, however, Bunting et al. (2007, 49) suggest lack of *interest* is the real barrier for lower socioeconomic groups, but for higher socioeconomic groups lack of *time* is more important. It is difficult to avoid the conclusion that it is a reflection of a class divide, which in turn creates a "participation divide" that affects social and civil engagement across the board, not just in the arts (Bunting et al. 2007, 49, 62). This seems to be a partial return to the views of Bourdieu (1984) on the capacity of the higher social classes to dominate cultural opportunities that are supposedly there for all. The results of more recent research in the UK by Bennett et al. (2009) support this view, while acknowledging that factors including age, ethnicity, and gender render matters more complex than Bourdieu suggested.

Reaching out to marginalized communities

While it can also refer to building deeper relationships with existing audiences, most museums associate the concept of audience development with broadening their audience base by reaching out to non-users, particularly those who are on the margins of society. As such, they have focused on the issue of relevance, the second of the three reasons for non-visiting highlighted by Aust and Vine, and sought to look beyond leisure choices and class issues to consider potential underpinning factors. In the process, they have used the same market segmentation practice that established the characteristics of "traditional" museum visitors, to define who does not visit, with the UK used as an example in Box 6.5.

Box 6.5   Under-Represented Audiences at UK Museums and Galleries

Disabled people: People defined by themselves as having any longstanding illness, disability, or infirmity that limits their activities in any way.
Black and minority ethnic groups: People defined by themselves as Asian or British Asian (Indian, Pakistani, and Bangladeshi; Other Asian Background); Black or British Black (Black Caribbean; Black African; Other Black Background); Mixed Ethnicity; Chinese; and other ethnic groups. For reasons of space, Black and minority ethnic is sometimes shortened to "BME" in charts and tables.

Lower socioeconomic groups: Using the National Statistics Socioeconomic Classification (C2, D, E), that is those in supervisory and technical roles, semi-routine, or routine occupations, or who have never worked.

(after Bunting et al. 2007, 12–13)

The concept of "barriers" – physical, social, cultural, intellectual, environmental, and within the museum structure – was developed to examine why these segments believe museums lack relevance, a reflection of core issues relating to inclusion, representation, and equality of participation. For example, when UK researchers explored usage of museums by the local black and Asian community for the Yorkshire Museums Council, they saw attitudes and assumptions to be a key factor:

> "They don't do activities that interest me."
> "Not enough black culture."
> "Doesn't relate to me."
> "Don't feel included." (Woroncow 2001, 2)

The conclusion reached was that museums must work with communities to break down barriers to use:

> Audience development is about breaking down the barriers which hinder access to museums and "building bridges" with different groups to ensure their specific needs are met. It is a process by which a museum seeks to create access to, and encourage greater use of, its collections and services. (Dodd and Sandell 1998, 6)

There is nothing new to museums seeking to broaden their audiences. In the USA, one can look at the work of John Cotton Dana, founder in 1909 of the Newark Museum, New Jersey (Dana 1917) and at Theodore Low's 1942 publication *The Museum as a Social Instrument.* The United States also led the world in the development of community and neighborhood museums. Danilov (2009) listed 622 museums, galleries, historic sites, and other facilities founded and operated by ethnic groups, with the oldest operating example dating back to 1868 and more in the process of being created. Community museums became particularly important in the USA from the 1960s, with growing demand by marginalized communities for recognition both of their contribution to wider society, and of the value of differing perspectives on the past. Holo (2009) speaks strongly in favor of community-created museums: "They fulfilled an emerging need … determined by cultural insiders, representatives of living and evolving communities, for there to be museums that were demonstrably relevant – on terms set by communities themselves" (Holo 2009, 41).

Mainstream museums learned from these examples. Anacostia, the influential museum in a black district of Washington, DC, was set up in 1967 in a small disused cinema with the help and financial backing of the Smithsonian, under the leadership of a 30-year-old black youth worker, John Kinard: "What he envisaged was something which had not existed previously, a museum which grew naturally from the life of the district, a museum with a creative flow of ideas, exhibits and people between itself and the outside world" (Varine 1993, unpaginated).

In the 1970s and 1980s, institutions such as the Philadelphia Museum of Art and New York City Museum began what became known as "outreach" activities, staging festivals and exhibitions in poor neighborhoods both using their collections and exploring themes including drugs, violence, and sexually transmitted diseases. Alexander commented on the success of the outreach program begun in Philadelphia in 1970: "It has observed well the basic principles of community-oriented programmes: to respect the wishes and ideas of the groups, to help them whenever feasible, provided assistance is asked, and to keep the museum in the background" (Alexander 1979, 224).

By 1972, the American Association of Museums had already produced a major report on these new museums and potential new audiences (AAM 1972). Alexander's description of the criticisms that gave rise to this new movement bears a striking resemblance to comments still being made today:

> the criticism that they (museums) appealed only to the educated few and collected objects valued by wealthy leaders, that the immigrants, blacks, and other deprived minorities as well as the poor had been ignored, their cultural contributions and needs forgotten. (Alexander 1979, 14)

This same drive toward community engagement can also be seen in resolutions by ICOM's General Assembly in the late 1960s and early 1970s which focused on the contributions museums could make to the cultural, social, and economic life of their communities. It underpinned the Round Table on the Development and the Role of Museums in the Contemporary World held in Chile in 1972, with its long-lasting impact on museums across Latin America, particularly through the concept of the Integrated Museum – linked directly to its community and, particularly, to the most urgent problems faced by its inhabitants which would, in turn, form the themes of its exhibitions and programming (Silverman 2010, 12). An example can be seen in the Union of Community Museums of Oaxaka, Mexico. The European equivalent is the community involvement at the heart of the ecomuseum movement, whose defining project, the ecomuseum of Le Creusot–Montceau-les-Mines, was created in France between 1971 and 1974 (Davis 2008).

While community museums and outreach programs are now a relatively common feature of the US museum world, they could still not be defined as part of the mainstream. Equally, in Western Europe, while the rise of social history and indus-trial museums from the 1970s was based on a groundswell of support within local communities, and while the concepts of community museums and outreach have been present since the same period (see, for example, Merriman 1991), they were rarely seen as a priority by public sector museum services. What changed in the 1990s was the rise of a political agenda that committed museums to playing a role in tackling social issues within society, based on the concept of social exclusion. The term was first used in France in 1974 in relation to groups and communities believed to be excluded from mainstream society, and reflected growing under-standing of the complexity of social disintegration in which poverty was only one element. In the UK, it was defined by the then New Labour government as follows:

> Social exclusion is something that can happen to anyone. But some people are significantly more at risk than others. Research has found that people with certain backgrounds and experiences are disproportionately likely to suffer social exclusion. The key risk factors include: low income; family conflict; being in care; school problems; being an ex-prisoner; being from an ethnic minority; living in a deprived neighbourhood in urban and rural areas; mental health problems, age and disability. (Cabinet Office 2001, 11)

In 2001, the government asked the museum sector to explore how UK regional museums could best support the tackling of social exclusion. The report, *Renaissance in the Regions* (MLAC 2001), led for the first time to central government grant aid to regional museums, closely linked to enhanced access, social inclusion, and learning, with the latter seen by the government as the key route out of social exclusion. Thanks to this funding, UK museums were able to develop the range of learning activities they could offer to all visitors, their structured educational work, their collaboration with local communities and their own expertise in community engagement.

Over the last decade, longevity and sustainability of engagement with commu-nities have become core ambitions and some leading institutions such as Tyne and Wear Museums and National Museums Liverpool, and smaller locations like Hackney Museum, have transformed their missions and organizational structures to become community-focused. There are many examples of effective audience development going on in museums large and small which reach out to local audiences; such as the Potteries Museum in Stoke, which works with families (Figure 6.3). The development of a multiperspectival approach has become central to audience development work. New collections have been created, mostly through outreach programs in which museums have worked in partnership with minority communities combining oral histories with collecting, while existing collections have been re-assessed for their relevance to communities. Organizations like The Network (The Network n.d.) have encouraged participants to

FIGURE 6.3   The Potteries Museum in Stoke holds the finest collection of British ceramics in the world. It is also a leader in working with families who have children under five years of age. (For a color version of this figure, please see the color plate section.)
Courtesy of Stoke Potteries Museum.

share information and ideas, and there has been a gradual emergence of best-practice recommendations:

- commitment by the governing body and senior management to placing community at the core of what the museum does;
- a clear mission, a long-term plan and goals, and a collective sense of purpose across the service – with the entire organization involved;
- an approach based on working *with* individuals and communities in partnerships where authority is shared;
- good planning and evaluation;
- clear principles and standards;
- staff and community training and development needs identified and met;
- issues and tensions understood and addressed; and
- over time, the workforce – front and back of house – should come to reflect the audiences for the museum.

What is more, UK central government funding brought with it a need for museums to prove their effectiveness as learning and socially inclusive environments by establishing ways to measure the outcomes for those involved. This led to the development of the Inspiring Learning for All initiative (MLAC n.d.) which in turn produced learning impact assessment criteria (Generic Learning Outcomes or GLOs), now a norm in UK museum evaluation. An attempt to establish criteria for generic social outcomes (GSOs) was first piloted in the UK in Newcastle and Bristol (AEA Consulting 2005), giving some sense of the scale of the social impact that museum projects could have on individuals, but has never been commonly used.

This type of evaluation, however, is not just a UK development. An equivalent model of outcome-based evaluation by grantees of the Institute of Museum and Library Services in the USA is used to measure and document "achievements or changes in skill, knowledge, attitude, behavior, condition, or life status for program participants" (IMLS 2007). O'Neill (2010) surveys the growing academic research evidence now available worldwide that general cultural attendance, including at museums, has a significant health benefit. Research by the Working Group on Museums and Sustainable Communities in Canada points to changes not only within individuals but within communities, and the effect this can have within museums themselves (Worts 2006).

One impact of the continuing emphasis on community engagement and participation has been a growing willingness among museums to operate beyond their walls. A museum committed to partnership with its communities will break the stranglehold of its physical site and restricted opening hours and reach outward, beyond its walls, housed collections, "safe" history, and traditional audiences. As such, museums can become "third places," non-threatening environments in which they can work with their communities to develop partnerships that promote dialogue, build community capacity, and support civil engagement (Bodo, Gibbs, and Sani 2009, 23). Phil Nowlen (2009), Director of the Getty Leadership Institution, spoke of this when he challenged museums to "move beyond their comfortable street addresses … the better to advance society's culture, capacity for compassion, sense of community and strength of democracy."

A major starting point has been the way local history museums in the USA have increasingly encouraged their communities to investigate their own pasts, share their experiences, and enthuse museum visitors to go out and actively explore the locality, using local voices (live or audio) to reach below the surface patina. Oral and written testimonies, short films, soundscapes and images contribute to a wider understanding of a locality's complex culture and history, for example, in the collaboration between Missouri History Society and the communities of St. Louis in exploring the cultural landscapes of the city (Missouri History Society n.d.) and in the Levine Museum of the New South Changing Places project (Levine Museum n.d.).

From such initiatives has come a growing recognition that museums can act in a wider capacity, in supporting marginalized communities to engage with civil society and with civic institutions. In the USA, a national Museums and Community Initiative led to the publication of *Mastering Civic Engagement* (AAM 2002). This outlined core principles of greater civic engagement, democracy, and community building, and challenged US museums to strengthen their community bonds. One sees it also in the Animating Democracy initiative of Americans for the Arts (Americans for the Arts n.d.). As an example, the Centre for Cultural Understanding and Change at the Field Museum in Chicago has created a program of activities and exhibitions that respond to common concerns across its region, defined through over 100 conversations held with communities and organizations in 2007. Its website (CCUC 2008), in outlining current projects and programs, highlights the museum's commitment to the promotion of civil dialogue and social change:

> The Centre for Cultural Understanding and Change (CCUC) at the Field Museum uses problem-solving anthropological research to identify and catalyse strengths and assets of communities in Chicago and beyond. In doing so, CCUC helps communities identify new solutions to critical challenges such as education, housing, health care, environmental conservation and leadership development. Through research, programs and access to collections, CCUC reveals the power of cultural difference to transform social life and promote social change. (CCUC 2008)

However, while a minority of museums have transformed their relationships with local communities, the jury is definitely out on the ability of most to make serious inroads into non-user groups. As Robert Janes writes, "the majority of museums, as social institutions, have largely eschewed, on both moral and practical grounds, a broader commitment to the world in which they operate" (Janes 2009, 13).

Building partnerships that can change lives

The third key reason given by Aust and Vine (2007) for non-use of museums was poor health, to which one should add some disabilities. To make a valuable contribution in this area, museum staff must develop their expertise and professional relationships. In such an environment, they can truly change lives. Over the past decade the Heritage and Arts Services in Leicester and the county of Leicestershire in the United Kingdom have become national exemplars for working with communities, seen, for example, in the Moving Here project (Figure 6.4), at the New Walk Museum, Leicester, which recorded personal experiences of migration. In Leicestershire, the service is now located within the local authority's Communities and Wellbeing Department, and has established partnerships with social service and mental health professionals. In 2011, it became part of a county-wide Culture, Health and Wellbeing Partnership. One recent project: Opening Minds: Mental Health, Creativity and the Open

FIGURE 6.4   Local participants in the Moving Here project visit New Walk Museum, Leicester.
Courtesy of City of Leicester Museums and Heritage Service.

Museum (Leicestershire County Council 2011) brought with it close collaboration with mental health professionals and added local weight to the growing body of evidence for the positive impact that museums can have within mental health contexts (see, e.g., O'Neill 2010). Another, Sharing Stories, was an intergenerational project that brought together a group of local care-home residents and teenagers with behavioral problems (Bridge and Atkin-Barrett 2011). However, to date, its most extensive work has been with Special Educational Needs (SEN) and dementia.

In 2006 the service commissioned a report that identified the barriers that specialist SEN schools in Leicestershire faced in using museums. Since then the service's learning team, working in partnership with both SEN practitioners and specialist advisory teams within the Children's Services Department, has built up a significant body of expertise that is now being applied to creating new services. The Held in the Hand project represents a culmination of work to date and addresses one of the main challenges – that of moving from projects to services. By creating a set of dedicated and flexible resources that can be used on an on-demand basis by any SEN school in Leicestershire, the learning team now offers a sustainable service that can be further developed. In themselves the Held in the

Hand resources crystallize what has been learned, namely that for this audience group the quality of the learning derives from the engagement potential of the museum objects used. Objects must be able to draw participants in; to instill a desire to handle and question; and to allow children to imprint their own feelings, experiences, and memories onto the objects used. In this regard it is imperative to use objects that properly reflect these characteristics. The lessons learned with the Held in Hand boxes have now been applied to an additional resource called Touch Tables which are more secure, more robust, and, although developed for older people with late-stage dementia, can also be used effectively with young adults with learning disabilities and children with SEN.

Another program, Memory Plus, was researched, developed, and launched during 2012 to support vulnerable adults with dementia in both care homes and in day care. Up to 60 care homes a year will benefit from the project, which is both a training program and a set of dedicated themed resources that together assist care staff in the delivery of meaningful and engaging activities. Memory Plus aims to address key issues in the UK's National Dementia Strategy 2009, namely:

- fifty-four percent of carers reported that their relative did not have enough to do in a care home;
- the availability of activities is a major determinant of quality of life but these activities are seldom available;
- care staff enjoy providing activities and would like to be able to do more of it.

The training given to care staff includes:

- object handling skills and how to use the resource boxes;
- how to use object alongside other creative forms such as music and dance;
- how to evaluate the impact of the resources and activities;
- a toolkit of activity ideas to take away with them;
- training updates every three months covering specific skills, for example, drama, music, movement, art, or poetry;
- mentoring, support, and guidance.

The impact on the adults in care has been dramatic. One care resident commented that "It made us feel like real people and so valued. Thank you so much" (Care resident 2012).

But specialist partnership working is also essential for other vulnerable groups, and even the smallest institutions can make a difference. The independent Sir John Moore Foundation (Sir John Moore Foundation n.d.), in Northwest Leicestershire, UK, has been in existence since 1697. It gained a new lease of life in 2003–2004 with a local campaign to restore its seventeenth-century building, originally designed by Sir Christopher Wren, and keep it in use as the home of the village primary school.

Today the foundation has four areas in which it works: Heritage (and conservation), Learning (for all), Community (and social wellbeing), and Enterprise (and innovation). Despite its small size, village location, and heavy reliance on volunteers, the Foundation has gained national recognition for its work, in partnership with its local authority, with teenagers in challenging circumstances, including young offenders, those with emotional, social, and behavioral difficulties, those in care, who are at risk of exclusion from school or who are NEET (not in education, employment, or training).

Using the site's social history to demonstrate links between lives in the past and the challenges faced by the participants ignites their firm, occasionally unconventional and often vociferous view of fairness and morality. Examples such as the site's nineteenth-century punishment log, which recorded every cane stroke and the reasons for them, reveals to today's youth that their less acceptable activities are nothing new; a fact often met with incredulity. The site's wide range of original eighteenth- and nineteenth-century graffiti invites them to consider their own vandalism. For example, the measures taken by the nineteenth-century school governors to separate rich pupils from poorer village children who were forced to attend after the Education Act 1872 stimulate comparisons with today:

> the punishment book is cool. Caning them didn't work though because the same boys are in it again and again. They were done for the same things as me! I got done for vandalism. And for bullying people. They took money off smaller boys. I swore at a teacher and got excluded. (Matthew)

Conclusions

This chapter began with a reference to the slow, uneven, but real growth in museum-visiting in the United States over the past four years, with museum directors putting this down largely to better exhibitions and marketing. In the United Kingdom, there has been a decade of growth. In the first *Taking Part* survey, for 2005/2006 (DCMS 2005–), 42 percent of the adult population of England visited museums at least once a year (Aust and Vine 2007). In 2012/2013, this had risen to 52 percent. This period saw not only the provision of central government revenue funding to local museums, noted above, but also very substantial capital funding from the Heritage Lottery Fund (HLF), a body charged with investing part of the income from the UK's national lottery in relevant heritage projects. Major new and refurbished museums have become a feature of the arts landscape nationwide. So, as in the USA, better museums and museum experiences, supported by better marketing has made a major difference.

But, does this mean that English museums successfully attracted previous non-user groups? Stuart Davies, in his research on UK museum visitors since 1991,

TABLE 6.4   Shifting proportions of
socioeconomic classes visiting UK museums

	ABC1 (%)	C2DE (%)
1991	55	45
1994	56	44
1999	66	34
2003	75	25
2005/2006	72	28

Source: Davies 2007, 366

suggests that there is evidence of a substantial shift to a greater proportion of higher occupational class visitors (ABC1) compared to those from lower occupational classes (C2DE), shown in Table 6.4.

Davies discusses potential reasons for this apparent failure in what has been a major museum and government agenda in the UK to broaden the audience base. He points out that the population as a whole has become more middle class but also that the table charts proportions, not actual numbers. Davies further suggests that there is a possibility more C2DEs are visiting, but even more ABC1s are doing so.

So, an enhanced museum experience, supported by better marketing, *will* make a real difference to visitation – although this may not be sustainable in the UK, in the face of average cuts to revenue budgets of 20 percent since 2010, with more to come (Steel 2013). If the vision and funding can be sustained, however, the development of increasingly participative museum experiences that meet the needs and expectations of new generations could lead to a golden age for museums.

But this will not necessarily make a difference to use by those from lower socioeconomic groups, or from marginalized communities. Here, sustained commitment of a different kind is required. The attitude among communities that a museum "doesn't relate to me" will only fully disappear when those communities are not only welcomed into the museum but also become an inclusive part of it – in the collections; in the histories presented; in the programming; in the development of multiple perspectives within exhibitions; and in the staff. And representation means not only the presence of relevant objects, and the relationship that people can have with them through the museum, but a public recognition of the contributions communities have made to society at large. These issues cannot be combated in a piecemeal manner. They require a strategic response, seen for example in the approach to the Audience Development Plan promoted in the UK by the Heritage Lottery Fund (HLF 2010b). In doing so it is hoped that we may yet be able to develop audiences for the twenty-first-century museum.

References

AAM (American Alliance of Museums). 1972. *Museums: Their New Audience. A Report to the Department of Housing and Urban Development by a Special Committee of the American Association of Museums*. Washington, DC: American Association of Museums.

AAM (American Alliance of Museums). 2002. *Mastering Civic Engagement: A Challenge to Museums*. Washington, DC: American Association of Museums.

AAM (American Alliance of Museums). 2013. "American Museums Reflect Slow Economic Recovery in 2012." Accessed September 25, 2014. http://www.aam-us.org/docs/research/acme-2013-final.pdf.

ACE (Arts Council England). 2011. "Arts Audiences: Insight." Accessed September 25, 2014. http://www.artscouncil.org.uk/media/uploads/pdf/arts_audience_insight_2011.pdf.

AEA Consulting. 2005. "Tyne and Wear Museum, Bristol's Museums, Galleries and Archives: Social Impact Programme Assessment." Accessed September 25, 2014. http://tynewear2.sumodesign.co.uk/about/corporatedocuments/documents/Social_Impact.pdf.

Alexander, Edward P. 1979. *Museums in Motion: An Introduction to the History and Functions of Museums*. Nashville, TN: American Association for State and Local History.

ALVA (Association of Leading Visitor Attractions). 2013. "Visits Made in 2012 to Visitor Attractions in Membership with ALVA." Accessed September 25, 2014. http://www.alva.org.uk/details.cfm?p=423.

AMARC (Australian Museum Audience Research Centre). 2003. "Audience Research Unit." Accessed September 25, 2014. http://australianmuseum.net.au/Audience-Research.

Americans for the Arts. n.d. "Animating Democracy." Accessed September 25, 2014. http://animatingdemocracy.org.

Aust, Rebecca, and Lisa Vine, eds. 2007. *Taking Part: The National Survey of Culture, Leisure and Sport, Annual Report 2005/6*. London: Department for Culture, Media and Sport.

Baloglu, Seyhmus, and Muzzafer Uysal. 1996. "Market Segments of Push and Pull Motivations: A Canonical Correlation Approach." *International Journal of Contemporary Hospitality Management* 8(3): 32–38.

Bennett, Tony, Mike Savage, Elizabeth Silva, Alan Warde, Gayo-Cal Mosdesto, and David Wright. 2009. *Culture, Class, Distinction*. Abingdon: Routledge.

Bodo, Simona, Kirsten Gibbs, and Margherita Sani, eds. 2009. "Museums as Places for Intercultural Dialogue: Selected Practices from Europe. European Commission: MAP for ID." Accessed September 25, 2014. http://www.ne-mo.org/fileadmin/Dateien/public/service/Handbook_MAPforID_EN.pdf.

Bourdieu, Pierre. 1984. *Distinction: A Social Critique of the Judgement of Taste*. Translated by Richard Nice. Cambridge, MA: Harvard University Press.

Bridge, Andrea, and Jemma Atkin-Barrett. 2011. "An Evaluation Report of the Sharing Stories Intergenerational Project." Accessed September 25, 2014. http://www.leics.gov.uk/sharingstoriesintergenerationalprojectreport.pdf.

Bunting, Catherine, Jennifer Godleib, Michelle Jobson, Emily Keaney, Anni Oskala, and Adrienne Skelton. 2007. "Informing Change: Taking part in the Arts: Survey Findings from the First Twelve Months." Arts Council of England. Accessed September 25, 2014. http://www.artscouncil.org.uk/media/uploads/downloads/takingp.pdf.

Cabinet Office. 2001. *Preventing Social Exclusion: Report by the Social Exclusion Unit*. London: Cabinet Office.

CCUC (Centre for Cultural Understanding and Change). 2008. Field Museum, Chicago. Accessed September 25, 2014. www.fieldmuseum.org/ccuc.

Cohen-Gewerc, Elie, and Robert Stebbins. 2013. *Serious Leisure and Individuality*. Montreal: McGill-Queen's University Press.

Dana, John Cotton. 1917. *The New Museum*. Woodstock, VT: Elm Tree.

Danilov, V. J. 2009. *Ethnic Museums and Heritage Sites in the United States*. Jefferson, NC: McFarland.

Davies, Stuart. 2007. "Commentary 2: One Small Part. Taking Part and Museums." *Cultural Trends* 16(4): 361–371.

Davis, Peter. 2008. "New Museologies and the Ecomuseum." In *The Ashgate Research Companion to Heritage and Identity*, edited by Brian Graham and Peter Howard, 397–414. Aldershot, UK: Ashgate.

DCMS (Department for Culture, Media and Sport). 2005–. *The Taking Part Survey*. Accessed September 25, 2014. https://www.gov.uk/government/organisations/department-for-culture-media-sport/series/taking-part.

DCMS, Arts Council England, English Heritage, Museums, Libraries, and Archives Council, Sport England. 2010. "Understanding the Drivers, Impact and Value of Engagement in Culture and Sport." Accessed September 25, 2014. https://www.gov.uk/government/uploads/system/uploads/attachment_data/file/71231/CASE-supersummaryFINAL-19-July2010.pdf.

Destination Analysts. 2009. *State of the American Traveler Survey 2008*. Accessed September 25, 2014, www.destinationanalysts.com/SATSJuly2008.pdf.

Dodd, Jocelyn, and Richard Sandell. 1998. *Building Bridges*. London: Museums and Galleries Commission.

ETC Research Group. 2005. "City Tourism and Culture: The European Experience. A Report for the Research Group of the European Travel Commission and World Tourism Organization)." Accessed September 25, 2014. www.stnet.ch/files/?id=9490.

HLF (Heritage Lottery Fund). 2010a. "Investing in Success: Heritage and the UK Tourism Economy." Accessed September 25, 2014. www.hlf.org.uk/aboutus/howwework/Documents/HLF_Tourism_Impact_single.pdf.

HLF (Heritage Lottery Fund). 2010b. "Thinking about Audience Development." Accessed September 25, 2014. http://www.hlf.org.uk/HowToApply/goodpractice/Documents/Thinking_about_audience_development.pdf.

Holo, Selma. 2009. "Ethnic-Specific Museums: Why They Matter and How They Make a Difference." In *Beyond the Turnstile: Making the Case for Museums and Sustainable Values*, edited by Selma Holo and Mari-Tere Alvarez, 40–44. Lanham, MD: AltaMira.

Hood, Marilyn G. 1983. "Staying Away: Why People Choose Not to Visit Museums." *Museum News* April: 50–57.

Hood, Marilyn G. 1993. "After 70 Years of Audience Research, What Have We Learned? Who Comes to Museums, Who Does Not, and Why?" *Visitor Studies* 5(1): 16–27.

IMLS (Institute for Museum and Library Services). 2007. *Outcome Based Evaluation Overview*. Washington, DC: Institute for Museum and Library Services.

IOM (International Organization for Migration). 2010. "World Migration Report." Accessed September 25, 2014. http://publications.iom.int/bookstore/free/WMR_2010_ENGLISH.pdf.

Janes, Robert R. 2009. *Museums in a Troubled World*. London: Routledge.

Kelly, Lynda. 2007. "The Inter-relationships between Adult Museum Visitors' Learning Identities and Their Museum Experiences." PhD thesis, University of Technology, Sydney.

Leadbeater, Charles. 2009. "The Art of With: An Original Essay for Cornerhouse." Cornerhouse, Manchester. Accessed September 26, 2014. www.cornerhouse.org/media/Learn/The%20Art%20of%20With.pdf.

Leicestershire County Council. 2011. "Opening Minds: Mental Health, Creativity and the Open Museum." Accessed September 26, 2014. http://www.leics.gov.uk/opening mindsreport.pdf.

Levine Museum. n.d. "Changing Places." Accessed October 1, 2014. http://www.museumofthenewsouth.org/exhibits/detail/?ExhibitId=94.

Low, Theodore Lewis. 1942. *The Museum as a Social Instrument*. New York: Metropolitan Museum of Art.

McCarthy, Kevin F., and Kimberly Jinnett. 2001. "A New Framework for Building Participation in the Arts." Rand Corporation. Accessed September 26, 2014. http://www.rand.org/content/dam/rand/pubs/monograph_reports/2005/MR1323.pdf.

McKercher, Bob, and Hilary du Cros. 2002. *Cultural Tourism: The Partnership between Tourism and Cultural Heritage Management*. New York: Haworth Hospitality Press.

Merriman, Nick. 1991. *Beyond the Glass Case: The Past, the Heritage and the Public in Britain*. Leicester: Leicester University Press.

Missouri History Society. n.d. "History Happened Here." Accessed September 26, 2014. www.historyhappenedhere.org.

MLAC (Museums, Libraries, and Archives Council). n.d. "Inspiring Learning for All." Accessed September 26, 2014. www.inspiringlearningforall.gov.uk.

MLAC (Museums, Libraries, and Archives Council). 2001. *Renaissance in the Regions: A New Vision for England's Museums*. London: Museums, Libraries, and Archives Council.

MLAC (Museums, Libraries, and Archives Council). 2004. *Visitors to Museums and Galleries 2004*. London: Museums, Libraries, and Archives Council.

Museums Association. 2008. *Code of Ethics for Museums*. Accessed September 26, 2014. http://www.museumsassociation.org/download?id=944515,

National Trust. 2010a. *Going Local: A Guide to Our New Shape and Ways of Working*. Swindon: National Trust. Accessed September 26, 2014. http://asp-gb.secure-zone.net/v2/index.jsp?id=493/595/970&startPage=3.

National Trust. 2010b. *Going Local: Annual Report 2009–2010*. Swindon: National Trust.

National Trust. 2012. *Going Local: Annual Report 2011–2012*. Swindon: National Trust.

NEA (National Endowment for the Arts). 2009. *2008 Survey of Public Participation in the Arts*. Washington, DC: National Endowment for the Arts.

The Network. n.d. Accessed September 26, 2014. www.seapn.org.uk.

Nowlen, Phil. 2009. Video interview for Centre for the Future of Museums' *Voices of the Future*. Accessed September 26, 2014. http://www.youtube.com/watch?v=VzG1Iua_j7k.

O'Neill, Mark. 2010. "Cultural Attendance and Public Mental Health – From Research to Practice." *Journal of Public Mental Health* 9(4): 22–29.

OP&A (Office of Policy and Analysis). 2007a. "2030 Vision: Anticipating the Needs and Expectations of Museum Visitors of the Future." Smithsonian Institution. Accessed October 1, 2014. http://www.si.edu/content/opanda/docs/rpts2007/07.07.2030vision.final.pdf.

OP&A (Office of Policy and Analysis). 2007b. "Museum Visitation as a Leisure Time Choice." Smithsonian Institution. Accessed October 1, 2014. http://www.si.edu/Content/opanda/docs/Rpts2007/07.10.LeisureVisitation.Final.pdf.

Orend, Richard J. 1989. *Socialization and Participation in the Arts*. Princeton, NJ: Princeton University Press.

Pitman, Bonnie, and Ellen Hirzy. 2011. *Ignite the Power of Art: Advancing Visitor Engagement in Museums*. New Haven, CT: Yale University Press and Dallas Museum of Art.

Prentice, Richard. 2004. "Tourist Familiarity and Imagery." *Annals of Tourism Research* 31(4): 923–945.

Rabinovitch, Victor. 2003. "Museums Facing Trudeau's Challenge: The Informal Teaching of History." *Canadian Issues* October, 36–41. Accessed September 26, 2014. http://www.civilization.ca/research-and-collections/research/resources-for-scholars/essays-1.

Rainie, Lee. 2006. "Life Online: Teens and Technology and the World to Come." Paper presented at Annual Conference of the Public Library Association, Boston, MA, March 23.

Richards, Greg, ed. 2001. *Cultural Attractions in European Tourism*. Wallingford, UK: CABI Publishing.

Silverman, Lois H. 2010. *The Social Work of Museums*. London: Routledge.

Sir John Moore Foundation. n.d. Accessed September 26, 2014. http://www.sirjohnmoore.org.uk.

Stebbins, Robert. 2009. *Leisure and Consumption: Common Ground, Separate Worlds*. London: Palgrave Macmillan.

Steel, Patrick. 2013. "MA Warns of Museum Closures Ahead." Museums Association website. Accessed September 26, 2014. http://www.museumsassociation.org/news/18062013-museums-association-warns-of-museum-closures-ahead.

Tourism Research Australia. 2008. "Snapshot: Cultural and Heritage Tourism in Australia 2008." Accessed September 26, 2014. http://www.australiacouncil.gov.au/research/arts_sector/reports_and_publications/cultural_tourism.

US Department of Commerce and the President's Committee on the Arts and Humanities. 2005. "A Position Paper on Cultural and Heritage Tourism." US Cultural and Heritage Tourism Summit, Washington, DC. Accessed September 26, 2014. http://www.pcah.gov/sites/default/files/05WhitePaperCultHeritTourism_2.pdf.

Vargas, J. A. 2007. "Students Make Connections at a Time of Total Disconnect." *The Washington Post*, April 17, Metro: Special Reports 10.

Varine, Hughes de. 1993. "Tomorrow's Community Museums." Lecture in the Senate Hall, University of Utrecht, October 15. Accessed September 26, 2014. http://assembly.coe.int/Museum/ForumEuroMusee/Conferences/tomorrow.htm.

Wallace Foundation. 2009. "Engaging Audiences: Report on the Wallace Foundation Arts Grantee Conference, Philadelphia PA 1–3 April 2009." Accessed September 26, 2014. www.wallacefoundation.org/KnowledgeCenter/KnowledgeTopics/CurrentAreasofFocus/ArtsParticipation/Documents/Engaging-Audiences-Wallaconference.pdf.

Wilkening, Susie, and James Chung. 2009. *Life Stages of the Museum Visitor: Building Engagement over a Lifetime*. Washington, DC: American Association of Museums.

Woroncow, Barbara. 2001. "Heritage for All: Ethnic Minority Attitudes to Museums and Heritage Sites." Paper presented at the ICOM Triennial Conference, Barcelona.

Worts, Doug. 2006. "Measuring Museum Meaning: A Critical Assessment Framework." *Journal of Museum Education* 31(1): 41–49. Accessed September 26, 2014. http://douglasworts.org/wp-content/uploads/2010/12/Measuring-Museum-Meaning.pdf.

Further Reading

Bott, Val, Alice Grant, and Jon Newman. 2005. *Revisiting Collections: Discovering New Meanings for a Diverse Audience*. London: London Museums Agency.

Chamberlain, Gregory. 2011. *Museum Public: Audience Development, Marketing Strategies and Brand Identity*. Milton Keynes, UK: Museum ID.

Collections Management Network. 2010. "Stories of the World: Collections and Communities: Revisiting Collections Implementation Research Report." Collections Trust. Accessed September 25, 2014. www.collectionslink.org.uk.

Culture Unlimited. 2009. *Museums of the Mind: Mental Health, Emotional Well-Being and Museums*. London: Culture Unlimited.

Denniston, Helen. 2003. *Holding up the Mirror: Addressing Cultural Diversity in London's Museums*. London: Helen Denniston Associates for London Museums Agency.

Dodd, Jocelyn, Richard Sandell, Annie Delin, and Jackie Gay. 2004. "Buried in the Footnotes: The Representation of Disabled People in Museum and Gallery Collections." Leicester: Research Centre for Museums and Galleries. Accessed September 26, 2014. http://www2.le.ac.uk/departments/museumstudies/rcmg/projects/buried-in-the-footnotes/BITF2.pdf.

Weaver, Stephanie. 2012. *Creating Great Visitor Experiences: A Guide for Museums, Parks, Zoos, Gardens and Libraries*. Walnut Creek, CA: Left Coast.

Graham Black is a Reader in Public History and Heritage Management at Nottingham Trent University, where he teaches on the MA program in Museum and Heritage Management. Graham is also a professional consultant with extensive experience in interpretation, exhibitions, and audience development work in galleries, museums, and heritage organizations in the United Kingdom. He is the author of *The Engaging Museum* (2005) and *Transforming Museums in the Twenty First Century* (2012).

PART II

Resources

7 BALANCING MISSION AND MONEY
Critical Issues in Museum Economics

Ted Silberberg and Gail Lord[1]

Museums have become highly valued as providers of content, leisure destinations, community forums, magnets for knowledge workers, and a means of revitalizing communities large and small. There are an increasing number of museums being created in countries and communities that need civic building blocks for a knowledge economy and for cultural tourism. A growing recognition of cultural identity among formerly marginalized people has motivated many museums to develop new collections or interpret existing collections in new ways based on research and community consultation. Contemporary issues, such as human rights, climate change, and worldwide migration have stimulated novel programs and activities. All these initiatives have expanded the mission of many museums, which have historically been focused on preserving collections for future generations, conducting research on the collections, interpreting them for the public, and providing an educational resource for schools and the community.

Of course all this programming and activity requires funding. It is the recognition of their vital and widening mission that has enabled museums to merit financial support from funders who generally understand that operating costs associated with the long-term mission-related responsibilities of museums far exceed the revenues that may be generated from admissions and other earned income. However, the ability or willingness of government and private funders to offer adequate levels of support has varied in recent decades, depending very much on politics and economic conditions. The worldwide economic recession in 2008–2009 added to governmental debt loads, which in turn has led to debt crisis in several countries, and major spending reductions and austerity measures in many other countries, states/provinces, and cities. Museums have not been immune from these cuts. Staff layoffs, a greater burden on remaining staff, reductions in operating hours, and less money allocated to exhibitions, public programs, and

The International Handbooks of Museum Studies: Museum Practice, First Edition.
Edited by Conal McCarthy.
© 2015 John Wiley & Sons Ltd. Published 2020 by John Wiley & Sons Ltd.

marketing, have all become increasingly commonplace. During these periods of financial restraint, museums have been forced to respond with strategies to boost earned income and control operating costs while seeking to meet their goals, both old and new. Museum economics is thus very much about achieving a balance between mission-related and financial imperatives.

In this chapter, our objective is not to explore every aspect of the economics of museum operations but rather to focus on what we consider to be some of the critical issues facing museum professionals today. The selected economic issues include admission charges, issues associated with various operating revenue centers and expenses, and the opportunities and risks of collaboration. The analysis reflects the substantial experience of the authors as consultants working in different types of museums in various parts of the world. The chapter focuses on practical operational matters. This is due in part to a recognition of the limited literature on museum economics, at least within museum studies itself.

The broader field of cultural economics has developed a more substantial literature, which touches on aspects of museum work, and applies tools of economic analysis to problems in the arts. Most noteworthy for the economics of museums are Feldstein (1991), Towse (1997), and Throsby (2001), while there has been some work on the economics of cultural heritage (Rizzo and Mignosa 2013). The revised edition of Ruth Towse's *A Handbook of Cultural Economics* (2011) covers topics such as museums, heritage, creative industries, and the economic impact of the arts. Bruno Frey's *Arts and Economics* (2003, Part II) describes museums and performing arts, collections use and access, superstar museums, special exhibitions and festivals, and the appearance of private museums. As Frey and Meier point out, cultural economics "applies economic thinking to the arts," and does not concern itself only with financial matters but "uses an economic model of human behaviour to understand social aspects of the arts" such as how staff actions are guided by the institutional setting, the main source of funding, and so on (Frey and Meier 2006a, 398). Museums, they argue, can be seen as an economic unit where inputs and outputs can be analyzed, as in this chapter, in terms of supply and demand. However, much remains to be done in terms of specific studies of the microeconomics of museums, and research in future should aim to explore in greater depth how museums will adapt to changing conditions in terms of government support and leisure patterns (Frey and Meier 2006b).

The paucity of research and writing about museum economics is perhaps not surprising given that it is only in the past 25 years that economists have begun to focus on the not-for-profit or "third" sector of the economy. Even though that sector is growing rapidly, museums and culture are a very small part of it compared to healthcare and education. Nevertheless, the work of economist Richard Florida (2002) has demonstrated the economic benefits of the cultural and creative sectors to economic competitiveness. Some publications deal more directly with practical aspects of financial management in museums (Lord and Lord 2009). For practical advice on budgets, financial planning, and other management and business matters, the reader is referred to Lord and Lord (2012). Our approach in this chapter has been to focus on museum economics as a distinctive topic of analysis in its own right, situated in relation to museum practice but reflecting, and not being reduced to, the wider context of the cultural sector and the economy as a whole. In critically reviewing current debates it is also important to emphasize that there is no categorically right or wrong answer because every museum is different. Trustees, senior management, and their advisors need to consider the special circumstances and objectives of their own museums to come up with solutions to meet their needs.

To charge or not to charge? The debate on admission charges

The question of whether or not museums should charge admission remains one of the most frequently debated issues in museum economics. Elaine Heumann Gurian has asserted that if museums really want to provide access to all then admission charges should be eliminated. Gurian wrote that museums "cannot argue that they hold the patrimony of all if only some can afford to see them." She continues "There is a fundamental disconnect between the mission statements we write and the act of imposing an entry fee" (Gurian 2005, 33). In this section, we survey the evidence on this issue, considering the effect and impact of free admission on other earned income, on membership, and on the audience profile, before looking at free admission museums and their visitors as well as trends among charged admission museums.

A common concern in relation to mission-related arguments for free admission is that implementation usually requires willingness by government and/or private funders to make up for lost admissions income. This occurred in the UK, for example, when national museums which charged admission in the 1980s reintroduced free admission in 2001. There are 67 national museums in the UK offering free admission, of which 25 are in London. As shown in the following table, from 2001 to 2010 the national museums in England that used to charge for entry reported an overall increase in attendance of nearly 151 percent (Table 7.1). However, research conducted for the Museum Association (Selwood and Davies 2005) showed that the increases were attributable not only to free admission but also substantial government investment into enhanced visitor experiences and facilities. Along with free admission came £1 billion in public lottery spending on museums. The Department for Culture, Media and Sport also increased funding to support operating costs by about £44 million each year to allow the former charging museums and galleries to offer free admission to their collections and displays (on cultural policy, see Selwood and Davies in this volume).

One criticism of free admission is that tourists from outside the UK, who account for about 25 percent of all visitors to the national museums, *expect* to pay

TABLE 7.1   Visits to museums that formerly charged admission (2010/11)

Museum	2000/2001	2010/2011	% change since 2000/2001
Imperial War Museum (London)	661,804	1,095,442	65.52%
Museum of Science and Industry (Manchester)	287,814	638,347	121.79%
National Maritime Museum	799,777	2,433,163	204.23%
National Museums Liverpool	710,210	2,622,228	269.22%
National Museum of Science and Industry (National Railway Museum)	485,785	630,396	29.77%
National Museum of Science and Industry (South Kensington)	1,366,879	2,766,994	102.43%
Natural History Museum (South Kensington)	1,630,466	4,682,783	187.21%
Natural History Museum (Tring)	61,272	126,864	107.05%
Royal Armouries	225,141	343,582	52.61%
Victoria & Albert Museum (South Kensington)	936,652	2,619,505	179.67%
Total	**7,165,800**	**17,959,304**	**150.63%**

Source: DCMS 2011.

admission and that British taxpayers should therefore not be subsidizing them. The counter argument is that the free admission policy helps to attract tourists, just as in the United States free admission to the Smithsonian helps to draw tourists to Washington DC. Others dispute this by asserting that a free admission policy for museums is not a primary motivation for selecting a country or city to visit (Travers 2006, 38). Another study in France concluded that free admission was a secondary consideration in decisions to attend museums (Le Gall-Ely et al. 2007, 23).

Is government funding of free admission sustainable in tough economic times? Some have suggested that with the economic downturn free admission among national museums "could become a thing of the past" (Haywood 2009, 13). However, this remains speculation as the government commitment to fund national museums appears to be holding, largely because of arguments based on mission (Dowd 2011, 3). The UK is not the only country to boost museum attendance through free admission. Although previous admission prices had been modest by western standards, the People's Republic of China introduced free admission to over 1800 museums in 2009. The result was that attendance levels increased on average by 50 percent to include visitors who had not previously attended (Xinhua English News 2012). The objective was to provide easy access to national heritage resources for all citizens and visitors. Some museums, however, have had to impose limits on the number of persons who may attend at one time in order to help limit the strain on facilities. As in the UK, the free admission policy in the PRC was accompanied by a massive program of building new museums and improving existing ones (Varutti 2014).

Whereas the main arguments that everyone should get free admission to museums are mission-related, there is an economic rationale too – that the free entry has a positive effect on other earned income through more spending for charged major exhibitions, retail, food, public programs, and entrepreneurial revenue centers such as pay-for photo/video opportunities. With admissions revenue generally accounting for only 10–15 percent of total operating income for charged admission museums, and sometimes less, a common argument is that larger numbers of visitors drawn to a museum as a result of free admission will lead to more income from these other revenue centers. Tate Modern and Tate Britain have consistently maintained free admission and earn a remarkable 50 percent of their revenue from charged special exhibitions, retail operations, rentals, and other earned income (Tate Report 2011–2012, 68–69).

There is some debate about whether free admission really leads to more ancillary spending. A study in the UK (Martin 2003) indicated that 47 percent of persons surveyed believed they would spend more money on different aspects of their trip to a museum or gallery than they would have spent when they had to pay admission. This of course only represents what people *say* they will do. The number of people who will *actually* spend more money on retail, food, special exhibitions, or other offerings when admission is free may be substantially less. Faye Steiner (1997) reported that visitors who did not pay an admission fee to a variety of museums were likely to spend substantially less on additional goods or services than the average visitor who paid a fee to enter. Her research indicated that total restaurant and retail purchases declined by almost 50 percent during a museum's free day despite a 300 percent increase in overall attendance. Since the purpose of the museum is primarily for people to engage with the exhibitions, while retailing is a secondary service, attracting more visitors is arguably more important; it would be more of a concern therefore if the opposite was the case.

When in 2006 the San José Museum of Art reinstated entry charges after five years of free admission, its rationale was that total gift shop and restaurant revenues had declined, despite a doubling of attendance to about 200,000. As Executive Director, Daniel Keegan, told a reporter, "When people know they don't have to open their wallets to get in, oftentimes they won't open them at all" (McFelter 2007). The ability to achieve higher non-admissions earned income as a consequence of larger numbers of visitors actually depends on how creative and entrepreneurial a museum is in taking advantage of larger visitor volumes. Satellite retail spaces may help to overcome the crowding in the gift shop that might have contributed to a decline in sales.

What effect does free admission have on membership in museums? Free admission is often stated to have a negative effect on both the total number of memberships, and the income generated from membership programs. While free admission very likely *does* reduce membership totals in most museums, it may not necessarily have a negative impact on membership income. This reflects the fact that there are generally two broad categories of membership, lower level and upper level. In lower level categories (individual, student, family) the motivation for membership is largely value for money; so the benefits of unlimited free admission, discounts on retail, food, programs and rentals, invitations to exclusive events, and other perks are considered a good deal. For some museums more membership income is derived from upper-level categories, which often have names like benefactor, sustainer, or patron. The primary motivation for upper-level membership is not value for money but rather philanthropy, based on civic pride and/or a belief in the mission and value of the museum. Among these members, who are in essence donors, free admission is often viewed positively because it provides access to people who need a museum the most.

This can be seen at the Baltimore Museum of Art, which eliminated general admission fees in October 2006. Over the next few years it experienced about a 10 percent decline in total memberships, but the museum saw substantial increases in revenue from upper-level members/donors, including contributions to an endowment whose funds are specifically earmarked to support loss of admissions income (Green 2011a). Art museums generally find it easier to attract upper-level members relative to zoos, science, and children's museums. However, some free admission art museums have large numbers of members (for example, the Cleveland Museum of Art and the Tate). Some museums in the United States actually experienced an increase in membership levels after introducing free admission, for example the Indianapolis Museum of Art and the Nelson-Atkins Art Museum in Kansas City (Green 2011a).

An important part of the argument for free admission is to increase access for people in lower education and income categories who are less likely to attend if they need to pay. But it is not clear that free admission really helps broaden the profile of those visitors attending museums. There is conflicting evidence. A UK study (Martin 2003, 4) reported that free admission had a very positive impact on attendance by people in all education, income, and age categories, but at the same time found that though there were a lot more visitors, the "profile of the typical population of museum or gallery visitors has remained relatively stable, and firmly biased in favor of the traditional visitor groups." More recent data indicates a growth in attendance by persons in lower-income categories (Youngs 2011). The Baltimore Museum of Art reported that free admission changed the profile of its visitors as African American attendance doubled from 10 percent to 20 percent of the total (McCauley 2007; Baltimore Museum of Art 2011). (On the issue of museums, audience, and social inclusion see Black this volume.)

In France the national museums set out to broaden their audience, both in the number and types of visitors, through a program trialed in 2008 in which 14 museums became free to all for a period of six months. It resulted in an average attendance increase of 52 percent. However, a report by the Cours des Comptes (national auditors) indicated that, even with free admission, the museums did not succeed in widening the audience to the extent anticipated (Cour des Comptes 2011). One of the key objectives of the free admission experiment was to increase the number of young people attending. In 2007, only 17 percent of national museum visitors were under 18 years of age. The goal of the Ministry of Culture and Communication was to increase this to 22 percent through free admission. Although there was an increase in the total number of young people, the increase in attendance among adults meant that the percentage of young people overall actually declined to about 16 percent. Following the six-month experiment of free admission for all, the government made a commitment the following year to offer free admission to young people on a permanent basis, not only for those 18 and under, but also for those 25 and under (Dowd 2011, 2).

Some corporate sponsors have recognized the value of free admission. Walmart, for example, donated $20 million to the new Crystal Bridges Museum of American Art in the company's headquarters of Bentonville, Arkansas, to cover admission fees for all visitors. "One of the greatest challenges for museums today is finding ways to remove barriers to community participation, including admission charges," said Don Bacigalupi, Crystal Bridges executive director. "Walmart has shown extraordinary vision and foresight in funding access to the museum, providing all that Crystal Bridges has to offer to all people at no cost," he said. "We know that this gift will allow the museum to become a daily resource in our community" (Philanthropy News Digest 2011).

In the debate over whether admission should be free to all visitors, what needs to be emphasized is that a substantial number of museums, even in the United States with its generally lower levels of governmental support, *do* offer free admission. Free admission museums are more common than perceived; many are federal, state, or university museums, or museums with large endowments, often established long ago specifically to enable free admission. Table 7.2 shows that in 2009 only about 59 percent of US museums charged admission fees of any amount. The table also shows that among art museums less than 48 percent charge and for history museums it is 49 percent. Also from 1989 to 2006 the trend was for more US museums to charge admission, but in 2009 there was a shift to lower charging. This may indicate the beginning of a trend, or it might be skewed by a somewhat smaller sample size that year. What is evident, however, is that median admission charges have been steadily and substantially increasing, even when taking rates of inflation into account.

For museums that charge admission there are sometimes categories of visitors who receive free entry, either as a requirement of funding support, or to seek to overcome a market weakness. For example, art museums, which often face challenges in attracting children, use free admission to encourage parents to bring their children. Other museums offer free admission to children and school groups, which is often an effective strategy for attracting corporate or other sponsorships. Among museums that charge, it is common to offer free admission days or evenings, whether once per week or month. At the Museo de Oro in Bogota Columbia there is free admission every Sunday, and free admission all the time for children aged 12 and under, and seniors aged 60 and older. The Art Gallery of Ontario in Toronto offers weekday free admission after 3 p.m. to high-school students. These free periods are popular and lead to much higher than average attendance levels during the designated time offered. They are also inexpensive to market, as potential visitors find out about them through word of mouth and social media. An alternative view is that free admission periods should be discouraged as they cause people who can afford to pay to wait for the free admission times.

For some museums free admission periods are offered only if sponsored by private or government sources. In Chicago, a specific number of free admission days are mandated by the municipality in return for receiving financial support. Lastly, the complicated revenue implications of free admission periods may be observed from the experience of the Los Angeles County Museum of Art. Free admission periods were so popular that admissions income declined to only 3.3 percent of total revenue (from a sector average of 10–15 percent), which raised the question of why admission should be charged at all (Green 2011b).

To conclude this section of the chapter, we consider some recent trends among museums which charge for admission. It appears that some museums have been eliminating admission charges altogether or else reducing them substantially, while others have been increasing charges to boost earned income during times of reduced government and private support. Increased charges are also intended to convey the substantial cultural value of what the museum offers to visitors, such as rare collections and spectacular architecture. When in 2006 the Museum of Modern Art in New York (which receives no government support) introduced a $20 admission charge it caused a major stir, but many others soon followed: the Metropolitan Museum of Art in New York announced in June 2011 that it was raising its suggested (and strongly encouraged) adult admission charge from $20 to $25, one of the first institutions to cross the $20 threshold for museum admission charges in North America.

Substantially higher admission charges generally result in lower attendance levels but higher revenue per visitor, and it also tends to increase the value of membership. Moreover, higher admission charges may help to demonstrate to private and government funders that a museum is doing all it can to boost earned income levels. It may even be argued that lower attendance as a result of high admission charges may have a positive financial impact on the bottom line because fewer visitors means lower staffing needs and reduced occupancy costs, with less wear and tear on the building. On the other hand, admission charges perceived to be excessive may suggest to funders that a museum is making too much money and thus, they may reason, needs less contributed and grant income.

With respect to specific admission charges, every museum is different and the key for each is to find the right balance that takes into account the nature and quality of the visitor experience, the size of the space and length of stay in the museum,

TABLE 7.2 Admission charges at US museums

2009 AAM profile	Art museum	Children's or youth museum	General museum	Historic home or site	History museum or historical society	Living collections	Natural History or Anthropology	Science or Tech	Specialized museum	Overall 2009 survey	Overall 2006 survey	Overall 1999 survey	Overall 1989 survey
Sample size	156	18	71	89	190	17	32	25	73	**671**	809	1080	8189
Median attendance	44,878	130,870	58,500	11,700	10,000	208,574	58,176	357,103	22,000	**26,500**	33,446	27,175	50,000
% charging admission fees	47.6%	94.1%	63.2%	77.4%	49.2%	64.3%	63.3%	96.0%	57.1%	**59.0%**	60.7%	56.5%	55.1%
Median adult admission charge (US$)	$8.00	$7.50	$7.00	$6.00	$5.00	$8.00	$8.00	$10.00	$7.00	**$7.00**	$6.00	$4.00	$2.00

Source: American Association of Museums (now called the American Alliance of Museums), Financial Surveys, 2009, 2006, 1999, 1989; https://www.aam-us.org/ProductCatalog/Product?ID=222.

admission charges at other museums in the community, and admission charges of the same museum type elsewhere. Regarding the issue of length of stay, a proposal for "pay as you go pricing" (Frey and Steiner 2010) suggests that museums should be free to enter, and that visitors should pay for time spent in the museum when they exit – this is akin to the scheme operating in parking lots in which people pay a varying amount when exiting according to how long they have parked there.

What comes in: other revenue centers

Having described the issue of revenue from admission charges, we now turn to look at the main ways in which museums earn income other than from charging at the door. With the exception of the United States, most museums around the world receive more financial support from government than from any other source of income, often in the range of 50–70 percent or more of total operating revenues. In the United States there is more substantial private support for museums, at 37 percent of operating revenue, with earned income at 28 percent, government grants at 24 percent, and 11 percent from endowment/investments (Merritt and Katz 2009). In Canada, the UK and the USA, it is common for museums to generate about 25–30 percent of their revenue from earned sources, with admission revenues often accounting for 10–15 percent of total operating income.

Earned income may be generated from visitors, including admissions and retail, and from other sources that do not depend on visitors. Most museums have strategies for increasing attendance levels, but it should be remembered that income from rentals, fundraising events, public and educational programs, and memberships is not directly affected by attendance levels. Increasing attendance is an important performance indicator of museums not only because of objectives of higher earned income but also because, as pointed out in their missions and policy, they are there to serve the public, and because many private and government funders wish to see a return on their investment in the form of high levels of attendance.

Strategies to increase attendance levels relate primarily to the visitor experience offered by the museum through its exhibits, programs, and events, and whether it is compelling enough to attract visitors or offers the variety needed to motivate repeat visitation. The drive to boost attendance levels also builds upon the museum's knowledge and understanding of the preferences and motivations of existing and potential audiences, seen in economic terms as "market segments." This in turn leads to the development of effective programming and "products" such as exhibitions, marketing and pricing initiatives, and other activities, all pitched at these target audiences (on this topic see Black and Davidson, both in this volume).

However, the focus in this section of the chapter is not on direct revenues from visitor attendance as such, but rather on other revenue centers in contemporary museums. Within each revenue category discussed below, we review the economic issues that repeatedly demonstrate the need for museums to balance mission and economic imperatives, and also to plan how to best meet their own particular objectives in relation to their particular context and circumstances. These revenue centers include:

- retail
- food service
- facility rentals
- public and educational programs
- fundraising events
- membership
- other earned sources
- private support (donations and sponsorships)
- endowment/investment
- government support.

The first such issue concerns retail, more specifically, the implications of retail product lines to mission and profitability. For many museums the income from retail sales is only exceeded by admissions and membership as an earned income source, and may sometimes exceed one or both of them. The amount that may be earned from retail sales depends primarily on attendance, but also on other factors such as the exposure of the museum store to non-visitors, the size of the public retail space, and the product lines offered, both within the store and increasingly online. One of the issues facing museum management is whether the store product line should extend to items with a questionable relationship to the mission and collection of a museum. The rationale for doing so is that the income generated goes to support the museum's other mission-related responsibilities.

There also appears to be an economic rationale for a mission-related product line, as seen in a survey of Museum Store Association members in 2009 that included the question: "What strategy or tactic was most successful in increasing your *sales*?" Low on the list of responses was "Product development based on the museum and collection." However, when questioned about strategies or tactics to boost *profits* it was reported that product development specific to the museum/collection ranked much higher. This suggests that a product line consistent with the mission and collections-focus of a museum is also important to profitability, largely because the uniqueness of the museum product line allows for higher prices to be charged and accepted (Museum Store Association 2009).

An innovative example of museum retail can be seen in Ghana where the Museum and Monuments Board operates the National Museum and former slave transit sites such as Elmina and Cape Coast Castles. Many of these national historic sites extend the benefits of attracting tourists to local merchants and craftspeople by featuring community bazaars in which farmers, merchants, and craftspeople sell all manner of items from food and clothes to craft and artwork. The historic sites benefit from the activity created by these bazaars.

Another key issue is whether museums should have a restaurant or café. Restaurants in the private sector are the business type with the highest rate of bankruptcy in the USA (Parsa et al. 2005). It is therefore not surprising that, unlike retail stores, which are primarily operated by museum staff, restaurant or café operations are usually contracted out to private operators, often for very little gain to the museum. Only 32 percent of the museums surveyed by the American Association of Museums (AAM) had food-service facilities in 2009 (Merritt and Katz 2009). This reflects the high capital costs of kitchen and servery equipment and space requirements, as well as the limited operating income available from food service. The AAM survey showed that among museums with food-service operations, food accounted for only 1.6 percent of gross operating income and 0.6 percent of net income, confirming that a museum café is primarily a visitor service and usually not a significant revenue generator.

Visitor service itself, however, is very important. There are alternative options: prepackaged foods and beverages, or discount arrangements with nearby restaurants (depending on the site), which may contribute to economic development through downtown revitalization. However, there are cultural differences. In Europe it would be generally unacceptable for a museum not to have a café or restaurant, and to expect people to walk to a nearby café then return. An exception is the Paris contemporary art museum, Fondation Cartier, which does not have its own café, but encourages visitors to eat at any of six commercial restaurants nearby.

Another issue to be considered is facility rentals, the fastest-growing museum revenue center. Although, as we saw above, cafés or restaurants are not revenue generators for most museums, evening events and other rental opportunities may be very substantial income sources as they enable a museum to generate funds from spaces that would otherwise not be used during hours in which the institution is closed. The trend over the past two decades is for museum buildings to incorporate space that can be hired out, for example larger, more elegant lobbies connected to chair/table storage and catering kitchens. The National Constitution Center in Philadelphia was built with rentals in mind and reported that 40 percent of earned revenue is from rentals business. Other institutions, such as the Indianapolis Museum of Art, have been expanded to include separate banquet facilities and secondary entrances, allowing them to offer evening openings for the general public while a private rental takes place, as well as private daytime events during opening hours. However, this adds to capital and operating costs for single-purpose spaces that are otherwise unused.

For the large majority of museums the lobby/foyer is the primary space to rent out, and so a choice must be made, for either evening corporate events, or remaining open to the public. The former is chosen primarily for economic reasons, since it would take the admissions and other revenue from a substantial numbers of visitors to equal the amount that may be earned from an evening rental. In Paris, museum rentals are increasingly important not only for banquets but also as venues for film and commercial use. Having the building seen in a movie is regarded as a marketing advantage that prompts some museums to offer much lower rates for film-makers than for banquets. For example, the Museum of Jewish Art and History in Paris charges an evening rental at €500 for the shooting of a documentary and €2,500 for a fiction movie, whereas the price reaches €10,000 for a private or corporate event.

The benefits of rentals are not limited to earned income. Private and government funders are more likely to be aware of a museum and its need for contributed income if they attend a rental event. One of the errors made by museums is to underprice private-sector hotel, banquet hall, and other facilities. This is inappropriate because museums receive financial support from government and private funders and it therefore constitutes unfair competition. It is better for museums to charge at rates the same or higher than private sector competitors for rentals business. Fewer rentals and more income per rental also reduce wear and tear on a building.

Another source of revenue that museums are exploring today is public programs, but this raises issues to do with what level to charge at. Obviously public programs are important to achieving the mission of a museum, and many are free with admission because of mission-related responsibilities. Some museums offer registered programs, sleepovers, summer camps, and other programs for which fees are charged. These programs may or may not generate substantial income, but they do add to the benefits of membership. Given the need to boost earned income, the trend has been to identify popular public programs which have the capacity to generate as much revenue as possible. Birthday parties, once exclusively organized by children's museums, are now offered by many different institutions. Some museums, especially smaller ones like the Galena Historical Society and Museum in Illinois, have eliminated all programs that are not profitable or at least break even.

However, it must be noted that reference to "break even" or "profit" in museums focuses on direct costs and usually does not take into account overheads and other indirect costs. Sometimes the relationship of revenue-focused public programs to a museum's mission is questionable. For example, some museums offer exercise classes or beer festivals because it helps to offset some of the costs associated with free programming. Some funders are positive about programming that is not mission-related, viewing management as entrepreneurial in seeking to maximize earned income, but for others the inconsistency with mission is troubling.

School field trips and other educational programs are particularly important to the mission of all museums and are often free. Museum management must decide whether special staff or docent-led programming, opportunities which go beyond standard gallery tours, should be charged or free, and if free whether sponsorship support should be sought to help offset the costs. In fact, sponsorship of educational programs is very common in North America and serves as an example of how museum mission can be lined up very well with economic considerations, because education is a primary motivator of contributed income, both public and private. For example the Newseum, which is located in the largely free admission Washington DC marketplace, has a current adult admission charge of $22.95 (Newseum 2014) but all regional school group admissions and programs receive free admission sponsored by a local newspaper and radio station.

One issue that often arises in relation to commercialized programming is the frequency of fundraising events. Unlike donations and sponsorships, which are contributed income, fundraising events are earned income. Gala dinners and other fundraising events are an essential source of annual operating income for many museums. However, there is debate about whether such events encourage donations or sponsorship support or are a substitute for it, that is to say, if donations income declines because funders have supported a fundraising event then the event will not have had the net positive impact desired. One problem with fundraising events, which we have encountered in our work with museums, is that they tend to wear out volunteers, so it is therefore becoming increasingly common for museums to limit major funds development initiatives to one per year or even every second year.

Museum foundations, "friends," or membership organizations are important for museums in terms of fundraising. Museums usually categorize all membership income as earned because a higher percentage of earned income is viewed by funders as a positive performance indicator. Membership revenue, however, is truly both earned and contributed. Lower-level categories (individual, family) generate earned income, while upper-level revenue is very much contributed, because the motivation for upper-level membership is primarily philanthropic, based on a love for the museum, its mission, and/or civic pride, which contrasts with a desire for value among lower-level members. Consequently, a critical issue for museums is whether they should focus more effort on attracting and retaining upper- or lower-level members. The argument in favor of focusing on upper-level memberships is that the revenues may be substantially higher, particularly among art, history, and specialized museums. Children's museums, science centers, and zoos attract mainly lower-level memberships but tend to lose them once children get older.

What are the other sources of earned income that museums are currently exploring? There are a variety of sources: these include charges for photo or video opportunities, sleepovers, publications, genealogy services, interactive donation boxes, and other entrepreneurial ideas. The amounts generated may not be substantial but they do help to convey the message to funders and stakeholders that a museum is doing all that it can to boost earned income levels.

As more and more cities seek to distinguish themselves through cultural offerings, museums have become sought-after partners in real-estate developments and mixed-use projects. Sometimes developers can get planning gains or tax relief as part of the project. In most instances, the museum benefits by receiving an infusion of capital for the building. An alternative that benefits operations is to negotiate an annual fee from the development for the added value that the museum brings. The Museum of Modern Art in New York still receives a regular stream of revenue from a "mixed-use" project that opened in 1984 when it sold its air-rights to a developer, who added about 46 floors of condominiums to the six-story museum. The initial sale paid for the museum's expansion and renovation, and the organization now gets a portion of the condominium-owners' annual fees. Mixed-use development involves a combination of residential, commercial, cultural, or industrial uses that are integrated into the same building or project, and have become increasingly important for museums because they may share capital costs with developers and potentially gain operating income from condominium fees or hotel room night surcharges.

What about contributed income? In many countries museums receive very little in the way of contributions, philanthropy, or private support in the form of donations, sponsorships, and board annual giving. This is in contrast to the USA where private support exceeds both earned income and government grants. In part this is because of favorable US tax laws, but it is also due to a long-standing tradition of private support for museums.

Private donations and sponsorship support in the USA and in some other countries are important for funding core operations, such as the replacement of permanent exhibitions, and also the temporary exhibitions program. This external funding helps to justify increased admission charges, but has other indirect benefits by making new exhibits possible, helping the museum boost first-time and repeat visitation levels, add value to membership, and expose more people to other revenue centers. Research in New Zealand points to the important intangible benefits that are part of a long-term relationship between the museum and the corporate organization, rather than simply a one-off financial deal such as sponsorship (Major and Sutherland 2007).

Many museums employ development staff to secure and maintain giving, donations, and sponsorships, and this appears to be a growing area of professional museum work. For these staff, there is a constant balance between the financial benefits of sponsorship and the price that sometimes has to be paid in terms of the sponsor's profile, their influence on decision-making, or other side-effects (see Chong in this volume). For the company involved in relationships with museums, their financial support turns philanthropy into investment and leads to expectations for high attendance levels in order for there to be a return on that investment. For most museums, agreeing to highly visible company brands is justified because it generates income to help fund other mission-related responsibilities. This affects museums at the level of governance as well. In most countries trustees are not expected to be donors to a museum, but in the USA, board annual giving is expected. There is debate, however, about the extent to which board members should be selected on the basis of their ability to donate money and whether they should really have to "give, get, or get off" to be considered valuable to the museum (on this point, see Lord in this volume).

Finally in this section, we consider another phenomenon, found largely in the USA, which is the development of endowment funds to support collections acquisition and operating costs. Some endowments were established many years ago and have grown to be valued at hundreds of millions of dollars. Investments, whether in equities or interest, are used to fund operations and help museums to offer free admission or other subsidized programs. For US museums the median figure for endowment income is about 11 percent of annual operating income. For art museums it is about 19 percent (Merritt and Katz 2009). In contrast to these private funds, in India an endowment, or "corpus" fund was established by the national government to support the development of seven free-admission museums intended to continue the message of Mahatma Gandhi. This fund accounts for about 80 percent of the total operating budgets of those museums (Chhabra 2010, 92).

In 2008–2009 when the value of equities and interest payouts plunged in the financial crises, endowment principals also declined, causing severe hardship for museums dependent on them. However, for new museums, and existing ones without an endowment, it is debatable whether it is worth establishing one, when it takes $1 million at 4 percent interest or return-on-investment to pay the salary and benefits of only one lower-level member of staff.

What goes out: operating expenses

In this section we turn to the other side of the ledger and examine operating expenses and the efforts museums are making to control their spending. In our experience, funders who themselves are reducing spending in a recession wish to see that museums are seeking to control their operating costs too. Most museums have responded to this challenge. A survey of institutional members of the American Association of Museums in April 2011 reported a variety of budget-saving measures to meet economic challenges throughout 2010. These included a freeze on hiring (reported by 35 percent of museums in the survey), relying more on volunteers (34 percent), deferring building maintenance (30 percent), and relying more on their own collections for temporary exhibitions (29 percent). The focus of cost-control strategies is very much on staffing, due to the fact that staffing costs generally account for 50–60 percent of museum operating costs and sometimes more (AAM 2011).

The survey results are probably applicable in many countries in which there have been reductions in governmental support for museums. They identify specific issues connected with various operating expense categories, which we discuss below. Museum-operating expense categories generally include:

- staffing
- building occupancy
- collections care
- exhibitions
- public and educational programming
- marketing
- retail cost of goods sold
- general and administrative.

Balancing staffing needs with cost-control imperatives

Without a talented and trained staff a museum will not be able to achieve its mission and serve the public. Yet staffing costs are the single largest expense item for a museum. Controlling these costs is usually the most important factor in achieving operational sustainability, and there are a variety of strategies used by museums to address the issue. Many museums are considering whether to increase the use of part-time and contract staff, who are seen as "cheaper" than full-time staff because of benefits, but the downside is that they are transient, have a high turnover, and therefore generate higher recruitment and training costs. As shown from the survey of AAM members above (AAM 2011), the most common cost-control methods often mean that remaining staff are forced to take on additional responsibilities and work longer hours without extra financial compensation. The ability to achieve mission-driven goals or excellence according to any set of criteria is very difficult under these circumstances; and museum trustees and directors therefore need to be judicious in finding the right balance between cost-cutting and maintaining staffing capacity.

Museums cannot go on demanding their staff do more with less: extra funding is require to make workloads more sustainable. More than ever, the need for senior management to identify and implement successful revenue generation initiatives is critical for the survival of the institution. This obviously demands a very different skill set for the museum professional, and a different organizational culture which supports earned and contributed income initiatives. What makes for an entrepreneurial museum? There is little detailed research on these issues, but Tony Gilmour's study of heritage in Australia suggests it is possible for business-like organizations to be commercially positive thereby "giving the past a future" (2007). One study of six museums in New Zealand found that the two main drivers of enterprise were, first, the entrepreneurial characteristics of the key individual or individuals in the museum's management structure, and second, the culture of the organization for which he or she works (Massey and Lewis 2003).

In-kind support for building occupancy costs

Occupancy costs generally include utilities, repairs and maintenance, insurance and security systems. For museums that are not situated in buildings that they own, the payment of rent is an occupancy cost too. These fixed costs generally account for 10–15 percent of total operating expenses and there is often little that can be done to control them. The AAM survey indicates that the most common method for museums to control the costs of building occupancy is to defer maintenance. The problem is that this may create a negative image for visitors, particularly if the maintenance required is for public spaces, while a lengthy deferred maintenance may potentially imperil the collections or the building itself and should be avoided where possible.

At times when governments seek to limit or reduce cash expenses, one way they achieve this while continuing to fund a museum is to provide in-kind services: using municipal staff to provide repairs, maintenance, gardening, and other professional services, adding museums to municipal insurance coverage and absorbing museum utilities costs. The experience in North America is that in-kind support for museums is much more likely to take place if the museum building is municipally owned, because the city or other authority already has an investment in the infrastructure and it is a relatively straightforward matter to offer other ancillary or service-level support, such as IT.

Paying for changes in permanent and temporary exhibitions

Exhibitions are what visitors come to see, and they expect them to change periodically. One of the challenges facing museum management in times of economic stringency is how long to wait before the core or permanent exhibitions are replaced, refreshed, or updated. The decision is often really about the ability to obtain funding from private or governmental sources and it is not surprising that during challenging economic times exhibitions remain unchanged for longer. Some museums, including the expanded and relocated Natural History Museum of Utah, have recognized the need to introduce a reserve to pay for exhibit replacement as part of their annual operating budgets. Allocation of a relatively small amount in the reserve every year builds up over time and allows for more rapid changes to the permanent exhibitions.

Compared with permanent museum exhibits, the changeover of temporary displays, or segments within them, obviously happens more frequently. When these kinds of shows are generated in-house, there are still high costs associated with them, even if they are offset to some extent by touring the exhibition and generating some income from other institutions that lease them. For those museums that take travelling exhibitions, while they are spared the costs associated with developing the exhibition, the obligations associated with bringing in hired exhibits are greater than simply the overall fee. Other costs include transportation, marketing, and insurance. Most often these costs exceed the revenues generated from visitors and so temporary exhibitions rely very much on sponsorship. However, when assistance from private and government sources is reduced in lean times, there are corresponding reductions in the number of temporary exhibitions. In recent times museums have tended to develop exhibitions from their own permanent collections, largely because it is cheaper to do so (AAM 2011; Wallach 2013).

Working together: collaborations

It is logical for museums to collaborate with each other, as they share a commitment to missions that focus on heritage preservation, collections care, and education. However, the reality is that most view other museums as competitors and do relatively little to collaborate for common benefit even when they are site neighbors. But now museums have been forced to collaborate because of the recession, proving that necessity is indeed the mother of invention. This section therefore considers collaboration as a response to, and an aspect of, museum economics.

More collaboration has taken place in recent years, often in response to financial challenges that all museums face, and the need to make their money go further. Collaborative initiatives may help to address some of the problems discussed above associated with admissions, and issues concerning operating revenues and cost-control needs. For example, it is relatively easy for neighboring museums to work together to offer ticket packages, passport, or value-added schemes to encourage visitation. It is very likely that there will be more formal collaborations, management service agreements, or mergers between museums in the future as they consider their options in making savings.

The different types of collaboration may be seen as stages on a continuum that moves toward greater integration, as follows:

- *Informal collaboration*: Cooperation takes place typically at the staff level as they work together on a project or event, to achieve cost savings (e.g., joint purchasing), or to achieve mutual benefits (e.g., joint ticketing or marketing).
- *Formal collaboration*: This entails a formal agreement among organizations and involves board approval. Most formal collaborations are of several museum-related institutions such as the Cleveland Cultural Collaborative (including the Cleveland Botanical Garden, the Western Reserve Historical Society, and the Cleveland Museum of Art), the seven museums in the Museums District or "Museums on the Boulevard" in Richmond, Virginia, and the Heart of Brooklyn (Heart of Brooklyn 2014). Formal collaboration often involves a member of staff, shared among the organizations, who is responsible for bringing senior personnel of the various entities together to identify and implement revenue generation and cost-control opportunities.

- *Management service agreement*: This takes place when one organization provides services to another for a fee or barter arrangement. Examples include the Cattle Raisers Museum relationship with the Fort Worth Museum of Science and History, in Fort Worth Texas, which operates as a "museum within a museum" (Cattle Raisers Museum 2014), or the more substantial management services provided by the Tennessee Aquarium to two museums in Chattanooga (Tennessee Aquarium 2014). The management services concept allows a smaller museum to have access to the professional staff of a larger museum and thus forego the need for, and cost of, various senior staff positions.
- *Merger*: This occurs when the decision is to become fully integrated, although there is a spectrum of options even within mergers, which might allow for brand independence of the merged organizations. For example, the Southwest Museum retained a separate identity as part of the Autry Center in California. Science Place and the Dallas Children's Museum disappeared as separate entities by merging with the former Dallas Museum of Natural History to become the rebranded Perot Museum of Nature and Science. Each previously had its own board, building, staff, and development or expansion plans and they all competed for markets and funding. The merger led to a single new museum building being constructed that opened in 2013 (Perot 2014).
- *Acquisition*: One museum acquires all of the assets of another museum, which ceases to exist as a separate organization.

It is very likely that there will be more formal collaborations, convergence, or mergers among museums in the future, as they consider how to do more with less. Certainly there seem to be many advantages and positive results from collaboration, not just between museums, but museums and other heritage institutions, and indeed between not-for-profits generally and the business world. However, there is debate about the long-term effects of these developments, and the danger that, when they do not take into account the goals and commitments of partnering institutions, they can lead to a degree of integration that is less than the sum of its parts, or even the kinds of corporate partnerships which may harm arts organizations (Zorich, Waibal, and Erway 2008; see also: Chong in this volume; Wellington and Oliver in this volume). Working together for the greater good seems reasonable when times are tough, but if economic rationalization is the sole driver for the coming together of museums, and museums with galleries, libraries, archives, and other like entities, then it is possible that less than positive outcomes may result (Wellington 2013).

Conclusion

The topics touched on in this chapter constitute some of the critical economic issues in museums that professionals face today. We have argued that these issues – admission charges, revenue centers, operating expenses, and collaboration – are essentially to do with balancing imperatives associated with mission and money. The need to do so in increasingly common periods of financial restraint puts pressure on staff to come up with strategies to attain the appropriate balance for their museum.

Looking at the larger picture of museums and museum studies, we believe there is a lack of economic thinking informing management strategies within museum practice, and a need for more direct attention to business and financial matters in general within academic research and writing on museums. We hope that this chapter, which draws on our work with museums in various countries, will contribute to the literature on what we have called museum economics through the analysis of the most important financial issues within contemporary museums. In doing so, it may further the task of stimulating additional research on the economics of museums, and challenging the current generation of museum professionals to engage in debates about money without losing sight of their mission.

Notes

1   The authors would like to acknowledge the research and input offered by a variety of staff of Lord Cultural Resources in Toronto and New York, Lordculture in Paris and Lord India. These include Joy Bailey Bryant, Camille Balmand, Gloria Bardi, Laure Confavreux Colliex, Ameline Coulombier, Amy Kaufman, Lindsay Martin, Batul Raaj, Marina Ramirez, and Barbara Taylor. Thanks also to AAM Accreditation Commissioner Terrie Rouse.

References

AAM (American Association of Museums). 2011. "Museums and the American Economy, 2010." April. Accessed October 15, 2014. http://www.aam-us.org/docs/research/acme12-final.pdf?sfvrsn=0.

Baltimore Museum of Art. 2011. "Free Admission at Baltimore Museum of Art and Walters Art Museum Begins October 1." Accessed October 15, 2014. http://thewalters.org/news/releases/article.aspx?e_id=23.

Cattle Raisers Museum. 2014. Website. Accessed October 1, 2014. http://www.fwmuseum.org/cattle-raisers-museum.

Chhabra, Deepak. 2010. *Sustainable Marketing of Cultural and Heritage Tourism*. New York: Routledge.

Cour des Comptes. 2011. "Les musées nationaux après une décennie de transformations 2000–2010." Paris: Rapport public thématique, March. Accessed October 15, 2014. http://www.ladocumentationfrancaise.fr/var/storage/rapports-publics/114000168/0000.pdf.

DCMS (Department for Culture, Media and Sport). 2011. "Maintaining World-Leading National Museums and Galleries, and Supporting the Museum Sector." Accessed October 1, 2014. http://www.culture.gov.uk/what_we_do/museums_and_galleries/3380.aspx.

Dowd, Vincent. 2011. "Museum Entry Fees: How the UK Compares." BBC. Accessed October 1, 2014. http://www.bbc.co.uk/news/entertainment-arts-15982797.

Feldstein, Martin, ed. 1991. *The Economics of Art Museums*. Chicago: Chicago University Press.

Florida, Richard. 2002. *The Rise of the Creative Class: And How It's Transforming Work, Leisure, Community and Everyday Life*. New York: Basic Books.

Frey, Bruno S. 2003. *Arts and Economics: Analysis and Cultural Policy*. New York: Springer.

Frey, Bruno S., and Stephan Meier. 2006a. "Cultural Economics." In *A Companion to Museum Studies*, edited by Sharon Macdonald, 398–414. Oxford: Blackwell.

Frey, Bruno S., and Stephan Meier. 2006b. "The Economics of Museums." In *Handbook of the Economics of Art and Culture*, edited by Victor A. Ginsburg and David Throsby, 1017–1047. Cheltenham: Elsevier.

Frey, Bruno S., and Lasse Steiner. 2010. "Pay As You Go: A New Proposal for Museum Pricing." CESIFO Working Paper No. 3045, May. Zurich: University of Zurich.

Gilmour, Tony. 2007. *Sustaining Heritage: Giving the Past a Future*. Sydney: Sydney University Press.

Green, Tyler. 2011a. "Does Going Free Hurt Membership Programs?" Blouin Artinfo: Modern Art Notes, May 2. Accessed October 1, 2014. http://blogs.artinfo.com/modernartnotes/2011/05/does-going-free-hurt-membership-programs.

Green, Tyler. 2011b. "Should LACMA (or Your Local Museum) Be Free?" Blouin Artinfo: Modern Art Notes, April 28. Accessed October 1, 2014. http://blogs.artinfo.com/modernartnotes/2011/04/should-lacma-or-your-local-museum-be-free.

Gurian, Elaine Heumann. 2005. "Free at Last: A Case for Eliminating Admission Charges in Museums." *Museum News* September/October: 33–35, 61–66.

Haywood, Felicity. 2009. "Is Free Thinking on the Way Out?" *Museums Journal* 109: 13.

Heart of Brooklyn: A Cultural Project. 2014. Website. Accessed October 1, 2014. http://www.heartofbrooklyn.org.

Le Gall-Ely, Marine, Caroline Urbain, Anne Gombault, Dominique Bourgeon-Renault, and Christine Petr. 2007. "An Exploratory Study of the Implications of Free Admission to Museums and Monuments: Perceptions and Effects on Visiting Behaviours." *Recherche et applications marketing* 22(2): 23–28.

Lord, Gail Dexter, and Barry Lord. 2009. *The Manual of Museum Management*. Lanham, MD: AltaMira.

Lord, Gail Dexter, and Barry Lord. 2012. *The Manual of Museum Planning*. Lanham, MD: AltaMira.

Major, Suzette, and Tamarisk Sutherland. 2007. "Strategic Partnerships between Museums and Corporate Organisations – The Marriage of the Museum of New Zealand Te Papa Tongarewa and TOWER." In *Museum Marketing: Competing in the Global Marketplace*, edited by R. Rentschler and Anne-Marie Hede, 250–256. London: Routledge.

Martin, Andy. 2003. "The Impact of Free Entry to Museums." London: MORI. Accessed October 15, 2014. https://www.ipsos-mori.com/DownloadPublication/541_sri-the-impact-of-free-entry-to-museums-2003.pdf

Massey, Claire, and Kate Lewis. 2003. "Exhibiting Enterprise: How New Zealand Museums Generate Revenue." *International Journal of Heritage Studies* 9(4): 325–339.

McCauley, Mary Carole. 2007. "Museums Enjoy Their Free For All." *Baltimore Sun*, September 30. Accessed October 1, 2014. http://articles.baltimoresun.com/2007–09–30/news/0709300210_1_baltimore-museum-walters-art-museum-of-art.

McFelter, Gypsey. 2007. "The Cost of 'Free': Admission Fees at American Art Museums." *Museum News* 86(1): 60.

Merritt, Elizabeth, and Phillip Katz, eds. 2009. *Museum Financial Information*. Washington, DC: American Association of Museums.

Museum Store Association. 2009. *MSA Retail Industry Report: Financial, Operations and Salary Data*. Denver, CO: Museum Store Association.

Newseum. 2014. Website. Accessed October 15, 2014. http://www.newseum.org.

Parsa, H., John Self, David Njita, and Tiffany King. 2005. "Why Restaurants Fail." *Cornell Hospitality Quarterly* 46(3): 304–322.

Perot (Museum of Nature and Science). 2014. Website. Accessed October 1, 2014. http://www.perotmuseum.org.

Philanthropy News Digest. 2011. "Walmart Awards $20 Million to Crystal Bridges Museum." August 1. Accessed October 1, 2014. http://foundationcenter.org/pnd/news/story.jhtml?id=347400025.

Rizzo, Ilde, and Anna Mignosa. 2013. *Handbook on the Economics of Cultural Heritage*. Cheltenham: Edward Elgar.

Selwood, S., and Maurice Davies. 2005. "Museums: After the Lottery Boom." *Spiked*. September 2. Accessed October 1, 2014. http://www.spiked-online.com/site/article/760.

Steiner, Faye. 1997. "Optimal Pricing of Museum Admissions." *Journal of Cultural Economics* 21: 307–333.

Tate Report. 2011–2012. "Who We Are." Accessed October 15, 2014. http://www.tate.org.uk/about/who-we-are/tate-reports/tate-report-2011-2012.

Tennessee Aquarium. 2014. Website. Accessed October 1, 2014. http://www.tennesseeaquarium.org/Home.aspx?gclid=CLyFquf2-r0CFUMGvAodZmQAgw.

Throsby, David. 2001. *Economics and Culture*. Cambridge: Cambridge University Press.

Towse, Ruth. 1997. *Cultural Economics: The Arts, Heritage and Media Industries*. Cheltenham, UK: Edward Elgar.

Towse, Ruth. 2011. *A Handbook of Cultural Economics*, 2nd ed. London: Edward Elgar.

Travers, Tony. 2006. *Museums and Galleries in Britain: Economic, Social and Creative Impacts*. London: National Museum Directors' Conference; Museums, Libraries, and Archives Council.

Varutti, Marzia. 2014. *Museums in China: The Politics of Representation after Mao*. Woodbridge, UK: Boydell.

Wallach, Alan. 2013. "The New American Art Galleries, Virginia Museum of Fine Arts, Richmond." *Museum Worlds* (1): 222–227.

Wellington, Shannon. 2013. "Building GLAMour: Convergent Practice between Galleries, Libraries, Archives and Museums." Unpublished PhD thesis, Victoria University of Wellington. Accessed October 1, 2014. http://hdl.handle.net/10063/2835.

Xinhua English News, 2012, "Grass Roots Enjoying Free Admission to Chinese Museums." Accessed October 15, 2014. http://news.xinhuanet.com/english/indepth/2012-01/13/c_131359259.htm.

Youngs, Ian. 2011. "Museums Enjoy 10 Years of Freedom." BBC. December 1. Accessed October 1, 2014. http://www.bbc.co.uk/news/entertainment-arts-15927593.

Zorich, Diane, Gunter Waibel, and Ricky Erway. 2008. "Beyond the Silos of the LAMs: Collaboration among Libraries, Archives and Museums." Dublin Ohio: OCLC Programs and Research. Accessed October 15, 2014. http://www.oclc.org/content/dam/research/publications/library/2008/2008-05.pdf.

Further Reading

Bowden, David. 2009. "Museums: The Impact of Free Admissions." September. Accessed October 1, 2014. http://www.ewriter.eu/documents/MuseumsWEBOct2009.ART.pdf.

Brodie, Ellie, David Kane, and Jenny Clark. 2012. "Income Generation in London's Non-National Museums." Accessed October 15, 2014. http://www.museumoflondon.org.uk/files/4313/7468/2647/Income-Generation-in-Londons-non-National-Museums-August-2012.pdf.

Genoways, Hugh H., and Lynne Ireland. 2003. *Museum Administration: An Introduction.* Walnut Creek, CA: AltaMira Press.

Museum of New Zealand Te Papa Tongarewa. 1994. *Admission Charges: The Issues.* Wellington: Museum of New Zealand Te Papa Tongarewa.

Silberberg, Ted. 2005. "The Importance of Accuracy in Attendance Reporting." *International Journal of Arts Management* 8(1): 4–7.

Ted Silberberg is the Senior Principal responsible for market and financial planning at Lord Cultural Resources, the world's largest firm specialized in the planning and management of museums and other cultural institutions. He has worked in the field for over 30 years, is a certified management consultant, and is the author of various articles associated with business planning for museums. He has spoken at a variety of conferences on issues associated with revenue generation, cost control, market analysis, site evaluation, and other related business planning topics.

Gail Lord is Co-President of Lord Cultural Resources, and has helped to plan numerous museums throughout the world. With her husband and partner, Barry Lord, she is co-author of the *Manual of Museum Management*, co-author of the *Manual of Strategic Planning for Museums*, co-editor of *The Manual of Museum Planning* and other volumes in their Manual series. She is most recently co-author of *Artists, Patrons and the Public: Why Culture Changes*. Gail has been a featured speaker at a wide variety of conferences around the world.

8 TATE AND BP – OIL AND GAS AS THE NEW TOBACCO?

Arts Sponsorship, Branding, and Marketing[1]

Derrick Chong

Museums may not be businesses, but their attempts to be business-like have led to problems, at least with some critics. As one book puts it, "there's no business that's not show business" (Schmitt, Rogers, and Vrotsos, 2004). Museums and galleries have been forced to raise more money, focusing their attention on sponsorship and marketing. These efforts to be commercially positive earn praise from some quarters and suspicion from others, especially the academic critics of museums. Commercial relationships between arts institutions and multinational enterprises – such as corporate sponsorship of art exhibitions – usually lead to two broad positions being adopted. On the one hand, there is a faith in the market and corporate sponsorship, particularly in the face of reduced public subsidy, and their commitment to engaging with diverse audiences (see for example Kotler, Kotler, and Kotler 2008; Lord and Lord 2009). On the other hand there is antipathy toward the corporatization of the museum, with the rise of marketing, the reliance on sponsorship, and private interests infiltrating what are deemed public spaces (see, for example, Wallis 1986; Schiller 1989; Rectanus 2002; Wu 2003).

Sponsorship, branding, and marketing in museums have undoubtedly become an important aspect of current practice, but are not yet a significant aspect of museum studies. Several books on these topics describe the broad parameters of contemporary practice in the museum (Janes and Sandell 2007; French and Runyard 2011). There is increasing attention to the study of these phenomena in the public sector, although the field is still small, and there is more work outside museum studies than within it. These publications usually take a pragmatic attitude and simply describe how to get on and do it (Schmitt, Rogers, and Vrotsos, 2004; Wallace 2006). This chapter takes a different and more critical approach and

The International Handbooks of Museum Studies: Museum Practice, First Edition.
Edited by Conal McCarthy.
© 2015 John Wiley & Sons Ltd. Published 2020 by John Wiley & Sons Ltd.

addresses the broader contestation of commerce and culture mentioned above. It argues that sponsorship and branding cannot be seen simply as techniques but must be understood and critically analyzed within a wider social and political context. I explore these issues by focusing on a particular event, namely Tate's decision to celebrate two decades of BP corporate sponsorship in 2010 at the time of a disastrous oil spill in the Gulf of Mexico. The murky specifics of the Tate–BP case provide an opportunity to move the current debate beyond a circular for/against argument about these commercial relationships, which tends to present them as either good or bad.

Are oil and gas the new tobacco, as the chapter title suggests? The simple answer is "no." Not necessarily an emphatic "no" as in "never," more like "no" as in "not now." In defense of the market, pragmatists could cite the fact that the FTSE, the index company behind the FTSE 100 index of the leading publicly listed firms in the United Kingdom, launched the FTSE4Good Index in 2001 as a series of benchmark and tradable indices for responsible investors. According to responsible global investment thinking, a small number of sector exclusions have been applied: tobacco producers; companies manufacturing either whole, strategic parts of, or platforms for, nuclear weapon systems; and companies manufacturing whole weapon systems. Oil and gas does not appear as an excluded sector.

Moreover, these pragmatists could point out that plural funding has become entrenched in government policy as far as museums are concerned, in other words they have had to seek other sources of funds as public funding has been reduced (see Selwood and Davies in this volume). Arts institutions in receipt of public money have had to develop and manage multiple income streams, all the while juggling these demands with increased responsibilities for social well-being and community engagement, to ensure institutional viability. The upshot is that, alongside contributing to social goals such as life-long learning, they also have to operate in a business-like fashion by raising more of their own income, making greater contributions to the economy and demonstrating efficient delivery of services that put consumers first (on cultural economics, see Silberberg and Lord in this volume).

How do art museums manage to balance these demands? This chapter looks at one institution and the tensions that arise from the ways in which it reconciles culture and commerce. Tate is one of the great art museums in the world, famous for its exhibitions and events staged at its spectacular building on the banks of the Thames in central London. To be specific: Tate's 2008–2011 Funding Agreement with the Department for Culture, Media and Sport (DCMS) has a range of performance indicators (or metrics) including access and audience profile (visitor data), learning/outreach, visitor satisfaction, income generation (including admissions, trading and fundraising) and regional engagement.[2]

On the other side of the sponsorship ledger, what about the oil and gas industry? Carbon-based consumption means that the oil and gas sector of the global economy is significant. For example, the Fortune Global 500 ranking of publicly listed firms in 2010 placed five oil and gas firms in the top 10 as measured by revenue; the top 10 of the FTSE 100 as measured by market capitalization tells a similar story of the size and stature of oil and gas.[3] The enormous profits earned in this sector naturally make it the target of public scrutiny, and at times outright hostility. But the level of public hostility varies a great deal. This can be seen in the varying levels of attention directed at oil and gas logos, such a prominent part of arts sponsorship arrangements, which may not necessarily be perceived as "toxic" branding.

But does this vacillating public opposition mean that we should all ignore criticism of this industry and its forays into cultural heritage? What about the opposition by artists and cultural critics – often deemed idealistic – to oil and gas as sponsors of arts institutions? What do these protestors have to say that may throw light on debates around museums and corporate money? In other words, do these activists help us to address some knotty questions in relation to the role of arts institutions, questions which scholars of arts marketing would do well to address? For example, what is the proper relationship between business and the arts? How do arts institutions know where to draw the line? What can be gained from considering the perspective of activist artists?

The perception of the Tate–BP sponsorship arrangement, discussed in this chapter, reflects a duel between pragmatism and idealism in terms of the contested relationship between business and the arts. This tension is reflected in the organization of the chapter. First we review the incident in which artists protested the 2010 summer party at Tate Britain. This is followed by a section which traces how both Tate and BP sought to manage their evolving institutional identities, or brands, including a commercial relationship. Then the chapter considers the current status of the art museum as civic institution with reference to its historical roots as a product of modern democracy. How does this museum ideal grate against the powerful new relationships between business and the arts which have emerged since the mid-1960s? I then consider contemporary artists operating under the banner of institutional critique who counter the arts–business nexus, concerned at the growing privatization of public culture by commercial interests and the way that institutions are being used as a "social lubricant" by multinational enterprises. Finally the chapter critically examines the institutional trust expressed in the pragmatic joint statement by leading arts institutions in the UK – including Tate – to support the role BP has played in the arts, and ends by reviewing the controversy one year later. The concluding questions raise issues both about corporate governance in arts policy and public opinion in the UK, and also about the approach to corporate sponsorship in research on museums.

Artists protesting Tate's summer party

Tate organized its annual summer party at Tate Britain on June 28, 2010 to celebrate the opening of Fiona Banner's *Harriers and Jaguars*, the Annual Duveen Commission sponsored by Sotheby's, and "BP British Art Displays, 1500–2010,"

FIGURE 8.1   Invitation to Tate Britain Summer Party, June 21, 2010.
From *Not If But When: Culture beyond Oil*, Platform, November 29, 2010. Accessed October 6, 2014.
http://www.platformlondon.org/carbonweb/documents/summerparty.pdf.

sponsored by BP (Figure 8.1). BP is one of Tate's eight long-term partnerships with business corporations. As its website explains: "Tate is proud to collaborate with a number of leading companies on a series of strategic long-term partnerships that provide mutual benefit on a long-term basis, across a number of different aspects of Tate's activity."[4]

On June 28, the same day as Tate's summer party, a letter of protest was published in a major daily newspaper. Artist Hans Haacke was the lead signatory of a group that included Caryl Churchill (playwright), Suzi Gablik (art critic and writer), Gordon Roddick (arts philanthropist and co-founder of the Body Shop), Lucy Lippard (writer and curator), and Martin Rowson (cartoonist). This group used the letters page of *The Guardian* to mount a protest against BP's arts sponsorship. The letter read:

> These relationships enable big oil companies to mask the environmentally destructive nature of their activities with the social legitimacy that is associated with such high-profile cultural associations.
>
> Many artists are angry that Tate and other national cultural institutions continue to sidestep the issue of oil sponsorship. Little more than a decade ago, tobacco companies were seen as respectable partners for public institutions to gain support from – that is no longer the case. It is our hope that oil and gas will be seen in the

same light. The public is rapidly coming to recognize that the sponsorship programmes BP and Shell are means by which attention can be distracted from their impacts on human rights, the environment and the global climate. (*The Guardian* June 28, 2010)

The protest in *The Guardian* was part of a wave of public action against the oil-industry sponsorship of the arts that materialized in response to the Deepwater Horizon spill. This was the largest accidental marine spill in the history of the petroleum industry when in April 2010 an oil rig in the Gulf of Mexico exploded with catastrophic environmental effects. One such arts group who joined the protest was Platform, an artist collective which describes itself as "promoting creative processes of democratic engagement to advance social and ecological justice" (Platform 2013). Platform launched a new campaign, Licence to Spill, with direct reference to the Tate–BP sponsorship agreement. This campaign included a public demonstration at Tate Britain, including a dramatic performance in which a naked man was covered in oil (see Figure 8.2). These actions drew attention to the way in which oil companies use their connection with arts institutions to create a kind of "social license" which covers up their less savory activities and facilitates their operations elsewhere in the world.

Artists critiquing Tate linked Platform's campaign to an earlier initiative, Liberate Tate. Liberate Tate was formed in 2010 following what was perceived to be censorship by Tate in connection with a workshop, "Disobedience Makes History," led by a group calling itself the Laboratory of Insurrectionary Imagination. Liberate Tate disrupted Tate Modern's 10th anniversary celebration in May (Liberate Tate 2013). There were other protests as well: environmental group Greenpeace mounted an alternative exhibition, and Art Not Oil, a project of Rising Tide UK committed to "creativity, climate, justice and an end to oil industry sponsorship of the arts," protested the BP Portrait Award celebration at the National Portrait Gallery (Art Not Oil website).

Of course, the timing of Tate's party, and the implied tribute to major sponsors such as BP, was extremely awkward – to say the least. The Gulf of Mexico catastrophe, a leading business news story of 2010, occurred on April 20 when the Deepwater Horizon drilling rig, one of BP's offshore rigs outsourced to Transocean and Halliburton, burst into flames. Eleven men died in what was the worst oil spillage in US history. The impact on the company was immediate and far reaching. BP's share price dropped 50 percent within a period of 10 weeks. The chief executive Tony Hayward faced a barrage of negative press for his crisis management performance. In an effort to placate a growing list of powerful critics, BP cancelled shareholder dividends for the remainder of 2010 and established a large compensation fund. When BP announced its second-quarter 2010 results at the end of July, it reported the largest quarterly loss *ever* of any publicly listed company in the UK. Eventually Hayward was forced to resign (BP website).

FIGURE 8.2 "Human Cost" by Liberate Tate, 2010.

Photo from front cover of *Not If But When: Culture beyond Oil*, Platform, November 29, 2010. Accessed October 6, 2014. http://platformlondon.org/p-publications/culutr. Photograph by Amy Scaife.

In early September, BP released a report on the cause of the Gulf of Mexico catastrophe, based on a four-month internal investigation. BP's outgoing CEO commented on the report:

> The investigation report provides critical new information on the causes of this terrible accident. It is evident that a series of complex events, rather than a single mistake or failure, led to the tragedy. Multiple parties, including BP, Halliburton and Transocean, were involved. (BP 2010)

BP was finally able to cap the oil well in mid-September 2010 (153 days after it started). At the time of Hayward's departure, at the end of September, BP's share price was 415 pence: still down nearly one-third from the precatastrophe level, albeit an improvement from the time of Tate Britain's summer party, during the worst of the spill, when shares plunged by half.

How did mainstream arts institutions respond to criticisms of corporate sponsorship? BP's arts sponsorship in the UK was defended by Tate and three other leading arts institutions in a prepared joint statement:

> The British Museum, National Portrait Gallery, Royal Opera House and Tate work with a wide range of companies who support the work of each organisation alongside government subsidy, commercial enterprise and philanthropy. The income generated through corporate partnerships is vital to the mixed economy of successful arts organisations and enables each of us to deliver a rich and vibrant cultural programme.
>
> BP has, for many years, made a very significant contribution to the arts and cultural life of this country including support for the Royal Opera House since 1988, the BP Portrait Award since 1990, Tate since 1990 and the British Museum since 1996.
>
> We are grateful to BP for their long-term commitment, sharing the vision that our artistic programmes should be made to the widest possible audience. (UK Sponsorship 2010)

Maurice Davies, head of policy and communication at the Museums Association, expresses a pragmatic approach to corporate sponsorship of the arts:

> Museums make judgements about who is a suitable sponsor.
>
> No one would take [money] from tobacco firms or arms companies. [However] BP has a long and distinguished record of sponsorship. No one will rush to judgement on a company that has been a loyal supporter for such a long time. I don't hear a national clamour for BP retail stations to be shut down. (*The Guardian*, June 24, 2010)

Indeed BP's record of collaboration for the public good is promoted on its website:

> We are committed to arts and culture, supporting several leading UK institutions for three decades.
>
> Our sustained support enables them to plan programmes and secure performers, artists and works of art well into the future. New performances, exhibitions, special events, awards, grants, lectures and access to works of art are made possible by our support.
>
> All of this is part of our broader contribution to society – promoting ideas, inspiring creativity and supporting the social and economic fabric of the UK. (BP 2010; www.bp.com)

BP also supports education and other community projects in countries – where it operates: Germany, China, the United Kingdom, the United States, Canada, Angola, and Azerbaijan. Such a declaration seeks both to address regulatory reporting requirements on sustainability and to counter perceptions, as suggested by Haacke et al. in *The Guardian*, that BP may be "environmentally destructive" with "impacts on human rights, the environment and the global climate" (*The Guardian*, June 28, 2010). A similar motivation may have lain behind an advertising campaign in January 2011, in which Tate Britain and three other major art institutions appear as framed pictures under a banner declaring "Four National Treasures: One Long History" ("Four National Treasures" 2011).

BP and Tate: two brands in partnership

Both Tate and BP are brands. At this point we should consider the links between them in light of the literature on branding (see, for example, Olins 1994; Pavitt 2000; Twitchell 2004; and on branding and museums see Scott 2000). A brand is an intangible asset; which in simple terms can be likened to "reputation." Branding – as the process of establishing and developing a brand – is a form of institutional storytelling (Twitchell 2004). In these narratives, the brands play the role of both author and protagonist (anthropomorphism has certainly been important to branding). In 2000–2001, the Victoria and Albert Museum mounted an exhibition *Brand.New* on the rise of brands and branding as a cultural phenomenon. "The brand is a prefix; the qualifier of character," Jane Pavitt argued in the catalog, "The symbolic associations of the brand name are often used in preference to the pragmatic description of a useful object" (Pavitt 2000, 16). This separation between an object and its symbolism is the subject of much critical commentary, for example Olins who in *Corporate Identity* (1994) cites the concept of "the invention of tradition" developed by Marxist historians Hobsbawm and Ranger. As Hobsbawm explained, an "invented tradition" is a "reference to a historic past … that is largely fictitious" (Hobsbawm and Ranger 1983, 1).

Tate and BP have sustained a partnership lasting two decades. They have much longer historical links, both being founded at a time of changing British identity in the late nineteenth century. Tate Britain was originally established in 1897 at Millbank as the National Gallery of British Art, a branch of the National Gallery (itself established in 1824), and became the Tate Gallery in 1932. The name Tate derives from sugar magnate Henry Tate, who was instrumental in establishing the new institution, an example of private patronage in the late Victorian period. A family brand name "Tate" was adopted in 2000 with the opening of Tate Modern at Bankside. The original Millbank site was rebranded as Tate Britain. Tate's brand includes Tate Liverpool and Tate St Ives. BP's origins date to 1908 as Anglo-Persian Oil (and then Anglo-Iranian Oil from 1935, following a request by the Iranian government that the country be called Iran not Persia). The name British Petroleum was adopted in 1954, then in 1998 the merger between British Petroleum and Amoco created BP Amoco, and finally BP was formally adopted in 2001 (BP website).

Nicholas Serota, who became Tate's director in 1988, was a driving force behind Tate's emergence as a premier international art museum. A starting point for Serota was the *New Displays* exhibition, which was first mounted in 1991 with BP sponsorship, an opportunity for a rehang of the permanent collection on an annual basis. As well as being an experiment in plural art histories, it drew attention to insufficient exhibition space. More significantly, Serota was already interpreting the institution's mission to manage a collection of British art from the sixteenth century to the present day and of international modern and contemporary art – within the original museum building at Millbank – as two distinct collections of art, which served to position London as an art center distinguished from Paris or New York.

The political agenda was quite clear and very successful. Serota (1996) argued that London needed a museum of modern art on a par with New York's Museum of Modern Art or the Centre Pompidou in Paris. The time was ripe, as the London of the 1990s was marked by the rise of the so-called Young British Artists. Eventually the project got the go-ahead and Tate Modern opened in 2000 to critical praise (mostly) and popular appeal, although there was much debate about the commercial aspects of the gallery, including the branding (Prior 2003; Phillips and O'Reilly 2007; McClellan 2008). Tate Modern was also said to reflect the trend in the UK to proclaim creative industries, which were seen as the drivers of economic growth (Holden 2007). However, with its popular success came large visitor numbers which in turn put pressure on existing facilities. Subsequently Tate Modern underwent a major capital expansion (at an estimated cost of £215 million at 2012 prices) with a new extension designed by architects Herzog and de Meuron (Tate website).

Were there any direct links between Tate Modern and its sponsor BP? Indeed there were. Lord Browne of Madingley, BP's chief executive from 1995 to 2007, was also chair of Tate's board of trustees at the time of BP's oil spill. According to the website, Tate's board "oversees management of the gallery, with Trustees acting as guardians of the public interest."[5]

Meanwhile under Browne's tenure at BP, its current identity as "bp" was launched. In this rebranding exercise, we can observe a shift from being perceived as a British-based oil and gas producer to being a socially responsible, global energy provider. The company described its brand as follows:

> Our brand is summed up by the phrase "beyond petroleum." BP recognizes that meeting the energy challenges of today and tomorrow requires traditional hydrocarbons and a growing range of alternatives. We are at the forefront of delivering diverse, material and real solutions to meet the world's needs for more secure, cleaner and affordable energy.

The BP logo was launched in 2000. According to BP:

> It is unlike any other energy identity, and symbolizes a number of things – from the living, organic form of a sunflower to the greatest source of energy ... the sun itself.

> The colours of the Helios – named after the Greek god of the sun – suggest heat, light and nature. It is also a pattern of interlocking shapes: like BP, a single entity created by many different parts working as one.

Like the British Museum, the National Gallery, the National Portrait Gallery, and the Victoria and Albert Museum, today Tate is a non-departmental public body (NDPB). As such it is funded in part by the DCMS. As a NDPB, Tate carries out functions on behalf of the DCMS; however, it is administered independently, allowing it to assert confidently that it is "able to focus entirely on its own objectives and make unbiased recommendations and decisions" (Tate website).[6]

Of course the reader will be aware that museum sponsorship arrangements in general have always been complex and contested, and measures can be taken to ameliorate their adverse effects. In the USA for example, sponsorship has been defined as a commercial transaction that is formalized legally with obligations on both sides. Cash and/or in-kind fees are paid to a property – in this case Tate – "in return for access to the exploitable commercial potential associated with that property" (IEG 2014). The Association of Art Museum Directors, representing the most prestigious institutions in the USA, Canada, and Mexico, recognizes "challenges to ensure that the museum's educational mission is not compromised by external commercial interests" (AAMD 2007, 1).

It is obviously a challenge for those in governance roles to maintain the public trust in art museums (on governance see Lord and Zigler in this volume). Any loss of trust naturally calls into question not just the reputation but also the viability of arts institutions. In the case of Tate, managing relationships with corporate sponsors was essentially a marketing issue of brand fit, congruence, or alliance, but with BP there were obviously special challenges which put their public image at risk. This raises a number of questions: Are BP's reputation, values, and products consistent with Tate and its community's standards of quality and integrity? Are there risks associated with the BP sponsorship agreement? Should these risks be acceptable to Tate? Lastly, we have to ask whether BP's sponsorship ultimately supports Tate's fulfillment of its mission, in terms of public perception and the museum's image? Clearly Tate does not emerge unscathed from this interrogation, and at the very least needs to address matters of corporate governance and integrity with frankness and transparency. Entrusted by the public to care for our shared artistic heritage, like all museums, a commitment to good stewardship is crucial to institutional viability.

The wider context of business and the arts

According to some scholars, the historical ideal of the museum was a civilizing temple of culture set apart from the social (Pointon 1994; Duncan 1995), whereas others argue that far from being aloof it has always been embroiled in wider economic relations (Witcomb 2003). Nevertheless the art museum has a close relationship with what Carrier calls "modern democratic culture" (2006, 15). Cuno writes that today it continues to be accorded status as a leading civic institution (2004). In recent times the role of "superstar museums" in urban regeneration, tourism, and cultural economics has been the subject of much research (Frey 1998). Frey argues that these institutions share the same attributes as the leisure industry: they have a reputation as a destination or site that is a "must" for tourists; a large number of visitors is used as a key headline figure of success; they boast "world-famous" artists and works of art; the museum building as a piece of architecture becomes an artistic feature; and commercialized spaces become more significant in the form of shopping and catering venues to satisfy visitors thereby making an impact on the local economy (Frey 1998).

Clearly this new commercial emphasis has to be balanced with the older cultural ideals of the art museum. In the USA relationships between business and the arts can be traced to the formation of the Business Committee for the Arts (BCA), now part of Americans for the Arts, in the late 1960s. The first meeting was held at the Metropolitan Museum of Art, where the first "Corporate Patrons Program" was established. At the time, David Rockefeller (in Gingrich 1969, xi), chairman of Chase Manhattan Bank, advocated business understanding and involvement in the arts: "The modern corporation has evolved into a social as well as an economic institution. Without losing sight of the need to make a profit, it has developed ideals and responsibilities going far beyond the profit motive." In the UK, the Association for Business Sponsorship of the Arts, now Arts and Business, was established in the mid-1970s – based on the BCA – to forge closer relationships among art galleries and other organizations and the corporate world.

Government policy under Margaret Thatcher (Prime Minister 1979–1990) promoted plural arts funding (or a mixed arts economy). The economist Friedrich Hayek (1944) in his book *The Road to Serfdom* provided an ideological framework for Thatcher's free market policies, just as Milton Friedman's (1962) *Capitalism and Freedom* did for Ronald Reagan. The idea was now that that minimal state involvement represents freedom from coercion, so government encouraged arts institutions to diversify the base of their financial support, in other words to rely less on a public funding (on this topic, see Selwood and Davies in this volume). Meanwhile, in the business world, companies were encouraged to take up "brand promotion" opportunities in association with sponsorship of the arts. All this may have been motivated by genuine public mindedness and philanthropy but some artists argue that sponsorship decisions are shaped by an attitude of self-interest, given the ego and lifestyle of senior corporate managers who view themselves as cultivated men and women. "I think a lot of the time the main motivation [of arts sponsorship] is to give their executives and clients a nice jolly and some privileged access," commented Grayson Perry. In 2003, Perry had won the prestigious Turner Prize, an award established in 1984 at the Tate which was funded by a group of patrons ("Crude Awakening" 2010).

Meanwhile the national and global economic situation changed dramatically after the 2008 recession. In 2010 following the UK general election, the austerity agenda of the coalition of Conservative–Liberal Democrats focused on reducing government expenditure, which meant that plural funding, such as individual philanthropy and corporate sponsors, became even more important. This situation reflected gradual changes in the arts funding environment in the UK during the previous several decades, but now the axe fell sharply. In 2010, the government announced a commitment to across-the-board cuts to public spending of 25 percent over four years (the biggest cuts in state spending since World War II) to address a budget deficit, including arts institutions in receipt of public subsidy ("EU Austerity Drive Country by Country" 2012). This austerity drive has already had impacts. In an unusual public statement, Tate's director described such cuts "as the greatest crisis in the arts and heritage since government funding began in 1940." Serota continued:

> With the ruthlessness of a blitzkrieg the coalition [government] is threatening the stability of an entire system of cultural provision that has been built up by successive Conservative and Labour governments: a mixed economy of public and private support that has made Britain a civilised place to live, where all have an opportunity to enjoy the arts or celebrate our heritage, and have been doing so in increasing numbers. (*Guardian* October 4, 2010)

In the face of austerity, arts commentators and artists have pleaded an economic argument that public subsidy to arts institutions represent an investment in the UK's creative industries sector (Bishop 2011). At the same time, the UK arts landscape has seen a greater emphasis on private giving (philanthropy) to reinvigorate the Victorian spirit of Henry Tate, including initiatives supported by Prince Charles (Prince of Wales Arts Philanthropy Medal). In addition, other earned sources of revenue, including corporate sponsorship but also membership dues, admission charges, and sales from retail, are deemed more and more essential for museums.

The chief executive of Arts and Business, Colin Tweedy is uncompromising in his pragmatic support of corporate giving as part of a mixed arts economy:

> There's always another needy mouth to feed if the arts don't want the money. And what happened [at the Tate party] was not helpful. Who's to say what's good or bad money?
>
> I don't think there's any way we can say that the arts scene has been distorted by corporate money; what distorts the arts scene is not having any money. We have to have private, public and earned income. (*The Guardian*, June 30, 2010)

How did Tate itself respond to this environment? Tate supplements the grant-in-aid (public subsidy) it receives from the DCMS with other revenue sources including commercial trading, corporate sponsorship, memberships, and admissions to temporary exhibitions (see Appendix A: Tate's consolidated statement of financial activity). In particular, at the time of the oil spill in mid-2010, Tate drew attention to the fact that it received less of its overall operational funding from the public purse: figures showed that grant-in-aid in relation to self-generated income has fallen from 78 percent in 2004/2005 to 60 percent in 2008/2009. Corporate sponsorship agreements are mutually beneficial, according to Tate. It promotes its value to corporate sponsors by offering the following benefits: "increased visibility and enhanced brand awareness"; "exclusive entertaining opportunities and access to leading opinion-formers"; "the opportunity to affiliate your company with world-class innovation and creativity"; and "tailored packages for your CSR agenda." At the same time Tate acknowledges that the economic value of "corporate contributions are essential to its ability to present exhibitions and public programmes" (Tate website). In response to questions about BP's arts sponsorship program including potential censorship, Browne has explained that:

> It's a way for companies to demonstrate they are alive and not just an entity working to extract profit. It's also cheaper than sport.
>
> I'm confident there is a complete separation between sponsorship and content; there is dialogue, but in the end, it is the museums and galleries who decide what goes ahead. (*Guardian*, June 28, 2010)

Hans Haacke and institutional critique

Put simply, the commercial activity reviewed above represents a highly pragmatic response by museums to a financial situation in which institutions have been encouraged to rely less on public subsidy and more on their own efforts to raise funds. However the scramble for philanthropists and sponsors in the arts sector comes with risks, whatever the reassurances of museum leaders. Critics of corporate sponsorship counter Browne's declaration of "a complete separation between sponsorship and content," citing examples of self-censorship in their own work.

These critics desire a greater separation between large business corporations and arts institutions, believing perhaps that if the creative and emancipatory role of art in society is constrained then it becomes merely utilitarian. In response to neoliberal agendas advanced during the 1980s, sociologist Herbert Schiller in his book *Culture, Inc.* described the state of affairs as "The corporate takeover of public expression" (1989).[7] This theme of the privatizing of public culture by corporate interests has recently been advanced by cultural critics: for example, in *Privatizing Culture* Wu examined "corporate art intervention since 1980" (2003); and Rectanus had a similar message in *Culture Incorporated*, which explored relationships amongst "museums, artists and corporate sponsorships" (2002).

A seminal figure in the attack on corporate arts sponsorship is Hans Haacke (b. 1936), who has been a longstanding critic of connections between business and the arts (see Wallis 1986). *Free Exchange*, the public dialogue between French sociologist Pierre Bourdieu and Haacke (1995), addressed corporate sponsorship as a tool for the seduction of public opinion (see Haacke 2002 and Fraser 2002 for tributes to Bourdieu). Bourdieu argued that "Museums need cultural respectability to be able to influence their sponsors," adding that they "need to be recognized as public authorities in order to have sponsors" (Bourdieu and Haacke 1995, 11). Drawing on Bourdieu's theory of cultural capital, Haacke distinguishes between "traditional notions of patronage and public relationships manoeuvres." He goes on to say that "The American term *sponsoring* more accurately reflects that what we have here is really an exchange of capital: finance capital on the part of sponsors and symbolic capital on the part of the sponsored" (Bourdieu and Haacke 1995, 17; emphasis in the original).

In the Haacke et al. letter to the *Guardian* attacking Tate's sponsorship agreement with BP some of the themes noted in *Free Exchange* are evident. They write that "social legitimacy" is sought by "big oil companies" with "high-profile cultural association" in order to distract public attention from the "environmentally destructive nature of their activities" (as tobacco companies did until quite recently when sponsorship bans were introduced) (*The Guardian* June 28, 2010).

Haacke's artistic practice is part of what has been called institutional critique. This emerged in the late 1960s and early 1970s as a form of resistance to the reproduction of relations of domination expressed and legitimized in the cultural field by public art museums and commercial galleries (Ward 1995). Yet it does not escape the observer that Haacke's oeuvre is represented by works in the permanent collection of Tate. One work, *A Breed Apart* (1978), plays on an advertisement for Jaguar cars, then owned by British Leyland. It critiques the company for supporting South Africa's apartheid regime through the sale of police and military vehicles. Works from this period also investigated what Haacke believed to be the dubious business dealings of Philip Morris, Mobil Oil, Deutsche Bank, Mercedes-Benz, Alcan, and Tiffany, all major sponsors of arts institutions.

Haacke feels that artists need to be aware of the sociopolitical determinants of artistic production. But in tackling contemporary issues, often with overt political references, he is not so naïve as to believe that change will come about as a direct result of his work. However, he seems determined to draw public attention to what he sees as the dependence of leading arts institutions on multinational enterprises, pointing out the potential conflicts of interest which may curtail them from fulfilling their artistic and social responsibilities. Haacke's institutional critique has influenced other prominent contemporary artists such as Andrea Fraser, Fred Wilson, the Guerrilla Girls, and Carey Young (who are all represented in Tate's permanent collection).

Other radical artists and activists clearly have affinities with Haacke, but he tends to distance himself from parts of the legacy of institutional critique (Alberro and Stimson 2009; Sholette 1999; 2000; Raunig 2008; Raunig and Ray 2009). Recent artist collectives and groups include Platform, Art Not Oil, and Liberate Tate. Whether or not they are part of the tradition of institutional critique, these groups are not content with dismantling the operation of the art museum from within, and seek to operate outside the art world. For example, Platform describes itself as "promoting creative processes of democratic engagement to advance social and ecological justice" (Platform 2013). For its part, Art Not Oil is a project of Rising Tide UK working "for creativity, climate, justice and an end to oil industry sponsorship of the arts" (Art Not Oil website). Liberate Tate, as its name suggests, was formed in 2010 to "liberate" Tate from oil-based arts sponsorship (Liberate Tate 2013).

These activist art groups employ tactical media strategies to intervene and transform. Liberate Tate disrupted Tate Modern's 10th anniversary celebration in May 2010 in dramatic fashion. They released helium balloons filled with dead fish in the Turbine Hall which forced Tate security staff to bring them down with air rifles. As described above, Platform's Licence to Spill campaign was launched to interrupt the 2010 summer party at Tate Britain celebrating two decades of BP sponsorship. The main site was picketed as guests arrived. Activists gained entry and simulated an oil spill in one of the galleries.

The artistic critique of arts and business forcefully argues that the art museum is no longer sufficiently committed to the *public* agenda that gave rise to it in the first place (Alberro and Stimson 2009). Institutional critique demands that museums change. In particular, critics want Tate to discontinue any partnership with BP as an immediate goal. This would help to situate oil and gas producers alongside tobacco manufacturers as inappropriate corporate sponsors of arts institutions. Ultimately, social change addresses a broader question of how, as citizens, we reduce our dependence on a carbon-based economy (Bradley and Esche 2007).

Despite these charges, a rebuttal has been aired to critics of corporate support. First, they argue, corporate sponsorship is a mutual agreement (not coercion) between business firms and arts institutions. A time frame is established, whether a one-off event, or a relationship over several years, which means that both sides can assess the outcomes. Second, corporate support is part of plural funding, which has been actively promoted as part of government policy in the UK and other liberal democracies for many years to control public spending. Third, it may be asked whether a greater reliance on public support is actually better for arts institutions or not. Calls for more public funding, not an uncommon refrain from the arts community (see playwright Mark Ravenhill in *The Guardian*, June 30, 2010) characteristically assume the intrinsic public value of the arts without making an evidence-based case to justify their funding (on this point see Scott in this volume).

Yet critics of public funding cuts continue to point to the negative effects for art, artists, and art institutions. Opponents in the UK such as Mirza (2006) point out that instrumentalization of the arts can be detected. Extra-artistic government policy objectives may be included as part of any arts funding agreement. For example, in return for its government funding, Tate needs to respond to and report on what has been interpreted as a social cohesion agenda of socioeconomic, ethnic minority, and disability metrics.[8]

One year later

To mark the first anniversary of the Deepwater Horizon spill in April 2011, a letter was published in *The Guardian* as a companion to the one by Haacke et al., reiterating that Tate should end its relationship with BP. Naomi Klein, best known for her book *No Logo: Taking Aim at the Brand Bullies* (2000), was lead signatory. The letter read:

> While BP continues to jeopardise ecosystems, communities and the climate by the reckless pursuit of "frontier" oil, cultural institutions like Tate damage their reputation by continuing to be associated with such a destructive corporation.
>
> The massive cuts to public arts funding in the UK have left hundreds of culturally important arts organizations in a position of great financial vulnerability, which means that that debate about the appropriateness of particular potential corporate sponsors like BP and Shell is more relevant than ever. As people working in the arts, we believe that corporate sponsorship does not exist in an ethical vacuum. In light of the negative social and ecological impacts of BP around the world, we urge Tate to demonstrate its commitment to a sustainable future by ending its sponsorship relationship with BP. (*The Guardian*, April 20, 2011)

This message had similar features to the earlier Haacke letter: the Tate–BP sponsorship is a high-profile target; "big oil" is labeled as destructive; and Tate damages its reputation as an ethical institution by lending legitimacy to BP. In addition, activism by artists continued to draw attention to what was presented as the unholy alliance of oil and art. As well as Platform's Licence to Spill intervention at Tate Britain's 2010 summer party, Liberate Tate used the first anniversary of the BP oil spill in 2011 to stage a performance, *Human Cost*, at Tate Britain. In this dramatic performance in the sculpture gallery the prone figure of a naked man was covered in an oil-like substance (see Figure 8.2; for a video of the work see *Human Cost* 2011). A striking image of this scene was reproduced on the front page of the *Financial Times* the following day ("Not If but When" 2011, 87).

But despite the critique, big business continued on its path of growth and expansion, and the public continued to consume oil despite its links to arts sponsorship. Bob Dudley, Hayward's successor as BP's chief executive, used an op-ed in the *Wall Street Journal* to highlight the continuing significance of a carbon-based economy:

> Looking ahead, it is important to keep in mind that the global demand for energy will rise inexorably in coming decades – nearly 40% by 2030, according to BP estimates. That's roughly twice the current energy consumption of the entire US. Even as energy companies develop alternatives, the world will still need a large volume of oil. (*Wall Street Journal*, April 20, 2011)

Concluding questions

Is oil and gas the new tobacco? The simple response to the chapter title may remain, as I suggested at the outset, a conditional "no." However, the opinions aired by Haacke, Klein, and other artists and critics are unlikely to go away. More disasters and perceived transgressions by oil and gas companies are bound to occur in future. What difference has all this made to the perception of art museums? It seems to me that Tate, as a leading cultural institution, should re-assess and re-affirm a commitment to good governance. At stake is the reputation of art museums as among the most trusted and respected public institutions in the world.[9]

What about the economic pressure on arts institutions? The political move to diversify funding sources with less reliance on public funding will continue to present a challenging constraint for museums and galleries. Is Colin Tweedy, of Arts and Business, right to ask "Who's to say what's good or bad money?" Or is the Museums Association's Maurice Davies correct when he says that "Museums make judgements about who is a suitable sponsor"? (Davies said no to tobacco but yes to oil and gas.) We may well ask: How should such judgments be made? What role should the FTSE4Good sector exclusions serve for Tate? Should Tate be able to argue that oil and gas is not an excluded sector in order to justify its sponsorship agreement with BP? Or are there additional benchmarks to assess whether the corporate sponsor is suitable?

Aside from these questions, we can conclude that activist artists do help arts institutions to clarify who is an acceptable relationship partner, not least for those professionals with roles in marketing and sponsorship. As we have seen, protest campaigns bring competing claims about these issues into the public domain and open them up for debate, whether or not arts institutions and corporates agree with the way they get the message across. Multiple perspectives on contested social issues are of course essential in a democratic society, and relationships between multinational capitalism and the arts will continue to be one of those issues. Even if corporate sponsorship *is* deemed a necessary compromise for all arts institutions, the critiques by artists serve as trenchant social commentaries and expose the topic to wider public scrutiny.

In examining the complexities of this issue through the protest and its aftermath, this chapter has assessed the study of museums and business that we began with. Despite the work on sponsorship, marketing, and branding in museums, we need more detailed and critical research on commercial relationships between cultural institutions and corporates. Museum studies needs to move beyond the classic positions of either faith or antipathy toward the market and museums, and embark on a more balanced and situated research agenda in order to explore more thoroughly the complex financial challenges facing the contemporary museum today.

APPENDIX A
Tate consolidated statement of financial activity

For the year ended March 31, 2009

	Total funds 2008/2009 (£1,000)	Total funds 2007/2008 (£1,000)
Incoming resources		
Donated works of art	64,017	63,132
Other voluntary income	27,037	16,892
Trading incoming (includes catering, retail, and publishing income)	29,386	26,511
Other activities for operating funds (including sponsorship and events income)	6,216	5,646
Investment income	8,605	9,118
Total Grant-in-Aid (to fund operations, for buildings and works of art)	53,954	45,929
Other income (from charitable activities)	10,388	8,253
Other income	636	598
Total incoming resources	200,239	176,079
Resources expended		
Costs of generating voluntary income (e.g., donations)	2,614	3,381
Trading costs	27,276	23,986
Other costs of generating funds (e.g., costs of general sponsorship)	2,795	2,547
Investment management costs	47	43
Charitable activities: public programs	52,322	40,924
Charitable activities: support costs	23,552	23,044
Governance costs	660	604
Other costs	636	597
Total resources expended	109,902	95,126
Net income	90,337	80,953

Source: Tate Report 2008/2009.

Notes

1   This chapter is based on "The Gulf of Mexico Catastrophe: Impact on Relationships between Business and the Arts," which won the 2011 John Molson MBA International Case Writing Competition hosted by Concordia University. A note on websites: In-text references are made to the London *Guardian* website, which served as a media vehicle. http://www.guardian.co.uk. Citations attributed to BP are from the BP website. http://www.bp.com/bodycopyarticle.do?categoryId=1&contentId=7052055. Likewise, Tate quotations including the *Tate Report* are sourced from the Tate website. http://www.tate.org.uk. Collectives of artists have disseminated their activities in various online forums. Platform's disruption of the summer party at Tate Britain (on June 28, 2010), as part of an agenda of "promoting creative processes of democratic engagement to advance social and ecological justice," is documented: "Licence to Spill – Full Report" at http://www.youtube.com/watch?v=vPpWPbEPspY&feature=related; see also http://www.platformlondon.org. Art Not Oil initiatives "for creativity, climate justice and an end to oil sponsorship of the arts," including Liberate Tate's performance *Human Cost* at Tate Britain (on April 20, 2011), are hosted at http://www.artnotoil.org.uk//index.php?option=com_frontpage&Itemid=1. All sites accessed October 2, 2014.

2   The 2008–2011 Funding Agreement between the UK Department for Culture, Media and Sport (DCMS) and Tate can be found on the Tate website at http://www.tate.org.uk/about/who-we-are/funding. Accessed October 2, 2014.

3   Fortune Global 500 top 10 as of July 20, 2010: Wal-Mart Stores (sales revenue $408,214 million), Royal Dutch Shell, Exxon Mobil, BP, Toyota Motor, Japan Post Holdings, Sinopec, State Grid, AXA, and China National Petroleum ($165,496 million). FTSE 100 top 10 as of September 15, 2010: HSBC Holdings (market capitalization £119,067 million), Vodafone, BP, GlaxoSmithKline, Royal Dutch Shell 'A', Royal Dutch Shell 'B', Rio Tinto, Lloyds Banking Group, AstraZeneca, and British American Tobacco (£47,023 million).

4   Tate's other current long-term partnerships are: Bloomberg and Interpretive Tools (Tate Modern); Tate and Lyle (Tate Britain); Sotheby's (Tate Britain); UBS Openings (Tate Modern); Unilever Series (Tate Modern); Laurent Perrier; and AXA Art.

5   See n.6 below. Tate's board of trustees has 14 trustees: 13 are appointed by the Prime Minister; one is a trustee of the National Gallery. In addition, three trustees must be practicing artists (Jeremy Deller, Bob and Roberta Smith, Patrick Brill's pseudonym, and Wolfgang Tillmans). The chair is selected by the other trustees from their own number. Sir Nicholas Serota is director of Tate, heads the senior management team and is aided by 15 senior managers.

6   For more on Tate governance, see the following section of the Tate website: http://www.tate.org.uk/about/who-we-are/governance. Accessed October 2, 2014.

7   The roots of Schiller's position include Hans Magnus Enzensberger (1982) on the so-called consciousness industry and the industrialization of the human mind, and Erik Barnouw (1978) on the role of advertising in radio and television, namely the role the broadcast sponsor serves as a potentate of our time.

8   See the Funding Agreement mentioned above, specifically "audience profile."

9   It is important to note that Serota was a leading signatory of an online petition, http://
www.change.org/petitions/call-for-the-release-of-ai-weiwei (accessed October 2, 2014),
started by the Solomon R. Guggenheim Foundation petitioning the Ministry of Culture
of the People's Republic of China (PRC) to release Ai Weiwei. Indeed Tate Modern
was exhibiting Ai's *Sunflower Seeds* (2010), in the Turbine Hall as part of the Unilever
Series, at the time of his arrest on April 3, 2011 by the Chinese authorities.

References

Alberro, Alexander, and Blake Stimson, eds. 2009. *Institutional Critique: An Anthology of Artists' Writings*. Cambridge, MA: MIT Press.

AAMD (Association of Art Museum Directors). 2007. "Managing the Relationship between Art Museums and Corporate Sponsors." AAMD: New York and Washington. Accessed October 15, 2014. https://aamd.org/sites/default/files/document/Corporate%20Sponsors_clean%2006-2007.pdf.

Barnouw, Erik. 1978. *The Sponsor: Notes on a Modern Potentate*. New York: Oxford University Press.

Bishop, Claire. 2011. "Con-Demmed to the Bleakest of Futures: Report from the UK." E-flux journal. Accessed October 2, 2014. http://www.e-flux.com/journal/con-demmed-to-the-bleakest-of-futures-report-from-the-uk.

Bourdieu, Pierre, and Hans Haacke. 1995. *Free Exchange*. Trans. R. Johnson. Cambridge: Polity Press.

BP 2010. "BP Releases Report on Causes of Gulf of Mexico Tragedy. September 8, 2010." Accessed February 10, 2015. http://www.bp.com/en/global/corporate/press/press-releases/bp-releases-report-on-causes-of-gulf-of-mexico-tragedy-.html.

Bradley, Will, and Charles Esche, eds. 2007. *Art and Social Change: A Critical Reader*. London: Tate Publishing in association with Afterall.

Carrier, David. 2006. *Museum Skepticism: A History of the Display of Art in Public Galleries*. Durham, NC: Duke University Press.

"Crude Awakening: BP and the Tate." 2010. *The Guardian*, June 30. Accessed October 15, 2014. http://www.theguardian.com/artanddesign/2010/jun/30/bp-tate-protests.

Cuno, James, ed. 2004. *Whose Muse? Art Museums and the Public Trust*. Princeton, NJ: Princeton University Press.

Duncan, Carol. 1995. *Civilizing Rituals: Inside Public Art Museums*. New York: Routledge.

Enzensberger, Hans Magnus. 1982. "The Industrialization of the Mind." In *Hans Magnus Enzensberger: Critical Essays*, edited by Reinhold Grimm and Bruce Armstrong, 3–14. New York: Continuum.

"EU Austerity Drive Country by Country." 2012. BBC. Accessed October 2, 2014. http://www.bbc.co.uk/news/10162176.

Fraser, Andrea. 2002. "'To quote', say the Kabyles, 'is to bring back to life'." *October* 101: 7–11.

French, Ylva, and Sue Runyard. 2011. *Marketing and Public Relations for Museums, Galleries, and Cultural and Heritage Attractions*. London: Routledge.

Frey, Bruno. 1998. "Superstar Museums: An Economic Analysis." *Journal of Cultural Economics* 22(2–3): 113–125.

Friedman, Milton. 1962. *Capitalism and Freedom*. Chicago: University of Chicago Press.

"Four National Treasures: One Long History." 2011. *The Spectator*, January 11. Accessed October 2, 2014. http://www.exacteditions.com/read/the-spectator/29-january-2011–8225/6/2.

Gingrich, Arnold. 1969. *Business and the Arts: An Answer for Tomorrow*. New York: Paul S. Erikson.

Haacke, Hans. 2002. "Public Servant." *October* 101: 4–6.

Hayek, Friedrich. 1944. *The Road to Serfdom*. Chicago: University of Chicago Press.

Hobsbawm, Eric, and Terence Ranger, eds. 1983. *The Invention of Tradition*. Cambridge: Cambridge University Press.

Holden, John. 2007. *Publicly-Funded Culture and the Creative Industries*. London: Arts Council England/Demos.

"Human Cost: Tate Britain Performance." 2011. Vimeo. Accessed October 20, 2014. http://vimeo.com/22677737.

IEG (Institute for Economic Growth). 2014. Lexicon and Glossary. Accessed October 15, 2014. http://www.sponsorship.com/Resources/IEG-Lexicon-and-Glossary.aspx.

Janes, Robert, and Richard Sandell, eds. 2007. *Museum Management and Marketing*. London: Routledge.

Klein, Naomi. 2000. *No Logo: Taking Aim at the Brand Bullies*. New York: Picador.

Kotler, Neil, Philip Kotler, and Wendy Kotler. 2008. *Museum Marketing and Strategy: Designing Missions, Building Audiences, Generating Revenue and Resources*, 2nd ed. San Francisco: Jossey-Bass.

Liberate Tate. 2013. Website. Accessed October 2, 2014. http://liberatetate.wordpress.com.

Lord, Barry, and Gail Lord. 2009. *The Manual of Museum Management*. Lanham, MD: AltaMira.

McClellan, Andrew. 2008. *The Art Museum from Boullee to Bilbao*. Berkeley, CA: University of California Press.

Mirza, Munira, ed. 2006. *Culture Vulture: Is UK Arts Policy Damaging the Arts?* London: Policy Exchange.

"Not If But When: Art beyond Oil." 2011. Platform: Arts, Activism, Education, Research. Accessed October 2, 2014. http://issuu.com/mellv/docs/cbo/87?e=1975852/2606665

Olins, Wally. 1994. *Corporate Identity*. London: Thames and Hudson.

Pavitt, Jane, ed. 2000. *Brand.New*. London: V&A Publications.

Phillips, Martha, and Darragh O'Reilly. 2007. "Major Case Study: Rethinking Tate Modern as an Art Museum 'Brand.'" In *Museum Marketing: Competing in the Global Marketplace*, edited by Ruth Rentschler and Anne-Marie Hede, 187–193. Oxford: Butterworth-Heinemann.

Platform. 2013. Website. Accessed October 2, 2014. http://www.platformlondon.org/carbonweb/documents/summerparty.pdf.

Pointon, Marcia, ed. 1994. *Art Apart: Art Institutions and Ideology across England and North America*. Manchester: Manchester University Press.

Prior, Nick. 2003. "Having One's Tate and Eating It: Transformations of the Museum in the Hypermodern Era." In *Art and Its Publics: Museum Studies at the End of the Millennium*, edited by A. McClellan, 51–74. Oxford: Blackwell.

Raunig, Gerald. 2008. "What Is Critique: Suspension and Recomposition in Textual and Social Machines." Transversal: European Institute for Progressive Social Policies. Accessed October 2, 2014. http://eipcp.net/transversal/0808/raunig/en.

Raunig, Gerald and Gene Ray, eds. 2009. *Art and Contemporary Critical Practice: Reinventing Institutional Critiques*. London: Mayfly.

Rectanus, Mark. 2002. *Culture Incorporated: Museums, Artists and Corporate Sponsorships*. Minneapolis: University of Minnesota Press.

Schiller, Herbert. 1989. *Culture, Inc.: The Corporate Takeover of Public Expression*. New York: Oxford University Press.

Schmitt, Bernd H., David L. Rogers, and Karen Vrotsos. 2004. *There's No Business That's Not Show Business: Marketing in an Experience Culture*. Upper Saddle River, NJ: FT Press.

Scott, Carol. 2000. "Branding: Positioning Museums in the 21st Century." *International Journal of Arts Management* 2(3): 35–39.

Serota, Nicholas. 1996. *Experience or Interpretation: The Dilemma of Museums of Modern Art*. London: Thames and Hudson.

Sholette, Gregory. 1999. "Counting on Your Collective Silence: Notes on Activist Art as Collaborative Practice." Gregory Sholette: Writings. Accessed October 20, 2014. http://www.gregorysholette.com/wp-content/uploads/2011/04/09_counting1.pdf.

Sholette, Gregory. 2000. "Some Call It Art: From Imaginary Autonomy to Autonomous Collectivity." Gregory Sholette: Writings. Accessed October 20, 2014. http://www.gregorysholette.com/wp-content/uploads/2011/04/06_somecallit1.pdf.

Twitchell, James. 2004. *Branded Nation: The Marketing of Megachurch, College Inc., and Museumworld*. New York: Simon and Schuster.

UK Sponsorship. 2010. "National Portrait Gallery, Tate, Royal Opera House and British Museum Issue Prepared Joint Statement on BP Sponsorship." June 24. Accessed October 2, 2014. http://www.uksponsorship.com/ukjun10.htm.

Wallace, Margot. 2006. *Museum Branding: How to Create and Maintain Image, Loyalty, and Support*. Lanham, MD: AltaMira.

Wallis, Brian, ed. 1986. *Hans Haacke: Unfinished Business*. New York: New Museum of Contemporary Art; Cambridge, MA: MIT Press.

Ward, Frazer. 1995. "The Haunted Museum: Institutional Critique and Publicity." *October* 73: 71–89.

Witcomb, Andrea. 2003. *Re-Imagining the Museum: Beyond the Mausoleum*. London: Routledge.

Wu, Chin-tao. 2003. *Privatizing Culture: Corporate Intervention since the 1980s*. London: Verso.

Further Reading

McCarthy, Kevin, Elizabeth Heneghan Ondaatje, Arthur Brooks, and András Szántós. 2005. *A Portrait of the Visual Arts: Meeting the Challenges of a New Era*. Santa Monica, CA: Rand.

McLean, Fiona. 2012. *Marketing the Museum*. London: Routledge.

Power, Michael. 1994. *The Audit Explosion*. London: Demos.

Rentschler, Ruth, and Anne-Marie Hede, eds. 2009. *Museum Marketing: Competing in the Global Marketplace*. Oxford: Butterworth-Heinemann.

Derrick Chong was Associate Dean (Education) between 2011 and 2014 in the Faculty of Management and Economics at Royal Holloway, University of London, where he taught a core first-year course, Markets and Consumption. He is originally from Canada where he read business administration and art history; his PhD is from the University of London. An earlier version of this chapter won the 2011 John Molson [Concordia University] MBA International Case Writing Competition.

9 FROM IDIOSYNCRATIC TO INTEGRATED
Strategic Planning for Collections

James B. Gardner

In the fall of 2001, in the weeks that followed the events of September 11, various staff at the Smithsonian's National Museum of American History (NMAH) in Washington DC began collecting objects related to the attacks and their aftermath. As Associate Director for Curatorial Affairs, I became concerned about the limited nature of what we were collecting. Operating independently, curators quickly collected artifacts that documented the engineering of the World Trade Center, the public response to rescuers after the attacks, and other important fragments of the day and its aftermath. Individual curators were doing admirable jobs collecting those items that fitted within their units' self-defined priorities, but no one was looking at the larger story that crossed collecting boundaries. In other words, museum staff were doing excellent work within the usual isolation of their individual collections, but they were not really thinking about the museum's larger responsibilities. What was absent was a museum-wide vision, providing the connective tissue and the sense of purpose and intentionality that makes the difference between collecting "things" and building a collection. So, after much thought, I decided to recruit a small group of staff to develop a plan for the museum to "collect September 11." Over the months that followed, they worked collaboratively, outside their normal specializations and their usual responsibilities. Together they built an important collection for the museum and for the nation (Gardner 2005).

The isolation I encountered at this particular historical moment was endemic of a larger problem with institutional collecting: business as usual often means being satisfied with the parts rather than aiming for the whole, for a more integrated and less fragmented collection. Concerned, I asked the American Association of Museums (AAM; now known as the American Alliance of Museums) for assistance in determining best practices in collections planning. I thought they could give me copies of good plans that I could revise and adapt for our purposes. But instead, AAM replied that from what they could tell there was surprisingly

The International Handbooks of Museum Studies: Museum Practice, First Edition.
Edited by Conal McCarthy.
© 2015 John Wiley & Sons Ltd. Published 2020 by John Wiley & Sons Ltd.

little good collections planning going on. Furthermore AAM's Accreditation Commission noted that over a fourth of negative actions regarding museum accreditation in the United States at that time cited inadequacies in collections stewardship (Sullivan 2004, 1; Merritt 2008; AAM 2014). The Accreditation Commission found a pattern of recurring problems connected to collections stewardship and institutional planning, including insufficient resources and collections unrelated to the institution's mission; and a lack of integration between planning for collections, interpretation, and facilities (Gardner and Merritt 2004b, 294).

Concerned about this situation, AAM proposed that we join forces in a collections planning initiative that would both provide the Museum of American History with the guidance and advice it sought and also initiate a larger profession-wide discussion of standards and best practices regarding collections development. So we did just that, convening in 2002 a national colloquium which provided the basis for further seminars and publications (see Gardner and Merritt 2004a for the report including discussion summaries, a glossary of terms, and other resources). The discussion that follows draws on this work, establishing the rationale for collections planning within the context of current museum practice, describing the planning process and the key components of a plan, explaining the critical role of an intellectual framework, and addressing the challenges to collections planning, both conceptual and organizational. This chapter is necessarily autobiographical to an extent, and it is important to acknowledge my central role as both author and subject positioned within the process described. Indeed, it is grounded in professional practice rather than a body of literature. Such is the importance of this topic which has rarely been discussed in the academic literature, that I feel a personal account of collections planning at the Smithsonian is justified, opening up this subject for wider discussion, much-needed research, and further debate.

Collections planning: what and why?

What is a collections plan? How is it different from other collections-focused policies and statements? First of all, a collections plan is not a policy. While in some contexts, the term "policy" is used to encompass some of what is addressed below (Knell 2004, 13), the focus in planning is not on principles, standards, or rules to regulate or govern collecting; rather it concerns overall strategies for *how* to collect. Thus a collections plan should not be confused with a collections management policy, which is "a written document, approved by the governing authority, that specifies the museum's policies concerning all collections-related issues, including accessioning, documentation, storage and disposition" (Gardner and Merritt 2004a, 69). Nor is a collections plan the same as a "scope of collections" statement, a document that only describes a museum's existing collections or what the museum collects or intends to collect, which is to say the basic parameters of the museum's collecting. Professionals sometimes use a "collecting plan," which identifies what a museum wants to actively acquire over time, but that usually does not address the larger strategic needs critical to sustaining the collections. A collections plan is strategic, guiding the content of the collections and providing "coordinated and uniform direction over time to refine and expand the value of the collections in a predetermined way." Rather than categorizing collections by type, topic, time period, geographical boundary, or other criteria, a collections plan focuses on the ideas, concepts, stories, or themes that provide the rationale for the museum's collecting decisions. Such a plan specifies how choices "will be achieved, who will implement the plan, when it will happen, and what it will cost" and addresses "deaccessioning, resource allocation, partnerships with other museum, and other aspects of building and sustaining the collections" (Gardner and Merritt 2004a, 69).

There is little literature to review on this topic, and in this section of the chapter I draw extensively on the published few works that have tackled the problems with museum collections development, including reports and one of my own publications which this chapter builds on. The call for a more strategic appraisal of collections is backed up by Knell in *Museums and the Future of Collecting*, when he calls for "a more long-term, holistic, inclusive, integrated, cooperative, sustainable, rational and thoughtful view of … institutional collecting" (2004, 15). He argues that collecting should be recognized not as simply "an act of accumulation" but as a larger responsibility that encompasses "every moment in the life of an object in the collections" (2004, 17). But apart from Knell, there is surprisingly little discussion of this need. In *Fragments of the World: Uses of Museum Collections*, Keene argues for a "more rational" approach to collecting and more attention to justifying collections and collecting but seems more concerned with access and use than strategic development (2005, 30, 177, 187). Indeed before beginning this initiative, AAM surveyed the field and uncovered little on the subject and few examples of good planning by museums. What has since been published has been derived largely from the work of Elizabeth Merritt and myself. In their 2012 chapter on collections planning, Meister and Hoff confirm, ten years later, the persistence of the problem. "Significant resources are devoted to acquisition, management and care of collections," they write, "so why do we not devote the same amount of effort to planning what goes into our collections and questioning how our collections serve our mission and audiences?" (2012, 110).

Apart from this, however, most of the literature on collecting that is not about collections management focuses on the meaning of objects and collections rather than the more practical challenge of planning. For example, rather than engaging in the on-the-ground problems of museums in regard to collections responsibilities and resources, Knell focuses largely on intellectual issues at a much higher level. That paucity of discussion is in stark contrast to the abundant literature on collections management, which focuses on practical, hands-on matters to the exclusion of the larger intellectual context for building or shaping collections (on collection management see Simmons in this volume). Collections planning bridges those debates, linking theory and intellectual frameworks with the day-to-day realities of collecting. Much of this chapter, therefore, explores current professional thinking going on below the academic radar, in which practice is pushing ahead of theory.

In arguing for thinking more strategically about collections, I am not concerned with the important discussions by Knell and others about why we collect or how different ways of knowing shape the *meaning* of collections (Knell 2004, 2–4, 15–32; Conn 2010; Weil 2004). Nor do I question whether we should collect at all (Gurian 2004), or question the idea of the perpetuity of collections (Knell 2004, 15–16). On the related issue of reviving active collecting see Merriman (this volume). While these writings provide a useful philosophical context for planning, they do not advance the actual work of planning as museum practice. Whether we agree with critics of museum collecting today or not, I would argue that collections planning simply makes good sense. As Knell (2004, 15, 37) and others argue, we need to collect better, and strategic planning for collections is the key (Young 2004, 188; Gagnon and Fitzgerald 2004, 15).

More specifically, collections planning makes it possible for a museum to gain intellectual control over its collections on an operational level, that is to say to align the rationale of collections and collecting with larger institutional priorities. While his proposal for "pruning" collections may be a bit extreme, Knell is certainly on solid ground in arguing that museum collecting needs to be rationalized within its institutional context and not rely on the individual subjectivities of staff (2004, 15–19). Of course individual curators usually have an impressive knowledge of the collections for which they are responsible, and often have interesting collecting initiatives underway, so that on the whole museum collections, whether small or large, have impressive quality and depth. But that comes at a price. At a museum the size of the Museum of American History at the Smithsonian Institution, you find a loose coalition of relatively autonomous curators, often with rather idiosyncratic goals, building on their predecessors' interests and work, adding depth and new topics. Too often that work is in isolation from other staff and other units. How can NMAH or any other museum be sure that it is making the right choices if it does not have a larger vision of what the collections should be?

Another advantage of collections planning is that it allows museums to better utilize shrinking resources. Few museums today can afford to simply continue doing what they have done, because of cuts to budgets and staffing levels. As Knell warns, "museums need to confront the resource implications of collections" (2004, 7). More problematic are orphaned or "dead" collections, that is to say collections which are not being actively used or added to, or for which no staff has been assigned at all. Space is another issue. As is the case with nearly every Smithsonian museum, NMAH's capacity to store and care for collections has been diminishing. The museum has filled up its existing collections storage, and it no longer has the staff or financial resources to conserve standing collections. Whether one agrees with the conservative growth projections proposed a decade ago by Weil (2004, 284–285) or the more alarming numbers reported by Šola (2004, 252–253), the reality is that few museums have the resources to collect and care for everything that might be of interest. For its part, NMAH has recognized that it needs to better focus collecting, to collect better and smarter, and to make difficult choices. The harsh reality, as Knell again reminds us, is that collecting is never free, even if an object is donated. The cost of care is "relentlessly cumulative" (Knell 2004, 37), constituting a financial burden on the future.

Lastly, collections planning enables museums to determine what they are *not* doing. During my tenure at the Museum of American History (1999–2011), I was less concerned with how to restrict collecting and more with how to focus it better. As Barbro Bursell persuasively argues, "Without ongoing collecting activity, museums will lose their memory function; they will cease to be living institutions, but rather fossilized monuments to a vanished age" (2004, 205). Indeed the reality is that, even though resources are tight, the issue for NMAH has not been whether the collections will continue to grow, but how. A related and thornier challenge has been determining what the museum does *not* have rather than what it *does*, in other words where the major gaps are, and therefore what it should be collecting to address those gaps.

While museums may be inherently conservative institutions resistant to change, widespread change is nevertheless challenging the ways that museums approach collecting. The original intellectual disciplines in which museums are rooted – art, history, science, anthropology, archaeology, or whatever – are evolving, and museums ignore that at their peril (Conn 1998, 2010; Keene 2005, 2006; see also Merriman in this volume).

But museums must also recognize that grounding collecting in new scholarship can challenge the very foundations for collections, the rationale for why an institution has what it has. Indeed the scope of institutions and collections may need to be rethought–in some cases to tighten and better focus, in other cases to broaden, recognizing that the world is becoming more complicated and interconnected (Keene 2005; see also Merriman this volume). Growing diversity in audiences and their expectations are a major issue for museums, as is demonstrated by several chapters in this volume (see Davidson, Black; see also Knell 2004, 20–37). As the world changes, or at least our understanding of it catches up, how do museums refocus collecting? In some cases, this means revaluing museum collections from a different perspective (Dominy 2004). But museums also need to think about *new* collecting. What is the intersection between the engagement of visitors and collections and collecting? Do the public have a role in reshaping collecting? And as we move into a virtual world, where the actual location of objects matters less, what impact will digital technology have on museum collecting?

Finally, we have to recognize that the vagaries of the economy are a significant factor even for collections. When the economy sours, museums, many of which struggle even in the best of times. are forced to retrench, and that mean making difficult choices about what to collect and what to forgo. As Bursell argues, in relation to Sweden, if a museum cannot explain why it collects what it does, then it will not be able to secure the resources it needs, jeopardizing its future (2004, 210).

Developing a collections plan

> *The written document is the least important part of collections planning; at best, it is a means of remembering the plan and communicating it to others. The planning process that brings that document into being and keeps it alive is far more important.*
>
> Merritt 2004, 27.

With all planning, as Elizabeth Merritt reminds us, the overall process is as important as the actual plan itself. Through the planning process, a museum's stakeholders reach agreement about what to do and how to do it in that specific context; that is the crucial element that determines success. Obviously, an institutional commitment to planning is critical. Collections planning must be a priority of a museum's leadership, with the appropriate commitment of human and financial resources. But how planning proceeds depends on what works within the culture of the particular museum. It is not important whether the work proceeds from the bottom up (an inclusive approach that begins with input from across the museum's community), from the top down (which focuses on leadership developing a draft that can then be the basis for broader discussion), or through some combination of both (see for example Gardner and Merritt 2004a, 27–32).

NMAH pursued a combination of both approaches. In this case the focus was on internal rather than external stakeholders. While management initiated the planning, the development of the collections plan was the responsibility of a task force of curators – not really a grassroots effort, since they were the curatorial leadership. The broader staff was engaged in and kept informed of the planning through oral and written updates, and the plan was then shared in draft electronically for comment and discussion. That process would not work at a smaller institution or where there is a stronger constituency of volunteers, users, or others who feel a greater stake in the collections than one finds in a national museum such as NMAH. Whatever the particular context, different from museum to museum, the main point here is that planning ideally should be organic, should grow out of the institution's culture.

While a collections plan can take different approaches and formats, in our case the National Collections Planning Colloquium in 2002, which Elizabeth Merritt and I later wrote up in a book published in 2004, identified the following as key components (Gardner and Merritt 2004a, 25):

- Executive summary – a short overview of the plan, recognizing that some stakeholders may not read the entire document.
- Preamble – basically a public relations tool, addressing (for internal and external audiences) the purpose of the plan and describing how it was developed, who participated, and who wrote it.

- Setting the stage – a discussion of the context, including the museum's mission or statement of purpose, its vision, and the relationship to other plans and policies.
- Intellectual framework – the vision for the collection, answering the question "Where is the museum going?" and identifying intended audience(s) for and users of the collections and the role the collections play in helping the museum fulfill its mission.
- Analysis of existing collections – answering the question "Where is the museum now?" through a comprehensive description of the collection, a history of the collection and collecting, a gap analysis (strengths and weaknesses in the context of the intellectual framework), and identification of connections to other institutions and their collections.
- Shaping the ideal collection – an outline of priorities, strategies, and criteria for acquisition and deaccessioning.
- Implementation strategy – answering the question "How is the museum going to get there?" through action steps that identify existing and needed resources (time, space, money), establish a timeline, and assign responsibilities.
- Evaluation – measures of success and methods of evaluation.
- Reviewing the plan – specifics of when and by whom the plan will be reviewed.

The intent of the National Collections Planning Colloquium was not to be prescriptive but rather to suggest the areas or issues that a museum should address. Thus NMAH adapted the list, collapsing the components into four groups:

- Setting the stage – including the executive summary and the preamble.
- Intellectual framework.
- Analysis of existing collections.
- Implementation strategy – including shaping the ideal collection, evaluation, and reviewing the plan.

NMAH then organized the work in four concurrent phases, establishing different time frames for developing each segment of the plan. The reasoning was that planning such as this would be more practicable if tackled in steps or phases, with a manageable and realistic agenda. For NMAH, writing the section on "setting the stage" was particularly important. Because this was new territory, the museum needed an internal document that would explain *why* the museum was developing an institutional collections plan, *what* its goals were, and *what* the process for developing it would be. Thus NMAH's "setting the stage" working group was charged with expediting its work so that the draft could be circulated within a couple of weeks to staff to help them get a better sense of what was going on and how it would affect their work. More specifically, the NMAH document was framed by a series of critical questions:

- Why does the museum need a collections plan?
- What does a collections plan include?

- What goals will a new collections plan help the museum accomplish?
- How should the collections planning process be defined and managed?
- How should reporting occur, and what elements should be included in the final plan?
- What larger institutional governing policies and regulations provide the context for planning?
- How does the collections plan relate to the current strategic goals and objectives of the museum?
- Who are the audiences for the museum's collections plan, and what forms should different parts of it take to reach each of those audiences?

Beginning its work at the same time, NMAH's second working group was charged with developing a new intellectual framework for collecting. Since they had the most critical and difficult assignment, they had the longest time frame, and that task ended up taking even longer than anticipated. They invested hours every week for months working on a new framework, and then the larger steering committee similarly debated and revised the framework before sending it to the director for review.

The initial direction to NMAH's "collections assessment" group was to pull together preliminary baseline data, with the complicated task of assessing the collections against the intellectual framework to come later. For all museums, the challenge in assessing the collections is to work from the themes to the collections, rather than from the collections to the themes. In order to re-center the discussion from what is already in the collections to what should be in the collections, a museum has to shift its focus from simply growing the current collection along preexisting lines to refining the collection within a clearer framework arising out of its broader institutional mission and vision.

For any museum, the most important working group in collections planning is the one charged with developing implementation strategies. NMAH jumpstarted this by identifying existing collecting models that could be the basis for "quick wins" that would be concrete demonstrations of how collecting could be changed through planning. The September 11 collecting initiative was the most important such "win" in demonstrating the potential of new perspectives, but the museum had other early successes such as an assessment across several units of collecting that focused on post-1945 home and family life, which yielded a small but significant new collecting initiative related to Korean adoption. Through these and other initiatives, the museum modeled new, collaborative collecting in support of its vision and immediately began building a foundation for the implementation that would follow.

Finally, dissemination and review are critical throughout the process. A plan presented to stakeholders as a done deal, developed and imposed from above or outside, will almost certainly fail. Just as planning should grow out of the culture of the specific museum, so should the format of the plan address the museum's different stakeholders. The same documents may not work for all. For example, NMAH knew that its board would not be interested in wading through the intellectual framework: they would want only an executive summary of the plan.

The intellectual framework

The key to collections planning is the intellectual framework. Essentially this is the "big idea" of a museum, on a par with the vision and mission that provide overall direction (see also Fleming in this volume). In providing the rationale for, or theory of, the collections and collecting, the intellectual framework establishes a compelling statement that defines the distinct role for a particular museum and provides the context for making decisions about the future of its collections. It is both the most critical piece of collections planning and the most difficult part of the plan to develop, requiring a long, hard look at where a museum is going.

Knell argues that, while most museums have policies regarding legal and ethical issues and the like, too few provide "a deeper intellectual rationale for collecting" (2004, 13). Likewise, Šola believes that museums, quite simply, need to articulate "the ends" of collecting and collections (2004, 253); furthermore the National Colloquium proposed that every museum should have an underlying conceptual structure that focuses the museum's collecting. More specifically, as I and my co-author Elizabeth Merritt reported in 2004, there was a call for museums to develop intellectual frameworks for their collections, addressing "the mission and the needs of the users," "often organized around ideas, concepts, stories, or interpretive themes that guide exhibits, programming, and research as well as collecting," and with enough specificity "to guide decision-making" (Gardner and Merritt 2004a, 70).

Many museums in the USA – especially those that collect history, art, or culture – continue to rely on relatively autonomous curators to develop the collections. Despite what the public may assume, and the guidance of policies and other objective controls, institutional collecting is a subjective process (Pearce 1989, 9), reflecting choices made by individual curators over time to collect some things and let other things go. Most museums today only have collecting plans that are little more than unit-by-unit lists of what is in the collections and what the priority collecting targets are. But the goal, as Richard Dunn (2004, 71) puts it so succinctly, should be "self-conscious collecting." An intellectual framework makes that possible, moving a museum from simply building or adding to its collections to actively shaping them. An intellectual framework shifts collecting from the personal, professional, or scholarly interests of individuals to a shared vision of the collections as a whole. That vision must be shared not only by the museum's staff but by the larger community of stakeholders, especially by audiences and users. Museums have different purposes and different audiences, and their collecting goals and frameworks should reflect that diversity. A museum's intellectual framework must reflect the disciplinary culture and the community context that defines it as an institution.

An intellectual framework is *not* just a summary statement of what a museum is about. It is also about where it is going. The framework can be crucial, for example, to the alignment or realignment of a museum's mission and collections. Consider the Museum of American History, which opened in 1964 as the Museum of History and Technology, with an agenda both broader and narrower at the same time. It did not explicitly narrow its focus to American history and did not more fully embrace social history until around 1980. How does such change in direction impact collecting? While arguably the idea of a museum should grow from its collections, the existing collections should not keep a museum from repositioning or even reinventing itself. An intellectual framework should therefore focus on what *can be*, not what simply is.

Developing an intellectual framework can also help formalize shifts in scope and direction. For example, national museums have long focused on the political contexts in which they were established: the nation state. But today many national museums are changing the scope of what they collect beyond the confines of the nation, broadening their agendas to encompass the messier and arguably richer side of human experience that pays little attention to national frameworks (Knell 2010). Some of this involves looking in new ways at what they already have, but it should also inspire new collecting, articulated in an intellectual framework. Maritime museums, on the other hand, have in one way or another long recognized and even collected global or international history, but many are now more explicitly embracing globalization as part of their scope. But does every maritime museum need to tackle this topic? Is there a difference between an individual museum's responsibility and the roles that museums can play collectively in collecting?

How does a museum develop an intellectual framework? The actual development of a framework begins with a museum's mission statement, but the latter is not likely to provide a clear enough vision for the collections in and of itself. For example, the mission statement of the Museum of American History reads: "The National Museum of American History, Behring Center dedicates its collections and scholarship to inspiring a broader understanding of our nation and its many peoples. We create learning opportunities, stimulate imaginations, and present challenging ideas about our country's past" (NMAH 2014). While it is important that the mission statement positions collections at the heart of NMAH's work, it does not establish even basic parameters of place, time, and subject. So the museum's challenge has been to "interpret" the mission and establish a bridge from that mission to the collections and collecting. Few museums do any better: generally speaking, mission statements do not establish the parameters or direction that are needed for an intellectual framework. Thus the NMAH's intellectual framework includes a collecting mission (why the museum collects), statements or assumptions about the role of collecting and collections in the museum, intellectual principles for future collecting, and eight themes. The eight themes do not constitute a classification scheme but are inter-related and intersecting, offering multiple perspectives on the museum's collections and collecting. They do not correspond to specific collections or units but are overarching, bridging the parts of the museum to establish larger goals for the whole:

- Creating culture.
- Experiencing home and community life.
- Interacting with the world.
- Peopling America.
- Shaping and using science, medicine, and technology.
- Shaping the economy.
- Shaping the political landscapes.
- Transforming the environment.

For each theme, active verbs are used to emphasize that these are not static concepts situated in the past but evolving and continuing into the present. Each is presented in three parts:

- A broad description of the theme.
- Topics that are included within the theme and that may or may not be represented in the collections.
- Suggested emphases or priorities for the future.

For example, "creating culture" is defined as follows:

> This theme is concerned with the development and expression of American cultural histories. It deals with the invention of and changes in the forms and media of cultural expression, shaped by identities and communities. It is concerned with how Americans create, learn, and express their cultural literacy.

Some of the topics included in this theme are the performance of identity and culture (i.e., how Americans perform their cultural identities); the business of culture (the buying and selling of culture) and ever-changing American patterns of cultural consumption; the politics of culture; the nature of and changes in American expressive culture. Obviously, this is rooted in current scholarship and the recognition of multivocal authorities and reflects the contested meaning of the past and the challenges that this particular museum faces in the changing global context. Each theme is similarly grounded, challenging the museum to collect in new ways.

Other museums might approach this task very differently – there is no single model or formula. A framework could consist of a series of statements or parameters, or it could pose questions to frame collecting. A framework might be more complex, perhaps a matrix or chart overlaying different themes or concepts with object types or priorities. The point is that a framework should be tailored to the museum – the end product really depends on such variables as the discipline of the museum, its function, and other defining characteristics. What should be avoided is any assessment of the collections (that is a different task in collections planning), and it should not include criteria such as provenance or value or address policies and procedures. But whether simple or complex, the point of a framework should be the same: to step away from a description of what the museum *has* and develop a vision for what the collections *should be*.

A framework should be detailed enough to guide collecting but not too restrictive or confining. Establishing focus should not curtail a museum's flexibility, as it should still be able to accommodate new collecting directions that respond to recent scholarship, evolving institutional goals, even new opportunities. For example, the NMAH had the opportunity to acquire an important group of firefighting artifacts, a collection of national significance in an area in which the museum had done limited collecting, but also a collection that would come with significant stewardship needs and require a sizeable commitment of scarce resources. While the particular topic had not previously been a high priority, the collections committee reviewed the idea within the context of the intellectual framework and concluded that it not only constituted a unique opportunity but also fitted well within the museum's collecting vision. In other words, the collections plan provided the critical context for decision-making that had long-term resource and stewardship requirements.

In arguing that an intellectual framework should not be too restrictive or confining, I also mean that it should not be viewed as a hard and fast rule that forces deaccessioning. What is important is that the framework provides the context for a discussion about what to keep and what to let go. A museum might decide to keep a legacy collection that is important for other reasons but not a good fit within the framework, and that is perfectly reasonable. The point is that the museum addresses such collections openly and makes decisions as an institution, and does not hold on to an object or objects through inertia.

Whatever the format or organization, the goal is the same: to provide a persuasive argument that establishes a single vision. An intellectual framework should be clear and understandable, free of jargon and scholarly digressions. What it looks like in terms of format is not important. A framework can be a discrete section of the larger plan, or it can be merged with other elements. The point is to establish a clear context for planning, for assessing and revaluing objects, initiating new collecting, and making difficult decisions about what to deaccession.

Challenges to planning

Strategic planning for collections is not easy, and museums that undertake it face a number of challenges or tensions, both intellectual and organizational, that have to be resolved. While the discussion can be unsettling, the issues are arguably foundational and should be on the agenda for any collecting institution. Collections planning foregrounds intellectual or conceptual tensions that are often just below the surface, such as that between legacy collections and new directions. If a museum decides to pursue new collecting directions, what happens to existing collections? Should the museum continue building them? What happens to historic, taxonomic collections, and synoptic series in a new world of thematically developed or focused collections? Does a commitment to the latter mean letting go of older collecting traditions? Are the two incompatible? Knell argues against assuming the significance of any objects just because a museum has had them for a long time. "All museum objects acquire histories which might suggest significance," he writes, "but there is a danger in valuing the object just because it has been a long-term resident in the collections" (Knell 2004, 28). Appropriately he points out that there is no "one-size-fits-all" answer. Each museum must work through this issue within the context of its culture and history.

Another tension arises between current and future needs. When setting priorities, museums have to sort out how to balance immediate needs and longer-term goals. A related issue is the potential conflict between passive collecting and planned collecting. Many history curators would argue that the best collecting is done after a certain period of time has passed, so that museums can wait and see from a historical distance what the public values and saves. But could such a strategy mean the risk of missing out on collecting opportunities in today's fast changing and increasingly disposable world? Can collections planning allow for the serendipitous while pursuing carefully worked out documentation strategies?

Institutional goals and collective responsibilities are another area of tension: every museum has a unique role or responsibility, reflected in its mission and goals, but that is not always fully reflected in collecting. While it may be obvious that the NMAH is a national museum, what is "national" in regard to collecting and what is not? What should a nation's history collection be? Should it be comprehensive to support a comprehensive interpretation of national history? Does that mean the history of nationhood, or should a national history museum address the more complex social history of a people, apart from politics and wars?

As part of the planning process, a museum should identify not only what makes it distinctive but also the areas where it is not unique, in other words areas where collecting responsibilities can be shared with other institutions. Knell argues that too often museums assume that there should be a "direct geographical match between funding body and the area from which the museum collects" (2004, 14). As an example of how rethinking this can change collecting, he points to the National Museum of Australia in Canberra, which recognized at its founding that:

> a distributed national collection already existed and that it needed to take this into account in its collecting. It can be a perspective less based on the possessive drive to acquire objects and more on the broader intellectual rationale of the museum, which encourages sustainability through shared values and shared collections, but which is so easily lost where local or singular perspectives dominate. (Knell 2004, 40)

But there are also more mundane organizational and management challenges to strategic planning for collections – resistance to change is a part of many if not most cultural institutions. Collections planning challenges curatorial autonomy, substituting a shared, museum-wide vision for the independent curator's vision and challenging many fundamental assumptions about curatorial roles and responsibilities. In order to take responsibility for collecting the broader stories that are critical to public outreach and engagement, in place of a loose coalition of independent curators, museums like NMAH need teams of curators committed to the museum's larger collecting interests. But how does a museum navigate the mismatch between larger planning goals and day-to-day care? That issue becomes even more complicated when planning moves beyond the individual museum to larger systems or collaborations. In the final analysis, I would argue that, as a participant at the National Colloquium put it, "It's not about me; it's about the museum" (Gardner and Merritt 2004a, 33).

Resistance may come from other quarters as well. Senior management may be supportive of strategic planning but not of developing an intellectual framework, which they may see as no more than an intellectual enterprise of marginal value to the museum. However, it is possible to persuade managers with cross-unit collecting initiatives that demonstrate how planning can lead to better use of limited resources. Governing boards too can be resistant, and in fact many museum staff do not really want board members involved in such discussions. The danger is that, faced with our silence, boards may discuss collections anyway but in terms that can lead to unfortunate outcomes. Board members who see collections as little more than financial assets are obviously a risk, but rather than wait in dread for such moments, museums can use the planning process to educate their boards about collections and collecting. For those of us with board members who are also potential donors to the collections, such discussion can lead to more productive discussion about what the museum should collect rather than what they want to give.

Strategic planning is hardly the exclusive property of the collections unit of a museum, and integrating collections planning with larger museum planning poses a different set of challenges. Most museums today engage in planning in different areas of their work (Houtgraaf and Vitali 2008). For example, more and more are developing interpretive plans, which are strategic plans for exhibits and other forms of museum interpretation. Collections planning should be considered within that context. Will collecting be tied to or driven by exhibition and program goals, or are collecting goals different? Should they be set apart? Is the intellectual framework solely for collecting, or does it also establish the foundation for interpretive planning, and if so which leads the process?

But sometimes it is not that easy. Consider, for example, the challenge faced by a curator working on the NMAH's *America on the Move* exhibition. He uncovered an impressive group of artifacts that documented the East/West migration of Americans during the Great Depression but needed only a few objects to tell the particular exhibition story in the museum. While the exhibition inspired the collecting, he concluded that he should collect more deeply, bringing to the museum a richer collection that would provide opportunities for study in a variety of areas unconnected to the museum's exhibition plans.

But while exhibition-driven collecting can be too limiting in focusing so much on current needs at the expense of the long term, a museum should also carefully consider whether it is responsible to acquire collections that it cannot conceive of exhibiting. Realistically, few museums today have the resources to invest in collections for mainly documentary or research purposes, which by definition must be more comprehensive than ones used largely for exhibition or interpretation, which generally rely on more representative, selective objects (on this topic see Merriman in this volume). The NMAH has a significant condom collection, an important part of a larger contraceptive collection. It is likely to remain a collection used mainly for research purposes. Even so, it requires care and that means museum resources, despite the fact that few may ever know of its existence let alone actually see it. The museum's September 11 collecting successfully straddled this issue. While it was a collection carefully assembled to document the events of that day, it was conceived with the expectation that it would be exhibited, whether in the short or long term.

Of course collections planning must be part of a museum's overall strategic planning, because collecting is so dependent on resources and because collections are really the heart of what museums do – they will remain while different styles of exhibits, programs, and other initiatives come and go. Collections must never be taken for granted, as though they are a given, and their needs must always be consciously addressed.

Conclusion: implementation and after

The reality is that careful attention to process is not enough. A museum must implement its plan, and that's where most planning fails. A collections plan can too easily end up in planning purgatory, sitting on a shelf, developed with the best of intentions but never quite implemented, never quite made real. Implementation begins with the language and tone of the plan itself. If a plan is fuzzy, unrealistic, or nothing more than wish lists, it will never lead to real change. It needs to articulate a compelling argument coupled with real benefits to the museum and its stakeholders. Furthermore it must identify success strategies, perhaps three goals or strategies that will be the museum's immediate priorities. For example, the NMAH focused on both documenting previous cross-unit initiatives that had been successful and developing new initiatives focusing on themes (rather than classes of objects or narrow topics). One new initiative began with a photo collection documenting guest workers in the United States in the mid twentieth century and expanded to include an oral history program, object collecting, and a traveling exhibition, led by a team drawn from the Division of Work and Industry and the Division of Home and Community Life and including non-Smithsonian museum and university partners. In ways that the collections plan alone could not do, this project quickly and concretely demonstrated that collaborative collecting in support of a shared vision benefits not only the museum but individual curators.

Even the most carefully crafted plan is useless unless it actually leads to changes in how museum staff work. Assuming a museum clears that considerable hurdle, how does it measure success? A critical element in collections planning is evaluation, assessing whether the museum has succeeded or not. Success can be as simple as re-centering resource discussion from curatorial units to the museum, or as ambitious as the implementation of new strategies for acquisition and deaccessioning. And a museum must also take steps to ensure that its plan does not fade into obscurity over time. An institution may have energy and commitment during the planning, but what happens ten years later, with new staff, facing new needs and new challenges? Even the best collections plan can too easily become a fossil like its predecessors. In order to keep a plan alive and relevant, the museum must not treat it as cast in stone. Collections planning is not something that can be completed, but should be seen as an ongoing process, subject to review, revision, and refinement.

Museums need to engage the future and embrace change. Rather than continuing to look back at how we've always worked, in this chapter I have argued that we need to turn around and face the future. Every museum must make difficult choices about what to collect and not collect, and those choices must be better informed and made within the context of integrated, strategic planning tied to institutional mission and thematic goals.

References

AAM (American Alliance of Museums). 2014. "Assessment Programs: Accreditation: Statistics." Accessed October 2, 2014. http://www.aam-us.org/resources/assessment-programs/accreditation/statistics.

Bursell, Barbro. 2004. "Professionalizing Collecting." In *Museums and the Future of Collecting*, edited by Simon Knell, 204–210. 2nd ed. Farnham: Ashgate.

Catlin-Legutko, Cinnamon, and Stacey Klinger, eds. 2012. *Stewardship: Collections and Historic Preservation. Small Museum Toolkit 6*. Lanham, MD: AltaMira.

Conn, Steven. 1998. *Museums and American Intellectual Life, 1876–1926*. Chicago: University of Chicago Press.

Conn, Stephen. 2010. *Do Museums Still Need Objects?* Philadelphia: University of Pennsylvania Press.

Dominy, Graeme. 2004. "The Politics of Museum Collecting in the 'Old' and the 'New' South Africa." In *Museums and the Future of Collecting*, edited by Simon Knell, 135–145. 2nd ed. Farnham: Ashgate.

Dunn, Richard. 2004. "The Future of Collecting: Lessons from the Past." In *Museums and the Future of Collecting*, edited by Simon Knell, 52–71. 2nd ed. Farnham: Ashgate.

Gagnon, Jean-Marc, and Gerald Fitzgerald. 2004. "Towards a National Collecting Strategy: Reviewing Existing Holdings." In *Museums and the Future of Collecting*, edited by Simon Knell, 215–221. 2nd ed. Farnham: Ashgate.

Gardner, James B. 2005. "Collecting Lessons from September 11th." *Samtid & Museer* 29(2): 6–7.

Gardner, James B., and Elizabeth Merritt. 2004a. *The AAM Guide to Collections Planning*. Washington, DC: American Association of Museums.

Gardner, James B., and Elizabeth Merritt. 2004b. "Collections Planning: Pinning Down a Strategy (2002)." In *Reinventing the Museum: Historical and Contemporary Perspectives on the Paradigm Shift*, edited by Gail Anderson, 292–296. Lanham, MD: AltaMira.

Gurian, Elaine Heumann. 2004. "What is the Object of This Exercise? A Meandering Exploration of the Many Meanings of Objects in Museums (1999)." Reprinted in *Reinventing the Museum: Historical and Contemporary Perspectives on the Paradigm Shift*, edited by Gail Anderson, 269–283. Lanham, MD: AltaMira.

Houtgraaf, Dirk, and Vanda Vitali. 2008. *Mastering a Museum Plan: Strategies for Exhibit Development*. Lanham, MD: AltaMira.

Keene, Suzanne. 2005. *Fragments of the World: Uses of Museum Collections*. Oxford: Elsevier Butterworth-Heinemann.

Keene, Suzanne. 2006. "All That Is Solid? Museums and the Postmodern." *Public Archaeology* 5(3): 185–198.

Knell, Simon. 2004. "Altered Values: Searching for a New Collecting." In *Museums and the Future of Collecting*, edited by Simon Knell, 1–46. 2nd ed. Farnham: Ashgate.

Knell, Simon. 2010. "National Museums and the National Imagination." In *National Museums: New Studies from around the World*, edited by Simon Knell, Peter Aronsson, Arne Bugge Amundsen, et al., 3–28. London: Routledge.

Meister, Nicolette B., and Jackie Hoff. 2012. "Collections Planning: Best Practices in Collections Stewardship." In *Stewardship: Collections and Historic Preservation. Small Museum Toolkit 6*, edited by Cinnamon Catlin-Legutko and Stacey Klinger, 108–131. Lanham, MD: AltaMira.

Merritt, Elizabeth. 2004. "The Planning Process." In *The AAM Guide to Collections Planning*, edited by James B. Gardner and Elizabeth Merritt, 27–32. Washington, DC: American Association of Museums.

Merritt, Elizabeth E. 2008. *National Standards & Best Practices for U.S. Museums*. Washington, DC: American Association of Museums.

National Museum of American History (NMAH). 2014. "Mission and History." Accessed October 15, 2014. http://americanhistory.si.edu/museum/mission-history.

Pearce, Susan. 1989. "Museum Studies in Material Culture: Introduction." In *Museum Studies in Material Culture*, edited by Susan M. Pearce, 1–10. Leicester, UK: Leicester University Press.

Šola, Tomislav. 2004. "Redefining Collecting." In *Museums and the Future of Collecting*, edited by Simon Knell, 250–260. 2nd ed. Farnham: Ashgate.

Sullivan, Martin. 2004. "Introduction: Collections Stewardship and Collections Planning." In *The AAM Guide to Collections Planning*, 1–3. Washington, DC: American Association of Museums.

Weil, Stephen. 2004. "Collecting Then, Collecting Today: What's the Difference? (2002)" Reprinted in *Reinventing the Museum: Historical and Contemporary Perspectives on the Paradigm Shift*, edited by Gail Anderson, 284–291. Lanham, MD: AltaMira.

Young, Linda. 2004. "Collecting: Reclaiming the Art, Systematizing the Technique." In *Museums and the Future of Collecting*, edited by Simon Knell, 185–195. 2nd ed. Farnham: Ashgate.

James B. Gardner is Executive for Legislative Archives, Presidential Libraries, and Museum Services at the US National Archives in Washington, DC. A trained historian, he formerly worked as Associate Director for Curatorial Affairs at the National Museum of American History at the Smithsonian. His publications include *The AAM Guide to Collections Planning* (with Elizabeth Merritt), *Public History: Essays from the Field*, and essays in *The Routledge Companion to Museum Ethics* and *Grassroots Memorials: The Politics of Memorializing Traumatic Death*.

10 COLLECTION CARE AND MANAGEMENT
History, Theory, and Practice

John E. Simmons

Collections management may be defined as *everything that is done to care for and document collections and to make them available for use*. Collections management encompasses the acquisition, accession, registration, cataloging, care, use (for exhibition, education, and research), and disposal of objects and specimens and their associated information, as well as collection security, conservation, storage environments, and access. The activities related to collections management may be the responsibility of one staff member or of many, depending on the organizational structure of the museum.

Although collections have been part of museums for hundreds of years, collections management is a relatively new profession, dating back to the concept of accreditation introduced in the early 1970s (care of the collections is a fundamental characteristic of an accreditable museum). Historically, the management of collections was a task handled by curators and minimally trained assistants (Matassa 2011). Over time, as collections became larger and more complex, the scope of collections care knowledge expanded to include material sciences, information management, preventive conservation, and complex legal considerations, resulting in the rise of professional registrars and collections managers.

Museums are collection-centered institutions concerned with the generation, organization, perpetuation, and dissemination of collection-based information (MacDonald and Alsford 1991); it is this concern with information that distinguishes museums from similar institutions. Specifically, it can be argued that:

- The *generation of information* results from the acquisition and use of collections and associated documentation. Information is generated directly from collection

The International Handbooks of Museum Studies: Museum Practice, First Edition.
Edited by Conal McCarthy.
© 2015 John Wiley & Sons Ltd. Published 2020 by John Wiley & Sons Ltd.

use as well as management activities. The kind of information generated is highly variable, depending on the type of collection and how it is used.

- The *organization of information* involves establishing relationships between and linking information to objects and specimens, and the classification and organizational schemes in collections. In the past, the quantity of information managed and how it was organized limited what was available to the users; with the advent of electronic data management museums now process more information in more categories.
- The *perpetuation of information* refers to the preservation of collections and their associated documentation (including that generated by use and management).
- The *dissemination* of information comes about through the creation of access to collections and related information directly and through exhibition, educational programming, research, publication, and other means.

Historical overview

Collections have existed for much longer than museums (Simmons 2010). Collection documentation probably began with the compilation of inventory lists not long after writing systems were developed in Mesopotamia around 3200 BCE. The concept of the modern museum – in which objects are associated with learning – originated with the Temple of the Muses, which flourished from around 330 to 30 BCE in Alexandria (Findlen 1989). After the collapse of the Roman Empire, most European collections were owned by the church (Impey and MacGregor 1985; Lewis 1992; Murray 2000), which was the most powerful public institution and the center of intellectual activity. During the Renaissance, cabinets of curiosities (also known as *Kunstkammer* or *Wunderkammer* and *studi*) began to appear in the homes and palaces of European "rulers, patricians, humanist scholars, lawyers, physicians, and apothecaries" (Findlen 2000, v). The cabinets contained mostly marvels – unusual or inexplicable objects and specimens – which seemed to reflect a divine order in the universe. By the close of the Renaissance, catalogs and object labels were being devised (Macdonald 2006a), but preservation technology was still primitive due to the lack of understanding of deterioration causes and processes.

By the late 1600s, collection organization was beginning to coalesce along modern lines; Macdonald (2006a, 84) has described organization schemes as coming from "the idea that there were multiple forms of resemblances, connected by complex and cryptic lineages" to be discovered from the study of collections. Collections continued to grow as unknown objects and specimens arrived in Europe from the Americas, Australia, Africa, and Asia (Simmons and Snider 2012). What had once been gatherings of the miraculous and the marvelous became comprehensive collections useful to understand the world at large, "indispensable for the preservation of the artifacts of history, the taxonomy of the natural world, the apparatus of science, and the legacy of great art from the past" (Orosz 1990, 13).

During the Enlightenment, organized collections became a rational tool of inquiry, and led to the emergence of modern discipline-based and national museums that helped define nationality and culture (Hooper-Greenhill 1992; Mason 2006; Murray 2000). By the eighteenth century, many of the basic principles of collections management were being developed even though it was not yet recognized as a profession. In 1727 the first comprehensive book on managing collections was published by Caspar Neickel (a pseudonym for Kaspar Freidrich Jenequel, a dealer in museum objects). Neickel's book provided guidelines on acquisition, organization, and collection care (Aquilina 2011; Murray 2000).

The issues of standards for education and training were not seriously discussed until the 1890s (Simmons 2006a). Until well into the twentieth century, museums were run by individuals who were trained in other fields of study but who happened to work with collections. As summarized by Boylan:

> scholar-curators undertook almost all of the museum's specialized work: acquiring collections, specimens, and works of art, researching, cataloging, and documenting their collections, and interpreting and communicating their significance through the museum's permanent display galleries, temporary exhibitions, publications, and educational programs such as lectures and guided visits. The "generalist" scholar-curators ... were in turn supported by a single category of non-professional support staff, lowly regarded manual workers mainly undertaking security, cleaning, and building maintenance duties. (2006, 418)

During the twentieth century, preparation for the museum profession diverged into three types of training: (1) on-the-job training in museums; (2) professional training offered through museum associations; and (3) museum training presented in a university setting (Simmons 2006a); the latter option led to the development of museum studies as an academic discipline. In the United Kingdom, Australia, New Zealand, and several other countries, museum associations played a major role in promoting formal training programs (the first standard museum diploma course was established in Great Britain in 1930), but in the United States, museum associations left the task of training largely to the universities (Simmons 2006a). The first formal museum training program began in the United States in 1908 (Cushman 1984; Glaser 1987), and the first university-based museum training program was established in 1910 (Cushman 1984; Glaser 1987). University-based museum training began in Czechoslovakia in 1921 (Lewis 1985), in Argentina and Brazil in the 1920s, in India in 1952 (Bedekar 1987), in Great Britain in 1966 (Lewis 1987), in Australia in 1975 (Hodge 1987), in Italy in 1984 (Fedi 1987), and in New Zealand in 1989 (McCarthy and Cobley 2009). The largest growth in museum studies programs in the USA occurred after the late 1960s (Simmons 2006a).

A necessary step in the professionalization of museum work was the formation of professional societies. From its founding in 1946, UNESCO (United Nations Educational, Scientific, and Cultural Organization) has had a museum division and provided partial support of the International Council of Museums (ICOM), and began publishing a journal (*Museum*) in 1948. The oldest organization for museum professionals is the Museums Association (UK), founded in 1889, which has published *Museums Journal* since 1901. In the United States, the American Association of Museums (AAM) was founded in 1906 and in 1970 began accrediting museums (Alexander and Alexander 2008). Since 1918, the AAM has published a journal, first *Museum Work* (1918–1926), then *Museum News* (beginning in 1923), now called *Museum*. In 2008 the AAM published voluntary standards and best practices (Merritt 2008); and in 2012 changed its name to the American Alliance of Museums.

The Art Galleries and Museums Association of Australia and New Zealand (AGMA) was established in 1937, with a separate New Zealand body (AGMANZ) breaking away in 1947 (McCarthy and Cobley 2009). In the UK, the Standing Commission on Museums and Galleries was established in 1931 and in 2000 merged with the Library and Information Commission to form the Museums, Libraries, and Archives Council (MLA). In 2012, the MLA functions were transferred to the Arts Council England and the National Archives. In the late 1980s, the *Management of the Collections of the English National Museums* report initiated the establishment of inventory control and documentation standards called the National Registration Scheme (Fahy 1995).

The word *registrar* (meaning a person responsible for keeping records) has been in use in English since at least 1571 (in reference to registrars in record-keeping institutions ranging from courts of law to universities), but the title does not appear to have been applied to museum workers until the latter half of the 1800s. The first use of museum registrar in the United States was in the US National Museum in 1881, followed by the Metropolitan Museum of Art around 1905, and the Museum of Fine Arts in Boston in 1906 (Buck 2010). McKenzie (2010, 14) noted that "Professional registration practices first developed in Australia in the mid-1960s and 1970s and emerged roughly a decade later in New Zealand." The first registrar in Australia was appointed in 1964 at the National Gallery of Victoria; the first in New Zealand in 1975 at the Auckland City Art Gallery (McKenzie et al. 2010). The title *collections manager* came into use in the mid-1970s in the United States (Simmons 1993). In some museums, the title registrar is reserved specifically for tasks involving record-keeping while collections manager is applied to other aspects of managing collections, but in most institutions the two titles are used more or less interchangeably. The Registrars Committee of the AAM was founded in 1977 (Buck 2010); in 1991, the first registrars' organization in Europe was the United Kingdom Registrars Group (Matassa 2011). The international Association of Registrars and Collections Specialists (ARCS) was established in 2012.

Prior to the mid-twentieth century, most museums had some sort of registration procedures, but there were no standards, sometimes not even among collections within the same museum. The standardization of collection management systems did not begin until after the institution of collection control systems in libraries (Buck 2010), and even now lags behind libraries. The advantages of the

Dewey Decimal System (developed between 1874 and 1877) for classifying, storing, and retrieving library materials caught the attention of museum personnel seeking better ways to manage their collections. Similarly, museums followed the lead of libraries with the introduction of computer systems for collections management. The introduction of electronic record management systems in museums transformed the way that documentation was carried out (Jones 2008).

Libraries began experimenting with computers in the 1960s (Jones 2008), but the expense of hardware and programming was prohibitive (Ellin 1968). In 1965, the first museum software program (for cataloging ethnographic collections) became available. The Museum Computer Network (MCN) was founded in 1967. By 1970, at least two museums (the Metropolitan Museum of Art and the Museum of Modern Art) were using computer-based collection catalogs (Jones 2008), and the Information Retrieval Group of the UK Museums Association had "under serious consideration a proposal for a museum cataloging system meeting the requirements of interdisciplinary searching for various types of data" (Bowles 1971, 176); the Inventaire général des monuments et des richesses artistiques de la France was working to establish a national museum inventory in France, and similar projects were beginning in Germany (Bowles 1971).

By the late 1970s, individual museums had begun to develop their own highly idiosyncratic systems, with no serious attempts at standardization (Marty 2008a). At the time, the way information was organized and recorded depended on the whims and interests of individual curators or registrars, so that what was recorded, and the way it was organized, was eccentric and specialized (it is still unusual to find systems in different museums that are exactly alike). As a result, in contrast to the situation in libraries, "Progress in implementing data management systems has persistently been hindered by a lack of agreed information standards within and between museums as well as access to hardware and the availability of software suited to the task" (Peacock 2008, 65).

Until the late 1970s and early 1980s, most software programs written for museums were run on large mainframe computers, which had high costs and limited access. When computerization first became affordable for museums, existing eccentric and specialized manual systems were converted to eccentric and specialized electronic systems, reflecting the organizational and occasionally non-rational ideas of the registrars and curators who drove system design. The standard for success was very low – if a system worked, then it was considered good; there was little questioning of how well systems worked or what they were supposed to do. By the mid-1980s, computers were at last sufficiently reliable and inexpensive to become widespread in museums large and small, and commercial relational databases were available – these changes required a "transformation ... of computer architecture: moving from mainframe computers to minicomputers to desktop computers and then client-server models, as museums were able to take advantage of market trends toward low-cost computing" (Jones 2008, 11); with this came more standardization of collections management systems. Current computer technology allows museums to share data on distributed databases even though their individual database structure may be different. (On this topic see Chapman in this volume.)

Literature review

Dorothy H. Dudley, a registrar at the Museum of Modern Art in New York, had a major impact on collections management with the 1958 publication of *Museum Registration Methods*, coauthored with Irma Bezold Wilkinson of the Newark Museum. The Dudley and Wilkinson book helped to define collections management in museums worldwide, as is reflected in its evolution – the first edition contained 225 pages; the fifth edition (published in 2010 and edited by Rebecca A. Buck and Jean Allman Gilmore) contained 516 pages with contributions from 68 authors. A number of other publications emphasizing practical aspects of collections management (with only tangential references to museological theory) have helped shape the profession, including *A Legal Primer on Managing Museum Collections*, first published in 1985 and now in its third edition (Malaro and DeAngelis 2012). Further practical advice has been provided in the USA by Burcaw (1997), Reibel (2008), and Simmons (2006b). In Europe, John Thompson (1992) addressed museums more comprehensively, particularly conservation and research concerns. Other significant European publications include Stansfield, Mathias, and Reid (1994), a compilation entitled *Collections Management* (Fahy 1995), and Matassa (2011).

Gary Thompson's *The Museum Environment* (first edition 1978, second edition 1986) had a profound impact on collections management by bringing the importance of maintaining and monitoring stable storage environments to the forefront. Thompson presented the first comprehensive discussion of the effects of light, humidity, and air pollution on museum collections and stimulated the incorporation of preventive conservation as a basic principle of collections management. Chris Caple's *Preventive Conservation in Museums* was published in 2011 reflecting the increasing importance of non-specialist collection care. During the past 25 years a number of museum studies anthologies have been published, but few of these have included contributions that address collections management, with the notable exception of Macdonald (2006b).

Two significant trends are evident in the recent literature – the establishment of standards and the development of museological theory. The AAM has taken the lead in establishing standards for collections care in the USA (Merritt 2008). In the UK, standards have been promoted most recently by the Collections Trust through the publication of SPECTRUM 4.0 (Collections Link 2014). Theoretical museology has shaped collections management by addressing the meaning of objects and specimens and its implications for how collections should be managed. Noteworthy in this respect were critical studies of material culture from the 1990s on (Pearce 1993; 1994; Maroević 1998) which stimulated the contextualization of collections in a cultural framework that shed light on the relevance of collections, the museality of objects and specimens, how collections are assembled and used, and the information that collections contain and generate.[1]

Theory: objects and meanings

The essence of collections in museums is the meaning-making that occurs as people interact with objects and specimens, which in turn depends on collections management systems that preserve the collections and associated information and make them available. In daily practice, it is easy to become overly focused on the individual objects or specimens, rather than on their meanings and multifaceted contexts (which go far beyond the physical aspects of the collections). As Wilcomb Washburn cautioned 30 years ago, "The object can become a fetish that, if we merely worship it, impedes our understanding of the object itself and its place in our society" (Washburn 1984, 15).

Susan Pearce (1993) has described the objects and specimens in collections as having a dual nature, both materiality and constructed understanding. Materiality refers to the physical characteristics and the concrete and intrinsic relationships an object or specimen has to its original context. Constructed understanding is the result of classification and interpretation – as Stephen J. Gould observed, "classification is truly the mirror of our thoughts, its changes through time the best guide to the history of human perceptions" (Gould 1986, 14). Mason (2006, 20) calls constructed understanding "the polysemic quality of museum objects" because of their multiple meanings and associations. In addressing how theory affects collections management practice, Maroević used the terms "idealist preservation" and "materialist preservation":

> Materialist preservation is what can be seen in the preservation of the materials of heritage objects and their characteristics. Idealist preservation is manifested in the conservation of the ideas stored in the material world by other media. With this distinction the importance of all forms of documentation comes forward. (Maroević 1998, 227)

A number of new terms have been introduced by museum theorists that, although not yet widely used in English, are in use in museum discourse worldwide (Desvallées and Mairesse 2009, Maroević 1998). *Museal* generally means "of museums," but more precisely refers to the field of reference in which the creation, development, and operation of museums as institutions takes place (Desvallées and Mairesse 2009). *Musealia* refers to objects and specimens that have undergone the process of musealization, and the sum of the meanings they thereby acquire. *Musealization* is the removal of an object or specimen from its natural environment and its transformation into musealia, or the process of recognizing and identifying the museality of the material world (Desvallées and Mairesse 2009; Maroević 1998). *Museality* refers to the characteristic features inherent in an object or specimen that document its specific relation to reality when it transcends functional reality to become a document in a larger context (Desvallées and Mairesse 2009; Maroević 1998).

In managing collections it is important to remember that in Western cultures, the value of the constructed understanding is perceived to be superior to material value (Pearce 1993). For example, an exhibit at the Robert J. Dole Institute of Politics at the University of Kansas in the USA includes two steel columns (each weighing more than 1000 kg) salvaged from the ruins of the World Trade Center in New York after it was destroyed in the terrorist attack of September 11, 2001 (Carroll 2003). An artist could have been hired to create two authentic-looking steel columns for less than the cost of obtaining and shipping the actual columns 2000 km across the country, and although the replica columns would have had material value, they would not have had the more highly esteemed constructed understanding of the authentic columns (*sensu*; Pearce 1993).

From a collections management perspective, the distinctions between data, information, and knowledge are significant – data is the raw facts that come from observation and measurements; information is generated by processing data to make it meaningful (e.g., via interpretation, reading, writing, speaking); information is converted to knowledge in the mind of the "knower," as each individual person builds knowledge using information and personal experience. In other words, knowledge comes from melding information and experience to produce meaning (Zorich 2008). It is the information associated with the objects and specimens that gives museum collections their special value – information may have value without objects, and objects may have value without information, but when there is a connection between the object and the information, the quality and significance of both are enhanced.

In the past, museums were limited in their ability to handle information generated by the multiple contexts of the objects and specimens simply because of the physical limitations of information storage and retrieval. Prior to the introduction of electronic databases, storing and accessing collection information was labor-intensive, slow, and often inadequate (for example, the card catalog for the collection in the Metropolitan Museum of Art in New York occupied a series of cabinets that were a full city block in length, but the information they contained was organized only by accession number). The introduction of computers has brought about a significant change as museums are now perceived as repositories of information as well as repositories of objects. The process of making museum information accessible electronically has not been simple (there are still problems stemming from the lack of standards), but managing information in the museum has become as important as managing the collections, which has created some interesting socio-technical interactions as human beings, technology, and information intersect (Marty 2008b). It is all too easy to allow the technological aspects of managing collections to consume so much of the resource base (including time) that little remains for collection care.

Museum information management creates *surrogates* and *aggregates* as the information is manipulated electronically – surrogates refers to the extraction of subunits of information; aggregates refers to creating new groupings of information from more than one source (Marty 2008a). Managing these surrogates and aggregates of collection information raises issues of the public trust and privacy. For example, not all information relating to the collection should be made available to the public (e.g., donor files and in-house appraisals should be confidential), but it is not always clear where to draw the line. Collection-based information can be used commercially, raising the question of whether or not the public institutions that collect and preserve the information should profit from it as well as the commercial user.

There have been many attempts to define museum collections. For example, "The objects, specimens, documents and data under a museum's care" (Case 1988) and "A group of specimens or artifacts with like characteristics or a common base of association (e.g., geographic, donor, cultural)" (Society for the Preservation of Natural History Collections 1994) are straightforward descriptions of what is in a collection, while "The collected objects of a museum, acquired and preserved because of their potential value as examples, as reference material, or as objects of aesthetic or educational importance" (Burcaw 1997) defines collections relative to their purpose. According to Pearce (1993), all collections have three things in common – they are made up of objects, the objects come from the past, and the collections have been assembled with some degree of intention (however slight) by someone who believed that the whole was more than the sum of its parts. Blending these ideas together, a more comprehensive definition of a museum collection was offered by Nicholson and Williams (2002):

1.   Collections consist of more than one object.
2.   The objects have order and organization.
3.   The objects are valued by people.
4.   The objects are collected with an intent to preserve them over time.
5.   Collections serve the institutional mission and goals.
6.   The integrity of the objects and their associated information are paramount.
7.   Collections are maintained in adherence to professional standards.

Ethics: best practices for museum professionals

Ethics is concerned with the distinctions between good and bad, right and wrong, and how this is applied to language, behavior, and thought. Ethics are not abstract opinions or beliefs, as morals are, but are based on experience and refined by testing. The primary purpose of a museum code of ethics is to raise the level of professional practice, which strengthens museums in society by setting standards of professional integrity (Edson 1997). Employee adherence to an institutional code of ethics is considered to be a best practice for museum professionals (Merritt 2008).

The first code of ethics for museum workers was proposed by the AAM in 1925 (with revisions in 1987 and 1994), but the *ICOM Code of Ethics for Museums* (first adopted in 1986; revised in 2004) is the most widely followed code of ethics for museum professionals worldwide. These codes reinforce the duty of managing the collections in ways that maintain the integrity of the collections and associated information (Besterman 2006; Edson 1997). The application of preventive conservation in collections management is an ethical duty, as preservation is included in both the ICOM and AAM codes as a function of museums (Williams 1997). Ethical standards directly related to collections management include those addressing collecting, the sale of objects and specimens, personal collections, confidentiality of collections records, access to and use of collections, conservation, conflict-of-interest, acquisition of deaccessioned objects, appraisals, and authentications (Simmons 2006b).

Legal aspects of collections management

There are many laws and regulations that affect the management of museum collections, ranging from how museums are legally organized to how museums treat their employees (Gerstenblith 2006; Malaro and DeAngelis 2012). The laws and regulations that cover acquisition, import, export, transport, and possession of collections are the most significant in the context of collections management. Museum professionals have an ethical duty to be aware of the laws and regulations that affect collections. As stated by Stephen E. Weil, "laws are too complex, and the consequences of misunderstanding them too grave, to make it thinkable that the legal aspects of museum management should be based on anything less than the best available professional advice" (Weil 1983, 133). A good summary of the laws affecting collections management in the USA is provided in Malaro and DeAngelis (2012); Matassa (2011) provides a summary of important UK museum collection legislation.

The most important international regulations affecting collections management include the UNESCO, Hague, UNIDROIT, and CITES conventions. The UNESCO Convention, (*Convention on the Means of Prohibiting and Preventing the Illicit Import, Export and Transfer of Ownership of Cultural Property*, 1970) makes certain cultural property subject to seizure if exported, imported, or transferred to or from a signatory country. The *Hague Convention for the Protection of Cultural Property in the Event of Armed Conflict* (1954) is an international agreement that protects cultural property during armed conflict. The *UNIDROIT Convention on Stolen or Illegally Exported Cultural Objects* (1995) strengthened the UNESCO Convention by making it easier to recover stolen cultural property. CITES (*Convention on International Trade in Endangered Species of Wild Fauna and Flora*, 1973) regulates the international trade in biological species threatened by commercial exploitation. The movement of a specimen of a species that is listed in a CITES appendix (including loans and transfers) across international borders or between institutions within a signatory country requires special permits; parts of protected species (such as feathers, teeth, and claws used in art objects or artifacts) receive the same protection as whole specimens.

Theoretical foundations of collections management

Collections management has a direct impact on all activities in the museum because all involve the collections at some level. An understanding of the theoretical bases of managing collections is fundamental to understanding the role of collections in museums.

Because collections have order, the objects or specimens in them must have definable properties, and thus a collection is a set of objects, which can be described as the set (C) containing the elements (a, b, c … z), or (a, b, c … z) ∈ C. Collections management has been conceptualized graphically in a three-dimensional model by Simmons and Muñoz-Saba (2003).

Historically, the most fundamental aspect of collections management has been establishing and maintaining order among the elements (objects or specimens) of the set (the collection). Collection order can be depicted on an x-axis (Figure 10.1), with increasingly chaotic situations to the left of the center point, and increasingly organized situations to the right. In a properly ordered collection, each object or specimen is assigned to a unique physical location (a cell) within the collection storage array. The cell is determined by the kind of object or specimen and the way the collection is organized (Table 10.1). For example, a natural history collection will probably be organized by class, order, and family and within these units, arranged alphabetically by scientific name. A history collection might be organized by the kind of object or function of the object (e.g., clothing or agricultural tools). An art collection might be organized by type of media, with artworks in order by the artist's name, or by accession number. In all cases, an organized

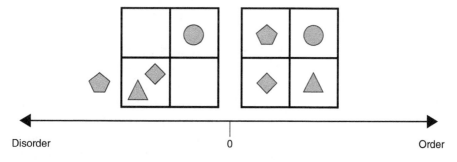

FIGURE 10.1   The x-axis (collection order and disorder).

TABLE 10.1   Organization systems used in museums

Type of museum	Ordering system
Art	Artist's name, period, medium, genre
Natural history	Hierarchical system based on Linnean taxonomy
Geology	Epochs, strata, chemical composition
History	Material, topical class (use), style, Chenhall system
Anthropology	Material, origin, cultural association

collection is one in which each element of the collection (each object or specimen) has a cell and each element is in its cell. To the left of the center point p (0) on the x-axis, the collection becomes unusable due to disorder (there may be more than one element per cell, elements that are not in their cells, or elements that do not have cells). To the right of the center point, the elements may be so organized so that the collection is unusable because the order is too complex or too expensive to maintain. An excess of either order or disorder can make a collection unusable. Because the x-axis extends to infinity in both directions, there is no limit to how disorganized or how organized a collection can be. The midpoint on the x-axis is the state in which each element of the collection is in its appropriate cell, in a usable order – the point where disorder ends and order begins.

Collection growth is depicted on the y-axis (Figure 10.2). The collection may be growing (increasing in size) as new objects or specimens are added, or may be losing elements due to neglect, deterioration, deaccession, or theft. The midpoint of the y-axis is defined as the point of stasis, at which the collection is neither growing nor losing elements. Most loss is due to the limitations of *preservation technology* (the materials and methods used to preserve objects and specimens). Preservation technology is represented on the z-axis (Figure 10.3). The midpoint of the z-axis is defined as the condition of the element when it arrives in the collection. Positive preservation occurs when an object or specimen is stabilized so that its long-term conservation status is improved (e.g., a silver teapot may be rehoused using inert materials and stored in a stable environment free of volatile acids). Negative preservation describes the deterioration of an object or specimen from its condition when incorporated in the collection (e.g., a circus poster that fades because it is exposed to ultraviolet radiation).

When the three axes are put together, they depict the primary considerations of collections management – order and disorder; growth and loss; and preservation and deterioration. The three axes intersect at their points of stasis, the point p (0, 0, 0).

Theory should serve as an analytical frame of reference for exploring ideas and meanings, and provide a perspective on new issues. A theoretical perspective therefore offers a framework for critically analyzing trends and making predictions. The importance of theory is reflected in the historic development of collections management in museums – for hundreds of years, collections care was

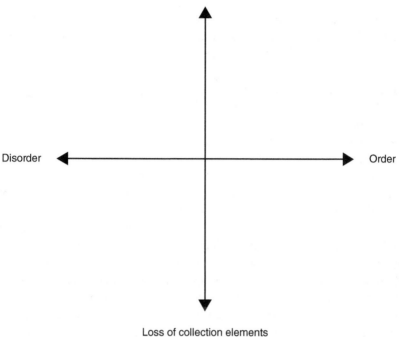

FIGURE 10.2 The x-axis (collection order and disorder) and y-axis (collection growth and loss).

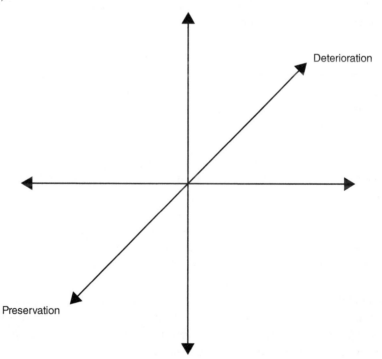

FIGURE 10.3 The x-axis (collection order and disorder), y-axis (collection growth and loss), and z-axis (preservation and deterioration).

based on oral traditions with little understanding of the factors that affected the useful life of collections – as a result, many of the objects and specimens in existence as recently as 100 or 200 years ago are now lost. Theory explains how the meaning of objects and specimens changes in different contexts, why meanings are different from different perspectives (Macdonald 2006a), and the significance of the fact that objects and specimens react continually with their storage environment.

The theoretical model presented above demonstrates that the cost of collections management increases *geometrically* as the collection size increases *arithmetically* because larger collections have more elements, more cells, and more ways that the elements can be displaced from their cells. The model shows that it is more efficient to allocate collection care resources to the initial stabilization of incoming elements than it is to try to stabilize them later. The model has predictive value – when the location of the collection elements are plotted relative to the three axes using the points p (x, y, z), the resulting cluster of points makes it possible to detect trends, such as a collection that is growing too fast and thus falling into disorder, or a collection in which insufficient resources (or misapplication of resources) is resulting in an increase of disorder that will lead to loss of objects or specimens. The amount of disorder and deterioration in the collection can be conceptualized as entropy (the quantitative measure of the degree of disorder – which is to say, the lack of order – in a system). The model shows that most of the cost of collections management is the cost of reducing the rate of entropy in the collection. There are three types of entropy in collections:

1. Disorder due to the lack of a system of order (the objects or specimens are placed randomly in storage).
2. Disorder due to an insufficient or dysfunctional system of order (including systems of order so complicated that they are unusable).
3. An acceptable (manageable) level of disorder.

Because the use of the objects or specimens displaces them from their cells, the presence of some entropy indicates that the collection is being used. An *acceptable level of entropy* in a collections management system is present when collection growth does not exceed the ability to assign each element to a cell, when there is order in the collection (each element has a cell), no single element is displaced from its cell for a prolonged period of time, each element can be found in the collection storage array with a minimum of effort, the deterioration of the collection elements is ameliorated, and the loss of elements is minimized. The only way to reduce entropy is to put energy into the system – for museum collections, energy is the time and money to care for the collection. The model also demonstrates that zero entropy comes at a cost that no museum can afford, because the lowest rate of entropy requires the highest costs to achieve.

The development of theoretical museology has had a significant impact on the practice of collections management as it has evolved from dominance by subject matter discipline specialties to functions-based operations (van Mensch 2004). The changes came about as a result of the theoretical understanding of the musealization of objects and specimens as they transition from their primary context to a museological context because "the act of isolating an object in a museum breaks the link between the object and its environment. Separation gives the object the status of evidence as a segment of the scientific documentation about the world that is created in the museum" (Maroević 1998, 226). Because knowledge is continually generated from museum collections (Maroević 1998), and because we now have tools to handle large amounts of information, "The past few decades have seen an important shift from the idea of museums as repositories of objects to museums as repositories of knowledge" (Marty 2008b, 4).

Documentation is the supporting evidence, recorded in a permanent manner using a variety of media (paper, photographic, electronic, etc.), of the identification, condition, history, use, and value of an object or specimen in the collection. Documentation is what gives value to a collection. Documentation enables a museum to record activities that affect the collection and fulfill its obligation to know at any time exactly which objects or specimens it is responsible for, where each is located, and to record information generated by the use of the collection, thus documentation is a continuous, open-ended process – as the collection is used, stored, and exhibited, new data is created and added to the records. Documentation must be carefully managed because if the link between the specimen or object and the documentation is lost, the value of the collection is greatly diminished.

The test of a documentation system is the ability to retrieve the information it contains. Although the format for records will vary from one museum to another, the documentation system must have clarity and permanence, be legible, and be comprehensive (complete). This means using simple prose in data recording, avoiding jargon and slang, but using defined technical terms and images. Documentation should be recorded in readable form, in an archival format, using stable materials. Electronic data is inherently unstable because it is susceptible to all of the agents of deterioration that affect paper (fire, heat, water, physical damage, and loss), as well as to static electricity, magnetism, power surges, equipment failure, and loss of retrievability due to software and hardware upgrades. Despite the quantity of electronic documentation currently being generated in museums, there are no means available to permanently preserve it at a rational cost:

> The notion that once something has become digital it has somehow been made permanent lingers, but in fact the strength of digital files is in such things as their transportability, or the ease with which they can be processed by computer or reproduced – and they are actually likely to face an early death. (Baca, Coburn, and Hubbard 2008, 120–121)

Preventive conservation

Collections management is not conservation, and conservation is not collections management, but the two are closely linked and share a large area of overlap in preventive conservation. Preventive conservation refers to the things that are done to prolong the useful life of an object or specimen in a collection. Preventive conservation became part of collections management beginning in the mid-1970s with the awareness that traditional object-directed practices were not addressing the deterioration of collections (Williams 1997). Preventive conservation includes risk management, responding to the agents of deterioration, use of archival-quality materials, and monitoring of the storage environment, making possible a holistic and integrated approach to collections management (Caple 2011). The practice of preventive conservation in collections management requires education and training in problem recognition, assessment (critical evaluation of preservation requirements), and management of conservation goals and strategic plans in conjunction with the overall collections management program (Williams 1997).

The goal of preventive conservation is to avoid deterioration (and therefore the need for resource-expensive treatments of individual objects) by providing quality care and a stable storage environment for the collection. It is far more cost effective (and much better for the objects and specimens) to prevent deterioration than to try to recover from deterioration. By understanding the factors that cause collections to deteriorate, better use can be made of collections care resources.

Risk management

A *risk* is the chance of an undesirable change occurring; *risk assessment* refers to the process of evaluating the chances of a risk occurring and the extent of the damage that could result; *risk management* is the application of resources to minimize the risk and potential damage.[2] Risk assessment frequently reveals that resources are invested in preventing risks that are rare, while ignoring risks that pose more immediate threats. For example, the rare risk of damage from high winds might get more attention than the likelier risk of excessive fluctuations in relative humidity. A theoretical and practical model for museum collection risk management can be found in Waller (2003). The basic steps in risk management are to:

1. Identify the risks the collection faces.
2. Assess the magnitude of each risk, should it occur.
3. Develop strategies to eliminate, ameliorate, or mitigate the risks.
4. Estimate the costs, benefits, and drawbacks of each risk strategy.
5. Set priorities for the risk management plan.
6. Implement the plan and evaluate its effectiveness.

Research work done primarily at the Canadian Conservation Institute (Canadian Conservation Institute 2014) is the basis for classifying the causes of collection deterioration into ten categories called the *agents of deterioration*:

1. Physical forces.
2. Thieves and vandals.
3. Dissociation.
4. Fire.
5. Water.
6. Pests.
7. Pollutants.
8. Radiation.
9. Incorrect temperature.
10. Incorrect relative humidity.

Physical forces include impact, vibration, abrasion, and pressure (e.g., seismic activity, sliding, or dragging an object). *Thieves and vandals* damage collections through intentional and unintentional actions. *Dissociation* refers an ordered system becoming disordered in a legal, intellectual, or cultural sense (e.g., missing numbers, illegible records, out-of-date software) resulting in the loss of data, objects, or value.

Fire may cause damage with heat, flame, ash, smoke, or the chemicals used to extinguish a fire and clean up. *Water* damage includes staining, chemical extraction, warping, oxidation, adhesive dissolution, and dimensional changes. *Pests* include arthropods, mold, and other organisms that cause damage or serve as food sources for pests. *Pollutants* include organic and inorganic gasses and acidic or abrasive particulates coming from cleaning agents, preparation chemicals, exhibit fabrication, and the external environment.

Radiation includes ultraviolet, visible, and infrared radiation. Radiation may cause disintegration or discoloration of materials; radiation damage is cumulative. *Incorrect temperatures* are temperatures that are too high, too low, or fluctuate excessively (cooler temperatures are preferred for collections storage; higher temperatures accelerate deterioration). High temperature may cause disintegration and discoloration; low temperature may cause cracking, flaking, dimensional changes, and fluctuations in relative humidity. *Incorrect relative humidity (RH)* is a problem at extreme highs and lows and excessive fluctuations. Relative humidity is the amount of moisture in a quantity of air compared to the amount that same quantity of air could hold if 100 percent saturated; RH is temperature dependent (warm air holds more moisture than cold air). Incorrect RH may affect chemical and physical stability, and may increase risks from other agents of deterioration. Critical values for temperature and RH depend on the materials in storage and the climate in which the museum is located (Ford et al. 2012).

Responses to the agents of deterioration are at one or more of five stages (in order from least expensive to most expensive in terms of collections care resources):

1. Avoid the source or the conditions that allows the agent to be present.
2. Impede or block the agent (this is the most practical stage of response).
3. Detect the agent through regular monitoring (either directly or by the damage it causes).
4. Respond by taking measures against the agent.
5. Recover/Recuperate after damage has occurred.

Acquisitions, accession, registration, and cataloging

The overall process by which an object or specimen becomes part of a collection is *registration*. Registration establishes the right of ownership and preserves the association of an object or specimen and its associated information. The registration system is used to identify and account for everything in the collection; an inadequate registration system will result in loss of collection value. The test of an accession system is that:

1. An intelligent person should be able figure out how to use the system.
2. Using the recorded documentation, it should be possible to produce any object or specimen from the collection.
3. Given any object or specimen, it should be possible to produce its associated documentation.

When an object or specimen is brought to a museum for consideration or evaluation, the museum accepts a certain amount of responsibility for its care and custody whether it is accepted for the collections or not. A receipt (with the donor's name and contact information) should be prepared and a copy given to the person bringing in the object. Donations should be examined for pests and, if retained, a condition report prepared.

*   An *acquisition* refers to an object or specimen obtained by a museum, but does not mean that a transfer of ownership has taken place.
*   An *accession* is an acquisition that the museum has taken legal ownership of.
*   *Accessioning* is the process of transferring ownership of an acquisition to the museum and recording it as part of the collection.
*   The *accession number* is a unique number assigned to an object or group of objects that comprise an accession. In some museums the accession number is the only number assigned to an object, in other museums a catalog number may be used to track the object. An accession number may also be called a *registration number*.

- The *accession record* documents the accession's origin and includes a brief description of it. Historically, accession records were hand-written in a bound ledger book or card file called the *accession register*; some museums now maintain accession records only in digital format.
- *Cataloging* is the process of organizing information by creating records related to the object or specimen ("to catalog" means to place in categories; the catalog is created by extracting data from the registration records).
- The *catalog* is a listing of object or specimen information that is separate from the accession register.
- A *catalog record* is created during the cataloging process.
- The *catalog number* is a number assigned to a particular object or specimen to provide a unique identification for it.

The accession or catalog number should be marked on the object or specimen in a reversible manner or inscribed on a tag attached to it. Some museums use only integers, but more commonly a compound, sequential number is used. A prefix may designate a collection (e.g., A7173); compound numbers may incorporate information such as date of accession. For example, 14/H212 is the 212th object in the history collection (H), part of the 14th accession. The AAM recommends using year, accession number, and object number, such that 1950.12.3 is the third object in the 12th accession of 1950. If an object has parts (for example, a knife and scabbard) lower-case letters may be used to identify them (e.g., the knife as 50.12.3a and scabbard as 50.12.3b).

Provenance (derived from the French *provenir*, to originate) refers to the history of ownership of an object or specimen. *Provenance research* is employed to differentiate authentic objects from fakes, to prove ownership, and to study the past use of objects. In museum terminology, provenance refers to the entire chronology of an object from its place of creation through its present ownership. A similar word, *provenience* (from the English word *provenance*) is used in archaeology to mean the physical location of objects in an archaeological site. In archives, *provenance* refers to the entity (individual, group, or organization) that created a set of records. Book collectors use *provenance* to refer to the chain of ownership or use, particularly evidence of who used a book and how it was used. In geology, *provenance* refers to the origin of rocks (e.g., how the rocks were formed). In botany, the term *seed provenance* is used to refer to the origin of the plants that produced the seed. *Provenance* is used in reference to computer data to mean where and how a data set was created and how it has been used and modified.

Standard nomenclature (taxonomy) is critical for classifying collections and reducing confusion (for example, there are at least 20 accepted variant spellings for the name of the composer Peter Ilyich Tchaikowsky, but to a computer, they would be 20 unique names). Near-universally accepted nomenclatural systems are available in the natural sciences. Many non-science museums use the taxonomic system developed by Robert Chenhall, later amplified by Blackaby and Greeno

(1988), and appearing most recently as *Nomenclature 3.0 for Museum Cataloging* (Bourcier and Rogers 2010) which provides names for human-made objects in a hierarchical structure. The current version contains more than 14,000 object names – the goal is not to propose a name for every object, but to provide a framework for cataloging.

The *collection storage array* refers to the system and arrangement of objects and specimens in storage, and is critical for reliable placement and retrieval. Collections are typically ordered by one of the schemes in Table 10.1. Ideally, objects should be arranged according to storage environment requirements, but more often they are sorted by size and shape because in practice the system of order is a compromise between the size of the collection, the space available, how the collection is used, and the resources available to maintain the collection. The test for a collection storage array is:

- Can each object or specimen be easily located in the collection?
- Can the collection be used efficiently and safely?
- Can the collection be maintained in order with a minimum of resources?
- Does the arrangement provide an appropriate, stable environment for each object or specimen?

As Freda Matassa has pointed out, "Exhibition and display are perhaps the most crucial means of access to and enjoyment of our cultural heritage" (2011, 201). It is important to remember that exhibition is at the same time a form of storage; the same requirements for security and environmental conditions should apply to both.

Traditionally, museums have limited access to collections and associated information, but it is now recognized that the public has a reasonable right of access to museum collections and data. Extenuating circumstances may affect access (e.g., the religious beliefs of the makers of artifacts), as will the museum's responsibility to care for its collections because access is a balance between conservation and use – increased access to the collections means increased handling, disruption of the stability of the storage environment, and a greater likelihood of loss. Access to collections data has been greatly facilitated by electronic data management systems, allowing information to be made available on websites or by request with minimal resource costs. Institutions should develop policies regarding what information is made available to the public and to researchers (Simmons 2006b).

Condition reporting provides a means of evaluating the impact of access and use through loans, display, and so on, by documenting the state of preservation of an object or specimen at a particular moment in time. Detailed directions for writing collections management condition reports and sample report forms are provided in Demeroukas (2010). Condition reports should be prepared for objects and specimens whenever they are moved on or off exhibit, sent or received on loan, or used in other ways that involve handling or environmental changes. Basic guidelines for object and specimen handling, packing, and transport can be found in Buck and Gilmore (2010).

The liability for the objects or specimens in a loan rests with the party that is the primary benefactor of the transaction (usually with the borrower). If the loan is for the sole benefit of the borrower, then the borrower is bound to great care or extraordinary diligence; if the loan is for the mutual benefit of both parties, both may be equally responsible; when the loan is for the sole benefit of the lender, the borrower is only bound to slight care and is liable for gross negligence (Malaro and DeAngelis 2012). A loan is a contract, thus the loan terms should be included in the loan documents, and the duration of the loan and the return date should be specified. The collections management policy should address such issues as which type of institutions the museum will or will not make loans to, image use rights, and insurance coverage (Simmons 2006b). By definition, a loan is a temporary arrangement because ownership does not change – there is no such thing as a "permanent loan." If an object is given to the museum, then it is a gift; if the object is not given to the museum, then it is a loan, not a gift.

Deaccessioning and disposal

Collections are dynamic, not static; as they grow and change over time, objects or specimens may need to be deaccessioned. *Deaccessioning* is the opposite of accessioning – it is the permanent removal of something from the collection. *Disposal* refers to what happens to the deaccessioned object or specimen after deaccessioning. The practice of deaccessioning is as old as collections, but legal and ethical implications have made it one of the most controversial practices in museums today. Because only specimens or objects that were accessioned can be deaccessioned, the first control over deaccessioning is a good accession policy.

Attitudes toward deaccessioning have changed over the years. In 1927, the executive secretary of the AAM, Lawrence Coleman, wrote that "On occasion, worthless material may be accepted and later thrown away rather than give offence by refusing it," but no museums should operate in that manner today. There are cultural differences regarding deaccessioning – European museums are more reluctant to deaccession than those in the USA. Most European museums follow the ICOM Code of Ethics, which states that "there must always be a strong presumption against the disposal of objects to which a museum has assumed formal title." By contrast, the AAM Code of Ethics states that "Museums must remain free to improve their collections through selective disposal … and intentionally to sacrifice objects for well-considered … purposes." A comprehensive consideration of deaccessioning concerns and practices is presented by Stephen Weil in *A Deaccession Reader* (1997).

Museums are accountable for the acquisition, conservation, and management of their collections as well as the content, nature, and quality of their scholarship, exhibits, and programs; this accountability is the context in which deaccessioning takes place. Weil (1997) makes three important points regarding deaccessioning decisions:

- the retention of each and every object in a collection involves an ongoing expense for the museum;
- deaccessioning may generate funds that can be used to acquire other objects more critical to the institutional collecting plan;
- deaccessioning an object to another museum (particularly a peer institution) may better serve the museum community, the discipline, and the object itself.

The future of collections management

One of the first important museums in the United States was founded by Charles Willson Peale (1741–1827) in Philadelphia in 1785 (Alexander and Alexander 2008). Peale's museum, based on the European model, was established on the principle that a museum should "amuse as well as instruct" the public. The museum was closed and its collections sold at auction in 1858 when admission income was no longer sufficient to sustain operations. The problems that forced the Peale museum to close still threaten museums today – inadequate funding, insufficient visitors, and failure to attract new audiences.

As collections grow ever larger (and older), overcrowding in storage is forcing many museums to either downsize collections or establish off-site storage facilities, creating new collections management and security problems as collections care staff size usually remains static (Simmons 2013). The growth of collections means that collections planning (unheard of in museums 15 or 20 years ago) is now widely considered to be a best practice (on this point see Gardner in this volume). In the future, museums must develop more efficient ways of managing off-site collections (for example, using archival quality support materials and building facilities that can maintain a stable storage environment are more expensive up front, but are more cost-effective in the long run). Future storage furniture should be configured for efficient monitoring of collections; database programs should incorporate environmental monitoring, collection use, and integrated pest management records. Storage arrays should be designed to provide the best environment and most efficient use of space, rather than be based primarily on classifications or taxonomies. The current trend in museum architecture to build stylized, energy-efficient buildings must be balanced with the need to provide appropriate environmental conditions for the storage of collections.

Museums are under pressure to be more socially responsible and better serve the public in ways ranging from increased access to collections and collection information to the repatriation of specimens or objects to their country or community of origin. The increase in demand for access, particularly electronic access, often means that fewer resources are available for collections care. One of the biggest challenges facing collections managers in the future will be finding cost-effective and efficient ways to preserve digital information (and in some museums, digital collection objects) for the future (Simmons 2013). Diane Zorich has compared the potential future loss of electronic data with the burning of the Library of Alexandria, noting that "Museums, often touted as memory institutions, now store much of their information on media that have notoriously poor preservation capabilities" (Zorich 2008, 85).

Emerging museological theory is affecting the perception, nature, and uses of museum collections, and consequentially how objects and specimens are stored and how information is linked to them. The impact of theory, coupled with the wider availability of university-based training for museum personnel, is changing preparation for the profession which has shifted from a focus on discipline-specific subject matter to a knowledge base grounded in museological theory and functions-based operations.

Notes

1   There is of course much work on institutional collections and collecting after the 1990s which falls outside the scope of this chapter. For references see Shelton (2006). "Museal" as an adjective refers to the museum aspects of something, but as a noun, it refers to the field of reference in which musealization takes place. By contrast, "museological" is an adjective that refers to the branch of knowledge that studies museums.
2   For information on developing disaster (emergency) preparedness and risk management plans, refer to Heritage Preservation (2013) and Matthews, Smith, and Knowles. (2009).

References

Alexander, Edward, and Mary Alexander. 2008. *Museums in Motion: An Introduction to the History and Functions of Museums*. Lanham, MD: AltaMira.

Aquilina, Janick D. 2011. "The Babelian Tale of Museology and Museography: A History in Words." *International Scientific Electronic Journal* 6: 1–20.

Baca, Murtha, Erin Coburn, and Sally Hubbard. 2008. "Metadata and Museum Information." In *Museum Informatics: People, Information, and Technology in Museums*, edited by Paul F. Marty and Katherine B. Jones, 107–127. New York: Routledge.

Bedekar, V. H. 1987. "The Museum Training Situation in India." *Museum* 39(4): 284–290.

Besterman, Tristram. 2006. "Museum Ethics." In *A Companion to Museum Studies*, edited by Sharon Macdonald, 431–441. Oxford: Blackwell.

Blackaby, James. R., and Patricia Greeno. 1988. *The Revised Nomenclature for Museum Cataloging: A Revised and Expanded Version of Robert G. Chenhall's System for Classifying Manmade Objects*. Lanham, MD: AltaMira/American Association for State and Local History.

Bourcier, Paul, and Ruby Rogers. 2010. *Nomenclature 3.0 for Museum Cataloging: Third Edition of Robert G. Chenhall's System for Classifying Man-Made Objects*. Lanham, MD: AltaMira/American Association for State and Local History.

Bowles, Edmund A. 1971. "Computers and European Museums: A Report." *Computers and the Humanities* 5(3): 176–177.

Boylan, Patrick J. 2006. "The Museum Profession." In *A Companion to Museum Studies*, edited by Sharon Macdonald, 415–430. Oxford: Blackwell.

Buck, Rebecca A. 2010. "History of Registration." In *Museum Registration Methods*, 5th ed., edited by Rebecca A. Buck and Jean A. Gilmore, 2–11. Washington, DC: American Association of Museums.

Buck, Rebecca A., and Jean A. Gilmore, eds. 2010. *Museum Registration Methods*, 5th ed. Washington, DC: American Association of Museums.

Burcaw, G. Ellis. 1997. *Introduction to Museum Work*. Nashville, TN: AltaMira/American Association for State and Local History.

Canadian Conservation Institute. 2014. "Preventive Conservation and Agents of Deterioration." Accessed October 15, 2014. http://www.cci-icc.gc.ca/resources-ressources/agentsofdeterioration-agentsdedeterioration/index-eng.aspx.

Caple, Chris, ed. 2011. *Preventive Conservation in Museums*. London: Routledge.

Carroll, Diane. 2003. "A First Look at a Remarkable New Building." *Kansas City Star* newspaper supplement, July 19–22, p. 2.

Case, Mary, ed. 1988. *Registrars on Record: Essays on Museum Collections Management*. Washington, DC: Registrars Committee of the American Association of Museums.

Collections Link. 2014. "Spectrum 4.0: The UK Museum Collections Management Standard." Accessed October 15, 2014. http://www.collectionstrust.org.uk/publications/spectrum-4-0.

Cushman, Karen. 1984. "Museum Studies: The Beginnings, 1900–1926." *Museum Studies Journal* 1(3): 8–18.

Demeroukas, Marie. 2010. "Condition Reporting." In *Museum Registration Methods*, 5th ed., edited by Rebecca A. Buck and Jean A. Gilmore, 223–232. Washington, DC: American Association of Museums.

Desvallées, André, and François Mairesse, eds. 2009. *Key Concepts of Museology*. Paris: Armand Colin/ICOM.

Edson, Gary, ed. 1997. *Museum Ethics*. London: Routledge.

Ellin, Everett. 1968. "An International Survey of Museum Computer Activity." *Computers and the Humanities* 3(2): 65–86.

Fahy, Anne, ed. 1995. *Collections Management*. London: Routledge.

Fedi, Fernanda. 1987. "Postgraduate Course in Museography and Museology in the Faculty of Architecture in Milan." *Museum* 39(4): 261–264.

Findlen, Paula. 1989. "The Museum: Its Classical Etymology and Renaissance Genealogy." *Journal of the History of Collections* 1(1): 59–78.

Findlen, Paula. 2000. "Introduction" to David Murray, *Museums, Their History, and Their Use: With a Bibliography and List of Museums in the United Kingdom*, i–xvii. Glasgow: James MacLehose. [2000 reprint of the 1904 edition. Staten Island: Pober Publishing.]

Ford, Patricia, Peter Herzog, Jeremy Linden, James Reilly, and Kristin Smith. 2012. *Sustainable Preservation Practices for Managing Storage Environments*. Rochester, NY: Image Permanence Institute.

Gerstenblith, Patty. 2006. "Museum Practice: Legal Issues." In *A Companion to Museum Studies*, edited by Sharon Macdonald, 442–456. Oxford: Blackwell.

Glaser, Jane R. 1987. "Museum Studies Training in the United States: Coming a Long Way for a Long Time." *Museum* 39(4): 268–274.

Gould, Stephen J. 1986. *Illuminations: A Bestiary*. New York: Norton.

Heritage Preservation. 2013. "Heritage Emergency National Task Force." Accessed October 3, 2014. http://www.heritagepreservation.org/PROGRAMS/TASKFER.HTM.

Hodge, John C. 1987. "Museum Studies Training in Australia." *Museum* 39(4): 249–251.

Hooper-Greenhill, Eileen. 1992. *Museums and the Shaping of Knowledge*. London: Routledge.

Impey, Oliver, and Arthur MacGregor, eds. 1985. *The Origins of Museums: The Cabinet of Curiosities in Sixteenth- and Seventeenth-Century Europe*. Oxford: Clarendon.

Jones, Katherine B. 2008. "The Transformation of the Digital Museum." In *Museum Informatics: People, Information, and Technology in Museums*, edited by Paul F. Marty and Katherine B. Jones, 9–25. New York: Routledge.

Lewis, Geoffrey D. 1985. "Museums." In *Encyclopedia Britannica*, 24: 480–492. Chicago: Encyclopedia Britannica.

Lewis, Geoffrey. 1987. "Museum, Profession and University: Museum Studies at Leicester." *Museum* 39(4): 225–258.

Lewis, Geoffrey. 1992. "Museums and Their Precursors: A Brief World Survey." In *Manual of Curatorship: A Guide to Museum Practice*, 2nd ed., edited by John M. A. Thompson, 5–21. Oxford: Butterworth-Heinemann.

MacDonald, George F., and Stephen Alsford. 1991. "The Museum as Information Utility." *Museum Management and Curatorship* 10: 305–311.

Macdonald, Sharon. 2006a. "Collecting Practices." In *A Companion to Museum Studies*, edited by Sharon Macdonald, 81–97. Oxford: Blackwell.

Macdonald, Sharon, ed. 2006b. *A Companion to Museum Studies*. Oxford: Blackwell.

Malaro, Marie C., and Ildiko P. DeAngelis. 2012. *A Legal Primer on Managing Museum Collections*, 3rd ed. Washington, DC: Smithsonian Books.

Maroević, Ivo. 1998. *Introduction to Museology: The European Approach*. Munich: Christian Müller-Straten.

Marty, Paul F. 2008a. "Information Representation." In *Museum Informatics: People, Information, and Technology in Museums*, edited by Paul F. Marty and Katherine B. Jones, 29–34. New York: Routledge.

Marty, Paul F. 2008b. "An Introduction to Museum Informatics." In *Museum Informatics: People, Information, and Technology in Museums*, edited by Paul F. Marty and Katherine B. Jones, 3–8. New York: Routledge.

Mason, Rhiannon. 2006. "Cultural Theory and Museum Studies." In *A Companion to Museum Studies*, edited by Sharon Macdonald, 17–32. Oxford: Blackwell.

Matassa, Freda. 2011. *Museum Collections Management: A Handbook*. London: Facet.

Matthews, Graham, Yvonne Smith, and Gemma Knowles. 2009. *Disaster Management in Archives, Libraries and Museums*. Aldershot, UK: Ashgate.

McCarthy, Conal, and Joanna Cobley. 2009. "Museums and Museum Studies in New Zealand: A Survey of Historical Developments." *History Compass* 7: 2–19.

McKenzie, Stephanie. 2010. "Link to Our Past, Bridge to Our Future: A Brief History of Registration in Australia and New Zealand." *Australasian Registrars Committee Journal* 59: 14–28.

McKenzie, Stephanie, Mary Faith, Charlotte Davy, and Anne Rowland. 2010. "Winding Back the Clock." *Australasian Registrars Committee Journal* 59: 8–13.

Merritt, Elizabeth E., ed. 2008. *National Standards and Best Practices for U.S. Museums*. Washington, DC: American Association of Museums.

Murray, David. 2000. *Museums, Their History, and Their Use: With a Bibliography and List of Museums in the United Kingdom*. Glasgow: James MacLehose. [2000 reprint of the 1904 edition. Staten Island: Pober Publishing.]

Nicholson, Emily G., and Stephen L. Williams. 2002. "Developing a Working Definition for the Museum Collection." *Inside Line* (fall): 1–4.

Orosz, Joel J. 1990. *Curators and Culture: The Museum Movement in America, 1740–1870*. Tuscaloosa: University of Alabama Press.

Peacock, Darren. 2008. "The Information Revolution in Museums." In *Museum Informatics: People, Information, and Technology in Museums*, edited by Paul F. Marty and Katherine B. Jones, 59–76. New York: Routledge.

Pearce, Susan M. 1993. *Museums, Objects and Collections: A Cultural Study*. Washington, DC: Smithsonian Institution Press.

Pearce, Susan M., ed. 1994. *Interpreting Objects and Collections*. London: Routledge.

Reibel, Daniel B. 2008. *Registration Methods for the Small Museum*, 4th ed. Nashville, TN: AltaMira / American Association for State and Local History.

Shelton, Anthony. 2006. "Museums and Museum Displays." In *Handbook of Material Culture*, edited by Chris Tilley, Webb Keane, Susanne Küchler, Mike Rowlands, and Patricia Spyer, 480–499. London: Sage.

Simmons, John E. 1993. "Natural History Collections Management in North America." *Journal of Biological Curation* 1(3/4): 1–17.

Simmons, John E. 2006a. "Museum Studies Programs in North America." In *Museum Studies Perspectives and Innovations*, edited by Stephen L. Williams and Catharine A. Hawks, 113–128. Washington, DC: Society for the Preservation of Natural History Collections.

Simmons, John E. 2006b. *Things Great and Small: Collections Management Policies*. Washington, DC: American Association of Museums.

Simmons, John E. 2010. "History of Museums." In *Encyclopedia of Library and Information Sciences*, 3rd ed., edited by Marcia J. Bates and Mary N. Maack, 2096–2106. New York: Taylor and Francis.

Simmons, John E. 2013. "Application of Preventive Conservation to Solve the Coming Crisis in Collections Management." *Collection Forum* 27(1–2): 89–101.

Simmons, John E., and Yaneth Muñoz-Saba. 2003. "The Theoretical Bases of Collections Management." *Collection Forum* 18(1–2): 38–49.

Simmons, John E., and Julianne Snider. 2012. "Observation and Distillation – Preservation, Depiction, and the Perception of Nature." *Bibliotheca Herpetologica* 9(1–2): 115–134.

Society for the Preservation of Natural History Collections. 1994. "Guidelines for the Care of Natural History Collections." *Collection Forum* 10(1): 32–40.

Stansfield, Geoff, John Mathias, and Gordon Reid, eds. 1994. *Manual of Natural History Curatorship*. London: Museums and Galleries Commission / HMSO.

Thompson, Gary. 1986. *The Museum Environment*, 2nd ed. London: Butterworths.

Thompson, John M. A., ed. 1992. *Manual of Curatorship: A Guide to Museum Practice*. Oxford: Butterworth-Heinemann.

van Mensch, Peter. 2004. "Museology and Management: Enemies or Friends? Current Tendencies in Theoretical Museology and Museum Management in Europe." In *Museum Management in the 21st Century*, edited by E. Mizushima, 3–19. Tokyo: Museum Management Academy.

Waller, Robert R. 2003. "Cultural Property Risk Analysis Model: Development and Application to Preventive Conservation at the Canadian Museum of Nature." *Göteborg Studies in Conservation* 13: 1–107.

Washburn, Wilcomb E. 1984. "Collecting Information, Not Objects." *Museum News* 62: 5–15

Weil, Stephen E. 1983. *Beauty and the Beasts: On Museums, Art, the Law, and the Market*. Washington, DC: Smithsonian Institution Press.

Weil, Stephen E., ed. 1997. *A Deaccession Reader*. Washington, DC: American Association of Museums.

Williams, Stephen L. 1997. "Preventive Conservation: The Evolution of a Museum Ethic." In *Museum Ethics*, edited by Gary Edson, 198–206. London: Routledge.

Zorich, Diane M. 2008. "Information Policy in Museums." In *Museum Informatics: People, Information, and Technology in Museums*, edited by Paul F. Marty and Katherine B. Jones, 85–106. New York: Routledge.

Further Reading

Ambrose, Timothy, and Crispin Paine. 2012. *Museum Basics*, 3rd ed. London: Routledge.

Catlin-Legutko, Cinnamon, and Stacy Klingler. 2013. *Stewardship: Collections and Historic Preservation*. Lanham, MD: AltaMira.

Keene, Suzanne. 2012. *Digital Collections*. London: Routledge.

Latham, Kiersten, and John E. Simmons. 2014. *Foundations of Museum Studies: Evolving Systems of Knowledge*. Santa Barbara, CA: ABS-CLIO.

John E. Simmons began his career as a zookeeper before becoming Collections Manager at the California Academy of Sciences, and later at the Natural History Museum at the University of Kansas where he also served as Director of the Museum Studies Program until 2007. Simmons' publications include *Foundations of Museum Studies: Evolving Systems of Knowledge* (2014, with Kiersten F. Latham) and *Fluid Preservation: A Comprehensive Reference* (2014). Simmons is currently a museum consultant and teaches museum studies at Juniata College, Kent State University, the Universidad Nacional de Colombia, the Northern States Conservation Center. He also serves as Adjunct Curator of Collections at the Earth and Mineral Sciences Museum and Art Gallery at Penn State University.

11

THE FUTURE OF COLLECTING IN "DISCIPLINARY" MUSEUMS
Interpretive, Thematic, Relational

Nick Merriman

There has been a considerable emphasis in recent years, in the United Kingdom at least, on the issue of disposal from museum collections. This has partly come about as a result of the Museums Association's "Collections for the Future" report (Museums Association 2005) and its follow-up "Making Collections Effective" (Museums Association 2007), and partly as a result of the financial pressures that museums have been under, which have led to a reduction in staff and resources to look after collections. The pages of *Museums Journal* and similar publications have seen extensive debate about disposals, especially on the acceptability of those which are financially motivated.

However, disposal is only one element in an overall approach to the development of collections, and was not the main emphasis of the documents cited above. What has been surprising is how little discussion there has been of the key recommendation of "Collections for the Future," which was that "all museums must enter into the debate about how collections can best be developed for the future, and reinstate active collecting as a crucial part of their activities" (Museums Association 2005, 17).

With the exception of art galleries, which are concerned with perennial issues relating to collecting contemporary art, and how to operate in the art market when there are almost no funds for acquisition, it is my experience that almost no museum in the UK these days sees collecting as a significant part of its work. This is quite a contrast to my experience as a Museum Studies student in the 1980s, when professionals seemed obsessed by collecting policies, and by bringing some order to what

The International Handbooks of Museum Studies: Museum Practice, First Edition.
Edited by Conal McCarthy.
© 2015 John Wiley & Sons Ltd. Published 2020 by John Wiley & Sons Ltd.

had been up till then some fairly haphazard and idiosyncratic collecting practices by museums. This was clearly a product of the huge expansion of museums in the 1970s and 1980s which characterized the development of the "heritage industry" (Hewison 1987; Arnold, Davies, and Ditchfield 1998). There were major debates on how to collect contemporary society, how to save the remnants of declining industries and cultures, and how to manage the large collections that were amassed (Lord, Lord, and Nicks 1989; Lowenthal and Binney 1981; Middleton 1990).

Since then, with the professionalization of collections management through the development of policies, the accreditation system, and the shift from an inward focus on collections to an outward focus on audiences, the rate of collecting seems to have slowed down, and with it the issue of collecting seems to have fallen off the agenda of many museums.[1] My own experience at the Manchester Museum is that I very rarely see proposals for new acquisitions, except occasionally when we are left a bequest.[2] Consultation among colleagues in the North West region of England shows that virtually none of them are actively collecting, with the exception of National Museums Liverpool, which is large enough to continue some traditional collecting in botany, in entomology (through commissioned research) and in anthropological fieldwork projects. This virtual cessation of collecting in most regional museums seems not to have occasioned any debate, possibly because it is seen as a luxury in a recession, and because so much attention has been given to disposal and sustainability.

However, in this chapter I argue that we *do* need to be concerned about the decline in collecting. It is not an "extra" to be considered when times are good, but one of the key functions of a museum when undertaken thoughtfully. Not engaging in active collecting programs diminishes the potential of museums. I examine why museums should restart collecting, with more ambition, and how they might go about doing so. I begin by looking at the distinctiveness of disciplinary museums and their collections, and focus on regional museums as these are experiencing a virtual stagnation in terms of their collecting ambition. Considering whether it is axiomatic that museums collect, I argue that we must make a distinction between collecting comprehensively (which is impossible) and collecting scientifically (which is desirable). A case is then presented for a new kind of collecting, which is thematic and "relational," and scientific in its execution. The chapter concludes by outlining an example of this new approach, the thematic project on trees which is being undertaken by the Manchester Museum as a pilot project.

Disciplinary museums

Simon Knell has usefully made a distinction between two basic types of museums or collections: those he calls "disciplinary," which were collected on a large scale for scientific purposes in support of disciplines such as anthropology, archaeology, botany, Egyptology, entomology, geology, paleontology, and zoology; and those he calls "identity-making," which comprise all of the others, from local history to biographical, from military to industrial, which were ultimately collected to say something about the identity of a place, person, or period (Knell 2004, 19–23). Traditionally it was the disciplinary museums which amassed large scientific collections for research purposes.

The national museums in general seem to retain an ambition toward systematic collecting, even though resources have somewhat limited the fulfillment of that ambition, and they continue to undertake fieldwork investigations allied to particular academic research projects. However, in this chapter I want to focus on the significant numbers of regional scientific collections that emerged in Britain from the latter half of the nineteenth century as a result of the country's imperial wealth. Museums such as those in Leeds, Sheffield, Bristol, Birmingham, Liverpool, Glasgow, and Manchester, and their slightly smaller counterparts in places such as Bolton, Ipswich, Lincoln, Truro, Maidstone, and Colchester, collected from around the world in the new and emerging disciplines and this century-long chapter of imperial collecting still constitutes the great bulk of their holdings.

I am interested in these regional disciplinary collections because they are large, primarily future-orientated (in that they form an archive for potential research), and are in a situation of virtual stagnation. Many regional museums have large and important collections in areas ranging from ethnography to geology and from archaeology to zoology, but have experienced a decline in expertise to bring the collections to life, and find that the material itself is often seen as a burden by funding bodies such as local councils which find themselves having to deal with huge reductions in their finances. In this situation it is perhaps not surprising that adding to the collections is not high on the strategic agenda, but I want to argue that ceasing to collect will begin to make these institutions moribund.

I think that there would be little dispute that the social and political context in which museums use and develop their collections has changed massively in recent decades, and that the former certainties around truth and objectivity in collections have been fundamentally challenged by postcolonial critiques, which have shown even natural history collecting to have been biased, partial, historically contingent, and deeply influenced by individual personalities (Hooper-Greenhill 1992; Cardinal and Elsner 1994; Pearce 1995; Gosden and Knowles 2001; Henare 2005; Macdonald 2006). What hasn't happened, in my view, is a review of the implications of the postcolonial critique for the future of these disciplinary collections in the very changed context in which we now find ourselves. Is the natural response to both critique and financial circumstances to conclude that disciplinary collections should cease to collect, or is there a different way of thinking about their future development?

Should we collect?

The first question, of course, must be to ask whether it is axiomatic that museums *should* collect. A perfectly legitimate argument can be advanced that we should treat the great collecting phase of disciplinary museums as a unique phenomenon, about a century long, from 1850 to 1950, and that further addition to this historic collection is not desirable. As several scholars have argued, meaning isn't inherent in objects, and "heritage" isn't about material things but about the values we imbue objects with and the questions we ask of them (Appadurai 1986; Vogel 1991; Merriman 1991; Clavir 2002).

As a result, it would be possible to treat disciplinary collections as a historic resource. Just as we don't generally make a case for adding to a historic monument such as a medieval castle, so too, this line of argument would go, we should not add to a superb Victorian and Edwardian collection that acts as a kind of time-capsule of a particular period of museum development. Should we not be content that these historic resources are continually reworked by different audiences and different generations, bringing forth new meanings suited for the times, strongly contrasting with those meanings made a hundred years ago (Conn 2011)? Future collecting could surely be undertaken digitally, and may often be done better by other organizations, from local archives to documentary film-makers (Keene 1998; 2005).

This is very much the situation at the Petrie Museum of Egyptian Archaeology at University College London, where legislation in Egypt and lack of resources means that the collection is effectively a closed one, with no new material being added unless it is by transfer from existing collections. This has led the museum to make a virtue of this situation by seeking to develop reciprocal relationships with Egyptian and Sudanese people in London and abroad, with people of African descent, with artists, and with hard-to-reach audiences such as prisoners, who have in turn interpreted the collections or worked with them in a variety of different ways and resulted in some outstanding audience development work (MacDonald and Shaw 2004).

So, collections development in the postmodern context *could* mean getting your collections in order through a program of rationalization and by making all information on it available on the web, but it doesn't *have* to involve collecting. In the Petrie's case, though, lack of collecting has really been enforced rather than a choice. As most museums still have the freedom to collect, should they do so when it can be highly fruitful just to work with the resources we already have? My view is that where museums have the ability to collect, they should do, so that their collection continues to develop and reflect contemporary interests and issues. However, the approach to collecting has to be different from that which formed the bulk of the historic collections. I think the difficulty about what this approach should be starts to resolve itself if we begin to challenge the notion that rigorous, scientific collecting has anything to do with comprehensiveness. Instead, we should be thinking of collecting as an interpretation of the world, but one which is conducted rigorously and scientifically.

Collecting comprehensively and collecting scientifically

The whole notion of disciplinary collecting in museums is still very much imbued with ideas of comprehensive recording, from Victorian and Edwardian notions of systematic classification (Mackenzie 2009), to post-war ideas of scientific recording of disappearing cultures, industries, and ways of life. Archaeology, from the 1960s until the present, has subscribed to the idea that it is objectively recording remains of past activity that can be preserved in a museum and somehow reconstructed from the resultant archives (Hodder 1999; Merriman 2004). In professional discourse about collecting there is still a great deal about filling in gaps in collections, as if it would be possible at some point to achieve a complete series. The notion of the "encyclopedic" museum exists as a kind of folk memory for museum professionals, as an ideal type that has since been discontinued.

In fact, the encyclopedic museum never existed, and all studies of the history of collecting, as well as professional experience, show that collections were never comprehensive but were shaped by the interests of the individuals who amassed them (for example for the Manchester Museum, see Alberti 2009). This has resulted in museum collections across the UK that are strong in certain areas, where collecting was undertaken on a rigorous basis by key individuals, with good comparative samples, and much weaker in other areas, with little scientific value. Museums have generally built on areas of strength, and continued to neglect weaker areas, unless a new curator with an interest in a new area began to build up collections in that field. In this way we can see, with hindsight, that collecting in the disciplinary field has always been an interpretation of the contemporary world. It is my contention that, instead of resisting this, we need to work with it as an assumption and help it shape our approach to collecting.

In thinking about this, we need therefore to distinguish between comprehensive collecting and rigorous or scientific collecting. Comprehensive collecting, and its notions of encyclopedic coverage, has never been achievable and should be dismissed from the professional mind set. Seeing collecting as an interpretive act, however, does not mean that collecting is serendipitous and subjective. In fact, rigorous, scientific collecting has always been the way in which the most valuable collecting has taken place. Scientific collecting – which can apply to all disciplines, from the humanities to technology and the natural sciences – is consciously structured, and gathers as much contextual information in as objective a manner as possible to support future investigation. The future for collecting is to accept that it is interpretive, then to collect scientifically within this framework, and as I suggest below, this scientific collecting should be selective rather than quasi-comprehensive, and thematic rather than disciplinary (see also Young 2004).

New scientific collecting: interpretive, thematic, and relational

What has hampered the development of collecting in disciplinary museums is that it has continued to be framed within the traditional disciplines themselves, with collecting being seen as in the service of disciplinary activity, within a peer group of fellow curators and academics. As a result, in my experience, collecting has been undertaken as a kind of sub-surface activity, entirely divorced from all of the other public work of the museum such as its exhibition program or its work with communities. It has been shaped by fairly standard collecting policies, derived from obligatory templates as part of the UK's accreditation scheme (aimed at raising the standards of professional practice), and has either been reactive, responding when opportunities come through donations or purchase, or it has been part of recording and research programs related to the curator's own disciplinary priorities rather than the wider work of the museum.

Partly as a result of this, as specialist curator posts have declined, along with resources for fieldwork, and as priorities have shifted toward public engagement and away from self-directed curatorial research, so collecting within the disciplines has gradually faded away: only a handful of museums which still manage to retain significant resources can realistically attempt to collect in this mode, such as the Natural History Museum in London. In some of the traditional collecting areas – such as Egyptology and many other branches of overseas archaeology – collecting has effectively ceased because of legislative changes. In other slightly larger museums which have retained some specialist staff, such as in the natural sciences, there is still a tendency to see the disciplinary peer group as the primary focus and the curatorial networks operate on primarily systematic disciplinary lines, with gap-filling still important. In many other museums – particularly those in local authority control – political priorities and funding cuts have often led to a loss of posts in more "exotic" areas (ethnography, Egyptology) and a renewing of focus on to the local, which has left the global and systematic collections in something of an anomalous position. These collections are represented in displays but no longer apparently central to the museum's mission, and valued as much for the local connection of the collector as for the global dimension of the material.

So, is it possible, from this current situation where collecting has faltered to nothing or at the very least become passive, to launch a more coherent approach to the development of these disciplinary collections? We can only begin to answer this, I think, by first setting out what this kind of collecting might look like. In response to the changes that characterize the postcolonial context, only in anthropology has a great deal of thought and action taken place with regard to collecting, clearly because of the pressing demands to address the issue in this particular subject area. In numerous instances abroad, and in the UK in the work of members of the Museum Ethnographers Group (2013; see their website Museum Ethnographers Group, and the *Journal of Museum Ethnography*), there has been some excellent practice in building mutual relationships with communities of origin, in sharing knowledge, and in recording that transaction through the collecting of objects, and the taking of photographs and video testimony (Brown 2001; Peers and Brown 2003; De Stecher and Loyer 2009; Herle 2008; Byrne et al. 2011).

Taking the lead from this approach, a future direction becomes clearer if we see collecting as a form of interpretation, which tells us something about the present, rather than as a systematic gap-filling exercise referring to the past. Of course, we can re-interpret our existing collections, but collecting today allows us to bring in contemporary perspectives on issues that can be illustrated both by historic material and new specially assembled collections. For example, the natural environment is such a crucial issue today that in the museum context it needs to be interpreted both with reference to existing material, and through new collecting now, which can act as a contrast or allow discussion of new issues.

If we begin to see collecting in traditional disciplines as an interpretive act, an exciting future for collecting begins to open up. Of course a critical understanding of the subjectivities of historical collecting in institutions, which is always already interpretive in nature, has been accepted in contemporary scholarship for some time (Vergo 1989; Cardinal and Elsner 1994), but this insight has not been translated into collecting practices in museums on a broad scale. This new self-reflexive kind of collecting would have a series of distinctive characteristics. It would have both a local *and* a global dimension in recognition of the fact that we live in a world of international communication, a global economy and networked relationships, where people and goods in a local community are part of an international system of trade and migration.

At the same time, the *process* of collecting would be highly significant, and one of the major outcomes would be the development of relationships between museum staff and members of particular communities. These relationships have the potential to be two-way and mutually beneficial, based on reciprocity, though naturally in practice community collaboration is a challenging process given the asymmetrical power relations. To borrow a phrase developed by the Pitt Rivers Museum in Oxford, the collecting institution would become a "relational museum" in which the specificities of context and the interaction between people is of fundamental significance in the collecting process (Gosden, Larson, and Petch 2007, 6–7). The collecting process could thus be as much about recording images, conversations, and thoughts alongside the collecting of objects and specimens. Crucially, though, the collecting would be undertaken *scientifically*. By this I do not mean to imply that it is objective, as science is of course as much constructed as other disciplines, nor that it is restricted to science or natural history – rather the word implies as I have argued above, a collecting that is rigorous, consciously structured, and thoroughly contextualized. Though the particular form it takes of samples of material and associated information may look quite conventional, I would argue that the breadth and holistic nature of the material, and the ways in which it is assembled rigorously and coherently to address a particular issue, makes what I have called scientific collecting distinctly different. As a result of this approach, digital preservation and distribution becomes fundamentally important: museums will therefore need to make common cause with archives and libraries and really think through these issues, and it will require a new kind of digital asset management and curation.

This new kind of scientific collecting will also be thematic or interdisciplinary rather than following the lines of traditional disciplines. One of the things that constrains us is that we still tend to think of collecting in terms of traditional collections areas and traditional nineteenth-century disciplines (Conn 1998; Shelton 2007). In the places they originated, the universities, these disciplines – for the most part – barely exist. If we are to revitalize collecting, we need to break out of this focus on the object and the discipline, and instead begin to focus on themes that are of relevance today, accepting that our legacy will not be comprehensive but selective, deep rather than broad in its particular focus. We should always be clear that what we choose to collect is partial and hence an interpretation of the world. As a result of all of this, collecting in these former systematic, disciplinary collections would move into a new phase where the focus is on relational, qualitative collecting, and the model of separate disciplinary and identity-making collections described by Knell (2004) begins to shift to a merged one.

Making it work in practice: the Trees project at Manchester Museum

To give a sense of how this might be realized in practice, this section provides a case study showing how thinking on these issues is developing at the Manchester Museum. Manchester Museum was established as part of the University of Manchester in 1890. It draws on the original collections of the Manchester Natural History Society, and today has about four and a half million objects and specimens from across all the major disciplines (Manchester Museum 2014a). At the moment the museum has a well-developed collecting policy which insists that the principal criterion for assessing new acquisitions has to be their potential *use*, in display, in public programs, in research, or in teaching.[3] For each acquisition a case has to be made as to how any particular item or group of items will actually be used – rather than simply added to a drawer. For disciplinary collections this can be a difficult question to answer, as distinctive use was not the rationale behind the collections, with the result that in recent years new acquisitions have declined to a trickle. This has been useful while we catch up on a backlog of documentation, but what needs to be added is an active vision for why we collect and a plan to implement it (see also Gardner in this volume).

A vision for the future is now emerging in that we have focused the museum on just two main objectives in the coming years:

1. promoting understanding between cultures;
2. developing a sustainable world.

So far this approach has been played out in programs which have re-examined the Museum's collections in new ways – such as the Revealing Histories project which looked at the slave trade and the *Myths about Race* gallery which surveyed how Victorian and Edwardian museums were complicit in racism through the classificatory schemes they used (Lynch and Alberti 2010). In these programs, community perspectives have been vital, particularly through our "Collective Conversations" method of working in which community members are filmed giving their personal perspectives on the meaning of a particular object to them.

We have more recently extended this overall vision to the development of web materials on, for example, biodiversity and climate change, and we are in the process of extending it to galleries. The old classificatory Mammals Gallery has been transformed into an issues-based exhibit called *Living Worlds* (McGhie 2012, 201); and our redeveloped archaeology and Ancient Egypt galleries, Ancient Worlds (Figure 11.1), highlight to a much greater degree issues of intercultural understanding and environment, for example different popular, academic, and African perceptions of ancient Egypt, as a product of extensive community consultation (Exell 2013; see also Manchester Museum 2014b).

What we have not done so far, though, is to extend this vision and approach to collecting, which remains something of a separate realm. The challenge for us is to see how the museum can integrate programs of relational collecting into its wider objectives around intercultural understanding and sustainability, while at the same time keeping hold of the notion that collecting has to involve some kind of public outcome. We have begun by instigating an interdisciplinary program of collections development which brings together a range of subject areas into an overarching theme of contemporary relevance which can be examined at both the local and the global levels, culminating in a major public output such as an exhibition. The first theme for this integrated collecting approach, which is in the pilot phase of what will be a three-year program, is called Trees.

Trees was chosen as a theme that includes most of our collections: botany, vivarium (where we have tree frogs), geology (for example fossilized trees), entomology, anthropology, and archaeology, with only Egyptology currently difficult to include. The long-term aim is to look locally and globally at issues relating to trees, such as forestation and deforestation in the Manchester region and in the Amazon; the uses to which trees are put; the effect of climate change and pollution; and the cultural meaning of trees to local people. This will result in a major exhibition and public program in over three years' time, with an interim small exhibition showing the initial results, funded by the British Ecological Society and mounted from summer 2013 (see Figure 11.2).

Work so far is at an early stage. We have undertaken "bioblitzes" in nearby Whitworth Park with members of the public and the Museum Youth Board participating with our natural-science curators recording tree species, mosses on trees, insects on trees, and so on, as well as recording people's thoughts and stories about the trees in the park (Figure 11.3). A highlight of the first bioblitz was the discovery of the horse chestnut leaf-mining moth, which attacks the leaves of horse chestnut trees. Originally from Macedonia, it was first recorded in the UK in 2002 and this was the first sighting in this part of the UK. This recording exercise therefore also contributed to a project called Conker-Tree Science, which is enlisting the public in trying to map the effects of these moths.

In addition, we have taken steps to make this project much more multidisciplinary and relational than a traditional collecting exercise. This has included working with Red Rose Forest, the Community Forest organization for central and western Greater Manchester, working with local communities, businesses and partners, to develop well-wooded, multipurpose landscapes and improve the quality of life in the area. Working with these partners, the museum has begun to look at the role of urban trees, videoing community members talking about the trees that are

FIGURE 11.1   The Ancient Worlds gallery, Manchester Museum. (For a color version of this figure, please see the color plate section.)
Courtesy Manchester Museum.

FIGURE 11.2   A botany assortment from the collections of the Manchester Museum.
Courtesy Manchester Museum.

FIGURE 11.3   A "bioblitz" or collecting expedition for the Trees project, Whitworth Park, Manchester.
Courtesy Lorna Davenport, Senior Youth Board, and Manchester Museum.

significant to them, and collecting examples of modern urban trees and seeds. A case in point is the recent series of demonstrations and occupations about the removal of large trees as part of the regeneration of Alexandra Park in Manchester – our curatorial team have been filming participants about their responses and motivations, and this material will be included in the interim exhibition.

The exhibition includes photographs and films of people talking about their relationship to trees, illustrated by specimens from the museum's collection and from material collected as part of the project. One area invites visitors to write down their thoughts on what trees mean to them on a paper leaf and hang it on a "tree." Here are a sample of some of these responses:

> As a teenager I got obsessed with bonsai trees after watching *The Karate Kid*. I dug up all the tree seedlings I could find.

> Alfie, Lacey, Alicia, Mummy and Daddy love trees. They are relaxing to watch in the wind.

> I get the Woodland Trust to plant trees for births, deaths, marriages etc. Better than "dead" flowers. They are important for the planet.

Another area asks what the museum should collect in the future:

> I think the museum should collect leaves. Leaves feel like they are under-represented and can be used in lots of different ways from medicine to preserving and presenting food. We often forget the importance of them.

> I don't think we should collect on the theme of trees as it's restrictive and not sustainable.

> I'm interested in how different communities use different trees.

Complementing the exhibition is a public program that explores the theme of trees, ranging from an after-hours event featuring an evening tree walk to an "Urban Naturalist" evening class focusing on identifying trees and associated flora and fauna. Following the exhibition, the scope of the project will be expanded by working both with our own Youth Board and the Manchester Youth Council on collecting sub-themes. Ideas include the ways trees are used for economic purposes locally (for example, the Moss Cider project in Moss Side where a group has bought a community cider press and has invited people to bring in apples from local trees to make cider); collecting objects made from local trees; and recording forms of life living in local trees, from insects to epiphyte plants. As we develop the project further it is planned to extend it internationally by undertaking the same approach in a rainforest such as in Ecuador or Costa Rica, where we have existing links.

As we refine our ideas through the experience of undertaking this pilot program, staff will inevitably begin to explore other collecting themes. One that has already emerged is the theme of Water, where again it would be possible to take a local area such as the Peak District and perhaps a desert area in Egypt, and look at water and its management; its cultural associations; the way changes in water availability have affect distribution of plants and animals. Another theme might be Cotton, which could be approached by looking at its cultivation in different parts of the world, its manufacture into clothing, and its retail in Manchester. Another might be the migration of people, plants, and animals, combining the global and the local. In each case, the program would involve humanities and natural-science curators working together in a local community project that would have a global dimension, and in each case all of the principles mentioned earlier about relationships, reciprocity, the virtual as well as the face-to-face, would pertain. Crucially, these programs would be part of long-term exhibition and public programs, and therefore at the heart of what the museum does, rather than peripheral.

However, these are only examples, and in the future we would expect collecting themes to emerge from close consultation with different communities of interest with whom we engage. Indeed, we expect the Trees theme to develop and become more focused as we work with a wider range of people. Indeed we have begun to refer to our approach as "dendritic," from the Greek word for tree, and referring to the branch-like projections of a neuron. Likewise the exploration of one "branch" of the topic, is followed by the branching off into another related area. This is collecting as a meandering journey without a clear route or a final destination, quite different from the preplanned totalizing schemes of previous generations.

Importantly, one of the keys to the realization of this vision must be for regional museums with global multidisciplinary collections to become more involved with their local universities. Museums have not really capitalized on the huge expansion that has been seen in higher education in the past 15 years, mainly because museums have been unable to find academic staff interested in traditional material culture and specimen-based work. There is now a huge opportunity to re-establish the link between museums and universities that Conn (1998) describes as being severed a century ago.

Universities are more and more seeking to play a civic role again as a way of demonstrating both the public impact of their research and the benefits they can bring to local education, culture, and economy, and university researchers are increasingly looking for ways to engage wider publics with their work. By focusing now on contemporary themes illustrated through objects, specimens and digital records, rather than just on the objects themselves, rich possibilities emerge for museums to develop partnerships with university researchers who may be able to bring new perspectives and a global dimension to the work. Finally, the thematic approach is also one which should encourage museums to work together in a collaborative and non-competitive way, sharing resources and the exhibition materials which emerge from these collecting programs.

Conclusion

In this chapter I began by observing a decline in collecting among nearly all disciplinary museums and consequently made the point that museums are not fulfilling their potential if they cease collecting. However, I have argued that we need to rethink the purpose and methods of collecting in these kinds of museums if they are to have a viable future. This includes seeing collecting not as comprehensive recording, but as contemporary interpretation, rigorously and scientifically undertaken. This new collecting will be multidisciplinary and thematic, and at the heart of the museum rather than at the periphery, taking the relationships between people and objects or specimens as the key focus of the collecting enterprise. In this relational approach, the process of collecting has a far greater role than previously, and is to be documented alongside the results of the collecting, which now include extensive digital records together with objects and specimens.

The Manchester Museum has developed a pilot collecting program on the theme of Trees which, though in its early stages, has demonstrated the viability of the approach. Involving the public in institutional collecting is obviously a very different method to the traditional internal museum process. It is taking a little time for the curators, who were recruited for their specific disciplinary backgrounds, to get used to collecting thematically, to working with other stakeholders, and to recording process as well as product, but they have been energized by the challenge and are continuing to develop their new practice. Issues have been raised that we have not yet solved, such as how the documentation of this thematic collecting is integrated into the traditional collections management system, and how the larger amounts of digital information are managed, but our approach is to learn by doing, and evolve solutions as we go along.

We plan to continue to develop this approach, and hold a conference on the theme of the future of disciplinary collections as a means of both eliciting responses to the work, and to develop with colleagues other strategies for these particular resources. Whether other museums decide to take up the challenge of reviving and rethinking collecting in "disciplinary" areas remains to be seen; in many ways it could be seen as a low priority at a time of severe constraints in terms of funding and personnel. However, in hard times one has to return to fundamental values. There is no better time to re-assert the vital importance of collecting.

Notes

1   For an international perspective on collections management in general, see Simmons in this volume. In the UK, the museum accreditation scheme has been operating since 1988 (originally under title of "registration") and is now managed by Arts Council England. See ACE 2014.

2 For information on the background, history, and operation of the Manchester Museum, see http://www.museum.manchester.ac.uk. For the acquisition and disposals policy, see http://www.museum.manchester.ac.uk/aboutus/reportspolicies/Acquisition-&-Disposal-Policy-2012.pdf. Accessed October 13, 2014.

3 See n. 2 above.

References

ACE (Arts Council England). 2014. "Accreditation Scheme." Accessed October 13, 2014. http://www.artscouncil.org.uk/what-we-do/supporting-museums/accreditation-scheme.

Alberti, Samuel J. M. M. 2009. *Nature and Culture: Objects, Disciplines and the Manchester Museum*. Manchester: Manchester University Press.

Appadurai, Arjun, ed. 1986. *The Social Life of Things: Commodities in Cultural Perspective*. Cambridge: Cambridge University Press.

Arnold, John, Kate Davies, and Simon Ditchfield. 1998. *History and Heritage: Consuming the Past in Contemporary Culture*. Shaftesbury: Donhead.

Brown, Alison. 2001. "Artefacts as 'Alliances': First Nations' Perspectives on Collectors and Collecting." *Journal of Museum Ethnography* 13: 79–89.

Byrne, Sarah, Anne Clarke, Rodney Harrison, and Robin Torrence, eds. 2011. *Unpacking the Collection: Networks of Material and Social Agency in the Museum*. One World Archaeology. New York: Springer.

Cardinal, Roger, and John Elsner, eds. 1994. *The Cultures of Collection*. Cambridge, MA: Harvard University Press.

Clavir, Miriam. 2002. *Preserving What Is Valued: Museums, Conservation and First Nations*. Vancouver: University of British Colombia Press.

Conn, Steven. 1998. *Museums and American Intellectual Life, 1876–1926*. Chicago: University of Chicago Press.

Conn, Steven. 2011. *Do Museums Still Need Objects?* Philadelphia: University of Pennsylvania Press.

De Stecher, Anne, and Stacey Loyer. 2009. "Practising Collaborative Research: The Great Lakes Research Alliance Visits to the Pitt Rivers Museum and the British Museum." *Journal of Museum Ethnography* 22: 145–154.

Exell, Karen. 2013. "Community Consultation and the Redevelopment of Manchester Museum's Ancient Egypt Galleries." In *Museums and Communities: Curators, Collections and Collaboration*, edited by Viv Golding and Wayne Modest, 130–143. London: Bloomsbury.

Gosden, Chris, and Chantal Knowles. 2001. *Collecting Colonialism: Material Culture and Colonial Change*. London: Berg.

Gosden, Chris, Frances Larson, and Alison Petch. 2007. *Knowing Things: Exploring the Collections at the Pitt Rivers Museum, 1884–1945*. Oxford: Oxford University Press.

Henare, Amiria. 2005. *Museums, Anthropology and Imperial Exchange*. Cambridge: Cambridge University Press.

Herle, Anita. 2008. "Relational Objects: Connecting People and Things through Pasifika Styles." *International Journal of Cultural Property* 15(2): 159–179.

Hewison, Robert. 1987. *The Heritage Industry: Britain in a Climate of Decline*. London: Methuen.

Hodder, Ian. 1999. *The Archaeological Process: An Introduction*. Oxford: Blackwell.

Hooper-Greenhill, Eilean. 1992. *Museums and the Shaping of Knowledge*. London: Routledge.

Keene, Suzanne. 1998. *Digital Collections: Museums in the Information Age*. London: Butterworth-Heinemann.

Keene, Suzanne. 2005. *Fragments of the World: Uses of Museum Collections*. London: Elsevier/ Butterworth.

Knell, Simon. 2004. "Introduction. Altered Values: Searching for a New Collecting." In *Museums and the Future of Collecting*, edited by Simon Knell, 1–46. Aldershot, UK: Ashgate.

Lord, Barry, Gail Lord, and John Nicks. 1989. *The Cost of Collecting: Collection Management in UK Museums*. London: HMSO.

Lowenthal, David, and Marcus Binney, eds. 1981. *Our Past before Us: Why Do We Save It?* London: Temple Smith.

Lynch, Bernadette, and Samuel J. M. M. Alberti. 2010. "Legacies of Prejudice: Racism, Co-production and Radical Trust in the Museum." *Museum Management and Curatorship* 25(1): 13–35.

MacDonald, Sally, and Catherine Shaw. 2004. "Uncovering Ancient Egypt: The Petrie Museum and its Public." In *Public Archaeology*, edited by Nick Merriman, 109–130. London: Routledge.

Macdonald, Sharon. 2006. "Collecting Practices." In *A Companion to Museum Studies*, edited by Sharon Macdonald, 81–97. Oxford: Blackwell.

Mackenzie, John. 2009. *Museums and Empire: Natural History, Human Cultures and Colonial Identities*. Manchester: Manchester University Press.

Manchester Museum. 2014a. Website. Accessed October 11, 2014. http://www.museum. manchester.ac.uk.

Manchester Museum. 2014b. "Ancient Worlds." Accessed October 11, 2014. http://www. ancientworlds.co.uk.

McGhie, Henry. 2012. "The Living Worlds Gallery at the Manchester Museum." *A Handbook for Academic Museums: Exhibitions and Education*, edited by Stefanie Jandl and Mark Gold, 222–253. London: MuseumsEtc.

Merriman, Nick. 1991. *Beyond the Glass Case: The Past, Heritage and the Public in Britain*. Leicester: Leicester University Press.

Merriman, Nick, ed. 2004. *Public Archaeology*. London: Routledge.

Middleton, Victor. 1990. *New Visions for Independent Museums in the UK*. Chichester: Association of Independent Museums.

Museum Ethnographers Group. 2013. Website. Accessed October 11, 2014. http://www. museumethnographersgroup.org.uk.

Museums Association. 2005. "Collections for the Future." Accessed October 11, 2014. http://www.museumsassociation.org/collections/9839.

Museums Association. 2007. "Making Collections Effective." Accessed October 11, 2014. http://www.museumsassociation.org/download?id=14112.

Pearce, Susan. 1995. *On Collecting: An Investigation into the European Tradition*. London: Routledge.

Peers, Laura, and Alison L. Brown, eds. 2003. *Museums and Source Communities: A Routledge Reader*. London: Routledge.

Shelton, Anthony. 2007. "The Collector's Zeal: Towards an Anthropology of Intentionality, Instrumentality and Desire." In *Colonial Collections Revisited*, edited by P. Ter Keurs, 16–44. Leiden: CNWS.

Vergo, Peter, ed. 1989. *The New Museology*. London: Reaktion.

Vogel, Susan. 1991. "Always True to the Object, in Our Fashion." In *Exhibiting Cultures: The Poetics and Politics of Museum Display*, edited by Ivan Karp and Steven D. Lavine, 191–204. Washington, DC: Smithsonian Institution Press.

Young, Linda. 2004. "Collecting: Reclaiming the Art, Systematising the Technique." In *Museums and the Future of Collecting*, edited by Simon Knell, 185–195. Aldershot: Ashgate.

Further Reading

Pearce, Susan. 1998. *Collecting in Contemporary Practice*. London: Sage.

Nick Merriman has been Director of the Manchester Museum since 2006. Prior to that he was Director of Museums and Collections, and Reader in Museum Studies, at University College London. He began his career at the Museum of London in 1986, as Curator of Prehistory and subsequently Head of the Department of Early London History and Collections. He was President of the Council for British Archaeology from 2005–2008. Nick studied Archaeology at Cambridge University, and his PhD on widening participation in museums was published as *Beyond the Glass Case* (1991). He has published widely on visitor studies, heritage management, and archaeology in museums, including the edited collection *Public Archaeology* (2004).

12 MANAGING COLLECTIONS OR MANAGING CONTENT?
The Evolution of Museum Collections Management Systems

Malcolm Chapman

Selma Thomas, in her Introduction to Din and Hecht's *Digital Museum*, writes that "the challenge inherent in digital technologies forces us to consider what it means to be a museum in the twenty-first century" (Thomas 2007, 1). This chapter addresses this challenge through an analysis of the evolution of museum collections management systems. Starting with a brief overview of the emergence of digital collections management systems (CMS), principally for internal inventory and audit purposes in the late 1960s and early 1970s, it surveys global innovations in collections and collections information management made possible by the latest generations of collections management systems, web developments, social media, and museological thinking. I examine how some museums have embraced and utilized new technologies to both improve internal management functions and to open up collections for greater engagement and interaction by users.

What is the position of a museum collections management system in the twenty-first century? At one time collections management systems were commonly referred to in the sector as CMS, however, with web-based innovations in social media and Web 2.0 this abbreviation is now more commonly taken to refer to *content* management system: that is, the procedures which "allow publishing, editing and modifying content as well as maintenance from a central interface ... procedures to manage workflow in a collaborative environment" (Wikipedia 2013). This simple abbreviation has occasionally caused some confusion within the museum

The International Handbooks of Museum Studies: Museum Practice, First Edition.
Edited by Conal McCarthy.
© 2015 John Wiley & Sons Ltd. Published 2020 by John Wiley & Sons Ltd.

sector; partly this is due to the increased professionalization of roles and experience in museums, with larger institutions employing technologists with external web-design and programming experience alongside, and in some cases instead of, the more traditional curatorial and collections-based documentation specialist. In response to the continually developing digital environment, collections management systems have become more than the simple inventory or descriptive catalog originally conceived – they are now a means of managing the collections, their intrinsic and associated knowledge, the risks they are subject to, their movement, lending, borrowing, disposal, and destruction, and their role in creating and sharing knowledge. A more useful phrase to use could be *museum* management system, although that in itself could imply other functions, and *information* management system has too much of a library and archives sound to it. However, on the whole I believe the confusion is a false one and there is no real difference between content management and collections management, because with online delivery, interpretation and creation of data *collections* have become *content*.

The early history of collections management systems

The history of electronic documentation systems in museums goes back to the late 1960s when large mainframe computers were developed in national and larger university museums with greater access to high-level computing support, such as the National Museum of Natural History at the Smithsonian Institution (Parry 2007; Williams 2010). Often based within the scientific functions of the museum, they were developed as one-off applications generally for internal use only and were essentially seen as inventory systems with the core function of bringing some order to the perceived chaos of large acquisitions. Parry notes that the Museum Computer Network in the United States was "born from the higher education sector and computing – not from museums and curatorship" (2007, 17). Given this, it was no accident that the focus was primarily on the larger collections within natural sciences and archaeology, particularly following the large growth in archaeological archives from the 1960s. Here there was a need to deal effectively with huge collections, but ones which required a less descriptive format for describing the object.

Consequently these disciplines were ideally suited to the introduction of computing processes not just for data recording but also for analytical processing; in the United Kingdom the Information Retrieval Group of the Museums Association, the predecessor of the Museum Documentation Association (MDA) had initially focused on the issues in natural sciences and humanities. The data in these collections are rarely in a descriptive form, neither is this desirable nor relevant, but tends to be short and succinct, and often only understandable or identifiable to a subject specialist. For example, in natural sciences the important data tends to cover taxonomy, site, collector, identification details, and form. The development of fields and structures in these systems were constrained by the capacity of the available computers, the MDA's own MODES system (Museum Object Data Entry System; http://www.modes.org.uk) launched in 1987 was limited to 254 fields in the data structure; "MODES, in other words, imposed a restriction on the developing standards themselves" (Parry 2007, 48). Consequently many abbreviations were used in place of full text for data fields such as geographic locality. At the Manchester Museum for example the code "Af1" was used to reference all finds from North Africa. As Parry notes, systems were developed in this way because "that is the way they needed to be for the computer to process the data" (2007, 48).

These systems predated the concept of national or international standards, partly as they were seen principally for internal management of the collections. It could also be argued that these were not really collection management systems at all but merely simple collection inventory systems. It was not until the Museum Documentation Association (now Collections Trust) introduced the MDA Data Standard in 1991, followed three years later by the first edition of SPECTRUM, that wider collections management practices and procedures began to be incorporated into the digital catalog (see Simmons in this volume). SPECTRUM introduced and formalized procedure in museums for the first time (Parry 2007, 105), however, collections management systems were not yet able to fully embrace these requirements and hybrid manual/digital systems were adopted. The mid-1990s also saw the widespread adoption of computer networks and personal computers and the development of client-server systems to replace the early systems, which tended to be based on large mainframe computers and accessed through "dumb" terminals. At this time the LASSI (Larger Scale Systems Initiative) consortium formed "to specify and procure collections management software that would meet all their various needs" (Keene 1996, 223). Two important elements of the project were that as a consortium of major local authority and national museums the system needed to cover "the needs of the whole variety of museum collections without compromising specialist requirements" (Keene 1996, 223) but, perhaps most significantly, for the first time it incorporated the developing standards from SPECTRUM into the search for an appropriate system, covering not just cataloging but also the "data requirements for actually managing museum collections: processes such as loans, object location and movement, conservation, reproduction and copying" (Keene 1996, 223).

The introduction and continuing development of SPECTRUM (version 4.0 being released in 2011) came about at a time when there was a significant shift in both technology and approach. It was a reflection of the changing nature of databases away from pure inventory and "museum catalog" to embrace wider issues and concerns. It was a move toward a full collections information management system – a system still often made by a combination of digital and paper-based procedures and recording methods, but essentially one aimed at improving how the museum works and how it records. Museum systems now embrace a developing range of processes, such as material sampling and integrated pest management, as well as narrative and descriptive data including online user-generated content. Collections data is now *descriptive* data rather than *pure* data; it is no longer simply a finding aid for professionals (curators and academic researchers). To be accessible and usable collections content now needs to be in a language that is understandable, relevant and useful to a wide range of audiences and users. Museum visitors, both physical and (especially) virtual, have changed their expectations of what a museum is and what their roles as audience and user are; they expect to communicate on an equitable level, with inclusive rather than exclusive language, to participate and where relevant to contribute their own knowledge and opinions.

Integrating collections management and pest management

Technological developments aimed principally at museum audiences can have unexpected spin-offs for the traditional collections care and management functions of a museum. Using a feature of their collections management system, KE EMu, the Natural History Museum (NHM; http://www.nhm.ac.uk) in London has developed an approach to managing pests that provides a visual representation of potential risks to the collections.

Integrated pest management (IPM) describes a holistic approach of using preventive methods to minimize the risks of pest infestation without resorting to the unnecessary use of pesticides and other interventive treatments. The main principles of an IPM program include the monitoring and identification of pests (or potential pests) and the subsequent development of any treatment or preventive program. Pinniger and Winsor have identified this approach as having "considerable advantages regarding health and safety, being less harmful to both humans and the environment, and once established is also likely to be more cost effective than a passive or reactive approach" (2004, 2). The key element in this approach to collections care is the "correct identification of pests and signs of their presence" (Pinniger and Winsor 2004, 13). Most sources of advice for recording this data suggest using simple software applications such as Microsoft Excel, while the Integrated Pest Management Working Group (IPMWG) has devised a free program to record and present this data (MuseumPests.net 2009). However, these databases ignore the purpose behind monitoring in the first place – the effect upon the stored collections themselves. The NHM has taken this concept of the pest management database and integrated it with KE EMu.

Having recently reviewed their IPM processes and introduced a series of "risk zones" identifying which pest infestations would cause the greatest risk to which collection area, the museum was now in a position to know which collections were at risk from which pest species and therefore could put in place more effective preventative measures to protect the collections in any particular zone. This new approach brought in consistent and regular trapping in both collection stores and exhibition areas, including greater reporting of pest activity throughout the museum. However, there was no centralized database monitoring this trap data with the effect that reporting and comparing activity across the museum, from collection area to collection area, or within exhibition spaces was problematic and led to individuals being aware of the issues within their own area but not elsewhere, such as adjacent areas which were the responsibility of another department. The solution was to make full use of features already present in KE EMu and adapt them to record, monitor, and display the trap data.

Pest data is recorded in three separate modules: location, trap, and trap event. The existing hierarchical structure of the physical location enabled complex and precise locations to be recorded, from building down to individual storage units thereby making it easy to retrieve all data relating to a particular room, floor, zone, or other specified criteria. Normally this would enable grouping of all objects and specimens stored in the specified area, and in this instance it enables retrieval of all insect traps in the location. The Trap module documents the type of trap (e.g. sticky, pheromone), a unique identification number, the associated department and specific location detail within the broader location (e.g. on the floor, on a window sill), together with proximity to potential risk factors such as opening windows, external doors, and food consumption and preparation areas. Using these fields, together with the broader location record, allows the museum to treat the trap as a physical object located within the building, thereby recording the spatial context of the monitoring and enabling the retrieval of data relating to traps in the same room, floor, or even similar proximity to food consumption areas (see Figure 12.1).

The data recorded as a trap event includes both common and taxonomic names, the eco type, life stage, and specimen count per species; each "event" being the inspection of a particular trap. To simplify the checking process for non-specialist staff across the museum these fields use controlled terminology linked to a hierarchical lookup list, there being only about 20 to 30 pest and indicator species commonly found within the museum. Each trap event has the trap-checking date and checker's name recorded, allowing the museum to now record temporal data and enabling seasonal trends and patterns to be recorded.

At first sight this is little different to the database developed by IPMWG and other pest management monitoring systems; indeed most of the fields being recorded map across to IPMWG recommended fields. However, what is different here is that by recording this within the collections management system it now becomes possible to view the likely impact of pests on the collection itself. Simple querying of the data can now resolve questions such as which specimens are most at risk from the presence of a particular pest at any given time. In addition to the usual comprehensive set of reports listing pest incidents over different periods and locations, the collections management system makes use of an "object locator" tool which can give a graphic presentation of the data. This tool was initially developed to enable visitors to build their own tours of exhibition areas, selecting objects to view in each gallery. However, applied to the pest management data it is possible to create a visual presentation showing the incidents of specific species

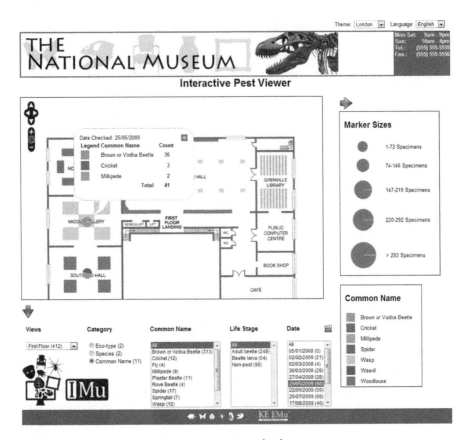

FIGURE 12.1   Interactive pest viewer, KE EMu database.
Courtesy of KE Software 2013.

during seasonal changes, for example, the spread of biscuit beetle (*Stegobium pani-ceum*) during spring once it leaves its larval form. Overlaying this display onto plans of different floors of the museum gives a real-time indication of the spread of pests through the museum and assists in targeting both collections at risk and the initial cause of an infestation. The end result for the NHM has been the ability to query the data across a large and complex historic building with large numbers of both staff and visitors. This has provided coherent hard evidence of the impact of pests on the collection and their spread throughout the museum, contributing to an improved strategic overview of pest management and collections care.

Collections management systems in the gallery

As mentioned earlier, there have been attempts to position collections manage-ment systems in the public galleries themselves. However, these can be seen as attempts to reveal inner workings of the museum rather than a sophisticated attempt to publish the content stored in the collections management system itself. Rather than repurposing content created in isolation from the management of the collection specifically for public consumption (see Wellington and Oliver in this volume) most museum users come across the collections management system through the obligatory web interface rather than in the gallery itself. This generally can be attributed to the perception of the role of the collections management system as purely a management tool rather than, as Gareth Salway and Mark Pajak at Bristol Museums, Galleries and Archives have put it, "the central repository and management mechanism for all collections-related information for the museum service" (Salway and Pajak 2011).

This approach is demonstrated most coherently at M-Shed in Bristol which opened in 2011 as a "museum dedicated to telling the amazing history of the city, through the objects and stories of the people who have made the city what it is today" (M-Shed 2011). Housed in a former transit shed on the city's historic dockside, the museum showcases the social and industrial history of Bristol in three main galleries with separate themes of Place, People, and Life. The linking theme through the galleries is the shaping of Bristol's identity and character through the involvement of its people in issues such as the development of free trade or human rights, connected to historic concerns such as the slave trade as well as contemporary globalization. Each of the three galleries is further broken down into specific active themes; for example Bristol People has the themes Creating, Trading, Challenging, Celebrating, Contributing, and Transatlantic Slave Trade.

These themes are supported by 57 in-gallery kiosks featuring additional, in-depth content sourced directly from the collections management system. Within the M-Shed interpretation strategy the kiosks are seen as central to the user experience with the CMS collections management system essential to its delivery. Each kiosk uses a common template with three top-level elements to reconstruct and publish the content for each theme: contextual narrative, an image or series of images and the relatively dry and impersonal key data from the catalog record itself: accession number, object title, and general storage location (e.g. museum building, in-gallery location). The contextualized content relates the object to the specific theme and offers users the opportunity to "explore and contribute ... your own experiences and opinions, and become part of the living record of a great city" (M-Shed 2011). User-generated content is encouraged through two elements: "Have your say," giving an option for short vox pops response to the theme and "Tell your story," allowing for a longer and more detailed contribution.

Within the back-end collections management system each contextual narrative record stores only the title and text for a single object or story. Using the inbuilt hierarchical structure of the collections management system the logical parent–child relationships between theme, sub-theme, story and object can both be maintained and altered if required. As this also allows for a one-to-many relationship, as you drill down through each theme a greater number of child records are available; in the gallery this translates to a greater number of viewable storylines. For example, the narrative theme "Defending the City" has four child records covering different historical periods "Civil War – Defence of the City," "Stephen and Matilda," "The French Prison," and "Iron Age Hill Forts." Each child theme could in turn connect to further sub-themes or directly to the record describing the object itself. This narrative record in turn is linked to the catalog record describing the object and a multimedia repository containing both the image and any associated rights.

User-generated stories and brief comments are uploaded from each kiosk into a separate content management system held locally rather than uploading to the main collections management system. However, there is no live link between this content management system, the kiosks and the collections management system – this ensures each kiosk operates independently and is not interrupted by any system maintenance or failure and ensures the availability of the in-gallery content at all times. An overnight data-load of changes to each record, or additional records and themes, makes any change live the next day. This gives the museum the ability to change the content in response to current events, particularly useful when referring to contemporary topics such as globalization. With each kiosk grouped around a theme, a series of data flags are used which ensure the content is delivered only to the appropriate kiosk and not to any other. By using a separate series of templates, the same data, both museum and user-generated, is made available on the M-Shed website (http://mshed.org) thereby fulfilling the ambition to "provide collections related content for publication via the museum's website and through gallery-based ICT … technologies, as well as being used in capturing and re-publishing content generated by our users" (Salway and Pajak 2011). This approach changes the focus and purpose of the collections management system; it is no longer concerned with museum procedures and has truly become a *content* management system. In consequence the curatorial staff no longer have sole authority to curate museum objects but this process also includes museum visitors drawing on their own knowledge.

Using a similar structure the Manchester Museum has produced a free smartphone and tablet application that delivers additional interpretive content for its redeveloped Living Worlds gallery in 2011 (see Figure 12.2). The content of the gallery is based upon the natural world and human relationships with it. In place of a sequential storyline, there are self-contained installations on a range of themes which are aimed at encouraging people to think rather than taking a didactic approach. Unlike the Bristol example, the Manchester content is published live from a number of different record types in the collections management system: media, specimen catalog and narrative contextual information. By connecting to a third-party source (http://www.arkive.org) the application provides a wide range of exhibit-specific content in the form of images of display cases, detailed catalog information, links to short films, and sign-posts visitors toward things to do next – either to "find out more" or to "get involved." While this content is too large to be delivered through 3G visitors can access it via the free Wi-Fi in the gallery. Delivering

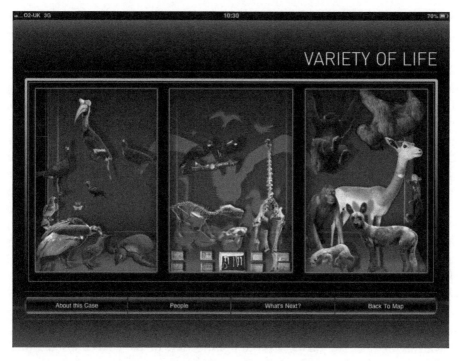

FIGURE 12.2   An example of interpretive content on the "Variety of Life," part of a free smart phone and tablet application for the Living Worlds gallery, Manchester Museum. Courtesy Manchester Museum, University of Manchester.

content in this way has connected the back-of-house documentation work with the visitor experience in the gallery, and, it is claimed, provides a mechanism for sustainable development and delivery of information. Although the visitor services staff in the gallery are provided with tablets to interact with and assist visitors without their own hardware, for some the experience is a purely visual one, there being little interpretation in the gallery other than that delivered through the application. If the application is essential for a full understanding of the gallery, rather than merely delivering additional and complementary information, it does raise the question of whether this approach leaves the visitor somewhat shortchanged.

Publishing collections management data online

While more museums are delivering dynamic collections content within galleries and exhibition spaces, this option can prove to be beyond the resources of many museums, or simply not deemed an appropriate interpretation method. For these museums a greater priority is the availability of collections data through online catalogs of varying simplicity and sophistication. Museums had a relatively early presence on the internet. ICOM issued a policy statement in 1995 that "museums should be active contributors of information to the Internet about their programs and collections in order to fully play their role in the service of society" (Parry 2007, 93). Unfortunately many of these early websites were little more than "brochure ware," offering information for potential physical visitors. Others, however, notably in larger and university museums, were making the collections data itself available; the Manchester Museum had an online catalog as far back as 1994, although this was aimed principally at academic researchers rather than a more general public and had no facility to publish images of the collections. The early 2000s in the UK was marked by an increase in digitization delivered through publicly funded sources such as the Heritage Lottery Fund (HLF), although as Parry notes the HLF's New Opportunities Fund would not pay for "the conversion of existing catalogues except where 'value is clearly added'" (2007, 135). Museum visitors now expect museums to have websites and for these websites to contain versions of their catalog, although there are still some major institutions without online catalogs. However, despite the development of new web technologies and the increasing sophistication expected by users of websites, many museums' online catalogs offer little more than a traditional catalog structure, not dissimilar to what one would expect from a printed catalog; that is, a long list of records or a single isolated image and short piece of text. A number of museums are breaking down this approach by taking a more holistic view of the collections and their accompanying data, seeing the collections data as part of a wider pool of content, both generated by the museum and also its users and partners.

The Museum of New Zealand Te Papa Tongarewa (Te Papa) uses the CIDOC Conceptual Reference Model (CIDOC CRM) to enhance their online collections by providing a framework to highlight how different categories of data relate to each other and to explicitly define these relationships. CIDOC CRM is the culmination of over ten years work within the sector and provides "a common and extensible semantic framework that any cultural heritage information can be mapped to … it can provide the 'semantic glue' needed to mediate between different sources of cultural heritage information, such as that published by museums, libraries and archives" (CIDOC 2006).

In common with some of the other case studies, Te Papa uses KE EMu as their collections management system, which has the ability to store images, video, and data relating to people, places, objects, specimen taxonomies, as well as the Getty Thesaurus of Geographic Names (TGN), and the Art and Architecture Thesaurus (AAT). Combining the full potential of the relational database structure inherent in the collections management system, the hierarchical structure from TGN and AAT and the "semantic glue" of CIDOC CRM, Te Papa has produced a dynamic online experience allowing full access across their collections and archives. It is the relationships within the database which produce the depth and range of content online. A search on "Captain Cook," for example (see Figure 12.3), brings up content from all relevant collections across the museum: scientific instruments from History; botanical specimens from Plants; engravings from Art; photographic

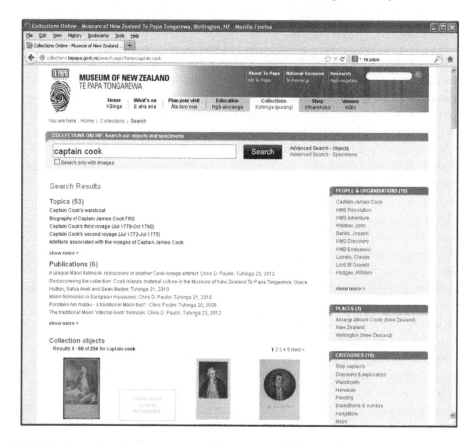

FIGURE 12.3 Results for a search on "Captain Cook" from Collections Online, Museum of New Zealand Te Papa Tongarewa.
Accessed October 6, 2014. http://collections.tepapa.govt.nz/search.aspx?term=captain%20cook.

prints from Photography; costume and textiles from Pacific Cultures. Because it is sourced from the catalog module of the collections management system, it contains basic collection information: title, artist, materials, dimensions, registration/accession number, acquisition source. However, by using the CRM and collections management system to drive the content more discursive and contextual content in the form of topics are returned by the search; for the Cook search this includes a biography, details of his voyages or the individual objects returned from the catalog search. Further context is provided by links to associated people, places and categories, the latter two searching content from TGN and AAT respectively. This approach places the object centrally in the delivery of content to the user, so that you are able to branch out and explore the collection through the relationships between the data.

The museum is also situated within the wider context of online resources; context specific to the initial request is provided by external links to Digital New Zealand (http://www.digitalnz.org) which is an aggregator sourcing digital content from museums, libraries, archives, government departments, television companies, universities, and more. The Te Papa collections are available directly through Digital New Zealand, in the same way that UK collections are harvested through Culture Grid (http://www.culturegrid.org.uk) and through Culture Grid to Europeana (http://www.europeana.eu). For Te Papa this means that the museum is no longer the sole publisher of relevant historical, scientific, or artistic knowledge but part of a wider democratized resource. This development is the logical result of the approach to integrating natural science, cultural, and art collections at Te Papa following the creation of the museum through the relocation and integration of the former National Art Gallery and Dominion Museum in 1998.

Looking at the collections management system as only one of a number of media repositories in the museum has led the Museum of London to develop what has been termed a Collections Information Integration Module (CIIM) to aggregate these disparate data resources. While the museum used a single collections management system, MIMSY XG (http://www.selagodesign.com/portfolio/mimsyxg.php), for all of its departments, the devolved development of online resources, which have often been linked to specific exhibitions and projects, had led to the re-creation or duplication of data, images, and content. Data from the collections management system was extracted to a separate SQL database which had appropriate templates applied prior to publishing online. This situation prevented searches across all online resources and also caused problems exporting resources to third parties such as Culture Grid and Europeana. The CIIM pulls in data from the collections management system and images from the associated media store, together with other relevant content from other internal sources, creating a central repository collating and indexing all object and contextual information from these sources and enabling their re-use both internally and externally. Within the CIIM is an editing sub-system built on the lines of a web-publishing content management system. Through this, the content from the collections management system and elsewhere can be brought together and edited appropriately for final publishing outside the CIIM, whether this is for collections online services, other more narrative-style pages on the website, in-gallery kiosks or for third-party web services.

The end result is similar to that of Te Papa with contextually related information and objects associated with each other. However, there is a different underlying philosophy; instead of the collections management system being central to the holding and publishing of collections-related data and content, here the collections management is the repository purely of collections management-related content and interpretation and other content are held elsewhere. This structure simplifies the import of data from other internal and external sources and enables the integration and augmentation of these in formats specific to the relevant publishing mechanism. However, the technical complexities of this approach require an in-house systems and information management team with sufficient skills and resources to maintain and further develop the content entering the CIIM, unless the museum is to rely on third-party developers. With the current funding position within the UK public sector this is increasingly problematic for all but the largest institutions.

A similar aggregator has been developed at Yale University in the USA, namely the Cross Collection Discovery (CCD) service (http://discover.odai.yale.edu/ydc). This enables users to search across the digitized cultural collections of the university, including the Centre for British Art, the Peabody Museum, the university art gallery, and the library, regardless of the different collections management and asset management systems in use across the university. Using open-source tools and the widely accepted schema and standards, including CDWA Lite, Darwin Core, Dublin Core, MARCXML, and OAI-PMH, metadata from across the cultural databases are harvested and published in a single return. Taking the Captain Cook example from Te Papa and applying it to Yale brings in results from over 30 databases across all six contributing repositories, including rare books, zoology, anthropology, and mineralogy. These results can then be refined further by applying any number of a range of filters including historical period, geographic area, topic, and type of record. Viewing a record in detail pulls in additional content harvested from the source database, and in some circumstances, such as in the search on Captain Cook, content sourced from third-party resources such as Wikipedia. Furthermore, the detailed view allows users to tag and comment on the individual records, these tags and comments remaining within the CCD and enhancing future searches rather than being returned to the source database. This approach to data interoperability places the disparate Yale collections in proximity to each other by virtue of their inherent relationships and makes full use of the "ability of the systems, procedures and culture of an organisation to be managed in such a way as to maximise opportunities for exchange and re-use of information, whether internally or externally" (Ashby, McKenna, and Stiff 2001, 63). Following this through to its logical conclusion it should be possible to search for a type specimen and also bring up the publication it appears in, or vice versa, thereby providing greater context for the collections; once again museum collections and data are no longer seen in isolation but as part of a wider pool of knowledge. As with the Museum of London example, maintaining and developing this approach requires input and resources beyond the scope of smaller museums. One alternative is to let a third party access and re-use data in an environment which they maintain at no ongoing cost to the museum itself.

Sharing data locally, nationally, and internationally

In the early days of the Museum Computer Network in the United States, there was an ambition to develop a nationwide information network of all museums, creating "a single information system which embraces all museum holdings …

including those of science and history museums" (IBM and Ellin quoted in Parry 2007, 17). As far back in the digital era as the first Museums and the Web Conference in 1997, Eleanor Fink, Director of the Getty Information Institute, in delivering the keynote address stated that

> the great collective repository of our cultural heritage scattered around the world in libraries, museums, and archives contains vast numbers of art objects and literary works from the past and present. These are fragments of the great mosaic of human civilization. To make sure these pieces can be accessed ... we need [to?] work together as collaborators. (Fink 1997)

While it has taken considerable time for such objectives to become a reality, the advancements in technology and development of the internet have made this a reality; new, and not-so-new, technology is now ubiquitous and integrated into everyday life, even in museums. However, some of the biggest barriers to achieving this are institutional and conceptual rather than technological. Many museums digitizing their collections have been internally focused on publishing their own collections rather than looking at how their collections and associated data fit within the concepts of distributed national or regional collections.

Early attempts at sharing data followed one of two distinct approaches. FENSCORE (http://www.fenscore.man.ac.uk) and Cornucopia (http://www.cornucopia.org.uk) were principally collection-level description databases aimed at others within the sector rather than the wider public. Though still available online, there is little or no future development planned for them, and while at least providing some information about which institutions hold collections relating to specific themes, subjects, or collection types they are slowly becoming redundant. The alternative approach was based around collecting data, mainly in the form of catalog records and images, and uploading them to a designated database allowing for dynamic object-level delivery based upon search results. A similar example, which is still maintained, is SCRAN (http://www.scran.ac.uk), originally developed in 1996 to provide access to Scottish collections data as an online learning resource. Aimed principally at a formal education audience it runs on a commercial subscription basis. While having a single database holding over 360,000 images and media from museum and other cultural collections, this data is separate to that held by the contributing institutions; it is not a dynamic link and is not updated as records are added or updated in the source institutions.

In 2002 a consortium of museums in Manchester launched Museums Unwrapped (an archived version of the site can be found at http://musunwrp.web.its.manchester.ac.uk) to demonstrate how disparate multidisciplinary collections could be search simultaneously. Users were able to search on the predefined themes of Manchester, People, Cotton, Plants, Animals, or a free-text search of their own choosing. For example, a free-text search on "Old Trafford" may result in football-themed wallpaper, trade union banners, paintings, costume, and even botanical specimens from the area. While this demonstrated that the technology worked, there was no institutional drive to connect this to the museums' end users. The data had been mapped according to broad Dublin Core Metadata Initiative elements of person, place, and date type, proving that there were no barriers formed by discipline- or object-specific data.

Libraries and archives had long-established standards and protocols for the exchange of information: MARC (Machine-Readable Cataloging) standard was developed by the Library of Congress in the 1960s and had been adopted as the international standard by the early 1970s, while in archives EAD (Encoded Archival Description) was developed in the early 1990s. However, museum standards, such as SPECTRUM, were focused on procedures rather than data sharing and compatibility, because museums were more concerned with internal consistency rather than the mechanics of finding objects and specimens from across the sector. It was not until the emergence of internet-specific protocols such as OAI-PMH (the Open Archives Initiative Protocol for Metadata Harvesting) from the late 1990s that the sharing of museum records and data developed further. The adoption of OAI-PMH within the cultural heritage sector has enabled the creation of web aggregators, online databases that harvest and index the contents of other databases and present them in a unified, consistent, and transnational format. The Europeana project harvests data from across the European Union. By April 2012 it provided access to over 23 million objects from over 2200 institutions in 33 countries (Europeana 2012). Unlike the earlier approaches, the data presented in a search result are still held in the original source database, enabling the collections to be searched from multiple angles. At the Hunterian at Glasgow University, as with many other UK collections, records are harvested first by Culture Grid, thereby placing them within the context of the UK national collection. Culture Grid, in turn, is harvested by Europeana (see Figure 12.4). This approach enables "bolt-on" applications to be offered; the Hunterian records are also available from the University Museums in Scotland portal (http://www.umissearch.org.uk), which likewise draws its results from Culture Grid.

This cross-sector searching has the capability of recreating the Enlightenment concept of encyclopedic collections. No longer divided by material type or academic disciplines and with little or no distinction made between the physicality of the collection and the knowledge stored within the accompanying manuscripts and publications, these large and diverse collections have the effect of "assembling a library in which each of these various forms was expected to complement the other" (McKitterick in Parry 2007, 34) whether they are distributed across an institution, as with William Hunter's collection at the University of Glasgow, or across institutions, as with Sir Hans Sloan's collection in the British Library, British Museum, and Natural History Museum. As Tomislav Sola has pointed out, "the inherited and developing diversity of institutions will, thanks to the possibility of virtual, informatics networking, become an integrated resource for data, information and messages" (Sola 2010, 423).

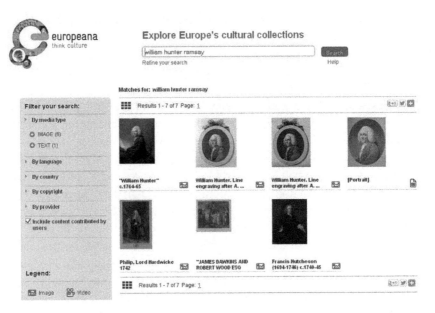

FIGURE 12.4   Matches for "William Hunter Ramsay" from the Europeana project, harvested from the UK's Culture Grid.

Accessed October 6, 2014. http://www.culturegrid.org.uk/search/#!culturegrid;hasThumbnail=true; query=william+hunter+ramsay.

Online cataloging and knowledge creation

The last few years has seen the development and growth of what has become known as "cloud computing," effectively the use of web services to access and store data. In terms of collections management systems this means using a web front end to access all the functions of the database: record creation, retrieval, management, report generation, etc. In some cases it can also mean remote hosting of the data: instead of the museum managing its own server, the data can be held remotely by a third party, often the suppliers of the web-based system itself. A number of these systems have recently been developed using open source software tools, which allow for easier integration with other web-based resources such as Wikipedia and Google Maps. By using a web browser these applications are platform independent: they do not require particular operating systems or backend database management systems to be functional.

A product called eHive (http://www.ehive.com), developed by Vernon Systems of New Zealand, is a simple to use, sign-up-and-ready-to-go option targeted toward smaller museums with little or no technical knowledge or resources. Once signed up, ready access is given to pre-defined cataloging screens for different collection disciplines and the opportunity to form online communities with other museums with similar collections, thereby giving access to a wider range of content for end users through a web portal. As a simple and relatively low-tech approach to collections cataloging, eHive's target market is the smaller independent museum with a small staff and limited resources, so the affordable pricing structure is based purely on the size of data and number of images uploaded. Following a simple-to-use, step-by-step process, small museums can now catalog their collections to basic standard. Online publication through eHive is quick and simple using a standard template, and because Vernon Systems hosts the data it is simple to create communities of collections and museums based around specific themes, such as the Rugby Moments community which allowed museums and private collectors to share their memorabilia and stories during the 2011 Rugby World Cup in New Zealand. By hosting both the system and its content, eHive reduces costs but this does place the data, some of it of a sensitive nature, out of the control of the museum and its IT support services. In the UK, local authority IT support services are often suspicious about giving online access to a database, and in some instances have concerns about installing systems which may require external providers to dial in. It would be difficult to imagine a local authority allowing a third party to host this data, making eHive a viable solution more suited to smaller museums in the charitable sector in other parts of the world.

At the other end of the spectrum of online cataloging systems are custom-built applications like Qi developed by KeepThinking (http://www.keepthinking.it). This was initially developed for the Public Catalogue Foundation (PCF; http://www.thepcf.org.uk) in the UK, which succeeded in photographing and cataloging all oil paintings in public ownership, not just museums and galleries, in the UK. As with eHive, the data-entry process was delivered through a web interface, principally because researchers and photographers were located throughout the country. As this was an external cataloging rather than collections management project the data held is minimal and has usually been supplied from existing catalog entries from museums and galleries. It could be argued that the PCF has, certainly for museum collections, merely replicated what is already in place and could have delivered some aspects of its aims through sourcing collections data from CultureGrid and already existing web-based resources. However, an interesting aspect of the project has been the inclusion of non-museum public collections, many held by schools, local authorities, fire services, etc.

Of most interest recently has been the appearance of the Your Paintings Tagger (see Figure 12.5), an innovative crowdsourcing aspect of the project which allows users to tag the paintings to generate relevant search metadata. Each registered user is presented with a random image of a painting and a simple box in which to enter tags based on what can be seen in the picture. With this project the tags only become searchable once a critical mass has been reached. Users are taken step by step through a series of tabbed screens categorizing tags by "things," "people," "places," "events," "types" and "subjects." Once the tags have been approved the paintings are searchable through their associated tags on the BBC Your Paintings website (http://www.bbc.co.uk/arts/yourpaintings).

Building on the earlier success of the BBC and British Museum project A History of the World (http://www.bbc.co.uk/ahistoryoftheworld) this visibly positions some of the work of museums in the public domain. However, one drawback, as with SCRAN, is that these tags are divorced from the source data held by the museums and galleries contributing to the project.

Another project to utilize crowdsourcing techniques to build up a catalog is Herbaria@home (http://herbariaunited.org/atHome), which grew out of volunteer work at the Manchester Museum. The aim of the project was to make use of the botanical knowledge held outside museums to help catalog large herbaria collections. Herbarium sheets are photographed and posted online and, as with the Public Catalogue Foundation, registered users log in and are allocated a selection of sheets from a specific collection. Basic data fields are available covering the same data as on the specimen label, such as taxon, collector details, site, herbarium. To date

FIGURE 12.5   Screen shot of the Your Paintings Tagger showing an oil painting of Sir Ian Colquhoun of Luss (ca. 1933) by Herbert James Gunn, from the collection of the West Dunbartonshire Council.

Accessed October 6, 2014. http://tagger.thepcf.org.uk/classify.

over 110,000 herbarium sheets have been catalogued in this way by online volunteers. However, while this is an interesting approach to documentation backlogs with relatively small and discrete collections, it is unlikely that this approach is applicable to larger museums with comparatively more resources. Of more interest to the mainstream museum is the growth of user-generated content, user comments and tags to create folksonomies, in other words taxonomies relevant and meaningful to the user community who created them. There is an argument that "allowing users to describe online content in terms that make sense to them, rather than relying solely on organising principles imposed by others, will make the content more retrievable, useful and meaningful to the audience" (MacArthur 2007, 58). The Powerhouse Museum in Sydney (http://www.powerhousemuseum.com) was an early adopter of this approach for its online collections with all users free to add any tag they thought relevant to the collections database. In this way online users can become "curators of meaning" (Pratty qtd. in Parry 2007, 55) while the museums themselves become "collectors of information" (Parry 2007, 55).

This in turn raises questions of legitimacy and authority. Witchey (2007) gives an overview of some ethical concerns raised by the introduction of new technologies including whether user-generated content needs to be clearly labeled as separate to that created by the museum. While most online participators are familiar with this type of content giving a voice to the "general public," within the context of museum knowledge it can create some concern among museum staff. Nevertheless, it is reflective of the general move toward participation, and the logical conclusion of new approaches to interaction which effectively break away from the traditional museum role of the single voice of authority and knowledge.

At the Manchester Museum these issues have been tackled with the Collective Conversations project funded by Renaissance North West. Building on existing relationships with community groups and its position within the university, the museum made a series of films, or conversations between academic researchers and community groups, exploring the relationship of the collection to themes such as the abolition of the slave trade, the origins of the wealth of the industrialists, the merchants who the collection came from, communities' own cultural history, personal experiences, and relocation from their home country to the center of Manchester. Taking the concept of the museum as a contact zone, a meeting point between cultures (Clifford 1997), the museum recreates this engagement in an environment where all voices have the opportunity to be heard, thus attempting to create reciprocal and sustainable relationships with communities based on mutual understanding and shared interests and benefits. As Culture Minister David Lammy put it "common ground cannot be staked out in a single narrative about who we were but only in a more intricate narrative about who we are" (DCMS 2006, 11).

Each conversation is fully documented on KE EMu, with the film being linked to a descriptive narrative of the conversation and relevant object catalog records. The first few films were posted online through the normal web front end of the collections management system. However, this limited access to those knowing about the project or stumbling across it while searching the museum's online catalog; it was not reaching newer audiences, certainly not those not already engaged with the museum. By posting the films on YouTube the museum has disseminated them in a wider context than that of the museum alone – they are reaching newer audiences and offering them an opportunity to respond directly with their own comments or to make links to other films of similar content or subjects. Here the museum has placed its knowledge, and the knowledge generated and shared by its communities, in a location and format where online participants feel most comfortable interacting with it. For example, in one series of films a Yoruba chief discussed traditional Yoruba religion, specifically the cult of Shango, the god of thunder and lightning. This series has been viewed over 27,000 times, with the two most frequently viewed films with high viewing figures in Venezuela and Cuba, both countries with religions incorporating elements of Yoruba beliefs and the worship of Shango. A significant number of these views came through the embedding of videos into third-party websites and social networks, evidence that the museum is engaging with online communities of interest in a way it could not have predicted at the start of the project. While such work can be seen as a "threat" to the authority of the museum, in giving voice to others "a process of self-discovery and empowerment will take place in which the curator becomes a facilitator rather than a figure of authority" (Witcomb 2003, 79).

It is only with the development of a new generation of collections management systems and new approaches to what constitutes museum data that museums are able to document and record "the other complex knowledge that surrounds the objects and collections" (Parry 2007, 105), what Nick Poole of the Collections Trust has called "crunchy knowledge" (pers. comm.); that is, the knowledge that makes you want to come back for more, the added ingredient that sticks in the memory and is sometimes unexpected. For example, in 2008 the Manchester Museum made a series of Collective Conversations films relating to Lindow Man, an Iron Age bog body found to the south of Manchester. It was to provide additional content for an exhibition about attitudes to the body while it was on loan from the British Museum. In one conversation about the finding of the body, Robert Connolly, a physical anthropologist from Liverpool University who carried out the first scientific examination of the body refuted the so-called "triple death" theory, where death had been caused by a blow to the head, garroting, and throat cutting. In the film (see Figure 12.6) he suggests the cut throat is a "modern artefact" carried out during the excavation and that a broken rib is also modern, contrary to the published reports which refer to a broken bone as happening during death, confessing:

> I did that actually … carbon 14 dating had been done with a fragment of bone from the leg and they wanted another piece from deep inside … I could break the rib because it was very fragile but I couldn't get it out because the soft tissue around it was like leather and so we couldn't get this bit of bone out and so we just left it there and when it was x-rayed the people who wrote up the x-ray report didn't know I had done that. (Connolly 2008)

FIGURE 12.6   Screen shot of YouTube clip on the investigation of Lindow Man, Collective Conversations project, Manchester Museum.
Accessed October 6, 2014. http://www.youtube.com/watch?v=zD6YPv4x9wQ.

Similar to Collective Conversations, the Museum Lives project at the Natural History Museum in London is a three-year collaboration between the museum and Kingston University. This oral history project is aimed at capturing the personal, and professional, memories of retired and soon-to-be-retired staff, including stories about the collection, collecting expeditions, the museum's history, and their own passion for their collection areas from childhood to retirement. This knowledge, which could also be termed "museum metadata," as it is knowledge about the museum itself which otherwise could easily be lost, will create an archive for both visitors and staff to draw upon. Like Collective Conversations, the filmed interviews will be permanently linked to the catalog records for the specimens mentioned in them. Previously curatorial knowledge has been seen as separate and sometimes invisible information, available only to internal users of systems, but now this curatorial memory "tucked away in curators' heads could be recorded and rendered accessible" (Parry 2007, 105). Having been captured and documented, this "contextual knowledge that has been accumulated over the years should enable subsequent generations to understand the significance of preserved digital heritage resources" (McCarthy 2007, 251) and form the nucleus of a continually evolving sustainable knowledge base.

At this point we might well ask how museum practice in this area relates to web developments in the wider world. While museums are delivering content individually through their own websites and collectively through portals and/or data harvesters such as Europeana, the style that data is delivered in is limited. There is still a tendency to think in terms of traditional printed publications, either a snapshot image with text as with a postcard, a list showing limited data fields as with a concordance, or a more detailed exhibition catalog style. The search interface itself tends to fall into one of two styles: a Google-like single search box searching data from a number of pre-defined fields; or a more detailed option which requires the user to know the meaning of museum- or discipline-specific concepts such as accession number, family, genus. A number of the examples discussed above are beginning to explore alternative means of searching and presenting the data and giving users the opportunity to browse and compare objects and concepts through association and linked facets. Instead of looking at traditional publishing methods these museums are looking at how users learn to navigate the web beyond the museum-sphere; parallels can be drawn with searching on shopping sites such as eBay and Amazon with filtering of results – comparing like for like, presenting related or alternative results, and offering the opportunity to review and give a rating are well established and familiar, understood and almost expected by their users. However, according to Parry, museum websites are still based on the "information management processes of the pre-standardised, pre-automated museum grew out from (and preserved) an unchallengeable authority of the curator [where] … curators were, in every sense, the authors of their collections" (Parry 2007, 107). Now these new commercial models offer the opportunity for users to author their own collections and curate exhibitions for themselves, to add their knowledge and share it with each other.

Developing a museum for the future: new initiatives at the Hunterian

For the past 20 years the collections of the Hunterian at the University of Glasgow have been catalogued and managed using a combination of in-house-designed and -maintained database and paper-based systems, a position not completely unique in the UK museum sector and compliant with SPECTRUM standards. As mentioned earlier, the Hunterian already provides web access to its collections, both in isolation on its own website and in wider collections contexts through CultureGrid, UMIS, and Europeana. However, we are now migrating all our systems to KE EMu and taking the opportunity to explore many of the developments highlighted in the preceding case studies. Internally this will allow us to manage the disparate curatorial areas as a single entity, bringing in unified and consistent approaches to loans and research management and creating a single repository for both data and images.

Improving the functionality and interface of the collections website is the first step toward integrating the collections with other research resources. Key aspects for this process include the ability to make onscreen comparisons between selected objects, onscreen sorting and filtering of results, linking between different result sets, and having reusable, downloadable, and interoperable search results. Front-end interoperability with other systems, especially the university library's discovery services and possible widget-based search functions within virtual learning environments will, it is hoped, bring greater awareness and use of the collections amongst the academic body. In addition to integrating the museum and gallery collections, which are documented in stand-alone databases, the use of the same database by the University Library Special Collections and Archives Service will reconnect all of Hunter's collections for the first time in over a century.

In partnership with Glasgow Life and the Scottish Screen Archive of the National Library of Scotland, the Hunterian has received funding for the development of the Kelvin Hall, located opposite both the main university campus and Kelvingrove Art Gallery and Museum. This will result, by 2016, in a unified storage facility for all the Hunterian collections, currently stored in seven locations across the campus and city, as well as improved visitor research and teaching spaces. Access to the collections in the Kelvin Hall will be provided via a new web interface where visitors will be able to request physical access to objects and specimens for research and close study. As the Kelvin Hall is a shared facility, it is essential that all collections and resources held within it are searchable through a single access point. Consequently we are developing a reliable, scalable, and low maintenance portal to the collections. In order to minimize ongoing maintenance and to provide a continually updated service, the portal site will harness automatic metadata harvesting from the Hunterian's KE EMu, Glasgow Life's MIMSY XG databases and the systems used by the Scottish Screen Archive. Searching large museum collections can, however, pose some problems in how results are returned to users, because many of the collections, particularly zoological and archaeological, contain many similar items that may not be distinguished in the catalog entries when users search on terms such as beetles, or flints. Searching on such terms could provide tens of thousands of results. In order to overcome this, we plan to provide initial search results at a collection or contextual level, with users then able to further refine their results by filtering accordingly.

Conclusion

After more than four decades of digital formats, technology is no longer an isolated tool consulted to accomplish specific tasks. Instead it has become infrastructure, essential to all aspects of museum operations and fostering better collaboration and access

(Thomas 2007, 1). It has brought new methods and ideas to museums, and these have resulted in fresh and innovative approaches to the use of collections themselves. Emerging approaches extend beyond the traditional functions of the museum, from the infrastructure and practices of the institution into the realm of the audience, who are now seen as participators and collaborators. Realizing the potential of the museum

> depends on how effectively and efficiently … knowledge resources are harnessed across the whole enterprise … the success of the museum depends on ensuring that this enterprise-wide knowledge and information management is *incremental* – that new activity generates new knowledge which builds on the body of knowledge that went before it. (Poole 2012; emphasis original)

Museums do not operate in isolation from the rest of the world. To be relevant and useful to their audiences they need to engage with them in ways which are familiar and current. This means investing in resources and ideas to deliver collections knowledge, the *content*, in the formats and locations where the user is. Museums need to be active in the digital world both as publishers and as participants in the creation and sharing of knowledge and ideas, bringing their "crunchy knowledge" with them.

References

Ashby, Helen, Gordon McKenna, and Matthew Stiff, eds. 2001. *Spectrum Knowledge: Standards for Cultural Information Management.* Cambridge: MDA.

CIDOC. 2006. "The CIDOC Conceptual Reference Model." Accessed October 13, 2014. http://www.cidoc-crm.org.

Clifford, James. 1997. *Routes: Travel and Translation in the Late Twentieth Century.* Cambridge, MA: Harvard University Press.

Connolly, Robert. 2008. "Lindow Man – Police and Coroners Investigation part 5." Accessed October 13, 2014. http://www.youtube.com/watch?v=Z0Webv4Z_jo.

DCMS (Department for Culture, Media and Sport). 2006. *Understanding the Future: Priorities for England's Museums.* London: Department for Culture, Media and Sport.

Europeana. 2012. "Facts and Figures." Accessed October 13, 2014. http://www.pro.europeana.eu/web/guest/about/facts-figures.

Fink, Eleanor E. 1997. "Sharing Cultural Entitlements in the Digital Age: Are We Building a Garden of Eden or a Patch of Weeds?" Accessed October 15, 2014. http://www.archimuse.com/mw97/speak/fink.htm.

Keene, Suzanne. 1996. "LASSI: the Larger Scale Systems Initiative." *Information Services and Use: Special Issue – British Library Treasures*, 16(3–4): 223–236. Accessed October 15, 2014. http://dl.acm.org/citation.cfm?id=249457.

MacArthur, Matthew. 2007. "Can Museums Allow Online Users to Become Participants?" In *The Digital Museum: A Think Guide*, edited by Herminia Din and Phyllis Hecht, 57–66. Washington, DC: American Association of Museums.

McCarthy, Gavan. 2007. "Finding a Future for Digital Cultural Heritage Resources Using Contextual Information Frameworks." In *Theorizing Digital Cultural Heritage: A Critical Discourse*, edited by Fiona Cameron and Sarah Kenderdine, 245–260. London: MIT Press.

M-Shed. 2011. Website. Accessed October 13, 2014. http://mshed.org.

MuseumPests.net. 2009. "Suggested Field List for Pest Observation Databases." Accessed October 15, 2014. http://museumpests.net/wp-content/uploads/2014/03/Updated-_Field_List_for_Pest_Observation_Databases.pdf.

Parry, Ross. 2007. *Recoding the Museum: Digital Heritage and the Technologies of Change*. London: Routledge.

Pinniger, David, and Peter Winsor. 2004. *Integrated Pest Management: A Guide for Museums, Libraries and Archives*. London: Museums, Libraries, and Archives Council.

Poole, Nick. 2012. "New Contexts for Museum Information." Accessed October 15, 2014. http://www.slideshare.net/nickpoole/new-contexts-for-museum-information.

Salway, Gareth, and Mark Pajak. 2011. "Using Emu for the New M-Shed Museum." Accessed October 13, 2014. http://emu.kesoftware.com/news-and-events/conferences/1590-1st-global-user-group-meeting-london-uk-12-14-october-2011.

Sola, Tomislav. 2010. "Making the Total Museum Possible." In *Museums in a Digital Age*, edited by Ross Parry, 421–426. London: Routledge.

Thomas, Selma. 2007. "Introduction." In *The Digital Museum: A Think Guide*, edited by Herminia Din and Phyllis Hecht, 1–7. Washington, DC: American Association of Museums.

Wikipedia. 2013. "Content Management System." Accessed October 13, 2014. http://en.wikipedia.org/wiki/Content_management_system.

Williams, David. 2010. "A Brief History of Museum Computerization." In *Museums in a Digital Age*, edited by Ross Parry, 14–21. London: Routledge.

Witchey, Holly. 2007. "New Technologies, Old Dilemmas: Ethics and the Museum Professional." In *The Digital Museum: A Think Guide*, edited by Herminia Din and Phyllis Hecht, 189–196. Washington, DC: American Association of Museums.

Witcomb, Andrea. 2003. *Re-imagining the Museum: Beyond the Mausoleum*. London: Routledge.

Further Reading

Bates, Marcia J. 2011. *Understanding Information Retrieval Systems: Management, Types, and Standards*. Boca Raton, FL: CRC Press.

Bearman, David. 2008. "Representing Museum Knowledge." In *Museum Informatics: People, Information and Technology in Museums*, edited by Paul Marty and Katherine Burton Jones, 35–59. London: Routledge.

Cameron, Fiona and Helena Robinson, 2007. "Digital Knowledgescapes: Cultural, Theoretical, Practical, and Usage Issues Facing Museum Collection Databases in a Digital Epoch." In *Theorizing Digital Cultural Heritage: A Critical Discourse*, edited by Fiona Cameron and Sarah Kenderdine, 165–191. London: MIT Press.

Chapman, Malcolm, and Gurdeep Thiara. 2010. *Collective Conversations, the New Museum Community: Audiences, Challenges, Benefits*. London: MuseumsEtc.

Collections Trust. 2011. "SPECTRUM." Accessed October 13, 2014. http://www.collectionslink.org.uk/programmes/spectrum.

Keene, Suzanne. 1998. *Digital Collections: Museums and the Information Age*. Oxford: Butterworth-Heinemann.

Keene, Suzanne. 2012. *Digital Collections*. London: Routledge.

Manovich, Lev. 2010 "Database as a Symbolic Form." In *Museums in a Digital Age*, edited by Ross Parry, 64–71. London: Routledge.

Marty, Paul. 2008. "Information Representation." In *Museum Informatics: People, Information and Technology in Museums*, edited by Paul Marty and Katherine Burton Jones, 29–34. London: Routledge.

Waibel, Günter. 2007. "Stewardship for Digital Images: Preserving Your Assets, Preserving Your Investment." In *The Digital Museum: A Think Guide*, edited by Herminia Din and Phyllis Hecht, 167–177. Washington, DC: American Association of Museums.

Malcolm Chapman is Head of Collections Management at the Hunterian, University of Glasgow. Malcolm has worked with collections and collections management systems in national and university museums for over 20 years, with a particular focus on improving users' access to collections and collections knowledge. While at Manchester Museum he initiated the Collective Conversations project, winner of the MLA Inspiring North West Awards 2006 for Innovation, which was published in 2010 with G. Thiara as *Collective Conversations, the New Museum Community: Audiences, Challenges, Benefits*. He has also published on human remains and regularly lectures at universities on current museum practice.

13 CONSERVATION THEORY AND PRACTICE
Materials, Values, and People in Heritage Conservation

Dean Sully

This chapter describes a personal conservation journey and, in so doing, reflects the changes that have become apparent to me in the conservation discipline. This journey has its beginnings in my training at University College London (UCL) Institute of Archaeology in the 1980s, within the department of Conservation and Material Science, through professional practice as a conservator, and currently extends to my work teaching conservation at UCL Institute of Archaeology in 2013, as part of the Heritage Studies Research Group.

The shifts in continuities of theory and practice, from materials science to heritage studies, including contradictory turns and revolutions in attitudes, are made real by the particularities of my time and place. In order to expose these shifts, I describe different conservation approaches as "materials-based," "values-based," and "peoples-based," which reflects a change in the focus of the conservation process, from the *materials* of heritage objects, to the *values* that cultural heritage holds for people. The chapter therefore considers external influences (social, political, technical, and economic) and the associated heritage, museum, and conservation responses. It advocates a shift in conservation practice from a specialist technical service aimed at preserving heritage, to a mechanism for the creation and re-creation of culture. The broadening of conservation into the notion of cultural heritage creation has resulted in many different challenges for professionals. As a consequence, a diversity of conservation responses is required to meet these challenges.

The International Handbooks of Museum Studies: Museum Practice, First Edition.
Edited by Conal McCarthy.
© 2015 John Wiley & Sons Ltd. Published 2020 by John Wiley & Sons Ltd.

Conservation practice

International, political, cultural, and legislative frameworks help to define what conservators do. These formal understandings are translated through state and institutional structures to affect professional codes and personal responses to conservation decision-making around heritage (Avrami 2009). Thus, we can trace influences from UNESCO (United Nations Educational, Scientific, and Cultural Organization) and its agencies ICOM (International Council of Museums) statutes, ICOMOS (International Council on Monuments and Sites) charters, and ICCROM (International Center for the Study of the Preservation and Restoration of Cultural Property) programs, through national legislation, to the mission statements of museums.[1] Guidelines for conservation practice have been laid down within codes of ethics from established professional bodies, those of ICOM-CC (International Council of Museums Conservation Committee), IIC (International Institute of Conservation), AIC (American Institute of Conservation), ECCO (European Confederation of Conservator-restorers' Organizations), and ICON (Institute of Conservation, UK), are a direct reflection of these influences.

Conservation has been defined as:

> All measures and actions aimed at safeguarding tangible cultural heritage while ensuring its accessibility to present and future generations. Conservation embraces preventive conservation, remedial conservation, and restoration. All measures and actions should respect the significance and the physical properties of the cultural heritage item. (ICOM-CC 2008).

Curating the "material" past has provided the foundation and universalizing justification behind heritage institutions (Shelton 2006). Conservators perform a specialist role in ensuring the continuing survival of objects and collections. The loss of physical fabric through deterioration equates to the loss of information and knowledge, and breaks a tangible link with the past. The product of materials-based conservation therefore lies in the preservation of the physical object and the information it "contains." As a consequence, conservation as a profession has been based on two main assumptions: the need to preserve the integrity of the physical object, and a belief in scientific inquiry as the basis for proper preservation and treatment of collections (Clavir 2002, 4).

Along with minimal intervention, authenticity, and reversibility, the concept of "object integrity" provides a framework for conservation decision-making. This refers to maintaining the "physical," "contextual," and "conceptual" integrity of objects within heritage collections (Sease 1998; Clavier 2002). Conservators – certainly those working in Western countries – have focused on the tangible aspects of the integrity of objects, which is to say physical stability. As a result, resources have been targeted to investigate the mechanisms of deterioration, and to develop techniques to prevent their effects (Clavir 2002; Appelbaum 2007). The use of scientific methodologies has provided a language for materials-based conservation to describe changes to objects through time, and has been used to guide technical interventions designed to mitigate these changes. There are many examples of the real benefits to the physical condition of collections as a result of conservation intervention.[2] In these cases, material culture that might have been lost has been conserved to provide a focus for the revitalization of cultural practices. (See Szczepanowska 2013 for an introduction to the materials of heritage conservation and Caple 2011 for an outline of preventive conservation processes.)

Recent shifts

Over the past 30 years, the impact of significant changes in other heritage specialisms, and the institutions that contain them, has become evident in the theory and practice of heritage conservation (Bennett 1995; Hodder 1999; Hooper-Greenhill 1989; Hooper-Greenhill 2001; Pearce 1990; Smith 2006; Vergo 1989). The primary focus of Western conservation on the preservation of the physical fabric of objects potentially isolates objects from other traditions and people that gave objects meaning, such as the living culture of descendants of originating communities (Clavir 2002, xvii). The dominance of the scientific model, and the right of heritage specialists to make decisions about the conservation of other peoples' heritage, has been challenged by social and cultural groups that are affected by the conservation process. Their diverse perspectives and responses have initiated a reconsideration of the "object-focus" of conservation, and conservation practice has progressively moved beyond defining the value of objects exclusively within the values system of the museum and academic disciplines (Kreps 2003, 149). Rather, the museum context is seen as merely one in a series of relevant cognitive frameworks that defines the effect of objects on people.

This has implications for the relevance of established working practices in the conservation profession (Appelbaum 2007; Ashley-Smith 1999; Richmond and Bracker 2009; Clavir 2002; Caple 2000; Muñoz-Vinas 2005; Pye 2001; Pye and Sully 2007). The assumed certainties of a conservation discipline, based on a technical understanding of the material world, have been changing – now the goals of the conservation process are less tangible, and are required to be negotiated within complex cultural systems (Clavier 2009). From the deterministic certainties of material science, the conservation process has turned toward a broader engagement with a community of stakeholders of diverse cultural perspectives. This acknowledges the need to justify conservation action to a broad range of people: general public, taxpayers, local people, artists, producers, original owners and users, heritage communities, and fellow heritage professionals and specialists. While a focus on the physical stability of heritage objects continues to be essential to conservation decision-making, increasing importance is given to the cultural significance of objects (Muñoz-Vinas 2005). The process is therefore seen to result in the *selection* of cultural values inscribed in the conserved object; as a consequence, evidence of certain values will be retained, maintained, or enhanced, while others will be diminished, altered, or removed. Conservators operating within a values-based conservation process are, therefore, unable to simply focus on the physical materials of the heritage places, spaces, and objects in their care.

Developing a working understanding of the object, one that is not limited to its materials, raises the question of how conservators are able adequately to assess these elements within the time, knowledge, skills, tools, and resources available in the conservation process. It is unlikely that this can be achieved without recognizing and gaining access to a diverse range of knowledge and opinion (Clavir 2002). As a result, contemporary conservation decisions are required to be collaborative in order to provide a broad base of support for the actions taken. Therefore, a clear aim and broad justification is required for good conservation decision-making (Varoli-Piazza 2007). Conservators are now required to "preserve the cultural significance of material heritage under their care," as, "it is due to this significance that the material is being preserved" (Clavir 2009, 145). Therefore, conservation should aim to enhance the preferred cultural values of material heritage, while maximizing the potential of people now and in the future to access their own preferred values (Muñoz-Vinas 2009, 56).

Careful management of change

The concept of conservation as a process of managing change, rather than as a process of arresting decay, affects how we understand the changes to physical materials, condition, meaning, use, expectation, and significance of heritage objects (Staniforth 2006, 35). The careful management of change involves interventive conservation (that seeks to alter places, spaces, and objects to maintain or enhance associated cultural values) and preventive conservation (aiming to mitigate adverse changes to these cultural values over time). The act of making conservation decisions about an object creates a conservation object, and affects the cultural value of the object. This highlights the tautology of cultural heritage and conservation; conservation is a cultural process and its actions *create* heritage, therefore we care for heritage not only because it is valued – it is valued because we care for it (Holtorf 2001, 266). Potentially this leads us to a definition of conservation simply as the work that conservators do!

The conservation of cultural heritage provides a catalyst for revealing the nature of social relationships that link peoples with both their pasts and futures. This leads us to reconsider the aims of the conservation process in terms of the "effect" on people, rather than in terms of preserving the physical "integrity" of the material past. It thereby presents an opportunity to see how the current processes of conservation practice can be affected by, and can have effect on, the relationships that surround the long-term use and care of cultural heritage. The artifact of conservation therefore is not the conserved object, but the social networks constructed between people and heritage that create meaningful objects, and sustain them into the future.

Simplifying the conservation object

The entry of objects into a museum redefines the interaction between objects and people in a way that reflects the needs of the institution that holds the collection. The act of conservation, regardless of specific decisions to retain an object's current form, or to restore to a preferred previous state, has the potential to separate an object from its previous use and development. Dedicated to a new heritage use, the conserved object is enclosed in this heritage frame, separated from the evolving present and situated in an imagined past. The object is conserved as a representation of an imagined past state in order to match expectations of what the authentic object should be. Instead it becomes a set of fragmentary memories or vestigial elements of a more complex web of meaning (Vergo 1989, 4). As Lowenthal has suggested, the heritage object's existence in the past is paradoxical, as it bears the cultural marks of the present from which it is supposedly demarcated (1985, xxv).

The conceptual separation of cultural objects from their present is a well-established technique of heritage conservation. Heritage professionals have used this to institute new frameworks of meaning and use for heritage objects, which arguably prioritize the needs of the heritage institution over other interests. It allows novel solutions to be developed for the care of cultural objects, and enables the conservator to sever the connection between objects in museums, and the people who made and used them prior to collection.

The changes that occur after an object enters into a museum collection are seldom considered valuable and therefore are rendered invisible by conservation action. Guided by ethical principles (for instance, minimal intervention and reversibility) within the scientific framework, conservators seek to define an objective physical "truth" in the conserved object (Muñoz-Vinas 2005, 188; Jokilehto 2009, 81). In the search for truth and authenticity, conservators may strip away the obscuring layers of history in order to reveal or retain the "true nature" of the object. Here there is a risk of cutting the threads that link objects with the present, which may reduce or limit the stories that can be told about objects (Denslagen 2003, 99). The conserved object is necessarily an edited version of all the interactions that link the current state of the object with its past states (Ashley-Smith 2009, 18). It presents a selection of certain truths, materialized as a conserved object, in a clear narrative that is distilled from the complex mass of individual stories that make up the past, its complexity reduced in order to render the object as a deliberately constructed representation of itself. Rather than being a neutral process conducted outside of history, conservation action is as much a part of the ongoing biography of the object as other interventions, in other contexts, which have created a trajectory for the object through time

(Gell 1998; Avrami 2009, 183). The object accrues new meanings and values as heritage: it is not artificially fixed in some imagined "original" state by being conserved and thereby "saved" from degeneration and the ravages of time.

The use of objects in the museum in reserve collections, permanent exhibitions, publications, research projects, short-term loan and exhibitions, unauthored access, handling sessions, outreach programs, digital access, and so on, lead to repeated cycles of decision-making about the appropriate care of the object in these situations. The conservation process requires arbitrary choices to be made about an object's care, in order to distinguish what physical states are acceptable, and what states require intervention. These encounters provide new opportunities to develop reciprocal relationships between the objects and the people who value those objects, and a device to reconnect an object's present with its past. The greatest value of museum collections may lie in their ability to physically endure, thus providing an ongoing opportunity to revitalize interactions between cultural heritage objects and people in a specific time and place. Due to the enduring nature of the physical materiality of heritage, people can invent and reinvent the cultural relevance of material culture in the present. The conserved object is judged by its relevance to the present, and justified by the credibility of the conservation processes employed in its treatment. Therefore, we can conceive of the successful product of conservation being a "plausible" rather than a "truthful" object (Wright 1985, 14).

Conservation concepts

Conservation, as a socially constructed activity, interacts with and is governed by the same economic, political, spiritual, religious, social, and cultural dynamics that influence other specialisms in the cultural environment. Many practicing conservators within museums claim little direct influence on their work from the supra-national codes of UNESCO and its agencies. Some may refer more directly to institutional aims (such as mission statements and management plans) to define the role of conservation, while the majority utilize the professional codes of practice of AIC, ECCO, or ICON to justify their conservation decisions (Ashley-Smith 2009, 12). The formulations of ethical codes and guidelines for practice are products of social processes mediated by the practical realities of taking action through specific events. They are designed to encourage agreed behaviors by stating aspirational aims for conservation responses reflecting a guiding philosophy of the conservation profession (Kemp 2009, 63). Central conservation concepts, such as "object integrity," "reversibility," and "minimal intervention," once used uncritically to guide decisions, have been re-examined and redefined as "cultural significance" (Clavir 2002), "re-treatability" (Appelbaum 2007), and "minimal meaning loss" (Muñoz-Vinas 2005).

A critical analysis of the meaning of such concepts is required in order to render them useful within modes of conservation practice. Recent shifts in the conservation discipline can be categorized in such a way that reflects a shift of focus from "materials" to "values," and toward a "peoples"-based conservation process.

Table 13.1 identifies the founding charters and conventions associated with each approach, and highlights the different foci provided by each framework of understanding in materials-, values-, and peoples-based conservation (this is considered further below). The shift in focus could be seen as an evolutionary sequence (as represented in Table 13.1), but, more usefully, it represents a broadening of the framework of theory and practice in heritage conservation in which these approaches are utilized to differing degrees, depending on the requirements of a particular heritage project. The reframing of conservation in this way encourages greater diversity in working practice. Furthermore, it provides the intellectual justification for challenging established norms of practice that limit appropriate solutions to the problems identified in conservation projects. It enables continuity of

TABLE 13.1 Materials-, values-, and peoples-based conservation approaches

Materials-based conservation	Values-based conservation	Peoples-based conservation
Universal values	Stakeholder values	Community values
Athens Charter 1931, Venice Charter 1964, World Heritage Convention 1972	Burra Charter 1979, Nara Document on Authenticity 1994	The Convention for the Safeguarding of the Intangible Cultural Heritage 2003
Heritage has "intrinsic value" decoded by experts	Heritage values are ascribed by experts in consultation with stakeholders	Heritage values are context-specific, defined by contemporary communities
Cultural significance based on expert values	Cultural significance guided by expert values that includes stakeholder values	Cultural significance is determined by community values
Decision-making by top-down closed linear expert systems	Decision-making by top-down integrated expert systems that seek stakeholder participation, consultation and dialogue	Decision-making by community-led, people-up systems that seeks locally appropriate questions, methods, and solutions
The welfare of the material heritage takes precedence over contemporary needs of people	The welfare of the material heritage is balanced with contemporary needs of stakeholders, but material heritage is the primary concern	The welfare of contemporary communities takes precedence over material heritage
Conservation aims to produce the "True" object	Conservation aims to produce the "Expected" object	Conservation aims to produce a "Plausible" object

Source: after Braillie 2009, 33.

established conservation practice, associated with a materials focus, where this is considered to be the most appropriate approach, and sanctions the incorporation of a community's cultural values into conservation decision-making, where relevant. Significantly however, it allows us to privilege the diverse ways that people think about, care for, and use their own cultural materials within the practice of heritage conservation.

Categorizing approaches as materials, values, and peoples-based conservation enables conservation professionals to re-interpret the core values of the discipline. So for example, we can consider how a definition of "minimal intervention" can be re-interpreted within each of these different frameworks of understanding (see Table 13.2).

Minimal intervention, along with other core conservation concepts, can therefore be re-thought. For example, minimal intervention can be used to justify significant changes to the physical fabric of a heritage object within a peoples-based conservation project, rather than minimal change within materials-based conservation. In the former, conservation interventions are aimed at maximizing the aspirations of the current generation of the community of users, rather than as in the latter, retaining the material authenticity of the heritage object (Sully 2007).

Materials-based conservation

Materials-based conservation has been a defining characteristic of the conservation profession and its evolution as a museum specialism. The adaptation of scientific discourse has given authority to the role of conservation within the

TABLE 13.2   Definitions of minimal intervention within materials-, values-, and peoples-based conservation frameworks

Materials-based conservation: minimal intervention
Whenever possible only the minimum treatment required to stabilize the object should be undertaken, and reassembly and restoration should be carefully limited. This is particularly important when introducing new substances, such as synthetic polymers, into objects since the long-term effects of these materials are difficult to predict.

Values-based conservation: minimal intervention
Whenever possible the minimum intervention required to maintain, retain, or enhance the cultural significance of the object should be undertaken. Any intervention should be carefully focused on the cultural values identified in the object to be conserved.

Peoples-based conservation: minimal intervention
Whenever possible the minimum intervention required to realize the aspirations of communities connected to the object should be undertaken. This should be led by the community in ways that are appropriate to local custom and practice.

FIGURE 6.1   Music in the foyer at Tel Aviv Museum of Art, Israel. A regular program of events is an important element in building a loyal audience in museums.
Photograph courtesy of Yael Borovich.

FIGURE 6.2   National Trust conservation in action: people watch while one of the sixteenth-century Gideon Tapestries is rehung at Hardwick Hall, Derbyshire. Whereas previously the gallery would have been closed to the public, now the Trust ensures that members and visitors are aware of the conservation work it carries out as part of its commitment to involving people in its work.
Reproduced with permission of the National Trust.

FIGURE 6.3 The Potteries Museum in Stoke holds the finest collection of British ceramics in the world. It is also a leader in working with families who have children under five years of age. Courtesy of Stoke Potteries Museum.

FIGURE 11.1 The Ancient Worlds gallery, Manchester Museum.
Courtesy Manchester Museum.

FIGURE 14.1   The exhibition *Sleeping and Dreaming* at Wellcome Collection in London, one of the new interdisciplinary cultural centers that is exploring different ways of making exhibitions. Image courtesy of Wellcome Collection.

FIGURE 17.4 "F is for Fire Engine" in *Minnesota A to Z*, Minnesota History Center Museum, St. Paul. Although alphabetical organizing schemas (or "hat racks") are rarely used, *Minnesota A to Z* was an exception that proved playful, engaging, and accessible to a broad audience due to its simple and instantly familiar structure.

Photograph courtesy of the Minnesota Historical Society.

FIGURE 18.1 Model of Professor Baldwin Spencer, biologist, anthropologist, and honorary director of the National Museum of Victoria (1899–1928) on display in the exhibition *Bunjilaka*, 2001.

Source: Museum Victoria. Photograph: John Broomfield.

FIGURE 18.3   Exhibition *Hitler and the Germans. Nation and Crime*, Berlin 2010. View of the section "Hitler and the Germans 1933–1945." Busts of the *Führer* as propagandistic mass products. © German Historical Museum 2010.

FIGURE 18.4   Exhibition *The Image of the "Other" in Germany and France from 1871 to the present*, Paris 2008, Berlin 2009. View of the contemporary section. In the center a model of the sculpture *The Foreigner* by Guido Messer, 1982. © German Historical Museum 2009.

FIGURE 18.6 *Rebecca Belmore*
Canadian, born 1960
Rising to the Occasion, 1987 – 1991
mixed media
Overall: 200 × 120 × 100 cm (78 3/4 × 47 1/4 × 39 3/8 in.)
ART GALLERY OF ONTARIO
Gift from the Junior Volunteer Committee, 1995
95/173
Artist
Art Gallery of Ontario, reproduced with permission of the artist.

FIGURE 18.7 Montreal Museum of Fine Arts, *Founding Identities* gallery, 2011.
Photograph by Tom Arban.

FIGURE 20.1 Dancers provide a traditional ceremonial "Welcome to country" upon the return of Larrakia ancestral remains, Mindil Beach, Darwin, Northern Territory, November 2002.

Photo: Michael Pickering, National Museum of Australia.

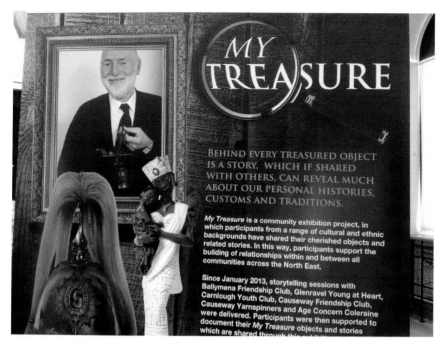

FIGURE 21.1　Detail of a panel from the *My Treasure* community exhibition (Mid-Antrim and Causeway Museum Service) displayed at Coleraine Town Hall, Northern Ireland, July–August 2013.

Courtesy Mid-Antrim and Causeway Museum Service.

FIGURE 23.1　The "Arrivals" display in the exhibition *Blood, Earth, Fire | Whāngai Whenua Ahi Kā*, which opened in 2006 at Te Papa, Wellington. Objects, design, and interpretation work harmoniously to deliver a purposeful experience for the visitor without relying on a lot of text.

Courtesy of the Museum of New Zealand Te Papa Tongarewa.

FIGURE 24.1 Formal education versus learning through participation: the Victorian classroom and teacher at the Ragged School Museum, London.
Photograph by Anna Robertson © Ragged School Museum Trust.

FIGURE 24.2 Two participants examining a traditional coffee pot as a part of the Asian Women's Documenting the Home project at the Geffrye Museum, London.
© Olivia Hemingway / Geffrye Museum.

FIGURE A2.1 *Walk among Worlds*, an installation by Máximo González, October 12 – November 10, 2013, at the Fowler Museum, UCLA. Photo: Anthony Alan Shelton, 2013.

FIGURE A2.2 Opening performance of the community-based collaborative exhibition *Death Is Just Another Beginning*, National Museum of Taiwan, Taipei.
Photo: Anthony Alan Shelton, 2012.

FIGURE A2.5 Exhibit Gallery, Kokdu Museum, Seoul.
Reproduced with permission of Sukman Jang.

FIGURE A2.6 *Box of Promises*, collaborative work between George Nuku (Māori) and Cory Douglas (Squamish/Haida) in the exhibition *Paradise Lost?* Great Hall, Museum of Anthropology, UBC, Vancouver.
Photo: Anthony Alan Shelton, 2013.

FIGURE A2.8 *Imprint*, choreographed by Henry Daniel and Owen Underhill. Great Hall, Museum of Anthropology, UBC, Vancouver.
Photo: Nicky Levell, 2010.

heritage institutions. The ability of conservators to intervene in the material remains of the past, to create something that is meaningful and useful in the present and future, is an important function of conservation. It provides a focus for the allocation of resources that are manifest in well-ordered stored collections, and exhibited objects that match the expectations of the museum as an institution, and presumably, the expectations of the audience of museum visitors.

A set of conservation core values can be linked to foundational documents such as the Athens Charter (1931) and the Venice Charter (ICOMOS 1964). These documents prioritized the materiality or monumentality of heritage as the focus for conservation action. This approach is based on principles of authenticity, and maintaining the historical and physical context of monuments, buildings, and sites. Conservation intervention is limited by concepts of anastylosis, minimum intervention, respect for historic evidence, avoidance of falsification, preservation of the original, and reversibility of interventions. The World Heritage Convention and its Operational Guidelines (UNESCO 1972) enshrined the idea of universal value, authenticity, and integrity within a shared responsibility for the stewardship of built heritage at a global level. As a consequence, other ways of conserving the past risk being considered "incorrect." The conservation associated with this approach is perceived as a technical process, aimed at resolving the instability of physical fabric, in order to preserve it for future generations. Consequently, significance is objectively determined, because values are considered qualities inherent in an object. Naturally this relies upon specialist knowledge of heritage materials and an understanding of how and why these materials change over time (Appelbaum 2007).

As a result, conservation practice and research has generally been based on an understanding of the vulnerability of the conservation object, and the actions required in order to mitigate these changes in the condition of the object. An assessment of object condition routinely provides a focal point for decision-making in the materials-based conservation process and provides a means to establish the impact of changes on the physical remains of the past, thus allowing the consequences to be evaluated. Physical condition, however, is not a secure reference point that can be found in the materials of heritage objects, nor is the assessment of condition an objective process of description, but a series of judgments constructed within the prevailing intellectual framing of the questions posed. So rather than a fixed reference point, the notion of the object's "condition" is contextual and understood in relation to other criteria, such as function, purpose, expectation, and use.

Claims about the role of heritage within political campaigns for social inclusion and diversity have encouraged heritage professionals to look for the benefits of conservation beyond the stability of heritage material (Jones and Holden 2008). The conserved object that results from a conservation process focused on an essentialized notion of an object, represented only by its material constituents, limits the multifaceted significance of the object and restricts ways of experiencing objects and the past. An acknowledgment that objects have cultural value *beyond* the materials from which they are made allows us to appreciate that conservation is not undertaken just because materials are damaged, but because cultural value can be maintained and/or revealed.

The object-centered lens of the conservation process has provided a unique method of investigation that can contribute to the debate about the past and the way it is understood in the present. Investigative conservation can expose traces of past practice within the object itself, which has the potential to reveal social relationships around the manufacture and use of conserved objects, made evident through decisions about the conservation and presentation of objects in museum collections. The tools, skills, and knowledge associated with conservation work therefore need to move beyond the scientific and technical aspects of the work, in order to consider the cultural interactions that are affected by the processes that are used to care for cultural heritage. The concept of cultural significance, considered further below, has been established as a mechanism for incorporating human values into conservation decision-making and the careful management of change.

Values-based conservation

The increased importance of engaging the public in heritage conservation reflects broader political developments evident in the latter half of the twentieth century (Avrami, Mason, and de La Torre 2000). Conservators have had to reconsider what they do and how they do it, and have moved gradually from the objective stewardship of heritage resources, to managing heritage in ways that reflect the multiple interactions between people and objects (Avrami 2009). A values-based conservation framework seeks to include a broad range of opinions within the decision-making process through engagement with multiple stakeholders (Avrami, Mason, and de La Torre 2000; de La Torre 2002; Clavir 2002; Muñoz-Vinas 2005).

A process of information gathering is required in order to incorporate human values into conservation decision-making. Values are dynamic, context dependent, and therefore contested, in flux, as communities construct and reconstruct meaning in response to the present cultural landscape (Ucko 2001, 304). The Charter for the Conservation of Places of Cultural Significance (the Burra Charter 1979), and its revisions up to the present, provides a foundational document for values-based conservation (Australia ICOMOS 1999). The Burra Charter directs the conservation process to an understanding of cultural significance through a sequence of collecting and analyzing information, prior to deciding conservation policy and management planning. The Nara Document on Authenticity (ICOMOS 1994) helped to introduce the concept of "cultural diversity" into conservation decision-making, recognizing that authenticity is rooted in specific sociocultural contexts and can only be understood and judged within the cultural context to which it belongs. The ICOMOS New Zealand Charter for the Conservation of

Places of Cultural Heritage Value (Revised 2010) provides a recent iteration of this approach (ICOMOS 2010).

The Burra Charter process is routinely used by heritage organizations in developing conservation management plans (Avrami, Mason, and de La Torre 2000). The process provides a decision-making model that incorporates stakeholder views through a process of consultation. It consists of three interrelated stages: understanding the significance; developing policy; and managing in accordance with policy (see Figure 13.1).

Values-based conservation decisions are premised on developing an understanding of cultural significance through physical examination, historical research, and community consultation (Kerr 1996). There are a number of tools that can be used to elicit cultural values as part of a heritage conservation project, including cultural and cognitive mapping, environmental and economic impact studies, contingent valuation studies, and ethnographic fieldwork (Avrami, Mason, and de La Torre

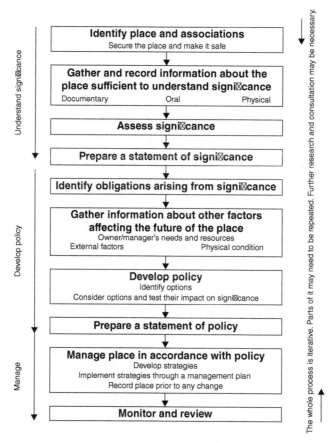

FIGURE 13.1   The Burra Charter process, with its sequence of investigations, decisions, and actions (Australia ICOMOS 1999, 10)

2000). There is, however, no universally applicable method for heritage assessments. The essential component is the involvement of the public – therefore a framework for assessment should be used as a departure point for discussion, and should be adapted for each project. Once these values are understood and recorded, they can be clearly expressed in a statement of significance.

The production of a statement of significance has the potential to provide a clear reference point from which to consider the impact of proposed conservation actions on the identified values of the object (Pearson and Sullivan 1995, chapter 4; English Heritage 2008; Australian Heritage Commission 2000). Compared to the function of a condition assessment/report for materials-based conservation, a statement of significance seeks to define cultural values at a specific time and place represented by the conservation moment. It flows from value assessments, understood as a summary of the cultural heritage values held by communities ascribed to cultural heritage, and should seek to incorporate commensurate and converging values, and emphasize the plural and often contradictory nature of significances, as interpreted by various stakeholders.

A first step in documenting cultural value for a heritage assessment is to establish a typology from which to categorize aspects of value. The values that are emphasized when writing statements of significance may include historic, aesthetic, scientific, research, educational/academic, technical, social, religious, spiritual, legal, economic, recreational, cultural, national, or political values that an object or collection has for past, present, and future generations (Kerr 1996).

A useful model for assessing significance for museum objects and collections is presented by Australia's Heritage Collections Council (Heritage Collections Council 2001). This was designed to enable Australian museums to make comparable decisions about conservation priorities across collections and museums. Four criteria are used to assess cultural significance: Historic, Aesthetic, Scientific (research or technical), and Social (or spiritual). The degree of significance in each category is evaluated using five comparative criteria (Provenance, Representativeness, Rarity, Condition/Integrity, and Interpretive Potential). The information gathered from this process is then summarized in a statement of significance, which provides a clear summary of the values, meaning, and importance of the object or collection (Collections Council of Australia 2009). A common methodology allows some standardization in significance assessment, and is attractive for heritage institutions that seek to compare the assessment of cultural value for different heritage objects.

The statement of significance, leading to a conservation assessment, and conservation management strategy and plan, provides a mechanism for the adaptation of existing modes of conservation practice within a values-based conservation project. Considered in association with condition assessment and external factors, statements of significance have become standard tools for the management of landscapes, sites, and heritage spaces, and are incorporated into the conservation of museum objects and collections (Avrami, Mason, and de La Torre 2000). The conservation proposal or management plan should identify the most appropriate way of caring for the object arising out of the statement of significance and other constraints (Kerr 1996). Ideally, it should identify ways of making cultural significance understandable in the fabric of the conserved object. Options for conservation intervention can be assessed in terms of the potential impact on cultural significance.

A materials-based approach to conservation practice sits comfortably within a values-based process, as one category of data amongst multiple sources of available information. Information generated from a materials-based focus can form a starting point for a dialogue between the heritage specialist and a community of "stakeholders," enabling the views of a community of users to be reflected in a values-based conservation response. The real advantage of this devolved decision-making process is that it helps to connect communities with the care of heritage, and broadens the focus of the heritage professionals managing the process.

Devaluing values-based conservation

A values-based conservation approach requires an assessment of cultural values and significance, in order to perpetuate these values in the conserved object, and prevent them from changing, emerging, or fading away. Cultural significance, however, is not an inherent quality waiting to be discovered – rather it is a product of the heritage process which is designated by heritage professionals. The use of strictly defined assessment criteria tends to reduce the complexity of culture down to a set of essentially objective things that can then be preserved. There is also the tendency to rank the importance of objects in relation to their cultural value assessment, a process that may be deeply offensive to people closely connected to certain heritage objects.

An assessment of cultural significance cannot possibly identify and represent *all* the values that heritage objects have for the individuals and social groups involved with a conservation object. All cultural value assessments are partial and incomplete, limited by the time resources, skills, and knowledge involved in the process. The statement of significance therefore cannot be expected to stand for the sum of all knowledge about an object. As a conservation document, its purpose is merely to guide a values-based conservation process. The degree to which the cultural significance of an object can be broadly justified and a consensus substantiated should provide a limiting factor to the extent of alteration considered acceptable during conservation treatment.

While stakeholder participation has become part of the general rhetoric, how this translates into a toolbox for conservation practice remains poorly developed (Avrami 2009). The top down, expert-led consultation that tends to underpin values-based conservation can be seen as an internally generated process that satisfies the requirements of the heritage professionals, but may not relate to the reality of people's experience of their heritage (Wright 1985, 14; Smith 2006, 12; Sully 2007,

226). Although such mechanisms supposedly make possible local community involvement in decision-making through accountability and transparency, the development of professional protocols that standardize practice can actually have the effect of prohibiting local responses to specific problems. Not surprisingly this has been criticized, especially when communities consider themselves not to be equally weighted stakeholders in the heritage process, but where they represent a privileged position in the use and care of their own cultural of heritage (Wijesuriya 2007). The authority to decide what is valued is largely the domain of heritage specialists as "insider" stakeholders. "Outsider" groups of other specialists, non-specialists and the public are likely to express values that diverge from those of the heritage specialists. These views may remain hidden to the conservation process, and excluded from it because of lack of opportunity, language, or incentive to participate. Obviously, this has implications for how decisions are made and ultimately how to conserve.

However, it is possible to plan a process of consultation which can feed into an appropriate conservation response that reflects the aspirations of the community of users. In order to do this it is necessary to critically examine the role of the conservation specialist within community-led heritage research and practice. Here the idea is that a community's traditional systems, skills, and knowledge are privileged over universalized concepts of heritage. Consequently the conservation specialist works within the custom, practice, and protocol of the communities involved, necessitating a reflexive approach in which the agency of all the participants, including the conservation specialist, are acknowledged (Kreps 2003; Sully 2007).

Peoples-based conservation

Treasured objects and heirlooms that once formed a focus for the social networks of their original owners can continue to perform this role following their encoding as heritage objects, it is just the nature of these relations that is different (Hoskins 1998). The old values and meaning are not erased, but are revealed through the ongoing encounters that people have with heritage objects. Some mechanism for understanding the effects that objects have on people therefore should be an essential element of the conservation of an object. But conservation action seeks to crystallize the presence of certain ideas within an object, along with the consequent removal of others. By doing this, conservators enhance evidence of particular interactions between objects and people, while diminishing others.

Such an approach is aligned to, but different from, the aims of a values-based conservation approach that seeks to maintain the cultural significance of the object to be conserved in a way that prioritizes the welfare of the material heritage as the primary concern. A peoples-based approach differs in that it prioritizes the welfare of the community over material heritage. Working within a "participatory process," consulting with a user community goes beyond simply evaluating a response to a predetermined expert-driven solution, but tries to develop an appropriate conservation response that reflects the aspirations of the community of users connected with those heritage objects. There is a difference between a people-up approach to community participation, and the expert-down process more commonly associated with consultation within what Smith calls the "Authorised Heritage Discourse" (2006, 37). Elements of this approach are evident within the International Convention for the Safeguarding of the Intangible Heritage (UNESCO 2003), the Faro Convention on the Value of Cultural Heritage for Society (Council of Europe 2005), and in the Living Heritage Programme and the People Centered Conservation Approach being developed at ICCROM (2012).

The Intangible Heritage Convention has helped to rebalance the focus of heritage professionals from the material authenticity of cultural heritage to the social process of capacity building and provision of social benefits for participant communities in the heritage process. A shift toward a peoples-based approach utilizes participatory processes to enhance the connection between a community and their heritage in ways that are appropriate to those people, seeking to empower communities to make their own decisions about the care of their heritage (Stovel, Stanley-Price, and Killick 2005; Wharton 2005).

How are heritage professionals able to support the aspirations of the community in this process, and how can the aspirations of the specialist be matched with those of the community? These are complex questions (Brown 2009, 155). The approach may involve drawing on conservation documents, such as a condition assessment and statement of significance, but, in addition, is likely to develop locally appropriate ways of expressing a community's aspirations for the use and care of their cultural material. Community-led conservation presents a range of challenges for the conservation specialist (Garton-Smith 1997/1998; Johnson et al. 2005; Wharton 2008, 2012). However, such a collaborative approach has the potential to create a new set of theories and practices for an ethically informed conservation process, in which the conservator is able to mediate between the various actors in the process. For the conservator, a balance between "educating the local" and "doing it like the local" may be struck so that the philosophical underpinnings of conservation are "stretched" to incorporate the diverse needs of local communities – expanding the goals of conservation and associated working methods, rather than limiting them.

Individuals, social networks, or community groups may not consider it appropriate to become involved in such heritage projects. Indeed active participation relies on the formation of reciprocal relationships between those involved as hospitable hosts and grateful guests. The nature of participation defines the relationships of people to cultural heritage and with each other, as an artifact of the heritage conservation project. As a result community-led projects may not offer easy solutions, but there is the very real prospect of different, and, possibly, better ways of working. The benefits of this work need to be assessed in terms of their effect on the people involved as measured through broader concepts of social welfare and human happiness, and may also be seen to provide a new set of questions about the role of conservation in developing a more humane heritage (Butler 2006; Sully 2007).

Heritage conservation has the potential to act as a lens through which to understand the realities of people's lives and relationships with each other and the material world. As part of this conservation work, museum professionals are able to see the performance of culture through the material traces left behind in the making of the world around us. The conservation process is able to reveal this journey, not as a singular moment frozen in time, but as a perpetual narration of moments up to the present, thereby revealing the traces of past networks constructed by people left behind in the making of the world around them (Nancy 2007). Finally I would argue, in line with much recent social theory, that a peoples-based conservation better equips us to investigate the artifacts of conservation that are created in the associations, networks, and relationships of things including people (Latour 2005; Henare, Holbraad, and Wastell 2007, 3).

Conclusion

The focus of "traditional" conservation on the physical fabric of heritage objects produced a degree of autonomy for conservators which is compromised when their work is refocusing on cultural significance. It is clear that this refocusing cannot be achieved without a broad-based conversation with the diversity of people affected by the conservation of their heritage. As a result, heritage conservation is a complex and constantly developing field that addresses key questions such as what is heritage, how it is used and cared for, by whom and for whom (Sully 2007, 39). Conservation does not simply privilege the past over the present in a benign act of stewardship that seeks to prevent change occurring. Rather, it is a means of creating and recreating cultural heritage, which risks the destruction of potential alternative futures (English Heritage 2008; Avrami 2009, 183).

Understanding conservation as the "careful management of change" suggests there are some enduring values that can be deployed in decisions about how the present becomes the future. In mitigating the effects of the ceaseless and unrestricted change of our cultural environment, whether objects, buildings, or landscapes, heritage conservation selects certain elements of the present that can be preserved and made available in a future assessment of cultural values. The assessment of cultural value has been institutionalized through the concept of significance, developed from the Venice Charter in 1964, through the Burra Charter in 1979 (Australia ICOMOS 1999), to the Intangible Cultural Heritage Convention in 2003 (UNESCO 2003). Systematic significance assessments can be used to develop an integrated understanding of an object undergoing conservation, beyond just a description of physical properties of its materials, required to ensure that the object, as crystallized during a conservation intervention, adequately reflects the multifaceted plurality of an object's transition through time.

Interacting in a continuum of past and present, things and people are agents within social networks through which identity, power, and society are produced and reproduced (Clavir 2009, 139). The survival of an object's physical properties makes possible this material and social agency over time. Material culture has the power to engage and re-engage people with aspects of their cultural identity. That is the heart of the museum's role in society, to use museum collections for sustaining culture in contemporary communities (Kaminitz et al. 2009). As the value of cultural heritage is produced by and entangled within multiple interactions between objects and people, then current conservation practice should aim to enhance and expand these interactions rather than reduce or limit them. Despite concerns about the ability of the conservation process to adequately assess contemporary values, it should nevertheless maximize the potential of current populations to use cultural heritage for their own purposes. A conservation aim that seeks to maintain the ability of future peoples to utilize heritage, is undermined by the need to make assumptions about the future, in the present. There is no reason why a future imagined by heritage professionals will have any credibility with the people whose heritage they conserve (Durie 1998).

In my view, what is required are conservation principles, policies, and guidelines that help conservators to engage people in decisions about their heritage. This chapter has therefore critically assessed the utility of a conservation profession bound by frameworks of restrictive theory and practice that create conserved objects separated from the present and from the people who provide them with meaning. I have called for a redefinition of the outcomes of the conservation process, determined by the impact on people's lives, rather than any physical quality in the conserved object. This balancing act is not easy, as is clearly demonstrated through the well-known difficulties of adopting participatory processes while utilizing conventional heritage materials-based conservation procedures.

Heritage conservation is a fundamentally local act, intensely subjective and political, engaged in privileging certain ideas within heritage and removing others. Conservation can mediate between the actors in the process, give voice to multiple narratives, empower communities, and negotiate change. It can play a role in community building by reinforcing shared histories, cultivating collective identities, and providing a sense of belonging. Alternatively, it can exclude, define difference, and prevent rather than manage change (Avrami 2009). As I have demonstrated in this chapter, new concepts, frameworks, and approaches leave open the possibility of creative and diverse solutions within the theory and practice of contemporary heritage conservation. The role of conservation professionals in the future is less likely to be as experts prescribing certain actions, and more as facilitators enabling people to engage with their cultural heritage.

Notes

1   For example, see Kaminitz et al. 2009 for Native American Graves Protection and Repatriation Act 1990 and the Smithsonian's National Museum of the American Indian, and Hakiwai 2007 for the impact of the Treaty of Waitangi on the development of biculturalism at Te Papa and the Historic Places Trust in New Zealand.
2   For example, the collaborative conservation research to stabilize black-dyed decoration on woven flax, organized between Te Papa, Victoria University of Wellington and the British Museum, provides new ways to curate and care for Maori taonga (Harris et al. 2008; Smith et al. 2011).

References

Appelbaum, Barbara. 2007. *Conservation Treatment Methodology*. Oxford: Butterworth-Heinemann.

Ashley-Smith, Jonathan. 1999. *Risk Assessment for Object Conservation*. Oxford: Butterworth-Heinemann.

Ashley-Smith, Jonathan. 2009. "The Basis of Conservation Ethics." In *Conservation Principles: Dilemmas and Uncomfortable Truths*, edited by Alison Richmond and Alison Bracker, 6–24. Oxford: Butterworth-Heinemann.

Australia ICOMOS. 1999. "The Australia ICOMOS Charter for the Conservation of Places of Cultural Significance (the Burra Charter)." Adopted 1979, with revisions in 1981, 1988, and 1999. International Council for Monuments and Sites. Accessed October 25, 2014. http://australia.icomos.org/publications/charters.

Australian Heritage Commission. 2000. *Protecting Local Heritage Places: A Guide for Communities*. Canberra: Australian Heritage Commission.

Avrami, Erica. 2009. "Heritage Values, and Sustainability." In *Conservation Principles: Dilemmas and Uncomfortable Truths*, edited by Alison Richmond and Alison Bracker, 177–183. Oxford: Butterworth-Heinemann.

Avrami, Erica, Randall Mason, and Marta de La Torre. 2000. *Values and Heritage Conservation: Research Report*. Los Angeles: Getty Conservation Institute.

Bennett, Tony. 1995. *The Birth of the Museum: History, Theory, Politics*. London: Routledge.

Braillie, Brigit. 2009. "Living Heritage Handbook." Unpublished report. Living Heritage Sites Programme. New York: ICCROM.

Brown, Deidre. 2009. *Maori Architecture: From Fale to Wharenui and Beyond*. Auckland: Penguin.

Butler, Beverly. 2006. "Heritage and the Present Past." In *The Handbook of Material Culture*, edited by Chris Tilley, Webb Keane, Susanne Küchler, Mike Rowlands, and Patricia Spyer, 463–479. London: Sage.

Caple, Chris. 2000. *Conservation Skills: Judgement, Method and Decision Making*. London: Routledge.

Caple, Chris, ed. 2011. *Preventive Conservation in Museums*. London: Routledge.

Clavir, Miriam. 2002. *Preserving What Is Valued: Museums, Conservation, and First Nations*. Vancouver: University of British Columbia Press.

Clavir, Miriam. 2009 "Conservation and Cultural Significance." In *Conservation Principles: Dilemmas and Uncomfortable Truths*, edited by Alison Richmond and Alison Bracker, 139–149. Oxford: Butterworth-Heinemann.

Collections Council of Australia. 2009. *Significance 2.0: A Guide to Assessing the Significance of Collections*. Canberra: Collections Council.

Council of Europe. 2005. "Faro Convention on the Value of Cultural Heritage for Society." Accessed October 14, 2014. http://www.coe.int/t/dg4/cultureheritage/Resources/default_en.asp.

de La Torre, Marta, ed. 2002. *Assessing the Values of Cultural Heritage: Research Report*. Los Angeles: Getty Conservation Institute.

Denslagen, Wira. 2003. "The Artificial Life of Heritage." In *The Sulima Pagoda: East Meets West in the Restoration of a Nepalese Temple*, edited by Erich Theophile and Niels Gutschow, 95–102. Weatherhill, MN: Kathmandu Valley Preservation Trust.

Durie, Mason. 1998. *Te Mana Te Kawanatanga: The Politics of Maori Self-determination*. Auckland: Oxford University Press.

English Heritage. 2008. *Conservation Principles: Policies and Guidance for the Sustainable Management of the Historic Environment*. London: English Heritage.

Garton-Smith, Jennifer. 1997/1998. "Discourse Conflict in Relation to Conservation in Local Museums." *AICCM Bulletin* [Australian Institute of the Conservation of Cultural Material] 22 and 23: 6–15.

Gell, Alfred. 1998. *Art and Agency: Towards an Anthropological Theory*. Oxford: Clarendon.

Hakiwai, Arapata. 2007. "The Protection of Taonga and Maori Heritage in Aotearoa (New Zealand)." In *Decolonising Conservation: Caring for Maori Meeting Houses outside New Zealand*, edited by Dean Sully, 45–58. Walnut Creek, CA: Left Coast.

Harris, Warwick, Suzanne Scheele, Guy Forrester, Kahutoi Te Kanawa, Margaret Murray, and Edna Pahewa. 2008. "Varietal Differences and Environmental Effects on Fibre Extracted from Phormium Leaves and Prepared for Traditional Maori Weaving." *New Zealand Journal of Botany* 46(4): 401–423.

Henare, Amiria, Martin Holbraad, and Sari Wastell. 2007. "Introduction: Thinking through things." In *Thinking through Things: Theorising Artefacts Ethnographically*, edited by Amiria Henare, Martin Holbraad, and Sari Wastell, 1–31. London: Routledge.

Heritage Collections Council. 2001. "Significance: A Guide to Assessing the Significance of Cultural Heritage Objects and Collections." Accessed October 14, 2014. http://www.collectionsaustralia.net/sector_info_item/5.

Hodder, Ian. 1999. *The Archaeological Process: An Introduction*. Oxford: Blackwell.

Holtorf, Cornelius. 2001 "Is the Past a Non-Renewable Resource?" In *Destruction and Conservation of Cultural Property*, edited by Robert Layton, Peter G. Stone, and Julian Thomas, 286–297. London: Routledge.

Hooper-Greenhill, Eilean. 1989 "The Museum in the Disciplinary Society." In *Museum Studies in Material Culture*, edited by Susan Pearce, 61–72. London: Leicester University Press.

Hooper-Greenhill, Eilean. 2001 *Museums and the Interpretation of Visual Culture*. London: Routledge.

Hoskins, Janet. 1998. *Biographical Objects: How Things Tell the Stories of People's Lives*. London: Routledge.

ICOM-CC (International Council for Museums – Conservation Committee). 2008. "Terminology to Characterize the Conservation of Tangible Cultural Heritage." Accessed October 14, 2014. http://www.icom-cc.org/242/about-icom-cc/what-is-conservation.

ICOMOS (International Council on Monuments and Sites). 1964. "The Venice Charter: International Charter for the Conservation and Restoration of Monuments and Sites." Accessed October 15, 2014. http://www.icomos.org/charters/venice_e.pdf.

ICOMOS (International Council on Monuments and Sites). 1994. "The Nara Document on Authenticity." Accessed October 14, 2014. http://whc.unesco.org/archive/nara94.htm.

ICOMOS (International Council on Monuments and Sites). 2010. "New Zealand Charter for the Conservation of Places of Cultural Heritage Value" (Revised 2010). Accessed October 14, 2014. http://www.icomos.org/charters/ICOMOS_NZ_Charter_2010_FINAL_11_Oct_2010.pdf.

ICCROM (International Centre for the Study of the Conservation and Preservation of Cultural Property). 2012. "Promoting People-Centered Approaches to Conservation: Living Heritage." Accessed October 30, 2014. http://www.iccrom.org/ifrcdn/eng/prog_en/4people-centered-appr_en.shtml.

Johnson, Jessica, Susan Heald, Kelly McHugh, Elizabeth Brown, and Marian Kaminitz. 2005. "Practical Aspects of Consultation with Communities." *Journal of the American Institute for Conservation* 44(3): 203–215.

Jokilehto, Jukka. 2009. "Conservation Principles in the International Context." In *Conservation Principles: Dilemmas and Uncomfortable Truths*, edited by Alison Richmond and Alison Bracker, 73–83. Oxford: Butterworth-Heinemann.

Jones, Samuel, and John Holden. 2008. *It's a Material World: Caring for the Public Realm.* London: DEMOS.

Kaminitz, Marian A., W. Richard West, Jr., with contributions from Jim Enote, Curtis Quam, and Eileen Yatsattie. 2009. "Conservation, Access and Use in a Museum of Living Cultures." In *Conservation Principles: Dilemmas and Uncomfortable Truths*, edited by Alison Richmond and Alison Bracker, 197–209. Oxford: Butterworth-Heinemann.

Kemp, Jonathan. 2009. "Practical Ethics v2.0." In *Conservation Principles: Dilemmas and Uncomfortable Truths*, edited by Alison Richmond and Alison Bracker, 63–72. Oxford: Butterworth-Heinemann.

Kerr, John Semple. 1996. *The Conservation Plan: A Guide to the Preparation of Conservation Plans for Places of European Cultural Significance.* Sydney: National Trust of New South Wales.

Kreps, Christina. 2003. *Liberating Culture: Cross-Cultural Perspectives on Museums, Curation, and Heritage Preservation.* London: Routledge.

Latour, Bruno. 2005. *Reassembling the Social: An Introduction to Actor-Network-Theory.* Oxford: Oxford University Press.

Lowenthal, David. 1985. *The Past Is a Foreign Country.* Cambridge: Cambridge University Press.

Muñoz-Vinas, Salvador. 2005. *Contemporary Theory of Conservation.* Oxford: Elsevier Butterworth-Heinemann.

Muñoz-Vinas, Salvador. 2009. "Minimal intervention Revisited." In *Conservation Principles: Dilemmas and Uncomfortable Truths*, edited by Alison Richmond and Alison Bracker, 47–59. Oxford: Butterworth-Heinemann.

Nancy, Jean-Luc. 2007. *The Creation of the World or Globalization*. Albany, NY: State University of New York Press.

Pearce, Susan. 1990. *Objects of Knowledge*. London: Athlone.

Pearson, Michael, and Sharon Sullivan. 1995. *Looking after Heritage Places: The Basics of Heritage Planning for Managers, Landowners and Administrators*. Melbourne: Melbourne University Press.

Pye, Elizabeth. 2001. *Caring for the Past: Issues in Conservation for Archaeology and Museums*. London: James and James.

Pye, Elizabeth, and Dean Sully. 2007. "Evolving Challenges, Developing Skills." *The Conservator* 30: 19–38.

Richmond, Alison, and Alison Bracker. 2009. *Conservation Principles, Dilemmas and Uncomfortable Truths*. Oxford: Butterworth-Heinemann.

Sease, Catherine. 1998. "Codes of Ethics for Conservation." *Journal of Cultural Property* 7(1): 98–115.

Shelton, Anthony. 2006. "Museums and Anthropologies: Practices and Narratives." In *A Companion to Museum Studies*, edited by Sharon Macdonald, 64–80. Oxford: Blackwell.

Smith, G. J., Y. Tang, J. M. Dyer, and S. M. Scheele. 2011. "Coumarins in Phormium (New Zealand Flax) Fibers: Their Role in Fluorescence and Photodegradation." *Photochemistry and Photobiology* 87(1): 45–50.

Smith, Laurajane. 2006. *Uses of Heritage*. London: Routledge.

Staniforth, Sarah. 2006. "Conservation: Principles, Practice and Ethics." In *National Trust Manual of Housekeeping: The Care of Collections in Historic Houses Open to the Public*. Amsterdam: Elsevier.

Stovel, Herb, Nicholas Stanley-Price, and Robert Killick, eds. 2005. *Conservation of Living Religious Heritage*. Rome: ICCROM.

Sully, Dean, ed. 2007. *Decolonising Conservation: Caring for Maori Meeting Houses Outside New Zealand*. Walnut Creek, CA: Left Coast.

Szczepanowska, Hanna M. 2013. *Conservation of Cultural Heritage: Key Principles and Approaches*. London: Routledge.

Ucko, Peter J. 2001. "'Heritage' and 'Indigenous Peoples in the 21st Century." *Public Archaeology* 1(4): 227–238.

United Nations Economic, Scientific, and Cultural Organization (UNESCO). 1972. *Convention Concerning the Protection of the World Cultural and Natural Heritage*. Paris: UNESCO. Accessed October 14, 2014. http://whc.unesco.org/en/conventiontext.

United Nations Economic, Scientific, and Cultural Organization (UNESCO). 2003. *Convention for the Safeguarding of the Intangible Cultural Heritage*. Paris: UNESCO. Accessed October 14, 2014. www.unesco.org/culture/intangible-heritage.

Varoli-Piazza, Rosalia, ed. 2007. "Sharing Conservation Decisions. Lessons Learnt from an ICCROM course." Accessed October 30, 2014. http://www.iccrom.org/ifrcdn/pdf/ICCROM_15_SharingConservDecisions-lt_en.pdf.

Vergo, Peter. 1989. "The Reticent Object." In *The New Museology*, edited by Peter Vergo, 41–59. London: Reaktion.

Wharton, Glen. 2005. "Indigenous Claims and Heritage Conservation: An Opportunity for Critical Dialogue." *Public Archaeology* 4(3): 199–204.

Wharton, Glen. 2008. "Dynamics of Participatory Conservation: The Kamehameha I Sculpture Project." *Journal of the American Institute for Conservation* 47: 159–173.

Wharton, Glen. 2012. *The Painted King: Art, Activism, and Authenticity in Hawai'i.* Honolulu: University of Hawai'i Press.

Wijesuriya, Gamini. 2007. "Conserving Living Taonga: The Concept of Continuity." In *Decolonising Conservation: Caring for Maori Meeting Houses outside New Zealand,* edited by Dean Sully, 59–70. Walnut Creek, CA: Left Coast.

Wright, Patrick. 1985. *On Living in an Old Country: The National Past in Contemporary Britain.* Oxford: Oxford University Press.

Further Reading

English Heritage. 2000. *Power of Place: The Future of the Historic Environment.* London: English Heritage/Department for Culture, Media, and Sport and the Department of the Environment, Transport, and the Regions.

Getty Conservation Institute. 1931. "Charter of Athens." Accessed October 14, 2014. http://www.getty.edu/conservation/publications_resources/research_resources/charters/charter04.html.

Szczepanowska, Hanna M. 2013. *Conservation of Cultural Heritage: Key Principles and Approaches.* London and New York: Routledge.

Wijesuriya, Gamini, Kazuhiko Nishi, and Joe King. 2006. "Living Heritage Sites Workshop: Empowering the Community." *ICCROM Newsletter* 32: 18.

Dean Sully is a Lecturer in Conservation at University College London, Institute of Archaeology, where he coordinates the MSc in Conservation for Archaeology and Museums. He joined UCL in 2000, after studying Conservation at UCL, and working as a Conservator for the National Heritage Board (Singapore), the Museum of London, the British Museum, and Monmouthshire District Council Museum's Service. Since 2001, as the National Trust's Conservation Advisor for Archaeological Artefacts, he has been involved with the conservation of *Hinemihi,* the Māori meeting house at Clandon Park, UK. This led to the publication of *Decolonising Conservation* in 2007, and the development of a peoples-based approach to heritage conservation.

PART III

Processes

14 FROM CARING TO CREATING
Curators Change Their Spots

Ken Arnold[1]

Curating: We'd better be careful about this one.

Fox and Higgie 2011, 158

I embark on this chapter fearing that there might not be very much original left to say. My extensive bibliography indicates just how much comment, some of it very insightful, has already been focused on my subject. It is, maybe, a feeling increasingly familiar to many, reflecting a broad cultural predicament. The easy, thoughtlessly easy, availability of so many ideas, so much comment, and the ever-burgeoning amounts of raw information – the plethora of essays, documents, pictures, films, interviews, as well as the over-abundance of undigested data – has brought us to a moment when the very notion of originality sometimes seems difficult to sustain.

It is the job of a considerable swathe of cultural workers to make sure all this material is available, as well as to track down and store yet more of it. They toil to maintain websites, databases, libraries, and museum collections. Until recently these cultural workers were broadly referred to as curators: people who gathered things and kept them safe. And we owe them much for their efforts to hold and make accessible large parts of our history, heritage, and culture; but fundamentally they do little to contribute anything culturally new. There are, however, others from broadly the same calling whose activities are, instead, undertaken precisely in an attempt to open up original ideas, by reassembling and sharing in public bits of our existing cultural landscape. These folk forage for, look at, and choose pre-existing things and then settle on refreshing and innovative ways of knitting them together. They too tend to be referred to as curators. At their best, they manage to stimulate human curiosity by activating or maybe just releasing an innate desire for self-discovery and fulfillment. It seems to me that curators have increasingly emerged as some of our most significant cultural leaders: impresarios with an acute ability to make relevant the dizzying world of stuff around us.

The International Handbooks of Museum Studies: Museum Practice, First Edition.
Edited by Conal McCarthy.
© 2015 John Wiley & Sons Ltd. Published 2020 by John Wiley & Sons Ltd.

This type of active and productive curatorship is now almost ubiquitous – it happens on the radio, behind the camera, in clubs, on stage, even in the kitchen and bedroom. But the notion of the museum is still essential to the definition of what curators do, providing the ultimate shibboleth for the term. Not for the first time in their history, however, museums are undergoing vast changes, taking up new social, cultural, and technological challenges. "The museum," James Clifford reminds us, "is an inventive, globally and locally *translated* form, no longer anchored to its modern origins in Europe" (Clifford 2010, emphasis original). And as a consequence, what professionals do in museums is being stretched, tested, and questioned. Curators are, it seems to me, set to continue their institution-defining role at the heart of museums and galleries; but what they do is likely to carry on altering and spreading. This then is a timely moment to explore the evolving nature of that job.

Museums on the move

Since the middle of the last century, the museum sector has proliferated from a limited range of traditional institutions to a great diversity of organizations (Boylan 2006), some having largely reinvented what it means to be a museum; others have more or less left the term behind as barely relevant to what they do. In a number of countries, the past couple of decades have witnessed something of a golden age for museums, with many reaching historic levels of popularity. In the United Kingdom, for example, government figures indicate that almost 50 percent of adults visited at least one museum in 2009, resulting in about 100 million visits to museums across the country (Schubert 2009, 9).[2] Each year has seen both the opening of brand new museums and the enhanced relaunching of others, across private, corporate, charitable, voluntary, and, especially, public sectors. This upturn in the fortunes of museums has coincided with the diversification of their shape and form, their mission, their content, as well as their look and feel. It is an irony of the museum mission that in order to continue to fulfill their role of preserving the material world around them they need continually to be updated, altered, and even reinvented. William Flower, the first Director of the Natural History Museum, pointed out that a museum was like "a living organism" requiring continual and tender care. Far from oases of calm in an ever-evolving world, then, they too are blown about by the storms of political, technological, and cultural shifts (Fowler 1972, 13; Schubert 2009, 11).

Furthermore, changes in museums come about from within as much as without. The so-called "new museology" that has swept the museum sector over the past quarter century has attracted new audiences with new attitudes and has displaced traditional methods of presentation; even more generally it has led to the idea of museums and galleries as the source of lively debate relevant to more than just those who work in them and a few passionate experts. Museums and galleries have never been more culturally significant and what happens in them has an increasingly widespread influence (Vergo 1989).

To get a handle on just what curators are doing these days, and why that matters, it is important initially to sketch out the recent developments affecting their institutional homes. Five specific aspects of change in museums and galleries suggest themselves for closer inspection: their physical space and place, how their collections are kept and displayed, the role of research and scholarship within them, the impact of new media, and finally their audiences: who the visitors are and the experiences they have.

Spaces and places

The past quarter century of building work in museums and galleries has reflected a self-conscious reconsideration of the core dilemma about whether museums are primarily about their collections or their visitors. Spaciously inviting and dramatically welcoming entrances and lobbies; architectural schemes envisaged primarily in terms of audience experience, visualized through virtual "fly-through" videos; the increasing footprint occupied by shops and cafes as well as marketing hoardings highlighting sponsorship partners; anxiously thought through way-finding systems; and an evangelistic insistence on lightness and brightness: these and other familiar tropes of consultations with architects, stakeholders, planners, and designers embody the dramatic conversion of the dominant place and space occupied by museums.

And when a new building is being considered rather than just an old one remodeled, it is increasingly assumed that the project will be led by a "star architect," anointed with considerable powers to make an uplifting visual experience, irrespective of the demands of the content, or indeed the potential future practical challenges that their audacious schemes might throw up. At the heart of this habit lurks the assumption that the museum building can itself become an institution's biggest and brightest exhibit: a public draw in its own right that not infrequently is captured in a silhouetted logotype. It is increasingly anticipated that these buildings will somehow deliver an emotional and even spiritual impact, an expectation that has led some to suggest that we are more and more looking to museums and galleries to perform a role within the built environment that previously was reserved for churches. Galleries then have been reinvented as places for secularized and humanized worship.

Inside the museum, beyond the entrance and foyer, the spaces in which displays and exhibitions are laid out have also been subject to much experimentation and theorization. Black boxes or white cubes, experimental laboratories, studios for active contemplation and creativity, domesticated interiors or theatrical backdrops: the informative and indeed performative role of these spaces has also been increasingly debated and deliberated. Often parceled up as outsourced contracts offered to professional experts, this aspect of the museum has become almost as important an ingredient in their planning as the exhibition content itself.

Such considerations are increasingly brought into play because of another shift in how museums use their spaces, namely a change from the notion that they function predominantly as a series of permanent galleries showcasing relatively unchanging displays, with a small space tacked on at the end for temporary displays; to a very different model based instead on constant refreshment and evolution, in which time-limited projects (exhibitions and events) are foregrounded. In the museum, rather than contemporary art world, the former model was virtually ubiquitous up until the 1970s, when major institutions started hosting big exhibitions and thereby adopting a more dynamic public image (Schubert 2009, 168). From that time on specific shows have had the potential to produce pivotal moments in an institution's history – blockbusters that focus publicity on a museum (the British Museum's 1972 Tutankhamen exhibition for example), or unexpected projects that reinvigorate an institution's reputation (such as Banksy's 2009 show at the Bristol City Museum); except, of course, when damaging contro-versy results instead (as with the Smithsonian's 1995 *Science in American Life* show). Whether displayed in permanent or temporary projects, the museum's artifacts are the same *things*; but somehow conceptually they assume a different presence within each. In the latter case, because the exhibits have been more recently handled and cared for, they seem almost more deserving of careful and inquisitive inspection. This eagerness to keep things alert and on the move – cleaned, conserved, re-analyzed, and re-curated – has gradually influenced the approach to permanent displays too, with corners and cases being changed and augmented more frequently.

After an era of new building projects, refashioned entrances, and glazed-in courtyards; and of exhibition spaces designed with an ever-greater focus on temporary programs – the temptation has been increasingly to focus on an institu-tion's architectural profile and the effectiveness of its program and somewhat less with their collections. But this concentration on the spaces in museums, reconsidered as sets of conceptual surfaces and volumes amenable to curatorial decision-making, has, in fact, gone hand in hand with shifting attitudes to the collections themselves.

Collections and exhibitions

Museums were once synonymous with their collections – conceptually, the permanent display *was* the museum, with rather little kept off display in storage ("in reserve"). And the curator's job was essentially to keep it safe, in reasonable repair, and, in theory at least, accessible. The idea of distinguishing between "study" and "public" collections – "typical" and "index" collections as some termed them – was already one that William H. Flower adopted in South Kensington at the end of the nineteenth century, with the former being aimed more at the general public and the latter at specialists and experts. This established distinction has evolved dramatically in the past decade or two, with permanent collections increasingly being viewed as a resource: a pool of things with meaning kept at the ready for use in loans and temporary displays or as an asset awaiting the financial wherewithal to be "digitized" and added to an online database.

It is no longer enough for museums just to keep precious and important things. The core asset of a museum – its collections – must, we increasingly insist, continually be of use. At rest, they begin to loom as inert drains on valuable resources, things that are expensive "to keep alive" and which, as stakeholders and investors increasingly assert, must be captured in some "outcome." Consequently, we have become increasingly embarrassed about objects that are held in storage, especially those that have not been used or shown or studied for significant periods. In museum terms, the invisible is dead, simply waiting to be buried.

But in this frenzy to make museums ceaselessly efficient, with their assets perpetually "paying their way," we run the risk of forgetting just how potent is the notion of museums affording opportunities for *rediscovery* after periods of benign inattention, and just how much the richness of "meaning" that adheres to important museum objects needs to be quietly and slowly left to ferment while at rest, often very much *out* of the public gaze. We need to be rather bolder about the fact that part of a museum's role is in fact, carefully to keep things out of sight, while not being hidden, so that they can be rediscovered and re-investigated. Without this, the whole routine of temporary exhibitions runs the risk of losing its potential to surprise and transfix – the daring, magic, and indeed delicious danger they have in exposing secrets.

Research and scholarship

In the "new museology," where much emphasis is placed on exhibitions, interpretation, and the visitor experience, the traditional and unquestioned values associated with connoisseurship and expertise have started to slip. The latest interpretation has come to be favored over and above the timeless factual information once inextricably associated with museum collections. The unchanging objects are seen as more loosely tied to a contingent understanding, one frequently up for grabs, swayed by insights from outside as well as within the institution. By no means embraced by all, these shifts have seen the erosion, if not permanent displacement, of the idea of specialist scholar-curators with independence delighting in, though not always sharing, their knowledge of what they keep. In the new museum, they find themselves instead as workers in an exhibition and display industry whose administrative and interpretive roles are mixed with that of others applying different professional skills far removed from traditional scholarship (Schubert 2009, 175).

For some, this shift from the traditional "keeping" of objects to an increasing emphasis on contributions to the creation of public spectacle has been decried as the beginning of the end for museums – a transformation orchestrated, they fear, by measurable "outcome-led" objectives that have squeezed out any time for genuine scholarship. Certainly, the nineteenth-century epistemological assumption that significant chunks of knowledge could be fashioned from the close analysis of classified collections has almost entirely been eclipsed by the competing idea of university-based research conducted in libraries, studies, laboratories, and on field trips (Conn 1998). More recently still, even this focus on academia as the likeliest source of new thinking has begun to give way to much more diversified online sources of knowledge, minted in digitized forms, produced in commercial contexts or indeed by lone individuals at their laptops. In the wake of these shifts, the types of job that people do in museums have changed significantly. In short, museums employ fewer natural historians, art connoisseurs, anthropologists, and other traditional subject specialists, and those who do hold on to that type of job are expected to devote increasing amounts of time to engaging with the public, raising money, and evaluating their effectiveness. What has almost entirely been eclipsed is the idea of a museum naturally being run by and for people whose time is devoted to researching collections (Conn 2010).

It is too easy, however, to indulge in an apocalyptic extrapolation from these changes, and effectively conclude that the traditional notion of a museum is doomed. For while it is undeniable that museum staff now have fewer scholar-hours to devote to their collections, much of their effort has simultaneously been applied to the question of how to provide multiple points of access to the collections. The advent of initiatives such as visiting scholar programs, students' rooms, visible storage, digitized collections within the context of social media, and handling collections all reflect an increasing eagerness to enable all sorts of access to collections by all sorts of people. It is too early to say whether the net result of all this emphasis on opening up access to objects, offset against the reduction of time devoted to them by museum experts, has increased or reduced the amount of interested investigative attention being focused on collections.

What has undeniably changed are the types of people that one expects to find examining a museum's holdings and why. Another unambiguous and linked trend is the inexorable ascendency of interdisciplinary research, of historians of science, for example, turning their attention to paintings and sculpture, and in the opposite direction, of design students concerning themselves with technological artifacts and maybe anthropologists turning to both. Here too, it would be premature to speculate about what will be the lasting legacy of this new investigative approach on the knowledge we have of museum displays and stores.

New and social media

One aspect of museological change that figures as both a category on its own and as an influence on all the others is the universal adoption of digital technology in general and new media in particular. Their impact is evident everywhere in museums from their spaces and collections, to exhibitions and scholarly activity, and on every activity undertaken in them from how curators spend their time to visitors' behavior. The virtual translation of old-fashioned reality, coupled with online investigation, communication, and interaction, now envelopes the entire experience of being in a gallery or museum.

Much thinking in and about museums has recently focused on the core institutional question of how they can best exploit the web in general and new social media in particular. As bastions of a particular part of established non-digital culture, it is not surprising that museums and galleries have also been trying to work out how much, but also just *how*, they can take additional responsibility for the newer less tangible culture that exists in computer-land. What are the implications of museums "digitizing" their collections? And can their efforts to embrace and exploit Facebook, Twitter, apps, and so forth promise a genuine democratization of museums, opening them up to anyone who wants to have their say? More pessimistic inquirers into these issues question what unique value will remain for museums as their contents become increasingly accessible to anyone, anywhere with access to a keyboard and screen, and whether galleries can do more than use a "dumbed-down" version of their significance belatedly to mimic radically socialized media that are essentially "happening elsewhere" (Henning 2006).

A particular focus of this dilemma has concerned the need within museums to colonize virtual space with digitized museum content. Actually, what mostly is meant by digitizing museum collections boils down to the production of an image, some accompanying catalog records and, if something has been on show, an interpretive label; plus, increasingly, indications of how many people have "liked" any associated comments and postings. Little wonder that many museum websites receive relatively modest traffic, with the bulk of those virtual audiences who do "click through" simply searching for information to help them visit the real space. The impact of museums, galleries, and indeed art via the internet has, to date, been muted, seemingly only able to play a semi-convincing game of catch up with the way computer technology has radically changed how we shop, chat, watch and listen, play, find, and check. Maybe Lauren Cornell is on to something when she suggests that art and the internet are somehow axiomatically polarized because "the art world is vertical whereas the web is horizontal," the latter thinning and spreading our attention, the former tending to do the opposite (Cornell 2011, 173).

Nevertheless, this idea of putting museums "online" has, for some at least, opened up innovative and exciting speculations about the potential long-term evolution of museum culture. In the world of art, for example, some boosters have wondered if museums could become significant nodes, as it were, for marshalling the emerging capabilities of new media to enable radical engagement with the body, space, and time (Cook 2003, 173–174). A more experiential approach to what museums and galleries might offer is envisaged here. And some even detect a revolutionary shift in the defining characteristics of museums, from a traditional notion of a place where collections are registered, selected, and presented within a narrative context determined by curators, to a very different paradigm where a gallery instead "catalyzes experiences" in more fluid models of production and reception, resembling instead laboratories, theatres, and even open-source software.

In this audaciously rethought version of museums (Graham and Cook 2010), digitized renditions of existing exhibits are added to by virtually limitless other new media "objects," which are then opened up in quantities previously unimaginable and to far wider audiences. Exhibitions too, we are invited to imagine, need boldly to be reconsidered, becoming more like interfaces and interactive tools than static showcases, personalized windows through with visitors can access material identified according to their own personalized preferences: "other visitors who chose that object were also interested in." The automated searching capabilities and the depth of computerized database structures promise a realm in which individual exhibition elements are freed from any particular meaning or significance prescribed for them by a "narrator," with visitors' access to collections no longer being constrained by the gate-keeping powers of curators. In this version of the "future of museums" innovations in applying new media have, eventually, the potential to make curators of all visitors (Cook 2003, 309).

For some, particularly those still troubled by the implied imbalance of expertise and power inherent in even the most "forward thinking" of new museums, this exponentially "opened-up" online museum represents a bold step in the direction of genuine cultural democratization. What remains to be seen, however, is how many potential visitors there are waiting to engage with this approach to museum and exhibition making. Personally, I wonder if this DIY version of putting on a show might just seem like too much hard work with too many degrees of freedom for people who rather like the more ready-made experience of pitching up at the entrance of a museum. It is also a fairly open question as to whether this radical technologically driven revision ends up representing a museum or gallery in a meaningful way at all. Many of these ideas can seem like an abstract redescription of what is already happening online in any case, without much tangible grounding in the routines of museums or galleries, or involvement of curatorial staff (Cook 2003).

Interestingly, an increasing impact of these cumulative virtual opportunities has been to encourage at least some museums and galleries to rediscover what it is that they uniquely offer. Seemingly just in the nick of time, we have realized that a rare pleasure and value can still be derived from visiting designated physical spaces, where the otherwise ubiquitously available virtual alternatives can, mercifully if briefly, be left behind at the front door. And, concomitantly, we have reminded ourselves that an inspirational and even spiritually uplifting experience can be conjured up by encountering "special" things in these places. Ultimately, many people still seem enthusiastically to seek out these relaxed, safe, and enclosed parts of the public domain where they can, in the company of other people seemingly enjoying the same basic experience, self-consciously apply an open frame of mind to a carefully pre-selected array of things that are real (often unique), precious, beautiful, meaningful, and important.

Audiences and evaluation

It is unimaginable these days that any self-respecting museum director could not, when asked, recite an account of her or his institution's audience profile – how many people visit and from where, what sorts of folk they are, what informs their choice to come, what their average dwell- or stay-time is, what kind of experience they enjoy, what their favorite bits are, and how much money they spend in the shop and café. Counting everything about our visitors is now a mandatory part of running a museum.

From the 1980s onward the core debate in and about museums concerned whether collections or visitors sat at the heart of their mission. The debate has now largely moved on, leaving behind a rather unsurprising conclusion, if one was ever reached, that it is precisely the perpetual negotiations between these two perspectives that defines these institutions. Arguably, science centers and some heritage venues have shown that it is possible to flourish with almost no regard for collections, or at least with an alternative primary concern with the "full experience"; while at the opposite end of the spectrum, some university museums continue to keep intact important, often unique collections, that are nonetheless only rather infrequently visited. More generally, the lasting momentum from this, occasionally heated, conversation has tilted in the direction of making sure that audiences are considered alongside other longer-standing concerns with objects, taxonomic research, display, and the like.

A significant number of interesting insights have been gained through the finer grained analysis of what happens (on a sociological, psychological, and even cognitive/neurological level) to people as they walk at an unnaturally slow pace around constrained spaces with the expectation of finding and experiencing things that might affect or even change their worldview. Few solid conclusions have yet emerged beyond some rather banal generalizations about things we already knew; but key questions posed about what happens in museums and how we can learn to make them more effective have been greatly sharpened. How should museums cope with the range of types of attention and learning-styles visitors are prepared to invest in museum visits? How directed or open should be the experiences offered? How long should we envisage visitors spending with each exhibit and cumulatively in each gallery and ultimately in the whole institution? How much information should be imparted, at what stage and in what form? How should that be mixed with opportunities instead to derive meaning and feeling from what's on show? How can curators accommodate all the different "starting points" that visitors arrive with? Are value-neutral shows possible or desirable? And so on.

The increasing focus on visitors and their active role in museums has also had a significant influence in operational terms. Larger and larger proportions of staff time and budgets are now devoted to communications and marketing, a type of activity inconceivable in earlier eras of museum management. While its most obvious manifestation has been the ubiquitous application of monitoring and evaluation techniques: up stream, front end, audience segmentation, qualitative and quantitative, exit poles, audience advocates, access criteria, target groups, secret shoppers, key performance indicators, and so forth. No museum or gallery can afford to ignore the thinking embedded in these ways of operating and their underlying vocabulary; while in some institutions, it has become inconceivable for any exhibition to be planned, any initiative conceived, almost any dollar spent without first attempting to find out what the potential audience response and impact will be.

Many museums have then fully signed up to a vox-pop culture that has, arguably, championed the known, safe and mediocre, over and above the innovative, bold and risky. The mantra of evidence-based activity and strategically driven initiatives has, maybe, emasculated the opportunities to be brave and authentic and to do things just because they have integrity and seem to be worth doing in themselves. Actually, such harsh words might well have fewer and fewer genuine targets, for there is an increasing realization that projects over-reliant on this type of second-guessing homework frequently fail to deliver to their own criteria of success; that visitors often do *not* really know how they might respond for real to hypothetical projects and experiences presented out of context; indeed, that sometimes they react most profoundly to precisely that which could *not* have been previewed and discussed in a focus group. It seems that many of us do not know what we like until we like it. It is not that knowing audiences, their tastes, and likely reactions is not an important ingredient in museum work; but that such knowledge can only, at best, provide an informed background against which the job of curating a good show or initiating a good project has still to be undertaken for its own sake. It turns out that a fail-safe recipe for a great new gallery or exhibition simply cannot be derived from any amount of museological research, no matter how sophisticated, and that the best curators are not necessarily the most audience focused.

New curatorship

Eternally in some state of flux, museums and galleries seem currently to be experiencing a particularly significant set of changes, ones which cumulatively are transforming the central role of curators. The evolution and proliferation of their job descriptions has, of course, just as much been shaped by their own instincts for innovation as by institutional and external factors. And while there are still a considerable number of people who call themselves "curators" doing a range of activities that their forebears would have easily recognized, a significant proportion of others are not.

In earlier centuries, wealthy collectors hired scholar-curators to care for their private museums, and expected them to focus on object-centered activities.

Non-professional support staff took care of anything and everything else that needed doing (Boylan 2006, 418–20). Throughout the twentieth century, as museums increasingly evolved into thoroughly public institutions, the variety of jobs done within them expanded to include education, conservation, management, fund raising, and marketing. Against this backdrop of spreading competences, the types of roles defined within museums diversified; and, as a consequence, the object-centered elements of a curator's role shrank proportionately. Directors of museums, who had pretty much always risen through curatorial ranks, started to emerge from other parts of a museum's workforce, and indeed outside the sector altogether. Initially in the art world, and particularly in association with the part of it that adopted the moniker "contemporary," professional museum curators saw packages of their job bundled up and contracted out to independent external figures: "guest curators." This increasingly significant band of freelancers operated as semi-detached adjuncts to institutions, paid to do time-limited, projects that often flirted with unexpected and improbable outcomes. And in other cast-breaking museum-like institutions – heritage and science centers – the term curator was often eschewed altogether, with labels like "exhibit developer," "audience advocate," "explainer," and "work-stream managers" being adopted instead.

Not surprisingly, many more traditionally minded curators have witnessed with alarm and disquiet the gradual erosion of their former status. The training offered to succeeding generations has tried to realign expectations amongst would-be curators; but it has, arguably, not quite caught up with the new business-oriented, project-centered contractual culture of the contemporary workplace. Cumulatively, the curatorial professions have become less certain of what they are expected to do, and, more challengingly yet, not always sure that it is still needed (O'Neill 2007b). Amongst the proliferation of roles that are now undertaken, specialists make choices between them, while generalists (often in smaller museums) adopt tailored variations of a hybrid job that adds to their traditional work as guardians of heritage, aspects of social work and political advocacy; entertainment and cultural trendsetting; and public investigation. In the rest of this chapter I will explore these emergent curatorial roles.

Before surveying recent curatorial innovations, it is worth reminding ourselves of the role's earliest history. Etymologically, as David Levi Strauss tells us, the title of curator originated in the Roman Empire, where it was "given to officials in charge of various departments of public works: sanitation, transportation, policing" (2007, 12). Kate Fowle (2007) finds a later version of the role in the medieval church, by which time a "caring" aspect had been added, with curators now particularly overseeing minors and lunatics. The implied migration of the role into the territory of medicine as well as the church left a lasting mark. Ever since, the practice of curators has fundamentally been split between the management of public works and the spiritual oversight of souls. And as Levi Strauss further puts it, "curators have always been a curious mixture of bureaucrat and priest," commanding, controlling, caring for and even curing certain aspects of culture. In

England, it was in the middle of the seventeenth century that the word began to be applied to the pioneer individuals who were given charge of various new cultural premises: libraries, menageries, botanical gardens, and museums (Fowle 2007; Levi Strauss 2007, 12).

As the role became professionalized, the definition of curatorship was inevitably increasingly codified, with a focus on the more technical aspects of collections care coming to the fore – valuation, acquisition, research, conservation, presentation, and interpretation. A range of national bodies, and then from the middle of the twentieth century the international agency ICOM, set about analyzing, defining, and then monitoring the professional calling of curators. Given the political and social inclinations of such bodies, it is not surprising that increasing emphasis was placed on the public service aspects of museums.[3] Core social and spiritual values of the curatorial role have endured, but modern curators have also developed an appetite for experimental, discursive, investigative, creative, collaborative, performative, as well as politically engaged work. Keepers (a job title with less and less currency except perhaps in zoos) have had to become more vigorous in their pursuits as political activists, artistic directors, and public investigators.

Curators as political activists

In many ways, the most radically different aspect of curating to have emerged in the past half century is highlighted in the political, social, and ethical judgments that are now invariably applied to their work. The question of how the power associated with collections, exhibitions, and museums should be distributed and exercised has generated more debate than any other single issue in contemporary museology. These "recent" trends, it turns out, have much older antecedents – a pre-history of sorts. For the tradition of curatorial undertakings (even when rather narrowly and technically applied) has been active in many indigenous cultures for a considerable time. To take just one example in New Zealand, Māori curatorial work in modern and contemporary art has been practiced since the postwar period, with the first significant exhibition to bring this work to the fore occurring in June 1958 (Mané-Wheoki 2010). In common with a range of "early" indigenous art projects, the focus of these enterprises was very much the home-grown heritage of indigenous curators who consequently found themselves leading something of a collectivist community practice (Ames and McKenzie 1996).

One of the most probing academic voices to emerge out of debates about the politics of curation (particularly in indigenous/settler contexts) is that of anthropologist James Clifford, whose insights are most tellingly captured in his 1997 essay "Museums as Contact Zones." His conceptual questions initially occurred to him during a consultative meeting with some Native Americans (the Tlingit) held in 1989 at Portland Art Museum. During the session, he was especially struck by the fact that the museum objects (which he had imagined might be a source of ill-feeling) were rather less the focus of direct attention than symbols employed "as *aides-memoires*, occasions for the telling of stories and the singing of songs." Adopting a term originally coined by the geographer Mary Louise Pratt, Clifford posited the notion that museums could in fact be conceived as *contact zones*: "the space of colonial encounters, ... in which people geographically and historically separated come into contact with each other and establish ongoing relations, usually involving conditions of coercion, radical inequality, and intractable conflict" (Clifford 1997, 189, 192).

The idea has, largely, stuck; and indeed has gradually become almost axiomatic in curatorial-speak. More than just the obvious manner in which any collaborative enterprise produces contact that requires negotiation, his specific insights focused on the political idea that "Contact work in a museum, ... goes beyond" "educating and edifying a public," "beyond... consultation and sensitivity, ... It becomes active collaboration and a sharing of authority." "All sites of collection," he went on, "begin to seem like places of encounter and passage." So that "more than ever before, curators reckon with the fact that the objects and interpretations they display 'belong' to others as well as to the museum." Curatorial practices emerge from this analysis as "a newly complicated and relational task." Focusing particularly on curating indigenous/native/first nations projects, Clifford insists that the ways in which they advise on, and often manage, decisions about "what to save and what to lose, what to remember and what to tell, what gets performed and what stays off-stage" are invariably *political* ones. There is, he wants us to acknowledge, no getting away from the "politics of curating" (Clifford 2010).

Clifford and the generation of curators whose work has focused on sometimes incendiary issues of identity politics have both highlighted and been caught up in the massive socioeconomic and cultural tides associated first with decolonization and then globalization. It is difficult to overestimate the impact that this politicized thinking has had on museums, especially those primarily concerned with anthropology and ethnology, and most acutely of all those in North America, Australasia, and other post-colonial regions. In questioning and redefining curatorial practice in terms of customary "native" notions of knowledge, partnership, and spiritual care, indigenous ideas have both gained a strong foothold in many very important institutions, and additionally have influenced many broader debates about curatorship, no matter what the disciplinary context (Kreps 2003, 2006).

The Museum of Anthropology (MOA) in Vancouver is just one amongst dozens of institutions affected by these realigned assumptions. As is almost universally the case in museums of ethnography and anthropology, it has become inconceivable for the institution to embark on a new project without trying, as thoroughly as possible, to think through its politics beforehand. The literature of museums studies is, by now, well populated with sorry tales of what can go wrong, sometimes badly wrong, if such considerations are naively overlooked. A key role for an institution like MOA (one explicitly captured in its "mission" that speaks of building and sustaining "relationships with diverse communities by encouraging their active engagement and honouring their contributions to our shared society") is to function as a forum in which first nation peoples can represent themselves (Museum of Anthropology 2012). The core question for these museums is one of who should represent whom, and for whom. In this new paradigm, research projects tend consequently to be formed in terms of participant action, with a vital imperative being to involve multiple voices reflecting diverse viewpoints, while (arguably) still crafting some sort of coherent curatorial narrative. Caught on the back foot, some curators have wondered about, and indeed given up on, their once-taken-for-granted responsibility for assuming some sort of authority (Schildkrout 2004; Shelton 2006).

At its most radical, this perspective has sought to explode any certainty about what might constitute an artifact, an exhibition, a museum, a key stakeholder, or indeed a curator, leaving some to despair of ever making this cultural practice non-exploitative. The instinct of those interested in exploring the life experiences of "others" to simply turn their backs on museums as hopelessly flawed enter-prises dates back at least to Franz Boas's resignation from the American Museum of Natural History in 1905. Even if stopping short of abandoning curatorship as either inherently exploitative or politically impotent, few have not re-thought the balance between intellectual and social imperatives for their work: have not, that is, asked themselves key questions about the ethics of their calling. Are they primarily there to help culturally engaged audiences investigate material culture and natural heritage? Or should they reassess their work in terms of its social responsibility, as a branch of social work and political activism? And should they therefore apply the institutions they shape as instruments with which to knit communities together or alternatively to right historical wrongs? Must their key imperative be to rebalance society by giving voice to the under-privileged and less-well-represented? Is their ultimate goal to make better and more critically-conscious citizens of their visitors?

Curators as artistic directors

Along with the politicization of the curator's role, another major recent shift has been an increased concern with the curator's ability to exercise creativity. It is strik-ingly common these days to come across curators eager to champion the place of aesthetic flair and cultural acumen in their *métier*, asserting a version of themselves as artistic practitioners. At the same time many artists seemingly want to be taken seriously as investigative intellectuals, practicing a different kind of curation. Most especially in the world of contemporary art, this has sometimes led to a fundamental struggle for cultural power between the artist and her or his "artistic" enabler: the curator. And while some artists have ended up attempting to be their own curators, a number of curators have focused their energies on finessing the "art" of curating.

This overlapping and intermingling of roles developed in part from the practice, common from the 1970s through to its zenith in the early 2000s, of artists being invited by traditional museums to act as guest curators, often with the aim of teasing or prodding an institution out of its perceived state of staleness and complacency. Andy Warhol's curatorial intervention at the Rhode Island School of Design in 1969 represents an early example of the trend; while in London, Eduardo Paolozzi's 1985 *Lost Magic Kingdom* exhibition at the Museum of Mankind had a similarly iconic influence. More recently, artists such as Fred Wilson and Mark Dion have become repeatedly associated with the habit of rethinking and re-working institutional collections as "artists in residence." Wilson routinely uses his practice to highlight the politics of race, class, and power that he finds submerged if not entirely hidden within a series of historic, decorative, and fine art collections; while Dion instead has donned the mantle of "artist-taxonomist," applying his subjectively idiosyncratic perspective to the public reordering of museums structured around scientific classification systems. Grayson Perry's much discussed exhibition *Tomb of the Unknown Craftsman* at the British Museum is just a recent example of the idea that an artist's inspired eye can provide fresh insight into established collections. Other guest curators, coming at the practice from an art-historical perspective, and drawing on more academic habits, have resisted this focus on the artistry of making a show. Robert Storr, for example – one of this generation's most respected art curators – is much more comfortable with the notion of using exhibitions to enact what he describes as "show and tell" sessions. While Miwon Kwon, this time with a background in architecture and photography, instead locates the core curatorial competency in terms of "critical services" (Corrin 1994; McShine 1999; Putnam 2001; Kwon 2004, 50; Storr 2001, 20).

Whether or not it actually counts as Art, champions of "creative curating" have managed permanently to lodge the notion that making an exhibition is fundamentally about staging an inspired show; with the implication that the manner in which exhibits are chosen, information and meaning imparted, and the visitor's thoughts, feelings, and experiences guided, effectively boils down to an elevated form of show business (Witcomb 2006). A common analogy invoked for this version of the craft – borrowed from Francois Truffaut's 1950s argument about how to categorize the role of a film director – is for curators to be championed as authors and directors in a different medium. Robert Storr again elaborates: "the exhibition organiser occupies, or should occupy a position analogous to that of a film director who works collaboratively with everyone else involved in the process of making a movie, but who is assured, in spite of all contrary pressures, of the final cut." "Showing is telling," he goes on, and "space is the medium in which ideas are visually phrased. Installation is both presentation and commentary, documentation and interpretation" (Storr 2001, 16, 23).

Two early exponents of this type of cultural practice were Swiss curator Harald Szeemann and the American Walter Hopps, who during the second half of the twentieth century, plied their trade as independent and self-consciously experimental art curators. Szeemann's first appearance as guest curator came in 1957, when he organized a show entitled *Painters-Poets/Poets-Painters*; but it was really 12 years later when he came to dramatic prominence with a landmark exhibition: *When Attitudes become Form: Works, Concepts, Processes, Situations, Information.* Szeemann's conception of exhibitions as ideas-based shows or performances, where audiences should have exhilarating experiences, has had a lasting influence on the conception of the curator. Meanwhile, on the west coast of America, Hopps similarly worked in unconventional, iconoclastic ways: his first exhibition organized in 1954 for example, involved renting the merry-go-round at the Santa Monica Pier and hanging on it some 100 paintings by 40 artists (Levi Strauss 2007).

By the 1990s, curating had by common consent become a creative and communicative craft: the verb "to curate" and the phrase "curated by" gradually gained mainstream gallery and critical currency (Harding 1997; McShine 1999; O'Neill 2007b; Witcomb 2003). As museums and galleries came to focus more on exhibitions than permanent collections, a particular set of core curatorial competencies emerged, most notably the conception, management, and presentation of short-term projects. There is, not surprisingly, a spectrum of approaches to this type of curating, with differing amounts of stress on the collaborative nature of the work. Despite what Storr suggests, much of it *is* in fact characterized by a dominant emphasis on individual practice, on first-person narratives, and a type of self-positioning. Hence the widespread notion of "uber-curators" – a cluster of jet-setting exhibition and biennale convenors – anointed with the mystique of single-minded-visionaries. Arguably the leader of the pack, Hans Ulrich Obrist – a self-conscious follower of pioneers like Szeemann – describes himself as a "negotiator of new forms of curating: a catalyst, someone who pedestrian bridges from the art to many different audiences" (Obrist in Thea 2001, 89).

Others of similar inclination nonetheless see themselves (depending on their cultural tastes) rather more as conductors or DJs, whose work involves a joint production through the art of mediation and the negotiated blending of contributions by artists, researchers, subject experts, designers, other "support staff" and, most radically of all, the visitors themselves. The traditional celebrity of the "auteur" structure is, in this version of the art of curating, softened with more involving practices, ones which ultimately posit visitors less in terms of cultural consumers, more as members of an engaged and interconnected participatory "community" (Greenberg, Ferguson, and Nairne 1996; Fowle 2007; White and Thompson 2008; Müller 2006, Thea 2001; Storr 2006; Rollig 2003; Birnbaum 2003; Nicks 2003).

Curators as public investigators

Not a few contemporary curators then have taken to their calling with a progressive zeal their predecessors would hardly have recognized; some seeing their work as essentially enabling political change, while others as a means to disseminate creative enterprises. Even curators who behave as neither activists nor artists, have nonetheless been redefined by playfully emancipated versions of their traditionally defined jobs. Almost all of them have found the character of what they do influenced, at times, by both reinvigorated social and aesthetic considerations. Furthermore, those trends have helped alter the manner in which they approach their core task of doing research into "charged goods" – the objects and exhibits that museums anoint with a "specialness." The evolving character of these investigative efforts – adroitly balanced between habits of study found elsewhere amongst connoisseurs, academics, journalists, cultural commentators, and literary critics – have gradually resulted in their increasingly refined ability to fashion a distinctive form of public knowledge. This idea of curators acting as public investigators is the third and final form of "new curatorship" to which I want to draw attention.

As with much that is new in curating, the world of contemporary art has here too been a strong influence. Captured in the writing of French sociologist Pierre Bourdieu, from the 1960s there was an increasing sense that the value and meaning of artworks was not purely determined by the "producer who actually creates the object in its materiality, but rather the entire set of agents engaged in the field" (O'Neill 2007a, 15). An especially powerful "agent" of course was the curator, whose gaze, as Paul O'Neill explains, turned away from a concern with "the artwork as an autonomous object of study... towards [instead] a form of curatorial criticism, in which the space of exhibition was given critical precedence over that of the objects of art ... Its discourse and subject matter went beyond discussion about artists and the object of art to include ... the role played by the curator in exhibitions" (O'Neill 2007a, 13). Drawing their vocabulary and philosophical presumptions largely from academic art history and especially from postmodern literary theory, their approach to art focused on the relationships between works that sat next to each other and on the notion of aesthetics and an understanding of meaning experienced in a real space. These ideas were most frequently articulated in catalog essays, which reflected but also cumulatively embodied the sense that putting art on show – curating it – was in and of itself a form of comment and discourse. This inclination to highlight the meaning invested in how art was brought into the public domain was further shored up by the range of curatorial studies programs established toward the end of the twentieth century, for example Whitney's Curatorial Program originally set up in 1968 and the Royal College of Art's Curating Contemporary Art MA established in 1992 (O'Neill 2007a; Townsend 2003; Lind 2011, 183).

A parallel but rather different version of this investigative and interpretive model of curating shows has more recently been found in a new cluster of curatorial projects and institutions concerned more with science than art, and frequently precisely with the bridge between these two fields. Whereas research-led art curators still seem predominantly concerned with questions circumscribed by the world of art, this new breed of science curators seems often intent on reaching out from their home territory into other domains. Certainly the considerable number of projects that champion an intermingling of science with art seem more likely to originate from the science than the art side of the divide. Drawing extensively on the legacy of earlier models of science museums where objects were held to embody moments of historical significance; but also absorbing some of the criticisms leveled at those institutions by educationalists seeking to replace them with phenomena-focused science centers, a new style of science-based museums and galleries seems to be emerging in the twenty-first century. The best-known examples are currently found in northern Europe and often in close proximity to the realm of tertiary education: Medical Museion in Copenhagen (part of a university), the Science Gallery in Dublin (part of Trinity College), the Charité Museum in Berlin (part of the teaching hospital), Laboratoire in Paris (the brainchild of Harvard professor David Edwards), and Wellcome Collection in London (part of the biomedical research charity the Wellcome Trust) are five notable examples.[4] Each demonstrates a commitment to contemplating and exploring science and medicine within a broad cultural context, rubbing shoulders with concerns emanating from the arts and humanities. Each also places emphasis on using short-term, ideas-led projects – temporary exhibitions and events – to bring into intriguing, sometimes iconoclastic, juxtaposition elements and demonstrations of real things, real expertise, and real experiences.

As described by Michael John Gorman, founder of Science Gallery and an articulate spokesman for many of the distinguishing features of these establishments, the new "cultural centres of science" (as he terms them) tend to be smaller than their science museum and center ancestors, and thereby more able to innovate with agility. They are more focused on the meaningful participation of experts and their tangible paraphernalia than the model of second-hand dumbed-down "interactivity" that had begun to go stale in the ubiquitous science center; and they more frequently seek to involve audiences in coproduction (providing creative platforms for them to share their own content and ideas) rather than simply providing finished products for visitors passively to absorb (Gorman 2011).

For Wellcome Collection, a further specific point of inspiration and departure came from the very first model of European museums: Renaissance cabinets of curiosities. This long reach back into the ancestry of museums is for this particular institution bridged within its own history by the activities of eponymous collector Henry Wellcome, who set up his own massive Edwardian wardrobe of wonders. Drawing directly on his material legacy as well as his almost scientific approach to collecting, this young (set up in 2007) cultural institution has fashioned a vigorous public program based on curiosity-driven curation. Itself a latter-day cabinet of curiosities (but one crucially pitched as much in terms of a place where people fueled with curiosity should gather and do things as the more static sense of a space in which to keep curious things), Wellcome Collection's fundamental aim has been to establish a lively public platform for investigations that cut across the traditional lines of opposition between lay and professional, contemporary and historic, as well as the arts and sciences (Arnold 2006; Kohn 2012; Arnold and Olsen 2003). The vision of medicine championed here is one where open-ended topics are explored not only in relation to science but a multitude of other perspectives too. Always partly about medicine and science, Wellcome Collection's projects are never exhausted by these perspectives. Exhibitions and events showcased in its first half decade of operation – looking at sleeping and dreaming (Figure 14.1), the heart, war, dirt, personal identity, skeletons, flesh, quackery, mind-altering drugs, human enhancement, the hand, and brains – have all leant themselves to the core idea of giving legitimate airtime to perspectives from history, geography, art, archaeology, science, design, and so forth, anticipating that new insights might emerge from the gaps between established bodies of understanding.

In Wellcome Collection, as in the rest of this new breed of self-consciously interdisciplinary cultural centers, there is both an ardent concern with the value of an intriguing topic (one worth probing and teasing out rather than just disseminating) and a desire to give curiosity-led curators a license to act as public researchers. Among these teams of programmers one finds curators acting as explorers, intent on constructing elegant and entertaining experiences through which people find things out in public – a kind of self-conscious "thinking out loud." In this particular form of new curatorship, a premium is placed on the idea of seeking and marshaling visual and material ideas in order finally, with an inspired flourish of showmanship, to just stand back and point.

FIGURE 14.1   The exhibition *Sleeping and Dreaming* at Wellcome Collection in London, one of the new interdisciplinary cultural centers that is exploring different ways of making exhibitions. (For a color version of this figure, please see the color plate section)
Image courtesy of Wellcome Collection.

Conclusion

Snowball-like, the work of curators has in the past few decades accumulated layer upon layer of ever more mediated activity – thrown up partly by the thorough modernization of museums increasingly aspiring to be expertly managed and visitor-focused; partly by the insistence that there is always a politics at play in the creation of culture; partly by the pervasive assumption that museums and galleries inevitably contribute to the sphere of "art"; and partly by the growing inclination to use them to find things out. The curator's role has, as a consequence, been thoroughly diversified and inexorably complicated; and there is a lurking danger that its fundamental focus could be dissipated. More than ever, maybe, there is a need to relocate the overarching idea of what defines this calling. This is, in part, provided by the evolving but distinctive, indeed unique, institutional context that gives them a home. Curators are still fundamentally creatures who inhabit museums and galleries. And within that setting, the essence of their task maybe ends up being as simple as the advice passed on to Hans-Ulrich Obrist by Anne d'Harnoncourt (former director of Philadelphia Museum of Art): "look and look and look, and then ... look again, because nothing replaces looking" (Cherix 2008, 4).

Notes

1   This chapter was prepared following the seminar *Curatopia: Museums and Curatorial Practice*, organized by Conal McCarthy on February 26, 2010. My thanks are due to the other participants on that day as well as to Bruce Phillips who provided research into the secondary literature.
2   Further statistical surveys relating to recent trends in UK museums presented by the Department for Culture, Media and Sport surveys can be found at: http://www.culture.gov.uk/publications/7386.aspx; and the Museum Association: http://www.museumsassociation.org/download?id=165106. Sites accessed October 20, 2014. See also Black in this volume.
3   See, for example, Museums Association 1983, 530–540; the AAMC 2007 Code of practice; Thompson (1984); Benton and Watson (2010).
4   Medical Museion (http://www.museion.ku.dk), Science Gallery (http://www.sciencegallery.com), Charité Museum (http://www.bbm-charite.de), Laboratoire (http://www.lelaboratoire.org), and Wellcome Collection (http://www.wellcomecollection.org).

References

Ames, Michael, and Mina McKenzie, eds. 1996. *Curatorship: Indigenous Perspectives in Postcolonial Societies*. Ottawa: Canadian Museum of Civilization.

Arnold, Ken. 2006. *Cabinets for the Curious: Looking back at Early English Museums*. Aldershot, UK: Ashgate.

Arnold, Ken, and Danielle Olsen, eds. 2003. *Medicine Man: The Forgotten Museum of Henry Wellcome*. London: British Museum Press.

Benton, Tim, and Nichola J. Watson. 2010. "Museum Practice and Heritage." In *Understanding Heritage in Practice*, edited by Susie West, 127–165. Manchester: Manchester University Press.

Birnbaum, Daniel. 2003. "The International Curator." In *Frieze Art Fair, Forum*. Frieze Talks, October 18, 4:40–5:15 min. Regent's Park, London: Frieze Art Fair. Accessed October 30, 2014. http://www.friezeprojects.org/talks/detail/the_international_curator.

Boylan, Patrick. 2006. "The Museum Profession." In *Blackwell Companion to Museum Studies*, edited by Sharon Macdonald, 415–430. Malden, MA: Blackwell.

Cherix, Christophe. 2008. "Preface." In *A Brief History of Curating*, by Hans-Ulrich Obrist, 4–9. Zurich: JRP/Ringier.

Clifford, James. 1997. "Museums as Contact Zones." In *Routes: Travel and Translation in the Late Twentieth Century*, 188–221. Cambridge, MA: Harvard University Press.

Clifford, James. 2010. "The Times of the Curator." Keynote address at *The Task of the Curator: Translation, Intervention and Innovation in Exhibitionary Practice*. University of California Santa Cruz Museum and Curatorial Studies, May 14–15, 2010. Accessed October 20, 2014. http://macs.ucsc.edu/conference/keynote.html.

Conn, Steven. 1998. *Museums and American Intellectual Life, 1876–1926*. Chicago: University of Chicago Press.

Conn, Steven. 2010. *Do Museums Still Need Objects?* Philadelphia: University of Pennsylvania Press.

Cook, Sarah. 2003. "Towards a Theory of the Practice of Curating New Media Art." In *Beyond the Box: Diverging Curatorial Practices*, edited by Melanie Townsend, 169–182. Banff, Canada: Banff Centre Press.

Cornell, Lauren. 2011. "In the Nostalgia District." *Frieze* 141: 170–175.

Corrin, Lisa G. 1994. *Mining the Museum: An Installation by Fred Wilson*. Baltimore, MD: The Contemporary.

Fowle, Kate, 2007. "Who Cares? Understanding the Role of the Curator Today." In *Cautionary Tales: Critical Curating*, edited by Stephen Rand, 23–34. New York: Apex Art.

Fowler, William. 1972. *Essays on Museums and Other Subjects Connected with Natural History*. London: Macmillan. (Originally published 1898.)

Fox, Dan, and Jennifer Higgie. 2011. Updated version of Raymond Williams' 1976 "'Keywords': A Record of an Inquiry into a Vocabulary... Concerned with the Practices and Institutions Described as 'Culture' and 'Society'." *Frieze* 141: 158–161.

Graham, Beryl, and Sarah Cook. 2010. *Rethinking Curating: Art after New Media*. Cambridge, MA: MIT Press.

Gorman, Michael John. 2011. "The Future of Science Museums: Ten Shifts Shaping our Cultural Institutions." In *Future Forecasting: The Challenge Facing Museums and Cultural Institutions*, 89–93. Dublin: National Gallery of Ireland.

Greenberg, Reesa, Bruce W. Ferguson, and Sandy Nairne, eds. 1996. *Thinking about Exhibitions*. London: Routledge.

Harding, Ann, ed. 1997. *Curating the Contemporary Art Museum and Beyond*. London: Academy Group.

Henning, Michelle. 2006. "New Media." In *A Companion to Museum Studies*, edited by Sharon Macdonald, 302–318. Oxford: Blackwell.

Kohn, Marek. 2012. *A Guide for the Incurably Curious*. London: Wellcome Collection.

Kreps, Christina F. 2003. *Liberating Culture: Cross-Cultural Perspectives on Museums, Curation, and Heritage Preservation*. London: Routledge.

Kreps, Christina F. 2006. "Non-Western Models of Museums and Curation in Cross-Cultural Perspective." In *A Companion to Museum Studies*, edited by Sharon Macdonald, 457–472. Oxford: Blackwell.

Kwon, Miwon. 2004. *One Place after Another: Site-Specific Art and Locational Identity*. Cambridge, MA: MIT Press.

Levi Strauss, David. 2007. "The Bias of the World: Curating after Szeemann and Hopps." In *Cautionary Tales: Critical Curating*, edited by Stephen Rand, 12–22. New York: Apex Art.

Lind, Maria. 2011. "Look and Learn: A Round-Table Discussion about Impact of Curatorial Studies Programmes." *Frieze* 141: 182–189.

Mané-Wheoki, Jonathan. 2010. "Titiro ki muri kia whakatika ki mua: Look to the Past to Proceed into the Future." Paper presented at the seminar *Curatopia: Museums and the Future of Curatorial Practice*, February 26, 2010, Victoria University of Wellington.

McShine, Kynaston. 1999. *The Museum as Muse: Artists Reflect*. New York: Museum of Modern Art.

Müller, Hans-Joachin. 2006. *Harald Szeemann: Exhibition Maker*. Stuttgart: Hatche Cantz.

Museum of Anthropology. 2012. "Mission Statement." University of British Columbia, Vancouver. Accessed October 30, 2014. http://moa.ubc.ca/about.

Museums Association. 1983. *Code of Conduct for Museum Curators*. London: Museums Association.

Nicks, Trudy. 2003. "Introduction." In *Museums and Source Communities: A Routledge Reader*, edited by Laura Lynn Peers and Alison Kay Brown, 7–25. Abingdon, UK: Routledge.

O'Neill, Paul. 2007a. "The Curatorial Turn: From Practice to Discourse." In *Issues in Curating Contemporary Art and Performance*, edited by Judith Rugg and Michele Sedgwick, 13–28. Bristol: Intellect.

O'Neill, Paul, ed. 2007b. *Curating Subjects*. London: Open Editions.

Putnam, James. 2001. *Art and Artifact: the Museum as Medium*. London: Thames and Hudson.

Rollig, Stella. 2003. "Contemporary Art Practices and the Museum: To Be Reconciled at All?" In *Beyond the Box: Diverging Curatorial Practice*, edited by Melanie Townsend, 97–107. Banff, Canada: Banff Center Press.

Schildkrout, E. 2004. "Ambiguous Messages and Ironic Twists." In *Museum Studies: An Anthology of Contexts*, edited by Bettina Carbonell, 181–192. Oxford: Blackwell.

Schubert, Karsten. 2009. *The Curator's Egg: The Evolution of the Museum Concept from the French Revolution to the Present Day*, 3rd ed. London: Ridinghouse.

Shelton, Anthony. 2006. "Museums and Anthropologies: Practices and Narratives." In *A Companion to Museum Studies*, edited by Sharon Macdonald, 64–80. Oxford: Blackwell.

Storr, Robert. 2001. "How We Do What We Do. And How We Don't." In *Curating Now: Imaginative Practice/Public Responsibility*, edited by Paul Marincola, 3–22. Philadelphia: Philadelphia Exhibitions Initiative.

Storr, Robert. 2006. "Show and Tell." In *Questions of Practice: What Makes a Great Exhibition*, edited by Joseph N. Newland. Philadelphia: Philadelphia Exhibitions Initiative.

Thea, Caroline, ed. 2001. *On Curating: Interviews with Ten International Curators*. New York: Distributed Art Publishers.

Thompson, John M. A., ed. 1984. *Manual of Curatorship: A Guide to Museum Practice*. London: Museums Association/Butterworths.

Townsend, Melanie. 2003. "The Trouble with Curating." In *Beyond the Box: Diverging Curatorial Practices*, edited by Melanie Townsend, xiii–xx. Banff, Canada: Banff Centre Press.

Vergo, Peter, ed. 1989. *The New Museology*. London: Reaktion.

White, Michelle, and Nato Thompson. 2008. "Curator as Producer." *Art Lies: Contemporary Art Quarterly* 59. Accessed October 30, 2014. http://turbulence.org/blog/2008/09/05/curator-as-producer-michelle-white-nato-thompson.

Witcomb, Andrea. 2003. *Re-Imagining the Museum: Beyond the Mausoleum*. London: Routledge.

Witcomb, Andrea. 2006. "Interactivity: Thinking Beyond." In *A Companion to Museum Studies*, edited by Sharon Macdonald, 353–361. Oxford: Blackwell.

Further Reading

Carbonell, Bettina Messias, ed. 2004. *Museum Studies: An Anthology of Contexts*. Malden, MA: Blackwell.

Macdonald, Sharon, and Paul Basu, eds. 2007. *Exhibition Experiments*. Oxford: Blackwell.

Marincola, Paul, ed. 2001. *Curating Now: Imaginative Practice/Public Responsibility*. Philadelphia: Philadelphia Exhibitions Initiative, Philadelphia Center for Arts and Heritage.

Marincola, Paul. ed. 2006. *What Makes a Great Exhibition?* Philadelphia: Philadelphia Exhibitions Initiative, Philadelphia Center for Arts and Heritage.

Martinon, Jean-Paul, ed. 2013. *The Curatorial: A Philosophy of Curating*. London: Bloomsbury.

O'Neill, Paul. 2012. *The Culture of Curating and the Curating of Culture(s)*. Cambridge, MA: MIT Press.

Smith, Terry E. 2012. *Thinking Contemporary Curating*. New York: Independent Curators International.

Ken Arnold is Head of Public Programmes at Wellcome Collection in London, and regularly curates exhibitions on medicine, art, and science. He completed a PhD in History at Princeton, and has worked in museums on both sides of the Atlantic. His last monograph about the history of museums was *Cabinets for the Curious* (Ashgate, 2006) and he is currently writing a book on exhibitions and public knowledge. In February 2010, he chaired an international seminar at Victoria University of Wellington entitled *Curatopia: Museums and the Future of Curatorial Practice*.

15 THE PENDULUM SWING
Curatorial Theory Past and Present

Halona Norton-Westbrook

The past generation has seen a steady rise in the number of scholarly critiques examining curating in the museum (Chambers 2006; Fowle 2007; Kreps 2010; Marincola 2001; Storr 2001; O'Neill 2007; Townsend 2003). The concerns of these publications are various: some center on an analysis of the curator's responsibilities in an increasingly interconnected global society, others consider how innovative media and technology have influenced the curator's presentation and interpretation of museum objects. Different emphases aside, these inquiries commonly begin by distinguishing between traditional definitions of curatorship and expanded contemporary understandings of curatorial practice. The conventional definition of a curator, we are often reminded, is that of a caretaker charged with the safekeeping of museum objects.[1] Today, however, such traditional interpretations of the profession must be viewed through a wider lens: one that allows for the incorporation of new meanings and purposes that serve to extend the boundaries and defining criteria of the curator's role. Indeed, the twenty-first-century curator may work within or outside of the museum infrastructure, and is just as likely to deal with the orchestration of ideas, concepts, and happenings as they are to spend time researching physical objects.[2] The need to initiate meaningful discussions of curatorial work with these juxtapositions is indicative of the extent to which the philosophical and institutional parameters of both museums and curatorship have been transformed in the past century.

It is with an awareness of these changes that this chapter explores the evolving nature and status of curatorial theory in the museum. Simply stated, curatorial theory may be understood as the complex compendia of ideas, beliefs, and critique that shape and inform curatorial work. As this investigation shows, theory and practice are not easily separated from one another: when we speak of one we necessarily invoke the other (see McCarthy in this volume). Therefore, rather than

The International Handbooks of Museum Studies: Museum Practice, First Edition.
Edited by Conal McCarthy.
© 2015 John Wiley & Sons Ltd. Published 2020 by John Wiley & Sons Ltd.

conceiving of curatorial theory as an abstract entity, it is useful to see it as an integral component of everyday curatorial work.

Endeavoring to balance philosophical reflection with historical overview, this examination draws upon a varied assemblage of sources, ranging from early twentieth-century museum literature to a survey and interviews conducted with contemporary museum directors, curators, and scholars. Reflecting my own research interests, the focus is primarily on institutions in Britain and the United States and also leans toward art museums. Yet, wherever possible, I have looked across the broader spectrum of museum typologies, aiming for diversity in terms of disciplinary attention. This is intentional: I am guided by the conviction that there is unexplored commonality to be found between the curatorial work performed in museums of art, science, history, and anthropology, and that disciplinary boundaries are often more fluid than they appear. As Ken Arnold aptly noted in the preceding chapter, museums are becoming increasingly interdisciplinary in their missions and programming. Institutions such as the Wellcome Collection in London and the Exploratorium in San Francisco, both of which attempt to integrate art and science into their exhibitions, serve as prime examples of this shift toward interdisciplinarity.

A consideration of curatorial theory must necessarily acknowledge the changes that have shaped past and present approaches to museum practice. The public museum is still a fairly young institution, emerging in its modern incarnation only after the Enlightenment (Bennett 1995). This relatively short lifespan has distinct consequences for how museological studies consider their subject. On the one hand, it is possible to conceptualize the institution's maturation as characterized by sweeping leaps and bounds of change. Indeed, a clearly discernible pattern of shifting attitudes to objects, display, and professional activities is readily apparent when the rapid growth that has shaped the museum field is surveyed.[3] On the other hand, the relatively condensed history of the museum lends itself to the scrutiny of individual institutions in micro detail. As a result, individual case studies often relay the developments, triumphs, and challenges of specific museums in extraordinary depth.[4]

Both perspectives are valuable and contribute to our collective knowledge of museums. This chapter seeks a middle ground between them, adopting an elongated view of curatorial theory's development both historically and across institutional boundaries. In so doing, it aims to highlight some of the subtle continuities (and discontinuities) that connect (and separate) the ideas and practices of museums to one another across space and time. The purpose of this undertaking, it must be stressed, is not to offer a comprehensive analysis of the content of curatorial theory as such. The reader can find a growing literature on this topic in a number of fields, especially the visual arts (Resnicow 1995; Ames and McKenzie 1996; Heinich and Pollack 1996; Ward 1996; Harding 1997; Crowther 2002; Thomas 2002; Rogoff 2006; Obrist 2008; Chandler 2009; Heumann Gurian 2010; O'Neill 2012). Rather, this chapter aims to stimulate thinking and further research on the current practice of curatorial theory that might bring us to a deeper and more nuanced understanding of a particularly abstract museological subject.

The discussion which follows is divided into four sections. First, the challenges inherent to a discussion of curatorial theory are acknowledged. Second, attention is given to the historical development of the curator's role from the late nineteenth century to the beginning of the twenty-first century. A third section summarizes the key findings of a survey of professional opinions about the status of curatorial theory in the present day museum field. Last, a final section reflects upon the constant and changeable aspects of curatorial theory and contemplates what the future might hold for those engaged in curatorial activities.

A challenging subject

A host of converging factors make curatorial theory a difficult subject to discuss. First and foremost, there is an intrinsic challenge in putting words to the motivation and causation that underlie our chosen approaches to professional activities. While this holds true for all types of work it seems particularly applicable to curating. As a professional pursuit, curating occupies a curious liminal space between cerebral endeavor and action-based activity. Generally speaking, curatorial workers are not only expected to be involved in research, but also in the acquisition and development of collections, the planning of exhibitions, the oversight of object installation within gallery spaces, and the presentation of public talks and lectures. This hybrid quality of curatorial work – caught somewhere between thinking and doing – makes it all the more challenging to examine.

Further complicating the matter is the complex nature of divisions of labor within museums. In her 1981 essay "Conflicting Visions in American Art Museums," Vera Zolberg discusses the nature of curatorship and notes that the work of the museum can be divided into governance, performance, and patronage. Yet, Zolberg observes, such tasks are rarely performed by mutually exclusive sets of players (1981, 104). Consequently, sites of authority within the museum are porous and the responsibilities and duties of curators, directors, and trustees are frequently entangled. As a result, the true origins of curatorial decisions, and their underlying rationale, are often obscured.

A lack of direct primary evidence also inhibits discussion of curatorial theory. Museums rarely maintain comprehensive records of the processes that result in significant curatorial activities such as acquisition, deaccession, or display. There are two primary reasons for this, as Charles Saumarez Smith explains in his essay on the history of display at the National Gallery, London (2008). First, such processes tend to go unrecorded as they are not considered worthy of documentation: the reasoning at the heart of the activity seems self-evident to those who are involved. Second, a dearth of comprehensive curatorial records may also be explained by the fact that the recording of such processes would reveal internal power struggles that could be detrimental to the interests of those who documented them.

Despite these obstacles, we can draw on a wealth of indirect primary evidence in our efforts to examine curatorial theory. Some sources, such as wall labels and catalogs, are readily apparent and easily accessible. Other sources, such as interviews and conference proceedings that document semi-public conversations between curatorial workers, are less so. It is these latter forms of evidence that this chapter focuses on as it turns to a consideration of how the ideas and beliefs that shape and inform curatorial work have developed in pace with the professionalization of the museum field.

Historical perspectives

In the first decade of the twentieth century, experienced museum workers, variously employed to care for collections ranging from fine art objects to natural history specimens, gathered together at the respective annual conferences of the UK Museums Association and the newly formed American Association of Museums.[5] They pondered and debated whether it was possible to train a curator and, if so, whether such training was best acquired through general education, practical job experience, or specialized training programs (the latter only recently proposed). In his address at the Museums Association's conference in 1906, William E. Hoyle, the organization's President, and Keeper of the Manchester Museum, spoke of the difficulties of devising a cohesive approach to curatorial training: "At the present moment there is no trace of any system even in theory, still less in practice, in regard to the matter. There is scarcely even an idea in the public that a special training of museum curators is conceivable, let alone desirable" (Hoyle 1906, 8). This sentiment was echoed by other senior figures within the museum field. In 1910, Frederick A. Lucas, President of the American Association of Museums and Chief Curator at the Brooklyn Institute of Arts and Sciences, concluded a roundtable seminar on the subject by asserting: "a curator is born and not made. I do not believe that you can train a man to be a curator. He is the result of natural ability and circumstance" (Crook 1910, 63).

Underlying these discussions were tensions about the nature of curatorial expertise and how it might be defined and differentiated across disciplines. While there was general consensus that the expertise required by an art curator differed from that required by a science curator, opinions varied as to what constituted these distinct types of expertise. In the face of such uncertainty, conference participants tended to speak of the qualifications and knowledge required of the curator in broad, all-encompassing terms. In 1902, F. A. Bather, of the British Museum, spoke of the model curator as: "a man of enthusiasm, of ideas, of strictest honour, of sincerity, with the grip and devotion of a specialist, yet with the wisdom born of wide experience, with an eye for the most meticulous detail, but with a heart and mind responsive to all things of life, art, and nature" (Bather 1902, 185). Hoyle offered a similar assessment in his 1906 address, describing the ideal curator as a man possessing qualities of "general culture, tact, and courtesy" coupled with "business-like and methodical habits" and an "artistic sensibility and appreciation of the beautiful" (1906, 11). Moreover, he should also have "an acquaintance, the more intimate the better" with subjects such as science, history, geography, and art, as well as "practical acquaintance with the use of ordinary tools for working in wood, metal and stone … experience in the management of assistants [and] the power to write correct, and if possible, elegant English" (Hoyle 1906, 12–14). Declarations such as these attest to the prevailing belief that the individual best suited for curatorial work was a well-educated generalist with some degree of inclination toward an area of specialism, who also possessed an expansive skill set that could be adapted to numerous aspects of the museum's organization and administration.

Reviewing these early conference proceedings a portrait emerges of a burgeoning professional field actively in search of self-definition and self-articulation. Permeating the records is an overwhelming emphasis on the acquisition, organization, classification, preservation, and physical presentation of museum objects, activities seen as central to the curator's purpose. The predominance of these concerns reflects the preoccupations of a rapidly maturing museum field where the unification of professional ideals and the standardization of practices were at the fore. This shift toward professionalization was born from a combination of circumstances: a spike in the growth of museum resources (both in terms of the number of institutions being founded and the availability of capital necessary to foster the expansion of collection holdings); a growing belief in the public good arising from the creation and support of public institutions; and a parallel movement to professionalize comparable fields of work, most notably library science (Norton-Westbrook 2013).

The march toward professionalization continued to be a defining characteristic of museums from the turn of the century onward, gaining notable momentum in the 1920s and 1930s. "Amateurishness," as Zolberg notes, "was becoming outmoded," replaced instead by an increasingly explicit understanding of what constituted curatorial expertise (1981, 110). In pace with this change, colleges and universities began to step up their efforts to provide training for those wishing to enter the museum field. These courses took different forms. Some were disciplinary and centered on molding individuals who would have specialist expertise within a given subject that was directly relevant to the types of collection that they hoped to care for. Curators of art, for instance, were increasingly expected to have completed formal studies in art history, a subject newly sanctioned as a recognized course of study in British and American universities (Norton-Westbrook 2013).

Other programs were more vocationally oriented, intended to impart knowledge of best practice and standard procedures within the museum. Beginning in 1908, the University of Iowa sought to engage future natural history curators through training in taxidermy and exhibition installation. Also notable, and more general in its scope, was the diploma course initiated by the Museums Association in 1932 which aimed to impart practical knowledge that was directly applicable to the everyday activities of museum workers (Boylan 2006).

Still other programs sought to combine disciplinary focus and vocational aims. The most sophisticated of these was Harvard University's renowned Museum Course, founded by the educator and collector Paul Sachs in 1921. Sachs' efforts to train a generation of what he called "connoisseur-scholars" through a combination of hands-on instruction, museum visits, and art-world introductions resulted in the cultivation of a generation of influential directors and curators who rose to the helm of leadership in mid-century American art museums (S. Duncan 2002).[6] Regardless of their varied approaches, the emergence of these structured training programs was meaningful. Their establishment contributed substantially to the notion of the curator as a highly skilled expert, an individual in possession of occupational specific skills and defined specialist knowledge that was legitimized through association with academia.

As time went on, both the general aims of museums and the parameters of the curator's role continued to evolve. Gradually, internal museum structures and protocols became more organized and systematic, and institutional focus began to turn outward. The post-World War II era also saw a large-scale reorientation of the museum's aims toward public service. During the war, this reorientation was visible in both individual institutions and professional museum organizations.[7] By the time that the International Council of Museums (ICOM) was established in 1945, public service aims had become part of established museum doctrine, in theory if not always in practice. For curators, this reorientation was significant. What had once been a decidedly inward-looking pursuit – defined primarily through a custodial relationship with objects – was now layered with expectations to work actively with museum audiences.

The postwar era also witnessed the diversification of occupations within the museum field. The emergence of three new types of professionals – the museum educator, the registrar, and the conservator – was of particular importance.[8] While education, registration, and conservation had long been recognized as important aspects of the museum's mission, these activities had traditionally been seen as falling within the general realm of curatorial responsibilities – existing as auxiliary duties in line with the curator's efforts to organize, classify, preserve, and present the objects within their collections (Boylan 2006, 418). The correlation between curatorial work and conservation and registration skills stretched back to the early nineteenth century, while a close association between the museum's educational objectives and the duties of the curator had also existed since that time. The creation of these new roles thus signaled at least a partial renegotiation of the boundaries of curatorial endeavors (Roberts 2004; McLean 2004).[9] This renegotiation was complex. On the one hand the opportunity to focus on activities beyond education, collection management, and care allowed curators to align themselves even more closely with object-based scholarship and research. On the other hand, curators were now displaced from their former role as the exclusive physical and intellectual caretakers of the collections that they oversaw. This new situation, combined with the growing expectation to engage the museum's publics, placed curators in a somewhat uncertain position.

The counter-culture movement of the late 1960s brought further changes for curators as museums found themselves at the center of a debate about institutional elitism (McClellan 2008, 42–46).[10] The 1969 publication of *The Love of Art*, Pierre Bourdieu and Alain Darbel's investigation into the audiences of French and European art museums, was indicative of a growing awareness that museums were not the impartial institutions that they presented themselves as (Bourdieu and Darbel 1991; Grenfell and Hardy 2007). Bourdieu and Darbel's study focused specifically on art museums and contended that rather than foster social inclusion for everyone these institutions actually served to "reinforce for some the feeling of belonging and for others the feeling of exclusion" (Bourdieu and Darbel 1991, 112). At the core of this debate were the politics of cultural authority and the extent to which museums might serve as instruments for redressing societal inequalities. These issues were not new. Indeed, John Cotton Dana, an early advocate for socially inclusive museums, had raised similar questions in his 1917 book *The Gloom of the Museum* (Dana 1917; DiMaggio 1991, 269–270; Pointon 1994; C. Duncan 1995). Yet the dialogue surrounding the museum's purpose that occurred in the late 1960s was unprecedented both in scale and in its connection to a wider cultural debate.

As the production of cultural knowledge was scrutinized, the authority of the museum and the curator to make decisions about the inherent worth and value of objects was viewed with mounting skepticism. This had both immediate and long-lasting consequences. A general trend toward the adoption of more inclusive, populist aims was visible across the museum fields of Britain and the United States from the late 1960s onward (Alexander 1999; Nairne 1999).[11] These aims manifested themselves not only in a more sensitive display and interpretation of objects but also in the physical architecture of newly constructed gallery spaces and museum buildings (Taylor 1999, 203–220).[12] Over the long term, the concerns raised during this time ushered in a gradual shift toward increased curatorial reflexivity: an awareness of the particular values, biases, and context governing curatorial decisions (Nairne 1999; O'Neill 2007).

Economic realities of the latter half of the twentieth century altered the financial pressures and expectations placed on museums. In both Britain and the United States, the first blockbuster exhibitions took place in the late 1960s, and gained prominence in the 1970s (Barker 1999, 127–146). These exhibitions held a double appeal as they reinforced the populist ethos of the museum at the same time that they generated much-needed funds. The 1980s rise of Reaganism in the United States and Thatcherism in Britain each served to make the economic position of the museum more tenuous (Wu 2002). It was in this environment that corporate sponsorship of the museum, particularly in relation to blockbuster exhibitions, became ever more commonplace (Alexander 1999; Deuchar 2002).

Strategies adopted in response to financial pressures necessarily influenced the way in which curatorial practice was approached. Increasingly, expectations were placed on those engaged in curatorial work to locate and secure funding for exhibitions and acquisitions, a situation that has persisted into the present and is seen by some as diverting the curator's attention away from research activities (Alexander 1999; Deuchar 2002).[13] Moreover, justified or not, there is a general unease that the museum's alignment with exterior funding sources, be they corporate or government sponsored, might influence the type of curatorial work produced in the institution (Alexander 1999).

The developments touched upon in this section do not represent an exhaustive list of the changes that have shaped the museum field or the curator's place within it. Instead, they highlight key factors that have converged to reorient thinking about curating over the course of the century. Surveying these factors, the pressures and tensions that today's curators workers are required to navigate become clear.

Curatorial theory now

The evolution of curatorship has been neither smooth nor predetermined. From the outset, curatorial work has been intimately entangled with wider sociocultural events and trends. Consequently, understandings and expectations of the curator's role and purpose have been continually molded by relationships and negotiations both within and outside the museum. The complex history of curatorship is worth bearing in mind as we consider the present and future state of curatorial praxis.

In conducting research for this chapter, I made contact with a broad range of professionals in the museum field, soliciting information about their experiences and their understandings of the role that critique and theory plays in curatorial work.[14] Assembled together, their responses hold a dualistic appeal. In one respect, they speak to deeply personal experiences – reflecting each individual's unique history, career path, interests, connections, and approach. In another respect, when reviewed in relation to one another, their responses speak to a collective experience that reveals trends and patterns shaping the contemporary museum field at large. It is this secondary aspect that warrants our attention.

Among the themes that emerged from my discussions with museum directors, curators, and scholars was a pervasive sense that curatorial theory and practice cannot be separated from one another. Indeed, the majority felt that theory and practice inform each other to the point of being essentially indistinguishable. As one curator put it, "My ideas aren't separate from my daily activities. At the same time my external activities can't help but be driven by my internal thoughts. Those thoughts are, in and of themselves, a combination of memory, reaction, sensory input and interpretation." Another curator observed, "It's not really an either/or type of situation. Theory and practice go hand in hand. They're really just two sides of the same coin."

Equally ubiquitous was a widespread belief that understandings of curatorial role and purpose evolve over the course of an individual's career. In line with this contention, it was frequently observed that mentors and colleagues play a critical role in the formation of both theory and practice. "My approach has been shaped by my peers and our shared experience of working together on projects" was a typical refrain. When asked directly whether individual relationships with mentors and colleagues played as significant a role as literature and formal study, the answer was a resounding yes. Indeed, most felt that these human relationships were of far greater importance.

Institutional politics and internal museum dynamics were also seen as significant in shaping curatorial values and approach. Time and again, the museum professionals that I talked to stressed the importance of the specificities of the context in which they operated. Individuals who had had the opportunity to work at both large and small museums were especially vocal in pointing out the degree to which variances in organizational structures impact upon curatorial duties and responsibilities. In turn, it was felt that these circumstances contribute substantially to the formation of the curator's ideas, beliefs, and sense of identity.

Moreover, nearly every respondent talked about the importance of the broader cultural climate. Many observed that perceptions and expectations of curators have changed in sync with broader social changes in recent decades and that, as a result, curation has become increasingly synonymous with interpretation. Some called this "a shift toward storytelling," while others referred to it as "a further reorientation toward audience acknowledgment and participation." Still others pointed out that the post-1980s movement toward greater reflexivity in curatorial work has resulted in a general consensus that the curatorial process needs to be as transparent as possible. This recurring sentiment transcended institutional typology and disciplinary specialty. For instance, curators of art spoke about the need for transparency in relation to object provenance, while curators of history and science mentioned a greater expectation to acknowledge past oversights and misconceptions within their disciplines. Several people noted that the most explicit call for transparency has been in relation to curatorial practices involving anthropological material (see Marstine, Dodd, and Jones this volume). As one individual explained, "The ideals embodied in NAGPRA [Native American Graves and Repatriation Act] have changed the expectations of how curators approach sacred objects. The need to be ethical and transparent has been embraced above and beyond the mandates of the law."

This increased focus on reflexivity and transparency is familiar to anyone who has been involved with museums in the past 30 years. People I spoke to were quick to point out that the movement toward openness reveals mounting tension within the museum field, which stems from a fear that efforts to champion inclusivity and collaboration may come at the expense of an appreciation of a curator's expertise and knowledge. However, I was struck by the extent to which the individuals that I surveyed expressed frustration with this kind of thinking. The observations of many are encapsulated in one particular statement, "In the past the pendulum has swung widely: curators have been seen either as experts isolated from the concerns of museum visitors or, in contrast, as impartial facilitators with no distinct knowledge base of their own. The time has come to reconsider this." Another individual noted, "The expert curator and the engaged and participatory audience are not fundamentally at odds with each other. Now is the moment to move toward the middle ground." Statements such as these were common, and their underlying sentiment suggests that the museum sector is gradually moving toward a more balanced conception of curatorial work. This new model places value on both official and unofficial knowledge, and recognizes that the way ahead may lie somewhere between staid traditionalism and radical innovation.

Conclusion: Reflections

The museum world is characterized by singularity. Institutions vary according to typology, scale, focus, and mission. Further, every museum is informed by its particular blend of history and politics. These factors converge, shaping internal mandates on everything from collections care to the hierarchy of personnel. Consequently, no two museums are exactly alike. Across the field, this same idiosyncratic quality is reflected in the ideas and beliefs that inflect curatorial work. Each curator's approach is distinctive, born out of a combination of individual expertise, personal, and cultural values, interaction with peers and colleagues, and institutional expectations.

Yet if singularity and distinctiveness are constant aspects of both museums and curatorial praxis, so too is an inclination toward continual innovation. This is not surprising. As we have seen, museums and curators have never been idle; rather, they are constantly engaged in a process of self-exploration that time and again questions the parameters and purpose of the curatorial role.

This tendency toward singularity, distinctiveness, and evolution is also one of the unifying characteristics within the curatorial profession. It raises an important question about the future of curatorship and how we might train curatorial workers. As we have seen, curators have long grappled with methods of practice and approach. Arguments about the best way to prepare an individual for a curatorial career are nearly as old as the profession itself. The issues underlying these debates and the solution are one in the same: when it comes to preparation for curatorship, there is no one answer.

Indeed, it is telling that in my conversations with museum professionals a number of individuals went out of their way to explain that their entrance into the field was "out of the ordinary" or "far from the norm." These statements are particularly fascinating because they were primarily voiced by professionals who had obtained university degrees with areas of disciplinary focus normally associated with their fields of interest. Thus, this shared experience of "otherness" is not inconsequential. Instead, it speaks to a broad discrepancy between how we train and how people actually enter the field and begin to acquire professional knowledge and skills.

So perhaps the time has come for a reconsideration. We are now in a new age of curating and have the opportunity to move away from traditional tensions: between academia and on-the-job-training, between disciplinary and vocational studies, between the expert and the novice. The future is wide open for collaborative ventures and the most effective training programs are likely to be those that balance practical instruction, disciplinary knowledge, and hands-on experience. I note the emerging trend for academic museum studies programs to take cues from the experiences of curators both past and present and hope that this will lead to the realization of the kind of model, discussed above, that recognizes the fluidity between curatorial theory and practice.

APPENDIX
Survey participants

Gail Anderson, Independent Museum Consultant; Gail Anderson and Associates; formerly Deputy Director of the Mexican Museum, and Chair of the Department of Museum Studies at John F. Kennedy University, California; author of *Reinventing the Museum* (2012).

Heather Birchall, Curator (Art); formerly Curator (Historic Fine Art) at Whitworth Art Gallery and Assistant Curator at Tate.

Mary Bouquet, Academic and Museologist (Anthropology); University Lecturer and Fellow at University College, Utrecht; author of *Museums: A Visual Anthropology* (2012) and *Academic Anthropology and the Museum* (2001).

Susan Casteras, Academic (Art); Professor, Art History Department, University of Washington; formerly Curator of Paintings at the Yale Center for British Art.

Kevin Coffee, Independent Museum Consultant, Chicago; Kevin Coffee Museum Planning.

Beryl Graham, Academic and Museologist (Art and New Media); Professor of New Media Art at the School of Arts, Design and Media, University of Sunderland; co-author of *Rethinking Curating* (2010).

Robin Held, Curator (Art); Museum Consultant; formerly Deputy Director of Exhibitions and Collections at the Frye Art Museum, Seattle, WA.

Rock Hushka, Curator (Art); Chief Curator, Tacoma Museum of Art, Tacoma, WA.

Tim Knox, Director (Art); Director of the Fitzwilliam Museum, University of Cambridge; formerly Director of the Sir John Soane's Museum, London.

Christina Kreps, Academic and Museologist (Anthropology); Director of Museum and Heritage Studies/University of Denver Museum of Anthropology and Associate Professor of Anthropology, University of Denver; author of *Liberating Culture* (2003).

Steven Lubar, Academic and Museologist (History); Professor, Departments of American Studies, History, and History of Art and Architecture; Director, John Nicholas Brown Center for Public Humanities and Cultural Heritage, Brown University; formerly Chair of the Division of the History of Technology at the Smithsonian's National Museum of American History.

Sandy Nairne, Director (Art); Director of the National Portrait Gallery, London; formerly Director of Programmes at Tate; co-editor of *Thinking about Exhibitions* (1996) with Reesa Greenberg and Bruce Ferguson.

Nina Simon, Museum Director (Art and History); Director of the Santa Cruz Museum of Art and History, California; formerly Curator at the Tech Museum of Innovation in San Jose, and the Experience Development Specialist at the International Spy Museum in Washington, DC; author of *The Participatory Museum* (2010) and the popular Museum 2.0 blog.

Rachel Souhami, Freelance Museum Consultant (Art and Science); Lecturer in Museum Studies; formerly Curator at the Science Museum, London.

Notes

1 The term "curator" stems from the Latin root, *curare*, meaning to care take. Traditionally, the title of curator has been applied as a label to an officer, keeper, or custodian charged with the caretaking of objects within an institution, such as a museum, gallery, or library. See definition in *Oxford English Dictionary*. See also Fowle 2007.

2 The opening chapter of Terry Smith's recent examination of contemporary curating offers a poignant and thoughtful discussion of how definitions of curatorship continue to expand (Smith 2012).

3 For notable full-length publications on the museum's historical development see Conn 1998; McClellan 2008; Waterfield 1991. Two essays also warrant mention: Alberti 2011; Shelton 2006.

4 For three prime examples of case studies of this kind, see Burton 1999; Abt 2001; Wilson 2002.

5 The Museums Association was founded in 1889 and the American Association of Museums in 1906.

6 The Museum Course was considered an experimental program during its first two years, becoming a permanent offering of the Harvard Fine Arts Department in 1923. Sachs oversaw the program until his retirement in 1948.

7 For instance, discussing the National Gallery's history during this period, Charles Saumarez Smith notes that the museum's relationship with the public was transformed during the war as the gallery repositioned itself as "a place of mass democratic culture" (Saumarez Smith 2009, 131).

8   The emergence of these professions was gradual. It was at the 1950 ICOM general conference, held in London, that conservators were recognized as a distinct category of museum professional. Educators received similar recognition at the 1965 ICOM general conference, which took place in New York City.

9   For more on the rise of the registrar and collection manager see Simmons in this volume. On education see Reeve and Woollard, and on conservation see Sully, both in this volume.

10   McClellan offers an excellent summary of the issues of the late 1960s debate surrounding the art museum (2008).

11   Alexander observes that, in the United States, the introduction of substantial state funding for special exhibitions and projects in the late 1960s served as an extra incentive in the adoption of a more populist approach. This form of funding persisted until the mid-1980s (Alexander 1999).

12   For instance, the 1968 opening of the Hayward Gallery on London's Southbank, a new permanent space for temporary exhibitions, serves as evidence of this more egalitarian approach.

13   For an early indication of this concern, see Alloway 1975.

14   The individuals I contacted came from diverse career paths and represent a broad cross-section of museum typologies. My interactions with them took various forms, ranging from surveys, email correspondence, and structured interviews, to more casual face-to-face conversations. See the Appendix for a complete list of participants. All the quotations in this chapter are taken from surveys and interviews with these participants.

References

Abt, Jeffrey. 2001. *A Museum on the Verge: A Socio-Economic History of the Detroit Institute of Arts, 1882–2000*. Detroit: Wayne State University Press.

Alberti, Samuel. 2011. "The Status of Museums: Authority, Identity and Material Culture." In *Geographies of Nineteenth-Century Science*, edited by David N. Livingstone and Charles W. Withers, 51–72. Chicago: University of Chicago Press.

Alexander, Victoria D. 1999. "A Delicate Balance: Museums and the Market-Place." *Museums International* 51(2): 29–34.

Alloway, Lawrence. 1975. "The Great Curatorial Dim-Out." *Artforum* 13(9): 32–34.

Ames, Michael, and Mina McKenzie, eds. 1996. *Curatorship: Indigenous Perspectives in Postcolonial Societies*. Ottawa: Canadian Museum of Civilization.

Barker, Emma. 1999. "Exhibiting the Canon: The Blockbuster Show." In *Contemporary Cultures of Display*, edited by Emma Barker, 127–146. London: Open University Press.

Bather, Frank Arthur. 1902. "The Man as Museum-Curator." *Museums Journal* 1(7): 185–188.

Bennett, Tony. 1995. *The Birth of the Museum: History, Theory, Politics*. London: Routledge.

Bourdieu, Pierre, and Alain Darbel. 1991. *The Love of Art: European Art Museums and Their Public*, trans. by Caroline Beattie and Nick Merriman. Oxford: Polity. Originally published as *L'Amour de l'art* (Paris: Minuit, 1969).

Boylan, Patrick. 2006. "The Museum Profession." In *A Companion to Museum Studies*, edited by Sharon MacDonald, 415–430. Oxford: Blackwell.

Burton, Anthony. 1999. *Vision and Accident: The Story of the Victoria and Albert Museum*. London: V&A Publishing.

Chambers, Elizabeth. 2006. "Defining the Role of the Curator." In *Museum Studies: Perspectives and Innovations*, edited by Stephen L. Williams and Catherine A. Hawks, 47–63. Washington, DC: Society for the Preservation of Natural History Collections.

Chandler, Lisa. 2009. "'Journey without Maps': Unsettling Curatorship in Cross-Cultural Contexts." *Museum and Society* 7(2): 74–91.

Conn, Steven. 1998. *Museums and American Intellectual Life, 1876–1926*. Chicago: University of Chicago Press.

Crook, A. R. 1910. "Training of a Museum Curator." *Proceedings of the Fifth Annual Meeting of the American Association of Museums*, 59–63. Charlestown, SC: American Association of Museums.

Crowther, Paul. 2002. "Against Curatorial Imperialism: Merleau-Ponty and the Historicity of Art." In *A Companion to Art Theory*, edited by Paul Smith and Carolyn Wilde, 477–487. Oxford: Blackwell.

Dana, John Cotton. 1917. *The Gloom of the Museum*. Woodstock, UK: Elm Tree Press.

Deuchar, Stephen. 2002. "Whose Art History? Curators, Academics and the Museum Visitor in Britain in the 1980s and 1990s." In *The Two Art Histories: The Museum and the University*, edited by Charles W. Haxthausen, 3–13. Williamstown, MA: Clark Art Institute.

DiMaggio, Paul. 1991. "Constructing an Organisational Field as a Professional Project." In *The New Institutionalism in Organizational Analysis*, edited by Walter Powell and Paul DiMaggio, 267–292. Chicago: University of Chicago Press.

Duncan, Carol. 1995. *Civilizing Rituals: Inside Public Art Museums*. New York: Routledge.

Duncan, Sally Anne. 2002. "Harvard's 'Museum Course' and the Making of America's Museum Profession." *Archives of American Art Journal* 42(1): 2–16.

Fowle, Kate. 2007. "Who Cares? Understanding the Role of the Curator Today." In *Cautionary Tales: Critical Curating*, edited by Steven Rand and Heather Kouris, 26–35. New York: Apex Art Curatorial Program.

Graham, Beryl, and Sarah Cook. 2010. *Rethinking Curating: Art after New Media*. Cambridge, MA: MIT Press.

Grenfell, Michael, and Cheryl Hardy. 2007. *Art Rules: Pierre Bourdieu and the Visual Arts*. Oxford: Berg.

Harding, Anna, ed. 1997. *Curating: The Contemporary Art Museum and Beyond*. London: Academy Editions.

Heinich, Nathalie, and Michael Pollak. 1996. "From Museum Curator to Exhibition Auteur: Forming a Singular Position." In *Thinking about Exhibitions*, edited by Bruce W. Ferguson, Reesa Greenburg, and Sandy Nairne, 166–179. London: Routledge.

Heumann Gurian, Elaine. 2010. "Curator: From Soloist to Impresario." In *Hot Topics, Public Culture, Museums*, edited by Fiona Cameron and Lynda Kelly, 95–111. Newcastle: Cambridge Scholars Press.

Hoyle, William Evans. 1906. "Presidential Address: The Education of a Curator." *Museums Journal* 6: 4–24.

Kreps, Christina. 2010. "Curating as a Social Practice." *Curator: The Museum Journal* 46(3): 311–323.

Marincola, Paula, ed. 2001. *Curating Now: Imaginative Practice/Public Responsibility.* Philadelphia, PA: Philadelphia Exhibitions Initiative.

McClellan, Andrew. 2008. *The Art Museum from Boullée to Bilbao.* Berkeley: University of California Press.

McLean, Kathleen. 2004. "Museum Exhibitions and the Dynamics of Dialogue." In *Reinventing the Museum: Historical and Contemporary Perspectives on the Paradigm Shift,* edited by Gail Anderson, 193–211. Lanham, MD: AltaMira.

Nairne, Sandy. 1999. "Exhibitions of Contemporary Art." In *Contemporary Cultures of Display,* edited by Emma Barker, 105–126. London: Open University Press.

Norton-Westbrook, Halona. 2013. "Between the Collection Museum and the University: The Rise of the Connoisseur-Scholar and the Evolution of Art Museum Curatorial Practice, 1900–1940." PhD thesis, University of Manchester.

Obrist, Hans-Ulrich. 2008. *A Brief History of Curating.* Zurich: JRP/Ringier.

O'Neill, Paul. 2007. "The Curatorial Turn: From Practice to Discourse." In *Issues in Contemporary Curating and Performance,* edited by Judith Rugg and Michele Sedgwick, 12–26. Bristol: Intellect.

O'Neill, Paul. 2007. *Curating Subjects.* London: De Appel, Centre for Contemporary Art.

O'Neill, Paul. 2012. *The Culture of Curating and the Curating of Culture(s).* Cambridge, MA: MIT Press.

Pointon, Marcia, ed. 1994. *Art Apart: Art Institutions and Ideology across England and North America.* Manchester: Manchester University Press.

Resnicow, David. 1995. "Everybody's a Curator." *Curator: The Museum Journal* 38(2): 74–75.

Roberts, Lisa C. 2004. "Changing Practices of Interpretation." In *Reinventing the Museum: Historical and Contemporary Perspectives on the Paradigm Shift,* edited by Gail Anderson, 212–232. Lanham, MD: AltaMira.

Rogoff, Irit. 2006. "'Smuggling': A Curatorial Model." In *Under Construction: Perspectives on Institutional Practice,* edited by Vanessa Joan Muller and Nicolaus Schafhausen, 132–135. Cologne: European Kunsthalle.

Saumarez Smith, Charles. 2008. "Narrative Display at the National Gallery London." In *Spectacle and Display,* edited by Deborah Cherry and Fintan Cullen, 137–153. Malden, MA: Blackwell.

Saumarez Smith, Charles. 2009. *The National Gallery: A Short History.* London: Frances Lincoln.

Shelton, Anthony Alan. 2006. "Museums and Anthropologies: Practices and Narratives." In *A Companion to Museum Studies,* edited by Sharon Macdonald, 65–79. Oxford: Blackwell.

Smith, Terry. 2012. *Thinking Contemporary Curating.* New York: Independent Curators International.

Storr, Robert. 2001. "How We Do What We Do. And How We Don't." In *Curating Now: Imaginative Practice/Public Responsibility,* edited by Paula Marincola, 3–22. Philadelphia, PA: Philadelphia Exhibitions Initiative.

Taylor, Brandon. 1999. *Art for the Nation: Exhibitions and the London Public 1747–2001.* Manchester: Manchester University Press.

Thomas, Catherine, ed. 2002. *The Edge of Everything: Reflections on Curatorial Practice*. Banff, Canada: Banff Centre Press.

Townsend, Melanie, ed. 2003. *Beyond the Box: Diverging Curatorial Practices*. Banff, Canada: Banff Centre Press.

Ward, Martha. 1996. "What's Important about the History of Modern Art Exhibitions?" In *Thinking about Exhibitions*, edited by Reesa Greenberg, Bruce W. Ferguson, and Sandy Nairne, 318–327. London: Routledge.

Waterfield, Giles. 1991. *Palaces of Art: Art Galleries in Britain, 1790–1990*. London: Dulwich Picture Gallery.

Wilson, David. 2002. *The British Museum: A History*. London: British Museum Press.

Wu, Chin-tao. 2002. *Privatising Culture: Corporate Art Intervention since the 1980s*. London: Verson.

Zolberg, Vera. 1981. "Conflicting Visions in American Art Museums." *Theory and Society* 10(1): 103–125.

Further Reading

Bouquet, Mary, ed. 2001. *Academic Anthropology and the Museum: Back to the Future*. New York: Berghahn.

Kreps, Christina F. 2003. *Liberating Culture: Cross-Cultural Perspectives on Museums, Curation, and Heritage Preservation*. London: Routledge.

Wade, Gavin, ed. 2000. *Curating in the 21st Century*. Wolverhampton, UK: New Art Gallery, University of Wolverhampton.

Halona Norton-Westbrook currently serves as the third post-doctoral Andrew W. Mellon Fellow at the Toledo Museum of Art. The fellowship program, underwritten by a grant from the Andrew W. Mellon Foundation, endeavors to train the next generation of museum leaders by giving them opportunities to learn the Museum's inner workings firsthand as part of the executive staff. Fellows not only take part in strategic planning for the institution but are also immersed in curatorial work.

Norton-Westbrook, who received her BA from Mills College in Oakland, California, holds an MA in Art History from the Courtauld Institute of Art in London and a PhD in Museology from the University of Manchester. Her doctoral research centered on the history of curating in American and British art museums. Norton-Westbrook has worked on a number of diverse curatorial projects at museums in the USA and the UK, with past engagements at the Georgia O'Keeffe Museum, the Mills College Art Museum, the Courtauld Institute of Art Gallery, and London's Garden Museum. Norton-Westbrook's curatorial focus at the Toledo Museum of Art is primarily in modern and contemporary art.

16 PLANNING FOR SUCCESS
Project Management for Museum Exhibitions

David K. Dean

This chapter begins with a story about developing an exhibition, which demonstrates the need for project management in museum practice. It concerns a new vertebrate paleontology exhibition in the Museum of Texas Tech University, Lubbock, a medium-sized general university museum well known for its science exhibits (Museum of Texas Tech University 2014). In 2001, the exhibition team were tasked with generating the concept and content for this gallery and contracting an exhibit design/build company to fabricate and install it. The problem was that the scope of the exhibition and its storyline (in other words, its content framework) varied greatly both in range and subject matter, and despite considerable negotiation, there remained some issues that the team members and the curator in particular could not fully agree on. The exhibition made little progress because the developers could not agree on the overall direction and concept, which meant that the development process seemed to go round and round in circles instead of moving forward. I was called in to clear the "road block." Working with the staff to review the storyline, we modified and further developed it so that a clear and consistent framework could be used to deliver the content and guide the designer's fabrication efforts. The whole team was now committed to the one vision for the space instead of being distracted by a fragmented and changing focus. The exhibition went ahead, and was successfully opened to the public on schedule in 2004 as *A Changing World: Dinosaurs, Diversity, and Drifting Continents* (Figure 16.1).

Looking back on this experience, we learned that it is essential to agree on a unified approach for developing an exhibition, otherwise there is a risk that subsequent work – design, promotion, outreach, and education – lacks any clear foundation upon which to grow. Reflecting on my own professional experiences working with exhibitions, I, therefore, set out to provide an overview of a clear pathway for planning exhibitions in order to guard against the problems that often

The International Handbooks of Museum Studies: Museum Practice, First Edition.
Edited by Conal McCarthy.
© 2015 John Wiley & Sons Ltd. Published 2020 by John Wiley & Sons Ltd.

FIGURE 16.1   A view of the vertebrate paleontology gallery after completion. The exhibition is titled *A Changing World: Dinosaurs, Diversity, and Drifting Continents.*
Image courtesy of the Museum of Texas Tech University.

arise when it comes to the messy realities of managing exhibition production. Though exhibitions can be and are developed very well in many different ways in various kinds of museums, a major problem with completing exhibitions success-fully is the lack of a clear, structured process, and in particular a need for project management (OP&A 2002a, 10–11).

What are exhibitions? Though they can take many forms, traditionally museum exhibitions can be seen as composite, three-dimensional visual products, usually created by a group of professionals as a public and physical expression of a muse-um's mission, collections, and research. By "composite" I mean that exhibitions are comprised of not only collection items and other material, but also the physical apparatuses (mounts and supports) that the objects rest upon or in, the outer protective containers (exhibit cases and vitrines) they are displayed within, the barriers and buffering agents that protect them, and the gallery environment in which they are installed and presented (Dean 1996).

The public only see the exhibition as a finished *product* in the public spaces of museums, but it is important that institutions have a carefully managed *process* for producing them and do not simply rely on goodwill, creativity, or luck. Usually the products of group activity (exhibitions are seldom the work of an individual), museum displays are *projects* involving coordination, information exchange, resource allocation and use, and interpersonal and communal effort. In many museums, exhibition teams are the preferred organizational structure for bringing together the appropriate expertise needed for the multiple elements of the project in order to assure a successful outcome. This chapter outlines a practical integrated model for successful exhibition production from theory to practice, tested out and refined through professional experience, an approach that has stood the test of time and met the many challenges that have to be surmounted in getting shows opened on time and under budget.

Exhibition development and project management

Preparing exhibitions is a complex and demanding task, which involves many subjects, disciplines, and terminologies (Dean 1996, 1; Serrell 2006). Despite these challenges, this chapter sets out to describe an ideal process of exhibition development in practical terms. The literature of museum studies contains much work on the history, theory, and politics of exhibitions, display, and design (Karp and Lavine 1991; Ferguson, Nairne, and Greenburg 1996; Macleod 2005), but the practice of exhibition development or production is not so well examined (for museum design and display, see Spock in this volume; for trends in exhibition practice, see Young in this volume). There are several publications on exhibition creation and reception from a philosophical or conceptual perspective (Macdonald 1998; Barker 1999; Macdonald and Basu 2007), as well as a number of manuals with practical guidance on the process of mounting exhibits in museums (Klein 1986; Belcher 1991; Dean 1996; Lord and Lord 2002; Ambrose and Paine 2012) and particularly science and natural history museums (Houtgraaf and Vitali 2008; Caulton 2013). Some particular design/exhibit issues are dealt with in a few books, such as physical access (Sartwell 1992; Holmes-Siedle 1996), and security (Liston 1993).

In the United States there has been some empirical research on current museum practice in exhibition-making (OP&A 2002a; 2002b) and a lively professional subgroup of AAM (American Alliance of Museums) called NAME (National Association for Museum Exhibition) has its own website with online resources and a journal *Exhibitionist* that explores trends in exhibition practice (Morris 2002). Of the authors who have written about the internal process of developing exhibitions, Kathleen McLean (1993; 1999) is probably the best-known. She continues to practice as an exhibit developer and to critically reflect on current practice (Exhibitricks 2008).

In the United Kingdom, Durbin (1996), Fritsch (2012), and McKenna-Cress and Kamien (2013) have documented developments in exhibition practice, including the move to teams, the stress on education and learning, and increasingly collaborative and audience-focused approaches. There have been a few in-depth studies of particular projects such as the British Galleries at the V&A in London (Wilk and Humphrey 2004). Recent work on museum and gallery exhibitions focus on planning (Bogle 2013), interpretation (Bridal 2013), and narrative (Macleod, Hanks, and Hale 2012). One area that has consistently attracted the attention of researchers is the visitor experience, and how knowing more about visitors can guide exhibition development, particularly in terms of participation, interaction, and interpretation (Serrell 1998; Roppola 2011; Christidou 2012; Simon 2013). (On interpretation and exhibitions, see Jimson in this volume, and on visitor research and exhibitions, see Davidson in this volume.)

However, this chapter takes a different approach, and concentrates on presenting a practical model for managing the development of exhibition as projects. This is a model that I have refined in my own professional practice over many years, building on proven ideas that – although they have been around for some time – are still very pertinent in the everyday reality of exhibition development. In doing so it draws on the field of project management, which is critical for everyday museum work despite the fact that it is often overlooked in academic museum studies (Tonquist 2009; Meredith and Mantel 2011).

Developing and presenting an exhibition is an organizational project. We can think of an organization as an institutional structure made up of roles and responsibilities through which individuals work together systematically to meet predetermined objectives. In the field of organization studies, an organization is defined as a "social entity" that is "goal directed," "designed as deliberately structured and coordinated activity systems," and is "linked to the external environment" (Daft, Murphy, and Willmott 2010, 10). A project is generally understood as a unique, specific, and temporary process with constraints of time, cost, and resources, which is quite different to the ongoing, business-as-usual management of an organization (Lester 2013, 1–2). For the purposes of this chapter, a project is defined as a finite set of activities aimed toward a specific, one-time goal that requires multiple disciplines to accomplish, and has a product for which the project agents are accountable.

All projects share some common traits. They all take time and personnel to plan, develop, and execute, and that time and those personnel are limited resources. Projects have definite beginning and ending points (bearing in mind, of course, that projects can linger on and overlap, making them difficult to manage). After running their course, they generate new approaches and ideas for future efforts. Projects are, therefore, cyclical in nature. Consider a temporary exhibition. Its installation and public presentation may be considered the project's product. A set number of dates dictate when the exhibition will be available to the public and when it will close. The life cycle of the exhibition project encompasses the time needed to plan, produce, present, terminate, and evaluate the exhibition. The gallery or space used to present the exhibition must be prepared, used, cleared, and prepared to receive the next exhibition. This cyclical, phased, and linear (or sequential) nature of a project has been widely utilized in many areas of endeavor (Daft, Murphy, and Willmott 2010). Industry successfully employs schema such as this for producing the everyday products we all consume and use. It seems logical, then, to frame exhibition development within a similar practical model.

For projects to meet their objectives, it is expected that participants fulfill consistent roles at various stages of the process that work toward a successful outcome. Early in the project, product-oriented activities focus on the actual exhibition product, such as object conservation and preparation, fabrication, preparation, presentation of educational activities that accompany the exhibition, and promotional and marketing efforts to entice the audience to participate. Management-oriented activities are also an important responsibility, which focus on providing and overseeing the resources necessary for accomplishing the project. These activities include procurement, accountability for funding, assignment and organization of tasks, quality and progress control, and dissemination and coordination of information between the different agents engaged in the project. Dutch academics Verhaar and Meeter define both organizational structures and management responsibilities as follows:

> In general, the management function deals with directing processes in organizations. An organization can be viewed as a group of people with the common objective of realizing a product or service with the available abilities and resources, in order to satisfy a certain need in society. The management function ensures that the creative process continues to be aimed at this objective. (Verhaar and Meeter 1989, 3)

Another set of activities of a supervisory nature might be called administration, and deals with keeping product and management activities coordinated and moving toward the same objectives and goals; it also includes decision-making and staff supervision. One of the main responsibilities of administration should be the selection and initial appointment of the exhibition team.

As a practical matter, for many smaller institutions, these responsibilities, both product- and management-oriented, may well be the purview of very few individuals. Some or all of the roles may be subsumed into one person's duties. However, it should be stated that, whenever possible, a division of tasks and responsibilities is preferable because it seems to me that combined talents usually produce a better result and furthermore relieves the stresses of project planning and development.

Team building for success

Over the last half of the twentieth century and into the current one, museums have shifted from an older curator-directed exhibition paradigm in favor of a more inclusive and broader team model (OP&A 2002a). As McLean states, "In the 1980s, museums embraced the 'team approach' to exhibition development as a way of improving exhibit quality and ultimately diversifying exhibition presentations" (McLean 1999, 93–94). This change was partly the result of museum professionals recognizing that no one person within an organization has the comprehensive knowledge and skill sets needed to effectively bring together the multifaceted components of modern public exhibitions. Professionals also recognized the short-comings of an open storage style of collections display, interpreted by subject specialists, that provides information more beneficial to colleagues with similar interests than to the casual museum visitor. For the most part exhibitions are still object-based, and, while acknowledging the advent of digital and other new media, and the range of presentation styles whether aesthetic, thematic, narrative, cognitive/didactic, or taxonomic in style, they are designed to provide accessible interpretation and interactivity accessible to a range of audiences (Verhaar and Meeter 1989; van Mensch 1992; OP&A 2002a). Nevertheless, debate continues about the team approach and the internal "dynamics of dialogue" between different museum developers, as well as the advantages of different styles of exhibitions (McLean 1999; Kamien 2002; Pekarik 2002).

A clear and detailed knowledge of the capabilities of each staff member, volunteer, or consultant is needed to properly assess and assign roles within a functional team. Team members must be stakeholders, meaning they have vested interest in seeing the exhibition project through to a successful conclusion. Obviously they should have the appropriate skill sets and attitudes needed for coherent team work and product or management roles. And, they must understand the interdependent nature of the team structure, realizing that all members must cooperate in working toward common goals and substantively share responsibility in the project's success or failure.

For many museums, the team is self-identifying, as the range of individuals from which to choose is limited and, normally, staff positions tend to dictate the membership of the exhibition team core – the two to five members who remain active on the team for the duration of the project. As an exhibition is *about* something (a subject), there is a need for a subject specialist, generally a curator, collections manager, subject expert, or researcher. In concept-driven or narrative exhibitions this is often referred to as a concept developer. The role of designer usually falls to the lead exhibits staff member in the museum. As the exhibition is a public educational presentation, a museum education or learning specialist, such as a teacher, interpreter, or museum educator, is needed. The registrar or collection manager may well be included if the exhibition requires collections items, loans, and shipping arrangements.

There is one other key role that may require a separate individual: the project manager or team leader. This person should be appointed as the central point of contact and decision-maker for the overall project so as to coordinate all the activities required to complete the exhibition. Industry has given us a model for a team leader known as the "Strong Project Manager" (Burstein and Stasiowski 1982, 11), who essentially is a sub-administrator having the authority and responsibility to establish the project team membership, set goals and objectives, develop timelines and deadlines, and to "hire and fire" team members depending on performance criteria. This model works well in manufacturing and similar commercial businesses, but is not usually the style adopted by educational and non-profit organizations such as museums, zoos, aquaria, and botanical gardens. For many, this strongly directorial mode of supervisory control harkens back to the earlier style of curator-centered exhibition development, but with the advent of the audience-focused exhibition described here, the project manager's role becomes much more that of a facilitator.

What is needed in an exhibition project manager or team leader? This role calls for someone who is very familiar with the organization and its mission; has a good understanding of the collections, best practices, and standards; works well within the organizational structure of the institution; and fully appreciates the needs of the other team members and the project. Skill sets should include: the ability to assess and appreciate the professional qualities of other team members; excellent communication skills; the confidence and tact to handle conflicts that inevitably arise; and the intellectual flexibility to make good decisions and to adapt to changing circumstances.

In the museum setting, the role of team leader can be described as "coordinating" project manager. They are vested with the authority and responsibility to facilitate the other team members in accomplishing their roles. To do this, the project manager must manage the resources available for the project, coordinate scheduling and meetings, expedite procurements, enforce deadlines, and act as the liaison between the team members, other staff, and the museum's administration or governance. These managerial duties fall into what Verhaar and Meeter refer to as the five aspects of an exhibition project: Time, Finances, Quality, Information, and Organization (TFQIO; Verhaar and Meeter 1989, 11).

In addition to the core exhibition team, some supplementary agents may serve for only a portion of the project's life span to assist with specific issues and objectives, and then, having fulfilled their roles, retire from the team: these may include visitor research, conservation, marketing, and fund-raising. The exhibition team should be configured to best fit the needs of the project. The caveat is: the larger the team, the more complex communication and consensus become.

Lastly, team building reflects the widespread trend to use the "expert generalist" (Verhaar and Meeter 1989, 11). These are museum professionals who are versed not only in the design principles and practices needed to plan and produce an exhibition conducive to information presentation and visitor use, but who also possess a broad and detailed understanding of subject matter, educational principles, and administrative skills required by project development. Kathleen McLean describes these individuals well:

> Most exhibit creators agree that organizing a good museum exhibition requires the passion, intuition, scholarship, and expertise of a wide range of people, and more professionals are becoming multilingual (or fluent) in the languages of environmental

psychology, aesthetics, learning theory, conceptual and spatial design, and interpretation. They are essentially "expert generalists," able to synthesize the variety of disciplines that inform the exhibit-development process – to recognize the importance of accurate and meaningful content, to comprehend and be able to manipulate the dynamics at play in the three-dimensional environment, and to be sensitive to the expectations and interests of a diverse audience. They are first and foremost communicators, dedicated to sustaining the relationships and enriching the conversations between exhibition and visitor. (McLean 1999, 99–100)

Through the vehicle of excellent professional training programs around the globe, such individuals are becoming more available to the field every year. These expert generalists often drift into the private sector as consultants in design/build firms, which are contracted by museums to produce exhibitions. However, many remain active in the museum profession as well. Whether paid consultants or employees, these individuals can be extremely beneficial to organizations as team members and communicators, as they possess a cross-section of the skills formerly held by specialists in various disciples. Though not a replacement for the collaborative structure of the exhibition team (two or more heads are generally better than one), the expert generalist can add significantly to the capabilities of the exhibition team as a valuable and capable member and, perhaps, even more so in the role of project leader.

The project model: structure and clarity

Projects, have characteristics that are shared. Among these are the finite nature of their time frames and the linear nature of their development. Although there are multiple models for project development and the literature concerning their inner workings is plentiful, many of these paradigms are more detailed and intricate than might be needed for our purposes (Tonquist 2009; Lester 2013). Some good expositions on project management may be found in Burstein and Stasiowski (1982; 1994); R. S. Miles's work (1982; 2012), which reviews a rather complex methodology called Critical Path Analysis employed by industry; and Belcher (1991, chapter 7), which surveys many similar concepts.

In my view, the models published by Jan Verhaar and Han Meeter of the Reinwardt Academie in the Netherlands are among the clearest and most easily assimilated (Verhaar and Meeter 1989, 4). They describe a simplified paradigm called a "life cycle of product/system" (see Figure 16.2).

The waveform structure of this life-cycle model delineates types of activities, a series of stages through which the project must progress, and the varied energy levels inherent in the progression. This model specifies five stages of development labeled sequentially as Conceptualizing, Developing/planning, Implementing/operating, Deteriorating/terminating, and Assimilating/innovating. Within these

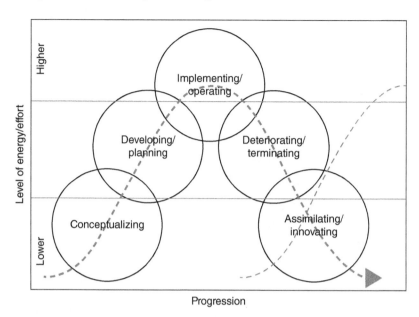

FIGURE 16.2   Life cycle of a product or system, 2011.
Based on Vehaar and Meeter 1989, 4.

stages are very brief allusions to the kinds of issues and approaches characteristic of each stage. One of the most revealing aspects of this model is the overlapping nature of the sine wave patterns, clearly indicating that projects, in actual practice, frequently overlap each other. Take for instance the way temporary exhibitions often occur in a museum: unless the organization has only one presentation space or gallery, usually its exhibitions begin and end at alternating intervals, meaning that the stages and energy levels inherent in the exhibitions' developmental cycles are alternating as well. A museum staff member might well be dismantling one exhibition while installing another and, at the same time, be in the planning stages of a third exhibition. Although projects do have definite beginnings and endings, the overlapping cyclical nature of their developments interweave to form a seemingly continuous level of energy required of the staff to successfully accomplish them all.

Another way of looking at this sharing feature of the life-cycle model is to note that the authors specify that overlapping should occur in the final Transformational stage of one project and in the Concept stage of the next. Within this shared period are listed Innovation Issues and an Innovation Approach, indicating that what is discovered and learned in the execution of one project will be a guide to innovation and improvement for the next and others that follow.

One other model examined by Verhaar and Meeter is the project in a "rolled out model" (see Figure 16.3). This paradigm derives from manufacturing projects in the industrial sector and describes in far greater detail the elements of conceptualizing, planning, producing, and "rolling out" a final product.

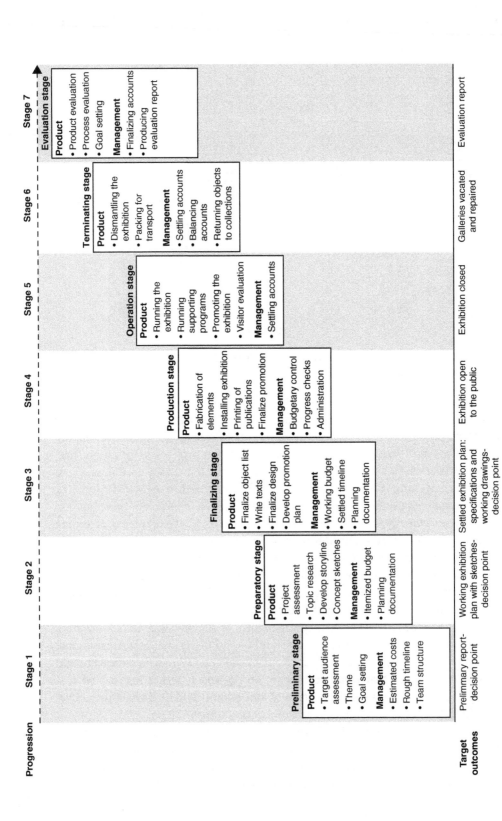

FIGURE 16.3 Rolled-out model, 2011.
Adapted from Vehaar and Meeter 1989, 34.

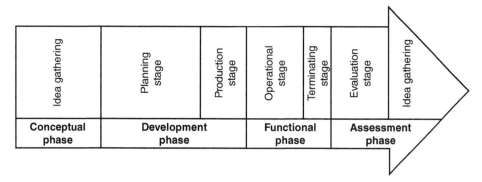

FIGURE 16.4   Linear model: Dean 1996, 9.

Verhaar and Meeter have modified this framework for exhibition development purposes and divided it into seven successive stages, each containing a description of several activities and outcomes to be achieved as the project progresses. For example, in the Preparatory stage, "problem formulation," "analysis diagram," "thematic research," "storyline," and "concept sketches" are specified as product-oriented activities, while "itemized budget" and "detailed planning" indicate the management-oriented responsibilities. The rolled-out model is highly segmented for planning and execution purposes, has clearly demarcated activities, and deline-ates specific tasks (or objectives) to be accomplished sequentially.

The model proposed by this author simplifies the project-oriented approach, while incorporating essential elements of the above examples and others in the literature. The "linear model" presented here (see Figure 16.4) is phased and sequential in nature, and should be envisioned as extending from either end, shar-ing the first and last elements (generation of ideas) with preceding and succeeding projects. This model identifies four phases for exhibition development and splits into stages within some phases, indicating the kinds of activities expected at any particular time during the project's life cycle.

The models described above clearly imply the progressive, orderly nature of exhibition project development. However, developing an exhibition in an actual institution is seldom so clearly hard-edged and defined – the real world is a messy place with much overlapping of efforts and activities and it should be readily acknowledged that a linear process is only an abstract ideal. Nevertheless, these models hopefully provide a structured template within which energy and creativity might flourish. The segments in these models allow for analysis and clarification of activities and roles, and establishes a flow for project maturation, while minimizing the normally very fluid nature of such endeavors in real museum environments. Of course, the reality for most institutions, depending on their size and organizational culture, lies somewhere between the highly structured model and the more informal everyday efforts needed to create successful exhibitions.

Phases and stages: reaching the goal

In this section I present the various steps of exhibition development. These steps follow, to a greater or lesser degree, the project models introduced in this chapter. It is hoped that the process is easy to understand when described as a sequence of phases and subordinate stages. Throughout development, and in each phase, there are three primary tasking orientations. These are:

- Product-oriented activities – efforts centered on the collection objects and their interpretation.
- Management-oriented activities – tasks that focus on providing resources and personnel necessary to complete the project.
- Administrative activities – keeping the product- and management-oriented activities working toward the same goal.

As stated above, it is important to note that the reality of exhibition development means the progression of elements and tasks is not always so clear cut; activities will overlap and morph from one into another along the way. Let us examine each phase and stage individually to clarify and generically identify the types of activities that might occur in each.

Conceptual phase

Exhibition development begins with ideas or concepts that arise from many and varied sources such as: staff, management, stakeholders, community, current events or issues, visitor research, or serendipitous opportunities. Brainstorming is one proven method of generating ideas. Since ideas are not always arrived at in an orderly sequential fashion, allowing the free flow of thoughts at the beginning of planning often provides surprisingly useful conceptualizations not only of the exhibitions themselves, but also how they can be structured and produced for best telling the story. Brainstorming can be defined as a collaborative technique for addressing specific issues, gathering ideas, and stimulating creative thinking to produce new approaches, typically accomplished in an unrestrained and sponta-neous discussion. An important element of this "blue skies" approach is to have someone designated to record the ideas, no matter how improbable, for later examination and reflection. The process of brainstorming and reflection can pro-duce remarkably good results that otherwise would never have arisen if left to one person staring at a budget sheet and artifact list (on this point, see Jimson in this volume).

The concepts for exhibitions are, of course, myriad and museum staff should be receptive to all ideas they receive from as many sources as possible. Collecting ideas costs nothing and can produce results from unexpected quarters. However, one approach museums should avoid is that of being motivated by the need to merely fill galleries. Traveling exhibitions are an attractive, packaged product that have become a feature of the museum sector in many countries. However, in recent years cash-strapped US institutions have increasingly relied on cheaper in-house exhibitions drawn from their own collections (Wallach 2013).

Ideally, the motivation for exhibition decisions should derive from an ethical responsibility to serve the public good. And, this is a worthy modus operandi to pursue. However, in my experience many exhibiting choices arise simply out of a mistaken notion that satisfying the public's appetite for the sensational and enter-taining is required. Novelty and name recognition do play important roles in many exhibiting decisions. The 1980s and 1990s emphasis on "blockbuster" exhibitions led many museums to expend large portions of their resources based upon the presumption that such mega-exhibitions provided a way to generate support, large visitor numbers, and increased revenues (Wallach 2003). While these goals may have been met in the short term, the legacy of the blockbuster treadmill remains controversial. As Janes and Conaty put it, blockbusters are like an "addictive substance … the impact is fast and undeniable, but quickly dissolves in the quest for more, and there is never enough" (Janes and Conaty 2005, 9). The thrust has now shifted more toward more social goals of relevance and educational signifi-cance while still seeking to appeal to a sense of wonder, curiosity, and novelty of experience. Koster aptly summarizes this movement:

> Our field's desire for record-breaking attendance is illustrated by the buzz over time-limited blockbuster exhibitions and their box-office performance … Museums should aim for the largest possible audience as the fruit of their labors. The caveat, though, is that the desire to be popular must responsibly be equaled by a determina-tion to be useful. To conceive, design and offer experiences that are both engaging and worthwhile must surely be the museum field's highest aim. (Koster 2006, 70)

In my view, ideas can come from anywhere, "seeping" in to the development process, but the main thing is to constantly sift them to identify those that meet the overall requirements of mission, public service, and education (Dean 1996, 12). In the end, there must come a time for making decisions about which concepts to pursue and which to discard. However a particular museum goes about making decisions, it is vital that they be made based upon a well-defined set of public-oriented criteria pertinent to that institution, or at least some consistent selection framework, rather than on the personal subjective biases of staff or trustees/governors.

As it proceeds into decision-making about which exhibitions to pursue, a museum should have on hand:

- Short- and long-range strategic plans integrated with the museum's mission.
- A strong sense of the museum's audiences and their expectations.
- A clear view of the museum's and community's educational goals.

- In-depth knowledge of the museum's collections and collecting goals.
- A firm grasp of available funding and personnel resources.

Ideally, museum management will have clear processes for selecting exhibitions which ensure that decisions made are underpinned by professional and institutional priorities and policies. An appointed committee to do initial research and provide advice about which exhibitions to focus on can be helpful as well. Following the preliminary consideration of exhibition ideas, the committee can refine the field of prospects to a list of exhibitions that is practicable for the museum staff to accomplish. This slate of potential exhibitions would then be reviewed by senior managers, and in some cases be presented to the museum's governing body, for approval. Following approval, the business of planning and implementation can begin.

In addition to the internally generated documentation discussed above, an in-depth knowledge of the museum's communities is of paramount importance. Museum staff should never make the mistake of assuming they understand community knowledge, needs, and expectations based upon their personal experiences alone. Visitor studies organizations, consulting firms, and other such resources exist to gather and provide pertinent and relevant information to a museum about its audience which can underpin exhibition development (see Davidson in this volume). If funding is not available to contract out to external providers, a staff member can gather this data themselves in an informal, "quick and dirty" approach. However it is obtained, visitor research is invaluable in helping developers make informed decisions about what exhibit subjects and content to develop and how.

Armed with this documentation and information, the task for museum staff now becomes one of evaluating the exhibition ideas that have been accumulated with the purpose of producing a schedule of exhibitions contained within the organization's particular time frame. The results of the Conceptual phase activities should be an exhibition that is scheduled for planning and production, and the identification of the resources needed to give it form and function.

Development phase

As implied by the life-cycle project model discussed above (Figure 16.2), energy levels increase at a great rate during the Development phase. This period is characterized by two distinct stages of activity: Planning and Production. While management activities are important and energetic at this juncture of the process, product-oriented activities are and remain more visible during the Development phase. Management duties are centered upon behind-the-scenes efforts such as procurement, distribution, and regulation of resources. These efforts involve the concept of TFQIO management activities, detailed below:

- Time management – timelines and deadlines.
- Financial management – revenues and expenditures.

- Quality control – product and process.
- Information – internal and external communication.
- Organizational control – assigning tasks and approvals of changes.

(Verhaar and Meeter 1989, 11)

At some point, either during the latter part of the Conceptual phase or early in the Development phase, the administrator decides the makeup of the exhibition team based on the disciplines and skills that are needed. Personnel and funding available will directly affect the scope and breadth of the job and time it takes to accomplish it – when only one or two people are available, obviously the duration of a project's life will need to increase to accommodate the team members' other simultaneous duties.

The team skills and knowledge required for the product-oriented tasks of planning and production include collections and subject knowledge, educational expertise, and visual/spatial design experience. Typically, these roles are filled by the time-honored disciplines of curator or keeper, museum educator, and exhibit designer, respectively. The curator (sometimes called a concept developer when carrying out this role in an exhibition team) or another expert in the subject matter and collections, generally does the research, provides scholarly information, and selects and curates the appropriate collection items to include in the exhibition – although this role is often contracted out. To guide interpretive planning and presentation, the museum educator, interpreter, or audience advocate advises about school curriculum, audience educational levels and needs related to the design and messages being communicated, develops and structures information for tours and programs, and creates training materials for docents and guides. These days, of course, educators often play a more general role in overseeing interpretation across the organization as well as being an integral part of the exhibition development process. The designer's role, whether in-house or contracted out, is to translate the subject matter, objects, and ideas into visual form within the spatial parameters of the gallery environment in both two and three dimensions and increasingly in digital environments as well. The designer considers the brief, utilizes the information provided by the other team members, and creates plans, models, and drawings for presenting the exhibition in a public space. (For curatorial theory and practice see the chapters by Arnold and Norton-Westbrook in this volume. For more on museum education see Reeve and Woollard, and on design and display see Spock, both in this volume.)

Meanwhile, the project manager is occupied with coordinating and overseeing all of the parts and activities of planning to keep efforts converging toward the short-term goal of production and the ultimate objective of opening the exhibition for public viewing. Consequently, this role can be very challenging and stressful with a heavy workload, the pressure to meet deadlines and balance the different levels of management and reporting: the person selected as project manager should ideally be an experienced professional, who is cool under pressure, capable of juggling a lot of tasks and handling difficulties if they arise. A part of the project manager's job may be periodically reporting on progress or complications to the museum's senior management or director. The project manager's responsibilities include:

- Encouraging and facilitating communication between team members and administration.
- Ensuring that information and resources are available as needed.
- Calling meetings and assigning tasks as required.
- Performing progress checks and seeking change approvals.
- Acting as a mediator between the other team members as necessary.

Planning stage

The planning stage sets the tone and mood of the remainder of the project. Standards for quality, behavior, and communication should be agreed upon within the core team. If this aspect of teamwork is neglected, the rest of the development process is in jeopardy of being confusing at best and, at worst, resulting in conflict and a poorly executed exhibition.

Drawing upon the pre-established standards and a suitable understanding of the subject matter, the collections, and the target audience's needs and expectations, goals and objectives for the exhibition can be formulated and written down. For our purposes, goals are defined as being desired outcomes relating to the museum's mission that are stated in broad terms, for example: "To increase visitor knowledge about the effects on humans of the global warming phenomenon, this exhibition from the textiles collection will present climate change's effects on clothing styles and accessories over the past 25 years."

While goals may be broad and somewhat abstract, objectives are results-oriented and specific in their construction. They give concrete, achievable tasks to perform, and contain information about whose tasks they are and when completion is needed. Therefore, objectives may contain information about how much funding, time, and personnel are available for a given task. An example of an objective might be: "The exhibition storyline is to be drafted by the curator, educator, and project manager for first review by the whole exhibition team by Feb. 28, 20--."

The objectives, then, relate to both the exhibition goals and the other targeted outcomes. They describe concrete, measurable tasks that drive the exhibition project toward its initial objective of opening the exhibition. Because they are quantifiable, objectives make excellent progress milestones and provide evaluative information about the viability of the project's processes.

A significant amount of time and discussion needs to be spent by the exhibition team in formulating the project goals and objectives. These will then guide the team with the more concrete, object-oriented work of research, storyline or scriptwriting, designing the gallery, and developing educational and promotional plans.

For the process of interpretation, cognitive and affective objectives may be framed to guide the communication of particular concepts, information, or moods and feelings that the team want to get across to visitors. It is important that both goals and objectives be written down and distributed to the team members, as well as kept in the exhibition's documentation to serve as an evaluative tool later. (On this point see Jimson in this volume, and for examples of this kind of documentation, see Serrell 2006.)

Following the establishment of goals and objectives, the planning can begin in earnest. Management activities are critical and centered on time, funds, and personnel. A timeline – a listing of the various objectives (tasks) to be performed and their deadlines – provides a framework for making decisions and distributing the resources needed to accomplish the exhibition's goals. Product-oriented planning involves assessing collections and developing lists of objects to be included. Other collections-related concerns might be condition assessment or reporting of items to determine what level of conservation treatment is needed prior to placing an object into an exhibit environment.

Early in the planning process, a timeline of specific tasks to be accomplished should be a top priority for the exhibit team under the guidance of the project manager. Such a document can take several forms. At its simplest it could be a checklist of items or objectives to be met. A more developed option would be a critical path or graphic chart illustrating the steps in a linear fashion, again indicating the principal milestones / deadlines or targets that lead to the opening of the exhibition. Whatever form it takes, these documents can be useful internally to focus the team on its common goals, and externally to report to management and governing board on the progress of the project.

The first few deadlines appearing on the project timeline should include the development and approval of exhibition planning documents, which typically include: a working budget; a concept, storyline, or script for the exhibition along with derivative text and label copy; an object list and collection management plan; a set of drawings and floor plans of the gallery space, exhibition layout, and casework; an educational plan; and a promotional or marketing plan. When these components are complete and have been approved through the relevant approvals process or committee, the exhibition project is ready to move into the next phase, which is the most energetic, and resource- and time-intensive stage: namely, production.

Production stage

In the production stage of the project the three elements of management that are most critical are quality, information, and organization (Verhaar and Meeter 1989, 11). Having determined which collection objects are to be exhibited, the actual work of preparing them for display commences. Alongside educational and marketing work, text copy and labels are written for the objects identified. Accompanied by gallery plans, the work of fabricating casework, preparing the gallery, creating graphics, text panels, and labels begins, culminating in the installation of the exhibition

Chiefly handled by the project manager, management activities during the production stage include budgetary control and account maintenance, arrangement and negotiation of loans and contracts, and procurement of materials, transportation, and insurance as appropriate, as well as reporting to management/directorial staff on expenditure and approval and monitoring of changes.

Installing exhibitions can be a long, tiring, and stressful process, and collaboration between the designer, collection specialist, and security staff should result in a checklist for frequent and periodic gallery inspections to assure object safety up to the opening and during the display time frame. Once the exhibition is open to the public, and the public programs are underway, a final outcome of development (sometimes overlooked) is that of a clearly understood (preferably written), and properly disseminated maintenance booklet or plan for collections, security, and custodial personnel to accompany the exhibition during its tenure.

Functional phase

The project continues after the exhibition opens, but now moves into a phase that is less energy and resource intensive though just as vital to the success of the overall endeavor. This is the functional phase, the period when the exhibition is available to the public and its various accompanying activities are in place and ongoing. This phase can be divided into two separate identifiable stages: operational and terminating. While the exhibition "operates" to fulfill its mission and established goals, product-oriented activities are less visible, but are nevertheless present and important. They include admissions and ticket sales, continuing exhibition inspections and maintenance, exercising safety procedures for both the collections on display and visitors, evaluation and visitor research, and checking conservation factors such as environmental controls and monitoring devices.

The terminating stage begins when the exhibition ends its publicly accessible period, and is concerned with closing out the exhibition. Product-oriented activities are once again elevated during the dismantling of the exhibition (although it normally takes less effort to dismantle than to assemble), documenting the transfer of collection objects, and preparing the collections for return to lending institutions, sending them to the next venue, or restoring them to the museum's own collections storage facilities. Management activities involve examining accounts and generating reports for fund granting agencies. The end results of termination are that the collections are safely moved to their appropriate venues, and the galleries are cleared and made ready for the next installation. Yet, the project has one more step before it can be properly be considered completed: the follow-up actions of the assessment phase.

Assessment phase

For many, when the gallery is closed and cleared of collections, the project is finished. However, one extremely important phase of activity still remains if the institution is to learn and progress in its exhibiting practices and improve its outcomes. Exhibition evaluation is very useful to a museum for determining whether or not goals and objectives set early in the development process were indeed realized by the final product. Evaluation or assessment should be an ongoing priority within any project cycle. Front-end or pre-project assessments help with determining audiences and their expectations and needs. In-progress or formative evaluation guides staff in determining what works and what does not. And finally, summative or after-action analysis provides the feedback necessary for pointing the way for future exhibitions and improvement in methodologies. The tools, techniques, and forms of evaluation are too broad a subject for this chapter (see Davidson in this volume), but it is sufficient to say that evaluation should be considered just as essential to the success of an institution's exhibitions as the skills and knowledge required to produce them.

An analysis of the outcomes can reveal how well the internal team process worked, what issues arose and how they were dealt with, and whether or not the planning, production, and functioning by the exhibition team produced the desired results. Often granting agencies that provide funding for exhibitions require an after-action report to show appropriate use of funds. Even if this is not formally required a summative report can provide, to the institution and its staff, invaluable information about the product (the exhibition) and the processes (the project) involved in producing it. Ideally, the assessment phase should be conducted shortly after the functional phase ends, so that memories are fresh and data is readily available. However, as is often the case, even if some time passes before assessment is done, the efforts and time expended to document the project's final outcomes will serve as a fertile seedbed for fostering new ideas and improving ways of doing things, or at least not repeating the same mistakes.

Conclusion

The linear project model presented in this chapter is theoretical, segmented, and somewhat idealized in certain aspects; nonetheless in my own experience the general principles and processes have proven successful despite different contexts and parameters. In practice, the phased and staged approach blends into a holistic process which can be adapted for different museums and their specific projects.

The project management approach advocated here has proven effective, not only for exhibition development, but for other projects within the museum profession as well, such as educational programming, marketing and promotion, publications, building projects, and collection-related and administrative tasks.

Although there are commonalities in the ways in which projects are managed, each application requires its own adjustment of the model to fit its particular use. Overall, however, the basic model provides a strong framework to guide the process of exhibition development. If approached without clear focus, with poor organization and proper planning, the outcomes are invariably less successful and often unsatisfying for both the staff and the audience. Quite simply, project management planning gives professionals a better chance of creating successful museum exhibitions.

References

Ambrose, Timothy, and Crispin Paine. 2012. *Museum Basics*. 3rd ed. London: Routledge.

Barker, Emma, ed. 1999. *Contemporary Cultures of Display: Art and Its Histories*. New Haven, CT: Yale University Press in association with the Open University.

Belcher, Michael. 1991. *Exhibitions in Museums*. Leicester: Leicester University Press.

Bogle, Elizabeth. 2013. *Museum Exhibition Planning and Design*. Lanham, MD: AltaMira.

Bridal, Tessa. 2013. *Effective Exhibit Interpretation and Design*. Lanham, MD: AltaMira.

Burstein, David, and Frank Stasiowski. 1982. *Project Management for the Design Professional*. New York: Whitney Library of Design, Watson-Guptill Publications.

Burstein, David, and Frank Stasiowski. 1994. *Total Quality Project Management for the Design Firm: How to Improve Quality, Increase Sales, and Reduce Costs*. New York: Wiley.

Caulton, Tim. 2013. *Hands-on Exhibitions: Managing Interactive Museums and Science Centres*. London: Routledge.

Christidou, D. 2012. "Does 'Pointing At' in Museum Exhibitions Make a Point? A Study of Visitors' Performances in Three Museums for the Use of Reference as a Means of Initiating and Prompting Meaning-Making." PhD thesis, University College London. Accessed October 21, 2014. http://discovery.ucl.ac.uk/1370989.

Daft, Richard L., Jonathan Murphy, and Hugh Willmott. 2010. *Organization Theory and Design*. Andover: Cengage Learning EMEA.

Dean, David. 1996. *Museum Exhibition: Theory and Practice*. London: Routledge.

Durbin, Gail. 1996. *Developing Museum Exhibitions for Lifelong Learning*. London: HMSO.

Exhibitricks. 2008. "Planning for People in Museum Exhibitions: An Interview with Kathleen McLean." Exhibitricks: A Museum/Exhibit/Design Blog. July 17, 2008. Accessed October 21, 2014. http://blog.orselli.net/2008/07/planning-for-people-in-museum.html.

Ferguson, Bruce, Sandy Nairne, and Ressa Greenburg, eds. 1996. *Thinking about Exhibitions*. London: Routledge.

Fritsch, Juliette. 2012. "Education Is a Department Isn't It? Perceptions of Education, Learning and Interpretation in Exhibition Development." In *Museum Gallery Interpretation and Material Culture*, edited by Juliette Fritsch, 234–248. London: Routledge.

Holmes-Siedle, James. 1996. *Barrier-free Design: A Manual for Building Designers and Managers*. Oxford: Butterworth-Heinemann.

Houtgraaf, Dirk, and Vanda Vitali. 2008. *Mastering a Museum Plan: Strategies for Exhibit Development*. Lanham, MD: AltaMira.

Janes, Robert R., and Gerald T. Conaty. 2005. *Looking Reality in the Eye: Museums and Social Responsibility*. Calgary: University of Calgary Press.

Kamien, Janet. 2002. "An Advocate for Everything: Exploring Exhibit Development Models." *Curator* 44(1): 114–128.

Karp, Ivan, and Steven D. Lavine, eds. 1991. *Exhibiting Cultures: The Poetics and Politics of Museum Display*. Washington, DC: Smithsonian Institution.

Klein, Larry. 1986. *Exhibits: Planning and Design*. New York: Madison Square Press.

Koster, Emlyn. 2006. "The Relevant Museum: A Reflection on Sustainability." *Museum News* 85(3): 67–70, 85–90.

Lester, Albert. 2013. *Project Management, Planning and Control: Managing Engineering, Construction and Manufacturing Projects to PMI, APM and BSI Standards*. Oxford: Butterworth-Heinemann.

Liston, David, ed. 1993. *Museum Security and Protection: A Handbook for Cultural Heritage Institutions*. London: ICOM.

Lord, Barry, and Gail Dexter Lord, eds. 2002. *The Manual of Museum Exhibitions*. Lanham, MD: AltaMira.

Macdonald, Sharon, ed. 1998. *The Politics of Display: Museums, Science, Culture*. London: Routledge.

Macdonald, Sharon, and Paul Basu, eds. 2007. *Exhibition Experiments*. Oxford: Blackwell.

Macleod, Suzanne. 2005. *Reshaping Museum Space: Architecture, Design, Exhibitions*. Oxford: Routledge.

Macleod, Suzanne, Laura Hourston Hanks, and Jonathan Hale, eds. 2012. *Museum Making: Narratives, Architectures, Exhibitions*. London: Routledge.

McKenna-Cress, Polly, and Janet Kamien. 2013. *Creating Exhibitions: Collaboration in the Planning, Development, and Design of Innovative Experiences*. Hoboken, NJ: Wiley.

McLean, Kathleen. 1993. *Planning for People in Museum Exhibitions*. Washington, DC: Association of Science-Technology Centers.

McLean, Kathleen. 1999. "Museum Exhibitions and the Dynamics of Dialogue." *Daedalus: Journal of the American Academy of Arts and Sciences* 128(3): 83–107.

Meredith, Jack, and Samuel Mantel. 2011. *Project Management: A Managerial Approach*. 8th ed. Oxford: Wiley.

Miles, R. S. in collaboration with M. B. Alt, D. C. Gosling, B. N. Lewis, and A. F. Tout. 1982. *The Design of Educational Exhibits*. London: George Allen & Unwin.

Miles, R. S., M. B. Alt, D. C. Gosling, B. N. Lewis, and A. F. Tout. 2012. *The Design of Educational Exhibits*. Rev. ed. London: Routledge.

Morris, Martha. 2002. "Recent Trends in Exhibition Development." *Exhibitionist* 21(1): 8–12.

Museum of Texas Tech University. 2014. Website. Accessed October 21, 2014. http://www.depts.ttu.edu/museumttu/index.html.

OP&A (Office of Policy and Analysis). 2002a. *The Making of Exhibitions: Purpose, Structure, Roles and Process*. Washington, DC: Smithsonian Institution.

OP&A (Office of Policy and Analysis). 2002b. *Exhibition Development and Implementation: Five Case Studies*. Washington, DC: Smithsonian Institution. Accessed October 21, 2014. http://www.si.edu/content/opanda/docs/rpts2002/02.08.exhibitioncasestudies.final.pdf.

Pekarik, Andrew. 2002. "An Advocate for More Models." *Curator* 44(2): 151–152.

Roppola, Tiina. 2011. *Designing for the Museum Visitor Experience*. London: Routledge.

Sartwell, Marcia, ed. 1992. *The Accessible Museum: Model Programs of Accessibility for Disabled and Older People*. Washington, DC: American Association of Museums.

Serrell, Beverly. 1998. *Paying Attention: Visitors and Museum Exhibitions*. Washington, DC: American Association of Museums.

Serrell, Beverly. 2006. *Judging Exhibitions: A Framework for Assessing Excellence*. Walnut Creek, CA: Left Coast.

Simon, Nina. 2013. "17 Ways We Made Our Exhibition Participatory." Museum 2.0. Accessed October 21, 2014. http://museumtwo.blogspot.co.nz/2012/06/17-ways-we-made-our-exhibition.html.

Tonquist, Bo. 2009. *Project Management: A Complete Guide*. Copenhagen: Academica.

van Mensch, Peter. 1992. "Towards a Methodology of Museology." PhD thesis, University of Zagreb, Croatia.

Vehaar, Jan, and Han Meeter. 1989. *Project Model Exhibitions*. Leiden: Reinwardt Academie.

Wallach, Alan. 2013. "The New American Art Galleries, Virginia Museum of Fine Arts, Richmond." *Museum Worlds* 1: 222–227.

Wilk, Christopher, and Nick Humphrey. 2004. *Creating the British Galleries at the V&A: A Study in Museology*. London: Harry M. Abrams.

Further Reading

Exhibitionist. 2014. National Association for Museum Exhibition online journal archive. Accessed October 21, 2014. http://name-aam.org/resources/exhibitionist/back-issues-and-online-archive.

Lord, Barry, Gail Dexter Lord, and Lindsay Martin. 2012. *Manual of Museum Planning: Sustainable Space, Facilities, and Operations*. Lanham, MD: AltaMira.

David K. Dean was Director of Information Services at the Museum of Texas Tech University until 2013, and teaches in the graduate-level Museum Science and Heritage Management programs of Texas Tech University. An experienced designer and museum professional who has overseen the development of many exhibitions on a range of topics, he authored the textbook *Museum Exhibition: Theory and Practice* (1996) and co-authored *The Handbook for Museums* (1994).

17 MUSEUM EXHIBITION TRADECRAFT
Not an Art, but an Art to It

Dan Spock

In his essay *Dinomania*, the paleontologist Stephen Jay Gould, who credited his own childhood visits to the American Museum of Natural History as the inspiration for his choice of career, asks rhetorically: Why are children so fascinated with dinosaurs? "To this inquiry, I know no better response than the epitome proposed by a psychologist colleague," he wrote, "'big, fierce, and extinct' – in other words, alluringly scary, but basically safe" (Gould 1993).

The observation is funny, but true, particularly when we look to the peculiar hold museums have on the imagination. Dinosaurs, being big, extinct, and fierce, do not merely inspire awe in the viewer. They cause us to wonder about our own vulnerability, our impending mortality, our place in nature, in the universe, in the track of time, and what it means to be human. This quality is not exclusive to dinosaurs; it holds for many other things contained in a museum's exhibition galleries. But we should consider another equally important aspect of Gould's observation. Museums can be both alluringly scary, but *basically safe*. And the safety of that context, in a secular temple where the imagination reigns supreme, where challenges can be encountered and mastered, a social space where strangers gather together without fear of each other to learn and have fun, are other keys to the museum's enduring allure. The tradecraft of making a museum that kind of special place is not art, but there is an art to it. If I might put it crudely, the least successful museum exhibitions have little allure. But what makes exhibitions alluring? As far back as the early seventeenth century one could read this imprecation, "Viewer, insert your eyes. Contemplate the wonders of Calozari's museum and pleasurably serve your mind" (Daston and Park 1998, 3).

Even then, the essentials were all there and accounted for: viewing, contemplation, wonder, pleasure, the mind. By 1961, the British designers James Gardner and Caroline Heller would see the allure this way, "Novelty, charm, ingenuity, movement,

The International Handbooks of Museum Studies: Museum Practice, First Edition.
Edited by Conal McCarthy.
© 2015 John Wiley & Sons Ltd. Published 2020 by John Wiley & Sons Ltd.

people doing things, tricks and mystery, something really big and clever: these are the ingredients of successful display" (Gardner and Heller 1961, 12). In this straightforward assessment, we can see that museums are never merely assemblages of objects and labels, but a series of exercises in making choices about creative design. People flock to them, not only to learn, but to speculate, to be enchanted, to remember, to share with others, to wonder, to unwind, for diversion from the routine. The degree of satisfaction a museum-goer is able to derive from these experiences is highly dependent on how they are designed.

Although design is an important factor in the success of museum exhibitions, unfortunately there are few useful published sources to guide designers on the specifics of exhibition design. *Planning for People in Museum Exhibitions* by Kathleen McLean (1993) is still the best guidebook for exhibition creation. Though not limited to design, it does have the advantage of situating design within the fundamental considerations of the museum-goer's experience and the team dynamics of exhibition creation. In contrast, the weighty manuals by Barry and Gail Lord (2002) contain a mass of detailed standards for everything from lighting to labeling, but afford scant attention to specific design considerations and assume that collections form the basis of everything in museum exhibitions. David Dean's readable and direct *Museum Exhibition* (1996) provides an abbreviated synopsis of the basics, and also some useful theoretical context, particularly in his chapter on audiences and learning, although the examples he uses to illustrate design concepts are somewhat prosaic. On the other hand there are a number of handbooks for fellow designers, for example *Exhibition Design* by Philip Hughes (2010), which is richly illustrated and informed by experience. Consequently, its recommendations, made from the perspective of a designer-for-hire, are often presented as received wisdom without the supporting rigor non-designers might desire, but it is nonetheless thorough, practical, and current. The same cannot be said for *What Is Exhibit Design?* by Jan Lorenc, Lee Skolnick, and Craig Berger (2010). It runs the gamut from museum exhibitions to retail to trade shows but provides little useful guidance for museums, tending to focus on pure style in selling the services of commercial design firms. *Museum Design: The Future* by George Jacob (2009) is unhelpful for similar reasons, despite its promising title. A recent book on collaboration in creating exhibitions provides more useful and up-to-date advice for professionals (McKenna-Cress and Kamien 2013).

There are dozens of useful books relevant to exhibition design, but where design itself is rather sublimated to some other overarching idea. Of this literature, Simon (2010) and Adair, Filene, and Koloski (2011) provide cutting-edge thinking of consequence for designers, specifically relating to the emergence in the twenty-first century of a new pluralism, propelled by both a public-centered ethos and the revolution in online participatory social media. Similarly current if rather dense, MacLeod, Hourston Hanks, and Hale (2012) have brought together a series of mediations on the emergent use of space and place-based multidisciplinary narrative strategies in museum design, which must be commended for its spot-on embrace of the affective dimension of the museum experience and the essential role of narrative in how humans make sense of their experiences. In an earlier book, Suzanne MacLeod laudably set out to bridge the gap between designers, architects, and museum professionals (2005).

In terms of visitor research, the works of Falk and Dierking, especially *The Museum Experience* (1992) and *Learning from Museums* (2000), provide critical tools for thinking about what makes an exhibition work, particularly as an environment for learning. However I find that they do little to correlate specific concrete design standards and decisions to the theories they espouse, leaving designers to interpret as best they can. Beverly Serrell makes a useful contribution through her volume *Judging Exhibitions* (2006), though this approach tends to treat the merits of design methodology post facto through an evaluative lens. One of the best design overviews, referenced to supporting research literature, is the indispensable *Universal Principles of Design* by Lidwell, Holden, and Butler (2003), though it is not museum or exhibition specific.

In the face of all this publishing, it is necessary for experienced professionals to critically interrogate the museum literature and decide what works for them in their situation. This chapter attempts to glean some useful ways of thinking about exhibition design from these and other sources. Most of all, however, it is based on my own extensive experience as an exhibition designer. Far from an academic argument, the chapter should be read as a guide to the professional *practice* of museum design and display distilled from many years of working at what I call exhibition tradecraft. As well as students, academics, and general readers, I hope that this chapter not only addresses designers, but also those professionals working in museums who are looking for an understanding of exhibition design and its place in the institution from a design perspective.

Faced with an infinite variety of potential approaches, I believe that good design is not about falling back on mere style preferences, but concerns the critical framing of judgments for various design decisions. Given the absence of a perfect model, how do we make sense of all of this? I believe that it is best to break the exhibition tradecraft down and approach it as a series of critical considerations, about the museum experience, the senses, styles of exhibition, coherence, and so on. In this chapter I employ a number of useful analogies that will hopefully aid the thinking process, and end with some thoughts about rules, and rule breaking, in the process of making exhibitions.

Tradecraft in a changing and complex field

Everything on the museum floor is your responsibility. You're even accountable for what you choose to leave out. It's your job to anticipate what [visitors] will want to know about the topic and when they will want it. You have to meet or exceed visitor expectations. If you don't, no matter how understandable the excuse, you didn't fulfil your responsibility. (Serrell 2006, 30)

As Don Hughes, the exhibitions director at the Monterey Bay Aquarium, put it above, exhibition developers have to be attuned to the visitor experience. The intentional anticipation of what museum-goers will do, think, and feel, ideally informed by research, evaluation, and experience, is at the heart of museum exhibition tradecraft. It is important, on the other hand, to acknowledge the fact that times have certainly changed since Calozari, and museums have been influenced by developments in technology and the rapid transfer of information and interaction made possible by it. At one time it was enough to stuff a museum with a myriad of oddities because knowledge of the world was encumbered by hazardous and slow modes of travel and communication, the rarity of books and literacy, and the primitiveness of specimen preservation. What makes a thing exotic is entirely different today. The sea creatures or crocodiles that once seemed miraculously strange to inhabitants of northern Europe are now readily available for viewing instantaneously through electronic media, mass-produced publications, or travel, and thus relatively commonplace. Now we are overwhelmed with the amount of knowledge at our disposal and an exhibition-maker must reach beyond objects and labels to a more nuanced and complex sense of what is important to sustain public engagement. The challenges of tradecraft grow more formidable all the time. Kathleen McLean helps by emphasizing that a museum is a medium of communication,

> In addition to words, communication takes place through every aspect of the environment. How an exhibition smells, sounds, and feels may be just as important as how it looks, or what it says. Exhibit planners should communicate with visual and sensual literacy, using all of the elements of an exhibition to appeal to all of the senses. (McLean 1993, 17)

Without a doubt the process of orchestrating museum exhibitions is a very challenging communication design task. If this seems like an exaggeration, consider the fact that every form of human communication can be exhibited in the gallery. The written or spoken word, the choice and display of symbolic objects of all kinds, be they art or ephemeral kitsch, tiny or colossal things, graphic design and images, information graphics and data visualizations are all possible choices. Electronic media now proliferates in the museum in the form of video, audio, and audio tours, *son et lumière* spectacles or "object theater," social media, mobile technology, interactive multimedia, and oral histories. Live interpretation may include docent tours, demonstrations, music, dance, drama, and facilitated discussion. Scale models, full-scale settings, immersive environments, dioramas, mechanical interactives, interactives involving gross motor activity, games, and simulations – these can all be used in exhibitions. To employ these techniques in the service of a coherent and memorable museum-going experience increasingly requires a great diversity of skills, most of which cannot possibly be mastered entirely by one person. While a small museum may only command one or two of these skills or the resources to acquire them, there are museums with the resources to do them all.

To make matters more daunting, the best exhibitions are not analogous to theater or film in the sense that the production begins with a pre-written script and some sense of clearly defined roles. Instead, the participants in the exhibition-making process must wrest meaning and form in dynamic and shifting co-creation activities, a collaborative process that may unfold over many years (on exhibition development see Dean in this volume). Because exhibition professionals each have distinctive professional and personal perspectives, this process is nearly always a contentious one. Moreover, the exhibition is inherently a public medium and with each exhibition a museum reveals its own intentions and values to a broader public. The museum-going public – and stakeholders – may care a great deal, or care not at all, not merely about what is exhibited, but *how* it is exhibited and the explicit or implicit meanings conveyed thereby, often detecting both sins of omission and commission, whether those perceived messages are intentional or inadvertent on the museum's part.

Increasingly, the public play a direct and even determinative role in exhibition curation and design as more museums, mirroring the trends in social media and crowd-curated sites such as Wikipedia, open themselves to pluralistic, participatory processes, challenging and transforming traditional notions of authority. Museums have never really been sheltered from the world outside their walls, but the old image of the authoritative museum seems more under threat than ever today (Simon 2010; Adair, Filene, and Koloski 2011).

The museum is an experience

The first consideration in exhibition design should always be the museum-goers' experience. A great deal of research has revealed patterns in human behavior essential to any practical understanding of the exhibition design process (Bitgood 1994; 2011; Falk and Dierking 2000; 2013). While a design team may be preoccupied with the detail of exhibition-making, the museum-goer is inclined to see the exhibition in the context of a day's activity. The visitor decides when to go to the museum, how they will do it, and whom to go with. They have to travel there and negotiate all of the other logistics associated with the visit: parking or walking from public transportation, the accommodation of the various and often conflicting needs in their social group, the purchase of tickets, the navigation through the space, all before the exhibition experience has begun (Falk and Dierking 2011).

Museum-goers also have a limited fund of human energy that can be applied to the visit, though they may not have the slightest idea how deep that reserve is at the start. "Museum fatigue" is a well-known factor in a visit (Falk and Dierking 2011, 56). Museums themselves can be wearying places, but the fund of energy is being drawn down well before the museum-goer makes it through the door. Details too often incidental to the museum loom large for the museum-goer: elusive information online or in the media, exorbitant and complex fee structures, muddled way-finding, confusing or daunting architecture, surly staff, dirty restrooms, crowding, a lack of seating, poor-quality food and shop merchandise. Even a slight frustration at any of these points can deplete the fund of energy available and sour the memory of the museum experience. Since the vast majority of museum visits are undertaken by social groups, the museum-goer in the group with the lowest fund of energy may well be the individual who determines the duration of the visit for the entire group. Museum exhibitions are almost by definition intense sensory experiences.

Once museum-goers enter an exhibition, a range of factors will hasten the duration of the visit by rapidly depleting the fund of energy they bring to the experience: for example a confusing or cacophonous environment; a lack of design or curatorial coherency; broken exhibition elements; hard floors; visual monotony; lighting that is too bright or too dark, or a lack of comfortable seating at intervals. Even the most captivating exhibitions may only hold a group's attention for 30 minutes or so, an entire museum for no more than a couple of hours (Housen 1987). It is no use complaining about this, as it is a matter of basic human needs and limitations. Setting a standard for optimizing the visit is therefore an important principle. Never waste a museum-goer's time and energy with problems and irritations that degrade the desirable experience either inadvertently or by design – reward them for their effort instead. In my experience, the better the experience is for the museum-goer, the longer the experience is liable to be.

The museal sensorium

For humans, the visual seems to dominate all the other senses. The poet and essayist John Berger expressed it succinctly when he wrote, "The visible has been and still remains the principal source of information about the world" (Berger 1984, 50). Despite recent research that shows that museums were and are multisensory environments (Classen 2007; Candlin 2010), my impression is that exhibition design assumes that museum-going continues to be an overwhelmingly visual experience. Of course this is not to diminish the importance of considering non-visual learning styles, or people with visual impairments, but, in spite of the advent of audio tours, interactivity, and of better accessibility strategies, in all but a few museums, sight dominates touch, hearing, and smell. What does the importance of seeing things in museums mean for exhibit developers? As Kathleen McLean states, exhibitions *show* things:

All exhibition ideas are embodied in things, whether they are "things" from a museum collection, or things designed to illustrate a principle, convey information (such as a multimedia component), or demonstrate a phenomenon. The types of things shown from one exhibition to the next may vary greatly, but the three dimensional environment demands three dimensional things. That means if a concept is too abstract, if it requires too much background information or attempts to present sophisticated arguments requiring volumes of words, it is probably not a suitable subject for an exhibition. (McLean 1993, 16)

Some might worry that higher-order thinking will vanish in the museum if we follow McLean's advice about avoiding abstractions too assiduously. But consider Alan Kay, the pioneering computer scientist who developed the Graphical User Interface (GUI), that now ubiquitous system of visual icons and window shades that we "click" to open or "drag" into the "trash" which ultimately liberated computers from inscrutable abstract code (making them universally useful and essential to non-computer literate laypersons). Kay understood how inherent aesthetic qualities were to the practice of science, explaining that "there are these internal impulses that are basically artistic even if you are trying to learn science" (Wurman 1989, 157).

Museums express ideas through *concrete* representations. The dynamic combination of things, places, and people in a museum stands as a complex representational system, an arrangement of objects in a designed environment that is intended to convey messages to the viewer. The design of elements in a museum exhibition often communicates ideas in symbolic terms, quite apart from whatever labeling and signage there is, and that information is not of the usual, didactic kind. On the contrary, much of what a museum-goer experiences has uniquely personal, affective dimensions, or plays out on an entirely sub-cognitive level (Falk and Dierking 2011). Stephen Greenblatt talks about the emotional resonance and wonder that museum objects can convey (Greenblatt 1991). All museum display is an *interpretive* act in the sense that it is the result of deliberate choices, but it is not limited in that sense merely to the sorts of interpretations that are expressed in words. Rather these are interpretations in the broadest sense of the term, as are pictures, songs, and dance (on interpretation see Jimson in this volume).

It is an old cliché that a picture is worth a thousand words, but it is also true in the crucial respect that pictures are *remembered* better than words, a phenomenon called the "picture superiority effect." In a series of experiments, psychologists determined that pictures alone were remembered by test subjects better than words alone, but that a combination of words and pictures were remembered best (Pavio, Rogers, and Smythe 1968). This has important implications for museum practitioners, both because it means that museums can play to their strength as powerful visual environments, but also that the visual representation of things strengthens the particular kind of pedagogy museums are adapted to provide. In this sense, museums must simultaneously work with, and build upon, a museum-goer's sense of what John Debes, Coordinator of Educational Products at Eastman Kodak Company, termed "visual literacy," or "a group of vision-competencies a human being can develop by seeing and at the same time having and integrating other sensory experiences" (Debes 1969, 27).

All museum-goers are visually literate to varying degrees and museums also build visual literacy. Similarly, stories are a profoundly important way that people make sense of their lived experiences. According to Benedict Carey in a review of recent psychological studies on the significance of narrative, "People tend to remember facts more accurately if they encounter them in a story rather than in a list" (Carey 2007).

Visual storytelling, therefore, should also be a critical consideration for any interpretive effort. Rather than continually reasoning with museum-goers using predictable didactic pronouncements in text only, museums must convey ideas through compelling display. Since museum-goers tend to rely on the visual sense of things above all else, they often use text only as a last resort when the puzzle of the first visual impression of things cannot be rendered meaningful. This is why curators can never count on the written label alone to make things intelligible, and why design and intention are such crucial factors in the success of exhibitions of all kinds.

High-context, low-context, anti-context

Just as museums themselves constitute an artificial context, so the contextual treatment of things within the museum is a matter of artifice, a matter of design choice. This is why the practice of contextualization in exhibition design cannot merely be regarded as a matter of design preference or style – rather it is absolutely critical to the museum's interpretive objectives. As a useful means of understanding the available choices, one can plot design styles along a continuum from high-context through low-context to anti-context (see also Kirshenblatt-Gimblett 1998, 19–23).

At the highest contextual end of the continuum stand the open-air living history museums and the more modern zoos and aquaria. In each instance the design is characterized by an attempt to totally immerse the museum-goer (as much as possible) in a completely realized spatial context. The open-air living history museum, as pioneered in the late nineteenth century in Scandinavia and emulated later in countless places, hoped to preserve, with nostalgic urgency and in material form, folk lifestyles seen to be vanishing under the weight of modern industrialization. Taken in experiential terms, however, the ultimate aim is to create an experience akin to time travel, a complete imaginative departure from, and immersion in, another historical period entirely (Kirshenblatt-Gimblett 1998). Consequently, historical objects are mostly shown in their original context. For example the museum-goer sees butter actually churned in the butter churn; it is not ensconced in a vitrine. In the case of zoos and aquaria, the experience is a kind of safari or submarine expedition in spatially condensed replica. In the highest-immersion, high-context presentation, there are few barriers or prosceniums. Interpretive labels are used sparingly lest they spoil the immersion effect; instead the preferred communication techniques are by naturalistic, live, person-to-person interpretation.

You stroll through it at will, as you would in the whole wide world. For a designer, that of course makes it a very tricky presentation technique to control.

One rung lower on the scale are the *trompe l'œil* natural history dioramas, as perfected by Carl Akeley, the anthropological "life groups" pioneered by curators such as William Henry Holmes and Franz Boas, and the period rooms, which see their epitome in the work of George Francis Dow and R. T. H. Halsey (Schwarzer 2006, 127–128). Here specimens are abstracted from their original context to a greater degree by locating them indoors and away from their point of origin. There are distancing strategies for the public employed too: protective railings and plate-glass windows. Still, the dominant design idea is to visually and spatially replicate in convincing fashion the original context in which these things were found, the better to help the museum-goer imagine it. So the butter churn is an artifact here, inert by the hearth, with at most a static mannequin clutching it eternally in mid-churn. But the framing devices and the railings are all contrived to stage and therefore effectively control the physical and visual interaction a museum-goer may have with the objects in the museum, so actual physical immersion is mostly precluded. Tellingly, such designs are very often accompanied by a great deal of textual interpretation which typically conveys information that further contextualizes the objects and specimens shown, variously relating them to anthropological observations, the study of the natural environment or decorative arts traditions.

High-context treatments, especially dioramas, remain popular with both the public and museum professionals. Dioramas have been with us a long time, precisely because they help us imagine the past, another culture or place, by showing us what those times and places were like in highly visual and experiential terms (Falk 1991). As research demonstrates, they are broadly intelligible and so accessible to a wide cross section of people (Korn 2003).

Lower on the rung of our ladder of context continuum, we find the familiar conventions of the omnibus art museum or antiquarian historical society. Objects are normally shown plucked entirely out of context. Textual information is generally brief, very often limited to the name of the maker, a date, the materials of manufacture, and place of origin. In other words, usually the only context provided is by labeling. The implicit aim of this approach is to strip the object of distractions so as to heighten a museum-goer's appreciation of the formal, aesthetic beauty or other manifest qualities of the thing. Its place in a particular culture or time is considered secondary, or entirely irrelevant. Also, there is a shift in emphasis. Objects are less often interpreted as examples of commonplace things and more often as unique artifacts of a high degree of inherent worth.

Still, within this form, objects in combination or in juxtaposition can be displayed in ways that create provocations or changes of perception, in effect, making a sum that is greater than its individual parts. In other words, an object may be contextualized to some extent through the choice of objects placed proximate to it. It was this technique that was so brilliantly used by artist Fred Wilson in the exhibition *Mining the Museum* at the Maryland Historical Society. By juxtaposing, for one example, a fine silver tea service with slave shackles and labeling them "18th and 19th century metalwork," he not only showed these objects, but provoked significant questions about the slave labor system that made the production of such fine silver possible, and the role of the museum's collecting in that system (Wilson and Corrin 1994).

Then there is the kind of context favored by many contemporary art museums and private galleries. A style pioneered in the 1930s by Bauhaus-inspired collector Katherine Sophie Dreier and Wadsworth Athenaeum director Everett "Chick" Austin (Schwarzer 2006, 122–132; see also Staniszewski 1998), here the objects are offered with little or no written interpretation against a stark backdrop of eggshell white, or similarly neutral, wall paint. Objects are displayed with distances between them, the separation meant to provide an isolated and focused viewing. As in the general art museum, the idea is to strip away all competing clutter so as to afford the museum-goer a more immediate and unmediated experience with the formal qualities of the object. But this approach is also characterized by a strong strain of connoisseurship. If the intentions of the artist, the maker of the thing, or the ideas of the curator seem obscure, well, the message seems to be: "This may not be for you."

Last of all, we have anti-context, in other words showing things devoid of context, or in such a way as to negate the conditions of the object's production and reception. Usually, there is no explicative attempt made to place the objects in any other context than that of the collection they end up in. An example is the cabinet of curiosities, a popular approach in the history of museums which seems to be making something of a comeback (Greenblatt 1991; Bann 2003; Arnold 2006). In this design approach, objects are treated almost as décor as in a salon hang, or as presented as curiosities meant to elicit an experience of mysterious wonderment as opposed to conveying any scholarly interpretation. In fact, the subtext of the collection of curios or oddities is that it first and foremost represents the character of the collector as exemplified by the trophies and mementoes of his conquests and travels. The typical design approach here is cluttered, expressive of *horror vacui*. The cumulative effect is to impress the viewer, not as much with the quality as with the sheer quantity of the collector's holdings and how those holdings represent the collector's passions.

In the 1988 exhibition *ART/artifact: African Art in Anthropology Collections* at New York City's Center for African Art, African tribal objects were shown in nearly all of the contexts described above (see Figure 17.1 and Figure 17.2). The visual differences from gallery to gallery were striking, showing that contextual choices dramatically change whether viewers perceive an object as an artwork or an anthropological artifact. Susan Vogel, the exhibition's curator, pointed out that:

> Acknowledging that the physical setting of an object was part of what made the audience identify it as art, the installation of *Art/artifact* played with art objects and non-art objects showing them in four different ways. We hoped this would raise the question implicit in the exhibition title and make the trickery of museum installations evident. (Vogel in Danto 1988, 198; see also Vogel 1991)

FIGURE 17.1   Image from *ART/artefact: African Art in Anthropology Collections*, Center for African Art, New York, 1988. In the middle of the contextual spectrum, objects in classical natural history exhibits, like the one depicted here, are grouped taxonomically by culture with further context provided by written labels and graphics. High context treatments, on the other hand, typically utilize objects in full scale dioramas displaying "life groups" of human figures or animals depicted in meticulous recreations of natural habitat. Installation photographs of exhibition.
Photo: Jerry L. Thompson.

FIGURE 17.2   Image from *ART/artifact: African Art in Anthropology Collections*, Center for African Art, New York, 1988. In the low-context art gallery display, the museum provides little if any context about the culture that created the objects. The design approach puts the visual emphasis on connoisseurship and the formal "beauty" and singularity of the objects instead. Installation photographs of exhibition.
Photo: Jerry L. Thompson.

The lower one travels on the contextual continuum, however, the more specialized, the more rarified a museum-goer's prior knowledge, sophistication, and experience must be to make sense of what they are seeing and, correspondingly, the more exclusive the museum will appear to be to the casual viewer (Latimer 2011). While all contextual treatments have some inherent validity, it is essential to ask who this exhibition will be for and whether the chosen conceptual schema will help or hinder a museum-goer's engagement and satisfaction with her experience. Many art museums are now cognizant of how the traditional low-context style can seem exclusive and are taking steps to address the problem (Whitehead 2012). As a case in point, consider the following interpretive principle gleaned from a list espousing a new spirit of pluralism endorsed by Tate Modern in 2004: "Works of art do not have self-evident meanings" (Wilson 2004).

Coherence

The coherence of an exhibition depends first on its conceptual framework and secondarily on how that framework is rendered in form. Although all museum-goers have unique motivations, it is fair to assume that most want to understand what they encounter. When a museum frustrates that desire for coherence, it may make a museum-goer feel inadequate and excluded. Serrell calls a coherent exhibition "reinforcing," arguing that it provides visitors with "abundant opportunities to be successful and to feel intellectually competent – beyond the 'wow' of engagement," and also that "the exhibits reinforce each other, providing multiple means of accessing similar bits of information that are all part of a cohesive whole" (2006, 30).

Designer Richard Saul Wurman has posited that all information is organized in just five basic ways, in conceptual scaffolding systems he calls "the five hat racks." The five hat racks are: Time (chronological sequence), Location (geographical or spatial references), Category (similarity relatedness), Alphabet (alphabetical sequence), and Continuum (magnitude; highest to lowest, best to worst). Humans have developed each of these organizational schemas for the purpose of structuring and interpreting information in ways that are coherent and practical (Wurman 1989, 59–72).

In the museum, we most commonly see the first three hat racks employed in schemes for exhibition concepts. Predictably, history museums and paleontological exhibitions most often fall back on chronology as the organizing strategy, even relentlessly forcing visitors down a circuitous linear pathway to keep people focused properly on the forward march of time. Zoos, aquaria, natural history museums, and art museums tend to resort to geographical organizing strategies. Zoos, aquaria, and natural history museums organize animal collections around certain biomes, nations and so forth.

Traditionally, the category hat rack has most often been represented in museums by taxonomical displays (Bennett 1995). Today the more common descriptor

FIGURE 17.3   "Taking Care" section of the *Families* exhibition. The design of the *Families* exhibition followed a number of universal themes as an organizing schema. In this approach, objects were clustered, irrespective of the historical time of origin or culture, under these familiar aspects of family life. The hanging quilt motif here acts as an "advance organizer" establishing the theme of the exhibit section as "Taking Care." Photograph courtesy of the Minnesota Historical Society.

in the field for the category style of display is "thematic" exhibitions (Lord and Lord 2002, 150–152). History museums wishing to break from the chronological tradition have successfully experimented with thematic conceptual frameworks (Leon and Rosenzweig 1989, 24–25). For example the exhibition at the Minnesota History Center *Families* (1996) (Figure 17.3) grouped sections by the universal things all families do: making a home, taking care of one another, getting along, and surviving loss; comingling objects of different time periods in each section.

Far less common are continuum and alphabetically structured exhibitions, but in 1992 the Minnesota History Center debuted a playful and popular exhibition called *Minnesota A to Z* in which objects were grouped according to the alphabet (Figure 17.4). More recently the Brooklyn Museum showed *Click! A Crowd-curated Exhibition* (2008) in which photographs were ranked favorite-to-least favorite, then displayed according to the online voting preferences of the public.

Exhibition-makers should always consider alternative conceptual frameworks before adopting the obvious choice. I would recommend a design experiment: take one of the hat racks and creatively apply it to an unfamiliar museum discipline. So for example, apply the "Location" hat rack and apply it to History, to

FIGURE 17.4   "F is for Fire Engine" in *Minnesota A to Z*, Minnesota History Center Museum, St. Paul. Although alphabetical organizing schemas (or "hat racks") are rarely used, *Minnesota A to Z* was an exception that proved playful, engaging, and accessible to a broad audience due to its simple and instantly familiar structure. (For a color version of this figure, please see the color plate section.)
Photograph courtesy of the Minnesota Historical Society.

create an exhibition around cultural geography. Or apply "Chronology" to Natural History to interpret ecological change. Choosing a particular hat rack at the outset of exhibition design cannot guarantee coherence for the visitor, however, and it must be emphasized that an exhibition organized without a consistent underlying conceptual structure will invariably come across as a muddle (on concept development see Jimson in this volume). Once a hat rack is selected, it should be consistently communicated in visual form throughout the exhibition, including through signage, a technique sometimes called "advance organizers" (Lidwell, Holden, and Butler 2003, 16). There is really no valid reason for keeping an exhibition's messages obscure, so a firm standard of clarity and transparency should guide the implementation of the framework.

In exhibition design, coherence equals proximity. Over the course of evolution, humans developed the capability for recognizing meaningful patterns. Since a conceptual framework is most useful when it is outwardly apparent to the museum-going public, it should be realized in concise, elegant terms. Because exhibitions are spatial in nature, this cannot be rendered in the linear way chapters in a book are organized. Rather things must be clustered into interpretive sections and subsections. To draw an analogy, we know that interpretive labels generally work better the closer they are to the object they are meant to describe. How many of us have struggled to correlate numbered objects to a distant list, or have sought to locate a label in weird disconnection to the object it describes?

On a larger scale, the objects and settings in a gallery become more coherent by being clustered according to common themes, geography, or time. Since most exhibitions have rather open circulatory patterns, and the public will serendipitously navigate even the most linear exhibition layouts as they please – and in the process defying all well-intentioned attempts to control their movements and choices – special attention needs to be paid to the relationships implied by the objects arrayed through the gallery and their proximity to one another. This is why, as research shows, planners should steer clear of pedagogies that rely on the progressive accumulation of knowledge by the museum-goer (Hein and Alexander 1998, 40–46). If one idea in a museum setting cannot be understood without understanding a preceding idea in the same display, chances are that it will not. As stated earlier, an exhibition is not a book on a wall and cannot be laid out as such. The goal of a designer ought always to be one of optimizing the experience of the information-seeker, to make it as natural, seamless, and easy as possible, removing barriers to appreciation and understanding. In the spatial context of the museum, proximity reinforces coherence.

Cynosures, scale, and chains of engagement

As we saw from Stephen Jay Gould's observation about children and dinosaurs, size matters. Visitor research reinforces the idea that large objects or elements within exhibits attract attention (Peart and Kool 1988; Falk 1991). Experienced practitioners understand this and use it as a communication strategy. When Marty Sklar became the president of Imagineering for Disneyland, he urged his staff to "Create a weenie: Lead visitors from one area to another by creating visual magnets and giving visitors rewards for making the journey" (Sklar 1987).

A "weenie" is what Disney called the large structures designed to anchor each of the "lands" comprising Disneyland: a castle for Fantasyland, a stockade fort for Frontierland, and so on. As intended, these "weenies" (which can be thought of as visual brands or icons) have the power, when seen from a distance, to pull guests through the theme park from attraction to attraction. Moreover, each of these landmarks also has a story to tell, a story any person can begin to understand just by looking at it. Not surprisingly, Disney drew some of his inspiration for Disneyland from museums, most notably the open-air Greenfield Village (now The Henry Ford) in Dearborn, Michigan (The Henry Ford 2005, 7).

As visitors navigate their way through exhibition galleries, they interact with things on a variety of scale levels. Some modulation of scale is necessary to create visual interest. Large objects and settings serve as landmarks, but also as cynosures guiding visitors through the museum and providing an unspoken, symbolic expression of the larger themes a museum hopes to represent. Here is an example from an exhibition at Minnesota Historical Society, *Minnesota's Greatest Generation*, in which a large landmark or "cynosure" element in the form of a crashed World War II aircraft foreshadowed a combat story told by veterans depicted in a multimedia show inside (Figure 17.5).

By definition, cynosures are "sticky," they attract and hold attention, a quality Peter Samis at the San Francisco Museum of Modern Art calls "visual velcro" (Samis 2007, 21). A large object can generate a lot of attention simply by virtue of its display in a museum, but size, in and of itself, is not necessarily an attractor, unless it is "sticky." Kinetic exhibition elements will nearly always draw attention over stationary things. Things that whirl, sparkle, twist, and blink, or iconic objects of great appeal and evident value, all have the potential for being cynosures

FIGURE 17.5   In *Minnesota's Greatest Generation*, designers introduced a large landmark or "cynosure" element in the form of a crashed World War II aircraft as a way to foreshadow a combat story told by veterans depicted in a multimedia show. The plane's position in the gallery gives it visual pull, while setting the stage for the story inside. Photograph courtesy of the Minnesota Historical Society.

without being especially large. Visually animated video screens, in particular, can dominate a room – a good reason for using them sparingly, for enclosing them, and for spreading them apart from each other in a gallery.

From my observation of museum exhibits, I believe that if chosen wisely, a sequence or pattern of landmarks can create an implied pathway, a sort of visual "breadcrumb trail," even suggesting a narrative arc. A cynosure can also ignite a chain of engagement down to the details of each exhibition section. Curiosity inspired by a colossal or kinetic landmark can cause a visitor to slow down, stop and attend to other, smaller features arranged around it, even inspiring label reading (see Ash 2004). In this sense, there is an experiential hierarchy at work. In my experience, a museum-goer in motion can "read" the space by scanning the larger symbolic features of the museum environment without even stopping and, if the space is well designed, get the gist of what an exhibition is about. If it is working well, the self-directed visitor begins "grazing" the details of the section one by one, that is, slowly wandering past the objects gleaning chunks of information. The chain of engagement therefore goes from strolling, to grazing, to reading. Reading is far more likely to happen if the exhibit is highly attractive at the strolling level, and so draws the viewer to the grazing level, and finally on down to the reading level (Rounds 2006).

One more observation I have made concerns "streaking" or moving quickly through exhibits without stopping. It is tempting to judge audience behavior. If a person "streaks" the gallery by strolling through it continuously without lingering, we really cannot declare that it was because they were stupid or incapable of digesting what was put before them. There could be many reasons for this inattention. Maybe the space was completely lacking in visual interest, or the visitors were trying to find a café or the rest of their group. In my view, a designer's primary concern should be that everyone should get something out of the experience, not just the patient museum-goer who devours every label but also the streaker, even if they don't stop moving for a second.

The Advent calendar, buffet table, and highlighter pen analogies

When I was a child, my mother used to buy an advent calendar every holiday season before Christmas. This was a simple piece of printed cardboard, often depicting a nativity scene or a building. I could open a door each day, in the month leading up to Christmas, to reveal a surprising scene. This ritual of revelation was so pleasing that I eagerly anticipated performing it every year. Museum visits unfold in much the same way, and this is one of the reasons why we find them so pleasurable. In a technique known as "progressive disclosure," a designer can stage tantalizing elements to be revealed in sequence (Lidwell, Holden, and Butler 2003, 154). If a designer deliberately conceals things that can be revealed through exploration, and if the revelatory process discloses delightful surprises, the result makes for a pleasurable museum experience.

Of course, not all museum-goers are alike. Howard Gardner has theorized that there are perhaps eight to ten "multiple intelligences," learning styles ranging over a wide variety of preferences (Gardner 1983). John Falk has provided us with five different profiles or museum-going "identities," a taxonomy for the distinct ways people prefer to use their museum experiences (Falk 2006). Museum visitor research provides further guidance for the designer (Kirchberg and Tröndle 2012). We know that children have different developmental needs than adults and there is developmental variety throughout childhood. Museum-goers have different levels of ability with respect to height, mobility, sight, hearing, and so forth. There are cultural differences. With this inherent diversity, the museum will be used very differently by different people, so museum designers are wise to plan accordingly, rather than adopting a one-size-fits-all approach.

A fruitful way of reconciling this problem is to conceive of the gallery layout as a buffet table of experiential variety. From a diner's perspective, the appeal of a buffet is that there is a range of dishes to choose from. If virtually all exhibition elements are made up of six general categories: objects, label graphics, environmental settings, media, interactives, and human interaction, then a designer can ensure that all media are accounted for, spaced throughout the exhibition gallery. Similarly, a designer can create experiential variety by including elements that encourage active physical participation, others that involve seated viewing that is more passive, some places for looking and reading, others for social gathering, sharing, and cooperation. Yet another dimension is to think about things along a cognitive/emotional spectrum: for example, this section has an upbeat quality, this one is sad and wistful, this one energetic and busy, this one reflective and thought-provoking, this one inspiring and reverential, this one funny, and so forth, in much the same way a film or musical piece progresses through an emotional narrative arc. To understand how the buffet is working, it is useful to plot the different elements by color code on the plan so all can see how the sum of parts works together and then assess whether the totality feels balanced and pleasingly modulated.

Another advantage of this way of thinking is that it avoids the tedious sameness that makes museums dreary. As an analogy, imagine a textbook a student has worked over with a highlighter pen. On occasion, turning to a two-page spread, or even an entire section of a book, he highlights every line. The absurdity is that when we highlight everything, we highlight nothing. Highlighting is only useful when we highlight selectively, its entire purpose is *contrast*, to reinforce a hierarchy of attention, or to favor one line's significance over another. An important discipline to learn in exhibition design is to resist the urge to pile things on. Too often museums become driven by a mad completism: the urge to get as much of the collection on view as possible, or the compulsion to cover as much of the content as can be jammed into the space. In this case, the exhaustive exhibition is exhausting for the viewer and comprehensiveness becomes incomprehensible.

To illustrate this point, here is an example from the Minnesota History Center, a large state history museum in the USA where I am the director and lead the design team (Minnesota History Center 2013). A few years ago we realized that, although we were working really hard to put experiential variety into every exhibit, the sum of the total experience was a flattening of pitch and a creeping monotony throughout. We started to change, introducing more, relatively small, areas that had distinctive experiential attributes: areas of contemplation and quiet, raucous areas, funny or somber places, some exhibits that are more playful and less content-driven, others that are more serious in nature. Since then, our research and other indicators suggest that visitors are responding well. We started to talk about the museum experience as one might a good drama, with emotional peaks and valleys, plot twists and surprises, and great, engrossing characters. Especially for larger museums, providing a buffet of experiential variety throughout is a good strategy for engaging broader audiences, but also for conquering the kind of monotony that too often characterizes museums of all kinds (Spock 2013).

Conclusion: Rules and rule-breaking

There are never hard and fast rules in museum exhibition design and development. The exhibition is the sum of an infinite variety of potential design choices and communication media. Those decisions require trade-offs, each with strengths and weaknesses. It can be tempting to become an ideologue about a particular approach to exhibition design, because each exhibition team comes from a different set of life experiences, levels and domains of expertise, and because the sheer range of choices can seem overwhelming at first. Mastery of tradecraft, however, does not entail a narrowing of perspective, nor does it mean ossification of perspective into a rigid set of rules. Instead, I would advocate a critical framework for exhibition design, which entails a full understanding of the theoretical and practical implications for the museum visitor experience resulting from each design choice. It means a relentless, forward-looking curiosity, especially about new media, societal trends and their potential for the practice of museum exhibition design.

A lot of store has been placed on the value of innovation to the museum field. While there is an element of creative destruction – and hence rule-breaking – in all innovation, it should be recognized that innovators themselves do not emerge in a vacuum but often have a deep knowledge of their discipline. Yes, innovators break rules, but rules should not be broken just for the sake of it. Innovators must have clear, well-conceived ideas – the more empirically grounded the better – about how breaking a rule will actually solve a problem at hand. A common pitfall for those designers straining to be innovative is to render an exhibition as an expression of the latest design style of the moment. Trendiness, or personal taste, may be appealing in the short term, especially to other designers and peers, but I would argue that designing exhibitions as a stylistic gloss over weak concepts can prove fatal to its communicative power – if the styling contributes nothing to the visual coherence or symbolic power of the exhibit, then it is not likely to work for most visitors in the long term. Worse, if the exhibition is to remain in place for many years, an up-to-the-minute styling, with time, will only become a dated embarrassment to the museum. Similar problems are engendered by new technology. While a designer must keep an eye out for an emergent technology that promises to enhance the museum experience, a rigorous skepticism is also appropriate whenever the employment of the latest technology in an exhibition is suggested. Designers need to ask early on: Who is this really for? Is this the only way to present the same information or are there more cost-effective alternatives?

In summary, a designer is always on firmer ground if she holds the museum-goer's experience as the paramount consideration. Sometimes designers arrive at poor solutions simply because they have failed to ask good questions. There are things that museums can do better than virtually any other medium. Excellent exhibitions deliberately optimize those strengths. To conclude this chapter, I would like to present the following guiding principles drawn from my own professional practice. Considering these five "Cs" is a useful exercise in framing design judgments:

1. Captivating: Museums must be engaging, marvelous, delightful too, not merely informative. A museum's good intentions alone are not sufficient to ensure an alluring experience. Does a design speak through experiential variety? Does it constitute a "buffet" offering a range of engagement opportunities for different tastes? Have "big weenies," chains of engagement, and "breadcrumb trails" been designed to attract and draw the museum-goer toward deeper attention? Does the design consider the whole person, not only a thinking person, but a feeling person with capacities for wonder and resonance?

2. Coherent: Museums are a communication medium. An exhibition design, therefore, must not be a confusing muddle. Does the conceptual framework – the chosen "hat rack" – suit the subject? Are related things clustered? Does the anticipated flow of traffic through things reinforce the intended messages or narratives? Does the overall design complement and support the concept or does it degrade coherency?

3. Concrete: Museums show "real" things in real places. Does the design communicate ideas symbolically and visually by showing concrete things, not merely by easily overlooked textual descriptions? Is the curation overly dependent on abstractions that cannot be supported by visualizations? What aspects of the subject lend themselves best to the concrete experiences that museums are best adapted to provide?

4. Condensed: Museums collapse time, geography, space, and information into an experience that is manageable in an afternoon. Just as rigorous curation requires

discernment in the choice of things, elegant design strives for the essential. Is the design a concise expression, ruthlessly edited to avoid the tiresome completism that makes museums tedious? Is it conceived in full acknowledgment of the limited fund of attention a museum-goer brings to the museum? Have some things been deliberately highlighted, others de-emphasized?

5.   Contextualized: Museums do not only explain and describe things, but also *show* things in relationship to other things. The museum itself is an artificial context where every choice has implications. High- or low-context design choices determine how things are understood in aesthetic, emotional, and cognitive terms. Have design options and their consequent power to communicate been fully explored? Are those choices made with the museum-goer in mind?

Rather than being rules or questions of style, these design considerations can bring focus to the most consequential aspects of a museum-goer's experience. If approached in a disciplined manner, the result may not always be innovative, but the exhibition design will be perceived by the visiting public as one that was worth the price of admission. If exhibition design tradecraft is an art, then this is the art to it.

References

Adair, Bill, Benjamin Filene, and Laura Koloski. 2011. *Letting Go? Sharing Historical Authority in a User-Generated World*. Walnut Creek, CA: Left Coast.

Arnold, Ken. 2006. *Cabinets for the Curious: Looking Back at Early English Museums*. Aldershot, UK: Ashgate.

Ash, Doris. 2004. "How Families Use Questions at Dioramas: Ideas for Exhibit Design." *Curator* 47(1): 84–100.

Bann, Stephen. 2003. "The Return to Curiosity: Shifting Paradigms in Contemporary Museum Display." In *Art and Its Publics: Museum Studies at the Millennium*, edited by Andrew McClellan, 117–132. Oxford: Blackwell.

Bennett, Tony. 1995. *The Birth of the Museum: History, Theory, Politics*. London: Routledge.

Berger, John. 1984. *And Our Faces, My Heart, Brief as Photos*. New York: Vintage.

Bitgood, Stephen. 1994. "Designing Effective Exhibits: Criteria for Successful Exhibition Design Approaches and Visitor Strategies." *Visitor Behaviour* 9(4): 4–15.

Bitgood, Stephen. 2011. *Social Design in Museums: The Psychology of Visitor Studies*. 2 vols. Edinburgh: MuseumsEtc.

Candlin, Fiona. 2010. *Art, Museums and Touch*. Manchester: Manchester University Press.

Carey, Benedict. 2007. "This Is Your Life (and How You Tell It)." *New York Times*, May 22. Accessed October 29, 2014. http://www.nytimes.com/2007/05/22/health/psychology/22narr.html?pagewanted=all&_r=0.

Classen, Constance. 2007. "Museum Manners: The Sensory Life of the Early Museum." *Journal of Social History* 40(4): 895–914.

Danto, Arthur, ed. 1988. *ART/artifact: African Art in Anthropology Collections*, 2nd ed. New York: Center for African Art.

Daston, Lorraine, and Katherine Park. 1998. *Wonders and the Order of Nature, 1150–1750*. Cambridge, MA: Zone Books.

Dean, David. 1996. *Museum Exhibition: Theory and Practice*. London: Routledge.

Debes, John L. 1969. "The Loom of Visual Literacy." *Audiovisual Instruction* 14(8): 25–27.

Falk, John. 1991. "Analysis of the Behavior of Family Visitors in Natural History Museums." *Curator* 34(1): 44–57.

Falk, John. 2006. "An Identity-Centered Approach to Understanding Museum Learning." *Curator: The Museum Journal* 49(2): 151–166.

Falk, John, and Lynn Diane Dierking. 1992. *The Museum Experience*. Walnut Creek, CA: Left Coast.

Falk, John, and Lynn Diane Dierking. 2000. *Learning from Museums: Visitor Experiences and the Making of Meaning*. Lanham, MD: AltaMira.

Falk, John, and Lynn Diane Dierking. 2013. *Museum Experience Revisited*, Rev. ed. Walnut Creek, CA: Left Coast.

Gardner, Howard. 1983. *Frames of Mind: The Theory of Multiple Intelligences*. New York: Basic Books.

Gardner, James, and Caroline Heller. 1961. *Exhibition and Display*. New York: Dodge Corporation.

Gould, Stephen Jay. 1993. "Dinomania." *New York Review of Books*, August 12. Accessed October 29, 2014. http://www.nybooks.com/articles/archives/1993/aug/12/dinomania/?pagination=false.

Greenblatt, Stephen. 1991. "Resonance and Wonder." In *Exhibiting Cultures: The Poetics and Politics of Museum Display*, edited by Ivan Karp and Steven Lavine, 43–56. Washington, DC: Smithsonian Institution Press.

Hein, George E., and Mary Alexander. 1998. *Museums: Places of Learning. Professional Practice Series*. Washington, DC: American Association of Museums Education Committee.

Henry Ford, The. 2005. Annual Report. Accessed October 29, 2014. http://www.thehenryford.org/images/AnnualReport05.pdf.

Housen, Abigail. 1987. "Three Methods for Understanding Museum Audiences." *Museum Studies Journal* 2(4): 41–49.

Hughes, Phillip. 2010. *Exhibition Design*. London: Laurence King.

Jacob, George. 2009. *Museum Design: The Future*. Charleston, SC: Booksurge.

Kirchberg, Volker, and Martin Tröndle. 2012. "Experiencing Exhibitions: A Review of Studies on Visitor Experiences in Museums." *Curator: The Museum Journal* 55(4): 435–452.

Kirshenblatt-Gimblett, Barbara. 1998. *Destination Culture: Tourism, Museums, and Heritage*. Berkeley, CA: University of California Press.

Korn, Randi. 2003. Unpublished summative evaluation, Draper Museum of Natural History. Cody, WY: Randi Korn & Associates.

Latimer, Sue. 2011. "Art for Whose Sake?" In *Museum Gallery Interpretation and Material Culture*, edited by Juliette Fritsch, 67–79. London: Routledge.

Leon, Warren, and Roy Rosenzweig. 1989. *History Museums in the United States: A Critical Assessment*. Urbana: University of Illinois Press.

Lidwell, William, Kritina Holden, and Jill Butler. 2003. *Universal Principles of Design: 100 Ways to Enhance Usability, Influence Perception, Increase Appeal, Make Better Design Decisions, and Teach Through Design*. Gloucester: Rockport.

Lord, Barry and Gail Dexter Lord, eds. 2002. *The Manual of Museum Exhibitions*. Lanham, MD: AltaMira.

Lorenc, Jan, Lee Skolnick, and Craig Berger 2010. *What Is Exhibit Design? Essential Design Handbooks*. Los Angeles: University of California, RotoVision.

MacLeod, Suzanne. 2005. *Reshaping Museum Space: Architecture, Design, Exhibitions*. Oxford: Routledge.

MacLeod, Suzanne, Laura Hourston Hanks, and Jonathan Hale. 2012. *Museum Making: Narratives, Architectures, Exhibitions*. London: Chapman and Hall Routledge.

McKenna-Cress, Polly, and Janet Kamien. 2013. *Creating Exhibitions: Collaboration in the Planning, Development, and Design of Innovative Experiences*. Oxford: Wiley-Blackwell.

McLean, Kathleen. 1993. *Planning for People in Museum Exhibitions*. Washington, DC: American Association of Science-Technology Centers.

Minnesota History Center. 2013. Accessed October 29, 2014. http://www.minnesotahistorycenter.org.

Pavio, Allan, T. B. Rogers, and Padric C. Smythe. 1968. "Why Are Pictures Easier to Recall than Words?" *Psychonomic Science* 11(4): 137–138.

Peart, Bob, and Richard Kool. 1981. "Analysis of a Natural History Exhibit: Are Dioramas the Answer?" *The International Journal of Museum Management and Curatorship* 7(2): 117–128.

Rounds, Jay. 2006. "Strategies for the Curiosity-Driven Museum Visitor." *Curator: The Museum Journal* 47(4): 389–412.

Samis, Peter. 2007. "New Technologies as Part of a Comprehensive Interpretive Plan." In *The Digital Museum: A Think Guide*, edited by Herminia Din and Phyllis Hecht, 19–34. Washington, DC: AAM.

Schwarzer, Marjorie. 2006. *Riches, Rivals and Radicals: 100 Years of Museums in America*. Washington, DC: AAM.

Serrell, Beverly. 2006. *Judging Exhibitions: A Framework for Assessing Excellence*. Walnut Creek, CA: Left Coast.

Simon, Nina. 2010. *The Participatory Museum*. Santa Cruz, CA: Museum 2.0.

Sklar, Martin. 1987. "Education vs. Entertainment: Competing for Audiences." Paper presented at the American Association of Museums annual meeting, Pittsburgh, June. Walt Disney Imagineering. Accessed October 29, 2014. http://www.tumblr.com/tagged/walt%20disney%20imagineering.

Spock, Dan. 2013. Comment online in response to Jen Oleniczek, "A Museum Experience Is Not a One-Size-Fits-All." *Art Museum Teaching: A Forum for Reflecting On Practice*, September 25. Accessed October 29, 2014. http://artmuseumteaching.com/2013/09/25/a-museum-experience-is-not-one-size-fits-all.

Staniszewski, Mary Anne. 1998. *The Power of Display: A History of Exhibition Installations at the Museum of Modern Art*. Cambridge, MA: MIT Press.

Vogel, Susan. 1991. "Always True to the Object, in Our Fashion." In *Exhibiting Cultures: The Poetics and Politics of Museum Display*, edited by I. Karp and S. D. Lavine, 191–204. Washington, DC: Smithsonian Institution Press.

Whitehead, Christopher. 2012. *Interpreting Art in Museums and Galleries*. London: Routledge.

Wilson, Fred, and Lisa G. Corrin. 1994. *Mining the Museum*. Baltimore, MD: New Press.

Wilson, Gillian. 2004. "Multimedia Tour Programme at Tate Modern." In *Museums and the Web 2004: Conference Proceedings*, edited by David Bearman and Jennifer Trant. Toronto: Archives and Museum Informatics. Accessed January 17, 2012. http://www.archimuse.com/mw2004/papers/wilson/wilson.html.

Wurman, Richard Saul. 1989. *Information Anxiety*. New York: Doubleday.

Further Reading

Bogle, Elizabeth. 2013. *Museum Exhibition Planning and Design*. Lanham, MD: AltaMira.

Bridle, Tessa. 2013. *Effective Exhibit Interpretation and Design*. Lanham, MD: AltaMira.

Monti, Francesca and Suzanne Keene. 2013. *Museums and Silent Objects: Designing Effective Exhibitions*. Farnham, UK: Ashgate.

Roppola, Tiina. 2011. *Designing for the Museum Visitor Experience*. London: Routledge.

Tilden, Freeman, and R. Bruce Craig. 2007. *Interpreting Our Heritage*, Rev. ed. Chapel Hill: University of North Carolina Press.

Wilkening, Susie, and James Chung. 2009. *Life Stages of the Museum Visitor*. Washington, DC: AAM.

Dan Spock is the Director of the Minnesota History Center Museum (MHS), in St. Paul, Minnesota. In the course of his 20 year plus museum career, Dan has worked as an exhibit designer, an exhibit developer, and a program administrator. After several years as Exhibit Designer at the Boston Children's Museum, he was Exhibit Developer at the Museum of Creativity, and then joined the Minnesota Historical Society as Head of Exhibitions. He has consulted and lectured at a variety of museum and learning institutions and has published widely on a variety of museum subjects in books such as *The Digital Museum: A Think Guide* (2007), and the journals *Exhibitionist* and *Curator*.

18 MUSEUM EXHIBITION PRACTICE
Recent Developments in Europe, Canada, and Australia

Linda Young, with Anne Whitelaw and Rosmarie Beier-de Haan

Museum exhibitions constitute the frontline of engagement between the public and the institution: they are the defining communicative medium of the museum. To grasp the key features of contemporary exhibition practice, it is necessary to survey their two forms: permanent and temporary. The older tradition of permanent galleries placed collections on display in long-term installations (Klonk 2009). Indeed, the enduring presence of permanent galleries constitutes a crucial element of the cultural authority of the museum (Duncan 1995; Shelton 2006). Yet this very permanence generates an inertia that makes it difficult to introduce change, because of the effort and expense needed to refresh or replace displays. Like turning an ocean liner, the revision of permanent exhibitions can be a slow project (Wallach 2013), although it recognizes and introduces new knowledges and exhibitionary paradigms to the museum, as this chapter demonstrates.

The museum calendar of changing exhibitions developed largely after World War II. It both challenges the static reputation of the museum and attracts ongoing visitation with something new and different throughout the year (Ward 1996; Staniszewski 1998; Barker 1999; Altshuler 2008). Further, temporary exhibitions are the medium by which staff can investigate topical issues, focus on specific works, and explore aspects of the collection. This chapter presents accounts of these kinds of transformative revisions through the "permanent" installations representing Indigenous cultures in Australia, exhibitions of native culture and fine art in Canada, and temporary exhibitions in museums in the heart of the European Union.

The International Handbooks of Museum Studies: Museum Practice, First Edition.
Edited by Conal McCarthy.
© 2015 John Wiley & Sons Ltd. Published 2020 by John Wiley & Sons Ltd.

It is not hard to demonstrate the impermanence of "permanent" galleries, for although revision tends to be infrequent, almost nothing *never* changes. Fashions, both intellectual and visual, eventually make long-established galleries look old-fashioned (Karp and Lavine 1991, 1). Relatively unchanging exhibitions, such as the typological format of the Pitt Rivers Museum in Oxford dating from the late nineteenth century, have become rare, and some are now conserved as period pieces. Many museums founded in the Victorian period, however, have a history of redeveloping their permanent installations every several decades (Taylor 1999; Abt 2002; McCarthy 2007; MacLeod 2013). It is not uncommon for "permanent" galleries to endure for 30 to 50 years (and more). For example, the history of the American Wing at the Metropolitan Museum in New York begins with the first dedicated exhibition space opened in 1924, 50 years after the museum itself was founded; the next redisplay took place in 1980; and the most recent in 2012. Each was hailed for its contribution to revising the public understanding of American decorative arts (American Wing 2014).

Of course our ways of knowing are subject to change over time, but museums are rarely at the forefront of representing these epistemological shifts, as shown by the long resistance to exhibiting Darwinian evolution in natural history institutions (Yanni 1999). In fact, it could be argued that new ideas and frameworks of knowledge are more likely to occur in new museums than in old ones, which find it difficult to change and update their paradigms.

The immediate relevance of geopolitical shifts, such as the transformation of nation states in post-Communist Europe and the expansion of the European Union, produced both new displays and new museums, not least to celebrate and legitimize new states (Ostow 2008). Thus the reunification of Germany in 1990 led to the merging of East and West historical collections into the Deutsches Historisches Museum and the construction of a large new wing on the historic Zeughaus (arsenal) in Berlin. Naturally, museums are often mobilized by state agencies to address the immediate demands of politics and policy through exhibitions whose material culture is popularly credited with demonstrating the "truth" of nations, peoples, and their identity. Aspects of contemporary museum exhibition practice can be explored through the new and revived national and transnational stories installed in these museums old and new (Knell et al. 2010). In this chapter, Rosmarie Beier-de Haan notes that the transnationalism of the European Union is musealized in a Museum of Europe and a new House of European History in Brussels, as well as the Musée des Civilisations de l'Europe et de la Méditerranée in Marseille (MUCEM 2014). Beier-de Haan introduces a number of temporary exhibitions which grapple with complex ideologies arising from both the Napoleonic and Nazi domination of Europe.

Meanwhile in postsettler nations of the new world the first generation of colonial museums remade themselves at the start of the twenty-first century, striving to exhibit bi- or multicultural perspectives on their national stories. These "old" museums originally modeled themselves on their imperial progenitors, privileging discourses of settler achievement and Indigenous inferiority (MacKenzie 2009). By the 1980s, museums were viewed by many as bastions of the symbolic suppression of native peoples (Karp and Lavine 1991). New exhibitions were both praised and criticized. *Te Maori* at the Metropolitan Museum in 1984 asserted customary protocols in the display of treasured Māori objects from New Zealand (McCarthy 2007). In Canada in 1988 *The Spirit Sings* at the Glenbow Museum drew Indigenous rage over sponsorship by an oil company despoiling the local environment (Phillips 2011). More recently in Paris, the Musée du Quai Branly, opened in 2006, was criticized for its "regressive" museology which aestheticized Indigenous cultures as fine art. The imperative to address Indigenous survival, creativity, and rights spurred a wave of revisionism, seen in the Canadian Museum of Civilisation in Ottawa, the National Museum of Australia in Canberra, and the Museum of New Zealand Te Papa Tongarewa (Te Papa) in Wellington. But, rather than new exhibits in new museums, this revision was more often observed in the process of replacing old galleries in existing museums with new exhibitions (Hendry 2005).

This theme is discussed below by Anne Whitelaw in her study of the transformation of Canadian art history within the displays of three great art museums, each now incorporating First Nations artists' work. Each deploys a different strategy of inclusion. Perhaps the most obvious technique is to display a comprehensive collection of the creative products of Indigenous people before colonization, but this risks a charge of ghettoization and the imposition of a misleading cultural essentialism. Another exhibitionary approach is to hang artworks of diverse Canadian cultures within a conventional chronology of national history, thereby re-presenting what had been classified as ethnography or colonial amateur art within the construct of high art, with its connotation of elite culture. A further strategy is the thematic narrative exhibition, which also risks the de-aestheticization of artworks.

Revisionist exhibition of Indigenous culture and history is also the topic of Linda Young's case study (in this chapter) of the transformation of the major metropolitan museums of Australia. Each started as colonial natural history museums, and among the resources they collected and exhibited were the inhabitants of the land, resulting in displays which are today seen as racist (Griffiths 1996; Healy 2008). It took ten years of protest and debate starting in the 1980s to assert Indigenous ownership of their cultures and their input into museum representations, which gradually shifted exhibitionary practice from scientific ethnography and paternalist history toward a more equal "authority to represent." Only when the country's political and legal structures acknowledged Indigenous rights in the 1990s, did the museums grasp the nettle of revising the galleries dedicated to Aboriginal Australia.

As in Canada, a remarkable variety of exhibitionary techniques was deployed to convey new understandings of Indigenous culture and identity, ranging from shared decision-making and Indigenous curatorial control to multimedia interactivity and the reclaiming of culture via contemporary creativity (Thomas 2001;

Healy and Witcomb 2006). Despite accusations of tokenism and "political correctness," this surge of new exhibitions championed the cause of Australian Aboriginality, a stance which was vindicated in overwhelmingly positive visitor evaluations (Delroy 2001).

Exhibitions remain important statements of the values and politics of the contemporary world, and reflect the wider processes of globalization, nationalism, and transnationalism. The case studies presented in this chapter depict major shifts in museum exhibitions, temporary and "permanent." The changes that eventually acknowledged Indigenous rights, history, and culture were slower than curatorial staff might have liked, but perhaps faster than the current of public opinion. Either way, they confirm the capacity of museums to represent profound changes in concepts of social justice via interpretive exhibitions.

Re-presenting Indigenous culture in Australian museums at the turn of the twenty-first century[1]

The manikin seated in a display of Aboriginal artifacts would not have seemed strange if he hadn't been white (Figure 18.1). This was evident not only from his well-barbered moustache, three-piece suit, and spindle-back chair, but also from his rendering in bright white plaster. To his left was a display of spears and digging sticks. He lent forward, elbow on knee, evidently thinking. Stenciled on the glass front of the display case were these words: "We did not choose to be enshrined in a glass case, with our story told by an alien institution which has appointed itself as an ambassador of our culture." The figure was Professor Baldwin Spencer, biologist, anthropologist, and honorary director (1899–1928) of the museum in which he was on show between 2000 and 2012. The exhibitionary tables had been turned. An earlier scheme for the display proposed a matching figure outside the case, looking in: Irrapmwe, an Arrernte man of Central Australia, who had been a major informant of Spencer's. Design problems ruled out his material installation, but Irrapmwe did appear, with Spencer, in a talking-head video piece nearby. They debated a modern argument about cultural rights, reaching an anachronistically tolerant, quasi-resolution about modes of knowledge.

The inversion of conventional museum representations described above opened at the Melbourne Museum campus of Museum Victoria in 2000, in *Bunjilaka* ("the place of Bunjil," a creation spirit). This new museum building showcased permanent galleries that represented a major revision of the old style of display seen in the museum's original building. *Bunjilaka* was grounded in colonial-era collections, reinforced by notable anthropological collections and a growing body of contemporary Indigenous social history. However, it was conceived as a deliberate break with previous exhibition conventions, being constituted as keeping place and cultural center, where Indigenous people would manage programs, hold

FIGURE 18.1   Model of Professor Baldwin Spencer, biologist, anthropologist, and honorary director of the National Museum of Victoria (1899–1928) on display in the exhibition *Bunjilaka*, 2001. (For a color version of this figure, please see the color plate section.)

Source: Museum Victoria. Photograph: John Broomfield.

meetings, and celebrate the survival and revival of Aboriginal cultures (Simpson 2006). The result was attacked in some quarters as "a propaganda unit, presenting a skewed and inaccurate account of our history and culture," with a hidden agenda to "make the white man look silly" (Bolt 2000). Others regretted what they called the decontextualization of Spencer as someone who was merely a man of his times and the so-called fiction of "a post-colonial ticking off" (Mateer 2000, 22; Russell 2000). The new exhibition questioned the expectations of what a museum ought to do, and showed how exhibition practice might be rejigged to articulate a new politics.

Archaeological antiquity, typically represented in Aboriginal displays by a great number of ancient artifacts dug up or collected by Europeans, was absent in *Bunjilaka* because of budget cuts which meant the usual object-rich display was not possible. The juxtaposition of the anthropological Other and historical and contemporary Aboriginality was nevertheless prominent: hundreds of historic photographs of Indigenous people, hitherto treated as institutional specimens, were transformed by their identification as named individuals, reasserting their humanity.[2] The confrontation between historical anthropology and modern life took shape in a number of contrasts. The most startling of these confrontations in *Bunjilaka* were adjacent displays of an ancient bark canoe bearing a burial bundle close to a 1976 Chrysler hearse purchased by the Aborigines Advancement League to take urban-dwellers on their final journey "back to country." This modernization of tradition asserted within the "authoritative" museum provoked a few attacks from conservatives, but significantly more interest and praise (Delroy 2001).

By 2010, the museum politics of Australian Indigenous cultures were changing again in response to a generally more conservative political climate. At Melbourne Museum, where exhibition development models had always moved back and forth along the spectrum from community consultation to curatorial control, the process reverted to the latter in a sometimes fraught collaboration. *Bunjilaka* was now constituted as an Aboriginal community cultural center, and was required to refocus from a critique of the museum to an instrument of its people's survival and revival. In an unusually rapid turnaround of a permanent gallery, *First Peoples* opened in 2013 (for a full review, see Young 2014). The exhibition that emerged from the Yulendj (Law and Knowledge) group shows an intense spiritual impulse uniting the ancient and modern history of Aboriginal people in southeast Australia. A central contemplative space houses a hypnotic sculpture of the powerfully feathered wings of Bunjil the eagle and Waa the crow. The traditional knowledge of Indigenous people informs the exhibits, which also draw on information provided by Western scholars of paleontology, archaeology, and contact history. Some exhibits have been criticized for applying contemporary beliefs that do not accord with scientific orthodoxies (Vines 2013). In contrast to the museological wit and startling juxtapositions of the initial exhibition described above, like putting the anthropologist himself on display, it seems that the gallery has now been toned down to a perhaps more muted and less risky style. It is less "cutting-edge," but at the same time probably more accessible to a wider range of visitors.

Bunjilaka's first iteration came at the midpoint in a decade of Australian museum exhibitionary revisionism. Since their foundations in the nineteenth century, museums had displayed Aboriginal ethnology amid natural history collections; each institution's particular exhibition style was conditioned by a vigorous and, at times, virulent cultural politics of race. By the 1990s, Aboriginal Australians were asserting an agenda of rights that reflected the changing cultural politics throughout the "fourth world" of Indigenous peoples (Graburn 1981; Attwood and Markus 1999). They began to win legal struggles for land rights in 1992 and demanded acknowledgment of the culturally and personally destructive policy of removing children from parents' care, which culminated in a high-profile government report on what had come to be called "the stolen generations" in 1997 (HREOC 1997). Australia's so-called "history wars" of the turn of the millennium were played out in the spate of new Indigenous exhibitions in museums across the continent (Macintyre and Clark 2003).

Relationships between Indigenous people and museums had been reshaped during the previous 20 years as part of a larger re-evaluation of the postcolonial legacies of anthropology and archaeology (Clifford 1988; Ames 1992; Simpson 2001). Australian museums responded to the challenge by developing strategies of repatriation, shared stewardship, and ways of working with Indigenous people in managing collections and exhibitions (Anderson 1995; Davidson, Lovell-Jones, and Bancroft 1995; Kelly, Cook, and Gordon 2006). As a result, some of the former displays of Aboriginal exhibits in natural history museums were revised in light of shifts in thinking. Informed by the politics of human rights and by a critique of institutional complicity in colonial domination, the new displays were scrutinized for evidence of a commitment to social justice in the museum. The new praxis stressed assertions of civil and political rights, collaborative development, cultural continuity, contemporary Aboriginal identity, and cultural recovery through art-making.

The first significant museum redisplay of the 1990s opened in 1997 at the Australian Museum, Sydney, entitled *Indigenous Australians: Australia's First Peoples*. Museum staff had been deeply engaged with the 1993 professional protocol *Previous Possessions, New Obligations*, which promulgated the right of Indigenous people to control their heritage (Sullivan, Kelly, and Gordon 2003). The museum already operated a busy outreach assistance program to Aboriginal heritage groups within New South Wales, and thus had regular active contacts with communities. A further strength was the Australian Museum's expertise in evaluation and visitor advocacy in exhibition development. Studies by Lynda Kelly and colleagues clarified the exhibition's communication goals which were firmly grounded in the contemporary, explaining Indigenous people's experience in recent times, and leaving a positive message for the future (Kelly and Sullivan 1997).

The chosen display themes were Spirituality, Cultural Heritage, Family, Land, Health, and Justice – a clear shift from the former exhibition based on the museum's disciplinary foundations in archaeology and anthropology. To realize the new themes, it was necessary to augment the museum collections with modern material, including contemporary artworks, hybrid objects, and evidence of historical oppression and resistance. The careful construction of an exhibition for specific audiences employed social research applied to marketing techniques. Prototype testing of exhibits and labels revealed divergent responses among the three target audience groups: Indigenous people believed the content was too "soft"; family visitor groups felt it was too confrontational; while teachers were positive about their ability to use the exhibition's concepts and objects, so as to mediate students' understanding of Aboriginal histories and culture (Specht and MacLulich 2000; Kelly and Gordon 2004). The response was to spread out the placement of confrontational topics in the exhibition layout, toughen up the "Stolen Generations" presentation, and reinforce an emphasis on the future. Thus the Australian Museum launched what was, for the time, a groundbreaking contemporary statement of Indigenous life in modern Australia.

By contrast, the continuity of culture, or, rather, the implication of deep time lying behind current lives, formed one axis of the *Katta Djinoong* ("to see and understand") gallery at the Western Australian Museum (WAM), Perth, launched in 1999. Its other axis was geographic, examining four regions of the state. The exhibits had a dual narrative, with museum science interwoven with – though not directly compared to – a contemporary Aboriginal comparison; for instance, Pleistocene beads signifying the human taste for ornament made a reference to a modern evening dress by a Nyoongar designer. The history of contact between black and white is more recent in Western Australia than in other parts of the nation, and many Indigenous people still live on or near ancestral lands, under the threat of white encroachment. It is a violent history, and *Katta Djinoong*'s presentation of a 1926 massacre of Aboriginal people provoked a further sally of the "history wars" (Macintyre and Clark 2003), bringing the museum to unaccustomed prominence in rightwing commentary.

Much of this critique was based on the assertion that published records constitute the only verifiable source of history, in contrast to oral tradition, dismissed by critics as "stories my Mum and Dad told me" (Moran 2002). Exhibition texts erred in certain factual details, but nevertheless expressed the reality of murderous experience in the collective memories of generations of Aboriginal people. Thus the WAM's affirmation of traditional Aboriginal knowledge brought the new permanent gallery into conflict with conventional expectations of the white man's history. By presenting the oral record as equally reliable as written records, the contested politics of the past were revealed.

Meanwhile, the South Australian Museum's (SAM) Australian Aboriginal Cultures Gallery opened in 2000. Contrary to the trend, its exhibition strategy focused on pre-contact, traditional material culture (of which SAM holds the largest collections in the nation), with dense hangs of specimens, carefully spot-lit in darkened galleries. The design highlighted the aesthetics of form, and echoed the traditional mode of historical ethnographic display. The object-dense exhibition in the nineteenth-century halls of the SAM inevitably evoked a primitivist atmosphere reflecting curatorial anthropologists' construction of knowledge rather than the agency and history of Aboriginal people. Small videos of modern people speaking of their lives and work (among them an Indigenous archaeologist) indicated the living presence of the Indigenous, but they are seen to be engaging with traditional heritage more than with contemporary issues and concerns. Even label texts tended to be in the past tense, emphasizing the distant past rather than the present of current Aboriginal issues. The "affirmative action" seen in museums in Sydney and Melbourne, and the pointed politics evident in Perth, prompted the (non-Indigenous) leader of the gallery development team at SAM to criticize these more politically engaged exhibitions as voguish and didactic. But other commentators accused the Australian Aboriginal Cultures Gallery of being aestheticized, de-historicized, and obfuscatory (Allen and Bulbeck 2000; Dauber 2005).

So far this account of exhibitionary processes implies a positive political climate for Indigenous rights and interests, which had indeed gained successes in the 1980s and 1990s under a center-left national government. Museums were not at the forefront of government policy, although they had cooperated on a national plan for cultural diversity in collections, exhibitions, and employment in 1990 (DASETT 1991). In addition, academic and professional awareness of Indigenous culture and history was certainly infiltrating museum practice (CAMA 1993; Baillie 1998). However, despite this progress, active official support for Indigenous interests began to wind back after a conservative win in the 1996 Australian general election. Nonetheless, the incoming government committed itself to open a new National Museum of Australia (NMA) in the capital city, Canberra, to mark the centenary of national federation in 2001.

The National Museum began to take shape, having existed in embryo for 20 years, with a constitution mandating a distinct gallery dedicated to Indigenous culture and history (Australian Government 1980). Generally the NMA was unburdened by institutional history, although it had absorbed an existing anthropological collection; but now it set out to develop public programs through the frame of social history and contemporary culture in exhibits making extensive use of new media. In the Gallery of First Australians, the living agency of Indigenous people was taken as the guiding concept. Major features included prominent videos of modern people introducing their respective cultural identities, some living traditional lives and speaking in local languages, others presenting themselves as normative white Australians. Intended to blur stereotypes, this gallery surprised visitors' expectations of a more exotic indigeneity, this author included (Young 2006). Artworks derived from or inspired by traditional skills constituted a high proportion of the NMA's material exhibits of modern Aboriginal people. They included non-traditional media: wool rugs and silk batik taught by mission managers; an (ephemeral) traditional ceremonial ground image worked in red sand and dried seed fluff; and the dot painting tradition that had transferred from traditional applications to large canvases in the 1970s. By 2001 this Central Desert painting form had been adopted into the art canon and market, validated by international shows and surging prices (Sutton, Anderson, and Jones 1989; Ryan and Batty 2011).

The NMA opening exhibitions were informed by current academic directions in Aboriginal history, including research on Indigenous dispossession, disease, coercion, criminalization, exploitation, and death. When the museum opened, it was applauded by many, but censured by others, including some critics connected to the highest echelons of the conservative government. Following the museum's opening, exhibits depicting aspects of massacre were subjected to a denialist critique that repudiated the oral record and claimed an inaccurate reading of historic documents (Windschuttle 2001). The exhibit became the focus of a "black armband v. white blindfold" debate about Australian history (Davison 2003). In 2003, just two years after opening, the NMA was subject to a formal government review process. The review's conclusions sidestepped the contests of black–white history but demanded a grander narrative of national progress (Trinca and Wehner 2006).

There is no longer an exhibit on massacre in the Gallery of First Australians, although the painful histories of the Stolen Generations are still shown. In changing content of the exhibition since opening, the NMA has refocused (in practice if not explicitly) on the display of art/craft objects produced as acts of cultural recovery, such as possum-fur cloaks engraved with designs on the skin side, and baskets worked of giant kelp seaweed. It represents a carefully presented theme foregrounding contemporary Indigenous identity while avoiding contentious history – perhaps the tenor of the cultural politics of the twenty-first century?

Transnationality and difficult history: new exhibition practice in German and European museums[3]

Despite progress toward European integration and international cooperation, the analysis and dissemination of European history frequently remains stuck in traditional national categories. However, it is increasingly possible to speak of European history and memory in other than national terms. Since the 1990s, European cities such as Turin, Berlin, Brussels, and Marseilles have begun to establish a museum of Europe (or to redesign an existing museum in this way). These mainly politically initiated projects have had varying rates of success (for Marseilles, see below). Besides these universalizing projects, museums professionals and professional networks are increasingly engaged in the Europeanization of the museum field (Kaiser, Krankenhagen, and Poehis 2014). Networks such as the Network of European Museum Organizations (NEMO), ICOM Europe, and the International Association of Museums of History (IAMH) provide representation and resources for the museum community of Europe; equally of note is Europeana, an EU-funded digitization project, aiming to make the cultural heritage of Europe accessible to everyone online (www.europeana.eu).

Among the first museums dealing with trans-European identity was the Musée de l'Europe in Brussels, a project initiated in 1997 to explore interdisciplinarity and Europeanness (Museum of Europe 2014). Now located in a grand warehouse building, the Musée presents a permanent gallery of maps and the exhibition, *It's Our History*, which constructs a story of pan-European histories. To address the span of European geography, the Musée also develops co-produced temporary exhibitions in other locations, beginning with *Belle Europe: The Age of the Universal Exhibitions, 1851–1913* in 2001.

A cultural-political project is the European Parliament's House of European History, which will open in Brussels in 2015. Conceived as "a reservoir of European memory," itself an innovative concept, the exhibitionary program rejects sharp geographical boundaries in favor of a Europe produced by various social and cultural characteristics and trajectories (European Parliament 2013, 31).

The world wars that periodically ruptured Europe have recently been reviewed as a transnational phenomenon via museums and exhibitions. The centenary of World War I generated interpretive commemorations in many countries. Transnational approaches to war are not confined to the twentieth century. The exhibition *Napoleon and Europe: Dream and Trauma* (shown at the Bundeskunsthalle in Bonn in 2010, and at the Musée de l'armée in Paris in 2012) explored European modernization brought about by Napoleonic rule. Looking beyond the veneration of Napoleon, the exhibition also marked the enormous cost in human lives of the years of war waged under his regime (Savoy 2010).

Meanwhile the Musée des civilisations de l'Europe et de la Méditerranée was inaugurated in Marseille in 2013, looking beyond European borders to connections across the Mediterranean basin (MUCEM 2014). Exhibitions focus not on national/international politics, but on four themes – agriculture, religion, trade, and citizenship – expressed across the geography of the Mediterranean world (Moore 2013).

Museums increasingly position themselves as fora for civic dialogue, where questions of the past, present, and future can be examined (Beier-de Haan 2006). Institutions of the public sphere can create space and time for visitors to ask questions, reflect, and participate in dialogue. This is particularly important in exhibitions that explore the legacies of "difficult history": that is, past events that divide people today, and that continue to cause pain within and between societies. They raise challenging themes for exhibitions in Germany, with its "burdened past" (Macdonald 2008). In this vein, the Deutsches Historisches Museum has addressed the dark history of the Holocaust through a long series of exhibitions, including *Holocaust – The National Socialist Genocide and the Motives of its Remembrance* (2002); *1945 – The War and Its Consequences: The End of the War and the Politics of Memory in Germany* (2005) and *Germany and Poland: Despair and Hope* (2009) (Beier-de Haan 2012).

The 2010 exhibition *Hitler and the Germans: Nation and Crime* (Figure 18.2) posed difficult questions. Why were so many Germans willing to accept and support the expulsion of Jews? How could Hitler and his regime count on the broad acceptance of the Germans up to the end of the war? The record attendance of more than 265,000 visitors to the exhibition suggests that people still have a great need to examine this difficult heritage. The exhibition focused on the relationship between Hitler and the German people, showing how his extraordinary rise to the position of Führer was only possible because he was able to incite popular fears and exploit a longing for collective power.

It is worth analyzing this exhibition as a commentary on the others discussed here. The task lay in repurposing objects and images produced by the Nazi propaganda machine to tell a different story (Figure 18.2). According to exhibition curator Simone Erpel (2011), it was a matter of avoiding the creation of either "devotional" or "demonized" objects, achieved by various display strategies. For example, mass-produced busts of Hitler were placed together in a narrow space in order to present them as sheer commodities, illustrating the Nazi strategy of

FIGURE 18.2   Exhibition *Hitler and the Germans. Nation and Crime*, Berlin 2010. View of
the section "Hitler and the Germans 1933–1945." Large-scale film, picture, and photo
panels counteract the propaganda objects.
© German Historical Museum 2010.

creating an "omnipresent Führer" (Figure 18.3). The massive sideboard from the
room known as the "Führer's study" in the New Chancellery of the Reich was set
up at a slight slant in order to undermine its impression of massive authority.
Hitler's speeches could be heard only on headphones; never out loud.

With its claim of totalitarian supremacy the Nazi dictatorship wanted to "coordinate" (*gleichschalten*) the outward appearance of the whole society; and thus a
dress code of uniforms signaled rank and status in the *Volksgemeinschaft*, the "community of the people." This uniform society was represented in a parade of more
than 30 Party, Wehrmacht, and civilian uniforms, showing how men and women
offered their services to the regime in order to secure social advancement, prestige,
and personal benefits. With this installation, the exhibition curators presented
groundbreaking research in women's and gender studies, linking National Socialist
ideology and constructions of femininity and masculinity (Frietsch and Herkommer
2009). Central to this was the question of women's participation in building and
maintaining oppressive structures and their actual scope of action, apparently in
contrast to the idealized image of the wife and mother propagated in the *völkische
Weltanschauung* (ethno-nationalist "folk" worldview).

Behind war lies the psychological history of nations, a topic that can be explored
in terms of national construction and differentiation via the "Other." This was the
theme of the exhibition *The Image of the "Other" in Germany and France from 1871 to*

FIGURE 18.3   Exhibition *Hitler and the Germans. Nation and Crime*, Berlin 2010. View of the section "Hitler and the Germans 1933–1945." Busts of the *Führer* as propagandistic mass products. (For a color version of this figure, please see the color plate section.)
© German Historical Museum 2010.

the Present (Werquet and Beier-de Haan 2009), shown first at the Cité nationale de l'histoire de l'immigration, Paris, in 2008/2009 (Amar, Poinsot, and Wihtol de Wenden 2009) and then in an expanded version at Berlin's Deutsches Historisches Museum in 2009/2010 (Figure 18.4). Created by German and French curators working collaboratively, and presented from a transnational perspective, this enormous exhibition traced historical divisions and continuities, as well as numerous ties linking Germany and France since the founding of the German Empire (in 1871) and the French Third Republic (in 1870). Its transnational approach (Haupt and Kocka 2009) focused not on the history of events, but on the history of the representation of the "Other," leading to the question how were (and are) concepts and images of alterity formed and circulated? The idea was explored through the legal, administrative and scientific practices that normalize the attitudes and beliefs of the majority toward marginal and minority groups, thereby reaffirming the self-definition of the majority (Figure 18.5).

Forward-looking exhibition concepts in Germany, like the ones sketched here, are distinguished by the fact that they are able to reflect upon, free themselves from, and/or critique traditional national categories. Twenty-five years after the fall of the Berlin Wall, museum exhibitions are attempting to locate national histories within a wider European frame. Innovative exhibitions and museums do not want to deliver definitive interpretations of history, but to represent it as complex

FIGURE 18.4 Exhibition *The Image of the "Other" in Germany and France from 1871 to the present*, Paris 2008, Berlin 2009. View of the contemporary section. In the center a model of the sculpture *The Foreigner* by Guido Messer, 1982. (For a color version of this figure, please see the color plate section.)
© German Historical Museum 2009.

FIGURE 18.5 Exhibition *The Image of the "Other" in Germany and France from 1871 to the present*, Paris 2008, Berlin 2009. View of the contemporary section. French and German history presented as parallel history (see center of picture).
© German Historical Museum 2009.

and multi-perspectival. Use of sophisticated scenographies assist in creating spatial environments that can inspire people to reflect on and reconsider perceptions of their own, and others', histories. Such exhibitions stimulate reconsideration of difficult heritage in a spirit of dialogue, rather than judgment (Beier-de Haan 2011).

Writing national art histories in Canadian museums[4]

The history of art in Canada is closely tied to its development as a nation. From the time the first Europeans landed on the territory now known as Canada, artists have depicted the landscape and its inhabitants. Early French colonizers used wood sculptures and paintings as visual aids in the conversion of Indigenous peoples to Catholicism; at the same time they commissioned self-portraits documenting their rise to middle-class status. After the conquest in 1763, British topographic artists mapped out the landscape of Upper and Lower Canada, while adventurous paint-ers accompanied fur-traders to record the expanding territory to the west. Confederation in 1867 furthered the growth of major cities and also spurred attempts to foster the development of the fine arts in the Dominion through the establishment of professional artists' exhibiting societies, such as the Royal Canadian Academy. By the beginning of the twentieth century, the push to create a national school of art was taken up by the members of the Group of Seven, whose colorful depictions of an uninhabited central Canadian landscape bolstered the political vision of Canada as the land of unending natural resources. After World War II, Canadian artists began looking outside the country for inspiration and community, and the resulting abstractions revealed close links between Quebec artists and Paris on the one hand, and between English Canada and abstract modernism on the other. These international linkages were fostered over the following five decades, through Canadian artists' membership in conceptual art networks and their participation in international contemporary art fairs.

The above could be considered the dominant narrative of Canadian art from con-tact to the present, and its triumphalist account of the development of art from provin-cial colonialism to international contemporaneity characterizes the major written histories produced up to the 2000s (Harper 1967; Reid 1973). What is missing from this narrative, however, is the considerable cultural production of the Indigenous inhabit-ants of the territory now known as Canada: a production that predates contact by many centuries and that until recently was largely relegated to ethnographic muse-ums.[5] Since 2003, however, Canadian art galleries have made a concerted effort to include objects of expressive culture from indigenous communities in their displays of Canadian art. Starting with the National Gallery of Canada in 2003, this rethinking of the display of Canada's national art history to include the work of Aboriginal peoples was taken up by the Art Gallery of Ontario in 2008 and by the Montreal Museum of Fine Arts in 2011. This section of the chapter will consider the work of museums in constructing national art histories by examining the varying ways that art galleries have negotiated the inclusion of Aboriginal art in their permanent displays of Canadian art.

The National Gallery of Canada (NGC) was the first national institution to take this step. The NGC was founded in 1880, at the same time as the Royal Canadian Academy, in order to foster the appreciation of art in Canada and to boost the professionalization of the country's artists. Contemporary Canadian art was always an important feature of the NGC's collection and it actively supported the nascent Group of Seven through purchases and by selecting their work for international exhibitions. With its move to a purpose-built facility in 1988, the gallery finally had adequate space and dedicated galleries for the display of its permanent collection of Canadian art, for which it employed a chronological hang that took viewers from the colonial period to the 1970s. This linear trajectory mirrored the narrative then common in such surveys as J. Russell Harper's *Painting in Canada: A History* (1967) and Dennis Reid's *A Concise History of Canadian Painting* (1973) – both standard texts for university courses on Canadian art history. In 2003, following extensive consultations with scholars and Aboriginal elders, the NGC unveiled its new installation of its galleries of Canadian art, now featuring the work of First Nations artists in every gallery (Whitelaw 2006). The chronological hang was retained, but baskets, beaded moccasins and garments as well as cedar bark hats and dancing blankets were interspersed among the paintings and wood or bronze sculptures. In juxtaposing the work of settler artists with the contemporaneous work of indigenous artists, the curators at the NGC aimed to expand the public's understanding of what constituted the country's aesthetic production over the previous 300 years. Another key aspect of the display was to add complexity to the stereotyping representations of Native peoples found in much settler art. The images of the noble savage or bloodthirsty warrior that populate much settler art are rebuked by the intricate designs of a porcupine quill embroidered vest or in the details of ceremonial masks that signal the active and creative presence of Indigenous peoples throughout colonization. Indeed, for some visitors, the Native-made objects provide greater visual interest than the colonial representations.

As the nation's repository of fine art, the NGC has always keenly sensed its responsibility to "preserv[e] and promot[e] the heritage of Canada and all its peoples … and [to] contribut[e] to the collective memory and sense of identity of all Canadians" (Government of Canada 1990). As First Nations demanded a more visible presence in national affairs along with the power to determine the nature of that presence, museums in general and the NGC in particular have been more aware of the importance of representing Aboriginal expressive culture within their displays. For the NGC, the inclusion of Aboriginal art meant the contemporaneous integration of objects within the galleries of Canadian art. Given their lack of collections in this area – the gallery abrogated responsibility for collecting the cultural production of Indigenous peoples to Canada's national ethnographic museum in the 1920s – the objects on display in the galleries of Canadian and Aboriginal art are on loan from institutions in Canada and abroad. While this presents an administrative headache, it also allows the NGC to renew its exhibition and present new works as the loan period expires. Though not completely unproblematic, the choice to display contemporaneous objects from both indigenous and settler cultures allows viewers to assess the breadth and diversity of cultural production throughout Canada's history, thereby creating a more complicated picture of the idea of "Canadian art" than might previously have been considered.

A second route to representation and inclusion was devised by the Art Gallery of Ontario (AGO) which unveiled the reinstallation of its Canadian art galleries in 2008, in conjunction with a major expansion of the building by Frank Gehry, to house the collection of newspaper magnate Ken Thomson. Presented separately from the Thomson Collection, the Canadian galleries feature the production of both Aboriginal and settler artists and are organized thematically rather than chronologically. Rooms explore such themes as relations of power and colonization, often bringing new perspectives on well-known works through unexpected juxtapositions. At the same time, certain canonical areas of Canadian art such as the work of the Group of Seven or the rise of abstraction in Quebec, are maintained as coherent units, and the AGO has retained the popular salon-style presentation of work from the late nineteenth century. These more traditional displays function as touchstones of the traditional art historical narrative and amplify the critical stance of the galleries' thematic displays.

At the AGO, the presentation of Indigenous expressive culture extends through much of the Canadian galleries. Unlike the NGC, however, many of these objects are works by contemporary artists placed in galleries alongside settler paintings and sculptures from the eighteenth, nineteenth, and early twentieth centuries. To give one example, the dress from Anishinabe artist Rebecca Belmore's performance *Rising to the Occasion* (1987) is displayed next to the painting *Guyasdoms D'Sonoqua* (1930) by British Columbia artist Emily Carr. Carr's painting is typical of her and others' oeuvre of the period, depicting what were perceived to be the vanishing Indigenous peoples of the North American west coast. Surrounded by the trees and moss of the British Columbia rainforest, a single totem rises, its arms outstretched, its mouth in a large O: a representation of the Dzunoqua or wild woman of the woods figure found in many northwest coast communities' stories. Belmore's dress was produced for the 1987 visit to Canada of Prince Andrew and Lady Sarah Ferguson, and incorporates multiple representations of the British Royal Family on china, tea towels, and other souvenirs. The dress also features an "Indian princess" crown and braids and a large hooped skirt made of branches and twigs, strongly reminiscent of a beaver dam. Occupying the center of the gallery, *Rising to the Occasion* (Figure 18.6) is a powerful reminder of First Nations' presence in and historical occupation of the land. While Aboriginal peoples' relationship to the Crown is signaled by the collection of cups and plates on Belmore's dress, the erosion of that connection over the years is also indicated in the combative stance suggested by the strong forward movement of the imagined figure. Seen next to the work of Emily Carr, whose paintings were praised for their supposedly accurate and intimate depictions of First Nations culture, *Rising to the Occasion* speaks back to the presumptions of such depictions and emphasizes the importance of Indigenous self-representation.

FIGURE 18.6 Rebecca Belmore, *Rising to the Occasion*, 1987. (For a color version of this figure, please see the color plate section.)
Art Gallery of Ontario. Reproduced with permission of the artist.

Yet another strategy for gathering the Indigenous into mainstream art exhibition took place at the Montreal Museum of Fine Arts (MMFA), where the Claire and Marc Bourgie Pavilion of Quebec and Canadian Art opened with great fanfare in 2011. The fourth pavilion of the 150-year-old institution is a five-story glass and marble cube that presents an almost chronological development of art in Canada in six separate galleries. Starting with the display of Inuit art on the top floor, the narrative proceeds downward, each floor dedicated to a particular period in the history of Canadian art from the colonial period to the 1970s (Whitelaw 2013).

The MMFA is the oldest art gallery in Canada, founded in 1860 by the anglophone elite that dominated the city's – and the country's – business and political spheres. By the 1970s, however, the balance of power had shifted as francophones assumed leadership in the city's corporate boardrooms, and Montreal's status as Canada's economic center was displaced by Toronto. Such changes resonated across the province's cultural institutions including the MMFA, and greater emphasis in acquisitions as well as exhibitions was placed on the contribution of Quebec artists to the development of Canadian art. The description of the new wing as the Pavilion of *Quebec and Canadian* Art is a key indicator of the exhibition's narrative focus on the work of artists from the province, and nowhere is this more evident than in the ground floor display.

Titled the Age of the Manifesto, this gallery presents the work of mostly francophone artists from Quebec of the 1940s and 1950s whose work revolutionized Canada's painting traditions. Influenced by André Breton and the French Surrealists' ideas of automatic writing, a group of painters, poets, dancers, and playwrights under the leadership of Paul-Émile Borduas founded Les Automatistes in 1947 and produced non-figurative works that rejected the dominant landscape traditions of the period and introduced Canada to abstraction. In addition, the group rebelled against the teachings of the Catholic clergy who relied on the support of the right-wing provincial government to control the education system in the province, and published the essay collection *Refus global* (Global Refusal). Borduas's titular essay in *Refus global* denounced both the church and the government, called for a revolution against authority and acquiescence, and advocated spiritual and intellectual freedom. The text is often cited as a founding document of Quebec's Quiet Revolution of the 1960s and thus has a central place in the historiography of Quebec nationalism. As a result, the MMFA's devotion of a whole floor to the work of Quebec artists is a clear indication of the museum's commitment to presenting the history of Canadian art from the perspective of Quebec in general, and Montreal in particular.

Even though much of the narrative focus of the MMFA's display of Canadian art is oriented to Quebec, the curators were equally sensitive to acknowledging expressive production of Indigenous peoples. The display of Inuit art on the top floor of the pavilion has already been mentioned, but the work of Indigenous artists can also be found in the *Founding Identities* gallery (Figure 18.7) on the fourth floor in a display that focuses on the work of settler artists from 1700 to 1880, and in a more limited way on the second floor's presentation of work from the 1910s through the 1940s. In its incorporation of the work of Indigenous artists, the MMFA occupies a *juste milieu* between the strategies employed by the National Gallery and the Art Gallery of Ontario. In the early-twentieth-century floor, paintings of northwest coast villages by Emily Carr and other settler artists share space with a magnificent Tsimshian dancing blanket of roughly the same period whose sheer scale provides a powerful counterpoint to the smaller oil paintings. In the *Founding Identities* gallery, the curators paired contemporaneous silverwork by Aboriginal and non-Aboriginal artists and gathered a selection

FIGURE 18.7   Montreal Museum of Fine Arts, *Founding Identities* gallery, 2011. (For a color version of this figure, please see the color plate section.)
Photograph by Tom Arban.

of works from the museum's northwest coast collection to contrast a series of paintings from the mid-nineteenth century depicting first peoples in stereotypical guises. Most striking on this floor, however, is the presentation of two contemporary works by artists of Aboriginal descent. Here, Nadia Myre's black-and-white video of an unidentified figure paddling a canoe and Kent Monkman's graphic depiction of an imagined beaver hunt contrast dramatically with the religious statuary and portrait paintings from colonial Quebec. As at the AGO, the juxtaposition of contemporary Aboriginal and historical settler works produces a site of contestation where Indigenous peoples are given an opportunity to "talk back" to colonization and its depictions of Native peoples. And while some viewers find the contrast jarring, others acknowledge the importance of contemporary views disrupting dominant narratives of settler aesthetic progress.

In the reinstallations of their permanent collections, the National Gallery, the Art Gallery of Ontario, and the Montreal Museum of Fine Arts have done more than any written survey text to include the cultural production of Indigenous peoples into the narrative of Canadian art history. While recent publications such as *The Visual Arts in Canada: The Twentieth Century* (Whitelaw, Foss, and Paikowsky 2010) have chapters addressing the work of Inuit and First Nations artists, it remains a separate narrative within the larger whole. As art historian Lynda Jessup (2000) reminds us, however, "hard inclusion" – the incorporation of Native-made objects into art historical narratives – requires a complete rethinking of the terms within which we understand cultural production in general and art in particular. Historical objects from Indigenous communities possess a visual aesthetic complexity that certainly places them on par with the objects that the discipline of art history has claimed for the canon.

However, objects of Aboriginal expressive culture also have strong non-visual aesthetic qualities that the frame of the art gallery is incapable of (or unwilling to) address. Sound, touch, smell, as well as movement, are central components of masks, blankets, and feast dishes – all historical objects by Aboriginal producers that are regularly featured in the NGC's display. Conventional art gallery modes of exhibition, however, emphasize the visual properties of objects, including those works from Western traditions such as altarpieces and statuary that would have necessitated elaborate rituals and public engagement. The art gallery's minimizing of the objecthood of the works in its collection in favor of their imagistic properties – an emphasis that is also a significant component of the discipline of art history itself – does a clear disservice to all works on display, but particularly to those that are not part of the western canon.

Given the nature of art galleries, such a rethinking of the dominance of the visual is unlikely to occur, which may explain why the AGO and the MMFA have opted to use contemporary art by Aboriginal artists as a way of disrupting the traditional narrative of Canadian art history. Produced in the same media and using the same formal vocabulary as that of settler artists, the work of Belmore, Monkman, and Myre fit more readily within a tradition of art history and can enter into dialogue with it. Indeed, Belmore was Canada's representative at the 2005 Venice Bienniale, and both Monkman and Myre have been featured in international exhibitions of contemporary art. Their inclusion in the museums' displays – while perhaps unexpected from the point of view of art-historical chronology – is more tenable within the aesthetic context of the art gallery. Furthermore, the contemporary works also provide an important link with the historical objects on display, reinforcing the continuity between the historical cultural production of Indigenous communities in Canada and that of their descendants in the present. Since many settler depictions of Aboriginal peoples were produced as records of what was viewed as a vanishing race, the paintings, videos, and installations by contemporary artists of Aboriginal descent put the lie to this view and reinforce the continuing place of First Peoples within the Canadian nation-state.

In an essay on *Meeting Ground*, the exhibition he curated in 2003 from the AGO's permanent collection, Cree art historian Richard W. Hill reflected on the challenges of incorporating Indigenous and settler art in the same display. His statement that "Aboriginal art off in a space of its own is not particularly threatening, but the notion that Aboriginal art might enter and trouble the established narratives of 'Canadian' art is something else" (Hill 2004, 54) expresses the importance of attending to the manner in which displayed objects are incorporated into permanent exhibitions. As the analysis of the NGC, the AGO, and the MMFA suggests, Aboriginal art will continue to be included in the display of Canadian art in the nation's museums; whether their inclusion changes the way scholars and the public think about what constitutes "Canadian" art and Canadian art history remains to be seen.

Notes

1 This section was written by Linda Young.
2 In a similar transformation, anthropologists' years of genealogical research were transmuted in 1987 into the Aboriginal Family History Unit at the South Australian Museum.
3 This section was written by Rosmarie Beier-de Haan and Linda Young, and translated by Stephen Locke.
4 This section was written by Anne Whitelaw.
5 I use the term "Indigenous" and "Aboriginal" to refer to all the original peoples of North America. This includes both Inuit and First Nations cultures.

References

Abt, Jeffrey. 2002. *A Museum on the Verge: A Socioeconomic History of the Detroit Institute of Arts, 1882–2000*. Detroit: Wayne State University Press.

Allen, M., and C. Bulbeck. 2000. Exhibition Review. *Australian Historical Studies* 31: 345–347.

Altshuler, Bruce. 2008. *Salon to Biennale: Exhibitions that Made Art History*, vol. 1, 1863–1959. London: Phaidon.

Amar, Marianne, Marie Poinsot, and Catherine Wihtol de Wenden. 2009. *À chacun ses étrangers? France–Allemagne de 1871 à aujourd'hui*. Arles: Actes Sud.

American Wing, Metropolitan Museum of Art. 2014. Accessed October 30, 2014. http://www.metmuseum.org/collections/new-installations/american-wing.

Ames, Michael. 1992. *Cannibal Tours and Glass Boxes: The Anthropology of Museums*. Vancouver: UBC Press.

Anderson, Christopher, ed. 1995. *Politics of the Secret*. Sydney: University of Sydney Press.

Attwood, Bain, and Andrew Markus, eds. 1999. *The Struggle for Aboriginal Rights*. St. Leonards, NSW: Allen and Unwin.

Australian Government. 1980. *National Museum of Australia Act*. Accessed October 30, 2014. http://www.comlaw.gov.au/Details/C2011C00274.

Baillie, A. 1998. *Taking the Time: Museums and Galleries, Cultural Protocols and Communities*. Brisbane: Museums Australia.

Barker, Emma, ed. 1999. *Contemporary Cultures of Display, Art and Its Histories*. New Haven, CT: Yale University Press in association with the Open University.

Beier-de Haan, Rosmarie. 2006. "Restaging Histories and Identities." In *Companion to Museum Studies*, edited by Sharon Macdonald, 186–197. Oxford: Blackwell.

Beier-de Haan, Rosmarie. 2011. "Outlook: National History Museums at the Beginning of the 21st Century. Thoughts on the Viability of Their Actions for the Future." In *Nationalmuseen: Gedächtnis der Nationen. National museums: The Memory of Nations*, edited by Hans-Martin Hinz and Rosmarie Beier-de Haan, 174–181. Berlin: Deutsches Historisches Museum.

Beier-de Haan, Rosmarie. 2012. "Rethinking German History against the Background of a Burdened Past and New Challenges for the 21st Century." In *Entering the Minefields: The*

Creation of New History Museums in Europe, edited by Bodil Axelsson, Christine Dupont, and Chantal Kesteloot, 55–70. Linköping, Sweden: Linköping University Electronic Press. Accessed October 31, 2014. http://www.ep.liu.se/ecp_home/index.en.aspx?issue=083.

Bolt, Andrew. 2000. "Museum of Spin." *Herald Sun*, November 20.

CAMA (Council of Australian Museums Associations). 1993. *Previous Possessions, New Obligations: Policies for Museums in Australia and Aboriginal and Torres Strait Islander People*. Melbourne: CAMA.

Clifford, James. 1988. *The Predicament of Culture: Twentieth-Century Ethnography, Literature, and Art*. Cambridge, MA: Harvard University Press.

DASETT (Department of the Arts, Sport, the Environment, Tourism, and Territories). 1991. *A Plan for Cultural Heritage Institutions to Reflect Australia's Cultural Diversity*. Canberra: Consultative Committee on Cultural Heritage in Multi-cultural Australia, Australian Government Printing Service.

Dauber, Christine. 2005. "Revisionism or Self Reflexivity at the South Australian Museum." *Journal of Australian Studies* 29: 113–125.

Davidson, Ian, Christine Lovell-Jones, and Robyne Bancroft, eds. 1995. *Archaeologists and Aborigines Working Together*. Armidale, NSW: University of New England Press.

Davison, Graham. 2003. "Conflict in the Museum." In *Frontier Conflict: The Australian Experience*, edited by Bain Attwood and S. G. Foster, 201–214. Canberra: National Museum of Australia.

Delroy, Ann. 2001. "Bunjilaka." *Australian Historical Studies* 116: 147–150.

Deutsches Historisches Museum (German Historical Museum), Berlin. Accessed October 31, 2014. http://www.dhm.de.

Duncan, Carol. 1995. *Civilizing Rituals: Inside Public Art Museums*. New York: Routledge.

Erpel, Simone. 2011. "Perpetrators on Display: Nazi Dictatorship and WWII Perpetrators in Exhibitions." Paper presented at the International conference *Museums and Difficult Heritage*, ICMAH: International Committee of Museums and Collections of History and Archaeology, Helsinki, June 16–18, 2011.

European Parliament. 2013. *Building a House of European History*. Accessed October 31, 2014. http://www.europarl.europa.eu/visiting/ressource/static/files/building-a-house-of-european-history_e-v.pdf.

Frietsch, Elke, and Christina Herkommer, eds. 2009. *Nationalsozialismus und Geschlecht. Zur Politisierung und Ästhetisierung von Körper, "Rasse" und Sexualität im "Dritten Reich" und nach 1945*. Bielefeld: Transcript.

Government of Canada. 1990. Justice Laws Website: Museums Act. Accessed October 31, 2014. http://laws-lois.justice.gc.ca/eng/acts/M-13.4/page-1.html.

Graburn, Nelson. 1981. "1, 2, 3, 4… Anthropology and the Fourth World." *Culture* 1(1): 66–70.

Griffiths, Tom. 1996. *Hunters and Collectors: The Antiquarian Imagination in Australia, Studies in Australian History*. Melbourne: Cambridge University Press.

Harper, J. Russell. 1967. *Painting in Canada: A History*. Toronto: University of Toronto Press.

Haupt, Heinz-Gerhard, and Jürgen Kocka, eds. 2009. *Comparison and Transnational History: Central European Approaches and New Perspectives*. Oxford: Berghahn.

Healy, Chris. 2008. *Forgetting Aborigines*. Sydney: University of New South Wales Press.

Healy, Chris, and Andrea Witcomb, eds. 2006. *South Pacific Museums: Experiments in Culture*. Melbourne: Monash University ePress.

Hendry, Joy. 2005. *Reclaiming Indigenous Culture: Indigenous People and Self-Representation*. New York: Palgrave Macmillan.

Hill, Richard W. 2004. "Meeting Ground: The Reinstallation of the AGO's McLaughlin Gallery." In *Making a Noise: Aboriginal Perspectives on Art, Art History, Critical Writing and Community*, edited by Lee-Ann Martin, 50–70. Banff, Canada: Walter Phillips Gallery/ Banff Centre Press.

HREOC ([Australian] Human Rights and Equal Opportunity Commission). 1997. *Bringing Them Home: Report of the National Inquiry into the Separation of Aboriginal and Torres Strait Islander Children from Their Families*. Accessed October 31, 2014. http://www. humanrights.gov.au/publications/bringing-them-home-report-1997.

Jessup, Lynda. 2000. "Hard Inclusion." In *On Aboriginal Representation in the Gallery*, edited by Lynda Jessup with Shannon Bagg, xi–xxviii. Hull: Canadian Museum of Civilization.

Kaiser, Wolfram, Stefan Krankenhagen, and Kerstin Poehls. 2014. *Exhibiting Europe in Museums: Transnational Networks, Collections, Narratives, and Representations*. New York: Berghahn.

Karp, Ivan, and Steven D. Lavine, eds. 1991. *Exhibiting Cultures: The Poetics and Politics of Museum Display*. Washington, DC: Smithsonian Institution Press.

Kelly, Lynda, Carolyn Cook, and Phil Gordon. 2006. "Building Relationships through Communities of Practice: Museums and Indigenous People." *Curator* 49(2): 217–234.

Kelly, Lynda, and Phil Gordon. 2004. "Developing a Community of Practice: Museums and Reconciliation in Australia." In *Museums, Society, Inequality*, edited by Richard Sandell, 153–174. London: Routledge.

Kelly, Lynda, and Tim Sullivan. 1997. "Front-End Evaluation: Beyond the Field of Dreams." *Museum National* 5(4): 7–8.

Klonk, Charlotte. 2009. *Spaces of Experience: Art Gallery Interiors from 1800 to 2000*. New Haven, CT: Yale University Press.

Knell, Simon, Peter Aronsson, Arne Bugge Amundsen, Amy Jane Barnes, Stuart Burch, Jennifer Carter, Viviane Gosselin, Sara A. Hughes, and Alan Kirwan, eds. 2010. *National Museums: New Studies from Around the World*. London: Routledge.

Macdonald, Sharon. 2008. *Difficult Heritage: Negotiating the Nazi Past in Nuremberg and Beyond*. London: Routledge.

Macintyre, Stuart, and Anna Clark. 2003. *The History Wars*. Melbourne: Melbourne University Press.

MacKenzie, John M. 2009. *Museums and Empire: Natural History, Human Cultures and Colonial Identities*. Manchester: Manchester University Press.

MacLeod, Suzanne. 2013. *Museum Architecture: A New Biography*. London: Routledge.

Mateer, J. 2000. "The New Melbourne Museum." *Art Monthly* 136: 16–18.

McCarthy, Conal. 2007. *Exhibiting Māori: A History of Colonial Cultures of Display*. Oxford: Berg.

Moore, Rowan. 2013 "Museum of the Civilisations of Europe and the Mediterranean (MuCEM) – review." *Guardian*, June 9. Accessed October 31, 2014. http://www.theguardian.com/ artanddesign/2013/jun/09/museum-civilisations-europe-mediterranean-mucem-review.

Moran, Rod. 2002. "The Paradigm of the Post-Modern Museum." *Quadrant* 46(1–2): 43–49.

MUCEM (Musée des civilisations de l'Europe et de la Méditerranée, Marseille). 2014. Accessed October 31, 2014. http://www.mucem.org.

Museum of Europe. 2014. Accessed October 31, 2014. http://www.expo-europe.be/content/view/58/81/lang,en.

Ostow, Robin. 2008. *(Re)visualizing National History: Museums and National Identities in Europe in the New Millennium, German and European Studies*. Toronto: University of Toronto Press.

Phillips, Ruth B. 2011. *Museum Pieces: Towards the Indigenization of Canadian Museums*. Montreal: McGill-Queen's University Press.

Reid, Dennis. 1973. *A Concise History of Canadian Painting*. Toronto: Oxford University Press.

Russell, Lynette. 2000. "Where Is the Past?" *The Artefact* 23: 3–8.

Ryan, Judith, and Phil Batty. 2011. *Tjukurrtjanu: Origins of Western Desert Art*. Melbourne: National Gallery of Victoria.

Savoy, Bénédicte, ed. 2010. *Napoleon und Europa: Traum und Trauma*. Munich: Prestel.

Shelton, Anthony. 2006. "Museums and Museum Displays." In *Handbook of Material Culture*, edited by Chris Tilley, Webb Keane, Susanne Küchler, Mike Rowlands, and Patricia Spyer, 480–499. London: Sage.

Simpson, Moira. 2001. *Making Representations: Museums in the Post-Colonial Era*. Routledge: London.

Simpson, Moira. 2006. "Bunjilaka." In *South Pacific Museums: Experiments in Culture*, edited by Chris Healy and Andrea Witcomb, 15.1–15.5. Melbourne: Monash University ePress.

Specht, Jim, and Carolyn MacLulich. 2000. "Changes and Challenges: The Australian Museum and Indigenous Communities." In *Archaeological Displays and the Public: Museology and Interpretations*, edited by Paulette M. McManus, 24–49. London: Archetype.

Staniszewski, Mary Anne. 1998. *The Power of Display: A History of Exhibition Installations at the Museum of Modern Art*. Cambridge, MA: MIT Press.

Sullivan, Tim, Lynda Kelly, and Phil Gordon. 2003. "Museums and Aboriginal Australians." *Curator* 46(2): 208–277.

Sutton, Peter, Christopher Anderson, and Philip Jones, eds. 1989. *Dreamings: The Art of Aboriginal Australia*. Ringwood, VIC: Viking.

Taylor, Brandon. 1999. *Art for the Nation: Exhibitions and the London Public 1747–2001*. Manchester: Manchester University Press.

Thomas, Nicholas 2001. "Indigenous Presences and National Narratives in Australasian Museums." In *Culture in Australia: Policies, Publics and Programs*, edited by Tony Bennett and David Carter, 299–312. Cambridge: Cambridge University Press.

Trinca, Matt, and Kirsten Wehner. 2006. "Pluralism and Exhibition Practice at the National Museum of Australia." In *South Pacific Museums: Experiments in Culture*, edited by Chris Healy and Andrea Witcomb, 6.1–6.14. Melbourne: Monash University ePress.

Vines, Gary. 2013. "*First Peoples* Exhibition, Bunjilaka Gallery, Melbourne Museum: A Reflection." *Museums Australia Magazine* 22(2): 24–26.

Wallach, Alan. 2013. "The New American Art Galleries, Virginia Museum of Fine Arts, Richmond." *Museum Worlds* 1: 222–227.

Ward, Martha. 1996. "What's Important about the History of Modern Art Exhibitions?" In *Thinking about Exhibitions*, edited by Reesa Greenberg, Bruce Ferguson, and Sandy Nairne, 451–464. London: Routledge.

Werquet, Jan, and Rosmarie Beier-de Haan. 2009. "Zur Einführung: 'Wer sind wir? – Wer die Anderen?'" In *Fremde? Bilder von den "Anderen" in Deutschland und Frankreich seit 1871*, edited by Rosmarie Beier-de Haan and Jan Werquet, 12–14. Dresden: Sandstein.

Whitelaw, Anne. 2006. "Placing Aboriginal Art at the National Gallery of Canada." *Canadian Journal of Communications* 31(1): 197–214.

Whitelaw, Anne. 2013. "A New Pavilion for Quebec and Canadian Art at the Montreal Museum of Fine Arts." *Journal of Canadian Art History* 34(1): 167–184.

Whitelaw, Anne, Brian Foss, and Sandra Paikowsky, eds. 2010. *The Visual Arts in Canada: The Twentieth Century*. Don Mills, ON: Oxford University Press.

Windschuttle, Keith. 2001. "How Not to Run a Museum: People's History at the Post-Modern Museum." *Quadrant* 45(9): 11–19.

Yanni, Carla. 1999. *Nature's Museums: Victorian Science and the Architecture of Display*. London: Athlone Press.

Young, Linda. 2006. "The National Museum of Australia." In *South Pacific Museums: Experiments in Culture*, edited by Chris Healy and Andrea Witcomb, 1–5. Melbourne: Monash University ePress.

Young, Linda. 2014. "First Peoples, Bunjilaka Aboriginal Cultural Centre, Melbourne Museum: Exhibition Review." *Museum Worlds: Advances in Research* 2(1): 213–216.

Further Reading

Deutsch-Russisches Museum Berlin-Karlshorst (German-Russian Museum Berlin-Karlshorst). Accessed October 31, 2014. http://www.museum-karlshorst.de.

Hobsbawm, Eric. 1990. *Nations and Nationalism since 1780*. Cambridge: Cambridge University Press.

House of European History, Brussels. 2014. Accessed October 31, 2014. http://europarl.europa.eu/visiting/en/historyhouse.html.

Murphy, Bernice. 2011. "Transforming Culture: Indigenous Art and Australian Museums." In *Understanding Museums: Australian Museums and Museology*, edited by Des Griffin and Leon Paroissien. Accessed October 31, 2014. http://www.nma.gov.au/research/understanding-museums/BMurphy_2011.html.

Linda Young trained as a historian and worked as a museum curator in Sydney and Perth before becoming a university lecturer in Canberra and Melbourne, Australia. Since 2005 Linda has been Senior Lecturer in Cultural Heritage and Museum Studies at Deakin University, Melbourne. She is a consultant, critic, a historian of heritage genres and practice, and a student of nineteenth-century Anglo domestic and personal material culture. She has published widely on house museums, suburban archaeology, heritage management, and museum collecting and display. Her latest book, on the history of historic house museums, *The Nation at Home*, will be published in 2015.

Rosmarie Beier-de Haan is a Head of Collections and Exhibition Curator at the German Historical Museum, Berlin, where she has curated many social and cultural history exhibitions. Rosmarie is also an Honorary Professor of Modern History at the Freie Universität Berlin and at the Technische Universität Berlin. She has published extensively on transnational history, historical culture in the second modern age, history and theory of the museum, culture of memory, history of mentalities, and intangible heritage. She has been a board member of ICOM and the International Association of Museums of History as well as of diverse scientific committees for new museums in Germany and abroad.

Anne Whitelaw is Associate Professor Art History and Associate Dean Research in the Faculty of Fine Arts at Concordia University in Montreal, Canada. Her research examines the history of art and cultural institutions in Canada, with a particular focus on practices of exhibition and collecting as a means of understanding the formation of nationhood. She has published extensively on the display of Canadian art at the National Gallery of Canada, on the writings of art historian John Russell Harper, and on the integration of Aboriginal art into the permanent displays of national museums.

19 A CRITIQUE OF MUSEUM RESTITUTION AND REPATRIATION PRACTICES

Piotr Bienkowski

Although the concept of the return of cultural property has been around for a long time, as testified by European treaties from the mid-seventeenth century (Greenfield 2007, 391–392; Vrdoljak 2006, 22), it is still or, even, increasingly divisive. Depending on whom you talk to, restitution/repatriation of human remains and objects to source communities and legitimate owners is either becoming the acceptable norm in the museum sector worldwide, or it should very clearly be the exception. In support of the former we can cite the increasing numbers of successful returns and ongoing claims, and a shift in attitude among museum directors and curators that this is a legitimate and morally correct thing to do, and that indeed museums should be more proactive. On the other hand, some feel it should be considered on a case-by-case basis, with a general institutional presumption against return, along with robust processes that challenge claimants to prove their legitimacy and rights to ownership.

Whichever camp the reader may fall into, it is the case that most current restitution/repatriation processes still tend to be adversarial (whether in a strictly legal or processual sense). They are also long-winded, and inequitable in so far as they are stacked in favor of the holding institution rather than the claimant. While this may be acceptable to those who feel that restitution/repatriation should be the exception rather than the rule, I argue in this chapter that such adversarial processes run counter to and impede the purposes of museums. Not everyone will agree with me when I declare that the key role of museums in our globalized and fractured world is to use their collections in innovative ways to foster understanding between

The International Handbooks of Museum Studies: Museum Practice, First Edition.
Edited by Conal McCarthy.

communities and cultures; but I hope all would agree that museums should be the forum for a discourse over the values and meanings of objects.

Restitution/repatriation are no more than a formal and practical recognition that there are different values for something that may be held as property, and the processes around restitution/repatriation should ideally create a framework through which those different values can be expressed, acknowledged, and accommodated (Coleman 2010). Yet current adversarial processes do not, on the whole, allow for such an open and equitable discourse about objects and their values – rather, they get mired in requests for proof of legitimacy and ownership, which too often create bad feeling and tension rather than dialogue. Where institutions have developed processes that allow for a fruitful, trusting dialogue with claimant communities, which often results in an ongoing, sustainable relationship beyond the immediate results of the claim, they have done so *despite* international conventions, legal frameworks, and laws of property.

That is essentially what this chapter is about. The first part analyzes current restitution/repatriation practices and their drawbacks. The second section reviews key issues addressed by recent research on restitution and repatriation. The third and last proposes a new way forward for dialogue and decision-making around restitution/repatriation that attempts to draw all those strands together, explicitly incorporating different voices, values, and forms of knowledge. This does not depend on legal frameworks. Rather it calls on museums to acknowledge their key purpose as a locus for a discourse over the values and meanings of objects to different communities, to set aside the fetish of perpetual ownership of objects and to open up that ownership for discussion, and to be prepared to act on the consequences of such a discourse.

Current practices

So far, I have referred to "restitution/repatriation," but the terms are distinctly different and I should make clear what I understand those differences to be (see Whitby-Last 2010, 36–37; Skrydstrup 2010, 61–66 for more extensive definitions). While the legal concept of restitution came out of UNESCO discussions in the late 1960s concerned with the illicit trafficking of antiquities, essentially it denotes the return of an object to its owner, based on an analysis of property rights. The term "repatriation" became popular in the 1980s and 1990s in North America and Australasia connected with the return of human remains and sacred objects to indigenous communities. While the term, strictly speaking, means to restore or return to *patria*, a native land (see Kowalski 2001, 163), it is used more broadly to refer to returns of human remains and objects to a country or to sub-state groups such as indigenous communities. Whitby-Last (2010, 36) notes that it is often applied where the claim is perceived as being moral rather than legal, and this is an important distinction. Thus, many claims from indigenous groups are claims for *repatriation*, phrased in terms of a moral obligation, rather than for *restitution*, which may be the case, for example, with Nazi looted art, which is based on an assertion of property rights. The definitions used in this chapter, therefore, are:

- Restitution: return to legitimate owner, based on property rights.
- Repatriation: return to country or sub-state group, based on ethical considerations.

Other terms are occasionally used, or proposed, such as the more general "return" (Greenfield 2007, 65; Skrydstrup 2010, 63). This essentially overlaps with the above definition of repatriation, being not a legal question but one of cultural, historical, or social judgment. Other terms include "cultural recovery" and "rematriation," both put forward by Canadian indigenous groups (Myles 2010, 54).

Claims for restitution or repatriation generally fall into one or more of the following eight categories (rather than the very generalized three proposed by Vrdoljak 2006, 2–4). However, there is overlap, and some (notably Greek) claims for the Parthenon (or Elgin) Marbles (see Greenfield 2007, 41–96), have a mixture of many of them. Restitution/repatriation can include:

1. Objects looted or wrongfully removed during colonial occupation. Such repatriation is sometimes referred to as reparation, defined as "substantive redress" in the sense of effectively realizing justice, especially in the colonial context of the loss of indigenous cultural heritage (Lenzerini 2008, 8–13; Vrdoljak 2008, 213–20).
2. Illegal acquisition, including Holocaust art. Gerstenblith (2011, 447) points out that, from a strictly legal point of view, art stolen during the Holocaust is no different from the issue of the return of art works stolen under other circumstances. However, the particularly tragic circumstances have brought considerable international attention to this issue (Nicholas 1994; Palmer 2000).
3. Trophy art.
4. Symbols of cultural identity.
5. Belonging to community (the link between people, land, and objects, and ancestral remains).
6. Border changes.
7. Reunification of objects.
8. Claims by individuals against the state over objects.

The arguments museums and galleries have used to resist claims for restitution and repatriation also fall into standard categories, and often – as with the British Museum's responses to Greek claims for the Parthenon Marbles – several arguments are used to reject a single claim. Legal constraints are commonly cited for example: that the objects were acquired legally by the institution, which has legal title, and that the institution is legally prevented from being able to return the claimed objects. For example, the British Museum argues that it is unable to return collections other than duplicates, since it is legally prevented from doing so by the terms of the British Museum Act of 1963 (Greenfield 2007, 103). The Human Tissue Act of 2004 relaxed that provision for human remains less than 1000 years old, allowing the British Museum and other national museums to repatriate human remains to source communities legally. Another frequent argument is that the objects have become part of the national heritage or even the universal heritage of mankind and do not belong to any one community or nation. This was underlined in 2002 with the Declaration on the Importance and Value of Universal Museums signed by major European and North American institutions.

Problems with claimants are also used to reject requests for return. For example, the legitimacy of claimants is challenged or the fact that there are multiple claimants which means that the conflicting claims cannot be adequately addressed through return. In 1991, the repatriation of the remains of William Lanne, believed to be the last full-blooded Tasmanian Aboriginal, was resisted on the grounds that Tasmanian Aboriginals were already extinct and that this was therefore an invented tradition with no cultural continuity and no connection with the claimed human remains (Fforde 2004a, 34–40; Fforde 2004b, 123–126). The Koh-i-noor diamond, now part of the British Crown Jewels, has been formally claimed by both India and Pakistan, and informally by Iran (Greenfield 2007, 129–131).

More generally, there is a fear of setting a precedent for further returns. The British Museum, for example, argues that the return of collections such as the Parthenon Marbles would constitute a precedent for further claims that, according to its former director Sir David Wilson, would "start to dismantle" the museum and "start a process of cultural vandalism" (Wilson 1990, 116; see Vrdoljak 2006, 87–95 for an historical perspective). When NAGPRA (Native American Graves Protection and Repatriation Act) was enacted in the United States in 1990, many museums, archaeologists, and scientists protested that it would result in the emptying of museums. This has not been the case (see McManamon 2004; Gerstenblith 2011, 453).

Other arguments used to reject requests for return are the inability of the claimant to properly house and conserve the objects; that the objects are too fragile to be returned; that the collections are needed for research; and that retaining objects in major Western museums makes them accessible to a larger audience. Often cited are issues of reciprocity, compensation, and reparation: for example, Russia and Germany continue to insist on reciprocal returns of works of art looted from each other's territories during World War II, and are generally unwilling to undertake restitutions unless reciprocal returns are negotiated (Greenfield 2007, 184–201).

Box 19.1   Mechanisms for returns

Negotiations/bilateral treaties between governments.
Negotiations between institutions.
Legal enforcement by courts or government agencies.
Voluntary returns by institutions or individuals.
Repatriation within a country.
Compensation or compromise agreements by museums.
Stolen and returned by individuals.
Buying back at auction or return through auction houses.
Private purchase by individuals.
Loans.
Exchange.
Sharing ceremonial access to iconic objects.
Visual repatriation.
Virtual repatriation.

The mechanisms for successful returns are surprisingly varied (see Box 19.1). Legal enforcement by courts or government agencies, or negotiations between governments, have proved to be extremely time-consuming and frequently adversarial: it often takes many years for a claim to be resolved. Some negotiations, though, have been carried out openly and in good faith. For example, the Miho Museum in Kyoto, Japan, returned a Buddhist Bodhisattva figure alleged to be stolen from the garden of a public building in Boxing, Shandong Province, China. What is unusual in this case is that the Miho Museum belongs to a non-denominational spiritual organization, Shinji Shumeikai, which believes that art plays a significant role in creating greater tolerance and peace in the world. Although the museum had purchased it from a dealer, it returned the carving to China for no payment. However, as a result of the very productive and informal process, the Miho Museum was able to keep exhibiting the carving on an extended loan (Sims 2001; Brodie 2006, 55; Greenfield 2007, 279–280).

Voluntary return by institutions and individuals is another non-adversarial process. A key institutional example is the return, as a gift, of the Haisla spirit pole, clandestinely removed to Sweden in 1929, from the National Museum of Ethnography in Stockholm to the Haisla people in British Columbia, Canada. After difficult initial negotiations, the pole was returned with no legal intervention, together with practical assistance and training for the Haisla, and the development of an ongoing dialogue and relationship (Greenfield 2007, 316–320; Bell et al. 2009, 380–381. (For other voluntary returns by institutions, see Reppas 2007, 116–118). Another process is returns by individuals. An inspiring example is the woman whose father bought a drawing attributed to Rembrandt in good faith in the 1970s, but that had in fact been stolen by the Gestapo from the Feldmann family in Czechoslovakia in 1939. Once she discovered the circumstances it was returned to the Feldmanns' grandson as a gift (Alberge 2004; Greenfield 2007, 295–297; for other voluntary returns by individuals, see Reppas 2007, 116–118).

Some solutions to claims for return do *not* in fact involve returning the objects permanently or relinquishing ownership – but can be achieved through loans. This is not without its drawbacks however. A complex example concerns Hawaiian objects in the Bishop Museum, Honolulu, which had been removed from a cave in Hawai'i in 1905. In 2000, the museum made a formal loan of the artifacts to a Native Hawaiian organization, which reburied them in the original cave and sealed the entrance. But other claimants then opposed the loan, alleging that, by calling the transaction a "loan" instead of a "repatriation," the museum had circumvented NAGPRA guidelines for repatriation. Following a lawsuit in 2005, a court ordered that the collection be returned to the museum, and it was retrieved from the cave in 2006. Twenty-five Native Hawaiian organizations have now formally laid claim to the collection (Pala 2008).

Another mechanism that does not involve actual return is sharing ceremonial access. In 2000, the Clackamas tribe in Oregon claimed the return of the 16-ton Willamette Meteorite from the American Museum of Natural History in New York. To the tribe, it was a sacred object representing the union of sky, earth, and water. Avoiding legal action, the museum and the tribe agreed to share the meteorite: today it continues to be on display in the museum, but the Clackamas have annual access for religious, historical, and cultural purposes (Thomas 2006, 226–235; Singer 2006, 415).

There is much discussion about new technologies creating expanded possibilities for virtual repatriation (see Brown 2007; Greenfield 2007, 437–441). For example, in response to requests to return the Lindisfarne Gospels to the northeast of England, in 1998 the British Library created a digital version that could be accessed in the northeast as well as London, and that is now available online (see British Library n.d.). Virtual repatriation does return something significant to source communities, in that it is an opportunity to reconnect to past and culture. Sometimes, though, use of new technologies can be interpreted as a cynical replacement for repatriation, denying the necessity for a real return, as with the computer simulation accompanying the display of the Parthenon Marbles at the British Museum, which has been accused of being an intervention in the repatriation debate (Gillen Wood cited in Henning 2011, 315). (On this point see Pickering in this volume.)

It is, perhaps, not surprising that, despite the plethora of international conventions, committees, and panels dealing with the return of cultural property (see the comprehensive list in Vrdoljak 2006, xx–xxviii), not a single one has been directly responsible for a successful return. There are good reasons for this. For example, the 1970 UNESCO Convention on the Means of Prohibiting the Illicit Import,

Export, and Transfer of Ownership of Cultural Property deals with both illicit trafficking and cultural return, which are often quite distinct in terms of the practicalities of return. The same two concepts were combined in the body UNESCO set up to deal with the issues, namely the Intergovernmental Committee for Promoting the Return of Cultural Property to Its Countries of Origin or Its Restitution in Case of Illicit Appropriation (which met between 1979 and 1983; Greenfield 2007, 222–229). Not surprisingly, the Intergovernmental Committee was unable to resolve any actual claims for the restitution of cultural property, since its remit and role were limited to promoting cooperation and mediation (Vrdoljak 2006, 215, 234–241). UNESCO has produced resolutions, recommendations, and conventions, but beyond creating some level of dialogue, they have been branded as "largely ineffectual" (Greenfield 2007, 368). On a national level, the same criticisms can be leveled at the Spoliation Advisory Panel set up by the British government in 1989, which could mediate and make recommendations, but had no power over actual returns from institutions (Greenfield 2007, 295). A systemic problem with the 1970 UNESCO convention is that it only recognizes states. As Whitby-Last (2010, 40) points out, this means that indigenous groups cannot utilize the convention unless the state is prepared to act on their behalf.

Furthermore, the convention applies only to those objects designated as cultural property by the state and stolen from a museum or public monument. Since this clearly excludes many cultural objects that are the subject of repatriation claims by indigenous groups, the UNESCO convention is of little or no use to indigenous peoples. NAGPRA in the United States is quite different, since it is a federal law that allows Native American tribes to petition for the return of human remains and sacred items, and requires museums that receive federal support to supply information about their collections and to respond to repatriation claims.

There is also growing acknowledgment that legal processes in restitution and repatriation cases are generally complex, bureaucratic, very long-running, expensive, time-consuming for all involved, and set up an atmosphere of conflict and mutual distrust that cuts across processes of dialogue, persuasion, and mutual understanding (Morphy 2010, 160; see also Boyd 2006). The Kennewick Man case in the USA clearly highlights the difficulties in asking the court system to resolve disputes involving cultural heritage and intellectual property rights, since the argument becomes one of "winners" and "losers," overshadowing the search for a relationship based on mutual respect and consensus (Thomas 2006, 248). Indeed, the lead attorney for the plaintiffs in that case, which lasted six years and cost up to US\$3 million, states that "little has been accomplished other than to provide an expensive example of poor decision making" (Schneider 2004, 202).

Of course, legal processes are not alone in being adversarial, and most museums put claimants – especially indigenous groups – through extensive tests and trials to prove their legitimacy, making assumptions about which groups are or are not legitimate claimants. These demands for proof are often offensive to source communities, and the criteria are almost invariably based on a genealogical model imposed by the museum itself, which ties the notion of a legitimate claim for ownership to tight definitions of descent, kinship, and cultural continuity (Bienkowski 2007, 118–121; Bienkowski and Coleman 2013, 95–97). In the USA, for example, NAGPRA's criteria for cultural affiliation create "countless possibilities for uncertainty and disagreement," and accept only federally recognized tribes within federal definitions of identity, explicitly marginalizing those tribes that nevertheless regard themselves as Native American but lack this federal status (Brown and Bruchac 2006, 202–203; Garroutte 2001).

Yet it should be noted that, in the list of examples of successful returns above, the cases that did not involve legal intervention (indeed, often deliberately avoiding it) were based on dialogue, respect, and a search for mutual understanding. In every case, they led to an ongoing relationship between institutions, or bonds of friendship with communities, that were reciprocal and mutually beneficial (in particular the returns of the Bodhisattva figure from the Miho Museum to China, the Haisla spirit pole from Sweden to Canada, and the case of the Willamette meteorite). Thomas (2006, 248–251) notes that the issue of the meteorite was resolved because both parties recognized the downside of a court battle, worked behind the scenes to find channels for mediating their differences, and explored alternatives in an atmosphere of mutual respect and common interest. He concludes that litigation and legislation are increasingly unattractive ways of settling conflicts over cultural patrimony. Some caution is necessary, however, because while voluntary return may now be more common, it is still the case that the threat of litigation is needed to persuade many museums to consider return in the first place.

Recent research on restitution and repatriation

The ethics of return and cultural equity versus the universal museum

In December 2002, 18 major European and North American museums issued the Declaration on the Importance and Value of Universal Museums (reproduced widely, for example in Greenfield 2007, 86–87). The declaration condemned the illegal traffic in archaeological, artistic, and ethnic objects, but insisted that "objects acquired in earlier times must be viewed in the light of different sensitivities and values, reflective of that earlier era." It stated that such objects had by now become part of the national heritage of the nations that house them. Referring to calls for repatriation, it argued that museums serve not just one nation but the people of every nation, and thus to narrow the focus of museums through returning objects would be a disservice to all visitors.

The concept of the "universal" (or "encyclopedic") museum, while controversial and much debated, has received considerable backing in the writings and edited collections of James Cuno. Cuno, formerly Director of the Art Institute of

Chicago and currently CEO of the J. Paul Getty Trust, was one of the original signatories of the declaration (see especially Cuno 2009; 2010; for brief synopsis, see Cuno 2006). These argue, essentially, that antiquities are the cultural property of humankind, not of the countries that lay exclusive claim to them, and that modern nation-states have, at best, a dubious connection to the ancient cultures they claim to represent, therefore antiquities need to be protected from looting, but also from "nationalist identity politics" (Cuno 2009, 1–2).

Challenges to the universal museum concept, and specifically to the declaration (which is not representative of the views of the majority of the world's museums), fall into three groups: philosophical; responses to particular issues; and an alternative model. Philosophically, Jeanette Greenfield (2007, 87–93, 411) argues that institutions cannot be universal unless they are universally constituted or universally accountable. The possession of objects of importance to world culture does not necessarily make the holding institutions sole keepers in perpetuity, so they cannot have universal holding rights. Museum claims of universality are suspect, because they cannot be invoked unilaterally but must be determined by the international community. Representative of specific responses is William St. Clair (2006, 94–95). He argues that the collections of the "universal" museums are not in fact representative of the world's cultures, and in any case they are not practically available to those citizens of other countries who are unable to visit them. He criticizes the constant repetition, in the declaration, of the word "universal," which has become ritual and meaningless, and is merely an attempt to legitimate the status quo and continued ownership of objects claimed by others.

On the other hand, Besterman (2011) has proposed "cultural equity" as an alternative to the ethic embodied in the declaration. Cultural equity describes the values of the sustainable museum, reflected in the transparency and democratic accountability of its conduct. It embodies a democratic principle of universal entitlement, of citizens participating in the museum, which does not presume to a monopoly on knowledge and authority, and which is concerned with the accountable exercise of power. In recognizing that museums and their collections derive from, and are emblematic of, unsustainable imbalances of power and consumption, the values of cultural equity become a symbolic means of redress. Besterman argues that museums send out a powerful message when they recognize their accountability to peoples, hitherto denied a voice, both within and beyond the borders of the nation-state.

Building relationships and knowledge exchange

In recent years there has been an increasing focus by museums on building relationships and ongoing engagement with source communities from whence their collections derived. Much of this focus has been on the facilitation of knowledge networks through co-sharing of information and access to objects. The mechanisms have included visual or digital means, loans, visits, handling workshops, and training, all employed to restore and strengthen Indigenous cultural knowledge that is embodied within museum artifacts. The advantages are mutual, of course, with community-based research feeding back into curatorial knowledge and museum databases. Although the focus has not been explicitly on ownership of artifacts, source communities have commented that they regard such work as fitting the definition of "restitution" in many ways.

By far the most extensively documented – and deeply reflective – of these knowledge exchange relationships has been the repatriation of photographs to the Kainai Nation (Brown and Peers 2006). In 1925, Beatrice Blackwood of the Pitt Rivers Museum in Oxford took 33 photographs of Kainai people in southern Alberta, Canada, to illustrate racial difference and cultural change. In 2001, Pitt Rivers Museum staff took copies of these photographs back to the reserve and worked with members of the community to understand their perspectives on the images and their importance today, creating a long-term reciprocal relationship based on sharing knowledge (Figure 19.1). Not only did the process of dialogue enable Kainai meanings and interpretations to emerge around the images, but it became obvious how important these images from their past were in providing

FIGURE 19.1   Alison Brown and Andy Black Water examining the draft manuscript of a book on the Kainai Photos Project. The collaborative nature of the project meant that interviewees checked all their quotes in context – here, the post-it notes in the manuscript mark all of Andy Black Water's quotes.
Photograph reproduced by permission of Pitt Rivers Museum.

guidance for their present and future, in reassessing their cultural traditions and survival. Discussions prompted by the photographs contributed to the more formalized teaching of history within the community, especially how colonization affected the Kainai Nation and how its members can respond to it today. The project involved a multiplicity of voices that contributed to historical narratives, creating a fuller understanding of Kainai contributions to the history and culture of southern Alberta. For the Kainai as individuals, the photographs – or the messages within the photographs – became part of their efforts to pass on their cultural and historical traditions to future generations. Some made it clear that they would like to see community educational resources as a primary outcome of the project; as a result Pitt Rivers Museum staff handed over copies of all interviews and photographs for the community to use as it wished and to develop its own educational materials. Among the key lessons learned from this project, and other similar ones, is the need to allocate sufficient time for work of this sort. It is essential to allow for consultation and for opportunities to participate (or not) without being rushed or without fully understanding the processes involved, and for individual and community responses to emerge over time, without feeling that they are fitting into a schedule and outcomes predetermined by the museum.

Acknowledging alternative kinds of values for objects

Heritage objects have different value to different individuals, communities, and institutions, depending on their worldviews, religions, and contexts. These varying values have been characterized in different ways: as tensions between scientific and spiritual needs, between universalist and symbolic importance, or between economic value and experiential value. While it is true that such tensions are not always in binary opposition, they can nevertheless be characterized as points along a spectrum, which can itself be characterized as a tension between utilitarian value at one end and social value at the other end.

Broadly, utilitarian value favors:

- the good of the greatest number of people
- economic productivity
- universal access to knowledge
- outputs of scientific research ("evidence"), in principle available to all
- measurable value, often in monetary terms
- preservation.

Social value favors:

- individual or community experience
- spiritual and religious meaning and experience
- connection to place, ancestry, and specific cultural practices

- sense of individual or communal identity
- subjective value that is difficult to measure or "prove"
- more openness to natural processes of decay.

Western museums are, on the whole, concerned with an object's attributes as evidence in terms of history, science, or cultural trends, its beauty, and its physical preservation. For many Indigenous communities, objects are not inert but animated with a life force and spiritual power (which goes beyond the anthropological attribution of agency to objects), and can be the living embodiment of an ancestor. Objects have meaning, function, and importance within the community (Kreps 2011). For example, when the sacred Ahayu-da figures of the Zuni of New Mexico are taken from their shrines, put into museums, and indefinitely conserved against natural decay, the Zuni perceive them as being partly destroyed. As a consequence, harm has been done to them as a people. But when the Ahayu-da are allowed to deteriorate physically in their sacred places, until they disintegrate completely and return to the earth, their sacred meaning for the Zuni is fulfilled (Colwell-Chanthaphonh 2009, 144–152). This demonstrates how conservation "in perpetuity" is a cultural construct and part of a value system peculiar to museums, but it is not a universal value shared by all (on this point see Sully in this volume). Yet such social value is often difficult to establish and demonstrate, as it is largely experiential, immeasurable, often within a timeless present – concepts that tend to be excluded by the rational and institutionalized decision-making processes of organizations such as museums.

Colwell-Chanthaphonh (2009) has explored these different ideas of value in an attempt to propose a middle way to determine claims and rights. He considers social value (calling it the argument of proximity), utilitarian value (calling it the argument of inclusivity), and a middle ground (which he calls the argument for rooted cosmopolitanism). The argument of proximity is based on the notion that those individuals and communities most closely connected, in social or cultural ways, to an object will have the most intense emotional experiences with it and as a result have the greatest rights to it. But Colwell-Chanthaphonh (2009, 152–153) cannot see that the way people *feel* connection to objects necessarily implies that they *ought* to have more rights to them. The fact of social proximity does not make a moral imperative. The argument of inclusivity states that we should maximize the preservation of cultural heritage objects for the good of the greatest number of people, even if such preservation might conflict with the cultural beliefs of a minority. But Colwell-Chanthaphonh (2009, 154–156) sees problems with this too, since such a principle disregards the reasons why we value heritage objects, that is, for the particular experiences they evoke and for their connections to their source communities. So he suggests a middle ground where the local and global might meet. This is the argument for rooted cosmopolitanism, that we should maximize the integrity of heritage objects for the good of the greatest number of people, but not absolutely (Colwell-Chanthaphonh 2009, 156–160). Taking into account the views and values of multiple stakeholders, museums should therefore assess the value of the heritage object for all humanity, but acknowledge particular feelings of affinity and connectedness.

Nevertheless, it is not at all clear what he is suggesting in practice, and perhaps, as Christina Kreps proposes, the aim is to redefine curation as a social practice which is "about cultivating harmonious relationships directed toward redressing historical wrongs, and showing respect for diverse worldviews and belief systems as they pertain to people's perceptions of, and relations to, objects" (Kreps 2011, 469). At the very least, museums must acknowledge that their own institutional value systems, which have developed as a result of a particular history and have been shaped by an Enlightenment philosophy excluding much that indigenous peoples experience (Hooper-Greenhill 1992), are not self-evidently true and universal. Particularly in restitution and repatriation cases, museums need to develop decision-making mechanisms that allow alternative value systems to be expressed, acknowledged, and taken into account on an equitable footing.

Challenging and redefining ownership and possession

Most research on ownership of cultural heritage, especially in relation to questions of repatriation, has focused on whether objects belong to humanity as a whole, or to nations, or to enclaves within nations, particularly Indigenous communities (see, for example, Merryman 1986; Watkins 2005; Cuno 2009; 2010). Carman (2005) has analyzed the shift in the meaning and value of cultural heritage when it is acquired by the state, and finds that the symbolic or social value of a community's sense of heritage is converted into a "national heritage." This has utilitarian value to the state, giving greater prestige and authority to the state as an institution, and leads to restrictions on access justified by the needs of preservation. Through such means the ownership of, and connection to, the object are removed from those people and communities who lay claim to it as their heritage.

While such theoretical perspectives are revealing, they rather miss the point in practical terms. Indeed, there is a suspicion that such debates are often used deliberately to cloud the essential issue. The essential issue of course is that, in all questions of restitution or repatriation that involve museum collections, it is ownership *by the museum* that should be at question. It is the individual museum that, through acquiring and accessioning an object (setting aside whether the object was legally acquired or not), owns the object and can decide whether to keep it or return it; not the nation, and not humanity. Museums are free to make their own decisions about continued ownership of their collections. They will often state that they are keeping objects and collections for the nation and for humanity as a whole (which is essentially the argument of the universal museum declaration); but this is no more than an elaborate justification for retention of their own collections, which are not and cannot be owned by nations or humanity but only by individual museums.

It is true that some museums, such as the British Museum, are legally constrained in terms of what kinds of objects they can dispose of (see Greenfield 2007,

103–110). However, even in those instances, solutions have been found as long as the will was there to find them, whether through imaginative use of loans, or through political pressure changing the legal instruments under which the British Museum and other national museums operate. An example is the 2004 Human Tissue Act enabling national museums to return human remains. It is salutary to note that the relevant section 47 of the Human Tissue Act is completely unconnected to the rest of the Act, which deals with the removal, storage, and use of human tissue less than 100 years old. Yet the political will, as well as support from national museums affected by legal constraints, was there to allow repatriation of ancestral remains, and so the section was inserted into the next available piece of government legislation, rather than cause further delay by waiting for separate dedicated legislation.

In most cases, mechanisms do exist for museums and their governing bodies to make their own decisions about retention or return. A good example of thoughtful decision-making that involved the museum, its governing body, indigenous claimants and the public was the return of the Ghost Dance Shirt by Glasgow Museums to the Lakota Sioux Indians (see Allen 2013). After an initial request for repatriation was refused in 1995, Glasgow City Council re-examined the case in 1998 and set up a working group to discuss the issues and procedures. A process of consultation with museum professionals and the public culminated in a public hearing at which the Lakota and the museum presented their views. Although the official museum position was that the museum legally owned the shirt and was under no legal obligation to return it, it acknowledged that other values may be more important than possession and that the Lakota's views should be taken seriously. As a result of these public deliberations, Glasgow councilors and the public favored return, and the shirt was repatriated to the Lakota in 1999, albeit with conditions regarding preservation and continued display (Figure 19.2). The Lakota made a replica shirt for the museum which was displayed in Glasgow with its full history and an account of the repatriation. Through this process, Glasgow Museums acknowledged that repatriation and relinquishing of possession and ownership were not incompatible with its remit of public display and education. Indeed, public interest and understanding of the shirt, its history and context were stimulated and increased, especially through direct engagement with the Lakota, and the public demonstrated its support for the repatriation.

A different challenge to ownership has been made by Coleman (2010), who analyzes the concept of "inalienable possession" which is central to many claims for repatriation by source communities on the basis that they have special kinds of "identity" relationships with certain objects, irrespective of whether or not they have legal title to them. It is this identity relationship which defines an object as "inalienable," as opposed to something that is property, and alienable. However, Coleman argues that determining something as inalienable defines a kind of value and constitutes a demand that the culture and values of a group remain frozen in time, denying them the possibility to change. This effectively means that, at some

FIGURE 19.2 Tom Tettleman and Richard LeBeau in front of the Ghost Dance Shirt after its return by Glasgow Museums to the Lakota Sioux, at South Dakota State Historical Society Museum, August 1999. The shirt had been worn at the Battle of Wounded Knee in 1890.

Photograph reproduced by permission of Culture and Sport Glasgow.

point in the future, they might no longer acknowledge those objects as an integral part of their culture (see Akerman 2010 for an example). Because it freezes the structure of their societies, it is therefore morally unsupportable. She comes to a cautious conclusion: the relationship between person and object that is generally termed "inalienable possession" justifies a claim for consultation about, and a significant degree of control over, what happens to certain objects, without necessarily justifying their possession as property. However, her analysis also brings out an important point about the process of repatriation. The process should be thought of as a *framework* through which different kinds of value about objects can be acknowledged, expressed, and accommodated, changing the power relations between museums and indigenous groups and other claimants, so that the process and criteria formally recognize that what indigenous people and others want for their cultural artifacts matters.

A new way forward: museums as loci of deliberative democracy

Where museums have responded to requests for restitution or repatriation through legal or bureaucratic processes, challenging claimants to prove their legitimacy and rights to ownership, the processes have been long-winded, costly, and have invariably created tensions between the two sides, which have not led to long-term relationships. In contrast, those museums across the world that are responding to requests for return through open dialogue and are managing to create respectful and sustainable relationships with the claimants, are doing so not as a result of international conventions, or legal processes or through asserting their strict legal rights, but despite them. They do so by working ethically, accountably, and non-adversarially, and seeing the bigger picture of what their essential role is. Moreover, the overwhelming focus of recent research around repatriation and restitution has been on ways of proactively developing relationships with source communities, particularly through their active participation and the development of museums as democratic and accountable spaces which acknowledge alternative value systems and facilitate their free and full expression.

So what does a model of museum practice look like that prioritizes the building of relationships and allows participation in, and some control over, decision-making? How can museums acknowledge alternative values, set aside bureaucratic processes that ask claimant communities to prove their legitimacy, and relinquish their *a priori* assumption of a right to ownership? It must be admitted that the track record of many museums that claim to be beacons of public participation and the sharing of authority is, in reality, poor and often exaggerated. Lynch (2011) has demonstrated that, in many museums with a reputation for public participation, the actual experience of communities can be quite different. Communities often feel marginalized from any effective participation and core decision-making. Many museums are, in reality, reluctant to cede any real control, and instead coerce decisions or manipulate a false group consensus, which often means rubber-stamping existing plans and effectively robbing supposed participants of their active agency.

Yet I believe that the best examples of respectful practice in repatriation and restitution, cited above, already include many elements of deliberative democracy, a concept which offers a practical and tested model for museums to follow. Deliberative democracy, also known as discursive democracy, is so called because deliberation is central to its form of democratic decision-making (Fung 2006). It offers a different, more inclusive model for museums to follow, through which those interested in or affected by repatriation or restitution issues, including the museums themselves, can be involved in reasoning and persuading one another about the values or course of action to be taken. Crucially, this deliberative view contrasts with decision-making processes that are adversarial or in which power is delegated to authoritative experts (Fung 2006, 17). It can be defined as recognition of the right to equal participation between conversation partners, which is to say all whose interests are actually or potentially affected by the courses of action and decisions that may ensue from such conversations (Benhabib 2002, 37).

This process of making joint decisions has been widely tested in different arenas, for example across the neighborhoods of Chicago, where residents, police officers, teachers, and community groups meet monthly to banish crime and transform a failing city school system (Fung 2006). These are challenging environments and issues – surely more so than those we confront in museums – but all voices are heard and the process has led to surprising improvements in the city's schools and to safer streets, making the organizations involved more fair and effective.

How might this work in cases of museum repatriation and restitution practice? Deliberative democracy comprises facilitation of a dialogue, involving all those affected in a decision (for example, claimants, multiple claimants, museum staff, researchers, government officials), based on fairness, in which all key issues have been delegated for decision to the group participating in the dialogue. It is not an easy process. The most effective deliberative democratic processes are based on several key factors: top-down legitimation, neutral facilitation, some training of the participants, and minimizing domination by or exclusion of some groups due to inequalities of power and voice. In particular it is important to take into account and minimize differences based on different communication styles and cultural norms of argument and discourse (for example, possibilities of dominating the discussion through educational differences, aggressive communication styles, claims to expertise, gender and racial differences, and privileging of analytical argument over more poetic approaches; Fung 2006, 71–72). All participants have an equal right to suggest topics of conversation, to introduce new points of view, questions, and criticism into the conversation, and to challenge the rules of the conversation in so far as these seem to exclude the voice of some and privilege that of others. The participants decide among themselves how to reach a decision. This seems to be a model for what a museum should be: a locus for open, respectful, egalitarian dialogue and participation about the values and meanings of objects, issues of interpretation of the past, personal and group identity, and rights to ownership of culture. It is also a model for the process that should be followed, that is, a conversation to which all those affected or even interested in a repatriation or restitution issue are invited on the basis of universal respect and egalitarian reciprocity.

The possibility of radical disagreement and conflict as a result of mutually exclusive and contradictory beliefs tends to make museums shy away from creating such open opportunities for dialogue. But agreement by everyone involved is not necessarily the product of such conversations. There is a problem that people from different cultural backgrounds do not share norms and values and might be unlikely to come to agreement (and this is particularly the case in restitution cases). But participants can still reach consensus based on reasoned disagreement by striving to understand the cultural tradition and/or conceptual framework of the other participants (Dryzek 1990, 42). Even when some participants disagree with group decisions, they may be more easily reconciled to the outcomes because others have justified the bases of their positions in good faith. It is a process of understanding through familiarization with other ways of thinking, and a struggle to reach mutual understanding, if not agreement, through discussion (Valadez 2001, 91; Fung 2006, 17). Surely this is more in keeping with the purpose of museums than adversarial and expert decision-making?

There are three key hurdles which museums need to overcome in order to make this work effectively. First, museums must learn the techniques of open and honest dialogue, both internally and with all their audiences and communities. It takes serious training and practice to learn and sustain this, especially to relinquish the easy assumptions of an expert culture that prioritizes its own values above any alternatives. Second, museums must be open to ceding decision-making to a group comprising staff, claimants, interested communities, and external specialists which has been tasked with making a decision on repatriation and restitution issues. Museums must be prepared to relinquish control, and set aside the fetish of ownership by recognizing that other values may be more important than possession. They must consider how the process is helping achieve their wider aims, and must be genuinely prepared to implement any decision made using deliberative democratic processes that explicitly incorporate different voices and values. Museum hierarchies, governance procedures, and the personalities of individual directors make this step a difficult one. Third, the process is resource-intensive, slow, and messy, but it is *the process of deliberation itself* that fulfills museums' essential purposes, not necessarily the final decision and outcome. The resource implications for museums embarking on such a process are mostly time, the expenses of bringing people together, training, and facilitation. In the long run, however, these resources are being invested into building sustainable relationships, and they are measurably cheaper than protracted legal proceedings.

Is this all too idealistic and unachievable? Well, if it works in Chicago's school and police systems, then there is no reason why it cannot work in museums! In my view, the principles underpinning such an approach are already present in the way some progressive museums work. A prime example is the Museum of World Culture in Gothenburg, Sweden. It describes itself as an arena for discourse and reflection in which many and different voices are heard, where contentious topics can be thrashed out. Crucially, the museum defines itself as an intermediary between collections, knowledge, and multiple communities. The essential principles and working practices of deliberative democracy are already embedded in this museum's approach (Museum of World Culture 2012).

Conclusion

This chapter has critiqued current practices of restitution and repatriation, arguing that most of them are protracted, expensive, adversarial, and actively alienate communities and prevent museums from carrying out their essential purpose – acting as fora for an equitable discussion over the values and meanings of objects. On the other hand, those museums which have returned objects through an open and trusting dialogue with claimant communities, eschewing legal and adversarial processes, have created goodwill and ongoing, sustainable relationships, which also benefit their own local audiences. Such examples of good practice reflect many of the principles and practices of deliberative democracy, and show a way around the problems inherent in legal and bureaucratic processes of restitution and repatriation. For museums involved in restitution issues, an open and transparent deliberative democratic process to resolve the claims would be more beneficial to their wider purposes than the bureaucratic and costly process of establishing criteria of ownership and rights, with its colonialist demands of proof and legitimacy. Such a process would be a genuine and open discourse over the value and meaning of objects and cultural identity that would be mutually enriching, building sustainable and non-adversarial relationships.

References

Akerman, K. 2010. "'You Keep It – We Are Christians Here': Repatriation of the Secret Sacred where Indigenous World-Views Have Changed." In *The Long Way Home: The Meaning and Values of Repatriation*, edited by Paul Turnbull and Michael Pickering, 175–182. Oxford: Berghahn.

Alberge, Dalya. 2004. "Gift of Art to Atone for Looting by Nazis." *The Times*, December 2. Accessed October 31, 2014. http://www.lootedartcommission.com/MOACGX53334.

Allen, Patricia. 2013. "Glasgow's *Ghost Dance* Shirt: Reflections on a Circle to Complete." In *Global Perspectives: Understanding the Shared Humanity of Our Ancestors*, edited by

Margaret Clegg, Rebecca Redfern, Jelena Bekvalac, and Heather Bonney, 63–80. Oxford: Oxbow.

Bell, Catherine, Graham Statt, Michael Solowan, Allyson Jeffs, and Emily Snyder. 2009. "First Nations Cultural Heritage: A Selected Survey of Issues and Initiatives." In *First Nations Cultural Heritage and Law: Case Studies, Voices, and Perspectives*, edited by Catherine Bell and Val Napoleon, 367–416. Vancouver: University of British Columbia Press.

Benhabib, Selya. 2002. *The Claims of Culture: Equality and Diversity in the Global Era.* Princeton, NJ: Princeton University Press.

Besterman, Tristram. 2011. "Cultural Equity and the Sustainable Museum." In *The Routledge Companion to Museum Ethics: Redefining Ethics for the Twenty-First Century Museum*, edited by Janet Marstine, 239–255. London: Routledge.

Bienkowski, Piotr. 2007. "Authority over Human Remains: Genealogy, Relationship, Detachment." *Archaeological Review from Cambridge* 22(2): 113–130.

Bienkowski, Piotr, and Elizabeth B. Coleman. 2013. "Contesting 'Claims' on Human Remains: Which Traditions Are Treated as Legitimate and Why?" In *Global Perspectives: Understanding the Shared Humanity of Our Ancestors*, edited by Margaret Clegg, Rebecca Redfern, Jelena Bekvalac, and Heather Bonney, 81–101. Oxford: Oxbow.

Boyd, Willard L. 2006. "Museums as Centers of Cultural Understanding." In *Imperialism, Art and Restitution*, edited by John H. Merryman, 47–64. Cambridge: Cambridge University Press.

British Library. n.d. "Turning the Pages." Accessed October 31, 2014. http://www.bl.uk/onlinegallery/ttp/lindisfarne/accessible/introduction.html.

Brodie, Neil. 2006. "An Archaeologist's View of the Trade in Unprovenanced Antiquities." In *Art and Cultural Heritage: Law, Policy, and Practice*, edited by B. T. Hoffman, 52–63. Cambridge: Cambridge University Press.

Brown, Alison, and Laura Peers, with members of the Kainai Nation. 2006. *Pictures Bring Us Messages/Sinaakssiiksi Aohtsimaahpihkookiyaawa: Photographs and Histories from the Kainai Nation.* Toronto: University of Toronto Press.

Brown, Deirdre. 2007. "*Te Ahu Hiko*: Digital Cultural Heritage and Indigenous Objects, People, and Environments." In *Theorizing Digital Cultural Heritage: A Critical Discourse*, edited by Fiona Cameron and Sarah Kenderdine, 77–91. Cambridge, MA: MIT Press.

Brown, Michael F., and Margaret M. Bruchac. 2006. "NAGPRA from the Middle Distance: Legal Puzzles and Unintended Consequences." In *Imperialism, Art and Restitution*, edited by John H. Merryman, 193–217. Cambridge: Cambridge University Press.

Carman, John. 2005. *Against Cultural Property: Archaeology, Heritage and Ownership.* London: Duckworth.

Coleman, Elizabeth B. 2010. "Repatriation and the Concept of Inalienable Possession." In *The Long Way Home: The Meaning and Values of Repatriation*, edited by Paul Turnbull and Michael Pickering, 82–95. Oxford: Berghahn.

Colwell-Chanthaphonh, Chip. 2009. "The Archaeologist as World Citizen: On the Morals of Heritage Preservation and Destruction." In *Cosmopolitan Archaeologies*, edited by Lynn Meskell, 140–165. Durham, NC: Duke University Press.

Cuno, James. 2006. "View from the Universal Museum." In *Imperialism, Art and Restitution*, edited by John H. Merryman, 15–36. Cambridge: Cambridge University Press.

Cuno, James, ed. 2009. *Whose Culture? The Promise of Museums and the Debate over Antiquities.* Princeton, NJ: Princeton University Press.

Cuno, James. 2010. *Who Owns Antiquity? Museums and the Battle over Our Ancient Heritage.* Princeton, NJ: Princeton University Press.

Dryzek, John. 1990. *Discursive Democracy: Politics, Policy, and Political Science.* Cambridge: Cambridge University Press.

Fforde, Cressida. 2004a. "Collection, Repatriation and Identity." In *The Dead and Their Possessions: Repatriation in Principle, Policy and Practice*, edited by Cressida Fforde, Jane Hubert, and Paul Turnbull, 25–46. London: Routledge.

Fforde, Cressida. 2004b. *Collecting the Dead: Archaeology and the Reburial Issue.* London: Duckworth.

Fung, Archon. 2006. *Empowered Participation: Reinventing Urban Democracy.* Princeton, NJ: Princeton University Press.

Garroutte, Eva M. 2001. "The Racial Formation of American Indians: Negotiating Legitimate Identities within Tribal and Federal Law." *American Indian Quarterly* 25(2): 224–239.

Gerstenblith, Patty. 2011. "Museum Practice: Legal Issues." In *A Companion to Museum Studies*, edited by Sharon Macdonald, 442–456. Oxford: Wiley-Blackwell.

Greenfield, Jeanette. 2007. *The Return of Cultural Treasures.* Cambridge: Cambridge University Press.

Henning, Michelle. 2011. "New Media." In *A Companion to Museum Studies*, edited by Sharon Macdonald, 302–318. Oxford: Wiley-Blackwell.

Hooper-Greenhill, Eilean. 1992. *Museums and the Shaping of Knowledge.* London: Routledge.

Kowalski, Wojciech W. 2001. "Repatriation of Cultural Property Following a Cession of Territory or Dissolution of Multinational States." *Art, Antiquity and Law* 6(2): 139–166.

Kreps, Christina. 2011. "Non-Western Models of Museums and Curation in Cross-Cultural Perspective." In *A Companion to Museum Studies*, edited by Sharon Macdonald, 457–472. Oxford: Wiley-Blackwell.

Lenzerini, Federico. 2008. "Reparations for Indigenous Peoples in International and Comparative Law: An Introduction." In *Reparations for Indigenous Peoples: International and Comparative Perspectives*, edited by Federico Lenzerini, 3–26. Oxford: Oxford University Press.

Lynch, Bernadette. 2011. *Whose Cake Is It Anyway? A Collaborative Investigation into Engagement and Participation in 12 Museums and Galleries in the UK.* London: Paul Hamlyn Foundation.

McManamon, Francis P. 2004. "Repatriation in the USA: A Decade of Federal Agency Activities under NAGPRA." In *The Dead and Their Possessions: Repatriation in Principle, Policy and Practice*, edited by Cressida Fforde, Jane Hubert, and Paul Turnbull, 133–148. London: Routledge.

Merryman, John H. 1986. "Two Ways of Thinking about Cultural Property." *American Journal of International Law* 80: 831–853.

Morphy, Howard. 2010. "Scientific Knowledge and Rights in Skeletal Remains: Dilemmas in the Curation of 'Other' People's Bones." In *The Long Way Home: The Meaning and Values of Repatriation*, edited by Paul Turnbull and Michael Pickering, 147–162. Oxford: Berghahn.

Museum of World Culture, Gothenburg. 2012. Accessed October 31, 2014. http://www.varldskulturmuseerna.se/varldskulturmuseet/om-museet/in-english.

Myles, Virginia. 2010. "Parks Canada's Policies that Guide the Repatriation of Human Remains and Objects." In *The Long Way Home: The Meaning and Values of Repatriation*, edited by Paul Turnbull and Michael Pickering, 48–56. Oxford: Berghahn.

Nicholas, Lynn. 1994. *The Rape of Europa: The Fate of Europe's Treasures in the Third Reich and the Second World War*. New York: Alfred A. Knopf.

Pala, Christopher. 2008. "Paradise Almost Lost: Hawaii's Bishop Museum Grapples with NAGPRA." *Museum* 87(2): 44–53.

Palmer, Norman. 2000. *Museums and the Holocaust: Law, Principles and Practice*. Leicester: Institute of Art and Law.

Reppas, Michael J. 2007. "Empty 'International' Museums' Trophy Cases of Their Looted Treasures and Return Stolen Property to the Countries of Origin and the Rightful Heirs of Those Wrongfully Dispossessed." *Denver Journal of International Law and Policy* 36(1): 93–123.

Schneider, Alan L. 2004. "Kennewick Man: The Three-Million Dollar Man." In *Legal Perspectives on Cultural Resources*, edited by J. R. Richman and M. P. Forsyth, 202–215. Walnut Creek, CA: AltaMira.

Sims, Calvin. 2001. "Japanese Agree a Stolen Statue Will Be Sent Back to China." *New York Times*, April 16. Accessed October 31, 2014. http://www.nytimes.com/2001/04/18/arts/japanese-agree-a-stolen-statue-will-be-sent-back-to-china.html.

Singer, G. R. 2006. "Unfolding Intangible Cultural Heritage Rights in Tangible Museum Collections: Developing Standards of Stewardship." In *Art and Cultural Heritage: Law, Policy, and Practice*, edited by B. T. Hoffman, 413–415. Cambridge: Cambridge University Press.

Skydstrup, Martin. 2010. "What Might an Anthropology of Cultural Property Look Like?" In *The Long Way Home: The Meaning and Values of Repatriation*, edited by Paul Turnbull and Michael Pickering, 59–81. New York: Berghahn.

St. Clair, William. 2006. "Imperial Appropriations of the Parthenon." In *Imperialism, Art and Restitution*, edited by John H. Merryman, 65–97. Cambridge: Cambridge University Press.

Thomas, David H. 2006. "Finders Keepers and Deep American History: Some Lessons in Dispute Resolution." In *Imperialism, Art and Restitution*, edited by John H. Merryman, 218–253. Cambridge: Cambridge University Press.

Valadez, Jorge M. 2001. *Deliberative Democracy, Political Legitimacy, and Self-Determination in Multicultural Societies*. Boulder, CO: Westview.

Vrdoljak, Ana F. 2006. *International Law, Museums and the Return of Cultural Objects*. Cambridge: Cambridge University Press.

Vrdoljak, Ana F. 2008. "Reparations for Cultural Loss." In *Reparations for Indigenous Peoples: International and Comparative Perspectives*, edited by Federico Lenzerini, 197–228. Oxford: Oxford University Press.

Watkins, Joe. 2005. "Cultural Nationalists, Internationalists, and 'Intra-Nationalists': Who's Right and Whose Right?" *International Journal of Cultural Property* 12(1): 78–94.

Whitby-Last, Kathryn. 2010. "Legal Impediments to the Repatriation of Cultural Objects to Indigenous Peoples." In *The Long Way Home: The Meaning and Values of Repatriation*, edited by Paul Turnbull and Michael Pickering, 35–47. Oxford: Berghahn.

Wilson, David. 1990. *The British Museum: Purpose and Politics*. London: British Museum.

Piotr Bienkowski runs a cultural consultancy specializing in organizational change, community engagement, and cultural planning. He developed and directs the Paul Hamlyn Foundation program "Our Museum: Communities and Museums as Active Partners," which supports organizational change to embed community participation and agency in museums and galleries in the United Kingdom. Previously he was Head of Antiquities at National Museums Liverpool, Deputy (and Acting) Director at Manchester Museum (where he was responsible for several repatriations), and Professor of Archaeology and Museology at the University of Manchester. His disciplinary background is in Near Eastern archaeology, and he is the co-director of the International Umm al-Biyara Project in Petra, Jordan.

20 REWARDS AND FRUSTRATIONS

Repatriation of Aboriginal and Torres Strait Islander Ancestral Remains by the National Museum of Australia

Michael Pickering[1]

In October 2011, the Australian Government released its first policy on the Repatriation of Aboriginal and Torres Strait Islander remains (Australian Government 2011). Although this policy communicates a philosophy, and is not legally binding on Australian Federal, State, or Territory agencies, it nonetheless marks a long-awaited commitment by the Australian Government and comes after many years of active repatriation of remains in Australia.

The National Museum of Australia (NMA) in Canberra, like many Australian museums, has been repatriating Aboriginal and Torres Strait Islander remains since its inception in 1980. Increased Federal government support from 2001, has meant that activities were accelerated, with commensurate improvements in methods, philosophies, protocols, and identification of issues. Over 30 years, the NMA has had many experiences that cover the full gamut of political, economic, social, cultural, domestic, international, scientific, philosophical, and ethical realms of repatriation.

In this chapter, I describe the repatriation activities of the NMA, where, between 2001 and 2013, I was the senior manager and advisor for the Repatriation program. The chapter first describes some aspects of the history of repatriation in Australia and the processes of repatriation as practiced at the NMA. I then turn to look at some of the dominant issues and concerns that have arisen through my experiences. The policies, processes, and outputs described in this chapter do reflect the museum's official approach. Many of the comments, opinions and recommendations are, however, mine, based on my experiences, and may not

The International Handbooks of Museum Studies: Museum Practice, First Edition.
Edited by Conal McCarthy.

reflect the views of the museum. I present these as part of the discussion in the belief that they will re-occur whenever museums engage with repatriation of Indigenous human remains.

The Australian context

Given the increasing level of repatriation activity in Australia since 2001, and with the occasional provision of extra government funding and increasing engagement with international collecting institutions, it is surprising, first, that more has not been written on the development of associated philosophies, processes, and issues, and, second, that institutions have not been more open on how they deal with repatriation internally. What literature is available usually falls into one of five areas: advocacy; opposition; case studies; history of the collections; and policy. As repatriation increasingly becomes approved philosophy and practice within the Australian heritage industry, open dissent becomes rarer. I see this not only as a result of convincing debate, and government and institutional support but also, it must be acknowledged, by a fear of ostracism for voicing anti-repatriation views. Unfortunately, much of the debate has taken place behind closed doors.

Certainly, whenever there is a repatriation event it is usually well covered in the media, usually as a good-news story. However, such journalism is characterized by short snippets or sound bites, a photograph or statement by the relevant minister, and by event description rather than presentation of the debates or more complex circumstances and histories behind the event. Such correspondence certainly communicates the sentiments of both the Indigenous Australians,[2] whose ancestors are being returned, and of the participating museums, but provides little information as to associated governance or strategic issues that would assist in the proactive development of philosophies and processes of repatriation.

There is a smattering of industry and academic articles leading up to the 2000s, though in many of these the question of repatriation is a side issue rather than the central focus. Repatriation had long been a concern among Aboriginal and Torres Strait Islander communities, but it was difficult for these communities to get a hearing within the major heritage industry publications. The opportunity for Indigenous advocates to be heard increased greatly following a high-profile event in Victoria in 1985 when Aboriginal leader Jim Berg recovered Aboriginal remains held by the University of Melbourne and oversaw their subsequent repatriation (Faulkhead and Berg 2010). This event, complemented by increasing employment of Indigenous curators and managers, changed the face of repatriation activity in Australia, from a quiet plea on the edges to a major debate in agencies and professions associated with Aboriginal and Torres Strait Islander Heritage.[3] The 1990s also saw increasing Indigenous activism directed at the return of ancestors, with several successful, high-profile returns of remains from overseas institutions, as well as greater onus being placed on Australian museums to explain and reconsider their relationships with Aboriginal and Torres Strait Islander peoples and cultures. Within museums, staff were forced to look at their historical practices.

Direct advocacy for repatriation of remains includes many newspaper articles and conferences where repatriation events, and the experiences of the Indigenous participants, are discussed. Recent writings by Aboriginal authors include Atkinson (2010), Cubillo (2010), Hemming and Wilson (2010), and Faulkhead and Berg (2010). Turnbull (for example, 1997, 2002) and Fforde (for example, 2004) are leading historians on repatriation issues and have written extensively on the history of collections. Their revelations of the motives and methods of collectors, infringements of the law, museological theories and practices of the time, and the biases within collections, have done much to support arguments for repatriation, through illustrating unethical and illegal collection processes. (For an overview of international debates in repatriation and restitution in relation to museum practice see Bienkowski in this volume.)

More recently in Australia there have been moves to reinvigorate debate through engaging more widely with other interdisciplinary perspectives, encouraging research about human remains and repatriation beyond the conventional disciplinary boundaries of anthropology and archaeology. In a recent anthology (Turnbull and Pickering 2010), a number of writers presented papers on a diverse range of repatriation themes, providing a welcome shift away from the familiar critical "rhetoric of allegation" and simple case studies toward wider philosophical, historical, and cultural considerations. (This chapter aims to support this shift by raising and exploring issues of applied repatriation.)

It must be acknowledged that, over the years, debate occasionally deteriorated into rhetoric, inhibiting debate and discussion. Conference sessions on repatriation were characterized by polarization, with museum-based supporters of repatriation being abused by Indigenous speakers for *not* supporting repatriation or indigenous empowerment in the process, and Indigenous people similarly attacked for not appreciating the "importance" of scientific research. Dogma, rather than discussion, prevailed on both sides.

Arguments against repatriation of Australian Indigenous remains, or criticisms of processes, while commonly heard at professional conferences (or over a drink at the local), are rarely captured in print. Yet it is essential that all views be heard and responded to by reasoned argument rather than by dogma, although I am convinced that pro-repatriation arguments will prevail. There is no doubt that many people are afraid to comment on repatriation in print, either due to the concern that their views will incur the ire of Indigenous Australians and/or professional bodies, or because their status as public servants makes comment on government policy and actions a potential breach of the code of conduct. However, professionals working in the public-service heritage sector, including museums, must be allowed to comment on policy and action when it affects the interpretation and management of heritage and history. Are we public servants first, and historians, anthropologists, and archaeologists second? Or vice versa? I am of the latter persuasion, and feel that, presumably, our employers engaged us because of our professional abilities first (see Pickering 2011).

The most influential and empowering statements, though, have come from the Federal government and from within the Australian museums industry. These engage directly with the practical aspects of policy and processes of repatriation by museums. The Australian Government has progressively reinforced its support for repatriation since 2001, following the joint declaration of then Prime Ministers of Australia and the United Kingdom, John Howard and Tony Blair that "The Australian and British governments agree to increase efforts to repatriate human remains to Australian indigenous communities. In doing this, the governments recognise the special connection that indigenous people have with ancestral remains, particularly where there are living descendants" (Australian Government 2000). Through its departments, the Federal government had also provided financial support to museums and communities for domestic and international repatriation activities since 2000. The Australian Government's continued support for repatriation, at least in philosophy, over a number of years was ratified by the announcement of a formal Australian Government Policy in that: "The Australian Government recognises repatriation helps promote healing and reconciliation for Aboriginal and Torres Strait Islander peoples" (Australian Government 2011, Part II.1).

However, since 2000, the support of consecutive Australian Federal governments for repatriation of remains reflected what was already happening within the Australian museum industry. By the time governments became vocal, repatriation was already a philosophy and practice within the local sector. Political support was following, not leading, a developing trend. Nonetheless, formal Australian Government support, at both Federal and State levels, provides an important degree of legitimization, and repatriation officers are now less likely to be accused of "crimes against science." That this has emerged after many years of debate, rather than as a short-term publicity grab, suggests support will continue well into the future.

The major Australian Federal and State museums have been advocates and practitioners of repatriation for over 30 years.[4] This work was slow and tentative at first, but as experience mounted, and as arguments were developed, tested, and refined, the commitment increased. By 1993, Museums Australia, the major representative body for Australian museums, was promoting repatriation and ethical use of Indigenous collections through its document "Previous Possessions, New Obligations" (Museums Australia 1993, 2000). In 2005, this document was subject to extensive review through a consultation process with Indigenous and non-Indigenous museum professionals, and then released as "Continuous Cultures Ongoing Responsibilities." Again, this important document effectively captured and consolidated prevailing industry philosophy and practice, specifically stating:

> 1.4.3 The community from which the ancestral remains originated needs to be involved in deciding what will happen to remains repatriated by museums.

1.4.4 Museums are to seek out the rightful custodians of ancestral remains and ask them whether they wish the remains to be repatriated to the community or held by the museum on behalf of the community.

1.4.5 If rightful custodians ask for the return of ancestral remains museums should agree. All requests for the repatriation of Aboriginal and Torres Strait Islander ancestral remains should be promptly and sensitively dealt with by museums, who must at all times respect the materials' very sensitive nature.

1.4.6 Museums must not place conditions on communities with regard to the repatriation of ancestral remains. (Museums Australia 2005, 18)

While not binding upon museums, this strong statement reflects the determination of major Australian museums to support repatriation. But with the exception of Tasmania, which has legislation that compels its two major museums to return remains to local Aboriginal communities (Tasmanian Government 1984), there is *no* legislation in Australia that specifically compels repatriation. There *is* State and Territory heritage legislation that prevents private ownership of Aboriginal and Torres Strait Islander remains, and heritage legislation and philosophy that returns newly discovered remains (through archaeological or development activities) immediately to relevant communities. There is also non-heritage medical legislation that prohibits ownership or trade in human tissue, such as State and Territory Anatomy and Transplantation Acts that can be used to prevent trade or collection of remains, though this was not their original intention (for examples, see Morgan 2010).

The Federal government's *Aboriginal and Torres Strait Islander Aboriginal Heritage Protection Act* (Australian Government 1984, Div. 3, S 20 and 21) allows for the return of remains to communities, but only when "discovered" remains are referred to the minister, a rare event as the return of newly discovered remains is well covered by policy and practices of the states and territories.

The National Museum of Australia

The National Museum of Australia has been returning remains to Aboriginal and Torres Strait Islander people upon request since its creation in 1980. The returns were initially slow but consistent over 20 years. In the 1990s funding was provided by the Aboriginal and Torres Strait Islander Commission (ATSIC) to facilitate the repatriation of remains returned to Australia in 1991. In 2001, extra support funding became available through the Return of Cultural Property Program and through a further ATSIC contract to repatriate remains returned from the University of Edinburgh Anatomy Department following Indigenous advocacy. This funding allowed the NMA to establish a specialized Repatriation Program Unit, of which I was the Program Director, with dedicated facilities and staff. Over the years, this unit's resources and activities have waxed and waned, dependent upon vagaries in external government funding. Nonetheless, even at its poorest, the NMA continues to be a committed advocate of repatriation.

The NMA's current holdings of remains derive from many sources. Most are from the old Australian Institute of Anatomy collections. The Institute was established in the 1930s and closed its doors in 1985, at which time the bulk of its collections of both Indigenous and non-Indigenous human remains, animal specimens, and ethnographic objects, were transferred to the NMA. Holdings of remains have grown further as the NMA was contracted to provide storage and/or repatriation services for remains returned from overseas. For example, collections from Edinburgh University, the Royal College of Surgeons, Manchester and Horniman Museums, all in the United Kingdom; the Bishop Museum and Michigan University in the United States; and Vienna University, among others, have been held by the museum while awaiting repatriation to communities.

While these remains have been temporarily deposited with the museum, the advocacy that resulted in the earliest returns was initially carried out through Indigenous representatives, and Indigenous organizations. More recently, this role has been taken over by repatriation managers located within non-museum government departments. The NMA itself has no formal authority to pursue the return of remains from overseas, although staff do take the opportunity to advocate for returns when possible, such as when attending conferences or meeting with overseas colleagues, and as this chapter attests.

The NMA's Repatriation activities are in accordance with its Aboriginal and Torres Strait Islander Human Remains Policy (National Museum of Australia 2011). The most significant characteristics of this policy are that it supports the unconditional return of remains to traditional owners and custodians upon request and that any other external access to the remains is permitted only with the approval of the relevant community.

Until recently, with the establishment of an Indigenous Advisory Group to guide the Museum's Indigenous engagements, the NMA did not have an internal Indigenous committee to oversee repatriation. The main reason for this was that the most important authorities and advisors remain, of course, the identified custodians themselves, those people or groups with the strongest biological and/or cultural affiliation to the remains. There is little advantage in imposing another level of management between the NMA and the primary custodial community. Further, if other advice was required, there were a number of Indigenous people on staff, in the adjacent Australian Institute of Aboriginal and Torres Strait Islander Studies (AIATSIS), at the Australian National University, and within the wider Indigenous heritage management community, who provide advice to the NMA on important issues as required.

The NMA returned the remains of over 1000 individuals over 25 years. When received by the NMA, all of these remains were accompanied by provenancing documentation that made their assignment to an Indigenous group possible. Provenancing material ranged from simple written descriptions of place of collection on the remains themselves, through to complete documentation providing descriptions of the name of the individual, cultural affiliation, cause of death, collectors, and donor(s). Once provenance was determined, it was possible to identify appropriate representative groups. This was facilitated through engagements with State and Territory heritage agencies and Indigenous representative bodies established under Federal or State legislation (for example, land councils, native title representative bodies, museums, Aboriginal Affairs, and heritage departments).

Although a federally created institution, with the authoritative title of "National Museum of Australia," the NMA has no overriding authority in any States or Territories. Nor does it necessarily have the local knowledge or networks that those State- and Territory-based agencies and organizations have built up over many years. Such organizations have a statutory responsibility to represent custodians, traditional owners, and native title holders. Their advice and support in the identification of such individuals and groups, based on cultural, anthropological, as well as legislative criteria, has assisted the NMA in fast-tracking the repatriation process with no subsequent major disputes.

This process also provides some protection for the NMA when, as a public service institution, it may be required to describe whom it dealt with and the basis for accepting that individual or group as being the appropriate custodians (for example, government audit, discovery of documents for legal process (native title), financial reporting, inquiries by other Indigenous representatives and senate inquiry). The NMA is as accountable as any other public service agency. It must show evidence of due process in its financial and management actions. Its activities and actions must also accord with the laws of the State or Territory in which the repatriations occur. The museum thus recognizes and uses the local knowledge that such organizations provide.

Once a prospective custodian, custodial group, or representative body has been identified, they are advised by phone and/or writing of the nature of the remains available for return to them. Research on provenance and consultation with State and Territory heritage agencies usually allows identification of groups with solid claims to remains. However, every effort must be taken to demonstrate both cultural and procedural title. On rare occasions, the NMA is approached by applicants who may not be recognized by the State or Territory or by Indigenous representative bodies as appropriate custodians. Competing claims can also be an issue. Prospective custodians are therefore asked for any information that may support their claim to remains, including:

- The identities of the persons, groups, or community on whose behalf the application is made.
- The specific remains requested.
- Letters of support for the application from representative organizations.
- Where an organization is making the application, a statement of support from members of the relevant group represented.

- A statement that the applicants are entitled by the traditions and customs of their community to make application for the remains.
- The relationship of the applicants to the remains requested.
- Contact addresses for other groups or organizations that support the application.
- Any other issues or information.

Provision of this information is not compulsory. Indeed, by the time the NMA approaches custodians their rights are usually very well demonstrated through the initial provenancing research. For example, local Aboriginal land councils in New South Wales, regional Aboriginal heritage organizations in South Australia, and land councils in the Northern Territory and Western Australia, are endorsed by Federal, State, and Territory governments and by relevant heritage departments. In other cases, certain individuals and local community groups have an extensive history of recognition, by Federal, State, and local government authorities, as the appropriate people to deal with over the care of ancestral remains. Such organizations, groups, and individuals are not required to provide extra information in support of their claim – indeed the rule of precedent facilitates future repatriations. What these basic criteria do is discourage frivolous or vexatious claims by people who may not be culturally acknowledged or authorized to make claim for repatriation. This is a critical issue when it is remembered that any repatriation is an empowering event, involving formal recognition by a major Federal institution of the claimant's rights and authority over remains. Mistakes can be hard to repair.

There are, on rare occasions, competing claims within and between groups for the return of remains where both factions have a basis for claim. In such situations, the repatriation officer does not take on the role of judge. If community members, with historical links and living in close proximity, cannot come to an agreement then it is unlikely that the museum repatriation officer – who is culturally, spatially, historically, and socially foreign – will be able to make an unchallenged determination acceptable to both groups. Further, it must always be remembered that repatriation involves respect for both the deceased ancestors and descendants. Museum repatriation officers should assist, but not interfere.

The repatriation officer continues to consult with the applicants and other parties with potential interests. The return of the remains, or alternative management outcome, then proceeds, whenever possible, in accordance with instructions from the custodians. With the exception of signing a receipt for remains, returns are unconditional and custodians may do with the remains as they see fit. While at the museum, remains are stored in a locked facility. Keys to this facility are kept in a special key cupboard requiring a personal code to access specific keys.

It is not difficult for the NMA to return remains (see Figures 20.1 and 20.2). But it can often be difficult for communities to receive and manage remains in the way they would like. Aided by extra government funding, the NMA has, on occasion, been able to offer some logistical and financial support, facilitating travel for

FIGURE 20.1 Dancers provide a traditional ceremonial "Welcome to country" upon the return of Larrakia ancestral remains, Mindil Beach, Darwin, Northern Territory, November 2002. (For a color version of this figure, please see the color plate section.)
Photo: Michael Pickering, National Museum of Australia.

FIGURE 20.2 Larrakia families welcome the remains of their ancestors, Mindil Beach, Darwin, Northern Territory, November 2002.
Photo: George Serras, National Museum of Australia.

applicants to view and collect the remains, visits to the community by repatria-tion officers to consult or deliver remains, associated ceremonies, and reports into the characteristics of the remains. Still, support funding has fluctuated consider-ably over the years, affecting the ability of the museum to provide a consistent service. Nonetheless, the NMA has continued to return remains and provide such support as its own internal resources allow when external funding has not been available.

Although the situation has not happened as yet, the NMA will also return remains provenanced only to State or Territory to a suitable representative agency within that State or Territory when the transfer is supported by an appropriate Aboriginal or Torres Strait Islander heritage advisory group. All Australian govern-ments have formally convened and recognized Indigenous advisory groups that represent their communities on issues of Indigenous heritage. These groups may convene within land councils, museum advisory boards, native title representative bodies, or similar groups. Nevertheless, remains with a more specific provenance still require instructions from the identified custodial group.

Where groups do not have the resources to receive remains, the NMA offers either to return them to a designated repository, or to store them temporarily on their behalf. Unlike older Australian museums, the NMA does not have a history of deliberate collection of Indigenous remains; nonetheless, it must share respon-sibility with the wider industry for this past practice. The holding of remains at request and at no charge is thus a small courtesy, and small recompense, for prac-tices of the past, provided to communities. The remains are the property of the community / custodians and the NMA claims no authority over the remains beyond keeping them safe and secure.

Though still holding provenanced remains from international returns facili-tated by the Australian government's international repatriation departments, the NMA now prefers not to store provenanced remains where legal possessory title remains with other museums or external government agencies. The exception is where the request is supported by the community with which the remains are associated. This is because a change of government sentiment, a change of NMA management, or a change of NMA council, could result in policy changes that would halt repatriation or impose conditions unacceptable to Indigenous com-munities (for example, compulsory research). Indeed, in 2007 John Hirst, then a member of the NMA's Council, argued for mandatory scientific research on remains prior to return, stating: "The human remains the National Museum holds and may acquire are an essential resource for the scientific study of the his-tory of humankind in Australia" (Hirst 2006). Hirst's advocacy led to a change in the museum's Aboriginal and Torres Strait Islander Human Remains Policy so that groups are advised that remains may be of scientific importance, although the museum still does not carry out the unapproved scientific research sought by Hirst. Ensuring that ownership of remains is vested as quickly as possible with a claimant community means that the NMA cannot claim control of, research, interfere with, or refuse to return remains that have become the legal property of Aboriginal or Torres Strait Islander people.

As noted above, the NMA is a statutory authority and is obliged to keep detailed records of its activities. Repatriation is no exception. The museum maintains a separate database of human remains and a repository of repatriation files. This provides further security for the information, which cannot be accessed by other staff. For the purposes of day-to-day operational requirements, they can only be accessed by, or with the approval of, repatriation officers. Such records can, of course, be requested at any time for official audits, legal discovery, or through Freedom of Information provisions. They cannot, however, be accessed by general NMA staff or visitors. In those instances where documents have been required for audit, the auditors have been very sympathetic and have not requested access to remains themselves or any images of remains, nor have they reproduced culturally significant or sensitive information in any of their reports.

The processes and policies governing the NMA's repatriation activities, along with selected references and publications, are also provided on the museum website.[5] The processes described above have served the NMA well in its repatriation activities. There have been few issues over the life of the program. Certainly, there are always individuals or small groups who express dissatisfaction with some aspect of any repatriation event, ranging from allegations that the wrong people were given the remains through to concerns that community support resourcing was inadequate. But complainants are usually in the minority, and no legal or political action has occurred, which lends support to the view that the NMA did consult with appropriately authorized and recognized groups. Continued government support, and the recognition by other museums and industry professionals of the NMA's expertise in the area of repatriation also provides a validation of the museum's processes.

Issues in current repatriation practice

In the following discussion, I address several specific areas that have consistently arisen in my engagements with funding agencies, researchers, custodians, and overseas agencies and institutions. These are: the definition of repatriation; problems in funding; failure to adequately research provenance before returns; the effectiveness of scientific provenancing; allegations of destruction of scientific knowledge; and the imposition of unrealistic criteria for affiliation. I believe these areas have received little overt attention in repatriation debates.

I must assert that *any criticisms of practice and philosophy that follow do not constitute arguments against repatriation*. Rather, my intention is to identify and interrogate such problems, and their consequences, and propose alternatives in the hope that they can be predicted, intercepted, and, where possible, avoided.

What is repatriation?

In 2000, the Australian Government announced the Return of Indigenous Cultural Property program (RICP). This program would resource the seven State museums and the NMA to return Aboriginal and Torres Strait human remains and secret/sacred objects from their domestic holdings. Following the announcement of finance for such activities there was a rush of other institutions claiming repatriation activities and seeking to access RICP funding. Thus, concepts such as "digital repatriation" – the provision of copies of photographs, films and digitized documents – entered the language.

Unfortunately, the use of the word "repatriation" to describe provision of paper, electronic, or sculptural copies belittles the philosophy, intent, and meaning of repatriation, as well as increasing demand on limited resources. I am of the opinion that provision of casts, photos of, or research reports on human remains would never constitute repatriation. Take, for example, the provision of information to a researcher, then the provision of the same information to an Indigenous group – one would be called "business as usual" while the other would be called "repatriation" under this philosophy. Other terms can be found for the provision of other materials to communities, be it "restitution," "reparation," or simply "business as usual," as digitization of all collections and documents becomes increasingly popular. In my view, "repatriation" must be reserved for the return of the original material, not duplicates.

Repatriation also involves the return of ownership and authority over use. Providing communities with copies of information does *not* give that community full control over the original information, nor the authority to fully manage use and disposition of that material. Through return of the original material, true repatriation acknowledges the repatriation of authority over the future management of that material. Similarly, some museums have proposed the return of remains on the condition that the remains be made available to researchers. That is not repatriation, in my view: that is free, off-site storage.

Funding

The NMA has been heavily reliant upon extra government funding for the return of remains. The Federal government departments responsible for funding repatriation have changed frequently and have been transferred through several agencies, each with different governance practices over the past 12 years (to refer to them specifically would merely make this chapter more confusing through acronym saturation). Their staff have also changed frequently. For a large part of the period described in this chapter, the repatriation of remains returned from overseas collections was funded by different agencies to that responsible for funding the NMA's existing domestic collections of remains.

The NMA was thus under two separate agreements with two different departments, both with different reporting requirements and different terms and conditions. Often, when returning remains from both sources to a single group, the NMA was required to draw on two funding sources proportionate to the split in remains between domestic and international, with two sets of reporting required and both agencies not wanting information on repatriations that were not funded by their grants. For example, in the return of 80 individuals to one community, the remains were initially collected by one collector who split his collection, with 50 remaining in Australia and 30 going to Scotland. When these remains were eventually returned, the costings had to be split approximately 70 percent and 30 percent between the two buckets of money, and the reports to each agency could only report on the return of 50 and 30 remains respectively. The larger return of a total of 80 was untrackable, except through the NMA and the community's own records.

It was only in 2011, and after a lot of advocacy by the NMA, that a decision was made to merge international and domestic repatriation funding. Theoretically, this should reduce unnecessary reporting and paperwork. The disproportionate level of reporting compared to resourcing demanded by funding agencies has been a considerable problem. Indeed, the excessive amount of "red tape" involved in accessing one government agency's support funding for Indigenous activities in general, including repatriation, was identified in an Australian government report of 2007.

As noted earlier, it is relatively easy for the museum to return remains. It is not as easy for a community to receive them. Receipt and culturally appropriate management of remains can involve community meetings, travel, ceremonial costs, and burial costs, among other expenses. Government funding in the first three years facilitated the provision of community support which assisted such activities though it did not cover everything. In recent years, however, funding was not only reduced, but breaks between funding periods were introduced, during which no money could be spent or committed. Funding arrangements were typically short-term and did not cover the extended periods sometimes required to see a repatriation event from initiation through to its conclusion. In 2012 the process changed to allow a multiyear funding arrangement.

A typical condition of past funding was that no money be expended or committed for payment after the expiry of the funding period, in recent years typically a year or less. This made it impossible to commit to providing financial support to communities. It also made it impossible to engage suitable consultants, people with much more experience than NMA staff with some of the communities involved, as we could not guarantee payment for services beyond a certain period, typically a financial year. Due to these problems, the NMA also lost suitably experienced and highly specialized repatriation staff whose positions were supported by external funding. After long advocacy by participating Australian museums, the government has now introduced five-year funding cycles, which will make long-term financial commitments more feasible.

The NMA has also been contracted to store and care for remains returned from overseas. On occasions, following expiration of storage agreements, the external department responsible either failed to renew the contract in a timely manner or deliberately refused to continue to support storage, expecting the NMA to cover all costs (climate control, security, lighting, pest control, documentation management, and so on). In 2009, the Department of Finance and Deregulation carried out a Performance Audit of the International Repatriation Program (Australian Government 2009) and identified and discussed many of the issues pointed above. Little has changed.

Historical provenancing

The lack of historical research expertise in government repatriation departments is notable, particularly with regard to provenancing of remains returned from overseas. Where remains are well provenanced, they are usually returned directly to the relevant Indigenous community. Where provenance information is lacking, remains have been sent to the NMA for storage. But there is repeated evidence that many remains could be provenanced if extra research was done earlier, both at the originating institution and at home in Australia. Many of the remains returned to Australia only hold the information that was attached to them or was noted in the accession registers. Other documentation, hidden in older files or stored away from the remains, is rarely accessed or provided.

For example, in June 2011 the repatriation department of the Australian Government's Office for the Arts negotiated the return of a number of individuals from institutions in Austria. The majority of these remains had specific provenancing information, in particular identifying the place of collection. This allowed identification of suitable custodians and their direct return to communities (Australian Government 2011). However, several more remains were assigned as unprovenanced and delivered to the NMA for storage. Information accompanying these remains was minimal. They were simply identified as Northern Territory with the tribal names of "Pongka-pongka," "Mud-puck," "Bring-Can," "Ami," "Coar Gite," and "Marra Mungga." An examination of the most commonly used references to Australian tribes, the maps and documentation of Tindale (1974) and Horton (1994a; 1994b), identifies some of these names as alternatives for extant groups, all located in conjoined lands in the Daly River region of Australia's Northern Territory. Reference to other sources (for example, Stanner 1933) further identifies the likely affiliations of these remains. Thus the "Ponga Ponga" are the contemporary Malak Malak (Horton 1994a; 1994b, Aboriginal Land Commissioner 1982), the "Bring-Can" are Marringarr (Horton 1994a; 1994b, ATSIDA n.d.). "Ami" are Amiyengal/Amijangal (Tindale 1974, 220), the "Marra Mungga" are the Maranunggu (Horton 1994a; 1994b).

While "Mud-puck" and "Coar-Gite" cannot be identified at this stage, the circumstantial evidence of the cultural co-location of the other remains and a common collector suggest they too derive from the Daly River region. For example, "Coar-Gite" may be Wagait. It also helps that from 1985 to 1988 I was employed as an anthropologist with the Northern Land Council, an Aboriginal representative body, with specific responsibilities for the Daly River region. I thus already knew many of these groups and their alternative names. Thirty minutes of research using widely available documents would have facilitated the direct return of at least some of these "unprovenanced" remains. The department was notified at the time but took no further action. There are similar cases of this issue. In one currently under investigation, remains returned as "unprovenanced" have since been provenanced by an independent researcher following inquiries into readily available documentary records held by the original repatriating institution in the UK.

In another case, "unprovenanced Torres Strait Islander" remains were returned from the UK in 2011 and, at the request of Torres Strait Islander community leaders, deposited with the NMA. The supporting documentation was minimal, but did identify the naturalist, J. Beete Jukes, as the collector during the 1842–1846 voyage of the HMS *Fly*. A quick online search shows that HMS *Fly* visited a number of islands in the Torres Strait and Beete Jukes observed a number of burial sites and remains on ceremonial display. Yet his report specifically and comprehensively refers to the circumstances of acquisition of remains only from Mer and Waier Islands in the eastern Torres Straits (Beete Jukes 1847, 195–201). This significantly narrows down likely provenance to a select group of islands and a single Torres Strait Islander cultural group.

By contrast, in 2000 a number of remains were returned from the Anatomy Department of Edinburgh University. Prior to their return extensive documentary research was carried out in the university's archives, enabling the amassing of excellent provenance information for many of the remains. The information ranged from identifying named individuals, to identifying disparate anatomical parts to allow their reunification, to maps and documents detailing the exact location where the remains were excavated. This detailed research greatly facilitated the prompt, and largely issue-free, repatriation of these remains to relevant communities and, on occasion, descendant families.

Every time remains are moved, some information is lost. The remains become more and more distant, not only from the time and circumstances of their collection, but from the physical location of associated records. Retrospective recovery of information is difficult and, in the case of remains from overseas, expensive. It is critical that thorough research as to collection history and provenance be carried out on-site in the repatriating institution, otherwise returned remains will simply languish in museum stores. That said, the term "carrying out provenancing research" cannot be used as an excuse to delay the return of remains, as is often the case with overseas institutions. Once accurate provenance is determined, then remains can be returned – extra historical research can continue after the return of the actual remains themselves.

Scientific provenancing

There are a number of approaches to provenancing remains, ranging from examination of historical documentation, to biometric analysis, to DNA testing. No method is perfect, many are expensive, and some are simply socially dangerous.

As noted above, historical documentation is the best approach to determining the source location and affiliation of remains. The web of relationships between collectors, donors, time of collection, source of collection, and other historical documentation allows for a cross-referencing and correlation of sometimes disparate data. Experience has shown this historical method to be the most effective and accurate method of identifying geographic and cultural provenance, as well as generating histories that themselves can be significant contributions to knowledge.

Biometric analysis – the non-invasive, non-destructive analysis of remains based upon observation and measurement – is proving useful in narrowing down provenance. However, from the viewpoint of a museum repatriation officer, untrained in biological anthropology, it is still not a sufficiently reliable technique unless supported by corroborating historical documentation-based information. A number of concerns surround biometric analysis. Probably the most significant is that large databases for comparison of information are few and disparate, with many technically out of date. The major difficulty is that data is unconsolidated, with every researcher who investigates a collection of remains usually retaining the information within their own private database. Of course, there are ethical issues in the sharing of such information. Professional ethics would require that data be made available to other researchers, but moral, and sometimes contractual, obligations to potential custodians would require that the information not be distributed, indeed even not retained, without their approval. The lack of information relating to groups and their nearest neighbors means that some comparisons are linking groups with closest neighbors from a limited and worldwide sample. Thus remains from, say, somewhere in southern Australia, may be linked most closely to remains from Papua New Guinea, simply because the researcher has an inadequate sample for the groups in between. Another researcher, on the other hand, may have excellent information. The ethics of information dissemination or centralization (perhaps to a central Indigenous authority), is something that the biological anthropology community could do well to consider.

Another problem is that although biometric analysis gives a measure of probability, they are never 100 percent accurate. Even with an accuracy rate of 80 percent (high) that would mean that potentially one in five remains is wrongly provenanced. Consultations with some custodians have already shown a reticence to accept remains if there is any risk of including the remains of someone else's ancestors. Further, as noted under "historical provenancing," there are examples of presumed unprovenanced remains being subsequently provenanced through further documentary research. If remains returned to one group are subsequently found to be associated with another group, serious problems and distress will result.

Of course, the biggest scientific provenancing issues revolve around the use of DNA. As a base line, there is no argument that DNA testing can be used to provenance remains to living peoples and to link living peoples to remains. However, this superficially attractive technique brings with it the potential for serious social damage. The problem with DNA is that it provides a biological genealogy at the expense of the social genealogy. Social genealogies accommodate historical perceptions of parentage and origins as well as social processes such as adoption or succession. On several occasions, custodians have inquired about having DNA testing of remains so that affiliation can be identified for the purpose of inclusion or exclusion of community members in native title claims. Few people making such requests are aware that DNA testing requires not only the testing of the remains but also the widespread testing of community members, a highly invasive activity. Similarly, there is the possibility that the tested remains are from an immigrant guest rather than a long-term member of the historical land owning group. Conventional historical research in land claims and native title claims has been known to identify circumstances of birth or parentage that were unknown to the particular claimant and their community. Such discoveries may be historically and biologically accurate, but they can also be at odds with historical cultural processes, perceptions of one's own history and identity, and a community's belief in its own structures. DNA testing can aggravate this distress through extending biological differences back through a greater period of time than documentary records. Most Aboriginal and Torres Strait Islander societies have self-correcting social mechanisms and rules that prevent the perpetuation of knowledge of socially inappropriate marriages and parentage. Such "skeletons in the cupboard" are quickly lost in time and memory, returning balance to the community. DNA tells us what we are but not who we are. That is provided through examining cultural processes.

Destruction?

It is a common allegation from anti-repatriation advocates that repatriation of remains constitutes destruction of scientific knowledge. Yet provenancing research on collections of Aboriginal and Torres Strait Islander remains repeatedly reveals that the bulk of destruction of scientific information inherent in those remains occurred in the process of their collection and subsequent management.

A museum is the penultimate stage in a long sequence of "destructive" events, defined by the increasing separation of the remains from their original cultural and locational contexts. Indeed, it is odd that the *return* of remains to their cultural descendants and to their place of origin should be seen by anti-repatriation advocates as an act of final destruction, rather than a return to cultural context. Most museum collections of Aboriginal and Torres Strait Islander remains consist of skulls or selected elements chosen because of unusual pathologies (injuries, genetic defects, disease). Often initially intended for medical research, the original cultural context was seen as irrelevant. Thus, location, stratigraphic context, or the cultural attributes of the burial were ignored. Then, typically, only the elements of specific interest were removed, such as the skull or long bones, and then only particularly interesting examples, such as those with unusual pathologies. The majority of excavated remains also have no great antiquity – intact whole skulls, those of mature adults, were most commonly collected. More decayed and friable remains, such as those of greater antiquity or of children where sutures have not yet closed, were discarded. Collections of remains are thus extremely biased, in both age of remains, age of individuals, and pathology.

The same trail of "destruction" applies to remains acquired through other means, such as deaths through police or vigilante action, or in hospitals or asylums. The remains from these sources were sometimes preserved as complete articulated skeletons, and exposed to organic and inorganic contamination. The result is that the remains sitting on museum shelves are already highly compromised with regard to their scientific potential. Even the modern research advocated by anatomical researchers usually requires destructive acts through sampling, dating, or testing. It seems that destruction by science is acceptable, destruction by practicing culture is not.

There is, however, the capacity for the "constructive use" of those remains through the act of repatriation. The research into the provenance and history of remains followed by engagement with Indigenous custodians provides opportunities to understand contemporary Indigenous cultures and perspectives. It could be argued that more new knowledge has been generated through repatriation activities – ranging from issues in museology, to governance, to anthropology and contemporary cultural studies, than has been generated through restricted biological analysis of the remains. If destruction that creates new knowledge is acceptable, then repatriation wins easily.

There is also, of course, the oft-recited "someday they'll thank us" position (see Hirst 2006). This advocates that in generations to come Indigenous people will accuse museums of allowing destruction of important remains without scientific investigation. Therefore, we will be doing them a favor by researching remains, regardless of the opinions of contemporary Indigenous peoples. A self-fulfilling argument in my opinion.

The most common response from biologically oriented researchers is that remains in collections are all that are available to researchers, and their return is an irreplaceable loss to humankind. But remains from traditional burials are uncovered at least weekly in Australia; some are reported in the popular press, but most are simply referred to the relevant heritage agency for management in accordance with the prevailing legislation. It is now common practice to consult with local Aboriginal representatives when remains are discovered. On occasion, custodians have permitted some research of what are well provenanced remains with their archaeological contexts intact. Access to such remains for future research is, of course, not guaranteed, and will always require a close and respectful agreement between the Indigenous custodians and the researcher. Nevertheless, it is still a possibility that will become more frequent the more researchers engage with and empower custodians.

Proving affiliation to remains

A basic principle of repatriation is that some mechanism of affiliation to remains must be proven. In Australian practice, affiliation to *place* is a primary criterion. Most remains have been collected from burial sites and, where documentation allows, these sites can be identified geographically and linked to a local Indigenous representative body. Overseas institutions, on the other hand, seek to impose more complex constructs of "cultural" or "biological" affiliation, where a claimant group must demonstrate an unbroken cultural connection to the remains, through demonstrable historical residence and descent, or else prove a direct biological descent from the remains. At times, this is simply a misguided use of textbook anthropological principles. On other occasions, it is a clear strategy by which to impose conditions that few groups would ever meet to the satisfaction of a holding institution, thus preventing, or at least delaying, repatriation.

The problem with the "cultural and biological affiliation test" is that it ignores social processes. All groups, all cultures, change, sometimes move, and sometimes die out, to be replaced by another social group, and Aboriginal and Torres Strait Islander groups are no exception. While remains can often be associated to a geographic place – the place of their exhumation or collection – the contemporary local Indigenous community in that area may not, in the opinion of the holding institution, be able to demonstrate that they have either cultural or biological links to the remains.

This does not, however, disqualify them from being recognized as the appropriate and rightful custodians to receive and care for the remains. Indigenous traditions, worldwide, typically include formal and informal processes of succession to place and transmission of responsibility. These can include links and rights obtained through:

- patrilineal and/or matrilineal descent;
- adoption, conception, or birth;
- long-term residence;
- marriage;
- use of lands and resources;
- religious, ritual, and historical knowledge;

- burial of family members;
- care of sacred sites;
- territorial defense;
- migration.

As a general principle, the more criteria a person can satisfy, the stronger their claims to lands. Succession, whether by local residents or immigrant groups, is a legitimate, and legitimizing, process following established and acknowledged principles, conventions, or rules. Peer acknowledgment, the acceptance and support of territorial claims, is an essential component in legitimizing claims to land. There is therefore no act of succession without a complementary acknowledgment and legitimization of that succession by neighbors. In the past, this would constitute support by contiguous groups. Today it will typically also include support from local communities, Indigenous representative groups, and mainstream government.

The extent of the lands claimed by a contemporary claimant group may therefore differ to those claimed by that group's ancestors in the past, a result of processes of succession. Nonetheless, local Indigenous land interest groups will see themselves as having rights and responsibilities to the "ancestors" associated with those lands, regardless of whether directly related or not. Further, the knowledge of migration and succession may be lost over time and in the absence of a western, "record-keeping" culture, but people will believe they have always been the traditional owners of the country on which they live. That is in accord with tradition.

In rare cases, biological affiliation can be proven and will override place. These are, typically, named individuals who can be identified as having died while away from their country (that is to say, their ancestral homeland), due to imprisonment, institutionalization, or forced removal (Pickering 2010). In such cases, the remains can be returned to descendants based on biological affiliation. However, where descendants cannot be identified, the remains can again be returned to the modern community most closely associated with the cultural affiliation and geographic homeland of the individual.

Conclusion

Repatriation debates are shifting in focus as Australia turns to pursuing repatriation of Indigenous remains from overseas. Within Australia the discussions have settled down and museums regularly return remains as "business as usual." But as we turn our attention to international repatriation, issues and arguments are resurrected that were bypassed, or at least uncaptured in writings, in early Australian repatriation debates. Because so much repatriation governance and advocacy is now assigned to government agencies, bound by diplomatic confidences, many of the issues are still being concealed and unaddressed, and debate, which could identify and resolve them, is at best ignored and, at worst, avoided. Further, resourcing and governance processes, at the government level, that should have been refined, have remained or have become unnecessarily complex. It is time for greater transparency and discussion as to what has and has not worked in order to inform debate and practice.

The repatriation of Indigenous human remains has paid its way, both through supporting social well-being in affected communities and through disciplinary and professional demands for the production of new knowledge. We understand contemporary Indigenous peoples and cultures just that little bit better and, hopefully, the engagements and benefits are reciprocal. Despite fears, the repatriation of remains has not "opened the flood gates" to collections. Museums do not have to fear that a generous act will expose them to abuse. Indeed, my own experiences with repatriation have helped me develop professionally, forcing me to address questions relevant to my professional practice in museum activities outside repatriation, such as ethics in collection or exhibition development.

Nonetheless, museums can expect increasing requests for the repatriation of both sacred and secular objects. This is not necessarily a direct consequence of the repatriation of human remains; rather it is an unavoidable consequence of Indigenous groups asserting their individual and/or national identities. It was, and is, inevitable. Current repatriation activities will be critical in informing discussions of future, object-focused repatriation, making it all the more important that issues be identified and addressed with a spirit of transparency and cooperation as soon as possible.

Notes

1   This chapter has benefited greatly from comments by David Kaus (Senior Curator NMA), Stephanie Bull (Manager, International Relations Policy and Strategic Risk, NMA), and the editor Conal McCarthy (Programme Director, Victoria University of Wellington).
2   The use of the singular term "Indigenous" in this chapter refers to Australian Aboriginal and Torres Strait Islander peoples. It is an Australian convention that upper case is used in this context.
3   Rather than provide voluminous references might we refer the reader to the Australian Institute of Aboriginal and Torres Strait Islander Studies library at http://www.aiatsis. gov.au/collections/muraread.html. Search under "Repatriation" for an excellent annotated sample of repatriation articles and books. Accessed November 4, 2014.
4   National Museum of Australia in Canberra, Museum Victoria in Melbourne, South Australian Museum in Adelaide, Western Australian Museum in Perth, Northern Territory Museum and Art Gallery in Darwin, Queensland Museum in Brisbane, Australian Museum in Sydney, Tasmanian Museum and Gallery in Hobart.
5   National Museum of Australia. Repatriation. Accessed November 4, 2014. http://www.nma.gov.au/collections/repatriation.

References

Aboriginal Land Commissioner. 1982. *Daly River Malak Malak Land Claim. Report by the Aboriginal Land Commissioner, Mr Justice Toohey, to the Minister for Aboriginal Affairs and to the Administrator of the Northern Territory.* Canberra: Australian Government Publishing Service.

Atkinson, Henry. 2010. "The Meanings and Values of Repatriation." In *The Long Way Home: The Meaning and Values of Repatriation*, edited by Paul Turnbull and Michael Pickering, 15–19. Oxford: Berghahn.

ATSIDA (Aboriginal and Torres Strait Islander Data Archive). n.d. Home page. Sydney: University of Technology. Accessed November 4, 2014. http://www.atsida.edu.au/archive/language-groups/marringarr.

Australian Government. 1984. *Aboriginal and Torres Strait Islander Heritage Protection Act.* Accessed November 7, 2014. http://www.comlaw.gov.au/Details/C2010C00807.

Australian Government. 2000. Department of Families, Housing and Community Services and Indigenous Affairs. "Background Notes: International Repatriation Appendix B – Joint Statement with Tony Blair on Aboriginal Remains." Accessed November 7, 2014. http://pmtranscripts.dpmc.gov.au/browse.php?did=11611.

Australian Government. 2007. Department of Families, Housing, Community Services and Indigenous Affairs. "Evaluation of Indigenous Coordination Centres: Final Report July." Accessed November 7, 2014. https://www.dss.gov.au/sites/default/files/documents/06_2012/icc_review_report_0.pdf.

Australian Government. 2009. Department of Finance and Deregulation: Office of Evaluation and Audit (Indigenous Programs). "Performance Audit of the International Repatriation Program." December 2009. Accessed November 7, 2014. http://www.docin.com/p-378581524.html.

Australian Government. 2011. "Indigenous Repatriation." August 2011. Accessed November 4, 2014. http://www.arts.gov.au/indigenous/repatriation.

Beete Jukes, J. 1847. *Narrative of the Surveying Voyage of H.M.S. Fly.* London: T. & W. Boone. Accessed November 4, 2014. http://www.archive.org/stream/narrativesurvey00blacgoog#page/n8/mode/2up.

Cubillo, Franchesca. 2010. "Repatriating Our Ancestors: Who Will Speak for the Dead?" In *The Long Way Home: The Meaning and Values of Repatriation*, edited by Paul Turnbull and Michael Pickering, 20–26. Oxford: Berghahn.

Faulkhead, Shannon, and James Roger Berg. 2010. *Power and the Passion: Our Ancestors Return Home.* Melbourne: Koori Heritage Trust Incorporated.

Fforde, Cressida. 2004. *Collecting the Dead: Archaeology and the Reburial Issue.* London: Duckworth.

Hemming, Steve, and Chris Wilson. 2010. "The First 'Stolen Generations': Repatriation and Reburial in Ngarrindjeri Ruwe (Country)." In *The Long Way Home: The Meaning and Values of Repatriation*, edited by Paul Turnbull and Michael Pickering, 183–198. Oxford: Berghahn.

Hirst, John. 2006. "New Approach to Old Remains." *The Australian*. January 2. A slightly revised version of this article was reprinted In *Ozhistorybytes*, National Centre for History Education, May 24, 2007. Accessed November 4, 2014. http://www.hyper history.org/index.php?option=displaypage&Itemid=763&op=page&printpage=Y.

Horton, David. 1994a. *The Encyclopaedia of Aboriginal Australia*. Canberra: Aboriginal Studies Press for Australian Institute of Aboriginal and Torres Strait Islander Studies.

Horton, David. 1994b. *Map of Aboriginal Australia*. Canberra: Australian Institute of Aboriginal and Torres Strait Islander Studies.

Morgan, J. 2010. "Expert Has a Bone to Pick with Auction House." *Sydney Morning Herald*, August 5. Accessed November 4, 2014. http://www.smh.com.au/nsw/expert-has-a-bone-to-pick-with-auction-house-as-skull-sale-called-off-20100804-11foc.html.

Museums Australia. 1993, 2000. "Previous Possessions, New Obligations: Policies for Museums in Australia and Aboriginal and Torres Strait Islander Peoples." Canberra: Museums Australia.

Museums Australia. 2005. "Continuous Cultures, Ongoing Responsibilities: Principles and Guidelines for Australian Museums Working with Aboriginal and Torres Strait Islander Cultural Heritage." Canberra: Museums Australia. Accessed November 4, 2014. http://www.museumsaustralia.org.au/userfiles/file/Policies/ccor_final_feb_05.pdf.

National Museum of Australia. 2011. "Aboriginal and Torres Strait Islander Human Remains Policy." Accessed November 4, 2014. http://www.nma.gov.au/about_us/ips/policies.

Pickering, Michael. 2010. "Where Are the Stories?" *The Public Historian* 32(1): 79–95.

Pickering, Michael. 2011. "Dance through the Minefield: The Development of Practical Ethics for Repatriation." In *The Routledge Companion to Museum Ethics: Redefining Ethics for the Twenty First Century Museum*, edited by Janet Marstine, 256–274. Oxford: Routledge.

Stanner, W. E. H. 1933. "The Daly River Tribes: A Report of Field Work in North Australia." *Oceania* 3(4): 377–405; 4(1): [10]–29.

Tasmanian Government. 1984. *Museums (Aboriginal Remains Act) 1984*. Accessed November 4, 2014. http://www.thelaw.tas.gov.au/tocview/content.w3p;doc_id=75++1984+AT @EN+20120323000000;rec=0.

Tindale, N. B. 1974. *Aboriginal Tribes of Australia: Their Terrain, Environmental Controls, Distribution, Limits, and Proper Names*. Berkeley, CA: University of California Press.

Turnbull, Paul. 1997. "Ancestors, Not Specimens: Reflections on the Controversy over the Remains of Aboriginal People in European Scientific Collections." *Electronic Journal of Australian and New Zealand History*. Accessed November 4, 2014. http://www.jcu.edu.au/aff/history/articles/turnbull.htm.

Turnbull, Paul. 2002. "Indigenous Australian People, Their Defence of the Dead and Native Title." In *The Dead and Their Possessions: Repatriation in Principle, Policy and Practice*, edited by Cressida Fforde, Jane Hubert, and Paul Turnbull, 63–86. London: Routledge.

Turnbull, Paul, and Michael Pickering, eds. 2010. *The Long Way Home: The Meaning and Values of Repatriation*. Oxford: Berghahn.

Michael Pickering is a Senior Curatorial Fellow with the National Museum of Australia in Canberra, and an Adjunct Associate Professor with the National Centre for Indigenous Studies, Australian National University. He is a member of the Australian Institute of Aboriginal and Torres Strait Islander Studies (AIATSIS) and is on the editorial boards of the journals *ReCollections, Museum Management and Curatorship,* and *Museums and Social Issues*. Pickering has a wide range of research interests and has published on topics including political cartoons, material culture, cannibalism, settlement patterns, exhibition, ethics, and repatriation. He recently coedited the collection *The Long Way Home: The Meaning and Values of Repatriation* (2010).

PART IV

Publics

21

THE "ACTIVE MUSEUM"
How Concern with Community Transformed the Museum

Elizabeth Crooke

A recent study of the connection between museums and communities in the United Kingdom concluded that, despite innovative practice in this area, community partners often feel that their role is one of "supplicant" rather than the more desired "active agent" (Lynch 2011b, 22). The research gathered experiences of museum staff and community partners in projects celebrated for their commitment to public engagement. The findings will disappoint those striving for a more engaged and responsive museum. Nevertheless, this study and the projects it reviews indicate the continued relevance and value of the association between museums and community and the constant need to reflect upon the nature and impact of connections, hierarchies, and working practices.

The sustained interest in the concept of community has had a major impact on museum practice. The 1992 collection of essays *Museums and Communities* (Karp, Lavine, and Kreamer 1992) debated the very political nature of museums. Seen as places that represented cultures, museums were encouraged to challenge established assumptions about museum practice, such as relationships with their audiences, the ownership of collections, and the authority to tell stories. The examples of practice described in that volume showed the ways in which community could be used as a means to introduce diversity into the museum and encourage museum staff to think beyond the confines of the building, existing collections, and established narratives. In using this approach, the notion of community provides an opportunity to uncover different stories about collections, enables new forms of engagement, and encourages the development of collaborative working practices that are more representative of the multitude of stories and experiences beyond the museum walls.

The exploration of community and museums has been a concern of museums across the globe – the practice, meanings, and consequences differing with context

The International Handbooks of Museum Studies: Museum Practice, First Edition.
Edited by Conal McCarthy.
© 2015 John Wiley & Sons Ltd. Published 2020 by John Wiley & Sons Ltd.

and the nature of engagement (Bennett 1995; Witcomb 2003; Crooke 2007; Golding and Modest 2013). The study of community is particularly useful because it crosses so many different aspects of current practice and means of connecting museums with people. In this chapter I shall reflect upon the phenomenon by first placing it within a threefold framework: the idea of museums as a symbol of community; the connections between museums and community policy; and the use of museums for community action. This framework emerges from the diversity of approaches to community and community practice, reminding us that community is understood in a myriad of ways and, although the word may be the same, the intention will differ with context. The framework then forms the basis of a review of significant movements that have informed museum practice in relation to community, namely new museology and the idea of the ecomuseum. I shall then consider the debate concerning museums as an "instrument" of social policy and, reflecting current concerns, the rise of new museum ethics. The latter has indicated a shift from ethics in connection with collecting practices and governance to a more all-encompassing range of ideas such as equality, diversity, and rights. This, I argue, demonstrates the continuing importance of framing museums according to their relationship with and impact on community. The call now is for the creation of what can be referred to as the "active museum." Rather than only being an institution that provides comment at a safe distance, to be meaningful a museum must actively co-produce with its community, effect change, and forge dynamic connections. It is this active museum that is the antithesis of the disconnected museum of old.

Community and museum studies

Community is often identified according to characteristics or attachments such as ethnicity, faith, abilities, language spoken, or particular interests (Delanty 2003). It may be constructed symbolically (Cohen 1985) or formed on the basis of a range of lived experiences (Amit 2002). Rarely passive, when called to action community is reactionary (Butcher et al. 1993), taking on a social or political purpose. There is also a strong case for a term like "community" to be reconceptualized with shifts in time and lived experiences of different groups, such as the experiences of young people, rising to a multitude of "vocabularies of community" (Yerbury 2011). The analysis shared in the pages of journals such as *Community Development Journal* or *Journal of Community Practice* reveals the complexity and diversity of community-based public policy, urban and rural development (drawing upon the appeal of community), and community as means of grassroots action. The language of community is now familiar within government and it is usual for policy emerging from central government departments to refer to cohesive, sustainable, or integrated communities that enhance learning, health, security, and social services (Sommerville 2011; see also Selwood and Davies in this volume). Furthermore, community can be the focus of specific forms of grassroots political action and is associated with campaigning in areas such as social justice or advocacy (Craig and Mayo 1995).

In terms of the history of museums in Western Europe, scholars argue that they had a hierarchical relationship with their communities. Museums are described as an "ideological force," which have the ability, as observed by Carol Duncan, to preserve "the community's official public memory" (Duncan 1995, 8). The national museums and galleries of the late nineteenth and early twentieth centuries were founded during the rise of nation-states and nationalism across Europe, and were to be united by a national history and awareness of national achievements and characteristics (Anderson 1991; Crooke 2000). Hooper-Greenhill describes the creation of this master narrative at the National Portrait Gallery in London as a means to "picture the nation" in a way that would "legitimate its character and to construct its past" (Hooper-Greenhill 2000, 28). In the museum rhetoric of the Victorian age there is reference to communities, but in this situation museums were a place apart that officiated over their audiences. The community in this practice was passive – it was a people that the museum spoke to, provided the expertise on, and did things to. This passivity was essential to the political project of the time, as noted by Duncan, "to control a museum means precisely to control the representation of a community" (1995, 8). Museums were one mechanism by which such control could be achieved, places of expertise and authority, in which the histories told were untouchable – objects were behind glass and the narratives unassailable. In recent decades, not surprisingly, scholars who have reflected on the foundation of public museums in the nineteenth century, and the practices that sustained museums in the twentieth century, have mounted a critical analysis of the controlling nature of these institutions (Lumley 1988; Karp and Lavine 1991; Bennett 1995).

Within museum studies today, community is conceptualized in diverse ways, and a range of practices have been documented (Watson 2007). Engaging with the question of community has inspired deeper thinking about museums as a means to construct local and national identities (Knell et al. 2010). Museums have been encouraged to collaborate with their "source communities" to create more meaningful experiences within museums (Peers and Brown 2003). By considering the museums and communities connection, in relation to identity, audiences, authority, and collecting, the deeply political nature of what is practiced within museums has been exposed (Karp, Lavine, and Kreamer 1992; Knell, MacLeod, and Watson 2007; Watson 2007). So, too, engagement with the issues of audiences, representation, and interpretation, contributes to a better understanding of the museum–community relationship (Corsane 2005; Kelly 2006; Lang, Reeve, and Woollard 2006). The framework proposed in this chapter develops these issues further by considering them within three perspectives, which encourage deeper understanding of the diversity of the museum-community connection (Crooke 2006; Crooke 2007). First: how museums are a means of symbolizing community, achieved by what is represented in museums through buildings, collections, exhibitions, and programs. Second: the association between museums and community in public life reflected in the ways in which government-led public policy has impacted on the work and funding of the museum sector. Third: how grassroots museums, whose origins lay with political or social movements, make a significant contribution to community action and challenge the status quo.

Museums symbolizing communities

Studies of heritage in Europe have established that museums make a significant contribution to creating a powerful image of a place and people. National museums provide a window on the place they are located – they are the means by which we make ourselves and then put that on view (Kaplan 1994). In such cases, museums and their collections are construed as tangible evidence of the "imagined community" (Anderson 1991; Crooke 2000; Knell et al. 2010). The values placed upon collections was recently emphasized by a British MP who described museums as places that "help create a sense of history and a sense of community," which is achieved by "preserving our culture … by being a visible sign of civic pride and social values … planted squarely in the heart of the community."[1] This description is the typical, fairly uncomplicated, view of museums as places that symbolize communities, have a connection with local people, and serve an important purpose. The statement sees museums as creating community; by inclusion in museum collections, exhibitions, projects, and workforce, people and their stories are brought together and represented. These are what Mason refers to as the "interpretive communities," which are defined by shared cultural or historical experiences, specialist knowledge, demography, or identity (Mason 2005).

This is not a benign process, as a museum will always embody the cultural, social, and political aspirations of those at the heart of its creation. That is the case whether it is a museum of the nation, a city museum, or a much smaller concern of local or regional significance. A museum forges and communicates a sense of belonging – it tells you who fits into the narrative it shares. Equally, by omission, a museum symbolizes those who do *not* belong. The exclusion of people and their histories from the museum narrative can have an equally significant impact. Even if included, it is the nature of that inclusion that can be telling of the priorities, functions, and desires of the museum and its governance.

For instance, it was an objection to how modern Australian history was interpreted, particularly the arrival of Europeans, that fueled the "history wars" associated with the National Museum of Australia in Canberra in the early 2000s. Accused of being too left-wing, the exhibitions were seen as potentially divisive by a review panel, believing it could stimulate conflict and cause disunity (Dean and Rider 2005). The director, however, was quite unapologetic for the museum's refusal to provide a master narrative – one she considered would be authoritative and deny the complexity of history (Casey 2001; McIntyre 2006). This controversy was a dispute about how history should be told; it was one that challenged community histories in museums, questioning whose stories were shared and from what perspective. It was also a debate about historiography and diverging perceptions of the method, interpretation, and presentation of history in a public space. The result was a deeply contested engagement with how a museum represents communities and their experiences.

Because of the growing awareness of the authority of museum representation, it seems to me that those working in the established sector are increasingly self-reflective. Contemporary curators are ever more prepared to challenge the foundational purposes of museums, to make known the limitations of their collections, contest traditional work practices, and find a means to experiment with new forms of engagement (Dodd and Sandell 2001; Kreps 2003; Chandler 2009; Heumann Gurian 2010). In the mid-2000s the Victoria and Albert Museum in London worked with local South Asian and Chinese communities to uncover hidden histories within the museum collections. By revealing these stories staff hoped to increase the diversity of audiences coming to the museum and create partnerships that would increase "heritage skills" among people of black, Asian, and minority ethnic communities (Nightingale 2006; 2009a; 2009b). By prioritizing a particular community, and shaping its initiatives to become a more engaging space for a group of people who did not usually visit the museum, the project had a positive outcome for the more established visitor (see Nightingale in this volume). The visitors who already feel at ease within the museum space, who are familiar with the collections and feel they have a connection with them, should also benefit from viewing new exhibitions and projects. This is the aspiration for every curator attempting to create the inclusive museum.

Museums and community policy

Internationally the relationship between culture and social policy has been a key issue, particularly the argument that engagement with arts and culture improves the welfare of individuals and communities (Sandell 2003; Jenson 2002). In the United Kingdom during the New Labour era (1997–2010) concern with social issues impacted on all areas of governance (see Selwood and Davies in this volume). As a result the UK had a decade of community-focused social policy influencing the cultural sector, which concentrated efforts of those in museums, archives, and libraries to respond to government policy. In key areas such as social cohesion, security, health, and public participation, museum managers were invited to demonstrate measurable results against such indicators (Levitt 2008, 223). This was reflected by Chris Smith, Secretary of State for Culture, Media, and Sport during the early years of New Labour (1997–2001), who presented museums as "agents of social change in the community" (DCMS 2000). Numerous reports and studies emerged from the sector that explored the potential of such links, such as: *New Directions in Social Policy* (MLAC 2004a; see also 2004b); *Bringing Communities*

Together through Sport and Culture (DCMS 2004a); and *Culture at the Heart of Regeneration* (DCMS 2004b). This literature and debate forged what Tlili, Gewirtz, and Cribb refer to the "community pedagogy" that used museums to "bring community members to consciousness about their community; to help the community become a community-for-itself" (2007, 275). With such policy direction museums were being asked to demonstrate their relevance to society through community projects, and so the sector responded (GLLAM 2000). Not to do so would risk giving the impression that museums were elitist, not promoting access, and disinterested in the life experiences and needs of their potential visitors. Alongside this, consultancy groups and academics contributed to the fervor for social inclusion by measuring and evaluating the success of such projects (Economou 2004; Wavell et al. 2002). By the end of the decade a cycle of policy, examples of practice, and evaluation of projects had had a radical impact on museum activity (Sandell and Nightingale 2012; Sandell 2007).

Beyond the United Kingdom, we can look to other places where community was an active strategy of government – in each case the exact character of that connection is based upon the legacy of previous policies, local experiences, and histories. In Australia the importance of arts, culture, and heritage has been explored in the context of social value and museums regarded as a means to enhance the welfare of communities (Scott 2006; see also Scott Chapter 5 in this volume). Here it was directly linked to social development goals, such as, "reducing exclusion, improving individual self-esteem, providing opportunities for life-long learning and contributing to community health" (Scott 2006, 48). Similar aspirations were voiced on the opening in 2012 of Te Takere, the Horowhenua Culture and Community Centre in Levin, New Zealand.[2] Described as a community "heart and hub," it is planned that the center should provide facilities for local community groups, families, and businesses. Resources include a library, exhibitions, and a family history resource center. The goals are "sustainable communities," "lifelong learning experiences," and encouraging "satisfying and healthy lifestyles." Local, family, and Māori histories will be "collected, created, conserved [and] digitised" with the hope of celebrating local achievements and promoting community pride and respect.[3]

The initiatives above, demonstrating the manner in which museums create social change among communities, have ascribed an expanded role for these institutions. It is not just a case of museums representing or symbolizing a community; now it is museums forging community identity, altering community experiences, and improving community life. This broader and more active approach has arguably brought a greater diversity of thinking into museum practice. It is no longer just innovative curators thinking about the value and importance of museums to their local communities, or community members who had connections with the collections. Now, it is those in local or national government, with a stake in community issues, who are recognizing the potential of museums. Although there are precedents for this practice, what has been quite new since the 2000s is the globalization of this approach among museums in industrialized Western countries.[4]

Museums and community action

A further perspective on the connection between museums and community relates to community action. In this section I focus on social transformation and social justice, more traditionally a concern of community movements such as civil rights campaigns. These tend to emerge from grassroots community organizations with an activist role that frequently challenges local and national government. There are a number of examples of such initiatives, some of which have resulted in the formation of new museums, such as the District Six Museum in Cape Town, South Africa (Rassool 2006), and others that have shaped programming in established museums, such as the campaigns for social justice promoted by contemporary museum professionals (Fleming 2010). Although these initiatives may have some aspects in common, use similar language, and in some cases appear to be heading in a similar direction, there are fundamental differences that mark them apart. The principle variance lies with the origins of the social or political engagement. It is worth distinguishing between social justice campaigns that include a museum as one of its tools and the established museums that, shifting with the times, are beginning to engage with social justice issues. The origin of the former is entirely grassroots; the source of the latter reflects an established museum becoming politically engaged. These different origins may well shape the character of the eventual projects, their impact, and their legacy.

Arguably, grassroots action is the most significant form of "community action." Generated by a campaign for social or political transformation, museums and heritage are used as a means to achieve change. In such instances the museum initiative is a *tool* for the campaign, rather than the principal objective. An example is the District Six Museum in Cape Town, which grew out of a land restitution campaign (Rassool 2006; 2010). Another is the Museum of Free Derry, which was the result of the work of the Bloody Sunday Trust and its truth campaign concerning an event during the Troubles in Northern Ireland (Crooke 2012). In both cases, the existence of the museum is entirely a result of the political campaign; it is one of a number of means to achieve the objectives of the community movement, a way to communicate these objectives and effect change. What makes these examples so significant is that they demonstrate, more clearly than any other, a belief in a museum's potential to influence, to have impact, and be a stimulus for action. Those outside museums, with deeply felt concerns in areas of social and political transformation, recognize the influence of museums. By creating their museum, the individuals are harnessing the authority associated with museums and using it for their particular purpose. The histories and objects held within the museum are embedded in that process. The examples that include a museum building are a reminder of the importance of a built presence, which may well have an iconic significance for the local community (Crooke 2012).

Museums resulting from community movements provide an alternative space. They are different to established means of political campaigning and a substitute for other forms of history making in authorized heritage sites. The museum building, exhibitions, and artifacts provide a tangible presence for political activism. The museum, its collections, and stories provide a venue and focus for meetings, validate arguments, and impress a message on visitors. In the cases of the two examples cited, this communication is with an increasingly international audience. In both Derry and Cape Town, the Museum of Free Derry and the District Six Museum challenge the established museums, funded either by the state or local authority. The community museum sets itself apart from other museums in providing a new narrative on the past. A further dimension to these museum initiatives is that they are not created or led by staff trained in the conventions of museum curatorship. The people working there rarely come into the position equipped with the professional heritage networks and cultural capital that go with training and a career in the museum sector. Rather, in the earliest stages of the initiatives, the practices of collecting, display, and interpretation are directed by activists, who learn museum skills "on the job," and gradually accumulate professional networks and standards of practice (Crooke 2005).

These three areas of museum-community connections provide a strong framework by which to evaluate the many ways that community can be understood and investigated in relation to museums. This structure can also be used to uncover the fundamental guiding principles of museums – the attitudes of museum curators, managers, and other staff to the people they represent, the histories they tell, the objects they collect, and the experience they attempt to provide. This analytical framework is also a means to reveal how others look upon museums. What does government think the role of museums is? How do community members – and community activists – look upon a museum, whether it is already established or one they wish to create? Investigating the complexity and diversity of the links between community and museums enables us to ask further questions about the essential nature of the histories, objects, places, and people represented within and by museums.

Community and agency within the museum

The three areas discussed above – museums symbolizing community, as a means to community policy, and as an opportunity for community action – though easy to tease out, are interlinked because they each draw upon the same essential feature of museums: the ability to communicate ideas and influence thinking. These three ways of framing the museum-community connection reflect the *agency* of the museum. The very fact that museums are valued as places that can represent and influence communities, as important to public life and as providing opportunity for community action, suggests they are places of relevance and impact. The recognition of museums as places of significance has long been evident in the writing and thinking about museums. But, compared to the history of museums discussed above, what has changed in recent times is the deeper exploration of that significance investigated through the networks between museums and their audiences and how those are created, structured, and carried out.

The critique of museums in the 1970s led to questions about how museums interact with their communities, triggered challenges to established methods, and demanded re-evaluation of the role of museums and museum practice. Davis describes this critique of museums as the early days of community museology (2008) that focused attention on the relationship with community, linked museums with community development, and encouraged a more democratic approach to museums. He describes a time of social unrest and political activism when society was undertaking a re-evaluation of its goals, which subsequently led those in museums to question their role in society. The goal was a museum more integrated with society that demonstrated greater engagement with communities and more account of the needs and expertise of the public (Davis 2008).

The community-focused museology of that period underpinned both the ecomuseum model and "new museology," and led to a radical change in how people thought about museums (Stam 1993). The ecomuseum ideal takes the community as its starting point, using heritage, territory, a sense of place and identity, as means to communicate across a landscape. Essential among ecomuseum indicators is management of the museum by community members so that the project brings benefit to the local community (Corsane et al. 2007). An important element of new museology is the consideration of the politics of the museum as an inquiry about cultural production. It is concerned with cultural authority, and whether that is negotiable, and draws upon debates in feminism, colonial studies, sociology, and cultural studies to propose a radical change in museum practice (Vergo 1989; Stam 1993; Macdonald and Fyfe 1996). Although there are differences between the origins, scope, and purpose of ecomuseology and new museology, they share a desire for increased democratization of museums and the aspiration to effect change via museums.

The aim to democratize museums, which sought to overturn the old paradigm of social exclusion and prestige, led to new approaches that were more inclusive, autonomous, and egalitarian (Sandell 2002). Back in 1999, the UK museum director David Fleming urged museums to "share their power with communities," encouraging a two-way process that transfers energy and authority between museums and community groups (Fleming 1999, 16). The change advocated by Fleming and others was not as radical as it may sound. Prior to this period, there are many examples of museums with well-established, meaningful relationships with their audiences. These museums engaged with local people in an effective way, encouraging them to shape collections, exhibitions, and programming. Nina Simon, for instance, gives the example of Oakland Museum California that she describes as a "radically democratic" institution since its formation as a community-focused museum in the 1960s (Simon 2010, 237, 276). What Fleming and others were encouraging was a wider uptake of this approach, so that it would become a typical working practice.

The adoption of this new way of thinking is perhaps most clearly demonstrated by the way in which anthropology and ethnography museums now work with source communities: those people from whom museum collections originate (Peers and Brown 2003). Peers and Brown describe an important change in relations of authority after decolonization. Source community members are now recognized as knowledgeable about their heritage, and in some cases demand co-management of it. The growing awareness of the museum as a constructive space not just for colonized peoples but all communities – one that has potential to be innovative and creative – has inspired much of the new thinking about how museums and communities should work together.

For some this has been underpinned by the writings of Clifford and his notion of the contact zone, a place of dialogue and exchange, where different cultures could interact (Clifford 1997, 188–219). The idea has been picked up in museum theory to emphasize "the interactive nature of the relationships between various communities, stakeholders and museums" (Mason 2006, 25). However, the application of Clifford's work has led to debate about the persistence of the museum's powerful position (Boast 2011) and the connection between community and government (Witcomb 2003; Dibley 2005). Yet Witcomb considers the strength of Clifford's contribution as the recognition of different experiences of culture and history associated with the diversity of community (Witcomb 2003, 88–91). Although Clifford recognizes the unequal relations among participatory communities, within his model the museum is also *part* of that community, with particular modes of practice and traditions, such as the "exchanges … push and pull" that attempts to negotiate and accumulate meanings (Clifford qtd. in Witcomb 2003, 89). Clifford's method has had a major influence on museum practice, inspiring greater inclusion of community stakeholders. Robin Boast, reflecting on this impact, gives examples of prominent museums whose new exhibition projects now incorporated community consultation, collaboration, and partnerships that in turn stimulated innovative collecting projects, as well as improving access to and research on collections. For some, this was regarded as a shift from the museum as collecting institution to that of "educational instrument," the purpose of which, as Boast describes it, is "the transformation of social practices through the transformation of the museum" (2011, 58).

Museums, community, and evolving practices

Just when museums were beginning to be recognized for their democratic and transformative potential, the social policy agenda in government, with its focus on community, gained a high profile. The policy initiatives referred to earlier in this chapter provided the funding, public support, and context for community projects within arts, museums, and heritage sectors. By the 2000s community-focused social projects based within museums, but funded via this broader political agenda, were commonplace. Reflecting on the UK context, Belfiore describes the period of "enthusiasm" during which "the government seemed, for the first time, to take arts and the cultural sectors seriously" (Belfiore 2012, 104). Museums had an unprecedented period of funding available for projects which focused on communities of need, whether that was in areas of high deprivation or those who, either because of youth, gender, disability, or ethnicity, had suffered exclusion. Many innovative examples of practice emerged, such as those listed in the report *Museums and Galleries: Creative Engagement* (NMDC 2004). They range from museum partnerships in local regeneration projects to programs for young people experiencing social exclusion (NMDC 2004).

There was, on occasion, a downside. Museum curators unfamiliar with the requirements of community practice, and associated theories and skills, had to find a means of developing projects of relevance. Some did not regard such projects as relevant to the museum profession, viewing it as more akin to social work. This debate, though well-trodden, persists. Reflecting on this period in the UK, Belfiore asks "whether the price for relevance, a higher profile and better levels of funding might in fact have been too high" (2012, 104). In the complex arena of cultural "instrumentalism" – the use of culture as a "means or instrument to attain goals in areas other than cultural" (Vestheim qtd. in Gray 2008, 210) – the work of museums and the arts became "attached" to activities of other sectors. In order to maintain funding, such policy attachment provides evidence of the positive impact of museums (Macnaught 2005) as well as added political credibility. Reactions to the role of museums in the social policy agenda were divided. On this point, Gray speculated:

> At the very least this indicates the rather obvious point that cultural services are seen as having an impact across more than their own sectorial concerns. At the worst it could mean that these exogenous effects are the only ones that are seen as being of importance in assessing organizational effectiveness in the museums and galleries sector. (Gray 2008, 210)

Belfiore and Bennett have argued that involving cultural practice with social policy has "come at a cost" (2007, 137). The situation they observe is one of assumptions, within government, of what arts and culture comprise, with no shared understanding and no sense of what should be measured or evaluated (on this point see Scott in this volume). Additionally, people's experiences of the arts were overgeneralized with a simplified expectation that arts "can transform lives and communities" (Belfiore and Bennett 2007, 137). For others there were tensions regarding the relationship between government, museums, and their communities, and how this period impacted on understanding the purposes of museums.

Tlili, Gewirtz, and Cribb describe this as a period when the priorities in museums shifted away from collections and toward "bringing about broad social policy objectives on the back of the museum's cultural remit" (2007, 281). This they interpret as government politicking that rolled back the state and redistributed tasks among other organizations and community groups. They recommend that those in museums should "avoid being carried away by the ethical glamour of social inclusion" and "take a critical distance from government agendas" (Tlili, Gewirtz, and Cribb 2007, 284).

Adding to the complexity of this debate, there are those who present instrumentalism in cultural policy as "nothing remotely new." In the mid-nineteenth century the development of museums in England was seen as a "healthy alternative" associated with education and industry (Hill 2005, 10–11). Is it reasonable to accuse the sector today of attaching itself to irrelevant policy by adopting a more democratic approach? The community and outreach programs, often linked to social initiatives, are now well established as core museum activities. West and Smith, both curators, responded with the point "museums are being asked to address the needs of the communities they serve, not to sacrifice their collections" (2005, 281). Their view is that museums are reasonably asked to focus on "needs" by way of a service to community. It is a matter of appreciating social, cultural, and economic prerequisites to engagement with museums. For many professionals this is not initiated by social policy change and advances in thinking about museums; rather it is an ethical imperative that should inform every aspect of museum practice.

Rethinking museum purposes in past decades has not only been driven by social policy agendas; it has also been stimulated by the changes in how we study objects and histories. Cultural theory has asked us to consider how meanings are made, how cultures are interpreted and represented, and the power embodied in cultural practice (Mason 2006). This is also part of how we have changed the way we think about, and practice in, museums. The debate concerning museums and social policy demonstrates that those working within the sector also drive interest in the museum-community connection. This approach, at least in its infancy, can be discussed in the context of shifting ideas about the purposes of museums and how they engage with audiences (see Black in this volume). Now, with increasing emphasis on evaluating the connection between museums and audiences, the nature of that relationship can be further explored, and established social hegemonies challenged. Within the museum sector, institutions have been confronted for what they have failed to do, whether it is collections, exhibitions, museum governance, or other areas that do not reflect the diversity of peoples, perspectives, and experiences (see Nightingale in this volume).

Community museum connections are vividly illustrated in the new discourse on museum ethics. Traditionally museum ethics was concerned with issues of collections management, professionalization of museum staff, and respect for local and national legal frameworks. While these fundamentals may still be relevant, the debate is newly informed by current thinking regarding museums and social change (Marstine 2011). The question for new museum ethics is now one of morality: the "moral activism" referred to by Sandell and Nightingale (2012, 2) or an investigation of institutional morality suggested by Hein (2000). This more "dynamic social practice" encourages greater openness about the structures within museums and more attention to social responsibility, whether that is acknowledgment of the accountability of museums, or their obligations and liabilities. Community is ubiquitous within this discourse: Marstine describes museum ethics as "contingent upon the connectivity of museums with their diverse and ever-shifting communities" (Marstine 2011, 10). The nature of this connectivity, she continues, rests upon the "moral agency of the institution" (Marstine 2011, 10). So this approach asks us to think more deeply about the museum's obligations to people and the potential to make an impact on their lives, whether or not they visit the museum. (On new museum ethics see Marstine, Dodd, and Jones in this volume.)

Perhaps an awareness of the weight of responsibility of museum work can make us more tentative about forging such connections. The call for museum–community collaboration may be simplistic and may well underestimate the process and its potential impact (which can also be negative). Lynch, in her analysis of museum–community partnerships, describes the idealization of this connection as disregarding "the museum's fear of others that flows like an undercurrent beneath these encounters." More fundamentally, she adds, it underestimates "the museum's need to exercise control, and its even greater fear of change" (Lynch 2011a, 150). The museum framework, with its generations of museum practices, assumptions, and knowledge, is not one that can be altered easily or, for that matter, lightly. Besides, the communities a museum staff member must interact with will all have their own power frameworks. This must also be appreciated and negotiated. It is not a matter of "us and them"; we are ourselves part of that community and our community of interest varies with time and context (Meijer-van Mensch 2011).

Within museums and museum studies the association between museums and community has been subject to critical review, both in relation to how community should be understood and the relationship between community and museum practice. Museum staff have moved away from a time when they were only concerned with the chosen people represented in collections, and it was for those outside the museum to learn from that – the visitor "good enough" to get it (O'Neill 2002). Increasingly curators critique their collections, practices, and knowledge systems, looking for a more democratic approach. Among those professionals, the complexity of community is understood better than ever before and a new language of community is familiar within the sector and museum studies. As the agency of museums gains recognition, there is more dialogue between museums and communities of interest. Institutions are encouraged to think creatively about the range of communities they can connect with and to do so in an egalitarian manner that recognizes the expertise and skills within the community.

Community engagement in museums is now a well-established practice and has taken on an almost predictable format, the outcome of years of practice that has explored the ways and means of making museums relevant. One example is the community-engagement strategy and action plan adopted at the Manchester Museum, UK. The aspiration is to work and collaborate with communities to enhance understanding between cultures. The tools of practice are listed as: consultation "to gather the opinions and feedback from a cross-section of communities"; collaboration and partnerships with "community partners"; and, "outreach and inreach programmes" that are "collaborative and participative approaches to working with communities" (Manchester Museum 2009).

During the 2000s the focus on social policy in museums, on both sides of the Atlantic, galvanized interest in community projects in museums. The resulting support and funding enabled museums to engage in projects that would otherwise have lacked political will. As a result, museums connected with various public sectors that, at another time, it would not have had the opportunity to do so. More recently, with a less prosperous UK economy, and tighter funding streams that are harder to justify, museums need their communities even more. Feedback on the impact of the Making Collections Effective project, led by the British Museum, included the importance of involving communities in collections review (Museums Association 2012). In this project the community contributed expertise to the museum, enabling staff to interpret and understand better the collections within the museum. The impact of such projects was more than sharing knowledge; it was also about giving a sense of ownership back to the community. Alison Shepherd of the National Mining Museum Scotland referred to the increased recognition of the "deep meaning the objects in our collection hold for the community" and how the project enabled the museum to expand their collections and become more representative (Shepherd cited in Museums Association 2012, 45).

Among museums in Northern Ireland, the community aspect of their work is perceived as the Holy Grail. More and more, community groups are sought, and museums are keen, almost to a point of anxiety, to connect with new and diverse groups. The Northern Ireland Museums Policy describes good museums as "rooted in community" (DCAL 2011, 5) and advocates a partnership approach in museums that is "cohesive and integrated" (DCAL 2011, 9). The range of such linkages is evident in the report *Learning and Access in Museums*, published by Northern Ireland Museums Council (NIMC 2009). In the face of an economic climate that jeopardizes funding for museums and their supporting bodies, this report adeptly records and celebrates local achievements. The value placed on community projects is a demonstration of the relevance of museums to "a wide range of different agendas" (NIMC 2009, 3). The initiatives examined focused on cross-border and community groups, older people, youth projects, traveler communities, and those experiencing disability. *Learning and Access* notes that such innovation is driven by the ability of those working in museums to secure funding from external bodies, such as the Heritage Lottery Fund (UK), and the European

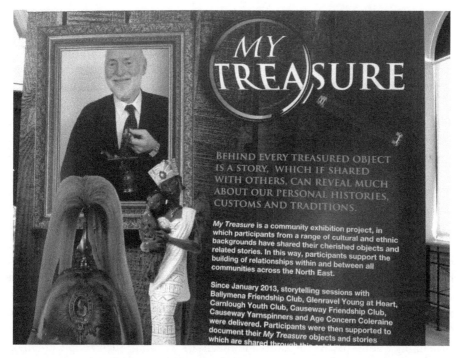

FIGURE 21.1   Detail of a panel from the *My Treasure* community exhibition (Mid-Antrim and Causeway Museum Service) displayed at Coleraine Town Hall, Northern Ireland, July–August 2013. (For a color version of this figure, please see the color plate section.) Courtesy Mid-Antrim and Causeway Museum Service.

Union (INTERREG; EU Programme for Peace and Reconciliation). These examples of practice in Northern Ireland's museums demonstrate that an engaged and audience-driven museum is also a living and surviving museum. The projects work because they are embedded in local needs; they make museums relevant to their communities and produce innovative projects that stretch museum staff (Figure 21.1). In so doing, these initiatives demonstrate that linking up with community groups is essential: it provides proof of relevance, evidence of meaningful service, adds authenticity to collections and exhibitions, and is almost a "must" when making a case for external funding. Curators, embracing this approach, find it highly rewarding and genuinely an essential part of their practice.

Conclusion: the "active museum"

For the purposes of this chapter, the debate concerning museums and agency, instrumentalism, and the rise of the new dialogue about museum ethics, provides opportunities for us to think more deeply about the significance of museums.

Each of these topics allows us to evaluate the purposes, meanings, and significance of museums, to consider how they operate, and ask questions about their influence and the nature of their authority. In addition, the three-part framework presented at the beginning of this chapter emphasizes that there are multiple ways of approaching the connection between museums and community. Despite this diversity, overall, museums have enhanced their role as important social institutions and their work is intimately connected to how we live our lives.

There is a key notion that unites this entire discussion of museum significance, as well as the framework of museum and community and the subsequent discussion of trends in museum practice. This is a belief in the "active museum." In the case of the museum and community connection, discussed in this chapter, the museum is revealed as an active participant. The museum is not passive; rather, it is an active agent that has been equipped with the authority to effect change. The word "active" has been used in the past with reference to active learning, interactivity, and the active museum experience, which reflects a growing interest with the museum as "active partner" and encouraging "active collaboration." In each case it is a reference to a form of engagement that is more dynamic, where people and the museum are more proactive and as a result the museum is more effective (Crooke 2007). We can also include the evidence of those in museums who are challenging traditional assumptions and means of working. Such people are making a deliberate choice to push the boundaries of museum practice, challenging themselves and others to embrace fresh ways of thinking, and taking an active approach to the habits of the workplace so that the museum is ever evolving and has greater relevance.

It seems to me that the active museum has become embedded in the museum sector, despite the problems mentioned above. This can be seen in the recent initiative focusing on museums and community engagement by the Paul Hamlyn Foundation (a UK-based charitable organization). Our Museum: Communities and Museums as Active Partners, launched in 2009, asks that museums consider "community needs, values, aspirations and active collaboration" as fundamental to their work; that communities are involved in core decision-making; that museums develop community skills; and that museums share new models of practice. Clearly in this kind of work museums are seen as places not only where people go to engage and participate, but as venues for communities to co-produce new meanings and experiences of significance (PHF 2013).

It is also noteworthy that this range of connections reveals that museums are recognized by others outside the sector. As a result we have government departments, concerned with public well-being and the economy, involving museums in that pursuit. Equally, community activists, engaged in grassroots work, are using museums as part of their strategies. Each is aware there is something in the process of collecting, displaying, interpreting, and engaging the public that has impact. It is undeniable that when people come from outside the sector, and wish to get involved in the processes that make museums, they are recognizing the influence of the active museum. Obviously its processes – such as meaning making, the authority of objects, and the politics of recognition – are encompassed in such projects. The significance of the active museum therefore lies in this political and social agency, as a place of identity formation, whether that is community, local, or national identity. In the active museum, place and people are recognized via the inclusion of stories, histories, artifacts, and engagement. In the final analysis, it is this politics of recognition that makes the active museum relevant to its local community.

Notes

1   Dan Jarvis, MP for Barnsley Central and Shadow Minister for Department Culture, Media, and Sport, cited on the Museums Association website as part of the Museum 2020 campaign. Accessed November 10, 2014 (http://www.museumsassociation.org/museums2020/m2020-dan-jarvis).

2   See "Welcome to Te Takeretanga o Kura Hau-Po," Te Takere (Te Takeretanga o Kura Hau-Po Horowhenua Culture and Community Centre) website. Accessed November 10, 2014. http://tetakere.blogspot.co.nz/2012/09/welcome-to-te-takeretanga-o-kura-hau-po.html. I am indebted to Belinda Hager, student on the MA Museum Practice and Management, University of Ulster, for making me aware of this example.

3   Te Takeretanga o Kura Hau-Po Horowhenua Culture and Community Centre Strategic Plan, 2012. Accessed November 10, 2014. http://www.tetakere.org.nz/assets/Plans/Te-takere-strategic-plan-full-document.pdf.

4   I am using this term to refer to countries such as the UK, USA, Canada, Australia, New Zealand, and France. I am aware that the interest in museums and social change goes beyond such places.

References

Amit, Vered. 2002. *Realizing Community: Concepts, Social Relationships and Sentiments.* London: Routledge.

Anderson, Benedict. 1991. *Imagined Communities: Reflections on the Origin and Spread of Nationalism*, Rev. ed. London: Verso.

Belfiore, Eleanor. 2012. "'Defensive Instrumentalism' and the Legacy of New Labour's Cultural Policies." *Cultural Trends* 21(2): 103–111.

Belfiore, Eleanor, and Oliver Bennett. 2007. "Rethinking the Social Impact of the Arts." *International Journal of Cultural Policy* 13(2): 135–151.

Bennett, Tony. 1995. *The Birth of the Museum: History, Theory, Politics.* London: Routledge.

Boast, Robin. 2011. "Neo-Colonial Collaboration: Museum as Contact Zone Revisited." *Museum Anthropology* 34(1): 56–70.

Butcher, Hugh, Andrew Glen, Paul Henderson, and Jenny Smith. 1993. *Community and Public Policy.* London: Pluto.

Casey, Denis. 2001. "Museums as Agents for Social and Political Change." *Curator* 44(3): 230–236.

Chandler, Lisa. 2009. "'Journey without Maps': Unsettling Curatorship in Cross-Cultural Contexts." *Museum and Society* 7(2): 74–91.

Clifford, James. 1997. *Routes: Travel and Translation in the Late Twentieth Century*. London: Harvard University Press.

Cohen, Anthony. 1985. *The Symbolic Construction of Community*. London: Tavistock.

Corsane, Gerard. 2005. *Heritage, Museums and Galleries. An Introductory Reader*. London: Routledge.

Corsane, G., P. Davis, S. Elliott, M. Maggi, D. Murtas, and S. Rogers. 2007. "Ecomuseum Evaluation: Experiences in Piemonte and Liguria, Italy." *International Journal of Heritage Studies* 13(2): 101–116.

Craig, Gary, and Marjorie Mayo, eds. 1995. *Community Empowerment: A Reader in Participation and Development*. London: Zed Books.

Crooke, Elizabeth. 2000. *Politics, Archaeology and the Creation of a National Museum in Ireland*. Dublin: Irish Academic Press.

Crooke, Elizabeth. 2005. "Dealing with the Past: Museums and Heritage in Northern Ireland and Cape Town, South Africa." *International Journal of Heritage Studies* 11(2): 131–142.

Crooke, Elizabeth. 2006. "Museums and Community." In *A Companion to Museum Studies*, edited by Sharon Macdonald, 170–185. Malden, MA: Blackwell.

Crooke, Elizabeth. 2007. *Museums and Community: Ideas, Issues and Challenges*. London: Routledge.

Crooke, Elizabeth. 2012. "The Material Culture of Conflict: Artefacts in the Museum of Free Derry, Northern Ireland." In *Narrating Objects, Collecting Stories*, edited by Sandra H. Dudley, Amy Jane Barnes, Jennifer Binnie, Julia Petrov, and Jennifer Walklate, 25–35. London: Routledge.

Davis, Peter. 2008. "New Museologies and the Ecomuseum." In *The Ashgate Research Companion to Heritage and Identity*, edited by Brian J. Graham and Peter Howard, 397–414. Aldershot, UK: Ashgate.

DCAL (Department of Culture, Arts, and Leisure). 2011. "Northern Ireland Museums Policy." Belfast: Department of Culture, Arts, and Leisure.

DCMS (Department for Culture, Media and Sport). 2000. *Centres for Social Change: Museums, Galleries and Archives for All*. London: Department for Culture, Media and Sport.

DCMS (Department for Culture, Media and Sport). 2004a. *Bringing Communities Together through Sport and Culture*. London: Department for Culture, Media and Sport.

DCMS (Department for Culture, Media and Sport). 2004b. *Culture at the Heart of Regeneration*. London: Department for Culture, Media and Sport.

Dean, David, and Peter E. Rider. 2005. "Museums, National and Political History in the Australian National Museum and the Canadian Museum of Civilisation." *Museum and Society* 3(1): 35–50.

Delanty, Gerard. 2003. *Community*. London: Routledge.

Dibley, Ben. 2005. "The Museum's Redemption. Contact Zones, Government and the Limits of Reform." *International Journal of Cultural Studies* 8(1): 5–27.

Dodd, Jocelyn, and Richard Sandell, eds. 2001. *Including Museums: Perspectives on Museums, Galleries and Social Inclusion*. Leicester: Research Centre for Museums and Galleries.

Duncan, Carol. 1995. *Civilizing Rituals: Inside Public Art Museums*. London: Routledge.

Economou, Maria. 2004. "Evaluation Strategies in the Cultural Sector: The Case of the Kelvingrove Museum and Art Gallery in Glasgow." *Museum and Society* 2(1): 30–46.

Fleming, David. 1999. "Viewpoint: Power to the People." *Museum Practice* (11): 15–16.

Fleming, David. 2010. "Museums Campaigning for Social Justice." Stephen Weil Memorial Lecture, ICOM conference, Shanghai, November. Intercom Documents. Accessed November 10, 2014. http://www.intercom.museum/documents/5thWeilLecture ShanghaiNov2010.pdf.

GLLAM (Group for Large and Local Authority Museums). 2000. *Museums and Social Inclusion: The GLLAM Report*. Leicester: Research Centre for Museums and Galleries.

Golding, Viv, and Wayne Modest. 2013. *Museums and Communities: Curators, Collections and Collaboration*. London: Bloomsbury.

Gray, Clive. 2008. "Instrumental Policies: Causes, Consequences, Museums and Galleries." *Cultural Trends* 17(4): 209–222.

Hein, Hilde. 2000. *The Museum in Transition: A Philosophical Perspective*. Washington, DC: Smithsonian Institution Press.

Heumann Gurian, Elaine. 2010. "Curator: From Soloist to Impresario." In *Hot Topics, Public Culture, Museums*, edited by Fiona Cameron and Linda Kelly, 95–111. Newcastle, UK: Cambridge Scholars Press.

Hill, Kate. 2005. *Culture and Class in English Public Museums, 1850–1914*. Aldershot: Ashgate.

Hooper-Greenhill, Eilean. 2000. *Museums and the Interpretation of Visual Culture*. London: Routledge.

Jenson, Jane. 2002. "Identifying the Links: Social Cohesion and Culture." *Canadian Journal of Communication* 27(2): 141–151.

Kaplan, Flora E. S. 1994. *Museums and the Making of "Ourselves."* Leicester: Leicester University Press.

Karp, Ivan, and Steven D. Lavine, eds. 1991. *Exhibiting Cultures: The Poetics and Politics of Museum Display*. Washington, DC: Smithsonian Institution Press.

Karp, Ivan, Steven D. Lavine, and Christine Mullen Kreamer, eds. 1992. *Museums and Communities: The Politics of Public Culture*. Washington, DC: Smithsonian Institution Press.

Kelly, Lynda. 2006. "Measuring the Impact of Museums on Their Communities: The Role of the 21st Century Museum." *New Roles and Missions of Museums ICOM: Intercom 2006 Symposium*. Intercom Documents. Accessed November 10, 2014. http://www.inter com.museum/documents/1-2Kelly.pdf.

Knell, Simon, Peter Aronsson, Arne Bugge Amundsen, Amy Jane Barnes, Stuart Burch, Jennifer Carter, Viviane Gosselin, Sara A. Hughes, and Alan Kirwan, eds. 2010. *National Museums: New Studies from Around the World*. London: Routledge.

Knell, Simon, Suzanne MacLeod, and Sheila Watson. 2007. *Museum Revolutions. How Museums Change and Are Changed*. London: Routledge.

Kreps, Christina. 2003. *Liberating Culture: Cross-Cultural Perspectives on Museums, Curation, and Heritage Preservation, Museum Meanings*. London: Routledge.

Lang, Caroline, John Reeve, and Vicky Woollard, eds. 2006. *The Responsive Museum: Working with Audiences in the Twenty-First Century*. Aldershot, UK: Ashgate.

Levitt, Ruth. 2008. "The Political and Intellectual Landscape of Instrumental Museum Policy." *Cultural Trends* 17(4): 223–231.

Lumley, Robert, ed. 1988. *The Museum Time Machine: Putting Cultures on Display.* London: Taylor and Francis.

Lynch, Bernadette. 2011a. "Collaboration, Contestation and Creative Conflicts: On the Efficacy of Museum/Community Partnerships." In *The Routledge Companion to Museum Ethics*, edited by Janet Marstine, 146–163. London: Routledge.

Lynch, Bernadette. 2011b. *Whose Cake Is It Anyway?* London: Paul Hamlyn Foundation.

Macdonald, Sharon, and Gordon Fyfe, eds. 1996. *Theorizing Museums: Representing Identity and Diversity in a Changing World.* Oxford: Blackwell.

Macnaught, Bill. 2005. "Commentary 3. Commentaries on John Holden's *Capturing Cultural Value: How Culture Has Become a Tool of Government Policy.*" *Cultural Trends* 14(1): 113–128.

Manchester Museum. 2009. "Community Engagement Strategy and Action Plan 2009–10." Accessed November 10, 2014. http://www.museum.manchester.ac.uk/community/communityengagement.

Marstine, Janet, ed. 2011. *The Routledge Companion to Museum Ethics: Redefining Ethics for the Twenty-First-Century Museum.* London: Routledge.

Mason, Rhiannon. 2005. "Museums, Galleries and Heritage: Sites of Meaning Making and Communication." In *Heritage, Museums and Galleries: An Introductory Reader*, edited by Gerard Corsane, 200–214. London: Routledge.

Mason, Rhiannon. 2006. "Cultural Theory and Museum Studies." In *A Companion to Museum Studies*, edited by Sharon Macdonald, 17–32. Malden, MA: Blackwell.

McIntyre, Darryl. 2006. "The National Museum of Australia and Public Discourse: The Role of Public Policies in the Nation's Cultural Debates." *Museum* 58(4): 13–20.

Meijer-van Mensch, Léontine. 2011 "New Challenges, New Priorities: Analysing Ethical Dilemmas from a Stakeholder's Perspective in the Netherlands." *Museum Management and Curatorship* 26(2): 113–128.

MLAC (Museums, Libraries and Archives Council). 2004a. *New Directions in Social Policy: Developing the Evidence Base for Museums.* London: Museums, Libraries and Archives Council, Burns Owen Partnership. Accessed November 18, 2014. http://webarchive.nationalarchives.gov.uk/20111013135435/research.mla.gov.uk/evidence/documents/ndsp_developing_evidence_doc_6649.pdf.

MLAC (Museums, Libraries and Archives Council). 2004b. *New Directions in Social Policy: Cultural Diversity for Museums, Libraries and Archives.* London: Museums, Libraries and Archives Council, Burns Owen Partnership.

Museums Association. 2012. *Making Collections Effective: Achievements and Legacy.* London: Museums Association.

Nightingale, Eithne. 2006. "Dancing around the Collections: Developing Individuals and Collections." In *The Responsive Museum*, edited by Caroline Lang, John Reeve, and Vicky Woollard, 79–92. Aldershot, UK: Ashgate.

Nightingale, Eithne. 2009a. *Capacity Building and Cultural Ownership: Working with Diverse Communities.* London: Victoria and Albert Museum.

Nightingale, Eithne. 2009b. "From the Margins to the Core." *Journal of Museum Education* 3: 255–270.

NIMC (Northern Ireland Museums Council). 2009. *Learning and Access in Museums: Case Studies from Northern Ireland.* Belfast: Northern Ireland Museums Council. Accessed November 10, 2014. http://www.nimc.co.uk/research-and-publications.

NMDC (National Museums Directors' Conference). 2004. *Museums and Galleries: Creative Engagement.* London: National Museums Directors' Conference. Accessed November 10, 2014. http://www.nationalmuseums.org.uk/media/documents/publications/creative_engagement.pdf.

O'Neill, Mark. 2002. "The Good Enough Visitor." In *Museums, Society, Inequality*, edited by Richard Sandell, 56–68. London: Routledge.

Peers, Laura, and Alison K. Brown, eds. 2003. *Museums and Source Communities: A Routledge Reader.* London: Routledge.

PHF (Paul Hamlyn Foundation). 2013. "Our Museum: Communities and Museums as Active Partners." Accessed November 10, 2014. http://www.phf.org.uk/page.asp?id=1125.

Rassool, Ciraj. 2006. "Making the District Six Museum in Cape Town." *Museum International* 58(1–2): 9–18.

Rassool, Ciraj. 2010. "Power, Knowledge and the Politics of Public Pasts." *African Studies* 69(1): 79–101.

Sandell, Richard, ed. 2002. *Museums, Society, Inequality.* London: Routledge.

Sandell, Richard. 2003. "Social Inclusion, the Museum and the Dynamics of Sectorial Change." *Museum and Society* 1(1): 45–62.

Sandell, Richard. 2007. *Museums, Prejudice and the Reframing of Difference.* London: Routledge.

Sandell, Richard, and Eithne Nightingale, eds. 2012. *Museums, Equality and Social Justice.* London: Routledge.

Scott, Carol. 2006. "Museums: Impact and Value." *Cultural Trends* 15(1): 45–75.

Simon, Nina. 2010. *The Participatory Museum.* Santa Cruz, CA: Museum 2.0.

Sommerville, Peter. 2011. *Understanding Community. Politics, Policy and Practice.* Bristol: Policy Press.

Stam, Deirdre. 1993. "The Informed Muse: The Implications of New Museology for Museum Practice." *Museum Management and Curatorship* 12: 267–283.

Tlili, Anwar, Sharon Gewirtz, and Alan Cribb. 2007. "New Labour's Socially Responsible Museum." *Policy Studies* 28(3): 269–289.

Vergo, Peter, ed. 1989. *The New Museology.* London: Reaktion Books.

Watson, Sheila, ed. 2007. *Museums and Their Communities.* London: Routledge.

Wavell, Caroline, Graeme Baxter, Ian Johnson, and Dorothy Williams. 2002. *Impact Evaluation of Museums, Archives and Libraries: Available Evidence Project.* Accessed November 10, 2014. http://www4.rgu.ac.uk/files/imreport.pdf.

West, Céline, and Charlotte H. F. Smith. 2005. "'We are not a government poodle': Museums and Social Inclusion under New Labour." *International Journal of Cultural Policy* 11(3): 275–288.

Witcomb, Andrea. 2003. *Re-imagining the Museum: Beyond the Mausoleum*. London: Routledge.
Yerbury, Hilary. 2011. "Vocabularies of Community." *Community Development Journal* 47(2): 184–198.

Further Reading

Waterton, Emma, and Steve Watson. 2013. *Heritage and Community Engagement: Collaboration or Contestation?* London: Routledge.

Elizabeth Crooke is Professor of Heritage and Museum Studies at the University of Ulster, Northern Ireland. As well as supervising PhD students, she is Course Director of the MA Cultural Heritage and Museum Studies and the MA Museum Practice and Management (distance learning). She has published *Museums and Community: Ideas, Issues and Challenges* (2007), *Politics, Archaeology and the Creation of a National Museum of Ireland* (2000), and many book chapters and journal articles. She is a member of the board of directors of the Northern Ireland Museums Council and the board of directors of the Irish Museums Association.

22 VISITOR STUDIES
Toward a Culture of Reflective Practice and Critical Museology for the Visitor-Centered Museum

Lee Davidson

Visitors have been central to public museums from their very beginning, but the relationship has not always been an easy one (Hooper-Greenhill 1994; Lang, Reeve, and Woollard 2006). In the nineteenth century museums served as sites of connoisseurship and class distinction, at the same time as civilizing and educating the masses; this created an ambivalence which resulted in conditions that were both "constraining and enabling" for different types of visitors and modes of visiting (Prior 2002). Prior argues that these tensions have persisted into the twenty-first century, as stalwarts of the museum as a bastion of cultural authority and discernment take fright at more recent notions of democratized and engaging spaces for the general public (Prior 2003). Within this context of debate about museums and their publics, the field of museum visitor studies, at the heart of which is the acknowledgment that museums should be responsive to the needs and interests of visitors, has only gradually gained recognition as an important facet of museum practice. Its emergence has been important not only for enhancing and sustaining the public functions of museums but also, increasingly, serving as an instrument for organizational change by contributing to a reshaping of fundamental ideas about the "what" and "why" as well as the "for whom" of museums.

Visitor studies today is widely accepted as a broad field encompassing various forms of research and evaluation relating to museums and their existing or potential visitors, and the wider communities they serve (Hooper-Greenhill 2006). It includes museum-based studies, conducted either by internal staff or external consultants, as well as university research. As such, visitor studies addresses a broad spectrum of questions relating to both practice-based issues and theoretical concerns. The term "museum audience research" is also widely

The International Handbooks of Museum Studies: Museum Practice, First Edition.
Edited by Conal McCarthy.
© 2015 John Wiley & Sons Ltd. Published 2020 by John Wiley & Sons Ltd.

used, preferred perhaps because it suggests a more inclusive remit, extending beyond those who actively cross the physical or virtual threshold of the museum (Loomis 1993). Audience research, however, can also relate more specifically to audience development and marketing functions (see Black in this volume). In this chapter I use the term "visitor studies" in the inclusive sense I have described, and "audience research" only where particular authors have adopted this term.

Visitor studies are most often conducted within education or marketing departments, but the potential range of museum functions and processes to which it applies is broad. Indeed Scott (1998), among others, advocates for a wider appreciation of the potential for visitor research and evaluation to act as "powerful tools" to inform a broad spectrum of museum functions including customer services, outreach programs, collection management, and volunteer programs. In a study of Australasian museums, Reussner (2004) found that visitor research had a wide range of impacts across entire organizations. Not only was it considered to be effective for improving visitor experiences through better exhibitions and programs, but museum staff also felt that it led to more informed decision-making in general and "appeared to be a driver for cultural change in that it is seen to increase visitor orientation [centeredness] within the institutions" (Reussner 2004, 19–20).

In this context Munley's (1986) five purposes of visitor studies remain apt. These include: *justification* of the value of the museum and its activities; *information-gathering* for long-term planning; the *formulation* of new exhibitions and programs; *assessment* of the effectiveness of current exhibitions and programs; and *construction of theories* to better understand how people use museums (cited in Hooper-Greenhill 1994, 69).

In this chapter, I first consider the history of visitor studies as a field of museum practice, charting its evolution throughout the second half of the twentieth century and touching on the key issues that it faces in the twenty-first. I then examine the basics of practice within the museum context, before looking at the growing body of theory on visitors and visiting based on empirical studies. Finally I review the key developments and challenges for visitor studies, and its future potential for enhancing a culture of reflective practice and critical museology.

A history of the field

Henry Hugh Higgins at the Liverpool Museum in the late nineteenth century, and Benjamin Ives Gilman at the Boston Museum of Fine Arts who famously coined the term "museum fatigue" in 1916, were among the early pioneers of visitor studies (Hein 1998; Loomis 1993). Today they are celebrated yet isolated examples, and very little systematic investigation of museum visitors occurred before the mid twentieth century, with the exception of the frequently cited observational studies carried out by Robinson and Melton in the 1920s and 1930s (Yalowitz and Bronnenkant 2009).

During the 1960s the "serious" study of museum visitors was becoming more common, with visitor surveys being conducted in the United Kingdom and the United States and the practice of exhibition evaluation gaining prominence in the USA following calls for accountability from funders (Hooper-Greenhill 2006; Shettel 2008). The dominant approach to evaluation at the time was to use an experimental-design strategy to assess educational objectives. While such studies generated useful ideas about how exhibitions could be improved, their aim of measuring the retention of exhibition content, informed by the transmission model of communication, was problematic (Hooper-Greenhill 2006) and formal conditions for experimental design were difficult to meet in an exhibition context (Hein 1998). From the 1960s onward, more holistic theories of education and the application of new "naturalistic" methodologies from the fields of anthropology and ethnography, gave greater consideration to the complexity of real-world settings and acknowledged the impact of context and researcher perspective on the research process (Hein 1998). By the 1980s, new approaches to museum education based on constructivist learning theory brought recognition that visitors had their own agendas and made meaning from experience according to their background and experience, and that these factors had to be taken into consideration in any assessment of the value of museum visits (Hein 1998; Hooper-Greenhill 2006). (On museum education and learning see Reeve and Woollard in this volume.)

The late 1980s through to the late 1990s saw increasing professionalism in visitor studies with the establishment of professional associations in North America, Australia, and the UK (see Black in this volume), as well as the first specialist conferences and the launch of the *ILVS Review: A Journal of Visitor Behaviour* by Harris Shettel and Chan Screven in the US (Bitgood and Loomis 2012). The appointment of marketing officers in UK museums led to more efficient visitor surveys and new methods linked to market research (Hooper-Greenhill 2006; McLean 1997).

The establishment of visitor studies as a facet of museum practice during the 1980s and 1990s coincided with the emergence of new ideas about the function and purpose of museums, and their wider social, economic, and political relationships (Stam 2005; Vergo 1989; Weil 1998). Encompassed within the "new museology" was what Hooper-Greenhill (2006) refers to as "the turn to the visitor," that is, a call for museums to be more democratic and give greater consideration to the communities they are charged to represent. The ICOM Code of Ethics, first adopted in 1986, acknowledged the responsibility of museums "to develop their educational role and attract wider audiences from the community, locality, or group they serve" (ICOM 2013, 8). Simultaneously, growing pressure to be more financially accountable and to maintain visitor numbers and generate income within a competitive leisure and tourism industry prompted many museums to seek to better understand their audiences (Galloway and Stanley 2004; Harrison 2005).

Publication of *The Museum Experience* by John Falk and Lynn Dierking in 1992 marked a milestone for visitor studies literature, which until then had consisted of "a discreet cluster" of journal articles (Spero 2013). This book was the first to offer a coherent framework within which to understand the visitor experience. Two years later, Eilean Hooper-Greenhill's *Museums and Their Visitors* (1994) sought to raise awareness and provide guidance for museums to connect better with their visitors. She argued for visitor research as "an essential management information tool," predicting its growing importance (Hooper-Greenhill 1994, 68).

In the same period, Loomis (1993, 13–14) wrote that with greater orientation toward audience had come an appreciation that visitors were not "an undefined mass" and that "[f]or the first time we are beginning to make significant progress in understanding the visitor." Yet in spite of the progress being made, Hooper-Greenhill (1994) noted that many museums still carried out very little, if any, visitor research, as staff often failed to see its relevance or usefulness, or failed to convince governing bodies to allocate the necessary funding. Hood (1992, 282) drew attention to additional problems, claiming that the majority of museum audience studies at this time were "poorly designed, implemented, analyzed, and interpreted" and "produced trivial results." Furthermore, the results often had no impact on practice, as museum staff were unaware of the findings of high-quality studies that did exist, or were put off by the magnitude of changes implied by the research findings.

Concerns and criticism about the inadequate application of visitor research findings in museum practice have persisted into the new millennium (Reussner 2008). In a survey of 119 Australian cultural heritage institutions, Reussner (2003) found that around one-third had commissioned or conducted audience research, with summative evaluations and visitor satisfaction and socio-demographics as the most popular research types. Barriers to the implementation of visitor studies included: perceptions of insufficient resources; no one taking responsibility for audience research within the institution; a lack of expertise in research methods; low awareness of audience research and its potential benefits; and a lack of interest, or belief, in its benefits.

In a later study of 21 museums across Europe, North America, and Australasia, Reussner (2008, 192) concluded that there were two main sources of resistance to museum visitor studies: concerns about its legitimacy as a "solid and trustworthy branch of research"; and its acceptance "as an instrument for reflection and development related to an evaluative culture that questions established ways of working and thinking and ... establishes audience orientation as an important value that needs to be considered in museum work."

Significantly, staff not working in front-of-house roles, with direct contact with the public, are less inclined to see audience issues as relevant to their work, and may fear they will lose their authority if visitor research is accorded too much weight, believing that it amounts to a crude give-'em-what-they-want style of market research (McLean 2004; Reussner 2003). The wider context of these fears is the new, customer-focused climate in which museums, like all other service providers, are "being required to smile" (Witcomb 2003, 59). This, according to Witcomb (2003, 60), has caused "intense pain and soul searching" as museums struggle to work out how to address audiences and how to reconcile this with their traditional functions.

In this environment, museums must position themselves somewhere along "a continuum between a product and a demand orientation" (Reussner 2008). Seagram, Patten, and Lockett (1993) articulate the issue as a tension between mandate-driven and market-driven models in terms of the delivery of museum exhibitions and programs, but argue that if museums adopt a "transaction approach" they can meet the needs and interests of visitors without undermining the core values and goals of the institution. Visitor studies has a critical role to play in negotiating this delicate balance. To be successful, research must be competently designed and executed. But it also relies upon the level of commitment and involvement of staff across the museum and a willingness to see it as an integral aspect of reflective practice, rather than undermining the function of the museum (Reussner 2008).

Basics of current practice

In this section, I focus primarily on visitor research conducted within museums for the purpose of meeting the needs of the institution by producing "actionable data," that is, findings that can provide solutions to practical problems (Hood 1992, 73). In this context, visitor research may or may not be theoretically informed, and may or may not contribute to the generation of new theories: its primary focus is to contribute to practice. I discuss the main types of research methods used, the contexts and considerations related to each of these methods, and the factors that contribute to the effectiveness of this research.

Visitor studies have been conducted using diverse research paradigms, from positivist to interpretivist (Lindauer 2005), and a broad spectrum of methods, from the quantitative to the qualitative. The ontological and epistemological differences underpinning these methodological choices have a long history of debate within the academy, and tend to divide along disciplinary lines. From the point of view of museum practice, the choice of paradigm and method may depend upon the professional training of individual researchers, but in a practical sense the most important consideration is which method is most appropriate and effective within any given research context.

The range of topics typically addressed by museum visitor research include visitation rates and patterns; visitor demographics and psychographics (including leisure habits and learning strategies); visitor motivations, behavior, experiences, and perceptions; non-visitors' perceptions and barriers to visiting; broader community needs and perceptions of value; and exhibition and program evaluation.

Hein (1998, 101) summarizes three broad categories of methods used in visitor studies as: observing what people do; talking with people about their activity or asking them to write about it; and examining some product of human activity. Counting visitors is perhaps the most basic method of collecting information about visitors. The analysis of visitation frequency data allows for the tracking of patterns of seasonal variation related to holiday periods and can also be correlated with exhibitions, events, and public programs to understand their impact on visitor flows (Davidson and Sibley 2011).

In addition to visitation figures, visitor surveys using structured questionnaires have become routine for many museums, especially larger institutions. These are used to collect the demographic, socioeconomic, and psychographic characteristics of visitors, as well as self-reported information about visiting behavior, motivations, and experiences. This information can be used to understand visitation patterns by audience segment, informing strategies for audience development, marketing, and issues of accessibility for underrepresented groups (see Black in this volume). It can also be used for reporting against performance indicators and to improve service delivery and for program development.

The Museum of New Zealand Te Papa Tongarewa (Te Papa) in Wellington, internationally recognized for its high levels of visitation and for having diversified its audience through innovative display techniques, public programs, and its family-friendly atmosphere, is an example of a large museum that systematically collects visitation and visitor profile data (Davidson and Sibley 2011; McCarthy 2013). Central to the planning of this new national museum in the mid-1990s was the establishment of a Visitor and Market Research unit (VMR) that undertook audience research and provided evaluation for exhibition concepts and designs in preparation for opening in 1998. Since opening, a core part of VMR's research program has been conducting regular on-site, face-to-face visitor exit surveys using its Visitor Profile Interview (VPI) to identify visitors' characteristics, behavior, and experience. As a result, a substantial and detailed database has been amassed, providing a rich source of information about the museum's audience. In the first decade of operation almost 30,000 interviews were carried out (Davidson and Sibley 2011).

Te Papa's VPI data are used on a routine basis for internal processes, such as exhibition evaluations and audience analysis, exhibition and event planning and development, retailing, marketing, sponsorship, fundraising, and to report on performance to external stakeholders and funders. In a recent study, university researchers analyzed the VPI data to assess the extent to which Te Papa had met some of the expectations of the new museology, including its success in attracting a demographically diverse audience and providing for a broad range of leisure and touristic functions (Davidson and Sibley 2011). A related study combined visitation data from Te Papa's VPI with data on tourism in Wellington city to obtain a quantitative indication of the impact of Te Papa on the capital city's tourism using an econometric methodology (Carey, Davidson, and Sahli 2013).

Quantitative survey data collected using closed questions allow for relatively straightforward analysis and reporting, and are appropriate for large samples. However, some of the data collected in this manner, such as satisfaction ratings, may be viewed as superficial and narrow measures of visitor experience, particularly if used as indicators of performance. Administering an ongoing, face-to-face exit survey, as Te Papa does, also requires resources that may be beyond smaller museums with low staffing numbers. A self-complete survey is a less resource intensive option, provided that visitors are invited to participate in a systematic way, thus ensuring an adequate response rate and as representative a sample as possible (Larkin 2011). Web-based surveys are another option for virtual visitors and for on-site visitors whose email contacts have been collected at the time of their visit (Parsons 2007; Storksdieck 2007; Yalowitz and Ferguson 2007).

General population surveys provide information about non-visitors and wider community museum-visiting behaviors, and perceptions of the value of museums. These surveys may be sponsored by local/national governments in order to evaluate publically provided services, and for policy purposes. For example, a nationwide household survey in 2002, conducted by Statistics New Zealand and the Ministry for Culture and Heritage, examined New Zealanders' cultural participation and spending, including their visitation to museums and art galleries and also perceived barriers to visiting (Ministry for Culture and Heritage 2003). Further research conducted by the Ministry of Tourism captured the trends and characteristics of international and domestic tourists visiting New Zealand museums between 2003 and 2008 (Ministry of Tourism 2009). Surveys in the UK in 2001 and 2004, published by the Museums, Libraries and Archives Council, examined museum-visiting and satisfaction levels (MORI 2001, 2004).

In contrast to surveys aimed at a broad understanding of museum audiences, evaluation has a problem-solving focus, asking questions "about specific processes or outcomes" (Hein 1998, 56). This form of visitor research is used throughout the conceptual and developmental phases of producing exhibitions, events, and programs to enhance their effectiveness, as well as to evaluate a final product and inform future development. The use of evaluation to engage visitors in a dialogue about the effectiveness of exhibitions corresponds with the transaction approach proposed by Seagram, Patten, and Lockett (1993). As such, learning more about the needs and interests of visitors is a tool for developers, curators, and interpreters, which complements other aspects of their professional expertise in the development process (see Dean in this volume).

A comprehensive model of exhibition evaluation was developed by Screven during the 1970s and 1980s (Bitgood and Loomis 2012; Screven 1990). The three key stages in this model are front-end, formative, and summative evaluation, with remedial evaluation as an additional option. Front-end evaluation begins with the early development of ideas for an exhibition, and can assist in deciding on the key goals for a particular exhibition, as well as "exhibit layouts, terminology, approaches to motivating visitor attention and interest, text formats, headlines, graphics and, particularly, to deal with distortions that occur from visitor preconceptions about an exhibit's topic" (Screven 1990, 38).

The formative phase involves the testing and modification of an exhibition as development progresses and ideally follows an iterative process with the increasing refinement of the exhibition design (Screven 1990). Formative evaluation can be particularly helpful for testing out the writing of exhibition texts and the development of interactive exhibits (Hooper-Greenhill 1994). Hein describes the range of forms a formative evaluation may take: "from informally trying out prototypes on the floor or asking a few visitors what they think about an exhibit component, to elaborate research studies, in which successive waves of exhibit components are subjected to relatively rigorous examination by visitors" (1998, 58–59). Remedial evaluation allows for the refinement of an exhibition after it has opened, when additional "occupancy variables" may produce problems unforeseen during the development process. These can include crowding, noise, social interaction, and circulation issues that can "generate headaches, fatigue, spatial disorientation, confusion, reduce concentration, distort thematic organization, reduce interest, and so on" (Screven 1990, 54). Many of these issues may be remedied by simple actions, and Screven (1990) recommends that the exhibition development period be extended to six to 12 weeks following opening in order to allow for remedial evaluation, while long-term exhibitions can benefit from periodic revision.

Although Screven (1990) argues that the front-end, formative, and remedial phases of evaluation are the most likely to contribute to exhibition effectiveness, Reussner (2003) found that, in Australia at least, evaluation occurred most often in the completion phase of projects. Summative evaluation seeks to describe the impact or outcome of a program or exhibition. In this phase, which questions to ask depends upon whether the exhibition or program was developed with predetermined, quantifiable objectives or "a more loosely circumscribed or open-ended stance" in terms of visitor outcomes, as well as for whom the evaluation is being done and what they consider as "value" (Lindauer 2005, 149). Summatives can be used to produce reports for funding bodies and/or for internal organizational learning, including ongoing exhibition planning and development (Kelly 2004; Screven 1990).

According to Shettel (2008), although there has been a significant increase in the usage of exhibition evaluation in the last 25 years, there are still a large number of museums that do not routinely conduct formal evaluations. One reason for this may be that unless museums have dedicated research staff, they may not feel they have the expertise to undertake evaluation. One option is to use external consultants. Independent experts may offer a higher degree of objectivity and breadth of experience from working across a range of institutions, but the downside is they may be so removed from day-to-day museum operations that their work has little impact (Hein 1998). Most important, according to Hein (1998, 62), is that evaluation should strive for a balance between "irrelevance and intrusiveness" and between "technical skills and social awareness of the professional culture of the museum."

Time and cost, of course, are key considerations. For evaluation to be a routine and effective aspect of museum practice, it must be integrated into the budgets and timeframes for exhibitions and programs, and be manageable in terms of time and cost (Hooper-Greenhill 1994; Screven 1990). In Shettel's (2008) view, it is false economy to spend significant amounts of money on developing exhibitions and not allocate a proportion of the budget to evaluation in order to ensure that the intended goals are achieved. Interestingly, Reussner (2008) found that although museums identify the availability of resources as a key factor in undertaking research, it is actually one of the least decisive factors in terms of determining the effectiveness of that research, with other aspects of the organizational culture, planning, and communication being far more important. It seems that where there is a will, there is a way.

Evaluations may be extensively planned and formalized, with rigorous research designs, or be quite informal processes where a few visitors are invited to comment on some aspect of an exhibition. Hein (1998) argues that summative evaluations in particular should follow formal research processes in order to produce useful results, but that even informal, ad hoc evaluations can be useful for improving exhibitions and concludes that it is better to try something out on a few visitors than to ask no one.

A range of social science methods are used in museum evaluation, with the appropriate choice depending on the particular question being asked and the method most likely to produce useful information (Screven 1990). The selection of research participants also depends upon the aim of the study. It is often most convenient to recruit current visitors as participants while they are on site. However, if the exhibition is seeking to attract new or infrequent visitors, it may be more appropriate to recruit participants from target groups outside the museum.

Observational methods are routinely used for evaluation. Usually focused on one exhibition, or a mock-up of exhibition components in the case of formative evaluation, timing and tracking studies produce useful and easily obtained information about the spatial and temporal aspects of actual visitor behavior, as opposed to reported behavior that might be gathered in a post-visit interview. In structured, unobtrusive observations, a researcher tracks a visitor through an exhibition space, recording the path and timing of the visit on a floor plan. Various categories of behaviors (reading, using interactives, engaging with other visitors), observable visitor characteristics (estimated age, gender, and social grouping), and other situational variables (crowding, presence of staff, or special events) can also be recorded (Yalowitz and Bronnenkant 2009).

Nurse Rainbolt, Benfield, and Loomis (2012) examined options for visitor self-mapping as an alternative to the more labor-intensive researcher observations. Results from two studies conducted at the Buffalo Bill Historical Center demonstrated that accurate data about circulation patterns and length of visit could be gathered using this method. They concluded that although there were limits to the type of data that could be collected and that it placed demands on visitors, which may affect the response rate, self-mapping is an acceptable compromise where time and cost are inhibiting factors. Another alternative is to capture and analyze video footage, although it can be difficult to get a view of a whole exhibition space. Other technologies such as mobile devices with GPS tracking, WiFi, and radio frequency identification show potential, but the initial cost investment may be prohibitive for most museums (Nurse Rainbolt, Benfield, and Loomis 2012).

Information about visitor orientation and circulation can help determine how spaces are being used and how time is spent within exhibitions, including the "attracting power" and "holding power" of various display components (Hein 1998, 106). Studies tend to show that paths through exhibitions are very individual and that most visitors stop at only a small percentage of displays and spend a very small amount of time looking at individual objects. Visitors generally become fatigued after about 15 to 20 minutes (Hein 1998). This has implications for "what visitors will see, where they focus their attention, and, ultimately, what they learn and/or experience" (Bitgood 2006, 463).

As Bitgood (2006, 464) points out, "visitor movement patterns through museums are influenced by both what the visitor brings to the museum (prior knowledge, interests, 'agenda') and the design of the museum (exhibit elements, architecture, open space)." However, a disadvantage of observational methods is that they do not gain access to visitors' thoughts and agendas, which can only be determined by asking questions. Adding a questionnaire or interview at the end of an observation is one way of ameliorating this limitation.

If a visit has a specific objective, such as for school groups on an educational program that is linked to a formal curriculum, pre- and post-visit questionnaires can be administered. However, Hein (1998) warns that short-term knowledge gains can be deceptive and long-term gains are arguably more significant, which suggests a longitudinal approach is more appropriate for assessing learning and lasting impact. At the same time, there is wider acceptance that the learning value of exhibitions lies not so much in conveying didactic messages, as in facilitating processes of meaning-making in which visitors are active participants (Hein 1998).

Personal Meaning Mapping is a method that has been developed to assess learning while taking into consideration visitors' prior experience and knowledge of a topic (Falk, Moussouri, and Coulson 1998). Visitors are recruited before they enter an exhibition and asked to complete a Personal Meaning Map (PMM) noting all the words, ideas, images, phrases, and thoughts that come to mind in relation to the exhibition topic. This is followed by an open-ended interview in which visitors are asked to expand on what they wrote and why. Next they are unobtrusively tracked through the exhibition, before being approached at the end of their visit and asked to complete a post-visit interview, including a second PMM. A third PMM can be conducted by telephone several weeks or months after the visit to determine long-term learning. The data gathered can be used to compare pre- and post-visit knowledge and feelings, in order to determine the change effected by the exhibition (Falk, Moussouri, and Coulson 1998).

Another variation on standard observations and interviews is the "accompanied visit." In a collaborative research project involving a university research center, an art museum, and an area museum council, Hooper-Greenhill et al. (2001) used this method to explore visitor interpretive and meaning-making strategies at the Wolverhampton Art Gallery. Researchers accompanied single, adult visitors on their visits around the museum, asking them to "think aloud" about what they "saw, thought and felt" as they viewed the exhibition, and recording this on an audio device. A questionnaire was administered at the end of the visit to capture basic demographic and additional related information.

A range of methods were used by the Museum Learning Collaborative to investigate learning in museums, including diaries, journals, experience sampling, and the analysis of recorded conversations among museum visitors (Leinhardt, Crowley, and Knutson 2002; Leinhardt and Knutson 2004). Paris and Mercer (2002), in seeking new methods to explore the relationship between objects and visitor identities, used structured interviews, stimulated recall, and the rating and sorting of photographed objects to determine various narrative associations and meaning-making.

Focus groups are an effective method for gaining a large amount of qualitative data on a specific topic relatively rapidly (Berg 2009). Widely used for market research, focus groups are most frequently used in museums for front-end studies (Hein 1998). Focus groups produce data that are collectively negotiated, rather than individual perspectives, and the quality of the data is more reliant on the skills of the facilitator/researcher than is the case for other methods.

Visitor books and comment cards, which are increasingly being made part of exhibitions, are simple and inexpensive ways for museums to gather information from their visitors. Macdonald (2005) outlines the various ways that visitor books are used, from being stored for possible future reference, to being actively scanned for positive comments or suggested improvements. The main limitation in their use for visitor research is the self-selecting nature of participation, meaning that the comments cannot be considered as representative of a wide range of visitors. On the other hand, they contain potential insights into visitors' views, experiences, and understanding of museums and exhibitions, and are relatively free of forms of bias associated with other methods. They may also be the only source of visitor data available for exhibitions that no longer exist (Macdonald 2005). In using this data, however, it is important to consider the context in which comments are made and to read them as "socially situated performances" (Macdonald 2005, 122). They may be particularly valuable if complemented with other data sources as part of a multi-method study, or to inform the design of other data collection instruments such as surveys or interviews.

Indeed, evaluations often combine multiple methods to achieve optimal results, as complementary methods compensate for their respective limitations. For instance, Kelly and Gordon (2002) describe a summative evaluation of the exhibition *Indigenous Australians* at the Australian Museum that utilized surveys (immediately pre- and post-visit), visitor tracking, focus groups (six months post-visit), and the monitoring of media reviews and visitor book comments. Front-end evaluation for the development of the exhibition included quantitative and qualitative visitor interviews, surveys and workshops with Indigenous people, focus groups, and prototype testing. In pursuing an agenda of social justice and inclusion, Kelly and Gordon (2002) highlight the value of visitor studies to help museums actively engage with stakeholder groups such as Indigenous Australians. They propose creating "communities of practice," involving people in decision-making around exhibition development, programming, and other matters related to the management of their cultural heritage through community meetings, workshops, and forums. (For more on museums as "active agents" engaging and collaborating with communities, see Crooke in this volume.)

The quality of visitor research relies upon a robust overall research design, including a clear articulation of the research questions and objectives, appropriate choice of method, effective design of the research instrument, sampling strategy, data analysis, and interpretation (Blaikie 2000; Reussner 2008). While these processes may be daunting for museum staff who lack the relevant professional training, a number of practical resources exist that can acquaint them with the basics in a museum context (for example, Diamond, Luke, and Uttal 2009; Dierking and Pollock 1998; Nichols 1999), while the general social science literature can provide more in-depth knowledge (for example, Blaikie 2000; Creswell 2013; Denscombe 2010).

Ideally, visitor research should be integrated within a planned and systematic program, rather than being undertaken in a sporadic manner (Hooper-Greenhill 1994; Seagram, Patten, and Lockett 1993). Indeed, Reussner found that the most important factor for ensuring the effectiveness of museum visitor research was its presence "as a continuous, integral function both of museum work in general and of specific lines of action such as exhibition development from a very early stage, instead of as a separate, add-on, ad hoc activity" and that "the person responsible for audience research is involved in the respective projects and project teams from the beginning" (2008, 192).

Reussner (2003) emphasizes that to ensure the success of visitor research the researcher has not only to be competent in the techniques and processes of their profession, but also to be "an advocate, a diplomat, a good communicator and a manager at the same time." Involving staff in the planning, execution, interpretation, and discussion of findings and their implications creates a sense of ownership and increases the chances that the findings will be applied in practice (Reussner 2008). Clear communication throughout the research process is critical, as is making its findings widely available and in an accessible format. Working across the institution and supported by senior management, museum staff responsible for visitor research have the best chance of ensuring the effectiveness of their work and having a broad impact on the organizational culture (Reussner 2008).

Literature review

Key to the new museology has been a shift from perceiving museum visitors as a "relatively homogenous and rather passive mass," to understanding them as "diverse, plural, and active" (Macdonald 2006, 8; McLean 2004). Underpinning this reconceptualization is a growing body of literature that seeks to theorize museum visitors and the act of visiting. The majority of these studies are being conducted by university-based researchers, often in dialogue with visitor research practitioners and with the intention of feeding into practice. Until now, empirical studies of visitors have not been prominent within the general museum studies literature, which has been dominated by "cultural, historical, or critical analyses of the museum as an institution" (Kirchberg and Tröndle 2012, 436). However, Hooper-Greenhill (2006, 374) notes the emergence of more studies driven by sophisticated, theoretically based research questions and adopting innovative, interpretive methods with the aim of "deep understanding rather than the improvement of practice." In contrast to the majority of museum-based visitor research, the researchers in these studies: "are very obvious throughout the discussion, positioned as reflective and responsive researchers; and the analysis of the museum event is placed within contexts that extend the analysis beyond the museums" (Hooper-Greenhill 2006, 374). Early literature focused on developing an understanding of who does and who does not visit museums and why. Demographic studies demonstrated that museum visiting is not spread evenly in the population, but rather that adult museum visitors tend to be younger, better educated, and more affluent than the general population, and to be drawn particularly from the "white professional classes" (Black 2005; Hood 1993a; Hooper-Greenhill 1994; Smith 2006). The implication drawn from these trends is that socioeconomic and demographic variables represent "structural" factors that influence whether or not people will visit museums in their leisure time (Kirchberg 2007). Merriman (1991) investigated this proposition with a survey of the general UK population and concluded that it was cultural values – an interest in the past and a certain image of museums – that were most influential in prompting decisions to visit, and that these were related to upbringing. To overcome this, Merriman (1991) proposed that museums needed to demonstrate their relevance to people's everyday lives, present content that they would find interesting, and become a more integral part of their communities.[1]

Hood (1992), frustrated by the lack of progress in audience research, concluded that typical demographic and participation studies did not explain why people do or do not visit museums. The answer to broadening museum audiences, she argued, lay in understanding the psychographics of both visitors and non-visitors, including their "attitudes, opinions, interests, values, concept of self, personality traits, goals, activities, group memberships, social position, and consumption behaviour" (Hood 1993b, 711). Her research is still widely cited as a breakthrough

in understanding who visits museums, who doesn't, and why, based on their leisure preferences and their perceptions of the extent to which museums meet these
preferences (Hood 1993a; 2004; see Black in this volume).

Falk's (2009; 2011) recent work, drawing on a longitudinal investigation of
learning at the California Science Center, proposes that museum visitors be
grouped into broad identity-related categories associated with different motivations for visiting: explorers (curiosity-driven); facilitators (socially motivated); pro-
fessional/hobbyist (specific content-related interests); experience seekers (the
museum as an important destination); rechargers (seeking contemplative, spiritual
and/or restorative experiences); respectful pilgrims (honoring the memory of
those represented by an institution/memorial); and affinity seekers (motivated by
particular content that speaks to their sense of heritage and/or personhood). Falk
(2011) argues that this model is more useful for museums attempting to attract
more visitors than traditional models based on demographics variables, such as
race/ethnicity, gender, or nationality.

The value of demographic and psychographic segmentation for understanding
museum-visiting was recently challenged by Dawson and Jensen (2011, 128) who
argue that grouping people according to certain characteristics, whether demographic or psychographic, is decontextualizing and essentializing, and creates "a
misleading portrait of visitors and their experiences." In their opinion, in order to
understand visitor experiences they must be placed within a "holistic and long-
term framework of individual life circumstances, relationships and trajectories"
(Dawson and Jensen 2011, 127).

Most literature supports the proposition that visitors seek a combination of
sociability, learning, and recreation from their museum visits (Black 2005; Falk and
Dierking 1992; Hood 1993a; Jansen-Verbeke and van Rekom 1995; Merriman 1991;
Packer and Ballantyne 2002; Thyne 2001). In the past learning and education have
received more attention because of their association with the traditional roles of a
museum, but now increasing attention is being paid to more general leisure and
social experiences as motivators, including learning as a shared activity. Social
experience has been found to be particularly important for those visiting in family
groups. Baillie (1996, 5), for example, found that family groups visiting the
Queensland Museum, in Brisbane Australia, were motivated to "do something
together, to share an experience with other family members and to have fun and
enjoy each other's company." Slater (2007) concluded that art gallery visitors
sought learning, but also the opportunity to escape everyday life and routines and
to spend time with family and friends. Similarly, Packer (2008) found that the
restorative and "unhurried" nature of museum visits are valued by visitors.

Other studies give a broader sense of the way in which museum-visiting is a part
of people's leisure lifestyles. In their study of museum-visiting in Manchester,
Longhurst, Bagnall, and Savage (2004) found that people "narrated" museums as
one of the "things to do in the city, especially with children"; and as part of a "day
out," "on a par with shopping, or visiting a theatre," that is, one of the

"contemporary consumption spaces" that comprise the city. Their participants also spoke about museum-visiting as being part of "the pattern of the weekend, or within the context of holidays, and special interests and enthusiasms." They concluded that museums were not "about cultural capital in any narrow sense," but that it was much more part of the "everyday," providing people with opportunities to "perform" parenthood and contributing to their sense of place. Museum-visiting is also increasingly viewed through the lens of cultural tourism as museums, along with a range of heritage sites, are recognized as important tourist attractions and an integral part of many holiday itineraries (Jansen-Verbeke and van Rekom 1995; Johanson and Olsen 2010).

In their survey of the literature on visitor experience in museums, Kirchberg and Tröndle found a kind of homogeneity, including a

> general idea of chronology and causality, perpetually using the same underlying schema. There are always social, personal, or physical characteristics (pre-visit parameters) that influence the visit experiences (satisfying, confirming, or aesthetic). Subsequently, the effects of the visit experiences are always some kind of utilitarian measures of post-visit satisfaction and reward consequences, either cognitive or emotional. (2012, 447–448)

The problem, they argue, is that the majority of research is underpinned by certain disciplinary biases and conceptual starting points such as learning and visitor satisfaction, with findings based on questionnaires. They advocate a move toward more interdisciplinary studies using different methodologies.

Silverman (1995) was an early advocate for a better understanding of visitor meaning-making in museums and heritage sites, and for the development of responsive museum practice. In a study exploring the meaning of heritage sites for visitors, Silverman demonstrates the value of qualitative methods for accessing meanings from a visitor perspective, rather than through the predetermined constructs of the researcher, as is the case with more structured and quantitative research (Masberg and Silverman 1996). Indeed there is a growing number of studies that seek to advance our theoretical understanding of visitor perceptions and meaning-making using qualitative interviews, the findings from which are interpreted in relation to wider social and cultural theories.

Smith's (2010; 2012) recent long-term, multi-site, international study examines the memory and identity work that visitors engage in at museums and heritage sites, using face-to-face exit interviews with a series of open-ended interviews. In an example of findings from interviews with visitors at the Old Melbourne Gaol and the Stockman's Hall of Fame in Australia, she found that visitors were engaged in "cultural work," "actively working out, remembering and negotiating cultural meanings" with implications for the definition of both "self" and "other" (Smith 2012, 230). Similarly, Bagnall (2003, 87) adopted a comparative case study methodology for a study of the Museum of Science and Industry in Manchester and

Wigan Pier in Wigan, from which she concludes that far from being "passive, uncritical consumers," visitors are engaged in practices of reminiscence, drawing on emotion and imagination as much as cognition, and demonstrating an ability to perform that is "related to the cultural literacy and competency of the visitors."

Building on Cameron and Gatewood's (2012) work on numinous experiences at museum and heritage sites, Latham (2013) used interpretive phenomenology, a form of qualitative interviewing aimed at generating a textual expression of lived experience, to investigate the nature of deeply meaningful experiences with museum objects. Other innovative methods in recent studies include Tzibazi's (2013) use of Participatory Action Research to explore the inclusion of young people in museums, and Everett and Barrett's (2009) use of narrative methodology to gain insight into sustained visitor–museum relationships.

Schorch (2013a; 2013b) also adopted narrative methods for his long-term study of global visitors to Te Papa, arguing that this relatively unstructured form of interviewing is an ideal method to access meanings constructed by visitors according to their own frames of reference and biographical experiences. His findings address the embodied experience of the physical space of the museum as one of the conditions of meaning-making, as well as the ways in which visitors experience the museum as a "contact zone" and the "cross-cultural encounters, translation and dialogue" (Schorch 2013a, 68 and 74) that it facilitates.

My own work with international colleagues investigates the role of traveling exhibitions as sites of transcultural encounter through a case study of the Māori exhibition *E Tū Ake: Standing Strong*, produced by Te Papa and exhibited in France, Mexico, and Canada. This long-term study uses in-depth, semi-structured interviews with museum visitors and staff to understand the co-construction of identity and meaning through the shifts that occur as exhibitions move across social, cultural, and political boundaries (Davidson and Crenn 2014). Very little previous research has examined the impact of touring exhibitions. The practical difficulties of examining exhibitions across international venues, and the conceptual challenges of taking into consideration cross-cultural contexts, have perhaps deterred work in this area. Nonetheless, visitor studies has a significant contribution to make to our understanding of this topic, as museums increasingly seek to establish themselves as global brands while participating in cultural diplomacy programs (Grincheva 2013) and the promotion of intercultural dialogue (UNESCO 2009).

There has been a growing interest in the long-term impact of visiting. In one example, Anderson and co-researchers (Anderson 2003; Anderson and Gosselin 2008; Anderson and Shimizu 2007) conducted a series of four case studies investigating visitors' long-term memories of experiences at World Expositions using in-depth, face-to-face interviews. These studies illuminate the factors that influence the vividness of memories, demonstrating that the experience of visiting can endure for decades after the actual visit, as memories are "rehearsed" over time (Anderson and Gosselin 2008).

These recent methodological innovations and their theoretical implications are an important development for visitor studies, strengthening its intellectual foundations and helping it to be taken more seriously within the field of critical museum studies. The ongoing challenge is to ensure a continuing dialogue between theory and practice, and to consider how this more sophisticated understanding of visitor experiences can lead to improvements on the ground.

Overview of key developments and challenges

The growing range and quantity of theoretically informed visitor studies bodes well for the future of the field. However, a key challenge, as I have mentioned, is for academic researchers to communicate their findings in ways that are relevant to museum professionals, and for them to stay in touch with the realities and complexities of museum work. For their part museums, Kelly argues, "need to move beyond an evaluative culture to a research one that focuses on visitor experiences and learning that, in turn, contributes to organisational learning and change" (2004, 62). She proposes developing a "community of practice" for museum audience research, which "means that research will be theoretically based; undertaken across a range of institutions; collaborative, both within the industry and the wider research community (especially universities); longitudinal; creative and innovative with wide ranging methods" (Kelly 2004, 67).

Kelly (2004) sees potential for innovative projects through collaboration between internal staff, external consultants, and university researchers, accessing funding not previously available.[2] Another area for possible collaboration is the development of outreach programs for smaller museums that do not have on-site professional expertise (Larkin 2011; Scott 1998). The pay-off would be the development of a field that is "truly strategic": demonstrating the value of museums, improving their performance, and contributing to organizational sustainability (Kelly 2004, 68).

A further challenge is to keep abreast of the implications of digital technologies for museum-visiting, including the potential for social media to help develop a more participatory culture in terms of the way museums engage their visitors (Fell 2011; Russo 2011; Russo et al. 2008) and to better understand how visitors engage with museum websites (Marty 2007) and virtual museums. There is also the potential to harness web-based technology for gathering, analyzing, and disseminating visitor research (Kelly 2004).[3]

Central to the future of visitor studies are perceptions of its value and role within organizations. Visitor research is most effective when it is supported by senior management, is viewed as a museum-wide function, and permeates the culture of the whole institution with a visitor-centered approach (Reussner 2008; Scott 1998). To achieve this, all museum staff should ideally have a general understanding of the theoretical and methodological principles of visitor studies so that they can engage with it in an informed way and apply it successfully to their practice, whatever their level of direct involvement (Pontin 2006).

It is important, therefore, that an introduction to visitor studies be considered a key aspect of museum training. Students on the Master's degree I teach take a research methods course, including a group project in which they design, conduct, and analyze a visitor research project with the support of the VMR staff at Te Papa. At the completion of the project the students present their findings to Te Papa staff. This gives them direct experience of conducting research in the museum setting, as well as articulating the value and applicability of that research to museum professionals. Whether or not these students are aspiring visitor research practitioners, they will nonetheless be equipped with an understanding of best practice and the strategic role of visitor studies. A number have gone on to conduct visitor research as part of dissertation projects on topics as diverse as social media in museums (Fell 2011), the representation of ethnic identity (Mey 2010), collaborative indigenous exhibitions (Sciascia 2012), and collection policy (Searle 2010).

Conclusion

Visitor studies has come a long way from its tentative beginnings in observational studies and educational evaluations. As an expanding field, it is now poised to make a significant impact on museum studies. It holds particular promise in its potential to create a bridge between theory and practice, in collaborations and dialogue between museums and universities. In this respect it is defining a space for itself as an integral and influential sub-field within museum studies, with clear theoretical implications and insights for practice across the whole organization.

By complementing critical, expert readings of exhibitions and museums as sites of cultural meaning with the notion of visitors as experts on their own cultural experiences and performances, visitor studies makes an important contribution to our understanding of the broad range of human needs that can be met by museums. Moving beyond a narrow view of an educational role, to a more nuanced understanding of the complexity of being "at leisure" in the museum, recent studies using interpretive methodologies have shown the various ways in which meanings are co-produced by cultural institutions and those that engage with them. This research has the potential to broaden the way in which we articulate and demonstrate museum value (see Scott in this volume) by informing the development of expanded value frameworks that include both traditional quantitative measures alongside qualitative indicators that represent a new language for narrating the social purpose of museums.

And yet, for the foreseeable future, museums need visitor studies that encompass quantitative management tools, along with evaluation processes that promote reflective practice, *and* cutting-edge studies that expand our ideas about what museums are and what they can do for – and with – their visitors. While there is still work to be done before visitor studies is fully embraced across the museum sector, the key ingredient is an openness to new ideas and a willingness to question ways of doing things which is surely the essence of reflective, research-led practice and a critical museology.

Notes

1   Other scholars working within a sociological tradition, and drawing on the work of Pierre Bourdieu, who examined the educational, social, and economic characteristics of visitors to French art museums in the 1960s, have considered the relationship between museum-visiting (among other practices) and notions of social class and cultural capital. Recent examples include Bennett et al. (2009) and Grenfell and Hardy (2007).

2   Examples of university–museum collaborations can be found on the Australian Museum Audience Research Unit's website (http://australianmuseum.net.au/Audience-Research), which lists a series of projects undertaken with university collaborators, related publications, evaluation reports, and other useful resources for visitor studies. See also the Research Centre for Museums and Galleries (http://www2.le.ac.uk/departments/museumstudies/rcmg), part of the University of Leicester's School of Museum Studies, which undertakes commissioned research and evaluations, and has its own independent research agenda. Both websites accessed November 11, 2014.

3   Examples of online resources include Lynda Kelly's audience research blog (http://audience-research.wikispaces.com), and the Learning Museum Network Project (http://www.lemproject.eu/library/books-papers/resouces-on-audiences-and-visitor-studies). Both websites accessed November 11, 2014. Online discussion groups for visitor research professionals include Committee on Audience Research and Evaluation, American Alliance of Museums, on Facebook and LinkedIn and the Visitor Studies Group Network on LinkedIn.

References

Anderson, David. 2003. "Visitors' Long-Term Memories of World Expositions." *Curator: The Museum Journal* 46(4): 401–420.

Anderson, David, and Viviane Gosselin. 2008. "Private and Public Memories of Expo 67: A Case Study of Recollections of Montreal's World's Fair, 40 Years after the Event." *Museum and Society* 6(1): 1–21.

Anderson, David, and Hiroyuki Shimizu. 2007. "Recollections of Expo 70: Visitors' Experiences and the Retention of Vivid Long-Term Memories." *Curator: The Museum Journal* 50(4): 435–454.

Bagnall, Gaynor. 2003. "Performance and Performativity at Heritage Sites." *Museum and Society* 1(2): 87–103.

Baillie, Ann. 1996. "Empowering the Visitor: The Family Experience of Museums – a Pilot Study of Ten Family Group Visits to the Queensland Museum." Paper presented at the Museums Australia conference, Sydney, October 30 – November 2.

Bennett, Tony, Mike Savage, Elizabeth Silva, Alan Warde, Modesto Gayo-Cal, and David Wright. 2009. *Culture, Class, Distinction*. London: Routledge.

Berg, B. L. 2009. *Qualitative Research Methods for the Social Sciences*. Boston, MA: Allyn & Bacon.

Bitgood, Stephen. 2006. "An Analysis of Visitor Circulation: Movement Patterns and the General Value Principle." *Curator* 49(4): 463–475.

Bitgood, Stephen, and Ross J. Loomis. 2012. "Chan Screven's Contributions to Visitor Studies." *Curator* 55(2): 107–111.

Black, G. 2005. *The Engaging Museum: Developing Museums for Visitor Involvement*. Abingdon, UK: Routledge.

Blaikie, Norman. 2000. *Designing Social Research: The Logic of Anticipation*. Malden, MA: Polity.

Cameron, Catherine W., and John B. Gatewood. 2012. "The Numen Experience in Heritage Tourism." In *The Cultural Moment in Tourism*, edited by Laurajane Smith, Emma Waterton, and Steve Watson, 235–251. New York: Routledge.

Carey, Simon, Lee Davidson, and Mondher Sahli. 2013. "Capital City Museums and Tourism Flows: An Empirical Study of the Museum of New Zealand Te Papa Tongarewa." *International Journal of Travel Research* 15: 554–569.

Creswell, John W. 2013. *Research Design: Qualitative, Quantitative, and Mixed Method Approaches*. Los Angeles: Sage.

Davidson, Lee, and Gaelle Crenn. 2014. "Intercultural Dialogue and the Touring Exhibition: A Case Study of a Maori Exhibition in the Northern Hemisphere." In *Understanding Each Other's Heritage – Challenges for Heritage Communication in a Globalized World*, edited by Henry Crescini and Ona Vileikis, 102–122. Cottbus, Germany: Brandenburg University of Technology.

Davidson, Lee, and Pamela Sibley. 2011. "Audiences at the 'New' Museum: Visitor Commitment, Diversity and Leisure at the Museum of New Zealand Te Papa Tongarewa." *Visitor Studies* 14(2): 176–194.

Dawson, Emily, and Eric Jensen. 2011. "Towards a Contextual Turn in Visitor Studies: Evaluating Visitor Segmentation and Identity-Related Motivations." *Visitor Studies* 14(2): 127–140.

Denscombe, Martyn. 2010. *The Good Research Guide: For Small-Scale Social Research Projects*. Maidenhead, UK: McGraw-Hill/Open University Press.

Diamond, Judy, Jessica J. Luke, and David H. Uttal. 2009. *Practical Evaluation Guide: Tools for Museums and Other Informal Educational Settings*. Lanham, MD: AltaMira.

Dierking, Lynn D., and Wendy Pollock. 1998. *Questioning Assumptions: An Introduction to Front-End Studies in Museums*. Washington, DC: Association of Science-Technology Centers.

Everett, Michele, and Margaret S. Barrett. 2009. "Investigating Sustained Visitor/Museum Relationships: Employing Narrative Research in the Field of Museum Visitor Studies." *Visitor Studies* 12(1): 2–15.

Falk, John H. 2009. *Identity and the Museum Visitor Experience*. Walnut Creek, CA: Left Coast Press.

Falk, John H. 2011. "Contextualizing Falk's Identity-Related Visitor Motivation Model." *Visitor Studies* 14(2): 141–157.

Falk, John H., and Lynn D. Dierking. 1992. *The Museum Experience*. Washington, DC: Whalesback Books.

Falk, John H., Theano Moussouri, and Douglas Coulson. 1998. "The Effect of Visitors' Agendas on Museum Learning." *Curator* 41(3): 107–119.

Fell, Georgina. 2011. "Going Social: A Case Study of the Use of Social Media Technologies by the Museum of New Zealand Te Papa Tongarewa." Unpublished MA dissertation, Victoria University of Wellington, Wellington. Accessed November 11, 2014. http://hdl.handle.net/10063/2555.

Galloway, Sheila, and Julian Stanley. 2004. "Thinking Outside the Box: Galleries, Museums and Evaluation." *Museum and Society* 2(2): 125–146.

Grenfell, Michael, and Cheryl Hardy. 2007. *Art Rules: Pierre Bourdieu and the Visual Arts*. Oxford: Berg.

Grincheva, Natalia. 2013. "Cultural Diplomacy 2.0: Challenges and Opportunities in Museum International Practices." *Museums and Society* 11(1): 39–49.

Harrison, Julia D. 2005. "Ideas of Museums in the 1990s." In *Heritage, Museums and Galleries: An Introductory Reader*, edited by Gerard Corsane, 38–53. London: Routledge.

Hein, George. 1998. *Learning in the Museum*. London: Routledge.

Hood, Marilyn. 1992. "Significant Issues in Museum Audience Research." *International Laboratory for Visitor Studies Review* 2(2): 281–286.

Hood, Marilyn. 1993a. "After 70 Years of Audience Research, What Have We Learned? Who Comes to Museums, Who Does Not, and Why?" *Visitor Studies* 5: 77–87.

Hood, Marilyn. 1993b. "Comfort and Caring: Two Essential Environmental Factors." *Environment and Behaviour* 25(6): 710–724.

Hood, Marilyn. 2004. "Staying Away: Why People Choose Not to Visit Museums." In *Reinventing the Museum: Historical and Contemporary Perspectives on the Paradigm Shift*, edited by Gail Anderson, 150–157. Walnut Creek, CA: AltaMira.

Hooper-Greenhill, Eilean. 1994. *Museums and Their Visitors*. London: Routledge.

Hooper-Greenhill, Eilean. 2006. "Studying Visitors." In *A Companion to Museum Studies*, edited by Sharon Macdonald, 362–376. Malden, MA: Blackwell.

Hooper-Greenhill, Eilean, Theano Moussouri, Emma Hawthorne, and Rowena Riley. 2001. *Making Meaning in Art Museums 1: Visitors' Interpretive Strategies at Wolverhampton Art Gallery*. Leicester: Research Centre for Museums and Galleries, University of Leicester.

ICOM (International Council of Museums). 2013. *ICOM Code of Ethics for Museums*. Paris: ICOM.

Jansen-Verbeke, Myriam, and Johan van Rekom. 1995. "Scanning Museum Visitors: Urban Tourism Marketing." *Annals of Tourism Research* 23(2): 364–375.

Johanson, Lisbeth Bergum, and Kjell Olsen. 2010. "Alta Museum as a Tourist Attraction: The Importance of Location." *Journal of Heritage Tourism* 5(1): 1–16.

Kelly, Lynda. 2004. "Evaluation, Research and Communities of Practice: Program Evaluation in Museums." *Archival Science* 4: 45–69.

Kelly, Lynda, and Phil Gordon. 2002. "Developing a Community of Practice: Museums and Reconciliation in Australia." In *Museums, Society, Inequality*, edited by Richard Sandall, 153–174. London: Routledge.

Kirchberg, Volker. 2007. "Cultural Consumption Analysis: Beyond Structure and Agency." *Cultural Sociology* 1(1): 115–135.

Kirchberg, Volker, and Martin Tröndle. 2012. "Experiencing Exhibitions: A Review of Studies on Visitor Experiences in Museums." *Curator* 55(4): 435–452.

Lang, Caroline, John Reeve, and Vicky Woollard, eds. 2006. *The Responsive Museum: Working with Audiences in the Twenty-First Century*. Aldershot: Ashgate.

Larkin, Casimar. 2011. "The Participation of Small Museums in Visitor Research." Unpublished MA dissertation, Victoria University of Wellington, Wellington. Accessed November 11, 2014. http://hdl.handle.net/10063/1841.

Latham, Kiersten F. 2013. "Numinous Experiences with Museum Objects." *Visitor Studies* 16(1): 3–20.

Leinhardt, Gaea, Kevin Crowley, and Karen Knutson, eds. 2002. *Learning Conversations in Museums*. Mahwah, NJ: Lawrence Erlbaum.

Leinhardt, Gaea, and Karen Knutson. 2004. *Listening in on Museum Conversations*. Walnut Creek, CA: AltaMira.

Lindauer, Margaret. 2005. "What to Ask and How to Answer: A Comparative Analysis of Methodologies and Philosophies of Summative Exhibit Evaluation." *Museum and Society* 3(3): 137–152.

Longhurst, Brian, Gaynor Bagnall, and Mike Savage. 2004. "Audiences, Museums and the English Middle Class." *Museums and Society* 2(2): 104–124.

Loomis, Ross J. 1993. "Planning for the Visitor: The Challenge of Visitor Studies." In *Museum Visitor Studies in the 90s*, edited by Sandra Bicknell and Graham Farmelo, 13–23. London: Science Museum.

Macdonald, Sharon. 2005. "Accessing Audiences: Visiting Visitor Books." *Museum and Society* 3(3): 119–136.

Macdonald, Sharon. 2006. "Expanding Museum Studies: An Introduction." In *A Companion to Museum Studies*, edited by Sharon Macdonald, 1–12. Malden, MA: Blackwell.

Marty, Paul F. 2007. "Museum Websites and Museum Visitors: Before and After the Museum Visit." *Museum Management and Curatorship* 22(4): 337–360.

Masberg, Barbara A., and Lois H. Silverman. 1996. "Visitor Experiences at Heritage Sites: A Phenomenological Approach." *Journal of Travel Research* 34, 20–25.

McCarthy, Conal. 2013. "The Rules of (Maori) Art: Bourdieu's Cultural Sociology and Maori Visitors in New Zealand Museums." *Journal of Sociology* 49(2–3): 173–193.

McLean, Fiona. 1997. *Marketing the Museum*. London: Routledge.

McLean, Kathleen. 2004. "Museum Exhibitions and the Dynamics of Dialogue." In *Reinventing the Museum: Historical and Contemporary Perspectives on the Paradigm Shift*, edited by Gail Anderson, 193–211. Walnut Creek, CA: AltaMira.

Merriman, Nick. 1991. *Beyond the Glass Case: The Past, the Heritage and the Public in Britain*. Leicester, UK: Leicester University Press.

Mey, Vera. 2010. "Commonplace: Towards a Post-Ethnic Understanding of Identity and Representation of Asian New Zealanders for Museum Practice." Unpublished MA dissertation, Victoria University of Wellington, Wellington. Accessed November 11, 2014. http://hdl.handle.net/10063/1545.

Ministry for Culture and Heritage. 2003. *A Measure of Culture: Cultural Experiences and Cultural Spending in New Zealand*. Wellington, NZ: Ministry for Culture and Heritage.

Ministry of Tourism. 2009. *Tourist Activity/Museum Tourism*. Wellington, NZ: Ministry of Tourism.

MORI. 2001. *Visitors to Museums and Art Galleries in the UK*. Birmingham, UK: Council for Museums, Archives and Libraries.

MORI. 2004. *Visitors to Museums and Galleries*. Birmingham, UK: Council for Museums, Archives and Libraries.

Munley, M. E. 1986. "Asking the Right Questions: Evaluation and the Museum Mission." *Museum News* 64(3): 18–23.

Nichols, Susan K. 1999. *Visitor Surveys: A User's Manual*. Washington, DC: American Association of Museums, Technical Information Service.

Nurse Rainbolt, Gretchen, Jacob A. Benfield, and Ross J. Loomis. 2012. "Visitor Self-Report Behavior Mapping as a Tool for Recording Exhibition Circulation." *Visitor Studies* 15(2): 203–216.

Packer, Jan. 2008. "Beyond Learning: Exploring Visitors' Perceptions of the Value and Benefits of Museum Experiences." *Curator* 51(1): 33–54.

Packer, Jan, and Roy Ballantyne. 2002. "Motivational Factors and the Visitor Experience: A Comparison of Three Sites." *Curator* 45(3): 183–198.

Paris, Scott G., and Melissa J. Mercer. 2002. "Finding Self in Objects: Identity Exploration in Museums." In *Learning Conversations in Museums*, edited by Gaea Leinhardt, Kevin Crowley, and Karen Knutson, 401–423. Mahwah, NJ: Lawrence Erlbaum.

Parsons, Chris. 2007. "Web-Based Surveys: Best Practices Based on the Research Literature." *Visitor Studies* 10(1): 13–33.

Pontin, Kate. 2006. "Understanding Museum Evaluation." In *The Responsive Museum: Working with Audiences in the Twenty-First Century*, edited by Caroline Lang, John Reeve, and Vicky Woollard, 117–127. Aldershot: Ashgate.

Prior, Nick. 2002. "Museums: Leisure between State and Distinction." In *Histories of Leisure*, edited by Rudy Koshar, 27–44. Oxford: Berg.

Prior, Nick. 2003. "Having One's Tate and Eating It: Transformations of the Museum in the Hypermodern Era." In *Art and Its Publics: Museum Studies at the End of the Millennium*, edited by Andrew McClellan, 51–76. Oxford: Blackwell.

Reussner, Eva M. 2003. *Audience Research in the Australian Cultural Heritage Sector. A Study Commissioned by the Museums Australia Evaluation and Visitor Research Special Interest Group (Evrsig). Final Report. May 2003*. Previously but no longer available online.

Reussner, Eva M. 2004. "Best Practices in Audience Research and Evaluation: Case Studies of Australian and New Zealand Museums." *Visitor Studies Today* 7(2): 17–25.

Reussner, Eva M. 2008. "Learning from the Best: Success Factors for Effective Audience Research." In *Heritage Learning Matters: Museums and Universal Heritage*, edited by Hadwig Kräutler, 186–197. Vienna: ICOM/CECA.

Russo, Angelina. 2011. "Transformations in Cultural Communication: Social Media, Cultural Exchange, and Creative Connections." *Curator: The Museum Journal* 54(3): 327–346.

Russo, Angelina, Jerry Watkins, Lynda Kelly, and Sebastian Chan. 2008. "Participatory Communication with Social Media." *Curator: The Museum Journal* 51(1): 21–31.

Schorch, Philipp. 2013a. "Contact Zones, Third Spaces, and the Act of Interpretation." *Museum and Society* 11(1): 68–81.

Schorch, Philipp. 2013b. "The Experience of a Museum Space." *Museum Management and Curatorship* 28(2): 193–208.

Sciascia, Ana. 2012. "Iwi Exhibitions at Te Papa: A Ngai Tahu Perspective." Unpublished MA dissertation, Victoria University of Wellington, Wellington. Accessed November 11, 2014. http://hdl.handle.net/10063/2513.

Scott, Carol. 1998. "The Long and Winding Road: Evaluation and Visitor Research in Museums in Australia and New Zealand." Paper presented at the Visitor Centre Stage: Action for the Future, Canberra, Australia. August 4–6.

Screven, C. G. 1990. "Uses of Evaluation before, during and after Exhibition Design." *ILVS Review* 1(2): 36–66.

Seagram, Belinda Crawford, Leslie H. Patten, and Christine W. Lockett. 1993. "Audience Research and Exhibit Development." *Museum Management and Curatorship* 12(1): 29–41.

Searle, Chloe. 2010. "Collecting for New Zealand: Examining What the Museum of New Zealand Te Papa Tongarewa Should Collect." Unpublished MA dissertation, Victoria University of Wellington, Wellington. Accessed November 11, 2014. http://hdl.handle.net/10063/1558.

Shettel, Harris. 2008. "No Visitor Left Behind." *Curator* 51(4): 367–375.

Silverman, Lois H. 1995. "Visitor Meaning-Making in Museums for a New Age." *Curator* 38(3): 161–169.

Slater, Alix. 2007. "'Escaping to the Gallery': Understanding the Motivations of Visitors to Galleries." *International Journal of Nonprofit and Voluntary Sector Marketing* 12(2): 149–162.

Smith, Laurajane. 2006. *Uses of Heritage*. London: Routledge.

Smith, Laurajane. 2010. "'Man's Inhumanity to Man' and Other Platitudes of Avoidance and Misrecognition: An Analysis of Visitor Responses to Exhibitions Marking the 1807 Bicentenary." *Museum and Society* 8(3): 193–214.

Smith, Laurajane. 2012. "The Cultural 'Work' of Tourism." In *The Cultural Moment in Tourism*, edited by Laurajane Smith, Emma Waterton, and Steve Watson, 210–234. New York: Routledge.

Spero, Susan B. 2013. "The Museum Experience Revisited." *Museum Management and Curatorship* 28(4): 430–432.

Stam, Deirdre C. 2005. "The Informed Muse: The Implications of 'the New Museology' for Museum Practice." In *Heritage, Museums and Galleries: An Introductory Reader*, edited by Gerard Corsane, 54–70. London: Routledge.

Storksdieck, Martin. 2007. "Using Web Surveys in Early Front-End Evaluations with Open Populations: A Case Study of Amateur Astronomers." *Visitor Studies* 10(1): 47–54.

Thyne, Maree. 2001. "The Importance of Values Research for Nonprofit Organisations: The Motivation-Based Values of Museum Visitors." *International Journal of Nonprofit and Voluntary Sector Marketing* 6(2): 116–130.

Tzibazi, Vasiliki. 2013. "Participatory Action Research with Young People in Museums." *Museum Management and Curatorship* 8(2): 153–171.

UNESCO. 2009. *Investing in Cultural Diversity and Intercultural Dialogue: UNESCO World Report*. Paris: UNESCO.

Vergo, Peter, ed. 1989. *The New Museology*. London: Reaktion Books.

Weil, Stephen. 1998. "When the Audience Takes Centre Stage." *Melbourne Art Journal* 3: 5–13.

Witcomb, Andrea. 2003. *Re-Imagining the Museum: Beyond the Mausoleum*. London: Routledge.

Yalowitz, Steven, and Kerry Bronnenkant. 2009. "Timing and Tracking: Unlocking Visitor Behaviour." *Visitor Studies* 12(1): 47–64.

Yalowitz, Steven, and Ava Ferguson. 2007. "Using Web Surveys in Summative Evaluations: A Case Study at the Monterey Bay Aquarium." *Visitor Studies* 10(1): 34–46.

Lee Davidson is a Senior Lecturer in the Museum and Heritage Studies program at Victoria University of Wellington, New Zealand. Her research interests include leisure (history, theory, and contemporary practice); visitor studies; narrative research methods; tourism; and natural/cultural heritage. She has published research articles in *Visitor Studies*, the *International Journal of Travel Research*, and *Leisure Sciences*, as well as contributing a chapter to *Intangible Natural Heritage* (2012) and coauthoring *Serious Leisure and Nature* (with R. A. Stebbins, 2011). Recent projects include the development of a national visitor research framework for New Zealand's museum sector (in association with Museums Aotearoa), and a transnational, collaborative study of Te Papa's exhibition *E Tū Ake: Standing Strong* on tour in France, Mexico, and Canada.

23 TRANSLATING MUSEUM MEANINGS
A Case for Interpretation

Kerry Jimson

"So, you're an interpreter? What do you translate?"

"Messages, concepts, stories… I try to get across the meanings of objects in museums so people can form their own understanding of them."

Well, at least that's how I think about my job. It is a grand aim and a challenge that can misfire, be misguided, patronize, or simply not work. But with the right approach, interpretation can open up worlds and meanings for people. It can excite, inspire, and motivate. It can galvanize perception, provoke action, and shift attitudes.

What is an interpreter? It can be difficult explaining your role to people outside museums, who naturally assume that the job involves interpreting languages. But actually, as I suggest above, this is not a bad analogy for what interpreters do in communicating meaning or getting across messages to people, hopefully in ways which allow them to make up their own mind about them. Often, brief answers to this question lean toward the reductive. Why? Although the interpreter has specific tasks, these are varied and potentially reach across an entire organization. In my own career, I have played a variety of roles in fulfilling the interpretive function of the museums I have worked in – concept developer, writer, audience advocate, educator – all involving an aspect of communicating, explaining, clarifying, facilitating, and opening things up to greater understanding.

While taking all the broad considerations of interpretation into account, I believe it is essentially a creative occupation. It may even seem mercurial or nebulous. Other museum practices, conservation for example, are more quantifiable and closely defined. Nevertheless an agenda for interpretation should still be set out, measured, and evaluated. In this chapter I attempt to do this, bearing in mind

The International Handbooks of Museum Studies: Museum Practice, First Edition.
Edited by Conal McCarthy.
© 2015 John Wiley & Sons Ltd. Published 2020 by John Wiley & Sons Ltd.

I am referring to the specific professional practice of museum interpretation, not the notion of interpretation in general.

So what exactly is the role of interpretation in museum practice? The American Association of Museums (Edcom 2005) defines interpretation as "the media/activities through which a museum carries out its mission and educational role." It then suggests how this can be done in three ways:

- Interpretation is a dynamic process of communication between the museum and the audience.
- Interpretation is the means by which the museum delivers its content.
- Interpretation media/activities include, but are not limited to: exhibits, tours, web sites, classes, school programs, publications, and outreach.

The broad scope of museum interpretative practice will be apparent already from this brief description. Similar definitions can be found in publications and on the websites of various interpretation societies (AHI 2014; INNZ 2013, IA 2014; Blockley and Hems 2006; Bridle 2013). For example, Interpretation Canada states: "Heritage interpretation is any communication process designed to reveal meanings and relationships of cultural and natural heritage to the public, through first-hand involvement with an object, artifact, landscape or site" ("Definition of Interpretation," 1976: qtd at InterpScan 2014).

The strategies, materials, and media used in interpretation are many and varied: they include the exhibitions, displays, and interactives, and the objects that thrill the imagination, that connect people to the outside world through understanding. Of course, as I hinted above, interpretation does not work for everyone every time, as the process of communication is far from simple and neutral. But when it works, these interpretive media can inspire, move, and provoke those who experience them. They *engage* viewers and visitors, and acknowledge them as active participants in the experience. They can also entertain, delight, and even be whimsical, depending on content and context.

At the outset, I should make it clear that I write as a practitioner, not as an academic: while drawing on scholarly sources, my aim is to elucidate what current museum interpretation is, how it works, and why it is an essential aspect of museum practice today. The chapter begins with a literature review and historical overview of interpretation in museums, followed by a description of the function of the interpreter and my key guiding principles for interpretation practice. The bulk of the chapter is then given over to an explanation of the role of the interpreter in exhibition development, including the process, concept, audience, story, planning, and related issues to do with comfort, safety and transparency, text, and access. After a brief case study of interpretation at the Museum of New Zealand Te Papa Tongarewa (Te Papa), the chapter concludes with an argument for the place and value of interpretation as an integral part of museum practice.

History and theory: a brief overview of interpretation

It was probably the growth of tourism that was the driving force behind the development of interpretation in the eighteenth and nineteenth centuries, with early examples of the practice including guides on the Grand Tours of Europe and those who showed visitors around their houses and private collections (Silberman 2013; Dewar 2000). Showing tourists around the sites was not just a European activity: in colonial New Zealand, Māori guides in the thermal village of Whakarewarewa were possibly the first "interpreters" in the country (Colquhoun 1995; Diamond 2007). In most cases, it seems reasonable to assume that guides operated in specific destinations: someone who could be questioned and who could supply relevant information that made sense to (usually) paying customers. In return, clients would be shown famous sites or objects, be informed (more or less accurately) about what they were looking at and often entertained. The guide presented an "insider's" view to outsiders. In the case of early museums, there is evidence that guides engaged visitors by allowing them to pick up and touch objects, as well as look at them (Classen and Howes 2006). By the early twentieth century in the United States, some public museums provided interpretation in the form of signage and tours by docents as part of an expanded range of visitor services designed to educate a broad cross-section of society (Hein 2013).

By the mid-twentieth century, many museums lagged behind the kind of interpretation that was increasingly familiar in natural environment settings. For example, the tour guides of the American National Parks from the 1950s are often acknowledged as the predecessors of contemporary interpreters (Merriman and Brochu 2006). These passionate advocates for nature and conservation worked on the premise that visitors' understanding and knowledge of the landscape, flora, and fauna in parks were closely linked to their enjoyment of these places.

Among these guides was Freeman Tilden, whose book *Interpreting Our Heritage*, first published in 1957, remains relevant today. Describing interpretation as an "art, which combines many arts" (2007, 14), he argued that interpretation was not about information, or the didactic teaching of facts, but about provoking and stimulating audiences to think for themselves. His famous dictum was: "Through interpretation, understanding; through understanding, appreciation; through appreciation, protection" (2007, 38). Tilden devised six principles of interpretation, as follows:

1. Any interpretation that does not somehow relate what is being displayed or described to something within the personality or experience of the visitor will be sterile.
2. Information, as such, is not interpretation. Interpretation is revelation based upon information. But they are entirely different things. However, all interpretation includes information.

3. Interpretation is an art, which combines many arts, whether the materials presented are scientific, historical, or architectural. Any art is to some degree teachable.

4. The chief aim of interpretation is not instruction, but provocation.

5. Interpretation should aim to present a whole rather than a part, and must address itself to the whole person rather than any phase.

6. Interpretation addressed to children (say, up to the age of 12) should not be a dilution of the presentation to adults, but should follow a fundamentally different approach. To be at its best it will require a separate program. (Tilden 2007, 14–15)

These are powerful and influential precepts that still resonate with contemporary interpretive practice, though they have been extended, expanded, and critiqued in recent studies (Beck and Cable 2002; Silberman 2013). Among those who have developed Tilden's work is Sam Ham, a specialist in communication psychology and conservation at the University of Idaho, who has trained interpreters, educators, and exhibit developers in the USA, Canada, Australia, and New Zealand, and whose practical guide (1992) is a leading text on applied interpretation. The revised edition, *Interpretation: Making a Difference on Purpose* (2013), refines Ham's theory of thematic interpretation, which argues that successful interpretation has four essential elements that can be encapsulated in the acronym TORE: that is, effective interpretation is Thematic, Organized, Relevant, and Enjoyable. Due to the work of Ham and other scholars, environmental interpretation has developed a distinct literature in the heritage management sector (Uzzell 1989; Howard 2003; Blockley and Hems 2006; West and McKellar 2010).

By the 1960s and 1970s, educators within museums, galleries, and aquariums had learnt from their colleagues in the heritage field, and increasingly perceived the need for their involvement in the development of displays, rather than being brought in at the end of the process. Their experience and understanding of how visitors responded to the museum's messages reinforced the view that exhibitions should *not* be the sole responsibility of curatorial staff if they were to communicate effectively with their audience (McLean 2004; Roberts 1997).

Such educators were advocates of the application of constructivist learning within the museum: that is to say, the idea originally championed by Jean Piaget (1896–1980) that learners construct meaning for themselves (Hein 2006; Hooper-Greenhill 1994; 2000; see Reeve and Woollard in this volume). Today, the discussion of interpretation in museum studies has similarly embraced the idea of active meaning-making (Mason 2005).

In recent years an important strand of critical heritage studies has debated Tilden's work, and raised questions about orthodox interpretation practices, calling for new theoretical orientations, greater diversity, a darker and "edgier" approach, and a more reflexive, dialogical practice (Staiff, Bushell, and Kennedy 2002; Frost 2005; Ablett and Dyer 2009; Winter 2013; Silberman 2013). Andrea

Witcomb in particular has critically analyzed public history, heritage sites, and museum displays (Witcomb 2006; 2013). In opposition to a style of interpretation that employs linear narratives, and conveys a nostalgic view of the past, she calls for an interpretation that destabilizes received ideas and establishes personal connections through emotions and affect (Witcomb 2011).

Today, the literature on interpretation encompasses general manuals (Catlin-Legutko and Klinger 2011), as well as interpretation in exhibition development (Bridle 2013), historic house museums (Donnelly 2002), and art galleries and museums (Whitehead 2012). Meanwhile, Fritsch's edited collection on museum and gallery interpretation provides an excellent overview of what might be called interpretation studies (2011a). Fritsch acknowledges that there is some ambiguity about the boundaries between interpretation, education, and visitor research, but argues that there is clearly "a place for interpretation strategy, development, production and reception in museums" (2011b, 1). Although interpretation is often associated with science and children's museums, successful new exhibits and displays have been developed in diverse institutions including: the British Galleries at the V&A (2001); Manchester Art Gallery (2002); Kelvingrove, Glasgow (2006); and the Detroit Institute of Arts Museum (2007) (Fritsch 2011b, 4–5).

Finally, it is important to draw attention to the growth of professional interpretation organizations in the USA (National Association for Interpretation), Canada (InterScan), UK (Association for Heritage Interpretation), Australia (Interpretation Australia), and New Zealand (Interpretation Network New Zealand). These organizations have produced a useful body of gray literature on many aspects of interpretation practice: the National Association of Interpretation maintains a journal (*Journal of Interpretation Research* 2013); Museums Galleries Scotland has a useful guide (Museums Galleries Scotland 2013); as does the American Alliance of Museums (Edcom 2005).

The function of the interpreter

In summary then, I would argue the function of the interpreter is to mediate between the curator, concept developer, or institutional knowledge-holder, and the visitor.[1] The interpreter translates museum meanings to audiences in such a way as to facilitate their participation in the process. They are, therefore, communication specialists, whose knowledge of museum production is combined with an understanding of how visitors respond to spaces and displays. This may involve devising ways of interacting with visitors by communicating the subject (the concept and content) through an object (also a place or experience). Following Tilden's first principle of interpretation, the essential factor is to find points of recognition and interest for the visitor.

It is more productive to consider interpretation as *function* rather than as a specific *role*. Although Fritsch writes that interpreters have varied job titles and find it hard to explain what they do, and the process and remit of interpretation varies enormously in different institutions, overall it can be thought of as a process rather than product (Fritsch 2011c). I think of it as a function because, in smaller institutions, many of the specialized roles that would be differentiated in a large museum will be conflated into single positions. For example, a concept developer and a curator and interpreter may be one and the same person – just as an interpreter may also be the writer and educator for an exhibition. Therefore, when I refer to the "interpreter" I am talking about the function of interpretation, regardless of whose responsibility it is. I also treat the terms "museum" and "exhibition" in the same way, as most of the principles and tools can apply equally to a heritage site, a gallery, an aquarium, or a zoo.

Interpretation has a key function within the exhibition process, with the twin goals of ensuring that it is engaging and relevant for visitors and that the conceptual and scholarly aims of the project are realized. Good interpretation ensures that the subject is presented accurately and clearly and visitors are stimulated to explore, investigate, and question. To this end, the interpreter acts as a "friend" to the concept or subject and an "advocate" for the diverse interests of audiences. Marstine makes this point in the context of the "post-museum": "the most significant indicator of the rise in the post-museum is the changing nature of the relationship between institution and audience ... the new attitude of respect for audience that puts the institution and the visitor on a more equal footing" (Marstine 2006, 30; see also Hooper-Greenhill 2000).

Part of the interpreter's function is to help clarify concepts and content, identify target visitor groups, and try to understand visitor interests, taking account of different learning styles. The ensuing interpretive plan will include communication objectives and proposed methods and media for the realization of those objectives. Learning styles are often divided into visual, aural, and tactile; most individuals use all three of these sensory inputs to learn, but tend to prefer one as being more effective for them (Fleming 2001–2012). Many models, such as VARK, an acronym for "Visual Aural Read/Write Kinesthetic," have been developed to evaluate these learning modes (Fleming 2001–2012). Although such models can be faddish, they are useful in analyzing the coverage of sensory input in an exhibition in its role of engaging visitors. As Beverly Serrell puts it, "[w]ithout engagement there is no learning" (2006, 113).

The delivery devices or media that interpreters have at their disposal employ a range of senses: verbal (signs, talks, audio-guides, as well as soundscapes that deliver aural information or texture); visual (films, graphics, images, which also includes design); tactile (feel boxes, textured surfaces, handle-able objects, which may include kinesthetic or active learning); olfactory (scent cannons, fragrance samples). Interpretation can also use: interactives, such as mechanical and computer interactives; websites, mobile, and social media; and physical spaces. Amid this array of media options, Uzzell reminds us that "we should be encouraging people to become interpreters themselves. When we interpret a site, inherent in the interpretation should be the communication of those skills which enable the interpretation in the first place ... interpreters should be giving away the skills of revelation" (Uzzell 1989, 9). Of course there are practical questions about how this can be effectively done, but the overall point here is that interpretation should be transparent so that visitors can evaluate the integrity of what is presented. This may also enable visitors to become aware of, and decode, the mechanisms of interpretation, thus making them self-conscious in the act of interpretation. It is a two-way process of active creation rather than the old idea of communication as a "silver bullet" going directly from producer to consumer (Silberman 2013).

Key resources for interpretation include the knowledge and experience of curatorial staff, educators, collection managers, designers, researchers, and – not least – an understanding of the community, groups, and individuals that the organization serves. This task becomes more complex as more communities and voices assert their right to a place within museum structures, both physical and conceptual. Opening up museums to public interpretation can be a messy business. As scholars have warned, the relationship between museums and communities is not straightforward:

> An acute moral dilemma is raised by the acknowledgement that museums have responsibilities to communities. What happens when one community makes a request that will inevitably oppress another community? Who actually speaks for a community? Are all demands equally valid? If not, what procedure should be set in place to adjudicate them? (Karp, Kreamer, and Lavine 1992, 10)

Interpreters cannot shy away from these debates: discussions about identity are at the heart of interpretation. Put another way: "museums are ... places for defining who people are and how they should act and as places for challenging those definitions" (Karp, Kreamer, and Lavine 1992, 11). Although it can be challenging, consultation and involvement can result in greater engagement with communities, as well as making exhibitions more relevant for a wider public, and, it should be added, the museum itself.

Interpretation is also about ensuring that the visitors' experience of a place is one that facilitates positive social interaction, including entertainment (Weil 1998). The interpreter, then, is aware of the many uses of their facility, as a forum, community space, meeting place, classroom, family destination, tourist amenity, and more. Contemporary museums are moving toward this, just as they are striving to address audience wants and needs in a holistic fashion. Barbosa and Brito have summarized their objectives in these terms: "sustained audience development should be considered a long-term goal of museums by improving the experience and the levels of satisfaction and commitment" (2012, 20). They argue that "museums have to design adequate responses to meet not only utilitarian and intellectual needs, but also hedonic and emotional needs" (Barbosa and Brito 2012, 20).

Taking account of these contexts, I have developed three functional principles for use in workshops on interpretive practice for students and museum staff (Box 23.1):

Box 23.1

1. Clarity – lucidly and briefly communicate key messages
The museum visitor is a "moving target" with a time budget. Well-constructed, focused messaging will benefit both the "speedster" as well as those who linger.

2. Transparency – be upfront about research, debate, and what under-pins the information within an exhibition, thereby exposing opinion, conjecture, and discursive content
The interpreter needs to show supporting evidence for concepts and develop a case that justifies the narrative. If there is reasonable doubt on a subject or cogent, dissenting voices, these too need to be clearly addressed and given expression.

3. Simplicity – for the broad appeal that engages "lay" visitor groups, employ simplicity without diluting scholarly complexity
Simple does not mean simplistic. It means unpacking concepts and ideas, and decoding jargon and complex language. In my own practice, it is key to the creative development of media and displays that enable visitors to understand and make meaning from unfamiliar or complex concepts.

Additionally the interpreter should aim to combine enjoyment with learning, whenever possible. If visitors are having a pleasurable time they are more likely to engage with the museum content. The same applies to the museum's own development process, which can employ tactics like brainstorming to find creative solutions. Developers should always be open to challenging, and even outlandish, ideas. Give people license to play, to let their imaginations roam around the topic, and not to censor themselves. I have found that fun and workable solutions often come from "bad" or "silly" ideas.

Interpretation in exhibition development

In this section, I describe the interpretive function within the process of exhibition development, by outlining the hypothetical development of a generic exhibition and related interpretive activities. Inevitably, this is a rather artificial scenario: the reality rarely follows a predictable path, although a roadmap is always useful. Readers should also refer to other sources for further discussion of exhibition practice (see especially Dean in this volume) and interpretation in exhibitions (Durbin 2004; Bridle 2013).

Describing the concept

The exhibition begins with an idea or concept. Usually this is articulated in a concept description, which is a brief document, often just a page, providing a broad brush-stroke picture of the exhibition and its essential components, including the target audiences and the projected visitor base – vital information for the interpreter.

The interpreter's responsibility is wide, and so it should be. In a multidisciplinary team model in a large museum, interpreters have relationships with the concept developer/curator, writer, any external suppliers (such as an interactive developer), filmmaker, educator, project manager, marketing, community groups, other subject specialists, stakeholders, and other exhibition contributors. Early in the process, the interpreter may well organize one or more focus groups to evaluate and provide feedback on the exhibition concept. Such discussions would usually involve the marketing team responsible for attracting, engaging with, and expanding the target audience.

Meanwhile, the interpreter needs to gauge the level of prior knowledge among the participants and their response to the concept, as well as to identify any risks or difficulties the exhibition may pose. Focus groups can reveal visitor expectations and interests, suggesting how to present the exhibition content most effectively. In addition, visitor research methods, such as front-end evaluation and consultation via social media, can provide further evidence of public perceptions and under-standings of the exhibition topic. Such information is invaluable feedback for con-cept development and preliminary interpretation; the beginning of many feedback loops that, ideally, inform the exhibition process (on visitor research, see Davidson in this volume).

Visitor research can also provide basic demographic profiling on existing and potential audiences for a particular exhibition. What age groups will it attract? Is it cross-generational? Does the exhibition appeal to couples? To teenagers? To solo visitors? Clubs? Religious or cultural groups? Scientific societies? Book clubs? Cyber communities? Where do these visitors live? Can the exhibition reach beyond the usual, well-heeled museum visitor to engage members of hard-to-reach groups? Visitor data can be further segmented into motivations for visiting the museum and associated visitor behaviors. Some people might be seeking new and cutting-edge experiences, some might be looking for an aesthetic encounter, and others a thrilling activity. It is the responsibility of the interpreter, as the audience advocate, to feed this visitor data into the process of developing the exhibition. This front-end visitor research then forms a basis for evaluation once the exhibi-tion has opened. (On audience segmentation, see Davidson in this volume; on audience development, see Black in this volume.)

The big idea

The early stage of development also requires the formulation of the single idea that informs the entire exhibition and determines whether the project has a strong and purposeful connecting thread. As Beverly Serrell explains "having a big idea does not make visitor's experiences in the exhibition more controlled, constricted, or less open-ended than an exhibition without one, but it does increase the likelihood that visitors will be able to decipher the exhibition's communication goal." She adds, "A big idea keeps the exhibition team accountable to their educational objectives, while allowing visitors to construct their own experiences freely" (Serrell 1996, 6–7). Formulating the main proposition of an exhibition or display in a single sentence, though difficult, reveals as much about what is excluded as what the visitor will eventually see (for examples, see Serrell 1996). The discussions around the formulation of this big idea can be fascinating, vigorous, and protracted, often providing a necessary filter for ideas that cannot – or should not – be included. Arguments against this approach are that it may confine the experience and the intellectual reach of the exhibition, and that it "dumbs down" and oversimplifies the subject (McLean 2004). I would argue that even very complex ideas can – and should – be stated clearly. As Albert Einstein, who once summarized his General Theory of Relativity in 11 words, is reported to have said: "Things should be made as simple as possible, but not simpler" (Quote Investigator 2011).

What's the story?

Focus groups and formative evaluation provide data on visitors' knowledge and understanding of, and interest in, a topic. This enables the interpreter, curator, and other team members to reflect on the exhibition concept and shape the exhibition narrative or story. This can be an actual story, such as a historical event or biography, or it can be a thematic framing of ideas, events, objects, and displays. The connections between these elements need to be effectively communicated to visitors; the narrative should have a clear purpose, logic, and coherence. In response to the charge that a narrative (or story) is reductive, historian Simon Schama has talked about developing a television program in these terms: "Writing a good script and filming a good program, which actually in the first instance tells a thrilling story but also always asks difficult questions without it seeming like homework for people, that is one of the most exacting disciplines that you can do" (Schama 2010). For the museum interpreter, just swap "script" and "filming a good program" with "exhibition."

Giving exhibitions a clear narrative structure is therefore one way of enabling visitors to create their own meanings, as well as having the power to draw people into a story, with all of its memorable qualities. Narratives are always present, even if the exhibition does not have an explicit storyline. Each visitor brings his/her own worldview, and creates his/her own story, in experiencing an exhibition (Kelly 2010). Anthropologists have made this point in relation to the museum visitor experience: "When people enter museums they do not leave their cultures and identities in the coatroom. They interpret museum exhibitions through their prior experiences and through the culturally learned beliefs, values, and perceptual skills that they gain through membership in multiple communities" (Karp, Kreamer, and

Lavine 1992, 3). In all this work, the interpreter has a valuable function in clarifying the concept and evaluating the developing narrative in relation to visitors' needs and interests. As well as the visitor research data, the interpreter uses his/her knowledge of visitors' learning styles and how they process material – emotionally, psychologically, and culturally. The interpreter does not need to be a specialist in the subject area, and, indeed, there is a compelling argument that he/she should *not* be. If the interpreter has the general knowledge of, say, a well-informed and curious person, he/she will ask intelligent, though sometimes basic, questions that tease out the complexity of the subject. I have certainly witnessed frustration from academics at this approach. However, the interpreter is merely voicing the very questions that visitors may ask, looking at the concept from their point of view. This benign interrogation is an excellent way to reflect on the strengths and weaknesses of the concept, to perceive how visitors might understand it, and help develop the concept so it can be realized with clarity, energy, and conviction to people who have some curiosity about, but a limited understanding of, the subject area.

Of course, the interpreter tries to understand as much as possible about the subject. Research is useful, but the conversations with curators, and those who have detailed specialized or community knowledge of the subject, are invaluable. In that face-to-face encounter, curators and other knowledgeable staff will often reinterpret difficult or complex ideas in a way that is comprehensible, by describing it through telling details, anecdotes, and examples that distil and clarify. This is the very conversation that the interpreter wants to bring into the gallery space for the visitor.

Taking the analogy of a conversation even further, an exhibit can be seen as a conversation within a drama. As in a drama or play, the audience actively participates by becoming immersed in the world of the exhibition and involving their imagination. This is why exhibitions in a "book-on-the-wall" style that rely on one-way, linear instruction rarely work. Instead, a more realistic communication model is at least two-way, and often interactive and dialogic (Witcomb 2003, 156; Burnham 2011, 86–87). Moreover, exhibition narratives should be explicit, rather than covert: the visitor can then consciously employ their "suspension of disbelief" just as they would in a play – or not.

By this stage, the growing exhibition concept becomes an ever-increasing series of feedback loops as the larger team becomes involved with the content and development. For example, the curator develops the elements that will form the sections of the exhibition, each of which should contribute to the overarching narrative and objectives. Objects are selected for each section. Often objects or props need to be sourced – bought or loaned – to support the concept and advance the narrative. But this is not a one-way process: objects can also feed back nuances that undercut, or divert from the concept and narrative, which may then necessitate reworking the concept and communication objectives. Object selection is usually the purview of the curator and/or collections staff. As with concept and narrative development, the interpreter has a valuable function in reflecting on these selections and interrogating each object and how it melds with the narrative and the big idea. Once the exhibition concept and objectives firm up, the choice of objects can be assessed in relation to them.

Interpretive planning and communication objectives

The development of communication objectives (sometimes called "learning objectives," "learning outcomes," or "key messages") is the next stage of realizing the exhibition's big idea. Communication objectives can be broken into three categories: cognitive, affective, and behavioral. Simply put, they relate respectively to visitors' intellect (what you want them to learn), emotions (what they feel), and practical responses (what they do) (Serrell 1996; McLean and McEver 2004).

In order to keep the focus tight, there should be a maximum of, say, three communication objectives for the exhibition as a whole. Communication objectives describe how the exhibition concept will be interpreted and represented, in principle and in practice (for example, through the use of particular media). Each section of the exhibition will have its own specific, more detailed and again, tightly focused, communication objectives. These need clearly to relate to the overall message of the exhibition. The communication objectives are shared among different members of the team, helping to keep everyone "on the same page," or, at least, discussing the same things. As David Dean makes plain in his chapter (in this volume) the reality of managing a complex project such as an exhibition, and refining the contents down to something that meets the space, budget, and mission, is an extremely difficult task; and tight communication objectives can help (for examples, see Serrell 1996).

A major task of the interpreter at this point is devising the interpretive plan, which goes hand in hand with object selection and placement, and spatial and graphic design (on this topic, see Spock in this volume). The interpretive plan includes the information architecture – including the texts, video, computer interactives, pictograms, cartoons, or other media – deemed to be most effective in engaging visitors with the exhibition topic and narrative. Given the importance of text in many exhibitions, the interpretive plan may well identify a text hierarchy or a structure of messaging. This usually begins with an exhibition title at the highest level and flows down through the big ideas articulated in introductory panels and on down to labels or signs that denote a specific theme or information about an individual object. From this, a detailed picture of each section and individual display within the exhibition, its objectives and proposed realization, begins to emerge.

At this point, the interpreter also proposes and develops the media, those diverse elements (whether text, graphics, images, interactives) that will help convey the key messages of the exhibition. The interpretive plan is then audited (as part of the larger exhibition plan) to ensure that it aligns with the overarching concept, communication objectives, and interest of the target audience. Pre- and post-opening audits are usually undertaken to check the ergonomics of the exhibition design, sound levels and "spill," media robustness, lighting issues, and so on.

Comfort, safety, transparency, and access

There are many practical issues that need to be considered in addition to clarifying and refining the concept, and realizing it in each component of the exhibition. One of these is visitor comfort, a term used to cover a great many things, from comfortable furniture for victims of "museum fatigue" to aspects of cultural safety. Because comfort is used so broadly, it has its detractors. For example, Therese Quinn writes that:

> Comfort includes a section about authorship and biases and another about welcoming people from different groups and classes. But I'm not satisfied with these: I think "comfort" is too weak a label to encompass everything from racism and bias to exclusion of disabled people and I still think that knowing who paid for an exhibit changes how I make sense of its messages. (Quinn in Serrell 2006, 23)

Arguably the cultural safety aspect of comfort requires the most care, thought, and discussion – and, often, stakeholder feedback. The aim is to ensure that visitors feel emotionally and psychologically safe within the exhibition environment, irrespective of their ethnicity, class, gender, or sexual orientation. In a general sense, the visitor trusts the institution and staff to uphold the social contract of hospitality. They will be welcome in the space; their rights will be respected. They will arrive and will leave safely. I should add that comfort and safety do not mean there should not be provocation, surprise – shock even – in the exhibition; but that this is managed in a way that cares for the visitor and mitigates harmful outcomes. This might involve warning signs, segregation of graphic content, and/or careful management of context and staging, so that visitors can navigate the space confidently and are prepared for what they may experience.

In order to uphold the values inherent in the concept of comfort, Serrell argues that exhibition developers have a responsibility to be transparent. For example, transparency should be evident in way-finding and conceptual orientation, in feeling welcomed and cared for, in the tone of signage, and more. In short, comfort aids learning while its absence inhibits learning (Serrell 2006, 112–114).

Factors that promote (or undermine) comfort can be very subtle. Similarly, cues that exclude are usually invisible to those who create them. Take the issue of the transparency of authorship, and specifically to the use of first person in exhibition text. For me, this is a natural way of speaking, and, I think, is meant to be inclusive. But is it? Does the use of "we" and "our" in a label indicate all people, or does it refer to the author, the team, or expert curators who hold particular opinions? Or could it even be the royal "we," which actually signifies "I"? If a reader disagrees with the text, the inclusive "we" is effectively excluding that person. It could be argued that the first-person usage can have a different function: namely, to promote a sense of inclusion among those "in the know" and to exclude those who are not.

By default, if not otherwise stated, *all* text is attributed to the institution that displays it: this is its "voice." The first person now gains even greater authority to include or exclude. In my experience, a general rule for the use of first person is positively to identify the author in question. This can be representative, as in the case of a cultural group such as an *iwi* (Māori tribe); it may be a personal opinion; it may be the specialist perspective of the curator, and so on. But if it is used, the identity of the speaker should be revealed.

A related issue is physical access. Ensuring that disabled visitors' needs are met is also part of an interpreter's work. Rather than treating this as a "tick box" exercise, staff should be aware that meeting the needs of disabled people can vastly improve the experience for all visitors (Samuels 2006). Everyone benefits from textural and aural stimuli and information for the sight-impaired, subtitles on films, succinctly written text, graphic information for the hearing impaired, and good access ways and lower sightlines for wheelchair users. Related to this, the needs of the elderly are often overlooked in museum settings. As people age, visual acuity and contrast perception lessens, and therefore more light is needed to view things clearly. Poorly lit signs, small typeface sizes, low contrast between colors, and reversed out white on black text create problems for many visitors, including some of the elderly. It is the role of the interpreter to check graphic design for readability prior to production for this basic need as well as to make sure that its presentation aligns with the communication objectives and overall aims of the exhibition.

Volume of text

Sheer volume of text can be an issue in exhibition design as in the aforementioned "book-on-the-wall" phenomenon. But while Janet Marstine criticizes texts that have been reduced to 75-word "scripts" (Marstine 2006, 12), I would provocatively suggest that some labels should not be longer than 30 words, depending on context. My principle is that the longer the text, the less it is read. However the interpreter should always work to find solutions, particularly between disparate views among the exhibition team. Here, the interpreter's first task is to ensure "messaging" is focused and succinct: that is, it communicates to the greatest number of people, while still being accurate. The second task is to layer depth and detail into the exhibition in a way that supports the main proposition and narrative, for those with an appetite to find out more.

In general, research suggests there is still a gulf between visitor-focused interpretation and exhibition practice, particularly in art galleries where the aesthetics of display inhibit the provision of more help for the visitor (Latimer 2011). McLean reflects on the "dynamics of dialogue" in exhibition development, and wonders if having been freed from the "curator's grip" the momentum has swung too far in the other direction: for example, has the separation between content and interpretation led to new problems, such as overly simplified exhibits with a reductive teaching style (McLean 2004, 208–209)? Surely, she declares, museums are *both* temple and forum. We should therefore be able to balance expert and public knowledge, and embrace the "tensions" inherent in different approaches through mutual dialogue.

Technology offers some tantalizing solutions to these issues. Links can be made to internal and external resources and communities that can facilitate greater learning. However, these still need to support the "case" presented in the exhibition before broadening out to a bigger picture or drilling down into a more finely detailed view. Linking visitors to an unmediated dump of information will have the same effect as a dense wall of facts.

Case study: *Blood, Earth, Fire | Whāngai Whenua Ahi Kā*

The long-term exhibition *Blood, Earth, Fire | Whāngai Whenua Ahi Kā* opened in 2006 at Te Papa in Wellington (*Blood, Earth, Fire* 2013). Its theme is human impact on the land of Aotearoa New Zealand and, in turn, how the land affects people. A key historical event in the exhibition narrative was the rapid introduction to the country of "alien" species by humans, mostly in the nineteenth and twentieth centuries. As visitors enter this part of the exhibition, they are confronted by a case crowded with these species which appear to be thrusting into the main body of the exhibition space (Figure 23.1). A taxidermied stag, antlers lowered, leads the charge of invading aliens. Close by is a flight arrivals board that ticks over with the names of the aliens and the date of their first arrival (for example, rabbits, opossums, rats) forming a relentless roll-call of invasion. A nearby mirror introduces another species that may also be considered alien: namely, people.

The display makes a dramatic point, however, the crowding of the case left little room for information about the many and varied species it contained. Standard solutions, such as text panels, label rails, or extended labels within the case itself, would take up too much space and would be visually intrusive.

A solution was found in the use of flat, touch-screen monitors through which visitors can access a database of extended object labels for each of the species. The home page displays a silhouette of each of the creatures in the same configuration as in the case, and the visitor simply taps on the silhouette to access the relevant label as well as contextual images (Figure 23.2). The monitor was carefully positioned so as to be noticeable, but not interfere with the visual impact of the display. It is a good example of how objects, design, interpretation, and curation can work together to deliver a visually arresting and informative experience for visitors.

FIGURE 23.1   The "Arrivals" display in the exhibition *Blood, Earth, Fire | Whāngai Whenua Ahi Kā*, which opened in 2006 at Te Papa, Wellington. Objects, design, and interpretation work harmoniously to deliver a purposeful experience for the visitor without relying on a lot of text. (For a color version of this figure, please see the color plate section.)
Courtesy of the Museum of New Zealand Te Papa Tongarewa.

However, one drawback of the touchscreen is that only a few people can read it at a time. On the other hand, this can also prompt positive group interaction, with perhaps one person reading for the group. This simple example, among many, has informed my own interpretive practice, particularly in understanding how a theatrical and immersive approach to presentation can clearly and effectively communicate a message. In this case, text is a supporting element, and the key message is conveyed visually and spatially. Interpretation does not have to be heavy-handed or preachy. It can be simple – even minimal – stylish, and imbedded into the design and mood of the exhibit.

Conclusion: a case for the interpreter

The question that continually arises in my work is: doesn't having a dedicated interpreter constitute an unnecessary extra step in the process? After all, the role of the interpreter was formerly covered by the curator, exhibition developer, or

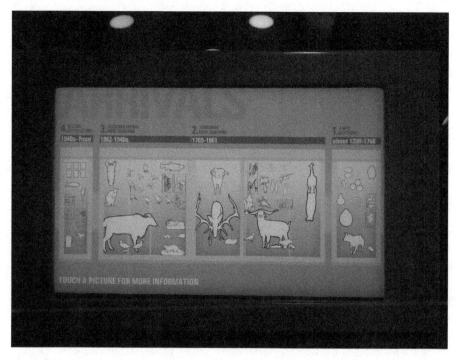

FIGURE 23.2   The computer interactive in the "Arrivals" display in the exhibition *Blood, Earth, Fire* | *Whāngai Whenua Ahi Kā*, 2006, Te Papa, Wellington.

educator – individually or collectively. And given that the curator has the specialist knowledge about the collection and topic, surely they are best placed to communicate with the museum's public?

My response is that, because interpreters operate *within* the institution and also figuratively stand *outside* it as audience advocates, they can act as a sensitive mediator and a reflective touchstone. Good interpreters employ their understanding of communication, engagement, and learning styles to serve both institutions and audiences. The function of the interpreter is essentially reflexive and creative, as I have tried to demonstrate in this chapter. Of course, interpreters also represent their own preferences and prejudices, but awareness of the problem is a good first step to addressing that natural bias. I have found that vigilance around one's own attitudes, robust processes with built-in feedback loops, strong communication between team members and visitors, continuous learning, and keeping an open mind and open ears are vital to effective exhibition development.

In this chapter I have made a case for interpretation, arguing that it is essential to the museum. In financially straitened times, museums can ill afford to shed or marginalize this important function. Interpreters represent the interface – a permeable membrane – between institutions and those they serve. The skills of the interpreter in mediating between multifarious groups to enable engagement and learning make for better exhibitions, and for better museums.

Note

1 I have chosen to avoid the much-used term "subject expert," as the word "expert" infers a sense of infallibility. To err is human, but to admit to it seems to be beyond the capability of many humans. Especially experts.

References

Ablett, Philip, and Pamela Dyer. 2009. "Heritage and Hermeneutics: Towards a Broader Interpretation of Interpretation." *Current Issues in Tourism* 12(3): 209–233.

AHI (Association for Heritage Interpretation). 2014. Website. Accessed November 12, 2014. http://www.ahi.org.uk.

Barbosa, Belem, and Pedro Quelhas Brito. 2012. "Do Open Day Events Develop Art Museum Audiences?" *Museum Management and Curatorship* 27(1): 17–33.

Beck, Larry, and Ted T. Cable. 2002. *Interpretation for the 21st Century: Fifteen Guiding Principles for Interpreting Nature and Culture*. Urbana, IL: Sagamore.

Blockley, Marion, and Alison Hems. 2006. *Heritage Interpretation*. London: Routledge.

Blood, Earth, Fire | Whāngai Whenua Ahi Kā. 2013. The Museum of New Zealand Te Papa Tongarewa (Te Papa). Website: Exhibitions. Accessed November 12, 2014. http://www.tepapa.govt.nz/whatson/exhibitions/pages/bloodearthfire.aspx.

Bridle, Tessa. 2013. *Effective Exhibit Interpretation and Design*. Lanham, MD: AltaMira.

Burnham, Rika. 2011. *Teaching in the Art Museum: Interpretation as Experience*. Los Angeles: Getty.

Catlin-Legutko, Cinnamon, and Stacy Klinger. 2011. *Interpretation: Education, Programs, and Exhibits*. Lanham, MD: AltaMira.

Classen, Constance, and David Howes. 2006. "The Museum as Sensescape: Western Sensibilities and Indigenous Artifacts." In *Sensible Objects: Colonialism, Museums and Material Culture*, edited by Elizabeth Edwards, Chris Gosden, and Ruth B. Phillips, 199–222. Oxford: Berg.

Colquhoun, Fiona. 1995. *Interpretation Handbook and Standard: Distilling the Essence*. Wellington: Department of Conservation Te Papa Atawhai. Accessed November 16, 2014. http://www.doc.govt.nz/Documents/about-doc/role/policies-and-plans/interpretation-handbook-complete.pdf.

Dewar, Keith. 2000. "An Incomplete History of Interpretation from the Big Bang." *International Journal of Heritage Studies* 6(2): 175–180.

Diamond, Paul. 2007. *Makereti: Taking Māori to the World*. Auckland: Random House.

Donnelly, Jessica Fay. 2002. *Interpreting Historic House Museums*. Lanham, MD: AltaMira.

Durbin, Gail. 2004. "The educational basis for the galleries." In *Creating the British Galleries at the V&A: A Study in Museology*, edited by Christopher Wilk and Nick Humphrey, 37–47. London: V&A.

Edcom. 2005. Booklet. American Association of Museums. Accessed November 16, 2014. http://www.aam-us.org/docs/default-source/accreditation/committee-on-education.pdf?sfvrsn=0.

Fleming, Neil. 2001–2012. VARK learning styles survey resource. Accessed November 12, 2014. http://www.vark-learn.com/english/index.asp.

Fritsch, Juliette, ed. 2011a. *Museum Gallery Interpretation and Material Culture*. London: Routledge.

Fritsch, Juliette. 2011b. "Introduction." In *Museum Gallery Interpretation and Material Culture*, edited by Juliette Fritsch, 1–12. London: Routledge.

Fritsch, Juliette. 2011c. "Education Is a Department Isn't It? Perceptions of Education, Learning and Interpretation in Exhibition Development." In *Museum Gallery Interpretation and Material Culture*, edited by Juliette Fritsch, 234–248. London: Routledge.

Frost, Warwick. 2005. "Making an Edgier Interpretation of the Gold Rushes: Contrasting Perspectives from Australia and New Zealand." *International Journal of Heritage Studies* 11(3): 235–250.

Ham, Sam. 1992. *Environmental Interpretation: A Practical Guide for People with Big Ideas and Small Budgets*. Golden, CO: Fulcrum Publishing.

Ham, Sam. 2013. *Interpretation: Making a Difference on Purpose?* Golden, CO: Fulcrum Publishing.

Hein, George E. 2006. "Museum Education." In *A Companion to Museum Studies*, edited by Sharon Macdonald, 340–352. Malden, MA: Blackwell.

Hein, George E. 2013. "'The Museum as Social Instrument': A Democratic Conception of Museums." In *Museum Gallery Interpretation and Material Culture*, edited by Juliette Fritsch, 13–25. London: Routledge.

Hooper-Greenhill, Eilean. 1994. *Museums and Their Visitors*. London: Routledge.

Hooper-Greenhill, Eilean. 2000. *Museums and the Interpretation of Visual Culture*. London: Routledge.

Howard, Peter. 2003. *Heritage: Management, Interpretation, Identity*. London: Continuum.

IA (Interpretation Australia). 2014. Website. Accessed November 12, 2014. http://www.interpretationaustralia.asn.au.

INNZ (Interpretation Network New Zealand). 2014. Website. Accessed November 12, 2014. http://www.innz.net.nz.

InterpScan "Our Work Defined." 2014. Interpretation Canada. Accessed November 12, 2014. http://www.interpscan.ca/our-work-defined.

Journal of Interpretation Research. 2013. Website. Accessed November 12, 2014. http://www.interpnet.com/nai/Publications/Journal_of_Interpretation_Research/nai/_publications/Journal_of_Interpretation_Research.aspx?hkey=4b57b935-c85e-4760-b5e3-449b613c827c.

Karp, Ivan, Christine Mullen Kreamer, and Steven D. Lavine, eds. 1992. *Museums and Communities: The Politics of Public Culture*. Washington, DC: Smithsonian Institution.

Kelly, Lynda. 2010. "The Role of Narrative in Museum Exhibitions." Australian Museum blog. Accessed November 12, 2014. http://australianmuseum.net.au/BlogPost/Museullaneous/The-role-of-narrative-in-museum-exhibitions.

Latimer, Sue. 2011. "Art for Whose Sake?" In *Museum Gallery Interpretation and Material Culture*, edited by Juliette Fritsch, 67–79. London: Routledge.

Marstine, Janet, ed. 2006. *New Museum Theory and Practice: An Introduction*. Oxford: Blackwell.

Mason, Rhiannon. 2005. "Museums, Galleries and Heritage: Sites of Meaning-Making and Communication." In *Heritage, Museums and Galleries: An Introductory Reader*, edited by Gerard Corsane, 200–214. London: Routledge.

McLean, Kathleen 2004. "Museum Exhibitions and the Dynamics of Dialogue." In *Reinventing the Museum: Historical and Contemporary Perspectives on the Paradigm Shift*, edited by Gail Anderson, 193–211. Walnut Creek, CA: AltaMira.

McLean, Kathleen, and Catherine McEver. 2004. *Are We There Yet? Conversations about Best Practices in Science Exhibition Development*. San Francisco: Exploratorium.

Merriman, Tim, and Lisa Brochu. 2006. *The History of Heritage Interpretation in the United States*. Fort Collins, CO: National Association for Interpretation.

Museums Galleries Scotland. 2013. "Introduction to Interpretive Planning." Accessed November 12, 2014. http://www.museumsgalleriesscotland.org.uk/research-and-resources/resources/publications/publication/316/introduction-to-interpretive-planning.

Quote Investigator. 2011. "Everything Should Be Made as Simple as Possible, But Not Simpler." Accessed November 12, 2014. http://quoteinvestigator.com/2011/05/13/einstein-simple.

Roberts, Lisa C. 1997. *From Knowledge to Narrative: Educators and the Changing Museum*. Washington, DC: Smithsonian Institution Press.

Samuels, Jane. 2006. "A Collective Responsibility: Making Museums Accessible for Deaf and Disabled People." In *The Responsive Museum: Working with Audiences in the 21st Century*, edited by Caroline Lang, John Reeve, and Vicky Woollard, 195–196. Aldershot, UK: Ashgate.

Schama, Simon. 2010. Transcribed from a discussion at the Writers and Readers Week, New Zealand International Arts Festival, Wellington, March 23.

Serrell, Beverly. 1996. *Exhibit Labels: An Interpretive Approach*. Lanham, MD: AltaMira.

Serrell, Beverly. 2006. *Judging Exhibitions: A Framework for Assessing Excellence*. Walnut Creek, CA: Left Coast Press.

Silberman, Neil A. 2013. "Heritage Interpretation as Public Discourse: Towards a New Paradigm." In *Understanding Heritage*, edited by Marie-Theres Albert, Roland Bernecker, and Britta Rudolff, 23–31. Berlin: De Gruyter.

Staiff, Russell, Robyn Bushell, and Peter Kennedy. 2002. "Interpretation in National Parks: Some Critical Questions." *Journal of Sustainable Tourism* 10(2): 97–113.

Tilden, Freeman. 2007. *Interpreting Our Heritage*, Rev. ed. Chapel Hill: University of North Carolina Press.

Uzzell, David L., ed. 1989. *Heritage Interpretation*, vol. 1, *The Natural and Built Environment*. London: Belhaven Press.

West, Susie, and Elizabeth McKellar. 2010. "Interpretation of Heritage." In *Understanding Heritage in Practice*, edited by Susie West, 166–204. Manchester: Manchester University Press.

Weil, Stephen. 1998. "When the Audience Takes Centre Stage." *Melbourne Art Journal* 3: 5–13.

Whitehead, Christopher. 2012. *Interpreting Art in Museums and Galleries*. London: Routledge.

Winter, Tim. 2013. "Cultures of Interpretation." In *Heritage and Tourism: Place, Encounter, Engagement*, edited by Russell Staiff, Robyn Bushell, and Steve Watson, 172–186. Abingdon: Routledge.

Witcomb, Andrea. 2003. *Re-imagining the Museum: Beyond the Mausoleum*. London: Routledge.

Witcomb, Andrea. 2006. "Interactivity: Thinking Beyond." In *A Companion to Museum Studies*, edited by Sharon Macdonald, 353–361. Oxford: Blackwell.

Witcomb, Andrea. 2011. "Unsettling Curatorial Practices in History Museums and Heritage Sites." Paper presented to the seminar *Curatopia: Museums and the Future of Curatorial Practice*, February 28. Wellington: Victoria University.

Witcomb, Andrea. 2013. "Using Immersive and Interactive Approaches to Interpreting Traumatic Experiences for Tourists: Potentials and Limitations." In *Heritage and Tourism: Place, Encounter, Engagement*, edited by Russell Staiff, Robyn Bushell, and Steve Watson, 152–170. Abingdon: Routledge.

Further Reading

InterpScan. 2014. National website of Interpretation Canada. Accessed November 16, 2014. http://www.interpscan.ca.

Staiff, Russell. 2014. *Re-imagining Heritage Interpretation: Enchanting the Past-Future*. Farnham, UK: Ashgate.

Kerry Jimson is a professional writer who has written for the screen, stage, and page. He has worked extensively in museums, art galleries, and zoos throughout New Zealand as a writer, editor, interpreter, and concept developer. Kerry began his museum career during the development of the new museum of New Zealand, Te Papa Tongarewa (Te Papa), in 1995, and in 1998 became its Senior Writer. He has worked on exhibitions in natural history, science, social history, *iwi* (Māori tribes), archaeology, and art. Since 2008, Kerry has been a Teaching Associate for the Museum and Heritage Studies program at Victoria University of Wellington.

24 LEARNING, EDUCATION, AND PUBLIC PROGRAMS IN MUSEUMS AND GALLERIES

John Reeve and Vicky Woollard[1]

In the past, curatorial authority, scholarship and professional judgment have been the drivers of the museum; today the driving position is shared with for example ... the educator.

Hooper-Greenhill 2000, 28

The role and place of learning in museums has been transformed in the past 20 years not only, though perhaps most distinctively, in the United Kingdom and the United States, but also through a shared global community of practice from Brazil to Japan. These transformations are both generic, in museological practice, and specific to local cultures and conditions. In many places learning has moved "from margin to core" (see Hooper-Greenhill 2000; 2007; Woollard 1998) and is now acknowledged as a central part of what a museum or gallery is. Leading progressive directors such as Sir Nicholas Serota of Tate have been emphatic supporters of this wider ambition for cultural learning: "Cultural learning feeds every part of our being – our minds, our imagination and our values" (Serota in Culture and Learning Consortium 2009, 2).

In this chapter, we ask why, and to what extent, expectations for museum learning have changed, whether by policymakers, museums, or their users. We review the last 20 years to identify the factors for change and how they have shaped current practice. Through examples from a range of museums and galleries worldwide, we will explore the possible characteristics of successful museum and gallery

The International Handbooks of Museum Studies: Museum Practice, First Edition.
Edited by Conal McCarthy.
© 2015 John Wiley & Sons Ltd. Published 2020 by John Wiley & Sons Ltd.

learning programs that are, for example: centrally placed in museum management and policy; audience-centered; reciprocally and responsively involved in partnerships with stakeholders at many levels; responsive to diverse needs of learners varied in appetites, learning styles, age, income, and ability; strategic in allocating resources and in planning programs; appropriately resourced for creative and active learning on site; using technologies and media creatively. The now extensive literature on museums and learning from many perspectives is itself an indication of this revolution in theory, discourse, and practice.

However, we recognize that, writing in 2014, we are in a difficult period, both economically and politically, where there can be no presumptions regarding the availability of financial support and the importance that culture will have in political debate. Against this backdrop, we ask whether more active audience participation and collaboration between the public and museum staff reduces the need for, or changes the role of, professional museum and gallery educators; and whether the requirement for assessing programs against measurable outcomes will continue to obscure the questions of quality, content, and delivery.

The core of museum and gallery learning

According to UK policy for museums, libraries, and archives, learning is at the heart of personal development:

> Learning is a process of active engagement with experience. It is what people do when they want to make sense of the world. It may involve the development or deepening of skills, knowledge, understanding, awareness, values, ideas and feelings, or an increase in the capacity to reflect. Effective learning leads to change, development and the desire to learn more. (Museums, Libraries and Archives Council 2010)

Screven observed that informal learning in museum settings is "non-linear, self-paced, voluntary and exploratory" (1986, 109). Museum and gallery learning therefore thrives where culture and learning are not just the preserve of the privileged, where the curriculum is not rigid and creativity is actively encouraged, where lifelong learning is an established concept in an ageing society, and where experiment and reflection are a normal part of professional life. Within the institution, it is vulnerable to changes of director, direction, and policy; from too much interference, but also from indifference. Effective learning programs are often characterized by sustained partnerships, robust evidence of impact and success, professional commitment, and political vision. They require flair, energy, and an unusually broad range of skills – including educational, fundraising, research, political and communication skills – and, above all, immense patience.

In the past 20 years there have been major changes in the contexts for museum learning; Cutler (2010) of Tate has summarized current shifts in practice (from a UK perspective) as:

> From the passive to participative.
> From standardized delivery to personalization.
> From the didactic to co-learning.
> From knowledge acquisition to knowledge application.
> From a single authorial voice to plural voices.
> From private knowledge to public access. (Cutler 2010)

Such a shift is evident in many museum environments. To take a recent example, the Nelson-Atkins Museum of Art (Kansas City) in 2011 appointed Judith M. Koke as the new Director of Education and Interpretive Programs. Koke argued that the museum should move from being a teaching institution to becoming a learning institution, embracing different learning styles and approaches to art (Nelson-Atkins Museum of Art 2011). The key distinction here is between education (as a modernist emphasis on delivering preordained forms of knowledge in structured groups) and learning (a postmodernist emphasis on individual and social meaning-making and more informal personalized activity and experience). In reality it is of course much more complex than that: for example, "education" is still commonly used in museum terminology, especially in job titles and departmental names.

Figure 24.1 illustrates the range of experiences offered by both formal education and participative learning. Modernist pedagogies enforce the authority not only of the curator but also the educator, favoring more deferential, passive, and bounded learning through, for example, the didactic exhibit, the lecture by an expert, the worksheet, and the guidebook. By controlling access, inclusion, responses, and behaviors of organized educational groups, museums may take little or no account of the diverse appetites and learning styles of their audiences. The effect is to reinforce the idea of the institution as the preserve of the privileged. In contrast, Postmodernism (especially "constructivist" learning theory) advocates active learning, engagement, personalized meaning-making, facilitation, and experience; in effect, sharing or undermining the authority of the museum voice in interpretation and learning (Hein 1998; 2011; Hooper-Greenhill 1991; 2000; 2007; Falk and Dierking 2000; 2011; Falk, Dierking, and Foutz 2007).

However, conventional modernist practices still prevail in many institutions where, for example, guides and teachers promote received opinions during adult tours. Elsewhere, change is evident: in the United States, docents (trained but often volunteers) and staff instructors now engage educational groups in discussion, problematizing and opening debate, rather than deliver a lecture or set tour format (Burnham and Kai-Kee 2011; Reeve 2006). Similarly the National Gallery in

FIGURE 24.1   Formal education versus learning through participation: the Victorian classroom and teacher at the Ragged School Museum, London. (For a color version of this figure, please see the color plate section.)
Photograph by Anna Robertson © Ragged School Museum Trust.

London disseminates nationwide a discursive approach, combined with practical art making, as a form of interpretation through its Take One Picture project (http://www.takeonepicture.org). The Great British Art Debate's collaborative strategy for developing self-help gallery learning and teaching techniques, instigated by Tate, involves debate, drama, role play, and art (http://greatbritishart debate.tate.org.uk).

Elsewhere, lack of resources and relatively low visitor numbers mean that it is not possible to provide learning activities for most, or any, groups. Teachers, families, and adults are therefore expected to operate on their own, with museum or gallery guides, including audio-tours and trails, to help them.

American science centers and children's museums have been highly influential on museum learning practice and programming worldwide (see Reeve 2006; Lord 2007, 54–61, on ZOOM in Vienna). In terms of pedagogy, the Getty Center for Education in the Arts' discipline-based art education (DBAE) program was influential on art teacher and art gallery education practice in the 1980s and was especially welcomed for its embrace of world art; although it was also seen as dogmatic and constricting by some (Burnham and Kai-Kee 2011, 43). In the United Kingdom (with a national curriculum and a more coordinated national museum and gallery framework) a different structure has evolved which seeks to balance the studio and the art history agendas in both schools and galleries as "critical studies" in the curriculum (see, for example, Taylor 2006). Within the education policy environment of Britain in 2013, art gallery education has assumed a renewed role, as in the United States, of compensating for what is increasingly missing or undervalued in the "mainstream" curriculum, with implications for provision in later lifelong learning also (see Rogers 2009; Bellamy and Oppenheim 2009).

US art gallery educators Burnham and Kai-Kee (2011) have described the museum's transition from a modernist model of imparting and sharing information to a constructivist model of encouraging perception, enhancing experience and even performance as part of the gallery visit. One critic of this shift commented that: "we could see that children were enjoying dancing in the gallery – but were they learning anything?" (Burnham and Kai-Kee 2011, 38). In response, Burnham stresses the value of shared experience:

museum teachers must be prepared to give up full control of the shared interpretive process … Museum instructors must always be able to step back, to step aside, or to step beyond the unfolding dialogue … . Adopt the various roles of: Player (being drawn in, absorbed, swept up just as students are), Mover, Follower, Bystander, Opposer … [t]o serve the needs of each group. (Burnham and Kai-Kee 2011, 131–132)

For some, the pendulum has swung too far. Veteran US gallery educator Danielle Rice has critiqued the approach of "visual thinking strategists," for whom all meanings are equally relevant, as too relativistic. We should not in her view "abdicate the responsibility of actually teaching visitors about the broader, consensual understandings that constitute an informed perspective" (Rice 2000, 224; Rice 2003, 91–92; see also Hooper-Greenhill 2000, 119). This is a profound issue at the heart of museum and gallery practice. The question is how far to facilitate or to direct; how to balance conventional "curatorial" agendas with broader social and developmental objectives. New approaches to collaborative learning are also reshaping the traditional role of the museum and gallery educator. Curators and freelance lecturers can lecture and freelance workshop leaders can facilitate; therefore core learning staff become program managers, learning consultants, and audience advocates.

Sometimes external or internal directives may replace or challenge more experimental and distinctive approaches. For example, the introduction of the UK national curriculum transformed museum use by schools from the 1980s (Reeve 1999). But one consequence of mirroring national and local curricula in museums and galleries is the danger of becoming (or remaining) just another classroom. Distinctive pedagogies have therefore developed in order not to be just another kind of schooling, but instead to adopt what Ivan Illich calls "de-schooled" approaches that are informal and personalized. For another influential theorist, the Brazilian Paulo Freire (1972), education is about empowering and liberating, rather than oppression by an established pedagogy of power and deference. Again, the emphasis is not on conveying bodies of knowledge, but on understanding concepts and processes, making meaning (Hein 1998; 2011; Hooper-Greenhill 2007), and above all on the museum and gallery experience as enhancing existing knowledge and understanding and motivating through other stimuli. Artists, actors, storytellers, dancers, designers may all contribute, as well as staff and volunteers, to create a polyvocal experience. Often a key element is the haptic learning (Pye 2008) that takes place in handling sessions for children and adults, including work off site, for example, in hospitals and prisons (Figure 24.2). The focus on engaging as many of the senses as possible derives from, and is a response to, an awareness of differing learning styles and multiple intelligences, as theorized by Gardner (1993).

Much of the core literature on learning in museums and galleries is influenced by art education and theory (for example, Burnham and Kai-Kee 2011; Cutler 2010; Xanthoudaki, Tickle, and Sekules 2003; Taylor 2006) and/or science education (Falk and Dierking 2000; 2011; Falk, Dierking, and Foutz 2007; Miles et al. 1988). The culture of the science museum and science center has generally been more interactive, but often also more didactic and output-driven, with a strong

FIGURE 24.2   Two participants examining a traditional coffee pot as a part of the Asian Women's Documenting the Home project at the Geffrye Museum, London. (For a color version of this figure, please see the color plate section.)
© Olivia Hemingway/Geffrye Museum.

mission to promote the public understanding of science. Science centers are often much more successful in engaging family audiences where other kinds of museum and gallery do not. Having said that, many areas of the curriculum can be enlivened and illuminated by a museum or gallery visit or access to a museum resource (Hooper-Greenhill 1991; 2007). Thus, over time, a fruitful relationship has developed between subject-specific disciplines, such as history and religious education, and museum and gallery practice (see Reeve 2012). Above all, the museum and gallery experience can often exceed the boundaries of the subject-specific curricula, not least by providing opportunities to apply and reconsider subject knowledge and to engage empathetically (Hooper-Greenhill 2007).

Improving the UK framework for museum learning

> *The biggest achievement of museums over the past two decades is the resurgence of their role in learning.*
>
> (Department for Culture, Media and Sport 2006, 7)

Museum learning professionals and responsive users have long understood the value of the museum experience: what was needed was greater investment in provision, sharper evidence of impact, with a wider understanding of informal learning and the audiences that benefited from it. From the early 1990s, the UK government began to acknowledge the educational role of museums, albeit through the provision of education services tailored to the new national curriculum. In turn, evidence of increased numbers of school visits and high satisfaction rates among teachers and pupils was required to legitimize the expanding field of practice (Hooper-Greenhill 2007). However, museum learning professionals also sought recognition for their work with diverse audiences, beyond the formal education sector. And this, argued Hooper-Greenhill, would require comprehensive strategic planning across and through all museum departments (1991).

From the early 1990s to 2010, successive Conservative and New Labour governments encouraged museums to generate new sources of income and become less reliant on state subsidy, for example through admission charges to many institutions and for temporary exhibitions. To meet "customer" expectations, greater attention was paid to improving physical and intellectual access, and to enhancing the appearance and interpretation of displays. Science museums often took the lead in developing better "customer care" and family-focused exhibits and programming (Lang, Reeve, and Woollard 2006; Miles et al. 1988). Government policies and museum learning agendas began to converge, but with strings attached.

Just as *Excellence and Equity* had provided an agenda for the changing role of museum learning in the United States (AAM 1992), so David Anderson's influential report *A Common Wealth* provided a similar call to action in the United Kingdom (Anderson 1999; summary in Lang, Reeve, and Woollard 2006, appendix 3).

Anderson's priorities were: to place education centrally in the mission of a museum or gallery with full endorsement at the highest level; to have a more holistic understanding of how a museum contributes to a visitor's learning; to develop a more skilled profession; and to undertake systematic research and evaluation on the delivery and impact of museum learning. The report reflected the New Labour mantra "Education, Education, Education" in 1997 and, in turn, provided a template for government policy for museums. Equally influential was Professor Ken Robinson, who argued in his report "All Our Futures" (NACCCE 1999), that young people would have to deal with an increasingly complex and diverse society, and that cultural education could make an essential contribution to this. The view thus emerged in government that museums, libraries, and archives could not only support the education agenda, but also contribute to cross-departmental policies for combating social exclusion by widening access to cultural participation (Lang, Reeve, and Woollard 2006: chapter 3). As a result, museum and gallery learning could be instrumentalized as a tool for social change, but to be assured of government funding, museums had to demonstrate its efficacy and impact.

By 2006, the number of visits by non-traditional museum audiences in the UK had increased by 6.8 percent since 2002/3, and major regional museums were attracting over 900,000 new non-traditional users per annum, thanks largely to new government funding channeled through the Museums, Libraries and Archives Council (MLA) and, specifically, the Renaissance in the Regions program (Hooper-Greenhill 2007, 72). Targeted "non-traditional" audiences included asylum-seekers, ethnic minorities, people on low income and the "working class" (though that term was no longer used), older people, families, young people who were "socially excluded" through homelessness or being outside mainstream education, and also prisoners and ex-offenders. However, as usual, the main recipients were schoolchildren who constituted the "key performance indicator" that attracted the largest proportion of funding based on evidence of a link between museum visits and improved exam results (see Hooper-Greenhill 2007, 15–30).

The case for learning was gradually won: a comparison between the situation described by, say, Hooper-Greenhill in 1991 and 2007 shows a palpable difference in terms of audiences, professionalism, research, and policy (1991; 2007). Equally if you compare Anderson's *A Common Wealth* with the situation 10 years later, the changes are clear: all 12 targets had, at least to some extent, been met in many UK museums and galleries (Bellamy and Oppenheim 2009).

A wider perspective

The context for US museum and gallery learning is different from that in northwest Europe. The United States does not have national systems for education or culture, and its taxation system encourages private and corporate philanthropy. In many US museums and galleries, there are named, sponsored/endowed posts for learning staff and centers, as there are for curators and directors, and the culture of evaluation took root in the United States when it was still a relative novelty in Europe. A number of advocacy documents and reports have provided a framework for practice, most notably *Excellence and Equity* (AAM 1992), which was subtitled *Education and the Public Dimension of Museums* and strongly advocated the value of partnerships, not least with audiences, "that respect the knowledge brought to the conversation by all the participants [and] … incorporate that collective perspective" (Lord 2007, 109). However, a recent review of US philanthropy by Sidford (2011) points out how little US funding for cultural learning is socially targeted and how big the challenges are that remain: participation in mainstream culture is falling and is still largely white, middle-class, and ageing, despite a demand for "active participation" elsewhere in the arts. Sidford identifies a tension between actual and target audience demographics, and also between new ways of interpreting collections and traditional canons of art history.

A pattern of institutional renewal through audience-focused learning and outreach work is now familiar in museums and galleries in many countries, such as Ireland (Bourke 2011; O'Donoghue in Xanthoudaki, Tickle, and Sekules 2003). For example, governments of some of the post-Soviet nations are gradually becoming more flexible in encouraging greater participation from adult learners, volunteers, and preschool children. Many Spanish museums have been reborn with energetic learning departments and programs, whereas change is slower in Portugal, where much of the initiative comes from foundations rather than government. In Denmark, change has resulted from a familiar mix of advocacy and innovation by museum professionals, increased government funding and policy change (Grøn 2011). Elsewhere, the value of museum learning has been embedded in Australia, New Zealand, and Singapore since the 1990s (Lord 2007, 3; Reeve 2012; Leong 2003), and more recently in Brazil, Japan, Korea, Hong Kong, Taiwan, and the Middle East. For example, the recently opened Museum of Islamic Art at Doha in Qatar defines its mission as "rooted in the belief that education is the founding stone for the future of any prosperous society" and the objective of its education center is to "become a 'knowledge hub' of the nation's arts learning. This is pivotal, in providing high quality, consistent and accessible teaching and learning opportunities for the Museum's key audiences: schools, students, scholars, families, adults and other community groups." When the museum opened, its website promoted its programs with the slogan: "DAZZLE THE EXPERT. INSPIRE THE CHILD" (http://www.mia.org.qa/en/learning).

Programming for leisure and learning

When learning is at the core of the museum's work and mission, its program will combine both pedagogical practice and audience development. A multiskilled learning manager needs to balance the following priorities: a knowledge of each audience group and its potential needs, interests, and incomes; an understanding of learning theory, practice, and styles; a knowledge of the collection and its multiple interpretations; and resource planning and management.

Rossman describes a program as "a plan or procedure for developing opportunities for individuals to participate in arts and cultural leisure experiences" (2008, 24). Programs may be single events or the museum's entire learning program across the year, and may involve activities (such as workshops), services (such as tours and audio-guides), and events (such as specialist conferences or performances by musicians/dancers); together and individually, the constituent parts of the program require clear aims and objectives. The form of the program may be determined by choices about scheduling (late-night openings, museum nights), delivery (hands-on, interactives, internet), location (hospital, prison, retirement home). These can take many different forms. Figure 24.3 shows dementia patients in a day

FIGURE 24.3   Older men with dementia in a day center using archive photographs of footballers to recall their past memories of playing and watching.
© Sporting Memories Network.

center using archive football photographs to recall their youthful experiences as players and spectators. Content may focus on supporting a major exhibition or new gallery, providing more information in a traditional way, or the program or event itself may become the focus in a more reflexive engagement with the form of the exhibition (for example, Black History Month, Day of the Dead, Chinese New Year). In this way the museum becomes a platform for performance and social interaction (Heumann Gurian 2010). In larger institutions, a separate program department (as at the Museum of London) or events team (as at the Victoria and Albert Museum) may work alongside the learning team which, in turn, focuses on conferences, lectures, gallery talks, and workshops.

A staple diet of "tried and tested" adult programming may help to streamline delivery and reduce uncertainties for both staff and visitors, but is unlikely to provide a creative experience for either. In many museums, greater progression is now offered through a range (in terms of depth and breadth) of adult learning events from free drop-in introductory tours, specialist gallery talks and lectures, through study days and short daytime courses to longer university-level courses. There is a new interest in events and conversations that focus on ideas and debates, given by authors, artists, scientists, critics, and historians, as well as social fora for discussion such as reading groups, science cafés, and salons. The typical learning department no longer aspires to interpret every aspect of the museum's collections from among its own staff members, but develops and delivers programs in conjunction with curators and external experts and practitioners. Meanwhile, learning staff may be specialists on, say, access, digital learning, and working with adults, families, schools, and teachers. In 2006, we summarized important considerations for programmers:

> Some audiences require special facilities (under-fives, schools, families, disabled people). Some services can be provided by hiring in (tourists, adult courses, practical workshops) or by using trained volunteers (introductory tours, craft demonstrations, stewarding at special events, accompanying severely disabled visitors, working with communities). Some audience roles require core expertise: policy and programme-making, audience and learning advocacy on gallery, exhibition and online projects, publishing for young and specialist educational audiences. Some programmes can sustain themselves through charging if key posts are already funded (schools, teachers, tourists, adult education); others need to be free if a museum is to be inclusive as well as responsive (under-fives, families, communities, youth, outreach). (Reeve 2006, 58)

Today's museum or gallery is not only part of the experience economy but is frequently a spectacle and destination in itself, a venue for dance and music, corporate entertaining, and audience interaction (Rees Leahy 2005). Museums and galleries host live performances by artists, storytellers, re-enactment groups, professional actors, and community performers. Film festivals are held on diverse themes, sometimes linked to exhibitions or new galleries. Museums are thus becoming more like arts and learning centers, working across many platforms, unconstrained by media and subject, and not just concerned with what happens to be in the collections. They cannot stay aloof from the pressures of the world outside, but are increasingly engaged, for example, with the tricky area of beliefs, faiths, dogma, and prejudice (see Reeve 2012). As safe places for unsafe ideas, the museum offers a platform where identities, ideals, and issues can be presented, shared, and disputed (Heumann Gurian 2010).

New programming approaches put increased demands on museum space (see Sharmacharja 2009) and learning centers have been constructed in many US museums (Lord 2007, chapter 8, with checklist for facilities). Meanwhile, in the UK, 650 museum and gallery learning spaces were created with support from the Heritage Lottery Fund and the Clore Duffield Foundation (Rogers 2004; Lang, Reeve, and Woollard 2006). For example, the Clore Centre at the British Museum (used as much for corporate hire and academic or adult education purposes as for schools) includes a Samsung digital discovery center alongside two auditoria, three seminar rooms and a studio, and school and family lunch rooms. At the British Museum, these facilities are tucked away in the basement, whereas, as a result of lengthy consultation with intended audiences, the V&A's Sackler Learning Centre is highly visible on the main floor of the museum. It comprises a lecture theatre and seminar rooms, publicly accessible studios for artists in residence, studios for computer-aided design and practical workshops, a small gallery space, and lunch rooms. Another trend is for "learning pods" to complement adjacent galleries, as in the Getty, with volunteer-run handling tables, terminals, and books. A similar idea is being introduced at Tate Britain to help remove the physical separation of gallery and learning spaces. Front-of-house staff in the galleries at the Museum of London combine learning and visitor service roles.

In *The Responsive Museum* (Lang, Reeve, and Woollard 2006), we noted the substantial investment in online technologies, although we queried the degree to which their learning potential had been evaluated, integrated, or realized (see also NMDC 1999; Selwood 2010, 3.4). Hawkey's extensive analysis of the literature (2004) confirms the need for a coherent pedagogy for museum learning that integrates digital learning and access. Often museums were, and still are, guilty of offloading catalogues of objects onto their websites or using the site solely as a marketing tool, thus missing the opportunity for real interaction with the collections (on this point see Chapman in this volume).

Approaches to digital resources and their use can vary dramatically, and this may reflect who is in charge of online media (see Wellington and Oliver in this volume). For example the Louvre online database Atlas provides information on 26,000 of the 35,000 works on permanent display, as well as high-resolution images. The British Museum has prioritized a comprehensive database with images for the majority of the millions of items in the collection, with separately originated strands for families and schools. Figure 24.4 shows secondary school students

FIGURE 24.4   Year 9 students (aged 13/14) in the British Museum using a Samsung tablet to access an interactive Augmented Reality activity investigating the ways postcolonial states drew on material culture from the past to forge national identities. Photograph: benedictjohnson.com © British Museum.

using PDAs (Personal Digital Assistants) in a British Museum gallery. By contrast, the V&A opts for limited collections coverage, but deeper engagement with specific target groups and their interests in inspirational designs (for example, makers of all kinds of textiles, especially knitters) or polyvocal interpretation (faith focus groups). Meanwhile, Tate Online invites virtual visitors to take an online course, explore material in its archive, use resources for visually impaired people, find in-depth information on artists and works in Tate's collection, or find video and audio from study days and artists' talks from a multi-voiced playlist of over 1000 items (Tate 2013). The Metropolitan Museum of Art site is more akin to a serious distance-learning course (Metropolitan Museum of Art 2014). The Prado, National Museums of Scotland, and the National Gallery London allow detailed inspection of their collection highlights, but do not provide depth of information. The Louvre, Prado, and the National Gallery London also offer online trails and the chance to construct your own collection. In the museum itself digital teaching resources are being used more flexibly: for example, at the Museum of London and V&A trolleys take ICT equipment into the galleries for design, research, and play (see Heritage Lottery Fund 2011).

Evaluation and research

Learning practitioners regularly evaluate their programs, and respond to the research data gathered by adjusting resources and redesigning activities (see Pontin 2006). Some UK museums now publish their evaluation data on exhibitions and galleries, revealing findings on interpretation, learning styles, stay time, and the use of multimedia (Natural History Museum 2013; Selwood 2010; Fritsch 2011). In the UK, this emphasis on evaluation and research has been partly driven by government performance targets tied to funding agreements. In this context, data from the formal education sector is easier to collect than from informal audience groups, such as families and adult learners, and is therefore privileged in terms of policy priorities (Lang, Reeve, and Woollard 2006).

Between 2000 and 2007 over 64,000 pupils and over 3000 teachers completed questionnaires and attended discussion or focus groups organized by the Research Centre for Museums and Galleries (RCMG) under the leadership of Professor Eilean Hooper-Greenhill (2007). The RCMG at Leicester University was commissioned by the MLA as part of its Inspiring Learning for All framework to develop Generic Learning Outcomes (GLOs) as a methodology for analyzing the impact of museum learning, providing qualitative, as well as quantitative, data for government and the sector. The evidence of the GLOs showed that museums are highly effective places for personalized learning in the formal education sector and for motivating learning, but were less effective in working with community groups (RCMG 2004a; 2004b). Cutler (2010) argued:

> that there is a set of repeated and identifiable similarities that frame cultural learning … Key findings … can be identified as increased confidence, a shift in attitudes and behaviours, improved motivation and sustained engagement. There is also evidence of an increase in critical thinking applied beyond the learning environment.

Regular evaluation of programs has long been part of US museum and gallery learning, and has influenced both practice and policy (Pitman and Hirzy 2011). Some UK museums have also established their own research culture around practice and learning, including Tate (Cutler 2010; Charman 2005) and the V&A (Sandell and Nightingale 2012; Fritsch 2011). Research partnerships with universities are increasingly common: for example, University College London is currently leading a study of the therapeutic use of handling cultural artifacts in hospitals, and the University of Newcastle is researching public understanding of art for the Laing Art Gallery Tyneside. The UK art gallery education organization Engage has also developed a substantial body of research in working with a number of university departments (Taylor 2006). Xanthoudaki, Tickle, and Sekules (2003) have documented examples of visual education research in museums and galleries in Canada, Greece, Finland, Ireland, Italy, and elsewhere.

A balancing act

Whatever the level of resourcing, learning departments have to be selective about targeting programs where they are most needed and have most impact. Flexibility is crucial, as is the ability to respond to the changing priorities of public, corporate, and charitable funders:

> If the overall aim is to create new generations of confident, engaged museum and gallery users having a high-quality experience, then resources need to be targeted at a combination of catching them young and making sure they are not put off by a parody of schooling; supporting them as parents; sustaining their interest as adult learners. As these new museum users make use of the improved facilities and the increasing range of learning tools on site and online, the core learning and access teams can then concentrate on the labour intensive groups and labour intensive roles. Streamlining for some and targeting for others does not inevitably mean a loss of quality. (Reeve 2006: 56–58)

In 2006 we reviewed the wider context for audience development beyond the policy initiatives and changes in museum learning philosophy that we have outlined above (see also Black in this volume). Factors included: more leisure time for many; more critical consumers; higher educational aspirations in a context of lifelong learning; significant demographic change, with increasing diversification of the population across the world through migration and growing diasporas; and ageing in the old world. By 2021 more than one-third of the UK population will be aged over 65, and similar patterns apply elsewhere in Europe and Japan (Social Trends 38 2008, 3).

Targeting communities demonstrates the challenges of balancing audiences, mission, and resources. The concept of community itself is problematic, but the museum's desire to work with, and for, communities is not new (see Crooke in this volume). For example, the Whitechapel Gallery in East London was founded in 1900 with the ambition of bringing culture to a poor, and especially Jewish, working-class neighborhood (Borzello 1987). Today, it manages to combine cutting-edge contemporary art while still fulfilling a community role. Similarly, Beth Schneider (1998) documents the revival of the founding purpose of the Houston Museum of Fine Arts (from 1924) of concerted community and outreach work made possible through substantial sponsorship. Elsewhere pioneering outreach work in US art museums did not survive because it was entirely dependent on ad hoc funding: embedding outreach work into the operational core of the museum, sustained through partnership rather than temporary funding, is a perennial challenge. Lynch (2011) concluded that recent funding in public engagement and participation in the UK's museums and galleries has *not* succeeded in shifting the work from the margins to the center of many organizations. On the contrary, by providing funding outside of core budgets, it appears to have helped keep the work on the organizations' periphery. Nonetheless, as examples of the pioneering community work and public programming in South Africa show, museums can work with communities at times of stress and upheaval as both anchors and platforms for participation and change (Lord 2007, 124–131).

Another way of thinking about priorities may be to ask the question "Where can museum learning make the biggest difference?" or in the jargon "Where can most value be added?" If museums are successful with, say, the very young, disaffected teenagers, and those in special schools for disabled children, should these not become major priorities? However, work with these audiences is very labor-intensive and therefore not likely to produce significant data against performance indicators. One can also ask "What can a museum uniquely do in relation to its collection or location?" Inclusiveness does not mean *all* museums aiming to provide programs for *all* audiences, and spreading their resources thinly as a result.

In the UK, museum audience priorities in 2006 appeared to be: schools (the primary audience measured by government and other funders) and families, rather than non-vocational adult learners or tourists (except as consumers); active rather than passive learners; and off-site, including online, learning, either as an adjunct to or substitute for a physical visit. The focus was also on targeting ethnic, gender, or special interest groups related to a specific exhibition, event, or collection, rather than sustained and truly intercultural programming or co-production (Lang, Reeve, and Woollard 2006). In the early 1990s at the British Museum, a balance was needed between the claims of different kinds of audiences and the delivery of content (for example, in relation to the national curriculum), between direct teaching by staff and the creation of teaching resources for others to use, and between time dedicated to the direct delivery of education services and contributing to exhibition design and interpretation (Reeve 1992; Hooper-Greenhill 1991). Today the Museum of London balances intensive, high-impact work (catering for early years and special educational needs) with high-volume resources for larger audiences (digital, families, schools). The learning team also acts as audience advocates on exhibition, gallery, website, and other cross-museum projects. In museums where the learning department is a cost center, income-generating work with adults and, sometimes, with schools, helps support outreach work and free programs, such as drop-in and community events.

There are also different responses to how the management of learning programs relates to the rest of the organization. For Cutler, Head of Learning at Tate, educators should be less compartmentalized and relieved of their custodial duties as "guardians of learning" and the "passers-down/on/across of information" in order to become learning facilitators who construct programs across the institution. Museum learning staff need to be more involved in more of the museum's activities but they also need an institutional base, body of evidence, and acknowledgment of their expertise, while avoiding an overly curatorial approach. There is a tendency for exhibition development teams in some museums to assume that their audience is somehow being addressed without audience advocates being part of the process. Underpinning all these recommendations is an understanding of the museum educator's role as facilitator, enabler, planner, and negotiator, working alongside both audiences and curators (on interpretation, see Jimson in this volume). Helen Charman of the Design Museum, London (2005) also believes that education curators need to rethink their role: knowledge of audience and policy contexts, learning theory and practice, subject disciplines, and organizations is no longer enough. She argues:

> It is in responsibility to audience that a distinctive quality of an educator's professionalism emerges, recast as a form of duty of care which embraces not just the intellectual experience of our visitors, but also cares for their emotional and physical well-being whilst at the museum, recognizing and respecting the embodied visitor who has physical and emotional needs as well as aesthetic and cognitive ones. (2005, 8)

Conclusions: a sustainable future?

What have we learnt about museum learning and public programs from the last 20 years? The UK experience of New Labour shows that government support for cultural learning can make a real difference to public participation and to raising professional confidence and standards. Publicly funded organizations now know that they have to address stakeholders' interests and that robust evidence is required to demonstrate that more people are included and actively engaged in museum programs. We have learnt that earmarked funding for projects can kickstart different methodological approaches, allow staff to acquire new skills, and help organizations to form sustainable partnerships. New forms of ICT (especially social media), more aggressive and targeted marketing techniques, and improved strategic thinking and leadership have helped to create more fully integrated learning organizations, with the goal of not only educating the public, but also sharing interpretation and authority in response to audience interests and opinions, through public forums, focus groups, and consultation. Figure 24.5 shows the young consultants group at the Geffrye Museum where the group contributes to exhibitions, leads guided tours, and runs public events. Effective lobbying, advocacy, better evaluation data, and campaigns such as "learning outside the classroom" and "kids in museums" have also contributed to this shift (*Transforming Education outside the Classroom* 2010; Kids in Museums 2014).

In many instances, learning teams are leading the way in forging new partnerships, embracing new audiences, attracting funding for promoting social inclusion, and interpreting collections in creative and imaginative ways that enable visitors (actual and virtual) to make connections with their own lives. However, there is much more work to be done. In the UK, it is clear from Arts Council England's review of research on museums and libraries (ACE 2011) that community engagement remains on the periphery of strategic planning and is not integrated into all aspects of museum activity. Museum learning departments must not be deflected by a focus on excellence rather than equity. Blackwell asks: "Why are community voices still unheard?" (Blackwell 2009;

FIGURE 24.5   Following government policy on including young people in decision-making, the Geffrye Museum in London among others set up a youth forum/paid young consultants group that encourages dialogue and contributions to exhibitions, interpretation, marketing, and event-planning.
© Geffrye Museum

Blackwell and Scaife 2006). The old equation of "formal" learning with "core" activity, and "informal" learning with "optional extra," must be rejected if museums and galleries are to have a sustainable future as learning experiences and providers. At the Museum of London, learning really *is* at the core and the learning team has contributed to re-interpreting several galleries with learners' needs in mind (Museum of London 2014).

The need to be flexible and entrepreneurial is a contemporary imperative. In the UK, mixed and unstable funding streams make core learning and community work particularly vulnerable at present (Selwood 2010). In the United States, philanthropy and other funding often needs to be re-targeted if museums and galleries are to realize their full impact for learning and engagement (Sidford 2011) rather than reinforce existing audiences for larger institutions.

Different models exist for sustaining learning services and expertise: for example, a small core of learning professionals working with a large rota of trained, diverse, and welcoming volunteers (such as American docents). The British Museum's volunteer "eye-opener" guides present informal introductory gallery tours to adults and families, thereby freeing up core education and curatorial staff for more specialist activities and work with more demanding audiences. Open-air museums and industrial or folk-life museums have always used volunteers for curation, conservation, and also programming and community engagement (Museum of East Anglian Life 2013). Many learning departments use freelance interpreters and performers on a contract basis, but this can be costly and there may be challenges when artists act as educators without appropriate training. Another model enables teachers, community activists, and other partners to co-teach, or ultimately run their own sessions, after training with in-house professionals. This system can work well with handling collections, as at the Horniman Museum, London, where the handling collection is easily accessed by a wide range of visitors. However, more work is needed to enable parents to feel more confident with their children in museums and galleries. Informal learning flourishes in informal settings, and it is useful to move out of the museum to get closer to people's daily lives. Museums have made tentative steps to place collections and run activities in hospitals, prisons, doctors' surgeries, community centers, schools, stations, airports, offices, and boardrooms. One current example is the pop-up, for example, a mobile oral history project run from a van outside a library or supermarket or a temporary art workshop in an empty retail space.

In 1999 the Anderson report showed that the majority of UK museums and galleries did not have education staff; that is no longer the case, but current funding constraints may require museums to work more collaboratively, both internally and externally. Thus, curators, conservators, and other members of museum staff may all contribute to museum learning programs. Many academic and professional training courses now take account of these wider roles for both curators and educators in the twenty-first-century museum. A growing number of freelance museum learning specialists work with museums that do not have in-house expertise in areas of work such as early years, diversity, new technologies, community, or evaluation. One UK initiative enabled self-directed learner groups to make use of museum and gallery spaces and resources to support their own learning interests, rather than those programmed by staff (Museums, Libraries and Archives Council 2010).

Heumann Gurian has recently outlined her vision for the sustainable museum, what she calls the "museum as soup kitchen." This needs to go beyond "business as usual" – not just "cloaked in the name of social good … but rather transforming currently less than useful local institutions into dynamic and community-focused 'clubhouses' for building social cohesion and incorporating social services usually delivered elsewhere such as job retraining, educational enhancements, and public discourse." In so doing, museums become "rated by many more as essential to their needs and their aspirations for their children" (Heumann Gurian 2010, 5).

When it comes to "teach the mind, touch the spirit" (the motto of Chicago's Field Museum), museum learning departments have a track record in knowing their users, knowing how to deliver, how to motivate and challenge, when to direct and when to hand back, what language or platform to use, when to structure and when to "let it all hang out." That kind of expertise does not come overnight or from a book or training course. Museum learning specialists should continue to expect and claim a major role in the increasingly multiskilled museum profession. They should themselves become more multiskilled and more willing to leave their comfort zones and education centers in order to advocate, campaign, curate, lead, direct – and to sustain what has been achieved. It should become a less uncertain profession, however uncertain the times.

Note

1   Our thanks to: Stephen Allan, National Museums Scotland; Christine Castle, Ontario, Canada; Gail Durbin, former Head of the V&A online museum; Pamela Glintenkamp, documentary media producer/director/editor; Karen Gron, Director of the Trapholt Museum Denmark; Litza Juhasz, Budapest Fine Arts Museum, Hungary; Caroline Lang, formerly V&A Learning Team; Beth Schneider, Royal Academy, author and museum educator.

References

AAM (American Association of Museums). 1992. *Excellence and Equity: Education and the Public Dimension of Museums*. Washington, DC: American Association of Museums.

ACE (Arts Council England). 2011. "A Review of Literature on Museums and Libraries." London: Arts Council of England. Accessed November 12, 2014. http://www.arts council.org.uk/publication_archive/museums-and-libraries-research-review.

Anderson, David. 1999. *A Common Wealth: Museums and Learning in the United Kingdom*. London: Department for Culture, Media and Sport.

Bellamy, Kate, and Carey Oppenheim. 2009. *Learning to Live: Museums, Young People and Education*. London: National Museum Directors' Conference. Accessed November 12, 2014. http://www.nationalmuseums.org.uk/media/documents/publications/learning_to_live.pdf.

Blackwell, Ian. 2009. "Community Engagement: Why Are Community Voices Still Unheard?" *Journal for Education in Museums* 30: 29–36.

Blackwell, Ian, and Sarah Scaife. 2006. "Networks and Partnerships: Building Capacity for Sustainable Audience Development." In *The Responsive Museum: Working with Audiences in the Twenty-First Century*, edited by Caroline Lang, John Reeve, and Vicky Woollard, 61–74. Aldershot, UK: Ashgate.

Borzello, Frances. 1987. *Civilising Caliban: The Misuse of Art 1875–1975*. London: Routledge.

Bourke, Marie. 2011. *The Story of Irish Museums 1790–2000: Culture, Identity and Education*. Cork: University of Cork Press.

Burnham, Rika, and Elliott Kai-Kee. 2011. *Teaching in the Art Museum: Interpretation as Experience*. Los Angeles: Getty.

Charman, Helen. 2005. "Uncovering Professionalism in the Art Museum: An Exploration of Key Characteristics of the Working Lives of Education Curators at Tate Modern." *Tate Papers Online Research Journal*. Accessed November 12, 2014. http://www.tate.org.uk/download/file/fid/7342.

Culture and Learning Consortium. 2009. *Get It: The Power of Cultural Learning*. London.

Cutler, Anna. 2010. "What Is to Be Done, Sandra? Learning in Cultural Institutions of the Twenty-First Century." *Tate Papers: Online Research Journal* 13. Accessed November 12, 2014. http://www.tate.org.uk/research/publications/tate-papers/what-be-done-sandra-learning-cultural-institutions-twenty-first.

DCMS (Department for Culture, Media and Sport). 2006. *Understanding the Future – Priorities for England's Museums*. London: Department for Culture, Media and Sport. Accessed November 12, 2014. http://webarchive.nationalarchives.gov.uk/+/http:/www.culture.gov.uk/images/publications/understanding_the_future_responses.pdf.

Falk, John, and Lynn Dierking. 2000. *Learning from Museums: Visitor Experiences and the Making of Meaning*. Walnut Creek, CA: Rowman & Littlefield.

Falk, John, and Lynn Dierking. 2011. *The Museum Experience*. Walnut Creek, CA: Left Coast Press.

Falk, John, Lynn Dierking, and Susan Foutz. 2007. *In Principle, in Practice: Museums as Learning Institutions*. Lanham, MD: Rowman.

Freire, Paulo. 1972. *Pedagogy of the Oppressed*. London: Penguin.

Fritsch, Juliette, ed. 2011. *Museum Gallery Interpretation and Material Culture*. Abingdon, UK: Routledge.

Gardner, Howard. 1993. *Frames of Mind: The Theory of Multiple Intelligences*. London: Fontana.

Grøn, Karen. 2011. "Empower the Audience! How Art Museums Can Become Enriching Creative Spaces for a Wider Audience through Deliberate and Strategic Use of Experience and Learning Theories." In *Museum Gallery Interpretation and Material Culture*, edited by Juliette Fritsch, 204–220. Abingdon, UK: Routledge.

Hawkey, Roy. 2004. *Digital Technologies for Learning in Museums, Science Centres and Galleries.* Bristol, UK: NESTA Futurelabs.

Hein, George. 1998. *Learning in the Museum.* London: Routledge.

Hein, George. 2011. "The Museum as a Social Instrument: A Democratic Conception of Museum Education." In *Museum Gallery Interpretation and Material Culture*, edited by Juliette Fritsch, 13–25. Abingdon, UK: Routledge.

Heritage Lottery Fund. 2011. "Digital Participation and Learning: 22 Case Studies." London: Heritage Lottery Fund. Accessed November 14, 2014. http://www.imagemakers.uk.com/wp-content/uploads/2012/09/HLF-Digital-Report-v9.pdf.

Heumann Gurian, Elaine. 2010. "Museum as Soup Kitchen." *Curator: The Museum Journal* 53: 71–85.

Hooper-Greenhill, Eilean. 1991. *Museum and Gallery Education.* Leicester, UK: Leicester University Press.

Hooper-Greenhill, Eilean. 2000. "Changing Values in the Art Museum: Rethinking Communication and Learning." *International Journal of Heritage Studies* 6(1): 9–31.

Hooper-Greenhill, Eilean. 2007. *Museums and Education: Purpose, Pedagogy, Performance.* London: Routledge.

Kids in Museums. 2014. Website. Accessed November 12, 2014. http://kidsinmuseums.org.uk.

Lang, Caroline, John Reeve, and Vicky Woollard, eds. 2006. *The Responsive Museum: Working with Audiences in the Twenty-First Century.* Aldershot, UK: Ashgate.

Leong, Jane. 2003. "Art Museum Education in Singapore." In *Researching Visual Arts Education in Museums and Galleries: An International Reader*, edited by Maria Xanthoudaki, Les Tickle, and Veronica Sekules, 49–64. Dordrecht: Kluwer.

Lord, Barry, ed. 2007. *The Manual of Museum Learning.* Lanham, MD: AltaMira.

Lynch, Bernadette. 2011. "Whose Cake Is It Anyway? A Collaborative Investigation into Engagement and Participation in 12 Museums and Galleries in the UK." London: Paul Hamlyn Foundation. Accessed November 12, 2014. www.phf.org.uk/downloaddoc.asp?id=547.

Metropolitan Museum of Art. 2014. "Learn." Accessed November 12, 2014. http://www.metmuseum.org/learn.

Miles, Roger, M. B. Alt, D. C. Gosling, B. N. Lewis, and A. F. Tout. 1988. *The Design of Educational Exhibits.* London: Unwin Hyman.

Museum of East Anglian Life. 2013. "About Us: Our Values." Accessed November 12, 2014. http://www.eastanglianlife.org.uk/about-us/our-values.html.

Museum of London. 2014. Website. Accessed November 12, 2014. http://www.museumoflondon.org.uk/london-wall.

Museums, Libraries and Archives Council. 2010. "Opening up Spaces – Bringing New People into Museums, Libraries and Archives by Supporting Self-Organised Groups." Accessed February 9, 2015.http://webarchive.nationalarchives.gov.uk/20110802101741/http:/www.mla.gov.uk/what/policy_development/learning/~/media/Files/pdf/2010/news/Opening_Up_Spaces.ashx.

NACCCE (National Advisory Committee on Creative and Cultural Education). 1999. "All Our Futures: Creativity, Culture and Education." London: Department for Culture,

Media and Sport; Department of Education and Employment. Accessed November 12, 2014. http://sirkenrobinson.com/skr/pdf/allourfutures.pdf.

Natural History Museum. 2013. "Visitor Research and Evaluation." Accessed November 12, 2014. http://www.nhm.ac.uk/about-us/visitor-research.

Nelson-Atkins Museum of Art. 2011. "The Nelson-Atkins Museum of Art Names Education Director." Press release. Accessed November 12, 2014. http://www.nelsonatkins.org/images/PDF/press/2011%2010%207%20Ed%20Director%20FINAL.pdf.

NMDC (National Museum Directors' Conference). 1999. "A Netful of Jewels: New Museums in the Learning Age." London: NMDC. Accessed November 12, 2014. http://www.nationalmuseums.org.uk/media/documents/publications/netful_of_jewels.pdf.

Pitman, Bonnie, and Ellen Hirzy. 2011. *Ignite the Power of Art: Advancing Visitor Engagement in Museum Experiences*. Dallas: Dallas Museum of Art Publications.

Pontin, Kate. 2006. "Understanding Museum Evaluation." In *The Responsive Museum: Working with Audiences in the 21st Century*, edited by Caroline Lang, John Reeve, and Vicky Woollard, 117–128. Aldershot, UK: Ashgate.

Pye, Elizabeth, ed. 2008. *The Power of Touch: Handling Objects in Museum and Heritage Context*. Lanham, MD: Left Coast Press.

RCMG (Research Centre for Museums and Galleries). 2004a. *Inspiration, Identity, Learning: The Value of Museums The Evaluation of the Impact of DCMS/DfES Strategic Commissioning 2003–2004: National/Regional Museum Education Partnerships*. Leicester, UK: Research Centre for Museums and Galleries.

RCMG (Research Centre for Museums and Galleries). 2004b. *What Did You Learn at the Museum Today? The Evaluation of the Impact of the Renaissance in the Regions Education Programme in the Three Phase 1 Hubs (August, September and October 2003)*. Leicester, UK: Research Centre for Museums and Galleries.

Rees Leahy, Helen. 2005. "Producing a Public for Art: Gallery Space in the 21st Century." In *Creative Space*, edited by Suzanne MacLeod, 108–117. London: Routledge.

Reeve, John. 1992. *Working in Museum and Gallery Education: Ten Career Experiences*, edited by Eilean Hooper-Greenhill. Leicester, UK: Department of Museum Studies, University of Leicester.

Reeve, John. 1999. "Making the History Curriculum." In *Making Histories in Museums*, edited by Gaynor Kavanagh, 228–239. London: Routledge.

Reeve, John. 2006. "Prioritising Audience Groups." In *The Responsive Museum: Working with Audiences in the Twenty-First Century*, edited by Caroline Lang, John Reeve, and Vicky Woollard, 43–60. Aldershot, UK: Ashgate.

Reeve, John. 2012. "A Question of Faith, Museums as Sacred and Secular Spaces." In *Museums, Equality and Social Justice*, edited by Richard Sandell and Eithne Nightingale, 125–141. London: Routledge.

Rice, Danielle. 2000. "Constructing Informed Practice." In *Transforming Practice: Selections from the Journal of Museum Education*, edited by Joanne S. Hirsch and Lois Silverman, 222–225. Bloomington: Indiana University; Museum Education Roundtable.

Rice, Danielle. 2003. "Museums: Theory, Practice and Illusion." In *Art and Its Publics: Museum Studies at the End of the Millennium*, edited by Andrew McClellan, 77–95. Oxford: Blackwell.

Rogers, Rick. 2004. *Space for Learning: A Handbook for Education Spaces in Museums, Heritage Sites and Discovery Centres*. London: Clore Duffield Foundation.

Rogers, Rick. 2009. "Get It: The Power of Cultural Learning." London: Culture and Learning Consortium. Accessed November 12, 2014. http://www.culturallearningalliance.org.uk/userfiles/files/2010/02/Culture-Learning-Printed-Report-Web.pdf.

Rossman, J. Robert. 2008. "Programming Approaches." In *Arts and Cultural Programming: A Leisure Perspective*, edited by Gaylene Carpenter and Doug Blandy, 23–36. Champaign, IL: Human Kinetics Europe.

Sandell, Richard, and Eithne Nightingale. 2012. *Museums, Equality and Social Justice*. London: Routledge.

Schneider, Beth. 1998. *A Place for all People*. Houston, TX: Museum of Fine Arts.

Screven, Chandler. 1986. "Exhibitions and Information Centers: Some Principles and Approaches." *Curator: The Museum Journal* 29(2): 109–137.

Selwood, Sara. 2010. "Making a Difference: The Cultural Impact of Museums." National Museum Directors' Conference. Accessed November 12, 2014. http://www.nationalmuseums.org.uk/media/documents/publications/cultural_impact_final.pdf.

Serota, Nicholas. 2009. "Museums and Young People: Where Are We Now?" In *Learning to Live: Museums, Young People and Education*, edited by Kate Bellamy and Carey Oppenheim, 21–29. London: National Museum Directors' Conference; Institute for Public Policy Research. Accessed November 12, 2014. http://www.nationalmuseums.org.uk/media/documents/publications/learning_to_live.pdf.

Sharmacharja, Shamita, ed. 2009. *A Manual for the 21st Century Art Institution*. London: Whitechapel Art Gallery; Koenig Books.

Sidford, Holly. 2011. *Fusing Arts, Culture and Social Change: High Impact Strategies for Philanthropy*. Washington, DC: National Committee for Responsive Philanthropy.

Social Trends 38. 2008. London: Government of the United Kingdom, Office for National Statistics.

Tate. 2013. "Online Resources." Accessed November 12, 2014. http://www.tate.org.uk/learn/online-resources.

Taylor, Barbara. 2006. *Inspiring Learning in Galleries*. London: Engage.

Transforming Education outside the Classroom. 2010. London: House of Commons Children, Schools and Families Committee.

Woollard, Vicky. 1998. "Fifty Years: The Development of a Profession." *Journal of Education in Museums* 19: 1–4.

Xanthoudaki, Maria, Les Tickle, and Veronica Sekules, eds. 2003. *Researching Visual Arts Education in Museums and Galleries: An International Reader*. Dordrecht: Kluwer.

Further Reading

Centre for Education and Industry. 2004. *Learning through Culture Is Working! Museums and Galleries Education Programme*. Warwick: Centre for Education and Industry, University of Warwick.

Eisner, Elliot, and S. Dobbs. 1986. *The Uncertain Profession: Observations on the State of Education in Twenty American Museums*. Los Angeles: Getty Centre for Education in the Arts.

Hawkey, Roy. 2006. "Digital Technologies and Museum Learning." In *The Responsive Museum: Working with Audiences in the Twenty-First Century*, edited by Caroline Lang, John Reeve, and Vicky Woollard, 115–116. Aldershot, UK: Ashgate.

John Reeve teaches on the Museums and Galleries in Education MA at the Institute of Education, London University, and was previously Head of Education at the British Museum, Chair of GEM, and Editor of the *Journal of Education in Museums*. He is also a museums consultant, working most recently in India and across Asia. He was co-editor and contributor to *The Responsive Museum* (with Caroline Lang and Vicky Woollard, 2006); and author of several books on Japanese and Indian art. He also writes on religions in museums, including in *Museums, Equality and Social Justice*, edited by Richard Sandell and Eithne Nightingale (2012).

Vicky Woollard is currently working as a researcher into museum visiting patterns, following a career in museum education and as a Senior Lecturer in the Department of Cultural Policy and Management, City University, London. She had 18 years' experience in working with museums in London such as the Geffrye Museum, the Museum of London, and the V&A, as well as running museum education and management training programs and consultancies for the British Council and several universities and organizations abroad. She was co-editor of *Museum and Gallery Education: A Manual of Good Practice* (1999), and *The Responsive Museum: Working with Audiences in the 21st Century* (2006).

25 REVIEWING THE DIGITAL HERITAGE LANDSCAPE
The Intersection of Digital Media and Museum Practice

Shannon Wellington and Gillian Oliver

In the Introduction to *Museums in a Digital Age*, Ross Parry aptly referred to the literature on digital heritage as a diaspora (2010, 3). Spread far and wide, this literature emerges from, and contributes to, the generation of new knowledge across a multitude of different domains (2010). Academic research, case studies, conference proceedings, project reports, and monographs are just some of the formats contributing to the corpus of this knowledge. Lurking in multidisciplinary domains, this corpus draws on the fields of information systems, computer science, museum and heritage studies, information management, media studies, and preservation management to inform our understanding of the intersections of all things "digital" and "heritage." According to Parry, this diaspora is not only entrenched in the domains in which digital heritage resides, but also in the professional identities of those people who engage with it: museum professionals, archivists, librarians, media specialists, content creators, preservation managers, educators, exhibition designers, and of course, by extension, the visitors to our cultural heritage institutions.

By utilizing multiple theoretical and conceptual frameworks, particularly the notion of digital heritage, we seek to understand and clarify the intersection/integration of digital media with core functions of the cultural heritage environment. Digital media in a museum construct can manifest in documentation through content management systems (CMS), through visitor engagement and interpretation, in the use of mobile technologies and through interfaces such as augmented reality, haptic technologies, and virtual reality. Digital media can support accessibility

The International Handbooks of Museum Studies: Museum Practice, First Edition.
Edited by Conal McCarthy.
© 2015 John Wiley & Sons Ltd. Published 2020 by John Wiley & Sons Ltd.

and visibility, facilitate user participation through social media platforms, as well as provide feedback and evaluation through the use of software designed to support museum analytics.

Digital heritage, however, is more than the sum of these digital media tools and platforms; the study of digital heritage aims to understand the engagement between cultural heritage and technology through the application of a broader sociocultural lens. The purpose of this chapter is not to align itself with, or promote the use of, or advocate for, certain digital technologies over others. It neither inflates the advantages to be had in the engagement between museums and digital media, nor does it seek to warn of the dangers of the digital to core museum function.

There is a transient aspect to digital architecture caused by rapid advancements in interface and application development. Accordingly the software used to design and capture digitally born or digital surrogates of collection objects is constantly changing, along with the multiplicity of platforms and interfaces used in the practice of collecting, curating, interpreting, and educating. We do not attempt therefore to provide platform or application specific evaluations for all things relating to "digital" and "heritage." Similarly, this chapter does not provide granular detail around specific applications and platforms currently used in cultural heritage environments. (We are moving beyond the concept of museum computing.)

In this chapter we step back to review the digital heritage landscape by re-enforcing the view of digital heritage as being embedded within a broad sociocultural context, firmly tied to the notion of practice *and* theory. Digital media in its various forms will come and go. As a digital preservation pioneer eloquently stated "Digital information lasts forever – or five years, whichever comes first" (Rothenberg 1995, 43).

The purpose of the chapter therefore is to provide a framework to help museum practitioners, students, and scholars understand the concept of digital heritage and its impact on the museum environment. The challenge to any successful integration/adoption of digital media by museum practitioners resides in being able to evaluate critically the emergence of, and future potential for, the platforms and software developed to support cultural heritage. An awareness of the inherent benefits and opportunities afforded through the intersections of "digital" and "heritage" will provide a solid foundation to the critical adoption, implementation, and evaluation of the multitude of digital media currently available for application in memory institutions.

In the Introduction to this volume McCarthy refers to the concept of practice-theory or theory-practice. By using the current body of knowledge to define the concept of digital heritage, historicize the emergence of digital heritage (both in theory and in practice), provide a concise overview of potential developments, and critically analyze key concepts, the structure and content of the current chapter reflect this framework. Through an examination of digital media in relation to the intersections and interactions between the people, organizations, information culture, education, entertainment, authenticity, artistry, and access, it aims to contribute to the growing sociotechnical understanding of the intersections of "digital" and "heritage."

Defining digital heritage

"Museum computing," a term used to describe the very new exploration of the use of computers in museums and supported by burgeoning interest groups, evolved as a sub-discipline of museum studies. The term "museum computing" features in much of the literature dealing with the intersections of automation and museum function (Bearman 1995; Parry 2007). Extended via the application of sociocultural theory through writers such as Parry (2005), Arvanitis (2010), and Van Heur (2010), museum computing has evolved into what we now understand as digital heritage.

UNESCO documentation defines the concept of digital heritage as "computer-based materials of enduring value that should be kept for future generations." These include "texts, databases, still and moving images, audio, graphics, software, and web pages, among a wide and growing range of formats. They are frequently ephemeral, and require purposeful production, maintenance and management to be retained" (UNESCO 2014). These materials, largely considered to be the digital outputs, platforms, and objects in a cultural heritage environment are arguably what spring to mind when we consider the concept of digital heritage. It is, however, impossible to conceptualize the outputs or objects (such as born digital or digital surrogates) without considering both the infrastructure that supports them (the digital architecture) as well as the way in which people engage with those objects and outputs (the sociocultural aspects).

The academic study of digital heritage wraps sociocultural frameworks around the digital objects, platforms, and outputs, and considers the theory and practice of the intersection of digital media in a cultural heritage environment (Parry 2010). Parry and Marty succinctly define digital heritage as the point where cultural heritage and digital media meet (2008). Given the focus of our chapter in a volume on museum practice, writers such as Parry and Marty provide a solid starting point from which to consider the construct of digital heritage.

"New media" is a term often used interchangeably with "digital media" and in some cases digital heritage (particularly in museum studies). As described by Manovich (2001), new media can be considered the result of a convergence between mass media and digital architecture. The concept of new media has its origins in the field of media studies, a field that exhibits strong interest for practitioners and academics working in and around museum interpretation and education. Henning, a prolific writer on the impact and engagement between new media and museums, draws on Manovich's definition to define new media as the platforms, objects, and architecture that support new media, platforms that are networkable, dense, compressible, and interactive (Henning 2006). Given that these features would be characteristic of most technologies today, we wonder how useful it is to continue to emphasize the "new." Parry suggests it is now time to acknowledge the prevalence of digital media in the museum, and thus enable both practice and research to move beyond concerns about the adoption of technology (Parry 2013).

Digital media by commonly accepted definition can encompass both new media as well as the ICT infrastructure (the hardware and software platforms). It can be found in what are traditionally considered the back-of-house functions of a cultural heritage institution, such as museum documentation and the preservation and access of collection objects – both digitally born and digital surrogates. (On this point see Chapman in this volume, on collection management systems.) Tangible manifestations of digital media can also be seen in the interpretive spaces, both physically and virtually, through the use of information layering such as pod casting and various types of digital information access points (for example, kiosks and QR codes), through the use of interactive technologies in exhibition and education, in outreach and in advocacy and audience engagement through social media. We therefore define digital heritage as the engagement, context, and agency of digital media within and around our cultural heritage environments. In other words, in analyzing digital heritage we are concerned with understanding the intersection of digital media with the sociocultural aspects of museum function, such as the people, the spaces, places, and the all-encompassing interrelationships between these entities.

The past is prologue: historicizing the field

In considering the interplay between today's digital media and current museum practice it is important to look back at the historical developments of museum computing in order to trace the journey through to our more nuanced understanding of digital heritage today. Williams (1987) provides an excellent overview of the history of museum computing. In historicizing digital heritage, this section provides brief and selective detail in order to frame our critical analysis of the interception of digital media and museum practice.

As was the case with the application of all early computing initiatives, initial adoption of automation in the museum sector first emerged through the advent of mainframe computing. This early automation was largely focused on back-of-house function in collection management and museum documentation (Williams 1987). Early museum computing initiatives required a large investment in infrastructure, funding, and people power: museum computing was undoubtedly a resource-intensive business. Very early on the Smithsonian set about establishing a project team to consider how best to harness digital opportunity and apply this new automation to museum practice. The Smithsonian led the way in the early adoption of automation in the form of mainframe computing through one early initiative called SELGEM (acronym for Self-Generating Master). SELGEM was a collection of programs designed for the management of museum registration and documentation. SELGEM, consisting of 33 individual programs using keypunch cards as input, was widely available to the museum community free of charge, and was promoted as a "generalized information management solution for museums" (Williams 1987, 17). Developed by the Smithsonian in 1967 (the date of the project's inception), by 1976 over 60 institutions were making use of the platform. Williams succinctly sums up the early information culture in relation to museum computing:

> As unwieldy as those early computers were, there was an aura surrounding them. They were perceived as magical: their operators, as wizards of the modern age endowed with extraordinary scientific prowess. Computers were status symbols – badges to be worn proudly, announcing to the world that the museum that owned one had finally entered the twentieth century. Museum staff members saw computers as electronic cornucopias, loaded with cures for the museum's every ill. (Williams 1987, 17)

The 1970s heralded the adoption of microcomputers and the reduction in costs and resources required to implement automation. Large mainframe computers required immense investment both in terms of finance and human resourcing, and their adoption and implementation was therefore carefully planned and largely successful (Williams 1987, 18). The rush to be both automated and technologically relevant, combined with the reduction in costs associated with micro-computing led to an increase in project implementation failure. These failures, according to Williams, were often due in part to poor planning and/or attempts to directly transpose analogue/manual systems to the new digital environment (1987). Throughout the 1980s a lack of standardized, "canned," out-of-the-box programs available for museums to use as a foundation of information architecture prompted a focus on standards development. This in turn resulted in early initiatives with IRGMA/MDA development of ICOM CIDOC.[1]

Given that digital heritage is concerned with conceptualizing and theorizing both the digital infrastructure as well as the way in which people engage with digital objects, it is useful to apply today's understanding of the digital to these early museum computing environments. The rise of museum computing can be traced back not only to the tangibles such as the use of hardware and software in museum practice, but also to the development of the first museum computing special interest groups – again the agency of people in the adoption of automation should not be understated. These early groups grappled with many of the same difficulties we do now in terms of understanding and best assimilating the integration of museum practice and automation – the Museum Computer Network, established in the United States in 1967, was one such group (Williams 1987).

The early adoption and use of these systems was contested ground. Debate ensued over the application and use of a quantitative data management framework to what was, at the time, considered a very different humanities ideology underpinning museum practice. Computing developments promoted an environment of standardization and formalization due to semantic rigidness of information organization and retrieval (Williams 1987). Early users expressed concern that museum computing would result in a situation whereby the practice of curation would essentially be reduced to codification. A clear progression can therefore be seen in the historical development of museum computing from back-of-house function through the development of standards, and on to museum experience and interactivity front of house, and then recursively back to informing practice behind the scenes again.

Museum computing and the "cultural turn"

While there has been a historical tendency to consider digital heritage as a purely conceptual, technological, and operational construct with scant regard for the agency of technology, Parry observed that digital heritage has experienced a "cultural turn" (2007). This cultural turn involved the recursive framing and informing of empiricism and practice with differing theoretical foundations, with the result that social and cultural dimensions started to permeate and provide a framework for critical reflection and analysis of the formerly technical foundations of museum computing.

The burgeoning interest in the development of museum computing has followed a trajectory common to many sub-disciplines. Early dissemination of much of the published literature in the field has been largely project-centric and heavily embedded in practice-based ideology (Parry 2005). Digital heritage is a comparatively young field, and the development of theory to frame and inform empiricism has been scant. Moreover, as Parry points out, "it is not too controversial to say that, as a body of work, museum computing has not consistently been predicated on clear theoretical models" (Parry 2005, 338). Parry advocates change management and a historicizing of the impact of new technologies on museum practice in order to frame our understanding of the digital heritage domain. The frameworks in digital heritage, Parry argues, on which the field of museum computing should draw include not only the historical foundations of museum computing, but also theoretical models from a range of cognate disciplines – for example, cultural studies, information management, and, we argue, information culture. Such application of theory has the ability to address challenging debates and issues about authority, authenticity, and commodification (Parry 2007). Given the diasporic foundations of the field, we extend this concept and argue for advancing digital heritage through a post-disciplinary or even transdisciplinary framework, one which acknowledges the plethora of knowledge that can be generated by bringing together theories and concepts from multiple fields, as well as drawing on the expertise of the academy, practitioners, policymakers, and the general public.

André Malraux's theories, in particular the idea of *Le Musée imaginaire* (1947), are often used in discussions about the impact of new media on the museum, particularly in relation to the capacity of new media to extend and reconceptualize how museums and their collections can engage with society. Parry succinctly refers to Malraux's thesis as the "the idea of technology liberating and reconfiguring the museum from its traditional modes of presentation" (Parry 2010, 119). The influence of Malraux's ideas can be seen in the concept of the virtual museum (see, for instance, Cameron and Mengler 2009; Giaccardi 2006; Styliani et al. 2009).

It is also useful to look to the cognate discipline of archival science for relevant theoretical innovations. In the last two decades of the twentieth century, concerns about the challenges of managing digital information in the archives and records community led to the development of "continuum thinking," drawing largely on Giddens' structuration theory (1984). Recursiveness, the ongoing influence of agency on structure and structure on agency considered against a backdrop of space–time distanciation, are at the heart of continuum thinking. Continuum theory represents a paradigm shift for the archival science discipline. The origins and development of the theory is documented by the three main architects, all of whom were academics at Monash University, Melbourne in the 1990s (McKemmish, Reed, and Upward 2009).

> Authenticity and reliability issues were also a particular concern in Australia in the early 1990s. At that time the findings of a number of Royal Commissions and major inquiries into a series of accountability crises in government and the corporate sector in the 1980s were released. They focused attention on the role of recordkeeping in supporting democratic and corporate accountability. (McKemmish, Reed, and Upward 2009, 4449)

Another key influence on continuum thinking came from David Bearman (see for instance Bearman 1994). Bearman was involved in the first major research project investigating digital recordkeeping (the University of Pittsburgh's *Functional Requirements for Evidence in Recordkeeping Project*) and worked closely with the Monash academics when he visited Australia in the early 1990s.

The initial and best-known articulation of continuum thinking is the records continuum model. The impetus for the records continuum model was the need to provide "new rules for a new game" (Upward 2000, 119) for recordkeeping in the third information age, when the accessibility of records has become more important than their location. Space–time dimensions are modeled as four continua: create, capture, organize, and pluralize. The records continuum focuses on the need to manage information as evidence, not surprising considering the crisis of accountability that was one of the key drivers for its development.

However, much less well known and scarcely documented are the other continuum models that have been developed. These include a cultural heritage continuum, which is very relevant to digital heritage in the museum context. Upward, the chief continuum proponent, provides a case study of the application of this particular model to a traditional museum setting (2005). Gibbons uses the model to demonstrate the need for a conceptual shift in practice by cultural heritage institutions collecting born-digital social media (2008). She concludes that using the cultural heritage continuum model allows insight into systems and structures of creative and collecting activities that point to the potential for "the development of powerful and innovative media tools for self and community expression for personal and shared community memory-making. These tools will be for individuals, groups, cultural heritage institutions and future researchers to engage with technologies as system of cultural production" (Gibbons 2008, 109–110).

The digital horizon: new technologies

Before we move on to a critical analysis of key issues in the digital heritage domain, it is important to reflect on the quote by Rothenberg used in the introduction to this chapter. These words remind us of the exponential changes we face in the development of digital media and the content which utilizes it: in other words digital information. We argue that there is inherent danger in anchoring any review of the digital heritage landscape to specific platforms or technologies, when the nature of those platforms and technologies is constantly evolving. However, no review would be complete without considering some of the digital media currently in use in our various cultural heritage institutions.

The NMC Horizon project (which began in March 2002) has produced a report series disseminating the results of a longitudinal study of emerging technologies likely to impact on education around the globe (Johnson et al. 2012). The Museum Edition Report outlines these emerging technologies and assesses their potential impact on, and use in, education and interpretation within museums. This report acknowledges that, while contextual factors affect the adoption and use of digital technologies, a number of issues transcend cultural heritage institutional and regional boundaries.

The Horizon report identifies six technologies to watch, which include mobile apps and social media, two platforms already well-established and evaluated as part of our socio-technical landscape. The ability of both platforms to support discovery, access, and content-sharing in museums is documented by writers such as Arvanitis (2010), Russo et al. (2008), and Sarzotti (2012). The interactivity of social media, in particular, potentially supports an open, recursive engagement between the museum and public. Moreover, the content-sharing, development, and engagement supported through the use of social and digital media creates opportunities to extend core museum function such as documentation outside of the area of registration. Drawing on society's collective cultural knowledge, information and content can be crowdsourced to contribute a rich layer of description and discovery to conceptualize and contextualize both digitally born and digital surrogate collection objects.

There have been many crowdsourcing initiatives instigated in museums over the past eight years. Oomen and Aroyo (2011) provide an overview of the different categories of crowdsourcing and include examples of projects relating to each category. While crowdsourcing relies heavily on participatory open platforms characteristic of social media, and a number of these platforms (such as Flickr) have been successfully implemented in this approach (see, for instance, Kalfatovic et al. 2008), not all crowdsourcing initiatives rely on the use of proprietary social media. One such New Zealand project includes the use of large flat-screens in New Plymouth district branch libraries to display changing photos from the Puke Ariki heritage pictorial collections, in particular the Swainson Woods Collection.[2] Puke Ariki[3] used this programming not only to make their heritage collections more visible to the wider community, but also as a mechanism for crowdsourcing metadata to strengthen the provenance of the pictorial series. The branch libraries were, according to the Manager of Service Delivery, a perfect venue for linking the wider community with their centrally managed cultural heritage (Wellington 2013).

The Horizon report notes that while augmented reality has been around for a while now, the integration of the technology with mobile platforms has exponentially increased its use and adoption in multiple domains. The layering of GPS, video, and pattern recognition allows users of the technology to experience new levels of discovery and interaction with gallery spaces and museum objects (Johnson et al. 2012). Natural user interfaces are another platform signaled by the Horizon report as key technologies to watch. While currently firmly embedded in gaming function and in some mobile technologies, the ability for users to interface with digital platforms through natural movement or voice recognition has vast implications for user engagement in cultural heritage spaces. Many of these emerging technologies are disseminated in conference forums such Museums and the Web.[4]

Key issues and controversies

The following section provides a critical analysis of important trends that are emerging from the intersections of museum practice and digital heritage. It considers the risks and opportunities inherent in digital curation, the skill sets required in the development of knowledge and expertise in our cultural heritage institutions to adopt and implement new media effectively, the omnipresent digital imperative, the risks and opportunities of content representation and control through digital media, and the implications of collaborative and convergence models of digital representation of cultural heritage across our gallery, library, archive, and museum (GLAM) domains.

Digital curation

The issues faced in collecting and curating digital heritage are enormous. Given the ever-increasing complexity and diversity of technology, ensuring that digital information can be accessed over time is one of the grand challenges of our age. The sheer volume of digitally born materials is overwhelming; there appears to be no end in sight as storage capacity exponentially becomes more expansive and cheaper. Taken in conjunction with the digitization imperative, in which museums and galleries feel they have to digitize their collections and put them on their websites, cultural heritage institutions appear to be actively contributing to the digital landfill that threatens to engulf us all. This point is reiterated by Henning who states:

> All media produce problems of storage: an ever growing archive of photographs, recordings, films and so on, has to be stored somewhere. This is not just a crisis in storage, it is a crisis in knowledge – in how to make sense of the unimaginable mass of stuff accumulating in museums and archives. (Henning 2006, 308)

Attracting the right people with the right expertise to work with digital heritage is another conundrum. If the established museum studies educational programs fail to consider the need for specialist expertise as a matter of urgency then curatorial specializations will become siloed. This may well have a negative impact on strategic development, and will pose threats to the future of the museum professional. Concerns about future access to digital information led to the development of a new discipline in the 1990s: digital curation (Higgins 2011). In this context, the term "curation" is used in a very specific way, encompassing not only the management of collections, but also the concept of preservation: that is to say, making sure that digital information can be retained and accessed in future. This successful model of "curation" adopted by the digital preservation community, to signal a new discipline and to attract support from funding agencies has been a successful move, informed by multinational research projects principally and supported by North American and European resourcing.

The trajectory of digital curation as a new discipline cuts across the traditional libraries, archives, galleries, and museums space as is evidenced by the development of specialist curricula. Starting in 2006, efforts to develop a digital curation curriculum have been led by a team at the University of North Carolina, Chapel Hill (DigCCurr 2014). The most recent manifestation of curriculum-building activity has focused specifically on the needs of current practitioners curating digital objects with the Digital Curator Vocational Education Europe Project.[5]

However, these initiatives to develop a new discipline focused on the management and preservation of digital objects, in all types of cultural heritage institutions, raise questions about existing professional skills. In particular, are museum practitioners who are accustomed to working with museum objects capable of bringing their professional skills and expertise to bear on virtual objects in the digital environment? What happens next is not clear: will a parallel set of competencies be developed, one for those people working with digital information, the other for those working in the analogue paradigm? This division of professional competencies has become apparent in the area of preservation and conservation. There appears to be a tendency for those responsible for preservation to restrict their attention to physical problems, with a whole new specialty developing around digital preservation. Specialization is of course not a problem, but the concern is when this occurs without a shared basis and understanding of fundamental principles. It seems that the increasing rhetoric about the convergence of practice, seen in the cultural heritage institutions of galleries, libraries, archives, and museums, may in fact mask a more fundamental and divisive split between the responsibilities of those curating physical and digital objects. The consequences of that for a single, coherent vision for the museum mission do not augur well.

The digital imperative

When we defined digital heritage we elevated the concept of agency and its relationship to new media. Many argue that it is dangerous not to maintain vigilant awareness of digital or technological determinism in any use and implementation of digital heritage (Parry 2005; Van Heur 2010). Often in our rush to remain digitally relevant, we become guilty of adopting and rolling out products/platforms without full consideration of the affordances of such platforms. Parry refers to Sola's concept of the technology trap in the context of digital heritage as the pursuit of "technology for its own sake" and "what catches us when we allow technology to become self-serving and let ourselves be guided by it" (Parry 2005, 333).

Rather than considering the risks and opportunities inherent in the actual bounded functionality of digital media, adoption and use is best served by critical analysis through a digital heritage framework. We believe a comprehensive assessment of digital media and ICT infrastructure within a sociocultural lens can be achieved by ensuring the answers to questions such as the following are considered:

- Does this product/platform meet our specified needs?
- Do we have the infrastructure to support the product/platform in an ongoing sense?
- Is this product/platform compatible with our strategic direction/operational plan?
- How will this product/platform impact on current organizational process and/or products?
- Do we have the skill, expertise, *and* willingness to manage this product/platform adequately in the future?

- Does this product/platform match the culture of our organization?
- What does the adoption of this product/platform say about our information culture?

There is close alignment between the concept of digital determinism and the digital imperative. Two spectrums of technological determinism (hard and soft) each differ in the varying degrees of agency they afford to technology (Smith and Marx 2001). Agency conceived as "soft technological determinism is deeply embedded in the larger social structure and culture" (Smith and Marx 2001, xiv). A soft deterministic approach acknowledges elements of human agency in the use and application of technology (Smith and Marx 2001) and reflects the sociocultural foundations of the digital heritage domain. The concept of technological determinism nurturing a digital imperative can be seen in project development in many cultural heritage institutions. One such project is examined in an article written by Van Heur, who reports on the lifecycle of a cultural heritage project commissioned in Maastricht, Netherlands. Van Heur employs Wyatt's concept of a digital imperative, defined as "a belief that the future is digital and that current practices need to digitize in order to make this future a reality." Wyatt also believes that a strong sociocultural pressure exists to engage in the "act of being digital" (Wyatt qtd. in Van Heur 2010, 406).

Van Heur draws on institutional theory and the sociology of expectations to show how a digital imperative can shape media development through the interplay between project members and the organizational and institutional dynamics in play in the development of a heritage project in the Netherlands. What starts out as a content-driven project (a cultural biography to conceptualize the city of Maastricht) becomes increasingly influenced by a growing digital imperative. The availability of ICT funding, ICT dominance in the skill set of the project group members, and the adoption of ICT external frameworks for content delivery resulted in the product being determined by the technological infrastructure available to support it (Van Heur 2010). Case studies such as this reinforce the importance of maintaining a critical awareness of the powerful agency of new media in museum practice; the implication of technology driving digital projects creates many problems for professionals.

The interplay between systems and context (people, places, culture, and society), and the use of new media and other ICT as cultural capital is often influenced by a digital imperative mindset. Museums are very much in the business of purchasing both proprietary and custom-built systems. The resource-intensive products and frameworks needed to support digital media adoption and implementation potentially draw many institutions toward use of and reliance on commercial sponsorship and branding in order to maintain digital relevance. Henning noted that this interaction between commerce and cultural capital was creating a form of cultural power play between museums as they increasingly compete with one another for digital prestige (Henning 2006).

Is there a digital divide? Does the implementation of digital information layering such as Qcodes and other mobile technologies limit access to a particular interpretative / knowledge layer for those who possess the digital technology and digital literacy to access it? We argue that layering digital initiatives over and in conjunction with analogue technologies to ensure equitable access to and experience of cultural memory is an important ethical and operational mandate for cultural heritage institutions. The multiplicity of backgrounds, technical literacy, and contexts with which users approach digital media in museums can both enrich and constrain the adoption, success, and use of those platforms. The principles of the new museology to which many cultural heritage institutions now aspire, demand democratized access. Museums have a fundamental obligation to cater to those who may not possess the digital capital to access or use digital media products and platforms. Lest we forget, there are audiences *not* interested in all things digital: those who are consciously concerned with the resonant power of the physical object and the sensory experience. Wyatt refers to this digital demographic as the resisters and rejecters, respectively those who do not have the means to digitally engage, and those who have the means but voluntarily reject engagement (2008, 9). For some, love is, consciously and validly, purely analogue.

Content, representation, and control

Issues of ownership, content representation, and control through the open, participatory affordances of digital media create both challenges and opportunities for museum practice; these are reflected in issues of ownership and access, institutional visibility, and what web developers call "information appropriateness," that is to say the appropriateness of selected digital media channels for the sociocultural needs of the information being transmitted.

The in-house development of digital content for use in exhibition spaces can be operationally challenging, both financially and in a human resource capacity. The development and implementation of in-house content and platforms allows the control and development of digital content to be carefully managed, but resource investment is intensive. Drawing on digital content sourced or developed by other organizations outside of the physical institution is often an alternative solution, yet a solution with pros and cons. The incorporation of material from a Digital Heritage Archive (DHA) to layer information around collection objects or support exhibition function can be mutually beneficial. For its part, the museum has an arsenal of material available to it to support core function and, on the other side, the institution managing the DHA receives additional exposure through outreach. However, curating such content for inclusion in education or exhibition programs requires the careful management of relationships with outside providers. Initial agreements aside, the permanence and lack of internal control of third-party content can generate difficulties for museum personnel. There are serious challenges for nodal institutions if DHA platforms are upgraded and compatibility problems result, or if content is remediated leaving the museum information layer obsolete. While the impact of these issues are context-specific to environment and museum function, they are worth considering early on at concept development stages and in the negotiation of contract access with outside media providers.

The issue of ongoing resources to support digital initiatives is another difficulty in terms of content control and representation. Research into integrated memory institutions shows that often digital initiatives are adopted and implemented under extraordinary operational environments such as the re-engineering of permanent exhibition galleries or the development of new organizational forms generated through building projects, mergers, or dissolution. The operational reality that follows often sees the initial investment in digital infrastructure deemed too resource- or financially intensive to continue. Consequently the initial investment is lost and, in the case of one interactive information kiosk, the forgotten piece of the interpretation jigsaw is left languishing unrefreshed in gallery spaces or relegated to a forgotten corner of a collections storage area (Wellington 2013).

The concept of information appropriateness needs to be applied to museum practice in terms of engagement with digital platforms. The digital media tools we use speak volumes about the way we chose to manage and represent digital information in a cultural heritage environment. There are undoubtedly inherent characteristics and vices in all platforms and there is inevitably an information culture associated with new media platforms. This culture is embedded in the characteristics, in the constraints, and in the ways in which people and organizations engage with the medium. Parry states: "As a cultural product, media (such as new digital media) is imbued with specific ideas and meanings and to use this media is to be implicated with those values" (2005, 343). To tout an often overused but still important turn of phrase, if the medium is the message (McLuhan 1964) then our adoption and use of that medium in museums and cultural heritage organizations must maintain an element of information appropriateness – not only must our choices to adopt and/or engage demonstrate a digital technology fit for purpose, but also a digital heritage fit for the purpose of cultural representation.

Social media can reach out to audiences through its wide dissemination and participatory communication culture, but, paradoxically, it also creates challenges in representation and control of both a museum's brand and also their digital objects. While the idea of controlling content is unpopular in the new museology and the post-museum (Hooper-Greenhill 2007), the ubiquitous open ideology of social media creates an environment that sometimes necessitates new layers of control for museum practitioners. A case study of the use of social media in the Holocaust Museum, Washington, DC, shows how affordances of particular forms of new media can be at odds with the message and the content we aim to deliver. Wong discusses the tension and synergy of new media in relation to modern museum practice, particularly with ethical considerations such as transparency, censorship, preservation, and privacy. The Holocaust Museum's experience of negotiating the information culture of YouTube required close monitoring of their YouTube channel and, in some cases, censorship of free comment, due to the gravity of the content sometimes posted by the museum (Wong 2011). The infotainment culture of "hating" on You Tube required more intervention and mediation by staff to maintain the ethical mandate of the museum's memorial function.

Photo-sharing sites such as Flickr also created issues for the Holocaust Museum (Wong 2011). The ease with which digital manifestations of collection objects were disseminated and repurposed beyond their original function called for additional intervention and control to manage the ownership and appropriate use of their material. Wong, commenting on the use of social media, noted that "if the medium is part of the message, museums are limited in what messages they can relay, especially by the architecture of social media sites" (2011, 102). Wong's statement reinforces the importance of information appropriateness in the adoption and use of new media in the museum.

The so-called new media, by general definition a subset of digital media, has promised much, delivered some, and influenced many. Henning states that it has been considered both a panacea designed to liberate the museum from its stuffy confines as well as the enabler of the vulgarizing of museums through edutainment (2006). The reality, proposed by Henning, sits somewhere in between. One of the key qualities of new media is its ability to reconfigure and recombine traditional content delivery. The haptic, mechanical, peep show and non-linear exhibition which encouraged the user to interact with the exhibit was a precursor to the virtual, media-heavy experiences we often have now. The difference, historically, is that the pre-digital exhibition still required a visitor to move through space and time in a gallery in a collective experience defined by place. Today's technology has the potential to disengage the visitor from the collective experience and transcend physical space. New media as a transformative power influences "the hierarchies of knowledge" (Henning 2006, 303) and contains the capacity to dissolve divisions between front- and back-of-house practice.

Digital media can be both a remediation platform and a platform for engagement, decentering curatorial practice, democratizing access, and inviting the formation of participatory cultural heritage. Digital media provides an opportunity to explore information layering and multifaceted representation of objects. Digital platforms and carefully considered metadata can bring objects together from disparate collections, institutions, and locations. Digital manifestations of objects add value to the museum experience by opening up a new way of looking at collections, recombining elements, and allowing us to see possibilities that are not apparent in the physical manifestation, and re-engineering from what Robertson and Meadow (2000) call a digital cabinet of curiosity through to the realm of the virtual multi-verse gallery.[6]

Both Hooper-Greenhill and Henning see digital heritage as a vehicle for moving into the post-museum domain. New media supports Hooper-Greenhill's idea of the post-museum (2007) which moves beyond the sole curatorial voice and iconic institutional building that transmits information and authority to the visitor, into a landscape of engagement and mutuality where knowledge is constructed and transmitted freely and the curatorial voice becomes only one of many. According to Henning, new media provides a platform for returning to a more flexible, fluid representation of knowledge, one that predates modern museum structure (2006).

The use of new media in interpretive spaces facilitates multimodal learning by transcending physical gallery engagement and extending out through audio, video, touch, and so on, thus supporting a variety of learning styles. However, the mere act of visitor engagement with digital interactivity does not necessarily signal success in terms of designated knowledge acquisition as determined by the exhibition design. As Henning (2006), Macdonald (2002), and Witcomb (2006) note, while it is possible to measure time spent engaging at interactive terminals, it is impossible to measure the amount of learning taking place and/or pleasure derived from the interactivity.

As we have noted, digital media and, in particular, new media can negate physical differences such as size and dimension, enabling the digital manifestation of multiformat collections to be accessed from one homogeneous platform by users outside institutional walls. There are multiple representations of online collections hosted through web interfaces and internal information portals in many cultural institutions all over the world (see Chapman in this volume). Other interfaces such as DigitalNZ,[7] aggregate this content; in other words these interfaces bring together collection records from a variety of different GLAM institutions and provide a federated searching layer that sits on top of institutional specific collection management systems. Moreover, creating these federated search interfaces for the representation of cultural objects from a diverse range of institutions, allows for the easy access, reconfiguration, ordering, and structuring of content by users.

However, the mere act of choosing what to digitize and make available through online interfaces is not a value-neutral activity. In essence we argue that a controlling curatorial element is still maintained. This controlling curatorial element exists in the digital paradigm applied through the use of digital curatorial filters. These digital filters are embedded in the features of the digital infrastructure, such as the functional restrictions of the platform, the information culture associated with the use and participants of that platform, along with the digital context or metadata associated with that object. This may potentially democratize the physical limitations of traditional museum practice through the open participatory nature of the electronic delivery, but it is still a heavily curated process. This is particularly reflected in the virtual exhibition, where the amount of resourcing available to develop and digitize collection objects, the functionality of the platform used to host the exhibition and metadata associated with the exhibition, all contribute to a heavily mediated digital experience for the end user.

If we consider digital heritage within a sociocultural framework it is clear that there are intrinsic differences in the use of collection management platforms within a museum environment, compared to other cultural heritage organizations. While work on the interoperable metadata and descriptive standards to facilitate management and discoverability continues, such standards may do little to address the different underlying value propositions that curators, registrars, exhibition developers, educators, and visitors place on their documentation systems (Wellington 2013). A museum CMS, as an information management tool, has an occupational/professional culture associated with its use and function that is historically embedded in museological practice; documentation and intellectual control are central to the value propositions placed on a museum CMS by staff, while access and discoverability dominate the value propositions placed on a library management systems.

The museum online presence can provide a voice of authority in a sea of unmediated opinion. While the notions of authority and authenticity are contested constructs in a digital world, memory institutions, such as GLAM institutions, still resonate with the general public as institutions of authoritative knowledge. The literature we have examined, and the issues discussed in this chapter so far, support the idea that visibility is power, and collection and institutional access enabled through digital platforms can enhance visitor engagement and increase physical museum visitation. New media increasingly provides complex and functionally rich platforms on which to build virtual exhibition and digital spaces for collections management and in the development of an online presence. Audience engagement, advocacy, and outreach can be greatly enhanced by the use of information appropriate digital infrastructure.

Collaboration and convergence

There has been a great deal of research directed at understanding the role technology plays as a catalyst for breaking down the traditional distinctions between GLAMs. This chapter draws on theories and literature from across the GLAM domain to discuss the digital heritage landscape. As we have noted, the homogeneous digital manifestation of cultural artifacts, from documents to three-dimensional objects, along with new media infrastructure, has seen an increase in the development and assimilation of virtual outputs between many GLAM institutions. Digital media has provided a catalyst for burgeoning GLAM collaboration initiatives and convergent practice. All GLAM entities are grappling with the provision of and access to digital representations of materials and increasingly, for libraries and archives, of digitally born materials.

The agency of digital media in converging practice between GLAM entities along with the impact of electronic formats of information on GLAM ideology was first raised by Rayward in 1998 (Marty 2009). Rayward stated:

> The increasing availability in electronic form of information generally and of new kinds of information more particularly will lead to a redefinition and integration of the different categories of "information" organisations. Traditionally these have been created to manage different formats and media such as print and its surrogates (libraries), objects (museums), and the paper records of organisational activity

(archives and records repositories). Differences in organisational philosophy, function and technique have arisen from the exigencies presented by these different formats and media. The exigencies no longer apply in the same way when there is a common electronic format. It is clear that if electronic sources of information are to be effectively managed for future access by historians and others, differences between libraries, archives and museums will largely have to disappear and their different philosophies, functions and techniques integrated in ways that are yet unclear. (Rayward 1998, 1)

While it may seem determinist to afford such agency to the digital, the role technology plays as a catalyst for GLAM convergence is undeniably important. Digital curation and new media suggest a move toward seamless integration, representation, and delivery of cultural heritage resources. Some argue that the digital representation of multifaceted collections is rendering the physical separation of collections across GLAM institutions by format obsolete, and in effect re-engineering the concept of cabinets of curiosity into a virtual space (Henning 2006; Robertson and Meadow 2000). The assimilation of multiformat collection objects – whether book, artifact, record, photograph, artwork – into digital manifestations strips away the differing treatments and delineations embedded in the respective GLAM sector collections management. Demarcations such as built environment, object size, preservation management, format type, and geographical boundaries are mitigated or marginalized. Technology levels the playing field by providing closely aligned digital formats and facilitates the use of one point of access for a multitude of cultural artifacts (Wellington 2013).

Wellington argues that the increasing development of integrated operational models for the management of cultural memory, seen in the way in which galleries, museums, and other entities are combined into one building, are, in part, an attempt to replicate the operational functionality provided by the digital space. Joining together the collections and services managed through GLAMs in a unified built environment attempts to replicate online information architecture in the GLAM digital domain, such as the seamless, format-agnostic transitions through hyperlinking from artifact to document, the online multiformat exhibition regardless of object institutional affiliation and the generation of platforms which layer a service/information model on top of GLAM silos (Wellington 2013).

Conclusion

As noted above, the digital heritage domain represents a diasporic body of knowledge. Rather than evolving through a single linear trajectory, it has emerged and grown through input from the professional and academic fields of museum and heritage studies, information studies, media studies, and information systems. This multidisciplinary input has enriched the study of digital heritage, as opposed to generating competing paradigms. The concept and theoretical foundation of digital heritage studies acknowledges the nuances in definition and application that exist in these various domains. Our contribution in this review of the landscape aims to bring together key considerations in the development of digital heritage and highlight the challenges and opportunities for museum practice. This review has been framed by our interdisciplinary understanding of information culture and information management, as applied to cultural heritage. In so doing, our purpose has been to present a balanced view of the engagement between museums and digital media, to advocate reflexive practice by historicizing the development of digital media and its impact on museology and to maintain critical awareness of theory and practice occurring in related disciplines.

In an age where it is possible to access digital manifestations of objects by visiting countless virtual museums, downloading content, manipulating content through reconfiguration, recombining and repurposing it through mash-ups, disseminating and discussing it via social media, and contributing metadata to it through crowdsourcing, the issues of authenticity and resonance appear to be foremost. In the day of "light touch" engagement with content and representation, the agency of the museum as place and the visit as physical sensory experience may take on an elevated importance. The ease with which we participate digitally with our cultural heritage, along with the transitory nature of that engagement, paradoxically places more emphasis on, and, perhaps surprisingly, elevates the notion of the physical.

We must embrace the opportunities inherent in bringing together digital media and museum practice, but be mindful of doing so within the wider sociocultural constructs of digital heritage. Digital heritage studies should take into account not just the intersections of "digital" and "heritage," but also how those intersections engage with past, current, and future practice.

Notes

1   The IRGMA is the acronym used for the Information Retrieval Group that was active from 1967 to 1977 as part of the Museums Development Association (MDA). The CIDOC/CRM is a conceptual reference model for describing concepts and relationships used in cultural heritage documentation. The CIDOC/CRM provides a framework for information-mapping and data-sharing that can be applied across multiple cultural heritage domains, for instance, galleries, libraries, archives, and museums. In 2006 the CIDOC/CRM became an ISO standard.

2   The Swainson/Woods Collection, donated to Puke Ariki in 2005, is a nationally significant collection that traces both the lives of Taranaki people and the development of photography from 1923 to 1997. Accessed November 13, 2014. http://pukeariki.com.

3   Puke Ariki is an integrated museum, library, and visitor information center located in the New Zealand city of New Plymouth in the Taranaki region. Accessed November 13, 2014. http://www.pukeariki.

4   For Museums and the Web see http://www.museumsandtheweb.com. Accessed November 13, 2014.
5   See DigCurV website. Accessed November 13, 2014. http://www.digcur-education.org.
6   For a physical representation of the Multiversity Galleries, see the Museum of Anthropology at the University of British Columbia in Vancouver. http://moa.ubc.ca/experience/exhibit_details.php?id=1161. For the catalog, see MOA CAT at: http://collection-online.moa.ubc.ca. Accessed November 13, 2014.
7   See DigitalNZ website. Accessed November 13, 2014. http://www.digitalnz.org.

References

Arvanitis, Kostantinos. 2010. "Museums outside Walls: Mobile Phones and the Museum in the Everyday." In *Museums in a Digital Age*, edited by Ross Parry, 170–176. New York: Routledge.

Bearman, David. 1994. *Electronic Evidence: Strategies for Managing Records in Contemporary Organizations*. Pittsburgh, PA: Archives and Museum Informatics.

Bearman, David. 1995. *Multimedia Computing and Museums: Selected Papers from the Third International Conference on Hypermedia and Interactivity in Museums*, San Diego, California, October 9–13. San Diego: Archives and Museum Informatics.

Cameron, Fiona, and Sarah Mengler. 2009. "Complexity, Transdisciplinarity and Museum Collections Documentation Emergent Metaphors for a Complex World." *Journal of Material Culture* 14(2): 189–218.

DigCCurr. 2014. "About our Projects." Accessed November 13, 2014. http://ils.unc.edu/digccurr/index.html.

Giaccardi, Elisa. 2006. "Collective Storytelling and Social Creativity in the Virtual Museum: A Case Study." *Design Issues* 22(3): 29–41.

Gibbons, Leisa. 2008. "Testing the Continuum: User-Generated Cultural Heritage on YouTube." *Archives and Manuscripts* 37(2): 90–113.

Giddens, Anthony. 1984. *The Constitution of Society: Outline of the Theory of Structuration*. Berkeley: University of California Press.

Henning, Michelle. 2006. "New Media." In *A Companion to Museum Studies*, edited by Sharon Macdonald, 302–318. Malden, MA: Blackwell.

Higgins, S. 2011. "Digital Curation: The Emergence of a New Discipline." *The International Journal of Digital Curation* 2(6): 78–88.

Hooper-Greenhill, Eileen. 2007. *Museums and Education: Purpose, Pedagogy, Performance*. New York: Routledge.

Johnson, L., S. Adams Becker, H. Witchey, M. Cummins, V. Estrada, A. Freeman, and H. Ludgate. 2012. *The NMC Horizon Report: 2012 Museum Edition*. Austin, TX: New Media Consortium.

Kalfatovic, Martin. R., Effie Kapsalis, Katherine P. Spiess, Anne Van Camp, and Michael Edson. 2008. "Smithsonian Team Flickr: A Library, Archives, and Museums Collaboration in Web 2.0 Space." *Archival Science* 8(4): 267–277.

Macdonald, Sharon. 2002. *Behind the Scenes at the Science Museum*. Oxford: Berg.

Manovich, Lev. 2001. *The Language of New Media*. Cambridge, MA: MIT Press.

Marty, Paul F. 2009. "An Introduction to Digital Convergence: Libraries, Archives, and Museums in the Information Age." *Archival Science* 8(4): 247–326.

McKemmish, S., Barbara Reed, and Frank Upward. 2009. "The Records Continuum Model." In *Encyclopedia of Library and Information Sciences*, edited by Marcia J. Bates and Mary N. Maack, 4447–4459. New York: Taylor & Francis.

McLuhan, Marshall. 1964. *Understanding Media: The Extensions of Man*. New York: McGraw-Hill.

Oomen, J., and L. Aroyo. 2011. "Crowdsourcing in the Cultural Heritage Domain: Opportunities and Challenges." In *C&T '11 Proceedings of the 5th International Conference on Communities and Technologies*, 138–149. New York: ACM.

Parry, Ross. 2005. "Digital Heritage and the Rise of Theory in Museum Computing." *Museum Management and Curatorship* 20(4): 333–348.

Parry, Ross. 2007. *Recoding the Museum: Digital Heritage and the Technologies of Change*. London: Routledge.

Parry, Ross. 2010. "The Practice of Digital Heritage and Heritage of Digital Practice." In *Museums in a Digital Age*, edited by Ross Parry, 2–7. New York: Routledge.

Parry, Ross. 2013. "The End of the Beginning: Normativity in the Postdigital Museum." *Museum Worlds: Advances in Research* 1: 24–39.

Parry, Ross, and Paul Marty. 2008. "Introduction to Digital Heritage." *Museum Management and Curatorship* 23(4): 307–308.

Rayward, W. Boyd. 1998. "Electronic Information and the Functional Integration of Libraries, Museums and Archives." In *History and Electronic Artefacts*, edited by Edward Higgs, 207–226. Oxford: Clarendon.

Robertson, Bruce, and Mark Meadow. 2000. "Microcosms: Objects of Knowledge." *AI & Society* 14(2): 223–229.

Rothenberg, Jeff. 1995. "Ensuring the Longevity of Digital Documents." *Scientific American* 272(1): 42–47.

Russo, Angelina, Jerry Watkins, Lynda Kelly, and Sebastian Chan. 2008. "Participatory Communication with Social Media." *Curator: The Museum Journal* 51(1): 21–31.

Sarzotti, Michela. 2012 "Sharing the Museum: Social Media and Curatorial Practice." *Interventions Journal*. Accessed November 13, 2014. http://interventionsjournal. net/2012/01/26/sharing-the-museum-social-media-and-curatorial-practice.

Smith, Merritt Roe, and Leo Marx, eds. 2001. *Does Technology Drive History? The Dilemma of Technological Determinism*. Cambridge, MA: MIT Press

Styliani, Sylaiou, Liarokapis Fotis, Kotsakis Kostas, and Patias Petros. 2009 "Virtual Museums, a Survey and Some Issues for Consideration." *Journal of Cultural Heritage* 10(4): 520–528.

UNESCO (United Nations Educational, Scientific and Cultural Organization). 2014. "Concept of Digital Heritage." Accessed November 13, 2014. http://www.unesco. org/new/en/communication-and-information/access-to-knowledge/preservation-of-documentary-heritage/digital-heritage/concept-of-digital-heritage.

Upward, Frank. 2000. "Modelling the Continuum as Paradigm Shift in Recordkeeping and Archiving Processes, and Beyond: A Personal Reflection." *Records Management Journal* 10(3): 115–139.

Upward, Frank. 2005. "Continuum Mechanics and the Making of Culture." *Archives and Manuscripts* 33(2): 18–51.

Van Heur, Bas. 2010. "From Analogue to Digital and Back Again: Institutional Dynamics of Heritage Innovation." *International Journal of Heritage Studies* 16(6): 405–416.

Wellington, Shannon. 2013. "Building GLAMour: Convergent Practice between Galleries, Libraries, Archives and Museums." Unpublished PhD thesis, Victoria University of Wellington. Accessed November 13, 2014. http://hdl.handle.net/10063/2835.

Williams, Paul. 1987. "A Brief History of Museum Computerization." *Museum Studies Journal* 3(1): 58–65.

Witcomb, Andrea. 2006. "Interactivity: Thinking Beyond." In *A Companion to Museum Studies*, edited by Sharon Macdonald, 353–361. Oxford: Blackwell.

Wong, Amelia. 2011. "Ethical Issues of Social Media in Museums: A Case Study." *Museum Management and Curatorship* 26(2): 97–112.

Wyatt, Sally. 2008. "Challenging the Digital Imperative." Inaugural Lecture KNAW Extraordinary Chair in Digital Cultures in Development. Maastricht University, Netherlands, March 28. Accessed November 13, 2014. http://www.virtualknowledge studio.nl/staff/sally-wyatt/inaugural-lecture-28032008.pdf.

Shannon Wellington is a Lecturer in the School of Information Management and a Teaching Associate for the Museum and Heritage Studies Programme at Victoria University of Wellington, New Zealand. She holds a Master's degree in Information Studies and a PhD in Museum and Heritage Studies, and currently teaches in the fields of Archival Science and Preservation Management. Her current research examines aspects of integration between galleries, libraries, archives, and museums with a particular interest in advocacy, outreach, and exhibitions in documentary heritage institutions. Shannon also consults for organizations looking to build collaborative or convergent frameworks for the delivery of their cultural heritage resources.

Gillian Oliver is Senior Lecturer at the School of Information Management, Victoria University of Wellington. Gillian's PhD is from Monash University, Australia, and her professional practice background spans information management in the UK, Germany, and New Zealand. She is Honorary Research Fellow at the Humanities Advanced Technology and Information Institute, University of Glasgow and at the Open Polytechnic of New Zealand, and was Visiting Scholar at Tallinn University, Sweden, in 2009. Her research interests reflect these experiences, focusing on the information cultures of organizations. She is a member of Archives New Zealand's Archives Council. She is Editor of *Archifacts* and co-Editor-in-Chief of *Archival Science*.

AFTERWORD
The Continuing Struggle for Diversity and Equality

Eithne Nightingale

At the time of my job interview at the Victoria and Albert Museum in 1998 I had planned to take photographs of an Irish Traveller family living on a site that has since been destroyed to make way for the Olympic Park in East London. This was for an exhibition run by the Travellers' Education Unit in the London borough of Hackney. When I rang Maria, the mother of the family, to apologize and explain why I would have to rearrange our appointment she interjected, "I will pray for you."

So I often reflect that it is Maria that I must thank for the incredible journey that I travelled during my 15 years at the V&A: visiting gurdwaras up and down the country to talk about the exhibition, the *Arts of the Sikh Kingdoms* in 1999, which attracted over 119,000 people of whom over 60 percent were of Sikh origin; supporting research initiatives that uncovered over 4000 objects that related to African Caribbean diaspora despite the museum, initially, saying it "did not collect Africa"; developing museum-wide policies and implementation plans related to access, inclusion, and diversity initiatives across all equality strands and leading on a major program, Capacity Building and Cultural Ownership – Working with Culturally Diverse Communities, funded by the Heritage Lottery Fund (HLF), which contributed to an increase in culturally diverse audiences from 8 percent in 2001 to 16 percent in 2009 (Nightingale 2010).

Yet when I arrived at the V&A I experienced significant culture shock. I had spent the previous 30 years working in community education, inner-city regeneration, and organizations working toward equality, often at grassroots level. I had worked with Bangladeshi clothing workers in Brick Lane, East London; with recently arrived Kurdish or Vietnamese refugees in Hackney, North London; with young people at risk, pensioners, the long-term unemployed, and people with disabilities including mental health service users. When I went to the V&A, the world-class museum of art and design, located in an affluent part of West London, I entered a different world.

The International Handbooks of Museum Studies: Museum Practice, First Edition.
Edited by Conal McCarthy.
© 2015 John Wiley & Sons Ltd. Published 2020 by John Wiley & Sons Ltd.

It was often a rocky ride at the V&A as I progressed from running "community" programs to developing cross-museum equality and diversity policies. At first I missed working in East London, much to the surprise of many who envied my position at the V&A. I decided the only way I could resolve my feelings of loss and culture shock was to bring something of East London into the V&A and, indeed, working with colleagues within and outside the museum, significant strides were made between 1998 and 2013, the year I left the V&A, in making the museum more inclusive and diverse. The territory was not new to the V&A. Both the Asia Department and the Education Department had developed programs and initiatives that brought in British South Asian and Chinese communities based primarily, but not exclusively, on the South and Southeast Asian collections. Of particular note had been *Shamiana*, the Mughal Tent project led by my predecessor, Shireen Akbar, which involved communities across the country in making panels for the Tent, inspired by the collections in the Nehru Gallery of Indian Art, which was exhibited at the V&A, in the regions, and internationally. When I arrived at the V&A I felt it important to build on this tradition but to broaden the audiences we worked with and to develop cross-museum approaches to diversity and equality, which is, after all, everyone's responsibility.

I was fortunate, I now realize, that New Labour (1997–2010) came to power just before I started at the V&A. Selwood and Davies (this volume) point out that Labour, even before winning the 1997 election, affirmed the capacity of the cultural sector to "promote our sense of community and common purpose" (Labour Party 1997, 9). Labour's establishment of DCMS (Department for Culture, Media and Sport) and the publication of *A New Cultural Framework* (DCMS 1998) made it clear that New Labour saw the cultural and heritage sector as a key instrument of government working with other departments such as the Department of Education and the Social Exclusion Unit. There followed a new emphasis on the "public" rather than the "producer." Annual Funding Agreements with government obliged museums to both set and deliver on key performance indicators such as the number of audiences from social classes C2, D, E (lower socioeconomic classes), from black, Asian, and minority ethnic backgrounds and then, later, from people with disabilities. From 2002 New Labour, recognizing the need to go beyond targets, increasingly referred to the notion of public value and the need to "best capture the value of culture" (Jowell 2004). It was not just that; "Policy certainly endorsed the actions of those museums – or more specifically, those museum leaders – who sought a wider role in society, through social inclusion and purposefully working with the disadvantaged" (Selwood and Davies in this volume). Such policies also empowered me and other members of my team, often working at the margins, to argue the case for our work within the V&A. There was both strategic and genuine interest in the work we carried out in broadening audiences. We were regularly asked to provide case studies that were sent to central government as evidence of our commitment to fulfilling our broader societal role and as outlined in our Funding Agreement on which the museum's resources depended.

Also significant was the support from the HLF and its interest in our work in diversity. The aforementioned Capacity Building and Cultural Ownership – Working with Culturally Diverse Communities had a grant of almost £1 million over three years with a cross-museum brief to work over three sites of the V&A: at South Kensington, the V&A Museum of Childhood in Bethnal Green, and the Theatre Collections in Covent Garden, which has now been incorporated into the South Kensington site. A clear aim of this program was to embed diversity and equality across the museum and to leave a lasting legacy, something that happened to some degree but that external funding rarely achieves. Indeed as Selwood and Davies (in this volume) point out, the HLF, along with the Renaissance in the Regions, and its commitment to make more people, and a wider range of people, take an active part in and make decisions about heritage has been the mainstay of museum development for nearly 10 years (Selwood and Davies in this volume). Yet, as Lynch, cited by Crooke in this volume, has shown, external funding for public engagement work from such bodies as the HLF and the charitable sector in the United Kingdom has not succeeded in shifting such work from the margins to the core.

I have now left the V&A and am carrying out research into children who migrated to East London between 1930 and the present day. This is a collaborative PhD between the Queen Mary, University of London, and the V&A Museum of Childhood. It is based on research I carried out with colleagues at the V&A Museum of Childhood for the World in the East End gallery initiative, drawing on both tangible and intangible heritage of culturally diverse communities. I am glad to be working in East London again, perhaps bringing back to the area something of what I have learnt at the V&A.

So it is with some excitement that I read the chapters in this book. Several of the issues explored in this excellent volume are those that I encountered during my work at the V&A. Many of the arguments reflect my own views developed through my experience, not only within the museum sector but outside of it, at grassroots level with diverse communities who may or may not have visited a museum, and who may not see its relevance to their lives. Like the black and Asian community in Yorkshire, many of the diverse communities with whom we worked at the V&A shared the view that it (the museum) "doesn't relate to me" (Black in this volume).

I was gratified to read in McCarthy's Introduction to the book about the need to bridge the gap between museum theory and practice. He quotes the work of Andrew Dewdney who, I know, writes from experience of the anger of museum professionals at academics "who know little of the practical pressures and exigencies of making an art museum 'work' successfully" (Dewdney, Dibosa, and Walsh 2013, 16). Dewdney encountered this anger at a major international conference organized at the V&A in 2010, "From the Margins to the Core: Exploring the Shifting Roles and Increasing Significance of Diversity and Equality in Contemporary Museum and Heritage Policy and Practice," organized in partnership with the University of Leicester (V&A 2010). Many attendees reacted strongly to Dewdney's critique of the work of people who had been at the forefront of trying to make institutions more inclusive. They did not need this criticism from inside the hallowed halls of academia, based on little understanding of the challenges they encountered on a day-to-day basis. Yet it was clear, throughout this exchange, that both sides needed each other. Theory needed to be more embedded in museum practice, and museum staff to be more open and self-reflective.

McCarthy (this volume) talks of museums having "little sense of unified professional identity." This was certainly my perception when I started at the V&A, the first and only museum where I have been employed. In Hackney adult and community education, where I worked previously, there was a sense of shared values on the importance of education, of furthering equality and widening participation despite significant challenges and disagreements. What I found at the V&A was that this united professional identity was elusive if not absent. Frequently the educators had to fight for their voice to be heard and to be, as Reeve and Woollard (in this volume) clearly state, at the core rather than at the margins of the museum's mission and purpose. Despite the expertise of educators and the multiskilled nature of their roles it was the curators who seemed to carry more prestige and political weight within the organization. Of course, there were individual curators who understood the need to be more audience-focused, who had excellent relationships with external stakeholders and individual members of diverse communities; but a shared sense of direction or underpinning values between educators and curators was not always evident.

The same applied to those who were leading on equality and diversity and who, placed within the Learning Department, sometimes felt even more marginalized and unable, from this position, to exercise the necessary influence across the museum whether that be on research, visitor services, collections, gallery development, marketing, public programs, or staffing, for example. And yet, as Gary Younge puts it, the margins "in no small part define the core … what we insist is marginal has in fact been simply marginalized" (Younge 2012, 107). It is a question of relative power positions that are in constant flux. As Younge reminds us, the core needs to take account of the margins, which is often where innovation and creativity take place:

> The journey between the margins and the core is one that most of humanity makes every day … the best we can do is travel from A to B safely and intelligently, with due regard for our fellow passengers, in the knowledge that without A there would be no B and that neither A nor B will necessarily be in the same place when we come to make the return trip. (Young 2012, 112)

It is not always easy within large national institutions, with layers of hierarchy and bureaucracy, to make such journeys but the benefits, when that interaction and respect are in place, can be significant. When those with power and influence in the museum did listen and take account of those at the margins then change could happen – and sometimes speedily. One case in point is when the Collections Policy was changed to incorporate objects of relevance to the African diaspora once it was established that, contrary to belief, there were over 4000 within the V&A's collections.

McCarthy (in this volume) also talks of "the tendency to freeze professional work in rules." There were many rules and codes at the V&A but, new to the profession and the V&A, I was not always aware of them and, when they were brought to my attention, I could not always understand their rationale. On one occasion the Chinese Education Officer brought over Chinese watercolor paintings for a display during Chinese New Year. The artist, relatively well known in China, had rolled them in a tube for ease of transport. When they were unfurled we were told they should be flattened for six months. We had a problem. The display was meant to go up within weeks. We rang the artist who insisted that we should roll the paintings in the opposite direction. This was unacceptable to staff internally so we outsourced the work to a local framer and the display, much enjoyed by Chinese and non-Chinese families alike, went ahead. There were other occasions when we circumvented procedures, often unwittingly but sometimes out of sheer frustration and in order to ensure an event went ahead.

I was often impressed by the way the V&A Conservation Department, operating within UNESCO and ICOM guidelines, respected the traditions and views of diverse cultural and faith communities. They did not use animal products in the preservation of Jain objects; they consulted with members of the Sikh community over the display of religious texts and with members of the Jewish community over conservation of the Torah. But I was surprised, even delighted, to read Sully (in this volume) outlining the need for equal stakeholder participation in decisions on conservation. Terms such as "equitable partnership," "capacity building," or "empowering communities" were not current when I started at the V&A although they were themes that later became central to the HLF-funded initiative Capacity Building and Cultural Ownership – Working with Culturally Diverse Communities (2005–2008). The attitude in many parts of the museum was more akin to what O'Neill, cited by Lang (2006) calls the welfare model with a focus on "outreach," educating those as "having 'deficiencies' to be corrected for their welfare" rather than a social model that "subverts power hierarchies as it generates co-creation and facilitates informed debate" (Marstine, Dodd, and Jones in this volume).

Yet the challenges inherent in such approaches should not be underestimated, particularly within a sector and a profession where I am not convinced the majority are aware of, let alone subscribe to, such principles. I am therefore surprised that they have, as Sully (this volume) suggests, become part of the general rhetoric in some quarters. But either way it is certainly true that there is some way to go in developing a related practice. Those involved in community development in other fields have long been aware of the barriers that work against equal participation and of the problems of top-down led consultation. The skills needed to negotiate the "contact zone" are not achieved overnight. This is a concept first articulated by

Mary Louise Pratt, and then by James Clifford as "the space of colonial encounters, the space in which peoples geographically and historically separated come into contact with each other and establish ongoing relationships, usually involving conditions of coercion, racial inequality and intractable conflict" (Clifford 1997, 188–219).

Of course conservators are not the only, or indeed the main, advocates for empowering communities or stakeholder participation within museums. As Crooke states "[t]he exploration of community and museums has been a concern of museums across the globe" (Crooke in this volume). She makes reference to a threefold framework: the role of museums as a symbol of community; the connections between museum and community policy; and the use of the museum for community action but now calls for a more "active museum" that will "actively co-produce with its community, effect change, and forge dynamic connections" (Crooke in this volume). She believes many organizations and people, recognizing the power of museums, are keen to be involved in this co-production, quoting impressive recent examples of work in Northern Ireland and elsewhere. Indeed from my own experience at the V&A I am aware that many external organizations are keen to collaborate.

But, in this climate of reduced resources, some museums seem to be retreating from such innovative practice and, indeed, other museums have never fully embraced it. This is shortsighted as there are many benefits to partnerships, such as the maximization of skills and resources as well as enhanced ability to draw down external funds from sponsors keen to see museums look outward. But as Lynch points out, we should not underestimate "the museum's fear of others that flows like an undercurrent beneath these encounters" nor the "the museum's need to exercise control, and its even greater fear of change" (Lynch cited in Crooke this volume).

The examples of indigenous communities influencing mainstream institutions in the United States, Canada, New Zealand, and Australia, some of which are illustrated in this volume, are impressive. Yet is the situation not significantly different where collections, with which diverse communities have a connection, have been taken from where the majority of the community live and been dispersed across the world? May not the physical distance between source communities and the collections make influencing and steering institutions more challenging? There are, for example, many Sikhs residing within the UK who have an interest in the Sikh-related objects at the V&A, and these and other collections from South and Southeast Asia have been the stimulus for work with British Asian communities for several decades. But the majority of Sikhs live outside the UK.

New technology, of course, opens up opportunities for remote democratic participation as with the initiative described by Basu on "'reanimating cultural heritage' through a digital access initiative among five UK museums and archives and collaborating institutions in Sierra Leone" (Marstine, Dodd, and Jones in this volume). So, while there are undoubtedly parallel issues of shared guardianship

(Marstine, Dodd, and Jones in this volume) are there not also differences between a museum in Australia working with Indigenous communities who have lived within its borders for centuries, and the V&A or British Museum working with Asian communities, a minority of whom live in the UK, and who, for the most part, have arrived since World War II? This is not to say that British Asian or other communities cannot or have not influenced UK museums, but that the diasporic element brings a different dimension.

In 2012, funded by the European Union, a colleague and I from the V&A Museum of Childhood ran a two-day training course for staff from the Archaeology Museum in Diyarbakir, a walled city in southeast Turkey to where many Kurdish refugees have fled from the conflict between the PKK and the Turkish government. This had been jointly planned with colleagues in Turkey through hours of conversations on Skype mediated through a translator. The first day of the training focused on the societal role of the museum and developing new audiences. This was followed by a "training the trainers" session in preparation for a week's participatory project for refugee children living within the walled city. With our help the archaeology curators rolled out the participatory project with the children who made mini Museums of Me with images, objects, and drawings of their families, their environments, and their personal journeys. There was a parallel project with Kurdish children in East London, culminating in a display of work from both Turkey and the UK at the V&A Museum of Childhood followed by a larger exhibition in Diyarbakir opened by the town's mayor. Needless to say we learnt as much, if not more, than the staff we trained, who also spent a week visiting museums in London. What was particularly heartening was to see the archaeology curators, encouraged by their enlightened woman director, willingly pull up their sleeves to help children use cameras, stick down their pictures, and assemble their museums.

During the training day on the societal role of the museum we reviewed several mission statements from British museums along with their own mission statement before they redrafted their own. We were worried about imposing what we thought of as good practice from a UK or European perspective that might be inapplicable in such a different context. Yet it was the mission statement of the National Museums of Liverpool, with its commitment to social justice and its confident assertion that it could change lives, that inspired the Turkish staff and was evident in their redrafted statement. Fleming (this volume), the Director of National Museums Liverpool, is well known for his commitment to social justice and his success in both Tyne and Wear and in Liverpool in transforming the museum services and changing the class profile of audiences. When New Labour came to power in 1997 it both drew on, and was inspired by, his work in Tyne and Wear quoting it as an example of good practice. But what is impressive about Fleming is that his commitment to social justice predates New Labour and unlike others, whose commitment to change has been proved to be skin deep since the change of government in Britain, will not waver. "[W]e will adhere to our values," he asserts (Fleming in this volume). For Fleming, progressive practice cannot operate in isolation but should be underpinned by its mission statement that truly reflects the museum's vision and purpose. It is this vision that inspired colleagues in Diyarbakir as well as New Labour and indeed others both in the UK and internationally. In the UK the Museums Association's 2012 vision for increased social impact of museums is outlined in their document "Museums Change Lives." But such claims need to be unpicked as well as evidenced. As one member of the National Museum Directors Council asked, "but what does it mean and how might we investigate it? What is the nature of the impact that museums have on individuals and how does this play out in communities, societies and even nations?" (Unidentified NMDC member in Selwood 2010, 4; cited in Scott in this volume).

Merriman (this volume) believes there should be a renewed focus on collecting, an area that has been neglected in a time of diminishing resources. For Gardner (this volume), collection planning should link to the institutional mission, be integrated into individual performance plans, monitored, and evaluated. It should also, within an increasingly interconnected world, be informed by intellectual rigor. For both Gardner and Merriman curators should not be autonomous individuals who seek to fill gaps in collections, but instead move from ad hoc to strategic planning. Collections "were never comprehensive but were shaped by the interests of the individuals who amassed them" (Merriman in this volume). Merriman talks of the need for "relational collecting," citing impressive examples of developing two-way beneficial relationships with members of particular communities. Any vision with regards to collections should be shared with different stakeholders and take account of changing demographics. Gardner asks profound questions about the ability of museums to build relationships with communities who have no reason to trust them and to move from a white male default position given the lack of diversity within the sector.

Such approaches are a symphony to my ears. They echo aspirations outlined in the Access, Inclusion and Diversity Policy agreed by the V&A trustees in 2003 and being presently redrafted. It stated, for example, that the V&A collections should not only incorporate objects that "inspire and broaden people's experience" but "relate to people's social and cultural heritage, particularly in relation to target audiences, taking care to ensure the heritage of diverse audiences is reflected in the collections." There should be work by "diverse practitioners including people from different social and cultural backgrounds and people with disabilities." Consultation is also mentioned: "Where appropriate, curators will consult and engage new and potential audiences when making acquisitions" (V&A 2003, Policy statement 3.12.1).

During training sessions on equality and diversity rolled out to all departments there was some resistance by curators that decisions about collecting should take into account anything other than their respective expertise. As we discussed how to implement the Access, Inclusion and Diversity Policy a not insignificant number of senior curators muttered, "but that is not how we collect" (despite curators having been involved in the drafting of the policy and it being the official policy of the museum). But one problem was that the Access, Inclusion and Diversity Policy did not always dovetail with the collection plans of the different departments, or indeed with the museum's overall collecting plan and certainly not with the practice of every curator. Of course there were notable exceptions. The Collecting Plan of the Prints, Drawings and Paintings at the time was the most in tune with the Access, Inclusion and Diversity Policy and, ironically, it was sometimes when a curator went out on a limb, a practice criticized by Gardner and Merriman, that work was acquired that was of resonance to diverse communities. In the introductory chapter of the book *Museums, Equality and Social Justice* (Sandell and Nightingale 2012) reference is made to the work of Rosie Miles at the V&A who made a concerted effort to collect paintings and prints by artists of African and Caribbean origin despite the overall policy at the time being that the V&A did not collect Africa. Clearly there was a problem, not only on how different plans related to each other, but on involving other stakeholders including audiences, diverse communities, or non-users in any collecting plans.

There was one program, however, where the V&A did set out to involve other stakeholders in decisions on collections. *Staying Power*, funded by the HLF under the Collecting Cultures initiative, is a partnership between the V&A and Black Cultural Archives. The funding is for the collection of photography that reflects the black British experience from 1950 to 2000 that is to be accessioned into the V&A's national collection of fine art photography. An exhibition both at the V&A and at the Black Cultural Archives' new premises in Brixton, South London opened in early 2015. This will include a selection of the images, along with excerpts from oral histories collected from photographers and members of different communities.

What was not apparent in this very successful exhibition were the challenges faced by both partners throughout this project – in respecting each other's viewpoints, developing collaborative ways of working, and coming to joint decisions on what should be collected. There is no doubt the partnership element strengthened our application to the HLF and indeed, as someone involved in drafting the application, I felt such a partnership could be beneficial. If we were to collect work that reflected the black British experience surely we needed the expertise, not only of the photography curators to ensure the aesthetic merit of the work, but also the expertise of people who knew about the black British experience, something that is mainly lacking within the curatorial departments as a whole and among photography curators specifically. The largest body of black staff at the V&A is employed within the security department. To have Black Cultural Archives (BCA) on board would seem to be the perfect partnership. As Marstine, Dodd, and Jones point out, "communities hold knowledge about collections of equal status and value to that of the museum, and that authority should be shared" (Marstine, Dodd, and Jones in this volume).

The partnership between the V&A and Black Cultural Archives was not an easy two-way relationship. My own perspective is that the curators, perhaps wary of the criticisms of peers or colleagues, have found it difficult to have their autonomy challenged and to give equal weight to both aesthetic considerations and the need to "ensure the narrative experience is representative of Black people and the Black experience" (Keith 2012, 56). Keith, who interviewed several leading community heritage practitioners with experience of working in partnership with museums, is a trustee of BCA and is on *Staying Power's* steering group. It seems there is still a problem with art and community engagement. As Marstine points out (Marstine, Dodd and Jones in this volume) many of the "ethical challenges endemic in art museums and galleries" result from "judgments of quality" that reinforce a canon, thus operating as "an exclusionary sifting device that delineates boundaries between insiders and outsiders, the core and the margins." It is this that can also prejudice against the showing of visitor-, community-, or user-generated creative work within the museum or online.

Yet the experience of *Staying Power* is not unique. Keith identified common concerns among those she interviewed about "the power of the curator, who is often perceived as difficult to access and holding tight control over the museum's narrative" (Keith 2012, 47). As Crooke states, it is the narrative of a museum that dictates who and who does not belong. "A museum symbolizes a sense of belonging," she writes, "it tells you who fits into the narrative it shares. Equally, by omission, a museum symbolizes those who do *not* belong" (Crooke in this volume).

Keith found that collaborations between museums and heritage partners are often fraught. They are dependent on time-limited funding and on individual relationships that are not enfolded into the organizational and operational culture of the museum or the heritage partner. There is little recognition of the free time expected of the community heritage partners. Such partners, however, have other motivations for wanting to collaborate besides influencing the narrative of the museum… "Whilst it [community heritage partner] may work on a 'budget of love', it is also working with the world's premier museum of art and design thus deriving a certain amount of cachet and kudos from funders and heritage sector peers" (Keith 2012, 56).

Keith goes on to say that equitable collaborations can "be best achieved through developing shared values and clear objectives and through open dialogue employed in a reciprocal partnership" (Keith 2012, 57) and their success can be "evidenced in their ability to endure despite the tensions that are involved" (Keith 2012, 57). With *Staying Power* there was not only tension between curators and community heritage partners and curators. Diversity practitioners and educators involved in the project also disagreed with the curators on occasion. But it says something of the power of the core that those at the margins both within and outside the organizations often find it difficult to make their voice heard. Following Younge's analysis, the journey between A and B both within and outside organizations is long and hard, and requires an active willingness to share power, build respect, and develop shared values.

I am aware that many of the examples I have quoted here relate to work with black, Asian and minority ethnic audiences and partnerships with black and Asian organizations. It is true to say that the V&A, over the period I worked there, was successful in increasing the ethnic diversity of its audiences and in delivering related programs and initiatives that influenced the narrative of the museum. It had less success in increasing audiences from a lower socioeconomic class despite the introduction of free admission, a strategy that was "originally identified as those whom the department initially classified as C2DEs (that half of the population comprising skilled, semi-skilled, and unskilled manual workers, state pensioners, with no other earnings)" (Selwood and Davies in this volume). The percentage of those from NS-SEC 5–8 at the V&A has hovered around 11 percent, a figure far less than the percentage of the population. The museum has seen a massive increase in visitors over the past decade a high proportion of them overseas visitors and of socioeconomic classes NS-SEC 1–4 (Nightingale 2010). It is they who, in the main, are benefiting from free admission.

The V&A is not unique in its difficulty in having a real impact on this target group as, while free admission has increased numbers across all groups, "free admission has not succeeded in attracting the groups for whom it was originally intended" (Selwood and Davies in this volume). The government target of an 8 percent increase in visits by lower socioeconomic classes came and went with little sense of museums making an impact or being made accountable and the Department for Culture, Media and Sport "has never publicly reflected on whom was encouraged to visit, and whether or not they were its original target audience" (Selwood and Davies in this volume). To some it was always evident that "free admission on its own is unlikely to be effective in attracting significant numbers of new visitors from the widest range of socio-economic groups" (HOC 2002 Para. 60 qtd in Selwood and Davies, this volume). Black (this volume) rightly believes "the jury is definitely out on the ability of most to make serious inroads into non-user groups" and this could not be truer than for those of lower socioeconomic background. What is needed is a "sustained drive over a considerable timeframe, and required regular evaluation against targets" (Black in this volume).

The problem, of course, with targets is that they are a crude instrument and it is regrettable that performance indicators and measurements required by government were, and increasingly have become, so narrow. And yet one of the prerequisites for sustainability is "selecting, rigorously measuring and powerfully articulating the value and impact of the sector" (Stanziola 2008, 317, qtd in Scott, this volume). As Selwood and Davies (this volume) state "Museums and galleries in the UK are relatively lightly legislated or regulated."

The year prior to moving to the V&A I led a project on compiling and presenting evidence on how Hackney Community College had delivered on its equality objectives and widened participation (FEFC 1996). This was a huge exercise gathering together strategies, project plans, evaluations, and written evidence from different stakeholders, including learners, staff, and partner institutions. The inspection entailed visits to programs both on- and off-site, stakeholder focus groups, and individual interviews. We were awarded a Grade 1 for Responsiveness, the highest category possible (FEFC 1996, 1, 3–6). But the strongest driver of all was that a proportion of the funding was dependent on the profile of our students as determined by postcode addresses (FEFC 1996). It would be interesting if a similar scheme were applied to museums with their funding dependent on the postcodes of their visitors. In comparison to other publicly funded sectors museums get off lightly.

It would be comforting to be assured that new museum ethics could be a discourse that could be a powerful framework to inspire change in museums. (Marstine, Dodd, and Jones in this volume). But alongside a revised ethics there has to be leadership that is prepared to listen to the margins, a vision that incorporates all stakeholders, more strategic planning across all parts of the museum, clearer accountability, and evidence that we can contribute to public value, equality, and social justice. There needs to be more collaboration between academia and museums; equitable partnership work with health and social services, local government, and the community and voluntary sector; a responsiveness, flexibility, and openness about different ways of working, allowing other voices to influence the narrative and preparedness to take risks; a sustained approach to becoming more relevant to, and attracting, non-users and particularly those from lower socioeconomic classes.

But this needs staff with skills not regularly found in museums, including policy and planning, audience and community development, and with a sense of empathy that Pickering believes is a "particularly 'under-rated' professional stance in museums" (Marstine, Dodd and Jones in this volume). If museums are to understand how to meet the needs of audiences and to become more relevant they also need to reflect diversity throughout their staffing structure including at senior management and governance level. One of the casualties of the expenditure cuts in the UK has been the Diversify program that had led to the employment of talented black and Asian minority ethnic staff within the sector. But we should no longer be reliant on targeted programs to diversify our workforce.

I apologize for any criticisms that may be implied in the above. I hope I am allowed my moment of "outrage" as recommended by Selwood and Davies. Times are hard but it is now more vital than ever to be clear and assured of our relevance for the future. Meanwhile, back to my research.

References

Clifford, James. 1997. *Routes: Travel and Translation in the Late Twentieth Century.* Cambridge, MA: Harvard University Press.

DCMS (Department for Culture, Media and Sport). 1998. "A New Cultural Framework." London: Department for Culture, Media and Sport.

Dewdney, Andrew, David Dibosa and Victoria Walsh. 2013. *Post Critical Museology: Theory and Practice in the Museum*. Oxford. Routledge.

FEFC (Further Education Funding Council). 1996. "Hackney Community College: Report from the Inspectorate." Accessed November 13, 2014. http://dera.ioe.ac.uk/3053/1/hackney_community_cyc1.pdf.

Jowell, Tessa. 2004. "Government and the Value of Culture." London: Department for Culture, Media and Sport.

Keith, Kimberley. 2012. "Moving Beyond the Mainstream: Insight into the Relationship between Community-based Heritage Organizations and the Museum." In *Museums, Equality and Social Justice*, edited by Richard Sandell and Eithne Nightingale, 45–58. Oxford: Routledge.

Labour Party. 1997. "Create the Future: A Strategy for Cultural Policy, Arts and the Creative Economy." London: Labour Party.

Lang, Caroline. 2006. "The Public Access Debate." In *The Responsive Museum: Working with Audiences in the Twenty First Century*, edited by Caroline Lang, Vicky Woollard, and John Reeve, 29–40. Aldershot, UK: Ashgate.

Nightingale, Eithne, ed. 2010. *Capacity Building and Cultural Ownership: Working with Culturally Diverse Communities*. London: V&A.

Sandell, Richard, and Eithne Nightingale. 2012. *Museums, Equality and Social Justice*. Oxford: Routledge.

V&A. 2003. "V&A Access, Inclusion and Diversity Strategy." London: V&A.

V&A. 2010. "From the Margins to the Core: Exploring the Shifting Roles and Increasing Significance of Diversity and Equality in Contemporary Museum and Heritage Policy and Practice." Victoria and Albert Museum, Sackler Centre, March 24–26. Accessed November 13, 2014. http://www.vam.ac.uk/content/articles/f/from-the-margins-to-the-core-2010-conference.

Younge, Gary. 2012. "The Margins and the Mainstream." In *Museums, Equality and Social Justice*, edited by Richard Sandell and Eithne Nightingale, 105–113. Oxford: Routledge.

Eithne Nightingale has worked in the community, education, and cultural sectors including as Head of Equality and Diversity at the V&A. She left this post in 2013 to pursue a PhD in Children, Migration and Diaspora at Queen Mary, University of London, part of the Child in the World AHRC-funded Doctoral Collaborative Programme with the V&A Museum of Childhood. She has written extensively on the arts and diversity, coediting a recent publication, *Museums, Equality and Social Justice* (2012). She lives in Hackney, East London, and is also a writer and photographer. See http://www.eithnenightingale.com; eithnenightingale.wordpress.com.

MUSEUM PRACTICE AND MEDIATION
An Afterword

Anthony Alan Shelton

For over three decades museums have experienced tempestuous and rapidly changing conditions that, one might have thought, their origins had left them ill equipped to navigate. They have been challenged by fierce intellectual critiques, destabilized by transformative political and market conditions, and repudiated by different sectors of increasingly non-consensual publics. Changes, originating from neoliberal policies, have challenged formerly established national, social, and cultural alignments, and engendered critical questions about the instrumental, intrinsic, and positional values inherent to the public domain and their public worth (Scott, Fleming, Selwood and Davies in this volume). These vast social transformations have destabilized art and cultural institutions to be re-evaluated in relation to the "new" knowledge and creative economy, and have fostered the museum's redefinition, foci, the classification and management of its resources, modes of content delivery, financial networks, and social relationships. The implications of new media (Wellington and Oliver in this volume) and the demands to conform to emergent civic, national, and international aspirational standards have provided additional challenges.

Taken together, these forces and circumstances have made museums into one of the most intense reflections and expressions of the wider social changes and economic crises that have transformed, and continue to transform, local, national, and global societies. The characteristics of Victorian and mid-twentieth-century museums have been thoroughly interrogated and critiqued, and, in many cases and in different ways, transformed. From the institutional husks of a small number of historically specific models, a multitude of variations in organization, philosophy, and practice have emerged, which, if not all thriving, have at least proliferated, enriched, and are helping to redefine the public and private spheres. These institutions are often, in a global world, unable to transmit the common values, community ethos, or shared purposes traditionally ascribed to them. Instead, they represent a plethora of socially constructed creative positions and knowledges

The International Handbooks of Museum Studies: Museum Practice, First Edition.
Edited by Conal McCarthy.
© 2015 John Wiley & Sons Ltd. Published 2020 by John Wiley & Sons Ltd.

that increasingly inform our decentered and fragmented worldly sense of being. The notion of museums as monolithic state-sponsored and narrow disciplinary institutions has been superseded by new operational strategies that have transformed many of them into open institutions which stand as bulwarks against closed society (Nightingale in this volume).

I focus my comments in this Afterword firstly on some of the primary problems that hinder discussion on museums and their related practices. I argue that the fragmentation of formerly coherent museum models (science and art), and forms (encyclopedic, disciplinary, thematic, or regional), disallow attempts at generalization whether based on their operation, exhibition genre, subject specialization, political, or cultural/scientific orientation. Museums now inhabit intellectually, aesthetically, and ethically complex landscapes littered by increasingly divergent and differently positioned institutions. The Tuol Sleng Genocide Museum (Phnom Penh) and the Kigali Genocide Memorial (Kigali); the Staatliche Kunstsammlungen [State Art Collections] (Dresden), the Zentrum für Kunst und Medientechnologie [Center for Art and Media] (Karlsruhe), the Canadian Museum for Human Rights (Winnipeg), the Alutiiq Museum (Kodiak), or the U'mista Cultural Centre (Alert Bay), have little organizational, scalable, or managerial consistency and even less connection to a common body of internationalized theory or philosophy that can equally or convincingly draw from universal or consensus-based principles.

Yet, despite these differences, such institutions still sometimes collaborate in unexpected ways. Instead of focusing on museums, we must, I shall argue, look at museum networks and the practices that emerge from the specific and distinct positions occupied by institutions and practitioners within them. The second part of this Afterword will discuss one institution where I am the director, UBC MOA (University of British Columbia Museum of Anthropology), and how during the last 30 years it has adapted and responded to this changing landscape through the development of a number of successive and more inclusive critiques and practices, or what Clifford (2003, 45) has called core "articulations." Attention will specifically be concentrated on diversifying exhibition practices, which now include not only practices solely focused on specific non-Western artists and communities, but new genres of display that give greater attention to the issues raised by modern and contemporary art and the implications of the emergence of global art on the established institutionalization of the world's sociologies, histories, arts, and other cultural expressions.

Problems and possibilities: rethinking museums in a globalizing world

Nowhere are differences between museums more clearly visible than in their exhibitions and programs. Many museums have moved from old, static long-term displays to rotating temporary exhibitions, which constantly re-engage with changing realities and multiple viewpoints (see the chapters by Arnold, Young in this volume). Kovach (2009, 30) in *Indigenous Methodologies* is clear: "Indigenous methodologies are guided by tribal epistemologies, and tribal knowledge is not Western knowledge. Knowledge is neither acultural nor apolitical." Some museums as well as science centers and heritage parks function hardly using collections at all (Arnold in this volume), while others have repositioned their usages away from passive, supposedly neutral didactic displays, to re-align them politically. Collections and exhibitions have been used to fortify indigenous identities and self-governance strategies (Hoobler 2006, 451; Stó:lō Nation and the Reach Gallery 2012, 56–57), or to articulate an indigenous interpretation of the relation between themselves and the wider society to express "pragmatic sovereignties" (Clifford 2013, 273–275).

Other museums have partly eschewed the need for permanent premises, as demonstrated by the pop-up exhibition concept implemented by the California-based Santa Cruz Museum of Art and History. This museum advertises a theme and venue and invites collectors to bring their objects together with a label for a period of a few hours or days, during which they are collectively exhibited. The program of pop-up exhibitions expresses the museum's broad commitment to foster participation, democratization of relations between insider/outsider, interdisciplinarity, experiential immersion, and the exploration of diverse life-worlds (Santa Cruz Museum of Art and History 2014).

The Denver Museum of Contemporary Art also values innovation and originality, as represented by its infamous "Black Sheep Fridays." This program combines absurdity, humor, trivia, and chance to produce such recent events as "a night of crochet, beer, and witchcraft" ("The Craft"), "Sock Puppet Karaoke" and "Icky-bana, The Japanese Art of Poisonous Plant Arrangement" (Denver Museum of Contemporary Art 2014). Today's museums and galleries are multifaceted and are variously defined as places of assertion, contestation, mediation, commemoration, learning, research, as well as increasingly profiled as hubs of sociability and sometimes even fun. In many places, exhibitions based on collections, classified by formal Western, disciplinary knowledge systems, no longer wholly monopolize museum displays. New exhibition mandates and informal programming are transforming at least part of museum operations into social clubs that, when at their most confident and flamboyant, have metamorphosed some august institutions like Toronto's Royal Ontario Museum's Friday Night Live, into culture lounges that share the floor alongside laboratories or galleries of "things." The term "museum" as it is used today, might easily hide the heterogeneity of these institutions, I fear, under allusions of their abstracted commonalities.

A second concern I have in discussing museum practice is the problem of comparison, which is often hindered by the imprecision ascribed to fundamental museological terms and categories. This is endemic to the vocabulary that divides French from English museology (Desvallées and Mairesse 2010), as well as widespread throughout the latter's lexicon. Culture itself, the irreducible category enshrined, protected, transmitted, and sometimes supposedly governed by museums, has multiple characterizations and definitions (Kuper 1999, 19); it can be defined as either things or processes; it can be conceptualized in its singularity or plurality; it can carry universalist, governmental, or positional agency and authority; and it can be represented as stable or conflictive; neutral or political. Museology/museography; interpretive mediation; property; ownership; repatriation/restitution; the public, and identity are core categories that are fundamental to issues concerned with the operation of museums, yet the considerable and contradictory literatures that lie at each of their roots is too often ignored in favor of reductive generalizations (Black, Bienkowski, Crooke, Jimson in this volume). Even preservation-based conservation practices, once protected by technical logic, can be viewed as involving unethical reconstitutive practices, which are no longer able to offer any sureties to guide practice (Sully in this volume).

Further, in the last decade museums have lost part of their semantic monopoly over a subject position, that of the curator or keeper, which, in both professional and public understanding, provided one of the most powerful tropes through which they were imagined. Freed, partly at least, from the obligation to care, research, and develop specialist collections within museums, the term has been increasingly appropriated and conflated in its external use with that of programmers, organizers, and stylists (Arnold, Norton-Westbrook in this volume). "Curator" may now be used to describe planners of film festivals, digital content developers, fashion shows, and culinary events, window dressers, and lifestyle advisors (see O'Neill 2012, 89). By distancing its designation away from scholarly or disciplinary collection-based functions to an organizational and design role, the term comes to fulfill a much hungered-for palliative to legitimate prestige production in the new cultural economy.

Despite the imprecision of some of the basic terms in the museological lexicon, "museums" of one sort or another continue to flourish. Although it is clear that museums and galleries have grown and prospered most in liberal capitalist democracies, they have also been preserved or reconstructed in communist-governed countries; widely copied in developing nations – originally under colonial duress; modeled in local communities; and widely mobilized to encourage the public consumption of culture in indigenous and internally colonized societies like those in Mexico, the USA and Canada. Museums have proliferated in all parts of the world and have achieved a universality of a kind of which those who expressed their early rhetoric could only dream.

Despite their initial ill-preparedness to adapt to change, fostered by international organizations such as UNESCO and ICOM, nation-states and professional associations, and forced by ethical interdictions and the recently asserted voices of marginalized peoples, museums and their practices have over the past three decades changed enormously, as the chapters in this volume demonstrate. Museums have been transformed by the move from curatorial amateurism to specialist regulated professionalism (Norton-Westbrook, Simmons in this volume); from

preserving closed internal groupings to more social and governmental responsiveness (Scott, Fleming in this volume); from internally unregulated institutions to
accountable, integrated, and audited operations (Scott, Gardner in this volume);
and from institutions that once disavowed social interests and inflections to those
that sometimes celebrate in their revelation (Marstine et al., Arnold, Young et al.
in this volume). Moreover, the decolonization of curatorial knowledge (Phillips
2012, 229–230); the incorporation of community-based or indigenous perspectives on conservation ethics and practices (Clavir 2002; Sully in this volume); and
the collaborative reconstruction of museum infrastructures (Bergstrom et al.
2011) have notably increased the transparency and public responsiveness of
museum practices.

Part of these challenges, changes, and ellipses in museum practice might not
have occurred so quickly without the critical, theoretical, and reflexive attitude
nurtured by the kind of scholarship described in McCarthy's Introduction to this
volume. While museum scholarship has undoubtedly suffered under the twin
insufficiencies of theoretically or critically uninformed curators (curatorial naivety)
and the generalizations of ill-informed and ill-situated academics (self-fulfilling
academicism), many exceptional exponents of both kinds of scholarship have
indisputably made outstanding contributions to reinvigorate each other's discourses and practices.

Their efforts have been further advanced by non-museum organizations and
practices such as biennales, kunsthalles, expos, cultural festivals, Documenta, private touring exhibition companies, and other sectors of the heritage industry,
which have created new ways of thinking about collections, exhibitions, and public
programming and have increased the interactions between academics and exhibition and museum practitioners (see O'Neill 2012, 51). There are 100 biennales
alone in the world, which, with their networks of visiting artists, curators, and
patrons, have stimulated the emergence of completely new art worlds (Belting and
Buddensieg 2013, 29).

Museum directors including Manuel J. Borja-Videl, Jean de Loisy, Martin Roth,
Jette Sandahl, Bernd Scherer, and Boris Wastiau are critically oriented and their
practices informed by the kind of theoretical scholarship that brings an originality
to project ideas, distinct from the bland managerial cadre preferred by, for example, successive British governments during the latter part of the twentieth century.
Their reflexive and critical approaches echo the earlier writings of museum professionals such as Michael Ames, Ken Arnold, Mary Bouquet, Fernando Estévez
González, Jacques Hainard, Charles Hunt, Jan Jelínek, Javier Gómes Martínez, and
Nuno Porto. Their work clearly expresses the maturity of approaches to the practice of theory and the theoreticization of practice developed over the past 30 years
(Shelton 2013, 8). Norton-Westbrook (this volume) describes the new style of
curating, an assessment widely supported by many other writers and practitioners.
Many of these theoretician/practitioners had or occupy joint museum/
university positions, which helped to unsettle and destabilize the old division

between theory and practice and release the potent agency that had been effectively neutralized by institutional separation.

The problem for museum practice, as McCarthy (this volume) concurs, is not over-theorization, but working through the implications of theory and criticism to help redefine museum operations, purposes, resources, as well as, following Simmons (this volume) and Shelton (2013, 14), providing perspectives on new issues. Marla Berns, Director of UCLA's Fowler Museum believes that museums can play an innovative role by questioning stabilized disciplinary boundaries and demonstrate through compelling visual expression, new narratives and ways of understanding and seeing the world (Figure A2.1). Her own museum has exhibited or incorporated art by José Bedia, John Cage, Máximo González, and Amalia Mesa-Bains to create active dialogues with "ethnographic" pieces and installations, and fracture the institutional borders that separate different genres (Fowler Museum 2014). Continued separation between the academy and museum and between their different traditions of scholarship is no longer justifiable or desirable and the division between practice and theory needs to be flatly rejected.

Germany provides noteworthy innovative approaches to exhibition practices, heavily influenced by a critical and theoretically informed turn (Beier-de Haan in this volume). The Rautenstrauch-Joest-Museum in Cologne has long pursued an independent approach to ethnographic exhibitions through the use of comparative perspectives to scrutinize contemporary European situations. Gisela Völger's *Ecstasy and Reality: Drug Use in Cultural Comparison* (1981), and ensuing gender-centered exhibitions (*The Bride in Cultural Comparison* 1985; *Male Secret Societies: The Role of Men in Cultural Comparison* 1990; *Him and Her: Masculine Strength and Feminine Leadership in Cultural Comparison* 1997), provide landmark examples in developing this genre.

The reinstallation in 2009 of the museum's ethnographic collections in a newly constructed building, allowed for the expansion and development of a series of modular based comparative themes that, by including European and non-European presences, emphasized the similarities between life-worlds over their differences (Rautenstrauch-Joest-Museum 2014). The importance of situated knowledge in constructing one's view of the world is affirmed throughout the museum. Difference invokes fascination and danger and is approached cautiously through curiosity and intellectual debate. Museum displays examine the colonial context, which mingled romanticism with exploration, collection, classification, and order. The section on Africa does not attempt to present indigenous interpretations of artifacts, but lays bare changing European conceptions and prejudices to introduce debates on xenophobia, racism, and genocide. One exhibit, the World in a Museum, creates an idealized museum within the museum. At its center is a large baroque interactive table, lit by overhanging chandeliers, surrounded by black walls, punctured by doorways that lead to obliquely angled presentations on culturally specific groups of artifacts (a Syrian merchant's room; a Tuareg tent, a Plain's Indian tipi and an Asmat male house). Authority and power is deliberately expressed

FIGURE A2.1   *Walk among Worlds,* an installation by Máximo González, October 12 – November 10, 2013, at the Fowler Museum, UCLA. (For a color version of this figure, please see the color plate section.)
Photo: Anthony Alan Shelton, 2013.

through the large size of the stylized antechamber in comparison to the smaller display areas; a relation that maps directly on to the antechamber as a repository of digitized maps, photographs and data, the evocation of the colonial archive, and the "closets" in which the artifactual remnants of the Other have been reduced to signs and domesticated meanings. The museum describes these areas under the theme of "Living Together," places of sociability that structure social relations within specific cultural contexts; but these are spaces that are also internally and hierarchically interrelated.

This German museum also presents indigenous cultural interpretations of some of its works, thereby setting up a problematic dichotomy between what it distinguishes as European ideologically mediated knowledge systems and what, it appears to assume, are "purer," apparently less problematic forms of knowledge external to European conceptions. Exhibition modules on the afterworld, religion, and ritual narrate comparative cosmologies and practices, and each of the ethnicized zones in "Living Together" incorporates recorded interviews to voice indigenous perspectives. The module "Art," intended as a changing exhibition, self-consciously and critically uses a Western category as its organizing principle, reinforced by an impressive, aestheticized presentation, while providing counter, culturally specific descriptions of the original significances and uses of works. "Art" thereby crosses Western visual codes with non-Western "authentic" narrative interpretations. This deliberate strategy helps draw attention to the epistemological and visual faultlines through which the tensions and contradictions between a Western modernist worldview, based on universalism and claims to political, economic, and cultural hegemony, are contrasted with the specificities of non-Western articulations of locally and globally located identity formation (Marcus 1998, 221).

The new Rautenstrauch-Joest Museum mobilizes sophisticated epistemological shifts to provide an intense and innovative, but sometimes lop-sided, intellectual journey between European, ideologically mediated ways of conceiving the world, and other cultures' perceptions of themselves. Using a full range of slick exhibitionary technologies, optical effects, and spectacle, the museum turns part of the ethnographic collection into an exhibition about ourselves and the mechanisms and strategies we have adopted to incorporate and intellectually colonize the non-European world.

The organization of the museum raises further questions too, regarding the relationship between museums and universities and the future of the humanities. If anthropology is able to provide a framework for studies of the "here and now" of historical, as well as geographically removed cultures, then could it not also provide a new disciplinary architecture for the humanities as a whole? Furthermore, given the allure of museums such as the Rautenstrauch-Joest-Museum, UCLA Fowler, and UBC MOA, can they significantly increase the profile of the humanities in modern society? Moreover, along with all the other complex shifts in these intellectual fields, might not the humanities be better served by museums instead of university faculties?

My third concern with museum studies and debates on museum practice dwells on their often Anglo-centric focus on Britain, Canada, the United States, Australia, and New Zealand. There is an inexplicable lacuna in scholarship surrounding the

FIGURE A2.2   Opening performance of the community-based collaborative exhibition *Death Is Just Another Beginning*, National Museum of Taiwan, Taipei. (For a color version of this figure, please see the color plate section.)
Photo: Anthony Alan Shelton, 2012.

world's fastest-growing and most ambitious museum sectors in Asia. Even major Asian museum projects like Kowloon's waterfront development in Hong Kong, the reorganization and expansion of Singapore's National Museum, and Gwangju's Asian Cultural Complex in South Korea, receive little sustained attention in Western debates and museological literature and even less in many Western accredited university courses in museum studies.

The Taiwanese museum sector is especially diverse, integrated and well developed. The sector is unusual in that it includes an expansive network of 33 indigenous peoples' community-based museums, with national, as well as private museums (Shung Ye Museum of Formosan Aborigines, Taipei), sometimes adopting collaborative approaches. The National Taiwan Museum (Taipei) (Figure A2.2) and the National Museum of Prehistory (Taitung), have also involved indigenous people, artists, and community-based groups as part of their curatorial processes, yet Taiwan is seldom mentioned in the literature on indigenous and collaborative museology. The National Museum of Natural Science (Taichung), presents the history of science using original and model reproductions of instruments invented and developed by Chinese civilizations which provides a strong and impressive corrective to European and American science displays that usually elude alternative narratives of science. Regional Taiwanese museums (Lanyang Museum, Penghu Living Museum, Chia-Yi Museum) often display cross-sections of the local natural, economic, and cultural history that remain indifferent to Western separation and classification of these fields.

The sophistication and cosmopolitanism of Taiwan's museums is also reflected in the foci and practices of its heritage sector, which, despite colonial domination, incorporates and preserves the world's largest extant core of Japanese imperial style architecture; the renowned collections of Beijing's Palace Museum; Chinese

FIGURE A2.3   Museum, Academia Sinica, Taipei.
Photo: Anthony Alan Shelton, 2012.

epigraphic, manuscript and book collections housed in the Academia Sinica; and even small Javanese and North American Indian collections in the National Taiwan Museum. Pacific Island collections are displayed at the National Museum of Natural Science and minority peoples' collections from mainland China constitute an important section of the collections at the Academia Sinica (Figure A2.3). These cultural configurations are perhaps not surprising given Taiwan's attempt to culturally identify itself as an independent Pacific nation, which it justifies by the continued existence within its territory of a range of Austronesian languages. Some of these languages are still spoken in indigenous regions, and are linked to other language groups in southeast China. Current research attempts to further link the southeast language families with those spoken by minorities in southwestern China. Politically, this research might potentially enable Taiwan to combine tangible and intangible heritage to shape and strengthen its independent national identity at the center of a cosmopolitan, overarching, and ancient complex of civilizations that played a crucial role in the historical development of mainland China and Island Oceania.

There are ample examples in China (Figure A2.4) and Hong Kong in particular of grafting Western models and commissioning Western museum consultants to help grow and modernize the museum sector (Lord in this volume); however, as elsewhere in Asia – in India, Japan, Korea (Figure A2.5), Taiwan, and Southeast Asia – there is also extraordinary local creativity and new models of museums and practices that are independently being developed. Asian museums are evolving from Western-imposed models, through hybrid institutions, to new Asianized configurations. Though historically inflected by concerns familiar to museums elsewhere – colonialism, exploitation of natural, animal, and human resources, expression of prestige, and identity politics – Asian institutional and philosophical articulations are sometimes materialized differently. This emerging uniqueness is visible in contemporary museum architecture, and the spatial notions and social relations it engenders through exhibitions and programming themes, and the establishment of connections between different cultural and regional groups they have fostered. Such differences might provide critical insights and new criteria for comparative evaluations of the work and focus of some Western institutions.

Thinking through practice visually at UBC MOA

One region in which traditional museum methods, missions, and operations must be constantly revised and rewritten is British Columbia, the farthest western province of Canada. Due to internal colonization, First Nation dispossession of land, changing multicultural and intercultural populations, and the province's geopolitical position between Asia and the USA, consensus over the representation of its history, geography, landscape, art, and cultural expressions

FIGURE A2.4　Atrium, Capital Museum, Beijing.
Photo: Anthony Alan Shelton, 2011.

has long been contested and elusive (Clifford 1997, 109–110). Moreover, the public presentation of epistemological, optical, and ethical differences does not always neatly follow ethnic or cultural distinctions.

I focus here on the use of exhibitions as reflexive and interrogatory practices that have helped successively to renew UBC MOA's critical engagement with multiple and shifting audiences. Exhibitions can be seen as processes or articulations through which culture is endlessly created. "Articulation," Clifford argues, inevitably incorporates ambiguity, contradictions, and coherencies as key to this dynamic process. "Articulation is the political connecting and disconnecting, the hooking and unhooking of elements," writes Clifford, "the sense that any socio-cultural ensemble that presents itself to us as a whole is actually a set of historical connections and disconnections" (2003, 45). Since its foundation in 1949 under the directorship of Harry and Audrey Hawthorn, UBC MOA has aligned itself with the struggles of indigenous peoples and cultural communities, while gradually

FIGURE A2.5   Exhibit Gallery, Kokdu Museum, Seoul. (For a color version of this figure, please see the color plate section.)
Reproduced with permission of Sukman Jang.

articulating an array of collaborative and increasingly reflexive working practices that enable it to better respond to broader globalizing world forces.

Within these articulations, four different moments, or genres of exhibitions have settled, which despite instabilities in their formation and reproduction, nevertheless have left clear imprints. In the first period, 1949–1976, with few exceptions, exhibitions were usually small, student-oriented installations, organized according to then conventional display styles. However, this period also included two unusual spectacular Northwest coast First Nation displays mounted with the help of Bill Reid and Robert Davidson for the Montreal Exposition (1967), and the later *Man and His World* exhibition (1969–1970), also in Montreal. These two exhibitions marked the beginning of a more theatrical approach to display that was taken up again later in the museum's history. The second period, 1977–1989, coincided with the museum's move to its current modernist building designed by Arthur Erickson, and the appointment of Michael Ames as its second director. During this period, the museum curated or hosted 17 First Nation artist exhibitions. Following the lead of the Hawthorns and Ames, the museum challenged the exclusivity of established aesthetic canons with the dramatic installation of Northwest Coast sculpture into MOA's Great Hall, the incorporation of smaller pieces of carving and metalwork into its Masterpiece Gallery, and the inclusion of contemporary First Nation artists into its temporary exhibition program. The exclusion of indigenous Northwest Coast works from Western-dominated, geographically defined, linear, and narrow aesthetic canons, not only provoked UBC MOA to confront these biases by exhibiting First Nation cultural expressions as art, but also stimulated its early research and many of its publications.

A third exhibition genre, which emerged between 1987 and 2001, focused on issues in the politics of representation and the relations between anthropology museums and non-indigenous as well as indigenous artists. These exhibitions included: Richard Hill's *The Whiteman in North America* (1987–1988); Stephen Clark's *Ouroboros* (1985); Gerald McMaster's *Savage Graces* (1992); Judith Williams' *High Slack* (1994); and culminated in the group series of interventions *Raven's Reprise* (2000–2001) that were intended to interfere with, and generate disjunctions in, the museum's dominant narratives. The development of these genres followed a movement from the first and second genres where interpretation was subject to disciplinary curatorial authority, to the third which acknowledged multiple subject positions; an attitude that Marcus (1998, 234) elsewhere sees as a move from appropriation and exclusionary practices to more open democratic forums of engagement. This shift also acknowledges a new view of culture in which "there is no longer a standpoint from which one can claim to definitively administer or orchestrate, the textualization of 'identity,' 'tradition,' or, 'history'" (Clifford 2003, 28).

A fourth genre of exhibition, for which UBC MOA is perhaps better known internationally, is that derived from a broad range of collaborative methodologies aimed at working with originating source communities (Ames 2003, 174–175; Phillips 2003, 158–160). Such exhibitions were not fully developed until comparatively late in the museum's history. In 1986, a group of Coast Salish weavers curated an exhibition on the revival of Musqueam weaving, *Hands of Our Ancestors: The Revival of Salish Weaving at Musqueam*. This was followed the same year by *Robes of Power* and, in 1996, by two other Musqueam exhibitions *From under the Delta: Wet Site Archaeology from the Frazer Valley* and *Written in the Earth*. In the same genre in 2002, the museum co-facilitated *Káxláya Gvílá: The Ones that Uphold the Laws of Our Ancestors* (2002), and the following year, *Mehodihi: Well-Known Traditions of Tahltan People: "Our Great Ancestors Lived that Way"* (2003–2005). Collaborative methodologies were also adopted when working with non-aboriginal cultural communities as in the 1993 show *A Rare Flower: A Century of Cantonese Opera in Canada*, and later in the 2001 exhibition *Spirit of Islam: Experiencing Islam through Calligraphy* (Museum

FIGURE A2.6   *Box of Promises*, collaborative work between George Nuku (Māori) and
Cory Douglas (Squamish/Haida) in the exhibition *Paradise Lost?* Great Hall, Museum of
Anthropology, UBC, Vancouver. (For a color version of this figure, please see the color
plate section.)
Photo: Anthony Alan Shelton, 2013.

of Anthropology 2014). Collaborative practices vary considerably depending on
community values and politics and their relations to the museum, but they are
modified and embedded in many of the museum's photographic, artist-based, and
student exhibitions too.

The last three of the exhibition genres defined above have exercised a central
role at UBC MOA throughout 1976–2013. *Robert Davidson: The Abstract Edge* (2004–
2005); *Kesu: The Art and Life of Doug Cranmer* (2012); and *Signed without Signature:
Works by Charles and Isabella Edenshaw* (2010–2011), are example of exhibitions that
continue to support the construction of a genealogy of First Nation artists that
began in the solo-art shows in the mid-1970s. Similarly, the community research
dedicated to curating a large part of the museum's new multiversity galleries
opened in 2010; *The Story of Nulis, a Kwakwaka;wakw Imas Mask* (2010–2013), and
Mnúkvs wuwáxdi: One Mind, One Heart (2012–2013), two exhibition modules within
this gallery complex, have built directly on earlier established collaborative models
(Museum of Anthropology 2014). Lastly, critically based practices that continue
the work of Raven's Reprise still inform UBC MOA's installations and interventions. *Wheel Overlays* by Edgar Heap of Birds (2007), and *Meddling in the Museum:
Michael Nicoll Yahgulanaas* (2007–2008), were both intended to provoke critical con-
sideration on the museum's role and confront popular presuppositions of First
Nation art (Levell 2013, 114). Other interventions and exhibitions such as Nicholas
Galanin's *Raven and First Immigrant* (2010), Peter Morin's *Museum* (2011), and
Paradise Lost? Contemporary Works from the Pacific (2013; Figure A2.6) engaged

increasingly with wider political issues and marked a further turn from "ethno-graphic" to "world," to "global" art perspectives (Fillitz 2013, 222–223). None of these articulations is exclusive, but mark a series of advances that stem from successive contradictions between academic definitions of "non-Western art" and changing sociopolitical and geographic realities.

Since 2010, partly influenced by earlier practices, and seminal exhibitions such as *Magiciens de la terre* (1989), Peter Weibel's *Inklusion: Exklusion* (1996), and Documenta 11 (2002), MOA has attempted to develop a more comprehensive critique of museum practice through a broader reflexive rereading of modernism and the disciplinary boundaries it imposes on its subjects. Issues concerning institutional history and identity; the museum's urban and rural integrations, and future directions, have become critical. This more recent cluster of exhibitions can be subdivided into three groups:

1. *Border Zones: New Art Across Cultures* (2010); *Safar/Voyage: Contemporary Works by Arab, Iranian and Turkish Artists* (2012–2013), and *Without Mask* (2014).
2. *Man Ray, African Art and the Modernist Lens* (2010–2011); *Inuit Prints: Japanese Inspiration* (2011); *The Marvellous Real: Art from Mexico 1926–2011* (2013–2014).
3. *Hiroshima: Ishiuchi Miyako* (2011–2012); *Visions of Enlightenment: Buddhist Art at MOA* (2012); and *Speaking to Memory: Images and Voices from St. Michael's Residential School* (2013–2014). (Museum of Anthropology 2014)

The first group of exhibitions examined social and cultural processes, borders, trans-geographical populations, and globally constructed identities, through the medium of contemporary art. Instead of beginning with an "ethnographic" approach (what constitutes the "ethnographic" is an implicit question behind many of these exhibitions), the curatorial process began with a critical theme relating to contemporary globalized reality, articulated through the Vancouver locality. Contemporary art, religious objects, or photographs and narratives all provided clear mediums to explore these issues, conjoining art practice with cultural analysis.

This exhibitionary practice reconfigures and attenuates the complexity of UBC MOA's earlier articulation in the local museum landscape as described by Clifford (1997). Such a rearticulation has not exchanged ethnographic exhibitions for art installations, or politics for aesthetics, but it does reject certain categorical distinctions which function as ideological constructs that work to enforce binary oppositions of inclusion/exclusion, and maintain the separation of different cultural traditions, alternative national and ethnic experiences of modernity, and the neocolonial relations between Euro-Canadian and American hegemonic discourses. Modern and contemporary art provide current mediums through which cultural and social relations are materialized, worked out, and new positionalities are asserted, or as Weibel (2013, 22) perceptively notes: "The world of art offers a glance at these global rewriting processes through a magnifying glass, as it were.

The global world system has transformed the global art system." While art may be exhibited in art galleries for its aesthetic effects, or historical affinities, or archetypal associations, other museums might use it to raise and explore critical and issue-based processes and conditions or provide alternative readings of dominant views and perspectives. In these latter museums, exhibitions may be curated by persons from any number of subject positions or community affiliations, whether through mediated or direct knowledge; or by diverse linguistic or epistemological interlocutors. Aesthetics – like history, anthropology, archaeology – is experienced differently depending on the defining and distinctive personal, social, and cultural positionalities of makers, mediators, and recipients.

Exhibitions for MOA are gradually evolving into a praxis between theory and future practice. *Safar/Voyage* began by raising questions about the nomadic condition of artists who had originated from specific geographic regions – North Africa, Turkey, and the Middle East – but who now live between different territories, forms of government, languages, historical and cultural traditions, and types of social relations, without ever being either at home or in exile. The nomadic artist led us to identify large and increasing numbers of Vancouver's population who live under similar conditions, experiencing binary or multiple social, cultural, and geographic worlds. These are anthropological conditions imbued with enormous political significance and intellectual ramifications that seldom, if ever, get raised in ethnographic museums solely dependent on disciplinary-based collections.

Through working with a diverse volunteer advisory group, *Safar/Voyage* also made MOA aware of the responsibility of museums in a globalized world. Museums came to be seen not as solid, but as porous institutions, that transmitted and received ethical and political interdictions and that shaped, and were themselves shaped by external realities far removed from Vancouver or their point of origin. Cultures then, should not be represented as territorially bounded, and ethnically and linguistically closed and homogeneous, but as entangled and constantly mutating, a characteristic explored in different ways by all the exhibitions in this broad cluster.

The second group of exhibitions, on the other hand, were meant to explore issues in identity-construction, historical and contemporary consciousness, and the politics of representation. All were intended to address questions raised by globalization and its effects not only in mediating relationships and influences between the West and other parts of the world but between regions sometimes thought of as independent from Western influence. Thus *Inuit Prints: Japanese Inspiration* looked at the global flow of techniques and their mobilization by cultural intermediaries; *Man Ray, African Art and the Modernist Lens* explored popular European and American preconceptions of African art and aesthetics, and their association with primordial archetypes, strength, and sensuality as mediated through the photographic images of Man Ray and his contemporaries in the 1930s and 1940s – not an anthropology of the Other, but an anthropology of ourselves;

FIGURE A2.7   Entrance to *The Marvellous Real: Art from Mexico 1926–2011*, Audain Great Hall, Museum of Anthropology, UBC, Vancouver.
Photo: Randal Platt, 2013. Reproduced with permission.

while *The Marvellous Real* (Figure A2.7) sought to destabilize surrealist tropes of Mexico and established classifications and chronologies of Mexican art, by proposing the alternative view of Latin America offered by the Cuban writer and musicologist, Alejo Carpentier.

All three exhibitions were planned to combat cultural essentialism by acknowledging the presence of European, American, and *mestizaje* thought and practices in mediating images and aspects of other cultures. The museum itself, by commissioning or hosting such exhibitions, rejects the separation between Western and non-Western cultures, while refocusing attention away from a glib multiculturalism to the influence of intercultural relationships between different groups, communities, and nations. MOA has not moved away from ethnography to "world art," but from "ethnographic material culture" to an ethnography and archaeology of global art. This is an important distinction that, as Weibel (2013, 23) writes, involves a crucial shift from modernity's play on exclusion and inclusion, the "Other" and the "we," to a more nuanced, networked, and interconnected world. These kinds of practices play with the tensions inherent within exhibitionary articulations and place museums in constant and restless motion, equal but not commensurate to that taking place in societies around them.

The third category of exhibitions distinguished here focused on affect and the evocations and experiences of serenity (*Visions of Enlightenment*), empathy (*Hiroshima: Ishiuchi Miyako*), and trauma (*Speaking to Memory*) at a different level in which the visual is sometimes dependent on performative engagement to be fully effective. Ranging from the original musical compositions accompanied by mass choirs in the museum's Great Hall, and the play, *One Thousand Cranes*, composed

FIGURE A2.8   *Imprint*, choreographed by Henry Daniel and Owen Underhill. Great Hall, Museum of Anthropology, UBC, Vancouver. (For a color version of this figure, please see the color plate section.)
Photo: Nicky Levell, 2010.

and performed in memory of the victims of the bombing of Hiroshima, to First Nation visitors reading and examining files and photographs of their compatriots schooled at St. Michael's Residential School – inscribing the names of those still unidentified on the foils covering photographic prints and adding their own comments to those of others written in books or on blackboards – performance, as part of museum practice, provides a reflexive strategy that interrogates, rewrites, or pluralizes history. For *Safar/Voyage*, UBC MOA commissioned a composition (*Voyage-Piano Sonata*) by Iman Habibi, to reflect his reactions to the themes and works in the exhibition, while *Border Zones* opened with the performance of a newly commissioned contemporary dance piece, *Imprint* by Henry Daniel and Owen Underhill, that magically wove dances and large audiences throughout the gallery spaces (Figure A2.8). In the case of *The Marvellous Real* it was the curator who chose Federico Álvarez del Toro's contemporary symphonic piece *Ozomatli* (1982), richly layered with Maya spoken words, howler monkeys, and croaking frogs, to introduce the idea of the multivalent, excessive and sometimes jarring baroque qualities which the exhibition sought to evoke.

The destabilization and fragmentation of nation-states, communities, hinterlands, and landscapes, alluded to in the first part of this chapter, is replayed in the dislocation of the West's former disciplinary-bound subjects from their institutionalization in public museums. These conditions have created the culturally indeterminate spaces in which UBC MOA's practices, and those of other museums and galleries, have to be located. Museum crises were perhaps first and most acutely felt in ethnographic museums where Western disciplinary authority has been the quickest to be eroded. As anthropology refocused itself in the 1980s on the processes of globalization, abandoning former views of the relationship between culture, land, and people (Fillitz 2013, 221), many of the criteria on which ethnographic museums and exhibitions were based were thrown into crisis. Some ethnographic museums attempted to avert criticism by embracing the progressive banalities of world art, a modernist invention defined as the art of the historic and ethnographic Other that remains tied to cultural context and notions of heritage. Global art, the sudden worldwide eruption of art production in the 1980s, supposedly disavowed history and Western modernity (Belting 2013, 178; Weibel 2013, 21). However, in this new and quickly changing relational world, "world art" had already been made irrelevant by global art, which challenges even the necessity of reserving special institutions for its display. Global art, performance, digital media, installation, and soundscapes integrate themselves into the whole of our lived environments (Weibel 2013, 27). The theories developed around global art can be redirected and used to revise earlier understandings not only of "ethnographic material culture" but history collections, and decorative art too.

The implications of all these changes in exhibition practices for museums more generally are clear. If museums are to escape the ongoing crises that have beset many ethnographic museums, they must become more theoretically and politically conscious institutions embedded, like UBC MOA and UCLA's Fowler Museum, in and between communities. They must embrace contradiction and tension, and focus on their creative potentialities as what I would call "culture lounges" and laboratories within networks that link together traditional and newly emergent communities internationally. Neither technological nor elitist panaceas are sufficient to guarantee their viability. Museums must mobilize to present contemporary realities in all the complexity through which new technologies have enabled us to re-engage and imagine the world; as spatially multilayered, culturally relative, contingent, and contiguous, and historically non-cumulative and transformable hypermediations of the "real." However, museums cannot become new media, which, despite all its potential to imbue contingency and indeterminacy to reality, nevertheless reduces the narrative qualities of the world to mere instrumental data. The purpose of museums should be to return narratives, connected to visualities, to the world, to foster complex multicultural and sensorial understanding, and reawaken the wonderment of difference and being in all its multiple manifestations.

References

Ames, Michael. 2003. "How to Decorate a House: The Renegotiation of Cultural Representations at the University of British Columbia Museum of Anthropology." In *Museums and Source Communities. A Routledge Reader*, edited by Laura Peers and Alison Brown, 171–180. London: Routledge.

Belting, Hans. 2013. "From World Art to Global Art: View on a New Panarama." In *The Global Contemporary and the Rise of New Art Worlds*, edited by Hans Belting, Andrea Buddensieg, and Peter Weibel, 178–185. Cambridge, MA: Centre for Art and Media Karlsruhe and MIT Press.

Belting, Hans, and Andrea Buddensieg. 2013. "From Art World to Art Worlds." In *The Global Contemporary and the Rise of New Art Worlds*, edited by Hans Belting, Andrea Buddensieg, and Peter Weibel, 28-34. Cambridge, MA: Centre for Art and Media Karlsruhe and MIT Press.

Bergstrom, Krista, Nancy Bruegeman, Susan Buchanan, Shabnam Honarbakhsh, Heidi Swierenga, and Mauray Toutloff. 2011. "A Partnership of Peoples: Renewal of the Collection Infrastructure at the UBC Museum of Anthropology." *Collections: A Journal for Museum and Archives Professionals* 7(2): 163–200.

Clavir, Miriam. 2002. *Preserving what is Valued: Museums, Conservation, and First Nations.* Vancouver: University of British Columbia Press.

Clifford, James. 1997. *Routes: Travel and Translation in the Late Twentieth Century.* Cambridge, MA: Harvard University Press.

Clifford, James. 2003. *On the Edges of Anthropology: Interviews.* Chicago: Prickly Paradigm.

Clifford, James. 2013. *Returns: Becoming Indigenous in the 21st Century.* Cambridge, MA: Harvard University Press.

Denver Museum of Contemporary Art. 2014. Website. Accessed November 14, 2014. http://mcadenver.org/index.php.

Desvallées, André, and François Mairesse. 2010. *Key Concepts of Museology.* Paris, ICOM with Armand Colin. Accessed November 14, 2014. http://icom.museum/fileadmin/user_upload/pdf/Key_Concepts_of_Museology/Museologie_Anglais_BD.pdf.

Fillitz, Thomas. 2013. "Global Art and Anthropology: The Situated Gaze and the Local Art Worlds in Africa." In *The Global Contemporary and the Rise of New Art Worlds*, edited by Hans Belting, Andrea Buddensieg, and Peter Weibel, 221–227. Cambridge, MA: Centre for Art and Media Karlsruhe, and MIT Press.

Fowler Museum, UCLA. 2014. Website. Accessed November 14, 2014. http://www.fowler.ucla.edu.

Hoobler, Ellen. 2006. "'To Take Their Heritage in the Hands': Indigenous Self-Representation and Decolonization in the Community Museums of Oaxaca, Mexico." *American Indian Quarterly* 30(3/4): 441–460.

Kovach, Margaret. 2009. *Indigenous Methodologies: Characteristics, Conversations, and Contexts.* Toronto: University of Toronto Press.

Kuper, Adam. 1999. *Culture: The Anthropologists' Account.* Cambridge, MA: Harvard University Press.

Levell, Nicola. 2013. "Coppers from the Hood: Haida Manga Interventions and Performative Acts." *Museum Anthropology* 36(2): 113–127.

Marcus, Georg. 1998. "Censorship in the Heart of Difference: Cultural Property, Indigenous Peoples' Movements, and Challenges to Western Liberal Thought." In *Censorship and Silencing: Practices of Cultural Regulation*, edited by Robert Post, 221–246. Los Angeles: Getty Research Institute for the History of Arts and the Humanities.

Museum of Anthropology, University of British Columbia. 2014. "Past Exhibitions." Accessed November 14, 2014. http://moa.ubc.ca/experience/exhibits_archived.php.

O'Neill, Paul. 2012. *The Culture of Curating and the Curating of Culture(s)*. Cambridge, MA: MIT Press.

Phillips. Ruth B. 2003. "Introduction." In *Museums and Source Communities: A Routledge Reader*, edited by Laura Peers and Alison Brown, 155–170. London: Routledge.

Phillips. Ruth B. 2012. *Museum Pieces: Towards the Indigenization of Canadian Museums*. Montreal: McGill-Queen's University Press.

Rautenstrauch-Joest-Museum. 2014. Website. Accessed November 14, 2014. http://www.museenkoeln.de/rautenstrauch-joest-museum.

Santa Cruz Museum of Art and History. 2014. Website. Accessed November 14, 2014. http://www.santacruzmah.org.

Shelton, Anthony. 2013. "Critical Museology. A Manifesto." *Museum Worlds. Advances in Research* 1: 7–23.

Stó:lō Nation and the Reach Gallery. 2012. *Man Turned to Stone: T'xwelátse*. Abbotsford, BC: Reach Gallery.

Weibel, Peter. 2013. "Globalization and Contemporary Art." In *The Global Contemporary and the Rise of New Art Worlds*, edited by Hans Belting, Andrea Buddensieg, and Peter Weibel, 20–27. Cambridge, MA: Centre for Art and Media Karlsruhe and MIT Press.

Anthony Shelton has been Director of the Museum of Anthropology at the University of British Columbia since 2004. An anthropologist, administrator, curator, and teacher originally from Britain, Shelton has over 20 years of teaching, curatorial, and management experience. Of the 15 exhibitions he has curated or co-curated, some of the more innovative include *African Worlds* (1999), *Fetishism* (Brighton, Nottingham, Norwich, 1995), *Exotics: North American Indian Portraits of Europeans* (Brighton, 1991), and *Heaven, Hell and Somewhere in Between* (MOA, 2015). Shelton has published extensively in the areas of visual culture, critical museology, history of collecting, and various aspects of Mexican cultural history.

INDEX

Page numbers in *italics* denote figures, those in **bold** denote tables.

The International Handbooks of Museum Studies: Museum Practice, First Edition.
Edited by Conal McCarthy.
© 2015 John Wiley & Sons Ltd. Published 2020 by John Wiley & Sons Ltd.